STAGES OF SOCIAL RESEARCH
Contemporary Perspectives

Edited by
DENNIS P. FORCESE *and* STEPHEN RICHER
Carleton University, Ottawa

Prentice-Hall, Inc., *Englewood Cliffs, New Jersey*

P-13-840397-X
C-13-840405-4

Library of Congress Card Catalog Number: 74-113846

Printed in the United States of America

Current Printing (Last Digit):

10   9   8   7   6   5   4   3   2

PRENTICE-HALL INTERNATIONAL, INC., *London*
PRENTICE-HALL OF AUSTRALIA, PTY. LTD., *Sydney*
PRENTICE-HALL OF CANADA, LTD., *Toronto*
PRENTICE-HALL OF INDIA PRIVATE LTD., *New Delhi*
PRENTICE-HALL OF JAPAN, INC., *Tokyo*

To the forty-one authors whose book this really is

Contents

Preface

In any book, and especially in a book of readings, considerable selectivity is involved, which permits biases in perspective and gaps in treatment. But one has to begin somewhere. If any single tone can be discerned in this volume, it is one of criticism. Many of the papers included are critical of research techniques and research interpretations that are extant in the literature, and many of these papers, more than being negative, go on to suggest remedial innovations. The critical tone corresponds to our conception of the function of a supplementary text: to go beyond the blithe and idealized descriptions of "the way it is." We judge that instructors require readings which, while helping illustrate how to proceed in research, also point to pitfalls along the way.

Most authors generally reveal that a book has emerged out of long years of teaching in the area. This particular book has no such history. Its editors are recent graduates of sociology; we are just beginning our teaching and research careers. Our book has developed from our recently experienced dissatisfaction, and sometimes frustrations, with the way methods texts attempted to transmit sociologically relevant techniques of research. The book thus represents the kind of supplementary text we would like to have had as students. We would have liked a book, first of all, which illustrated each of the various stages of a research project. Moreover, we would have liked a book sufficiently honest to bring out the difficulties of research and to point out the sloppiness and inadequacy of much of what passes for research.

Consequently, we have organized our readings to correspond to the phases of a study. We begin with readings on general themes relating to all scientific enterprises, the relationship between values and science, the task of problem definition; the relationship between theory and research, and the tasks of conceptualization and hypothesis formulation. These considerations lead to a discussion of measurement, as one attempts to "operationalize" the concepts employed in the hypotheses. Then we turn to a broad description of the various types of studies one could carry out—the alternative "research formats."

After one has decided *what* is to be studied, and has some idea of a research format, one must decide *who* is to be studied. This produces a set of readings on various sampling techniques and their appropriateness to the testing of particular kinds of hypotheses. Once hypotheses and samples are set up, the next step is the *how* stage—the collection of relevant data. Going beyond general research format, here the various data collection options are discussed, including structured questionnaires, interviews, and observational techniques. The task then becomes one of data analysis, the process of statistical manipulation and organization that renders the data amenable to interpretation. The culmination of the research is the interpretative scheme which one imposes on the data. Interpretation, in the general sense in which we mean it, consists of making sense of our data, of translating statistical configurations and relationships into theoretically meaningful statements. Thus, this final stage should produce some measure of explanation and bring the research process full circle, returning to theory from whence it was derived.

We have attempted to select readings which clearly describe, illustrate, and critically assess the steps and options of research. In our judgment the papers which we have assembled are lucid and intelligent, providing the undergraduate and the graduate student both with practical discussions and illustrations from the working literature of the discipline.

1

The Scientific
Approach

Sociologists have always been explicitly concerned with the nature of science and with the difficulties of scientific endeavor. In considerable part this has been a reflection of relative immaturity—the self-consciousness of the "new boy." But it has also been a tacit recognition that the study of man must necessarily include the study of what some men have called science. Thus, methodology has come to refer not simply to techniques of data collection and analysis, but also to questions of problem selection and data interpretation.

The difficulties of bias and value intrusions, the distortions as well as the utility of preconceptions, assumptions, and models have been viewed not as just interesting, but as essential objects of study.

Chapter 1 is a partial reflection of these interests. Whether one speaks of the philosophy of science or the sociology of sociology, the papers selected for this first chapter manifest a preoccupation with analyzing what others take for granted: the nature of science itself or, in this instance, the nature of scientific sociology.

We begin with Alan Mazur's paper "The Littlest Science." Like so many critiques, Mazur's argument is an overstatement, with a penchant for polemic for the sake of effect. For example, to say as Mazur does "that the essential characteristic of a science . . . is that it is profound" is absurd. One might get away with saying this of religion, or of philosophy, but surely not science where reliability of observation and explanation is the distinguishing quality.

Yet, explanations that are reliable because the scientists have limited themselves to trivia and which therefore lack significant application to the difficulties of social life are hardly more valuable than the less precise and less reliable procedures of the informed layman. Here Mazur certainly has a valid point—in a sense an extension of C. Wright Mills' earlier critique of "abstracted empiricism."[1]

Mazur suggests that to be a science sociology needs more than declarations of intention or assertion, and more than simply dedication to techniques and those data for which we have techniques. In an argument no less telling for its exaggeration, Mazur contends that any science must produce. That is to say, then, in order to speak of a science of sociology, sociologists must produce a fund of information and explanation which enables human beings to extend their control over social phenomena—information, therefore, which is significant by virtue of its utility. Moreover, information which, were it not for the scientific procedures of sociology, would have remained undiscovered. It is in this regard, argues Mazur, that sociology has been deficient. We know little more than the layman. Hence, "sociology, the littlest science."[2]

Mazur calls for injection of massive doses of new data into the sociological mill. Then theoretical advances can be made. Some twenty years earlier, in what has become one of the best known papers by a contemporary sociologist, Robert K. Merton discussed the interdependence of empirical research and theory. It is testimony to the influence of Merton's paper that we now take for granted the interaction of theory and empirical research for which he argued. As Merton argued, research "does far more than confirm or refute hypotheses." It may suggest new theories, it will always refine theories, and often redirect theories, pointing up new and largely unexplored avenues of investigation. Necessarily, then, there is a continuous process of feedback, with theory preceding, guiding, and initiating research, and yet also being altered by that research. If this is not the case, then surely we do have "abstracted empiricism" or its antithetical extreme of "grand theory."[3]

As he elaborates the ways in which research does affect theory, Merton introduces the notion of "serendipity." We are perhaps less sensitive than we should be to anomalous data. Like all scientists, we too often succumb to the temptation to make things fit—fit our

[1] C. Wright Mills, *The Sociological Imagination* (New York: Grove Press, 1961), pp. 50-75.

[2] For reactions to Mazur's paper see *The American Sociologist*, 3 (1968), 292-96.

[3] Mills, The Sociological Imagination, pp. 25-75.

biases, our preconceptions, the existing theory which we favor. Perhaps it is inevitable that this be the case, that we be so bound by the existing paradigm that anomalous data are ignored—at least until they accumulate to such a degree that they must be considered.[4]

Yet, a sensitivity to the anomalous finding may permit theoretical breakthroughs. We pay lipservice to the importance of the deviant case, but too infrequently do we actually study it deliberately.[5] We must not only be attentive to the deviant case, we must fully explore the implications of findings which turn up in our research and which do not conform to our expectations.

Merton's consideration of serendipity—the accidental or unexpected finding—is explored by Bernard Barber and Renee Fox as they discuss "the case of the floppy-eared rabbits." It is because of the importance which we attach to the anomalous outcome that we included the Barber and Fox paper. The process of discovery or "act of creation"[6] is fascinating, but so too is the failure to discover.

[4] See Thomas S. Kuhn, *The Structure of Scientific Revolutions* (Chicago: University of Chicago Press, 1962).

[5] See S. M. Lipset, M. Trow, J. Coleman, *Union Democracy* (Garden City: Doubleday & Company, 1962).

[6] Arthur Koestler, *The Act of Creation* (New York: The Macmillan Company, 1964).

THE LITTLEST SCIENCE

Allan Mazur

The littlest science is sociology—the study of social behaviour. That it is little, no one can doubt. That it is a science may raise some question.

Every introductory sociology text I can think of addresses itself to that question within its first ten pages. They all conclude that it is a science. Most students, by the time they finish the book, conclude that it isn't.

Let's agree at the outset that the question isn't of any particular importance. Our concern with it is purely a matter of interest, not utility. But it is interesting, and I have found myself quite preoccupied with it; and it is the custom in academia that if you think about something for a little while, and get a few interesting ideas, then you write them down and try to get them published.

One current well-known sociology text lists four characteristics of a science. These are: "It is *empirical*; that is, it is based on observation. . . . It is *theoretical*; that is, it attempts to summarize complex observations in abstract, logically related propositions which purport to explain causal relationships in the subject matter. . . . It is *cumulative*; that is . . . theories build upon one another, new theories correcting, extending, and refining the older ones. . . . It is *nonethical*; that is, sociologists do not ask whether particular social actions are good or bad; they merely seek to explain them." (Johnson, 1960:2)

Another text, a better known one, uses the same four points in more concise form: "One is entitled to call sociology a science if theories are progressively refined and tested by observation, and if the ideals of objectivity and exactness guide inquiry." (Broom and Selznick, 1963:4-6)

The similarity in definitions is hardly surprising. After all, these are the same notions of science and "scientific method" we've been getting since high school physics. Everyone knows that this is what science is supposed to be.

Obviously I disagree.[1] The fact is that the essential characteristic of a science, for the vast majority of people, is that it is profound—it is a body of theoretical knowledge that is not trivial. The scientist must have better theories than the layman, or he's really not a scientist at all.

If physics is a science because it is empirical and theoretical, it is also a science because physicists' theories about the physical world work better than the non-physicists' theories. And if it is the biggest science it is because they work *so much* better.

Reprinted with permission of the author and publisher, The American Sociological Association, from *The American Sociologist*, Vol. 3 (August, 1968), 195-200.

I am grateful to Steve Richer, Alan Altschuler and Dale Rolfsen for their comments and advice.

[1] If I didn't, I'd hardly be making such a point of all this.

The "scientific method" alone does not make a science. Consider a very precise people-watcher researching social behavior. He objectively observes that people stop and talk to each other, and he notes that the frequency of conversations differs from one situation to another. He theorizes that *people interact at different rates.* As observation continues, he sees that people usually only talk to each other when they are close, so he improves his theoretical statement: *People are more likely to have a conversation when they're closer than when they're far apart.*

The people-watcher has been empirical, theoretical, has cumulatively refined his theory, and makes no ethical judgment as to whether it's good or bad to shout across the room. But is this science? No—because it's trivial. We all knew his result before he began his investigation, and there was no doubt of it. He could have used electronic recorders and high precision measures, but his finding would still be trivial—and therefore not science. If he had found out that people are less likely to talk when they are *closer*—then *that* would have been science.[2]

An empirical, theoretically connected body of knowledge is science *only when the people who know the theories know more about the real world than the people who don't know the theories.*

Is sociology a science?

No.

This does not imply that there is a particular lack of knowledge about the workings of society. In fact, we know a good deal about how people behave. It's just that the difference between what sociologists know and what everybody else knows is practically nil. This certainly isn't the state of affairs in the real sciences, such as physics.

Actually the physicists don't *really* know so much. They know very little about the nucleus of an atom. In fact, compared to what the sociologists know about society, the physicists know practically nothing about the atom. But the point is that physicists know much more about the atom than sociologists do, whereas sociologists know very little more about societies than the physicists do.

This is why I don't think sociology is a science. But many people vehemently disagree, so to avoid bitterness I'm willing to compromise and call it a little science—the littlest. Now everyone can be happy, which is, after all, the most important thing.

Can sociology ever be a big science? I think so. I believe it is in the incipient stages of becoming a real science in which theory will be non-trivial, but this belief is very much a matter of faith.

There are certain arguments which "prove" there can never be a real science of human behavior because it is intrinsically different than physical behavior, and these differences preclude scientific description. For example, I have often heard people note that physical phenomena are determinate and regular while human behavior is subject to whim and fancy and so is not at all regular and determinate, and therefore cannot be scientifically described.[3] This is nonsense. Human behavior may or may not be subject to whim or fancy—that is immaterial. The point is that science does not require determinism and

[2] Analagously, it is only news when the man bites the dog.
[3] Russel Kirk in his article "Is Social Science Scientific?" writes: "Human beings are the least controllable, verifiable, law-obeying and predictable of subjects." (Kirk, 1961:16)

regularity. The highly successful theories of probability and statistics specifically deal with phenomena that are not regular but are in fact quite random
in their behavior.[4] And the quantum theory—the current ultimate achievement
of physics—is not at all a deterministic theory; it is completely probabilistic. It
cannot describe the behavior of any single electron because the behavior of an
electron is currently considered to be much less determinant and regular than
the behavior of the most contrary of humans.[5] Quantum theory works
because it is always applied to a large collection of electrons—not just one.
And though there is no telling what any given electron will do, the physicists
can quite confidently say that some specific percentage of the collection of
electrons will do one thing, and the rest will do something else. For example,
electrons exist in certain "energy states." While there is no way of telling
which energy state any given electron is in, one can make a statement to the
effect that "at any given time 20 per cent of the collection of electrons will
be in energy state three."

Human behavior is quite analogous. While I cannot name for you the
specific American women whose social behavior will put them in the state of
pregnancy next year, I can rather confidently predict that 5 per cent of the
collection of American women will be in that state and 95 per cent won't.

It is not my intention to infer that everyone who denies that sociology can
ever be a science is a dimwit. This is certainly not the case. There is at least one
argument that deserves some very serious consideration. It is: *If* sociology can be
a real science, why isn't it? Now that's a good question.

Some writers have cavalierly dismissed this question by arguing that it is
preposterous to expect all sciences to progress at the same rate, and that physics
is simply moving ahead much more quickly than sociology. They generally point
out that today's sociologists are at the point where physics was shortly before
Newton, which nicely specifies the time lag at almost three hundred years.

This argument is really quite naive.

Today's sociology is hardly comparable to pre-Newtonian physics or even
pre-Middle Ages physics. The truly powerful basis of physics, the mathematical
description of physical phenomena, sets it totally apart from sociology (as well
as from many of the bigger sciences like geology or biology). When mathematics
became integrated into physics, then at that point it became preposterous to
compare physics and sociology. The integration came long before Newton.

In the second century A.D. Ptolemy compiled his thirteen volume *Almagest*
which is the climax of Greek astronomy. His scheme of the solar system had the
moon, the sun and five planets all moving around the earth on perfect circles.[6]
The scheme bears little resemblance to what we currently think of as the solar
system, but Ptolemy made no claim that his picture was a true one. His intent
was to represent the solar system mathematically so that the positions of the
planets at any future time could be predicted.[7] He accomplished this

---

[4]A statistician might say that there is a regularity in the randomness, but that is getting
far beyond the present point.
[5]In fact, a basic notion of quantum theory says that if you do know the precise position
of an electron, you cannot determine its momentum, and vice versa. (Heisenberg's
Uncertainty Principle.)
[6]Actually they moved on circles called *epicycles* which moved on circles called *eccentrics*.
[7]This attitude is, by the way, totally in the spirit of modern physics.

magnificently. We know of no scheme that made better predictions until the sixteenth century. At this writing there is no comparable achievement in sociology.

In the third century B.C. Archimedes noted, among other things, the mathematical-physical principle that when you put a solid body in a fluid, "the solid will, when weighed in the fluid, be lighter than its weight in air by the weight of the fluid displaced." This is, of course, Archimedes' Bathtub Principle of high school physics fame.[8]

The Law of Levers[9] is probably due to Euclid in the fourth century B.C. And the optical Law of Reflection[10] was probably known earlier. There were other mathematical principles of physics then. I'm just touching a few high points.

Pythagoras or his followers knew the relationship between the length of a vibrating string and the tone it produced. This brings mathematical physics back to the sixth century B.C. It seems to me that we have to go back before Pythagoras if we want to find some period when the physics of that day is comparable to the sociology of today. So if we care to estimate a "time lag," it should be closer to 3000 years than 300 years. But that's equivalent to saying that sociology never got started as a science at all, which is hardly much of a refutation.

The question, "If sociology can be a science, why isn't it?" deserves a considered answer. I will propose an answer shortly, and spend the rest of this essay considering it—in a leisurely manner and with many divergences.

First I must state my belief here that a *necessary* condition for the significant advance of a science is the input of *new, previously unobserved data*.[11] Old data will not do. Advance requires some kind of new research findings.

Sitting and thinking about the same old facts, generation after generation, does not produce anything significant that hasn't been produced before. You need a new, inconsistent fact to jog you out of an old theory and set you off looking for a better one. And you need a new fact to think about if you want a new theory that's better than the old one.

Physics has had a continual flow of new data—sometimes a flood of it. *Sociology has not, and that is at least one reason why it is such a puny science.*

There are at least three circumstances in which the introduction of new data can promote a major theoretical advance. The first circumstance is when the new data destroys an old theory. The realization that the existing theory is no good is usually a precondition for the appearance of an improved theory. Most

---

[8] "We are told (by the Latin writer Vitruvius) that, as Archimedes entered the tub, the more he submerged his body, the more the water spilled over the tub, and this led him suddenly to the method of determining whether the crown being made for King Hiero was pure gold, for it if was not the crown would displace a greater volume of water than a weight of gold equal to the weight of the crown, since the equal weight of gold would have a greater density or specific gravity and thus occupy less volume than the crown made of alloy. At any rate, according to Vitruvius, Archimedes '... without a moment's delay and transported with joy ... jumped out of the tub and rushed home naked, crying out in a loud voice that he found what he was seeking; for as he ran he shouted repeatedly in Greek, 'Eureka, eureka!' " (Clagett, 1955:97-98)

[9] The torque of a weight in a lever system is measured by the product of the weight and its horizontal distance to the vertical line running through the fulcrum.

[10] The angle of incidence equals the angle of reflection.

[11] Though perhaps not a *sufficient* condition.

philosophers of the Middle Ages seemed to have been quite happy with Aristotle's explanation of why, when a heavier and a lighter object are simultaneously dropped from the same height, the heavier object reaches the ground first.[12] The theory only becomes unsatisfactory once you know that the heavier object doesn't reach the ground first. That realization did finally come as a result of new data obtained by Galileo from experiments on falling bodies in the beginning of the seventeenth century.[13]

This particular function of new data, the destruction of old theories, is of crucial importance to the development of science. For a long time scholars have pointed to the 1543 publication of Copernicus' *De Revolutionibus* as an ultra-significant event in the history of science. We hear of "The Copernican

[12] Aristotle assumed that the speed of an object's fall was proportional to its weight. His system of physics was based on the notion that everything is made up of basic elements. These are the well known Big Four: earth, air, fire, and water. These elements are arranged in concentric spheres around the center of the world. The central sphere is made up of earth, which is surrounded by a shell of water, then air, and finally fire. There is a good deal of evidence supporting this ordering. If you swim down through the shell of water, sure enough, you find the sphere of earth. In the night sky you see points of the outer shell of fire twinkling through the shell of air.

One property of the elements was that if a piece was removed from its sphere, it tended to return to that sphere. If you pick up a piece of earth and let go, it falls back to its proper sphere—even if it must pass through the sphere of water on the way. If you exhale some air under water, it heads right up for its proper sphere above the surface. And if you light a fire, sure enough, the flames shoot skyward to join their kin in the outermost sphere of fire. Actually the system works pretty well!

[13] There is a great deal of misinformation on this point. First of all, not *everyone* was surprised to find that two bodies of different weight still fell at the same speed. The Greek atomist Epicurus (340-270 B.C.) held that all bodies of any weight would fall in a void with the same velocity. But most philosophers did seem to hold the Aristotelian view until the time of Galileo.

Second, the relevant experiments were *not* those in which Galileo climbed to the top of the Leaning Tower of Pisa and dropped two stones. In fact ". . . there is no positive evidence that he actually made any experiments from the Leaning Tower, and his manner of introducing them (in his essays) suggests that they were 'thought experiments.' Thus in attacking Aristotle's assumption that speed of fall is proportional to weight, he speaks not only of flinging two stones, one twice as big as the other, from a high tower, but also of dropping two lead spheres, one a hundred times as big as the other, from the moon." This latter experiment he clearly did not do.

"Two other Italian scientists, Giorgio Coresio in 1612 and Vincenzio Renieri in 1641, did actually make such experiments from the Leaning Tower, and they found that even with bodies of the same material the heavier weight reached the ground first, if they were dropped from a sufficient height. Coresio even asserted that the velocity was proportional to the weight, thus confirming Aristotle's 'law'; but Renieri, giving actual figures, showed otherwise. In fact he submitted his results to Galileo who referred him to his *Dialogue*. . . . Unimpressed by the disagreement of experiment with theory, Galileo made an abstraction from empirical actuality and said that the theory applied to free fall in a vacuum. In a resistant medium such as air, he said that a lighter body would be retarded more than a heavier one. Same results, different explanations! It has long ago ceased to be possible to regard the Leaning Tower experiment, even supposing Galileo made it, as in any sense crucial, or even new." (Crombie, 1959:149-151)

The experiments to which I referred in the text involved bronze balls rolling down an inclined plane. The inclined planes were used to slow the descent of the ball enough so that Galileo could time it with a rather crude clock based on water pouring through a hole in a bucket. The fact that these experiments were not on a free falling body did not prevent Galileo from generalizing his result to that situation. That the result is indeed generalizable we can chalk up to Galileo's extreme insight and/or luck.

Revolution." But the really significant factor was not the conception of a heliocentric universe—the Alexandrian astronomer Aristarchus (ca. 281 B.C.) had an astronomical system that included an earth which rotated on its axis while it revolved around the sun as a fixed center. "Aristarchus appears to have arrived at the basic assumptions of the Copernican system almost two thousand years earlier than Copernicus." (Clagett, 1963:115) The significant factor was the *destruction* of the old Aristotelian theory which had the earth at the center of the universe, and the stars, sun and planets rotating about the earth on perfect crystalline spheres.[14] But why was Copernicus successful in the destruction while Aristarchus was not? To a very large extent it was because of the introduction of new data in the form of four astronomical observations made in the years 1572 to 1610.

Here is the view of historian of science H. Butterfield:

It would be wrong to imagine that the publication of Copernicus' great work in 1543 either shook the foundations of European thought straight away or sufficed to accomplish anything like a scientific revolution . . . (It) was only a generation after the death of Copernicus—only towards the close of the sixteenth century—that the period of crucial transition really opened and the conflict even became intense. And when the great perturbations occurred they were the result of very different considerations—the result of events which would have shaken the older cosmos almost as much as if Copernicus had never even written his revolutionary work.

One of these (events) . . . was the appearance of a new star[15] in 1572—an event which one historian of science appears to me to be correct in describing as a greater shock to European thought than the publication of the Copernican hypothesis itself. This star is said to have been brighter in the sky than anything except the sun, the moon and Venus—visible even

[14]I mentioned earlier the highly successful mathematical system of the universe due to Ptolemy in the 2nd century A.D. The reader may wonder why, in the face of such success, philosophers still held to the older Aristotelian system which didn't predict astronomical events nearly as well. You must realize that the Ptolemaic system was considered no more than a mathematical device for calculating the positions of the sun and planets and was in no way considered to be a true picture of the universe. The true, if inaccurate, picture of the heavens was the Aristotelian view that the heavenly bodies were indeed imbedded in perfect crystal spheres which rotated about the earth—the home of Man, who was at the center of the universe. All motion was in "pure" circular orbits. These were the "sublime" heavens which knew no change. (The Christian version of Aristotle held that the universe was complete by the sixth day so there was no change after the seventh.)

If you think it strange that someone would believe that such an empirically inaccurate system could be the Truth, you must realize that Empiricism is a relatively recent criterion for Truth. An older criterion was that the Truth must be reasonable and in conformity with the perfect nature of God. Aristotle's system was much more "perfect" in that sense than Ptolemy's.

[15]The star was a supernova. This is something of a misnomer since *nova* means "new." Actually a supernova is an existing star that suddenly emits a huge outburst of light for some reason not known to astronomers, though it is known that at the time of outburst an outer layer of the star is ejected in the form of a shell of gas. A supernova flares up to hundreds of millions of times its former brightness, in contrast to an ordinary nova which only increases a paltry few tens of thousands of times. Three suspected supernova have been observed during the last ten centuries in our galaxy. They are: (1) the supernova of 1054 in Taurus (described in the *Chinese Annals*); (2) the "star" of 1572; and (3) the supernova of 1604 in Serpens, described by both Kepler and Galileo (Abell, 1964:441-444).

in daylight sometimes—and it shone throughout the whole of the year 1573, only disappearing early in 1574. If it was a new star it contradicted the old view that the sublime heavens knew neither change nor generation nor corruption, and people even reminded themselves that God had ceased the work of creation on the seventh day. . . .Now . . . men were meeting inconvenient facts which sooner or later they would have to stop denying.

In 1577 a new comet appeared, and Tycho Brahe, using the best astronomical instruments of the day, was able to show that it was beyond the sun, and that therefore its orbit must have passed through the solid crystal celestial spheres. . . . Brahe, conservative though he was in other respects, henceforward declared his disbelief in the reality of these orbs. . . .[16] Quite apart from any attack which Copernicus had made upon the system, the foundations of the (old) . . . universe were beginning to shake. (Butterfield, 1962:55—61)

The other two new discoveries were made by Galileo with the new telescope he had invented after hearing that ". . . a certain Fleming had constructed a spyglass by means of which visible objects, though very distant from the eye of the observer, were distinctly seen as if nearby" (Drake, 1957:29). He found first that "the surface of the moon was not smooth, uniform, and precisely spherical as a great number of philosophers believe it (and the other heavenly bodies) to be, but is uneven, rough, and full of cavities and prominences, being not unlike the face of the earth, relieved by chains of mountains and deep valleys." This completely contradicted the Aristotelian notion that the universe was made up of smooth, perfect shapes.

Galileo's second significant discovery was the existence of four moons which revolved *around Jupiter*. Here was proof that there were at least some heavenly bodies that did not revolve around the earth. With the publication of Galileo's results in 1610, the old concept of the universe was just about dead.[17]

I have said earlier that new data often bring theoretical advance in at least three circumstances, the first being the destruction of old and incorrect theories. The second circumstance is the creation of new theories. If new data killed the old universe, they helped create the new system which was to be the

---

[16]Tycho evidently thought that the head of the comet was a large, massive body similar to most of the other objects observable in the sky. Our current knowledge suggests that the largest particles in a "typical" comet are less than 50 miles across, which is submicroscopic by astronomical standards. If Tycho had our modern information he might have decided that celestial spheres were simply porous enough to allow the diffuse comet to pass through.

[17]There were some diehards. "One . . . , who admitted that the surface on the moon looked rugged, maintained that it was actually quite smooth and spherical as Aristotle has said, reconciling the two ideas by saying that the moon was covered with a smooth transparent material through which mountains and craters inside it could be discerned. Galileo, sarcastically applauding the ingenuity of this contribution, offered to accept it gladly—provided that his opponent would do him the equal courtesy of allowing him then to assert that the moon was even more rugged than he had thought before, its surface being covered with mountains and craters of this invisible substance ten times as high as any he had seen. At Pisa the leading philosopher had refused even to look through the telescope; when he died a few months afterward, Galileo expressed the hope that since he had neglected to look at the new celestial objects while on earth, he would now see them on his way to heaven" (Drake, 1957:73).

The new use of the telescope quickly led to the further discoveries of sunspots and the phases of Venus, which also helped destroy the old notion of the "perfect" universe.

replacement. In fact, Tycho Brahe's data, which were so consequential to the destruction, were even more important for the ensuing creation.

I'm sure that all of the readers of this essay are familiar with most of the scientists I have been, and will be, discussing—Copernicus, Galileo, Kepler and Newton, for example. But I suspect that relatively few of you know anything about Tycho Brahe, if you have indeed ever even heard of him. But Tycho had a crucial role in the development of modern science, and he certainly deserves a little more fame;[18] for the discovery of Kepler's famous three laws of planetary motion required astronomical observations of an accuracy which had only been achieved by Tycho in his observations of the motions of Mars.[19]

Arthur Koestler, in his biography of Kepler, has I think properly stated Tycho's significance: "Had Kepler not succeeded in getting hold of Tycho's treasure (i.e. his observations), he could never have discovered his planetary laws. Now, Newton was born only twelve years after Kepler's death, and he could not have arrived at his synthesis without the planetary laws. They could only be discovered with Tycho's help. . ."[20] (Koestler, 1960:80)

The work of Kepler and Galileo (and others) led in a straight line to Newton's three laws of motion, and his Law of Universal Gravitation which states that the attraction between any two bodies is inversely proportional to the square of the distance between them; these unified Kepler's planetary laws and Galileo's terrestrial dynamics. The publication date of Newton's *Principia*, 1687, must stand as the climax of the Scientific Revolution, if not the whole history of science.

The magnitude of Newton's genius cannot be denied. His most important contributions to astronomy, mechanics, optics, and mathematics were conceived by the time he was 24.[21] But his achievements would have been inconceivable had it not been for the preliminary work of Kepler and Galileo instigated by the new data.

I originally spoke of three circumstances in which new data are particularly significant for theoretical advance. The first and second were the destruction and creation of theories. The third circumstance is the *verification* of a new theory. In modern science, verification takes the form of a prediction based on the new

[18]Tycho's lack of fame may be due to his lack of a successful theory. That's not to say he didn't try. He was on the right track when he invented a scheme of the universe which also had the planets revolving around the sun. But he blew it when he set that whole system revolving around the earth.

[19]Kepler was trying to find some orbit for Mars which would fit Tycho's observations. Of course, he eventually realized that the proper orbital shape was an ellipse, and that is Kepler's First Law. But he made many wrong attempts on the way to that conclusion, and at one point he found a hypothesis which fit the observations to within eight minutes of arc, which was in that day practically negligible. But he discarded the hypothesis knowing that Tycho's data could not even have that much error. Kepler finally realized that the proper orbit was an ellipse and wrote, "Ah, what a foolish bird I have been."

[20]I have often thought that Tycho would have deserved to be famous even if his observations hadn't led to such monumental achievements. He is the only astronomer I have ever heard of who had a silver and gold nose. While a student, he fought a duel which is supposed to have originated in a dispute with his opponent over who was the better mathematician. During the fight, part of Tycho's nose was sliced off, presumably indicating that his opponent was the better mathematician. Thereafter he used an artificial silver and gold nosepiece.

[21]There is no documented basis to that apple business.

theory. The relevant datum is then observed, and if the prediction is correct then the theory is more acceptable—if it is incorrect, the theory is less acceptable. The circumstances around one of the observations which verified the Newtonian system are particularly interesting and will serve as an example. Realize, of course, that Newton's work was not completely accepted as soon as it was published. There were several difficulties with it, and the astronomer Clairaut was on the verge of modifying the mathematical form of the Law of Gravitation in order to account for some motions of the moon. Finally in 1749 he was able to solve his problem without this modification, but there were still reservations about the complete acceptability of Newtonian mechanics.

The story begins on March 13, 1781 when the great English astronomer William Herschel accidentally discovered Uranus.[22] He didn't know that the new object was a planet until some months later when enough observations had been obtained to calculate its orbit. As more observations were made, it became apparent that the planet did not quite follow its predicted course. The two most reasonable assumptions were: (1) there was another unknown planet which was perturbing the orbit of Uranus; and (2) Newton was wrong. There were people who were inclined toward each hypothesis.

John Couch Adams, a 22-year-old student at Cambridge, chose to assume the existence of the unknown planet, and he used the principles of Newtonian mechanics to solve the extremely difficult problem of calculating the orbit of this planet, based on its disturbing effects on Uranus.

Good telescopes were not a commonplace thing at that time, so Adams had to interest one of the few people with a satisfactory instrument in doing the actual sighting. In October, 1845, four years after he began the problem, he sent the Astronomer Royal, Sir George Airy, instructions as to where to look for the new planet. Today we know that Adams' prediction was correct to within two degrees. Unfortunately Airy seems to have reacted badly to having so young a theoretician tell him how to become the second discoverer of a new planet since ancient times, so he sent Adams a simple problem to test his ability. Adams did not bother to respond, and Airy let the whole matter drop.

In the meantime, a French mathematician named La Verrier, unaware of Adams' work, published the solution of the problem in June, 1846. Airy, noting that La Verrier's predicted position for the planet agreed to within one degree with Adams', posed the same test problem to La Verrier, who promptly returned the correct answer. Airy then suggested that Challis, director of the Cambridge Observatory, begin the search, but having no good star charts of the area, Challis proceeded in a rather imprecise way. Although he did actually see the planet, he did not recognize it.

In September, 1846, Le Verrier wrote to Johann Galle at the Berlin Observatory, giving him his predicted position for the trans-Uranian planet and asking him to look for it. Galle received the letter on September 23rd, and that night discovered Neptune, only 52 seconds of arc from Le Verrier's predicted position[23] (Abell, 1964:272–273).

[22]It later turned out that Uranus had been "discovered" on charts of the sky at least 20 different times since 1690 (Abell, 1964:270-271).
[23]A similar analysis of the residual perturbations of Uranus led to the discovery of Pluto in 1930.

This discovery solidly established Newton's gravitational theory—until the beginning of the twentieth century when new data dislodged it.

You may be thinking that for an essay on sociology, an extreme amount of space has been devoted to physical science.[24] My concern with physics and astronomy has been to demonstrate the extreme importance of new data for the development of profound theory. I would have preferred to use examples from sociology, but significant new data and profound theory are largely lacking, and this joint scarcity, of course, has been the major point of my essay.

In recent years an increasingly large proportion of sociologists has been concerned with empirical research in contrast to the more conjectural "armchair" approach. The results have been mixed. A good deal of the survey and experimental findings have bordered on the trivial, but at the same time some legitimately new material has been added to our information on social behavior. The contemporary world, with its highly mobile populations and rapidly developing societies, provides major study areas for new data, just as the rapidly changing Europe of 1848 provided a new data basis for Karl Marx' theories. Certainly new data are coming in, but much more are obviously needed.

The major question, of course, is: what sorts of new data should we look for?[25] Unfortunately I don't know, but I can't resist making a suggestion.

Assuming that any of a large number of areas could be empirically investigated to yield new data, and further assuming that we have no *a priori* knowledge about which of these areas will yield the most fruitful new data, then it seems reasonable to use some other criterion for selecting research areas—some criterion for which we *can* make an *a priori* judgment of worth—even though the worth may have nothing to do with theoretical advance. I suggest the criterion of social welfare.

Why not focus our empirical attention on social problems? These areas may or may not yield fruitful new data for theoretical advance. They are no more or less likely to do so than any other research areas. But they will at least be fruitful for the welfare of the society, and that alone is justification.

REFERENCES

Abell, George, *Exploration of the Universe*. New York: Holt, Rinehart and Winston, 1964.

Broom, Leonard, and Philip Selznick, *Sociology* (3rd ed.). New York: Harper and Row, 1963.

Butterfield, H., *The Origins of Modern Science*. New York: Macmillan, 1962.

Clagett, Marshall, *Greek Science in Antiquity*. New York: Crowell-Collier, 1963.

Crombie, A. C., *Medieval and Early Modern Science*, II. Garden City, New York: Doubleday, 1959.

Drake, Stillman, *Discoveries and Opinions of Galileo*. Garden City, New York: Doubleday, 1957.

[24]On the other hand, one might consider that for an essay on science, a lot of space has been devoted to sociology.

[25]It seems that topics for sociological research are usually selected for their "theoretical relevance"—whatever that is. That is epitomized in the selection of Ph.D. thesis topics.

Johnson, Harry, *Sociology: A Systematic Introduction.* New York: Harcourt, Brace & World, 1960.

Kirk, R., "Is social science scientific?" *New York Times* (June 25, 1961):Section 6, 16.

Koestler, Arthur, *The Watershed.* Garden City, New York: Doubleday, 1960.

THE BEARING OF EMPIRICAL RESEARCH UPON THE DEVELOPMENT OF SOCIAL THEORY

Robert K. Merton

History has a certain gift for outmoding stereotypes. This can be seen, for example, in the historical development of sociology. The stereotype of the social theorist high in the empyrean of pure ideas uncontaminated by mundane facts is fast becoming no less outmoded than the stereotype of the social researcher equipped with questionnaire and pencil and hot on the chase of the isolated and meaningless statistic. For in building the mansion of sociology during the last decades, theorist and empiricist have learned to work together. What is more, they have learned to talk to one another in the process. At times, this means only that a sociologist has learned to talk to himself since increasingly the same man has taken up both theory and research. Specialization and integration have developed hand in hand. All this has led not only to the realization that theory and empirical research *should* interact but to the result that they *do* interact.

As a consequence, there is decreasing need for accounts of the relations between theory and research to be wholly programmatic in character. A growing body of theoretically oriented research makes it progressively possible to discuss with profit the actual relations between the two. And, as we all know, there has been no scarcity of such discussions. Journals abound with them. They generally center on the role of theory in research, setting forth, often with admirable lucidity, the functions of theory in the initiation, design and prosecution of empirical inquiry. But since this is not a one-way relationship, since the two *inter*act, it may be useful to examine the other direction of the relationship: the role of empirical research in the development of social theory. That is the purpose of this paper.

Reprinted with permission of the author and the publisher, The American Sociological Association, from *The American Sociological Review*, Vol. 5 (1948), 505-15.

Paper read before the annual meeting of the American Sociological Society, Cleveland, Ohio, March 1-3, 1946. This may be identified as Publication No. A-89 of the Bureau of Applied Social Research, Columbia University. Manuscript received April 19, 1948.

THE THEORETIC FUNCTIONS OF RESEARCH

With a few conspicuous exceptions, recent sociological discussions have assigned but one major function to empirical research: "testing" or "verification" of hypotheses. The model for the proper way of performing this function is as familiar as it is clear. The investigator begins with a hunch or hypothesis, from this he draws various inferences and these, in turn, are subjected to empirical test which confirms or refutes the hypothesis.[1] But this is a logical model, and so fails, of course, to describe much of what actually occurs in fruitful investigation. It presents a set of logical norms, not a description of the research experience. And, as logicians are well aware, in purifying the experience, the logical model may also distort it. Like other such models, it abstracts from the temporal sequence of events. It exaggerates the creative role of explicit theory just as it minimizes the creative role of observation. For research is not merely logic tempered with observation. It has its psychological as well as its logical dimensions, although one would scarcely suspect this from the logically rigorous sequence in which research is usually reported.[2] It is both the psychological and logical pressures of research upon social theory which we seek to trace.

It is my central thesis that empirical research goes far beyond the passive role of verifying and testing theory: it does more than confirm or refute hypotheses. Research plays as active role: it performs at least four major functions which help shape the development of theory. It *initiates*, it *reformulates*, it *deflects* and *clarifies* theory.[3]

I. The Serendipity Pattern

(The unanticipated, anomalous and strategic datum exerts a pressure for initiating theory.)

Under certain conditions, a research finding gives rise to social theory. In a previous paper, this was all too briefly expressed as follows: "Fruitful empirical research not only tests theoretically derived hypotheses; it also originates new hypotheses. This might be termed the 'serendipity' component of research, *i.e.*, the discovery, by chance or sagacity, of valid results which were not sought for."[4]

[1] See, for example, the procedural review of Stouffer's "Theory of intervening opportunities" by G. A. Lundberg, "What are Sociological Problems?", *American Sociological Review*, VI (1941), 357-359.

[2] See R. K. Merton, "Science, Population and Society," *The Scientific Monthly*, XLIV (1937), 170-171; the apposite discussion by Jean Piaget, *Judgment and Reasoning in the Child*, London, 1929, Chaps. V, IX, and the comment by William H. George, *The Scientist in Action*, London, 1936, p. 153. "A piece of research does not progress in the way it is 'written up' for publication."

[3] The fourth function, clarification, will be elaborated in a complementary paper by Paul F. Lazarsfeld.

[4] R. K. Merton, "Sociological Theory," *American Journal of Sociology*, L (1945), 469n. Interestingly enough, the same outlandish term 'serendipity' which has had little currency since it was coined by Horace Walpole in 1754 has also been used to refer to this component of research by the physiologist Walter B. Cannon. See his *The Way of an Investigator*, New York: W. W. Norton, 1945, Chap. VI, in which he sets forth numerous instances of serendipity in several fields of science.

The serendipity pattern refers to the fairly common experience of observing an *unanticipated, anomalous and strategic* datum which becomes the occasion for developing a new theory or for extending an existing theory. Each of these elements of the pattern can be readily described. The datum is, first of all, unanticipated. A research directed toward the test of one hypothesis yields a fortuitous by-product, an unexpected observation which bears upon theories not in question when the research was begun.

Secondly, the observation is anomalous, surprising,[5] either because it seems inconsistent with prevailing theory or with other established facts. In either case, the seeming inconsistency provokes curiosity; it stimulates the investigator to "make sense of the datum," to fit it into a broader frame of knowledge. He explores further. He makes fresh observations. He draws inferences from the observations, inferences depending largely, of course, upon his general theoretic orientation. The more he is steeped in the data, the greater the likelihood that he will hit upon a fruitful direction of inquiry. In the fortunate circumstance that his new hunch proves justified, the anomalous datum leads ultimately to a new or extended theory. The curiosity stimulated by the anomalous datum is temporarily appeased.

And thirdly, in noting that the unexpected fact must be "strategic," *i.e.*, that it must permit of implications which bear upon generalized theory, we are, of course, referring rather to what the observer brings to the datum than to the datum itself. For it obviously requires a theoretically sensitized observer to detect the universal in the particular. After all, men had for centuries noticed such "trivial" occurrences as slips of the tongue, slips of the pen, typographical errors, and lapses of memory, but it required the theoretic sensitivity of a Freud to see these as strategic data through which he could extend his theory of repression and symptomatic acts.

The serendipity pattern, then, involves the unanticipated, anomalous and strategic datum which exerts pressure upon the investigator for a new direction of inquiry which extends theory. Instances of serendipity have occurred in many disciplines, but I should like to draw upon a current sociological research for illustration. In the course of our research into the social organization of Craftown,[6] a suburban housing community of some 700 families, largely of working class status, we observed that a large proportion of residents were affiliated with more civic, political and other voluntary organizations than had been the case in their previous places of residence. Quite incidentally, we noted further that this increase in group participation had occurred also among the parents of infants and young children. This finding was rather inconsistent with commonsense knowledge. For it is well known that, particularly on the lower economic levels, youngsters usually tie parents down and preclude their taking active part in organized group life outside the home. But Craftown parents themselves readily explained their behavior. "Oh, there's no real problem about

[5]Charles Sanders Peirce had long before noticed the strategic role of the "surprising fact" in his account of what he called "abduction," that is, the initiation and entertaining of a hypothesis as a step in inference. See his *Collected Papers*, Harvard University Press, 1931-35, VI, 522-528.
[6]Drawn from continuing studies in the Sociology and Social Psychology of Housing, under a grant from the Lavanburg Foundation.

getting out in the evenings," said one mother who belonged to several organizations. "It's easy to find teen-agers around here to take care of the kids. There are so many more teen-agers around here than where I used to live." The explanation appears adequate enough and would have quieted the investigator's curiosity, had it not been for one disturbing datum: like most new housing communities, Craftown actually has a very small proportion of adolescents—only 3.7%, for example, in the 15-19 year age group. What is more, the majority of the adults, 63%, are under 34 years of age, so that their children include an exceptionally large proportion of infants and youngsters. Thus, far from there being many adolescents to look after the younger children in Craftown, quite the contrary is true: the ratio of adolescents to children under ten years of age is 1:10, whereas in the communities of origin, the ratio hovers about 1:1.5.[7]

We were at once confronted, then, by an anomalous fact which was certainly no part of our original program of observation. This should be emphasized. We manifestly did not enter and indeed could not have entered upon the field research in Craftown with a hypothesis bearing an illusory belief in the abundance of teen-age supervisors of children. Here was an observation both unanticipated and anomalous. Was it also strategic? We did not prejudge its "intrinsic" importance. It seemed no more and no less trivial than Freud's observation during the last war (in which he had two sons at the front) that he had mis-read a newspaper headline, "Die *Feinde* vor Görz" (The *Enemy* before Görz), as "Der *Friede* von Görz" (The *Peace* of Görz). Freud took a trivial incident and converted it into a strategic fact. Unless the observed discrepancy between the subjective impressions of Craftown residents and the objective facts could undergo a somewhat similar transformation it had best be ignored, for it plainly had little "social significance."

What first made this illusion a peculiarly intriguing instance of a general theoretic problem was the difficulty of explaining it as merely the calculated handiwork of vested-interests engaged in spreading a contrary-to-fact belief. Generally, when the sociologist with a conceptual scheme stemming from utilitarian theory observes a patently untrue social belief, he will look for special groups in whose interest it is to invent and spread this belief. The cry of "propaganda!" is often mistaken for a theoretically sound analysis.[8] But this is clearly out of the question in the present instance: there are plainly no special-interest groups seeking to misrepresent the age-distribution of Craftown. What, then, was the source of this social illusion?

Various other theories suggested points of departure. There was Marx's postulate that it is men's "social existence which determines their conscious-

7Essentially the same discrepancies in age distribution between Craftown and communities of origin are found if we compare proportions of children under ten with those between 10 and 19. If we make children under five the basis for comparison, the disproportions are even more marked.

8To be sure, vested-interests often do spread untrue propaganda and this may reinforce mass illusions. But the vested-interest or priestly-lie theories of fallacious folk beliefs do not always constitute the most productive point of departure nor do they go far toward explaining the bases of acceptance or rejection of the beliefs. The present case in point, trivial though it is in any practical sense, is theoretically significant in showing anew the limitations of a utilitarian scheme of analysis.

ness." There was Durkheim's theorem that social images ("collective representa-tions") in some fashion reflect a social reality although "it does not follow that the reality which is its foundation conforms objectively to the idea which believers have of it." There was Sherif's thesis that "social factors" provide a framework for selective perceptions and judgments in relatively unstructured situations. There was the prevailing view in the sociology of knowledge that social location determines the perspectives entering into perception, beliefs and ideas. But suggestive as these general orientations[9] were, they did not directly suggest *which* features of "social existence," *which* aspects of the "social reality," *which* "social factors," *which* "social location" may have determined this seemingly fallacious belief.

The clue was inadvertently provided by further interviews with residents. In the words of an active participant in Craftown affairs, herself the mother of two children under six years of age:

> "My husband and I get out together much more. You see, there are more people around to mind the children. *You feel more confident about having some thirteen-or-fourteen-year-old in here when you know most of the people. If you're in a big city, you don't feel so easy about having someone who's almost a stranger come in.*"

This clearly suggests that the sociological roots of the "illusion" are to be found in the structure of community relations in which Craftown residents are enmeshed. The belief is an unwitting reflection, not of the statistical reality, but of the community cohesion. It is not that there are objectively more adolescents in Craftown, but more who are *intimately known* and who, therefore, *exist socially* for parents seeking aid in child supervision. Most Craftown residents having lately come from an urban setting now find themselves in a community in which proximity has developed into reciprocal intimacies. The illusion expresses the perspective of people for whom adolescents as potential child-care aides "exist" only if they are well-known and therefore merit confidence. In short, perception was a function of confidence and confidence, in turn, was a function of social cohesion.[10]

From the sociological viewpoint, then, this unanticipated finding fits into and extends the theory that "social perception" is the product of a social framework. It develops further the "psychology of social norms,"[11] for it is not

---

[9]For the differences between "theory" and "general orientations," see Merton, "Sociological theory," *op. cit.*, 464.
[10]Schedule data from the study provide corroborative evidence. In view of the exceptionally high proportion of young children, it is striking that 54 per cent of their parents affirm that it is "easier in Craftown to get people to look after our children when we want to go out" than it was in other places where they have lived; only 21 per cent say it is harder and the remaining 25 per cent feel there is no difference. Those who come from the larger urban communities are more likely to report greater ease in obtaining assistance in Craftown. Moreover, as we would expect from the hypothesis, those residents who are more closely geared in with Craftown, who identify themselves most fully with it, are more likely to believe it easier to find such aid; 61 per cent of these do so as against 50 per cent of those who identify with other communities, whereas only 12 per cent find it more difficult in comparison with 26 per cent of the latter group.
[11]Muzafer Sherif's book by this title should be cited as basic in the field, although it tends to have a somewhat limited conception of "social factors," *The Psychology of Social Norms*, New York, 1936.

merely an instance of individuals assimilating particular norms, judgments, and standards from other members of the community. The social perception is, rather, a by-product, a derivative, of the structure of human relations.

This is perhaps sufficient to illustrate the operation of the serendipity pattern: an unexpected and anomalous finding elicited the investigator's curiosity, and conducted him along an unpremeditated by-path which led to a fresh hypothesis.

2. The Recasting of Theory

(New data exert pressure for the elaboration of a conceptual scheme.)

But it is not only through the anomalous fact that empirical research invites the extension of theory. It does so also through the repeated observation of hitherto neglected facts. When an existing conceptual scheme commonly applied to a given subject-matter does not adequately take these facts into account, research presses insistently for its reformulation. It leads to the introduction of variables which have not been systematically included in the scheme of analysis. Here, be it noted, it is not that the data are anomalous or unexpected or incompatible with existing theory; it is merely that they have not been considered pertinent. Whereas the serendipity pattern centers in an apparent inconsistency which presses for resolution, the reformulation pattern centers in the hitherto neglected but relevant fact which presses for an extension of the conceptual scheme.

Examples of this in the history of social science are far from limited. Thus it was a series of fresh empirical facts which led Malinowski to incorporate new elements into a theory of magic. It was his Trobrianders, of course, who gave him the clue to the distinctive feature of his theory. When these islanders fished in the inner lagoon by the reliable method of poisoning, an abundant catch was assured and danger was absent. Neither uncertainty nor uncontrollable hazards were involved. And here, Malinowski noted, magic was not practiced. But in the open-sea fishing, with the uncertain yield and its often grave dangers, the rituals of magic flourished. Stemming from these pregnant observations was his theory that magical belief arises to bridge the uncertainties in man's practical pursuits, to fortify confidence, to reduce anxieties, to open up avenues of escape from the seeming impasse. Magic was construed as a supplementary technique for reaching practical objectives. It was these empirical facts which suggested the incorporation of new dimensions into earlier theories of magic—particularly the relations of magic to the fortuitous, the dangerous and the uncontrollable. It was not that these facts were *inconsistent* with previous theories; it was simply that these conceptual schemes had not taken them adequately into account. Nor was Malinowski testing a preconceived hypothesis—he was developing an enlarged and improved theory on the basis of suggestive empirical data.

For another example of this pressure of empirical data for the recasting of a specific theory we turn closer home. The investigation dealt with a single dramatic instance of mass persuasion: broadcasting at repeated intervals over a span of eighteen hours, Kate Smith, a radio star, sold large quantities of war-bonds in the course of the day. It is not my intention to report fully on the dynamics of this case of mass persuasion;[12] for present purposes, we are

---

[12] R. K. Merton, M. Fiske and A. Curtis, *Mass Persuasion*, New York: Harper, 1946.

concerned only with the implications of two facts which emerged from the study.

First of all, in the course of intensive interviews many of our informants–New Yorkers who had pledged a bond to Smith–expressed a thorough disenchantment with the world of advertising, commercials and propaganda. They felt themselves the object of manipulation–and resented it. They objected to being the target for advertising which cajoles, insists and terrorizes. They objected to being engulfed in waves of propaganda proposing opinions and actions not in their own best interests. They expressed dismay over what is in effect a pattern of *pseudo-Gemeinschaft*–subtle methods of salesmanship in which there is the feigning of personal concern with the client in order to manipulate him the better. As one small businessman phrased it, "In my own business, I can see how a lot of people in their business deals will make some kind of gesture of friendliness, sincerity and so forth, most of which is phony." Drawn from a highly competitive, segmented metropolitan society, our informants were describing a climate of reciprocal distrust, of *anomie*, in which common values have been submerged in the welter of private interests. Society was experienced as an arena for rival frauds. There was small belief in the disinterestedness of conduct.

In contrast to all this was the second fact: we found that the persuasiveness of the Smith bond-drive among these same informants largely rested upon their firm belief in the integrity and sincerity of Smith. And much the same was found to be true in a polling interview with a larger cross-section sample of almost a thousand New Yorkers. Fully 80% asserted that in her all-day marathon drives, Smith was *exclusively* concerned with promoting the sale of war bonds, whereas only 17% felt that she was *also* interested in publicity for herself, and a negligible 3% believed she was *primarily* concerned with the resulting publicity.

This emphasis on her sincerity is all the more striking as a problem for research in the molding of reputations because she herself appeared on at least six commercially sponsored radio programs each week. But although she was engaged in apparently the same promotional activities as others, she was viewed by the majority of our informants as the direct antithesis of all that these other announcers and stars represent. In the words of one devotee, "She's sincere and *she really means anything* she ever says. It isn't just sittin' up there and talkin' and gettin' paid for it. She's different from what other people are."

Why this overwhelming belief in Smith's sincerity? To be sure, the same society which produces a sense of alienation and estrangement generates in many a craving for reassurance, an acute will to believe, a flight into faith. But why does Smith become the object of this faith for so many otherwise distrustful people? Why is she seen as genuine by those who seek redemption from the spurious? Why are her motives believed to rise above avarice, and ambition and pride of class? What are the social-psychological sources of this image of Smith as sincerity incarnate?

Among the several sources, we wish to examine here the one which bears most directly upon a theory of mass persuasion. The clue is provided by the fact that a larger proportion of those who heard the Smith marathon war-bond drive are convinced of her disinterested patriotism than of those who did not. This appears to indicate that the marathon bond-drive enhanced public belief in her sincerity. But we must recognize the possibility that her devoted fans, for whom her sincerity was unquestioned, would be more likely to have heard the marathon broadcasts. Therefore, to determine whether the marathon did in fact extend this belief, we must compare regular listeners to her programs with those who are not her fans. Within each group, a significantly larger proportion of people who heard the marathon are convinced of Smith's exclusive concern with patriotic purpose. This is as true for her devoted fans as for those who did not listen to her regular programs at all. In other words, we have caught for a moment, as with a candid camera, a snapshot of Smith's reputation of sincerity in the process of being even further enhanced. We have frozen in mid-course the process of building a reputation.

But if the marathon increased the belief in Smith's sincerity, how did this come about? It is at this point that our intensive interviews, with their often ingenuous and revealing details, permit us to interpret the statistical results of the poll. The marathon had all the atmosphere of determined, resolute endeavor under tremendous difficulties. Some could detect signs of strain—and courageous persistence. "Her voice was not quite so strong later, but she stuck it out like a good soldier," says a discerning housewife. Others projected themselves into the vividly imagined situation of fatigue and brave exertion. Solicitous reports by her coadjutor, Ted Collins, reinforced the empathic concern for the strain to which Smith was subjecting herself. "I felt, I can't stand this any longer," recalls one informant. "Mr. Collins' statement about her being exhausted affected me so much that I just couldn't bear it." The marathon took on the attributes of a sacrificial ritual.

In short, it was not so much what Smith *said* as what she *did* which served to validate her sincerity. It was the presumed stress and strain of an eighteen-hour series of broadcasts, it was the deed not the word which furnished the indubitable proof. Listeners might question whether she were not unduly dramatizing herself, but they could not escape the incontrovertible evidence that she was devoting the entire day to the task. Appraising the direct testimony of Smith's behavior, another informant explains that "she was on all day and the others weren't. So it seemed that she was sacrificing more and was more sincere." Viewed as a process of persuasion, the marathon converted initial feelings of scepticism and distrust among listeners into at first a reluctant, and later, a full-fledged acceptance of Smith's integrity. The successive broadcasts served as a fulfillment in action of a promise in words. The words were reinforced by things she had actually done. The currency of talk was accepted because it was backed by the gold of conduct. The gold reserve, moreover, need not even approximate the amount of currency it can support.

This empirical study suggests that propaganda-of-the-deed may be effective among the very people who are distrustful of propaganda-of-the-word. Where there is social disorganization, *anomie*, conflicting values, we find propaganditis reaching epidemic proportions. Any statement of value is likely to be discounted as "mere propaganda." Exhortations are suspect. But the propaganda of the deed elicits more confidence. Members of the audience are largely permitted to draw their conclusions from the action—they are less likely to feel manipulated. When the propagandist's deed and his words symbolically coincide, it stimulates belief in his sincerity. Further research must determine whether this propaganda pattern is significantly more effective in societies suffering from *anomie* than in those which are more fully integrated. But not unlike the Malinowski case-in-point, this may illustrate the role of research in suggesting new variables to be incorporated into a specific theory.

3. The Re-Focussing of Theoretic Interest

(New methods of empirical research exert pressure for new foci of theoretic interest.)

To this point we have considered the impact of research upon the development of particular theories. But empirical research also affects more general trends in the development of theory. This occurs chiefly through the invention of research procedures which tend to shift the foci of theoretic interest to the growing points of research.

The reasons for this are on the whole evident. After all, sound theory thrives only on a rich diet of pertinent facts and newly invented procedures help provide the ingredients of this diet. The new, and often previously unavailable, data stimulate fresh hypotheses. Moreover, theorists find that their hypotheses can be put to immediate test in those spheres where appropriate research techniques have been designed. It is no longer necessary for them to wait upon data as they happen to turn up—researches directed to the verification of hypotheses can be instituted at once. The flow of relevant data thus increases the tempo of advance in certain spheres of theory whereas in others, theory stagnates for want of adequate observations. Attention shifts accordingly.

In noting that new centers of theoretic interest have followed upon the invention of research procedures, we do not imply that these alone played a decisive role.[13] The growing interest in the theory of propaganda as an instrument of social control, for example, is in large part a response to the changing historical situation, with its conflict of major idealogical systems; new technologies of mass communication which have opened up new avenues for propaganda; and the rich research treasuries provided by business and government interested in this new weapon of war, both declared and undeclared. But this shift is also a by-product of accumulated facts made available through such newly developed, and confessedly crude, procedures as content-analysis, the panel technique and the focussed interview.

Examples of this impact in the recent history of social theory are numerous but we have time to mention only a few. Thus, the increasing concern with the theory of character and personality formation in relation to social structure became marked after the introduction of new projective methods; the Rorschach test, the thematic apperception test, play techniques and story completions being among the most familiar. So, too, the sociometric techniques of Moreno and others, and fresh advances in the technique of the "passive interview" have revived interest in the theory of interpersonal relations. Stemming from such techniques as well is the trend toward what might be called the "rediscovery of

[13]It is perhaps needless to add that these procedures, instruments and apparatus are in turn dependent upon prior theory. But this does not alter their stimulating effect upon the further development of theory. *Cf*. Merton, "Sociological Theory," 463n.

the primary group," particularly in the shape of theoretic concern with informal social structures as mediating between the individual and large formal organizations. This interest has found expression in an entire literature on the role and structure of the informal group, for example, in factory social systems, bureaucracy and political organizations. Similarly, we may anticipate that the recent introduction of the panel technique—the repeated interviewing of the same group of informants—will in due course more sharply focus the attention of social psychologists upon the theory of attitude formation, decisions among alternative choices, factors in political participation and determinants of behavior in cases of conflicting role demands, to mention a few types of problems to which this technique is especially adapted.

Perhaps the most direct impact of research procedures upon theory has resulted from the *creation* of sociological statistics organized in terms of theoretically pertinent categories. Talcott Parsons has observed that numerical data are scientifically important only when they can be fitted into analytical categories and that "a great deal of current research is producing facts in a form which cannot be utilized by any current generalized analytical scheme."[14] These well-deserved strictures of a scant decade ago are proving progressively less applicable. In the past, the sociologist has largely had to deal with *pre-collected series* of statistics usually assembled for non-sociological purposes and, therefore, not set forth in categories directly pertinent to any given theoretical system. As a result, at least so far as quantitative facts are concerned, the theorist was compelled to work with makeshift data bearing only a tangential relevance to his problems. This not only left a wide margin for error—consider the crude indices of social cohesion upon which Durkheim had to rely—but it also meant that theory had to wait upon the incidental and, at times, almost accidental availability of relevant data. It could not march rapidly ahead. This picture has now begun to change.

No longer does the theorist depend almost exclusively upon the consensus of administrative boards or social welfare agencies for his quantitative data. Tarde's programmatic sketch[15] a half century ago of the need for statistics in social psychology, particularly those dealing with attitudes, opinions and sentiments, has become a half-fulfilled promise. So, too, investigators of community organization are creating statistics on class structure, associational behavior, and clique formations, and this has left its mark on theoretic interests. Ethnic studies are beginning to provide quantitative data which are re-orienting the theorist. It is safe to suppose that the enormous accumulation of sociological materials during the war—notably by the Research Branch of the Information and Education Division of the War Department—materials which are in part the result of new research techniques, will intensify interest in the theory of group morale, propaganda and leadership. But it is perhaps needless to multiply examples.

What we have said does not mean that the piling up of statistics of itself

[14]Talcott Parsons, "The Role of Theory in Social Research," *American Sociological Review*, III (1938), 19; *cf.* his *Structure of Social Action*, New York, 1937, pp. 328-329n. "... in the social field most available statistical information is on a level which cannot be made to fit directly into the categories of analytical theory."
[15]Gabriel Tarde, *Essais et mélanges sociologiques*, Paris, 1895, pp. 230-270.

advances theory; it does mean that theoretic interest tends to shift to those areas in which there is an abundance of *pertinent* statistical data. Moreover, we are merely calling attention to this shift of focus, not evaluating it. It may very well be that it sometimes deflects attention to problems which, in a theoretic or humanistic sense, are "unimportant"; it may divert attention from problems with larger implications onto those for which there is the promise of immediate solutions. Failing a detailed study, it is difficult to come to any overall assessment of this point. But the pattern itself seems clear enough in sociology as in other disciplines: as new and previously unobtainable data become available through the use of new techniques, theorists turn their analytical eye upon the implications of these data and bring about new directions of inquiry.

4. The Clarification of Concepts

(Empirical research exerts pressure for clear concepts.)

A good part of the work called "theorizing" is taken up with the clarification of concepts— and rightly so. It is in this matter of clearly defined concepts that social science research is not infrequently defective. Research activated by a major interest in methodology may be centered on the *design* of establishing causal relations without due regard for analyzing the variables involved in the inquiry. This methodological empiricism, as the design of inquiry without correlative concern with the clarification of substantive variables may be called, characterizes a large part of current research. Thus, in a series of effectively designed experiments, Chapin finds that "the rehousing of slum families in a public housing project results in improvement of the living conditions and the social life of these families."[16] Or through controlled experiments, psychologists search out the effects of foster home placement upon children's performances in intelligence tests.[17] Or, again through experimental inquiry, researchers seek to determine whether a propaganda film has achieved its purpose of improving attitudes toward the British. These several cases, and they are representative of a large amount of research which has advanced social science method, have in common the fact that the empirical variables are not analyzed in terms of their conceptual elements.[18] As Rebecca West, with her characteristic lucidity, put this general problem of methodological empiricism, one might "know that A and B and C were linked by certain causal connexions, but he would never apprehend with any exactitude the nature of A or B or C." In consequence, these researches further the procedures of inquiry, but their findings do not enter into the repository of cumulative social science theory.

But in general, the clarification of concepts, commonly considered a province

[16]F. S. Chapin, "The effects of slum clearance and rehousing on family and community relationships in Minneapolis," *American Journal of Sociology*, XLIII (1938), 744-763.

[17]R. R. Sears, "Child Psychology," in Wayne Dennis, ed., *Current Trends in Psychology*, University of Pittsburgh Press, 1947, pp. 55-56. Sears' comments on this type of research state the general problem admirably.

[18]However crude they may be, procedures such as the focused interview are expressly designed as aids for detecting possibly relevant variables in an initially undifferentiated situation. See R. K. Merton and P. L. Kendall, "The Focused Interview," *American Journal of Sociology*, LI (1946), 541-57.

peculiar to the theorist, is a frequent result of empirical research. Research sensitive to its own needs cannot avoid this pressure for conceptual clarification. *For a basic requirement of research is that the concepts, the variables, be defined with sufficient clarity to enable the research to proceed*, a requirement easily and unwittingly not met in the kind of discursive exposition which is often miscalled "sociological theory."

The clarification of concepts ordinarily enters into empirical research in the shape of establishing *indices* of the variables under consideration. In non-research speculations, it is possible to talk loosely about "morale" or "social cohesion" without any clear conceptions of what is entailed by these terms, but they *must* be clarified if the researcher is to go about his business of systematically observing instances of low and high morale, of social cohesion or cleavage. If he is not to be blocked at the outset, he must devise indices which are observable, fairly precise and meticulously clear. The entire movement of thought which was christened "operationalism" is only one conspicuous case of the researcher demanding that concepts be defined clearly enough for him to go to work.

This has been typically recognized by those sociologists who combine a theoretic orientation with systematic empirical research. Durkheim, for example, despite the fact that his terminology and indices now appear crude and debatable, clearly perceived the need for devising indices of his concepts. Repeatedly, he asserted that "it is necessary ... to substitute for the internal fact which escapes us an external fact that symbolizes it and to study the former through the latter."[19] The index, or sign of the conceptualized item, stands ideally in a one-to-one correlation with what it signifies (and the difficulty of establishing this relation is of course one of the critical problems of research). Since the index and its object are so related, one may ask for the grounds on which one is taken as the index and the other as the indexed variable. As Durkheim implied and as Suzanne Langer has indicated anew, the index is that one of the correlated pair which is perceptible and the other, harder or impossible to perceive, is theoretically relevant.[20] Thus, attitude scales make available indices of otherwise not discriminable attitudes, just as ecological statistics represent indices of diverse social structures in a given area.

What often appears as a tendency in research for quantification (through the development of scales) can thus be seen as a special case of attempting to clarify concepts sufficiently to permit the conduct of empirical investigation. The development of valid and observable indices becomes central to the use of concepts in the prosecution of research. A final illustration will indicate how research presses for the clarification of ancient sociological concepts which, on the plane of discursive exposition, have remained ill-defined and unclarified.

A conception basic to sociology holds that individuals have multiple social

---

[19] Émile Durkheim, *Division of Labor in Society*, New York: Macmillan, 1933, p. 66; also his *Les règles de la méthode sociologique*, Paris, 1895, pp. 55-58; *Le Suicide*, Paris, 1930, pp. 356 and *passim*. *Cf.* R. K. Merton, "Durkheim's Division of Labor in Society," *American Journal of Sociology*, XL, 1934, esp. 326-7 which touches on the problem of indices.

[20] Suzanne K. Langer, *Philosophy in a New Key*, New York, Penguin Books, 1948, pp. 46-47.

roles and tend to organize their behavior in terms of the structurally defined expectations assigned to each role. Further, it is said, the less integrated the society, the more often will individuals be subject to the strain of incompatible social roles. Type-cases are numerous and familiar: the Catholic Communist subjected to conflicting pressures from party and church, the marginal man suffering the pulls of conflicting societies, the professional woman torn between the demands of family and career. Every sociological textbook abounds with illustrations of incompatible demands made of the multiselved person.

Perhaps because it has been largely confined to discursive interpretations and has seldom been made the focus of systematic research, this central problem of conflicting roles has yet to be materially clarified and advanced beyond the point reached decades ago. Thomas and Znaniecki long since indicated that conflicts between social roles *can* be reduced by conventionalization and by role-segmentation (by assigning each set of role-demands to different situations).[21] And others have noted that frequent conflict between roles is dysfunctional for the society as well as for the individual. But all this leaves many salient problems untouched: on which grounds does one predict the behavior of persons subject to conflicting roles? And when a decision must be made, which role (or which group solidarity) takes precedence? Under which conditions does one or another prove controlling? On the plane of discursive thought, it has been suggested that the role with which the individual identifies most fully will prove dominant, thus banishing the problem through a tautological pseudo-solution. Or, the problem of seeking to predict behavior consequent to incompatibility of roles, a research problem requiring operational clarification of the concepts of solidarity, conflict, role-demands and situation, has been evaded by observing that conflicts of roles typically ensue in frustration.

More recently, empirical research has pressed for clarification of the key concepts involved in this problem. Indices of conflicting group pressures have been devised and the resultant behavior observed in specified situations. Thus, as a beginning in this direction, it has been shown that in a concrete decision-situation, such as voting, individuals subject to these cross-pressures respond by delaying their vote-decision. And, under conditions yet to be determined, they seek to reduce the conflict by escaping from the field of conflict: they "lose interest" in the political campaign. Finally, there is the intimation in these data that in cases of cross-pressures upon the voter, it is socio-economic position which is typically controlling.[22]

However this may be, the essential point is that, in this instance as in others, the very requirements of empirical research have been instrumental in clarifying received concepts. The process of empirical inquiry raises conceptual issues which may long go undetected in theoretic inquiry.

There remain, then, a few concluding remarks. My discussion has been devoted exclusively to four impacts of research upon the development of social theory: the initiation, reformulation, refocusing and clarification of theory. Doubtless

[21]W. I. Thomas and F. Znaniecki, *The Polish Peasant*, New York: Knopf, 1927, pp. 1866-70, 1888, 1899 ff.
[22]P. F. Lazarsfeld, Bernard Berelson and Hazel Gaudet, *The People's Choice*, New York: Duell, Sloan & Pearce, 1944, Chapter VI.

there are others. Doubtless, too, the emphasis of this paper lends itself to misunderstanding. It may be inferred that some invidious distinction has been drawn at the expense of theory and the theorist. That has not been my intention. I have suggested only than an explicitly formulated theory does not invariably precede empirical inquiry, that as a matter of plain fact the theorist is not inevitably the lamp lighting the way to new observations. The sequence is often reversed. Nor is it enough to say that research and theory must be married if sociology is to bear legitimate fruit. They must not only exchange solemn vows—they must know how to carry on from there. Their reciprocal roles must be clearly defined. This paper is a brief essay toward that definition.

THE CASE OF THE FLOPPY-EARED RABBITS: AN INSTANCE OF SERENDIPITY GAINED AND SERENDIPITY LOST

Bernard Barber and Renee C. Fox

As with so many other basic social processes, the actual process of scientific research and discovery is not well understood.[1] There has been little systematic observation of the research and discovery process as it actually occurs, and even less controlled research. Moreover, the form in which discoveries are reported by scientists to their colleagues in professional journals tends to conceal important aspects of this process. Because of certain norms that are strongly institutionalized in their professional community, scientists are expected to focus their reports on the logical structure of the methods used and the ideas discovered in research in relation to the established conceptual framework of the relevant scientific specialty. The primary function of such reports is conceived to be that of indicating how the new observations and ideas being advanced may require a change—by further generalization or systematization—in the conceptual structure of a given scientific field. All else that has occurred in the actual research process is considered "incidental." Thus scientists are praised for presenting their research in a way that is elegantly bare of anything that does not serve this primary function and are deterred from reporting "irrelevant" social and psychological aspects of the research process, however interesting these matters may be in other contexts. As a result of such norms and practices, the reporting of scientific research may be characterized by what has been called "retrospective falsification." By selecting only those components of the actual

Reprinted with permission of the authors and the publisher, The University of Chicago Press, from *The American Journal of Sociology*, Vol. 54 (1958), 128-36.

[1] For an account of what is known see Bernard Barber, *Science and the Social Order* (Glencoe, Ill.: Free Press, 1952), chap. ix, "The Social Process of Invention and Discovery," pp. 191-206.

research process that serve their primary purpose, scientific papers leave out a great deal, of course, as many scientists have indicated in their memoirs and in their informal talks with one another. Selection, then, unwittingly distorts and, in that special sense, falsifies what has happened in research as it actually goes on in the laboratory and its environs.

Public reports to the community of scientists thus have their own function. Their dysfunctionality for the sociology of scientific discovery, which is concerned with not one but all the components of the research process as a social process, is of no immediate concern to the practicing research scientist. And yet what is lost in "retrospective falsification" may be of no small importance to him, if only indirectly. For it is not unlikely that here, as every where else in the world of nature, knowledge is power, in this case power to increase the fruitfulness of scientific research by enlarging our systematic knowledge of it. The sociology of scientific discovery would seem to be an especially desirable area for further theoretical and empirical development.

One component of the actual process of scientific discovery that is left out or concealed in research reports following the practice of "retrospective falsification" is the element of unforeseen development, or happy or lucky chance, of what Robert K. Merton has called "the serendipity pattern."[2] By its very nature, scientific research is a voyage into the unknown by routes that are in some measure unpredictable and unplannable. Chance or luck is therefore as inevitable in scientific research as are logic and what Pasteur called "the prepared mind." Yet little is known systematically about this inevitable serendipity component.

For this reason it seemed to us desirable to take the opportunity recently provided by the reporting of an instance of *serendipity gained* by Dr. Lewis Thomas, now professor and chairman of the Department of Medicine in the College of Medicine of New York University and formerly professor and chairman of the Department of Pathology.[3] Then, shortly after hearing about Dr. Thomas' discovery, we learned from medical research and teaching colleagues of an instance of *serendipity lost* on the very same kind of chance occurence: unexpected floppiness in rabbits' ears after they had been injected intravenously with the proteolytic enzyme papain. This instance of serendipity lost had occurred in the course of research by Dr. Aaron Kellner, associate professor in the Department of Pathology of Cornell University Medical College and director of its central laboratories. This opportunity for *comparative* study seemed even more promising for our further understanding of the serendipity pattern. Here were two comparable medical scientists, we reasoned, both carrying out investigations in the field of experimental pathology, affiliated with

[2] For discussions of serendipity see Walter B. Cannon, *The Way of an Investigator* (New York: W. W. Norton & Co., 1945), chap. vi, "Gains from Serendipity," pp. 68-78; and Robert K. Merton, *Social Theory and Social Structure* (rev. ed.; Glencoe, Ill.: Free Press, 1957), pp. 103-8. Our colleagues, Robert K. Merton and Elinor G. Barber, are now engaged in an investigation and clarification of the variety of meanings of "chance" that are lumped under the notion of serendipity by different users of that term.

[3] Lewis Thomas, "Reversible Collapse of Rabbit Ears after Intravenous Papain, and Prevention of Recovery by Cortisone," *Journal of Experimental Medicine*, CIV (1956), 245-52. This case first came to our attention through a report in the *New York Times*. The pictures printed in Dr. Thomas' original article and in the *Times* will indicate why we have called this "the case of the floppy-eared rabbits."

distinguished medical schools, and of approximately the same level of demonstrated research ability (so far as it was in our layman's capacity to judge). In the course of their research both men had had occasion to inject rabbits intravenously with papain, and both had observed the phenomenon of ear collapse following the injection.

In spite of these similarities in their professional backgrounds and although they had both accidentally encountered the same phenomenon, one of these scientists had gone on to make a discovery based on this chance occurrence, whereas the other had not. It seemed to us that a detailed comparison of Dr. Thomas' and Dr. Kellner's experiences with the floppy-eared rabbits offered a quasi-experimental opportunity to identify some of the factors that contribute to a positive experience with serendipity in research and some of the factors conducive to a negative experience with it.

We asked for and were generously granted intensive interviews with Dr. Thomas and Dr. Kellner.[4] Each reported to us that they had experienced both "positive serendipity" and "negative serendipity" in their research. That is, each had made a number of serendipitous discoveries based on chance occurrences in their planned experiments, and on other occasions each had missed the significance of like occurences that other researchers had later transformed into discoveries. Apparently, both positive and negative serendipity are common experiences for scientific researchers. Indeed, we shall see that one of the chief reasons why Dr. Kellner experienced serendipity lost with respect to the discovery that Dr. Thomas made was that he was experiencing serendipity gained with respect to some other aspects of the very same experimental situation. Conversely, Dr. Thomas had reached a stalemate on some of his other research, and this gave him added incentive to pursue intensively the phenomenon of ear collapse. Partly as a consequence of these experiences, in what were similar experimental situations, the two researchers each saw something and missed something else.

On the basis of our focused interviews with these two scientists, we can describe some of the recurring elements in their experiences with serendipity.[5] We think that these patterns may also be relevant to instances of serendipity experienced by other investigators.

SERENDIPITY GAINED

Dr. Thomas.—Observing the established norms for reporting scientific research, in his article in the *Journal of Experimental Medicine,* Dr. Thomas did not mention his experience with serendipity. In the manner typical of such reports he began his article with the statement, "For reasons not relevant to the present discussion rabbits were injected intravenously with a solution of crude papain." (By contrast, though not called by this term, serendipity was featured in the accounts of this research that appeared in the *New York Times* and the *New*

---

[4]These interviews lasted about two hours each. They are another instance of the "tandem interviewing" described by Harry V. Kincaid and Margaret Bright, "Interviewing the Business Elite," *American Journal of Sociology*, LXIII (1957), 304-11.

[5]In this paper we shall concentrate on the instances of serendipity gained by Dr. Thomas and lost by Dr. Kellner and give somewhat less attention to elements of negative serendipity in Dr. Thomas' experiments and elements of positive serendipity in those of Dr. Kellner.

York Herald Tribune. "An accidental sidelight of one research project had the startling effect of wilting the ears of the rabbit," said the *Times* article. "This bizarre phenomenon, accidentally discovered . . ." was the way the *Herald Tribune* described the same phenomenon. The prominence accorded the "accidental" nature of the discovery in the press is related to the fact that these articles were written by journalists for a lay audience. The kind of interest in scientific research that is characteristic of science reporters and the audience for whom they write and their conceptions of the form in which information about research ought to be communicated differ from those of professional scientists).[6]

Although Dr. Thomas did not mention serendipity in his article for the *Journal of Experimental Medicine,* in his interview he reported both his general acquaintance with the serendipity pattern ("Serendipity is a familiar term. . . . I first heard about it in Dr. Cannon's class . . .") and his awareness of the chance occurrence of floppy-eared rabbits in his own research. Dr. Thomas first noticed the reversible collapse of rabbit ears after intravenous papain about several years ago, when he was working on the effects of proteolytic enzymes as a class:

> I was trying to explore the notion that the cardiac and blood vessel lesions in certain hypersensitivity states may be due to release of proteolytic enzymes. It's an attractive idea on which there's little evidence. And it's been picked up at some time or another by almost everyone working on hypersensitivity. For the investigation I used trypsin, because it was the most available enzyme around the laboratory and I got nothing. We also happened to have papain; I don't know where it had come from but because it was there, I tried it. I also tried a third enzyme, ficin. It comes from figs, and it's commonly used. It has catholic tastes and so it's quite useful in the laboratory. So I had these three enzymes. The other two didn't produce lesions. Nor did papain. But what the papain did was always produce these bizarre cosmetic changes. . . . It was one of the most uniform reactions I'd ever seen in biology. It always happened. And it looked as if something important must have happened to cause this reaction.

Some of the elements of serendipitous discovery are clearly illustrated in this account by Dr. Thomas. The scientific researcher, while in pursuit of some other specific goals, accidentally ("we also happened to have papain . . .") produces an unusual, recurrent, and sometimes striking ("bizarre") effect. Only the element of creative imagination, which is necessary to complete an instance of serendipity by supplying an explanation of the unusual effect, is not yet present. Indeed, the explanation was to elude Dr. Thomas, as it eluded Dr. Kellner, and probably others as well, for several years. This was not for lack of trying by Dr. Thomas. He immediately did seek an explanation:

[6]Further discussion of this point lies beyond the scope of this paper. But in a society like ours, in which science has become "front-page news," some of the characteristics and special problems of science reporting merit serious study. A recently published work on this topic that has come to our attention is entitled *When Doctors Meet Reporters* (New York: New York University Press, 1957). This is a discussion by science writers and physicians of the controversy between the press and the medical profession, compiled from the record of a series of conferences sponsored by the Josiah Macy Jr., Foundation.

I chased it like crazy. But I didn't do the right thing. . . . I did the expected things. I had sections cut, and I had them stained by all the techniques available at the time. And I studied what I believed to be the constituents of a rabbit's ear. I looked at all the sections, but I couldn't see anything the matter. The connective tissue was intact. There was no change in the amount of elastic tissue. There was no inflammation, no tissue damage. I expected to find a great deal, because I though we had destroyed something.

Dr Thomas, also studied the cartilage of the rabbit's ear, and judged it to be "normal" (". . . The cells were healthy-looking and there were nice nuclei. I decided there was no damage to the cartilage. And that was that . . ."). However, he admitted that at the time his consideration of the cartilage was routine and relatively casual, because he did not seriously entertain the idea that the phenomenon of ear collapse might be associated with changes in this tissue:

I hadn't thought of cartilage. You're not likely to, because it's not considered interesting. . . . I know my own idea has always been that cartilage is a quiet, inactive tissue.

Dr. Thomas' preconceptions about the methods appropriate for studying the ear-collapsing effect of papain, his expectation that it would probably be associated with damage in the connective or elastic tissues, and the conviction he shared with colleagues that cartilage is "inert and relatively uninteresting"—these guided his initial inquiries into this phenomenon. But the same preconceptions, expectations, and convictions also blinded him to the physical and chemical changes in the ear cartilage matrix which, a number of years later, were to seem "obvious" to him as the alterations underlying the collapsing ears. Here again, another general aspect of the research process comes into the clear. Because the methods and assumptions on which a systematic investigation is built selectively focus the researcher's attention, to a certain extent they sometimes constrict his imagination and bias his observations.

Although he was "very chagrined" about his failure, Dr. Thomas finally had to turn away from his floppy-eared rabbits because he was "terribly busy working on another problem at the time," with which he was "making progress." Also Dr. Thomas reported, "I had already used all the rabbits I could afford. So I was able to persuade myself to abandon this other research." The gratifications of research success elsewhere and the lack of adequate resources to continue with his rabbit experiments combined to make Dr. Thomas accept failure, at least temporarily. As is usually the case in the reporting of scientific research, these experiments and their negative outcome were not written up for professional journals. (There is too much failure of this sort in research to permit of its publication except occasionally, even though it might be instructive for some other scientists in carrying out their research. Since there is no way of determining what might be instructive failures and since space in professional journals is at a premium, generally only accounts of successful experiments are submitted to such journals and published by them.)

Despite his decision to turn his attention to other, more productive research, Dr. Thomas did not completely forget the floppy-eared rabbits. His interest was kept alive by a number of things. As he explained, the collapse of the rabbit ears and their subsequent reversal "was one of the most uniform reactions I'd ever seen in biology." The "unfailing regularity" with which it occurred is not often observed in scientific research. Thus the apparent invariance of this phenomenon never ceased to intrigue Dr. Thomas, who continued to feel that an important and powerful biological happening might be responsible. The effect of papain on rabbit ears had two additional qualities that helped to sustain Dr. Thomas' interest in it. The spectacle of rabbits with "ears collapsed limply at either side of the head, rather like the ears of spaniels,"[7] was both dramatic and entertaining.

In the intervening years Dr. Thomas described this phenomenon to a number of colleagues in pathology, biochemistry, and clinical investigation, who were equally intrigued and of the opinion that a significant amount of demonstrable tissue damage must be associated with such a striking and uniform reaction. Dr. Thomas also reported that twice he "put the experiment on" for some of his more skeptical colleagues. ("They didn't believe me when I told them what happened. They didn't really believe that you can get that much change and not a trace of anything having happened when you look in the microscope.") As so often happens in science, an unsolved puzzle was kept in mind for eventual solution through informal exchanges between scientists, rather than through the formal medium of published communications.

A few years ago Dr. Thomas once again accidentally came upon the floppy-eared rabbits in the course of another investigation:

> I was looking for a way . . .to reduce the level of fibrinogen in the blood of rabbits. I had been studying a form of fibrinoid which occurs inside blood vessels in the generalized Schwartzman reaction and which seems to be derived from fibrinogen. My working hypothesis was that if I depleted the fibrinogen and, as a result, fibrinoid did not occur, this would help. It had been reported that if you inject proteolytic enzyme, this will deplete fibrinogen. So I tried to inhibit the Schwartzman reaction by injecting papain intravenously into the rabbits. It didn't work with respect to fibrinogen. . . .the same damned thing happened again to the rabbits' ears!

This time, however, Dr. Thomas was to solve the puzzle of the collapsed rabbit ears and realize a complete instance of serendipitous discovery. He describes what subsequently happened:

> I was teaching second-year medical students in pathology. We have these small seminars with them: two-hour sessions in the morning twice a week, with six to eight students. These are seminars devoted to experimental pathology and the theoretical aspects of the mechanism of disease. The students have a chance to see what we, the faculty, are up to in the laboratory. I happened to have a session with the students at the same time that this thing with the rabbits' ears happened again. I thought it would be an entertaining thing to show them . . . a spectacular thing. The students were very interested in it. I explained to them that we couldn't really explain what the hell was going on here. I did this experiment on purpose for them, to see what they would think. . . . Besides which, I was in irons on my other experiments. There was not much doing on those. I was not being brilliant on

[7]Thomas, *op. cit.*, p. 245.

these other problems. . . . Well, this time I did what I didn't do before. I simultaneously cut sections of the ears of rabbits after I'd given them papain *and* sections of normal ears. This is the part of the story I'm most ashamed of. It still makes me writhe to think of it. There was no damage to the tissue in the sense of a lesion. But what had taken place was a quantitative change in the matrix of the cartilage. The only way you could make sense of this change was simultaneously to compare sections taken from the ears of rabbits which had been injected with papain with comparable sections from the ears of rabbits of the same age and size which had not received papain. . . . Before this I had always been so struck by the enormity of the change that when I didn't see something obvious, I concluded there was nothing . . . . Also, I didn't have a lot of rabbits to work with before.

Judging from Dr. Thomas' account, it appears that a number of factors contributed to his reported experimental success. First, his teaching duties played a creative role in this regard. They impelled him to run the experiment with papain again and kept his attention focused on its implications for pure science rather than on its potentialities for practical application. Dr. Thomas said that he used the experiment to "convey to students what experimental pathology is like." Second, because he had reached an impasse in some of his other research, Dr. Thomas had more time and further inclination to study the ear-collapsing effect of papain than he had had a few years earlier, when the progress he was making on other research helped to "persuade" him to abandon the problem of the floppy-eared rabbits. Third, Dr. Thomas had more laboratory resources at his command than previously, notably a larger supply of rabbits. (In this regard it is interesting to note that, according to Dr. Thomas' article in the *Journal of Experimental Medicine,* 250 rabbits, all told, were used in the experiments reported.) Finally, the fact that he now had more laboratory animals with which to work and that he wanted to present the phenomenon of reversible ear collapse to students in a way that would make it an effective teaching exercise led Dr. Thomas to modify his method for examining rabbit tissues. In his earlier experiments, Dr. Thomas had compared histological sections made of the ears of rabbits who had received an injection of papain with his own mental image of normal rabbit-ear tissue. This time, however, he actually made sections from the ear tissue of rabbits which did *not* receive papain, as well as from those which did, and simultaneously examined the two. As he reported, this comparison enabled him to see for the first time that "drastic" quantitative changes had occurred in the cartilaginous tissue obtained from the ears of the rabbits injected with papain. In the words of the *Journal* article,

> The ear cartilage showed loss of a major portion of the intercellular matrix, and complete absence of basophilia from the small amount of remaining matrix. The cartilage cells appeared somewhat larger, and rounder than normal, and lay in close contact with each other. . . . (The contrast between the normal ear cartilage and tissue obtained 4 hours after injection is illustrated in Figs. 3*A* and 2*B* of this article.)

Immediately thereafter, Dr. Thomas and his associates found that these changes occur not only in ear cartilage but in all other cartilaginous tissues as well.

How significant or useful Dr. Thomas' serendipitous discovery will be cannot yet be specified. The serendipity pattern characterizes small discoveries as well as great. Dr. Thomas and his associates are currently investigating some of the questions raised by the phenomenon of papain- collapsed ears and the alterations in cartilage now known to underlie it. In addition, Dr. Thomas reported that some of his "biochemist and clinical friends" have become interested enough in certain of his findings to "go to work with papain, too." Two of the major problems under study in Dr. Thomas' laboratory are biochemical: the one concerning the nature of the change in cartilage; the other, the nature of the factor in papain that causes collapse of rabbits' ears and lysis of cartilage matrix in all tissues. Attempts are also being made to identify the antibody that causes rabbits to become immune to the factor responsible for ear collapse after two weeks of injection. The way in which cortisone prolongs the reaction to papain and the possible effect that papain may have on the joints as well as the cartilage are also being considered. Though at the time may have on the joints as well as the cartilage are also being considered. Though at the time he was interviewed Dr. Thomas could not predict whether his findings (to date) would prove "important" or not, there was some evidence to suggest that certain basic discoveries about the constituents and properties of cartilaginous tissue might be forth-coming and that the experiments thus far conducted might have "practical usefulness" for studies of the postulated role of cortisone in the metabolism of sulfated mucopolysaccharides and of the relationship between cartilage and the electrolyte imbalance associated with congestive heart failure.

In the research on reversible ear collapse that Dr. Thomas has conducted since his initial serendipitous discovery, the planned and the unplanned, the foreseen and the accidental, the logical and the lucky have continued to interact. For example, Dr. Thomas' discovery that cortisone prevents or greatly delays the "return of papain-collapsed ears to their normal shape and rigidity" came about as a result of a carefully planned experiment that he undertook to test the effect of cortisone on the reaction to papain. On the other hand, his discovery that "repeated injections of papain, over a period of two or three weeks, brings about immunity to the phenomenon of ear collapse" was an unanticipated consequence of the fact that he used the same rabbit to demonstrate the floppy ears to several different groups of medical students:

> I was so completely sold on the uniformity of this thing that I used the same rabbit [for each seminar]. . . . The third time it didn't work. I was appalled by it. The students were there, and the rabbit's ears were still in place. . . . At first I thought that perhaps the technician had given him the wrong stuff. But then when I checked on that and gave the same stuff to the other rabbits and it *did* work I realized that the rabbit had become immune. This is a potentially hot finding. . . .

SERENDIPITY LOST

Dr. Kellner—In our interview with Dr. Thomas we told him that we had heard about another medical scientist who had noticed the reversible collapse of rabbits' ears when he had injected them intravenously with papain. Dr. Thomas was not at all surprised. "That must be Kellner," he said. "He must have seen it.

He was doomed to see it." Dr. Thomas was acquainted with the reports that Dr. Kellner and his associates had published on "Selective Necrosis of Cardiac and Skeletal Muscle Induced Experimentally by Means of Proteolytic Enzyme Solutions Given Intravenously" and on "Blood Coagulation Defect Induced in Rabbits by Papain Solutions Injected Intravenously."[8] He took it for granted that, in the course of the reported experiments which had entailed papain solution given intravenously to rabbits, a competent scientist like Dr. Kellner had also seen the resulting collapse of rabbits' ears, with its "unfailing regularity" and its "flamboyant" character. And indeed, our interview with Dr. Kellner revealed that he had observed the floppiness apparently at about the same time as Dr. Thomas:

> We called them the floppy-eared rabbits. Five or six years ago we published our first article on the work we were doing with papain that was in 1951 and our definitive article was published in 1954. . . . We gave papain to the animals and we had done it thirty or forty times before we noticed these changes in the rabbits' ears.

Thus Dr. Kellner's observation of what he and his colleagues dubbed "the floppy-eared rabbits" represents, when taken together with Dr. Thomas' experience, an instance of independent multiple observation, which often occurs in science and frequently leads to independent multiple invention and discovery.

Once he had noticed the phenomenon of ear collapse, Dr. Kellner did what Dr. Thomas and any research scientist would have done in the presence of such an unexpected and striking regularity: he looked for an answer to the puzzle it represented. "I was a little curious about it at the time and followed it up to the extent of making sections of the rabbits' ears." However, for one of those trivial reasons that sometimes affect the course of research—the obviously amusing quality of floppiness in rabbits ears—Dr. Kellner did not take the phenomenon as seriously as he took other aspects of the experimental situation involving the injection of papain.

In effect, Dr. Kellner and his associates closed out their interest in the phenomenon of the reversible collapse of rabbits' ears following intravenous injection of papain by using it as an assay test for the potency and amount of papain to be injected. "Every laboratory technician we've had since 1951," he told us in the interview, "has known about these floppy ears because we've used them to assay papain, to tell us if it's potent and how potent." If the injected rabbit died from the dose of papain he received, the researchers knew that the papain injection was too potent; if there was no change in the rabbit's ears, the papain was not potent enough, but "if the rabbit lived and his ears drooped, it was just right." Although "we knew all about it, and used it that way . . .as a rule of thumb," Dr. Kellner commented, "I didn't write it up." Nor did he ever have "any intention of publishing it as a method of assaying papain." He knew

---

[8] See, Aaron Kellner and Theodore Robertson, "Selective Necrosis of Cardiac and Skeletal Muscle Induced Experimentally by Means of Proteolytic Enzyme Solutions Given Intravenously," *Journal of Experimental Medicine*, XCIX (1954), 387-404 and Aaron Kellner, Theodore Robertson, and Howard O. Mott, "Blood Coagulation Defect Induced in Rabbits by Papain Solutions Injected Intravenously," abstract in *Federation Proceedings*, Vol. X (1951), No. 1.

that an applied technological discovery of this sort would not be suitable for publication in the basic science-oriented professional journals to which he and his colleagues submit reports of experimental work.

However, two factors apparently were much more important in leading Dr. Kellner away from investigating this phenomenon. First, like Dr. Thomas, Dr. Kellner thought of cartilage as relatively inert tissue. Second, because of his pre-established special research interests, Dr. Kellner's attention was predominantly trained on muscle tissue:

> Since I was primarily interested in research questions having to do with the muscles of the heart, I was thinking in terms of muscle. That blinded me, so that changes in the cartilage didn't occur to me as a possiblity. I was looking for muscles in the sections, and I never dreamed it was cartilage.

Like Dr. Thomas at the beginning of his research and like all scientists at some stages in their research, Dr. Kellner was "misled" by his preconceptions.

However, as we already know, in keeping with his special research interests, Dr. Kellner noticed and intensively followed up two other serendipitous results that occur when papain is injected intravenously into rabbits: focal necrosis of cardiac and skeletal muscle and a blood coagulation defect, which in certain respects resembles that of hemophilia.[9]

It was the selective necrosis of cardiac and skeletal muscle that Dr. Kellner studied with the greatest degree of seriousness and interest. Dr. Kellner told us that he is "particularly interested in cardio-vascular disease," and so the lesions in the myocardium was the chance observation that he particularly "chose to follow . . . the one closest to me." Not only did Dr. Kellner himself have a special interest in the necrosis of cardiac muscle, but also his "laboratory and the people associated with me," he said, provided "the physical and intellectual tools to cope with this phenomenon." Dr. Kellner and his colleagues also did a certain amount of "work tracking down the cause of the blood coagulation defect"; but, because this line of inquiry "led [them] far afield" from investigative work in which they were especially interested and competent, they eventually "let that go" as they had let go the phenomenon of floppiness in rabbits' ears. Dr. Kellner indicated in his interview that the potential usefulness of his work with the selective necrosis of cardiac and skeletal muscle cannot yet be precisely ascertained. However, in his article in the *Journal of Experimental Medicine* he suggested that this serendipitous finding "has interesting implications for the pathogenesis of the morphological changes in rheumatic fever, periarteritis nodosa, and other hypersensitivity states."

Thus Dr. Kellner did not have the experience of serendipity gained with respect to the significance of floppiness in rabbits' ears after intravenous injection of papain for a variety of reasons, some trivial apparently, others important. The most important reasons, it seems, were his research preconceptions and the occurrence of other serendipitous phenomena in the same experimental situation.

In summary, although the ultimate outcome of their respective laboratory encounters with floppiness in rabbits' ears was quite different, there are some

---

[9]See Kellner and Robertson, *op. cit.*, and Kellner, Robertson, and Mott, *op. cit.*

interesting similarities between the serendipity-gained experience of Dr. Thomas and the serendipity-lost experience of Dr. Kellner. Initially, the attention of both men was caught by the striking uniformity with which the collapse of rabbit ears occurred after intravenous papain and by the "bizarre," entertaining qualities of this cosmetic effect. In their subsequent investigations of this phenomenon, both were to some extent misled by certain of their interests and preconceptions. Lack of progress in accounting for ear collapse, combined with success in other research in which they were engaged at the time, eventually led both Dr. Thomas and Dr. Kellner to discontinue their work with the floppy-eared rabbits.

However, there were also some significant differences in the two experiences. Dr. Thomas seems to have been more impressed with the regularity of this particular phenomenon than Dr. Kellner and somewhat less amused by it. Unlike Dr. Kellner, Dr. Thomas never lost interest in the floppy-eared rabbits. When he came upon this reaction again at a time when he was "blocked" on other research, he began actively to reconsider the problem of what might have caused it. Eventual success was more likely to result from this continuing concern on Dr. Thomas' part. And Dr. Kellner, of course, was drawn off in other research directions by seeing other serendipitous phenomena in the same situation and by his success in following up those other leads.

These differences between Dr. Thomas and Dr. Kellner seem to account at least in part for the serendipity-gained outcome of the case of the floppy-eared rabbits for the one, and the serendipity-lost outcome for the other.

Experiences with both serendipity gained and serendipity lost are probably frequent occurrences for many scientific researchers. For, as Dr. Kellner pointed out in our interview with him, scientific investigations often entail "doing something that no one has done before, [so] you don't always know how to do it or exactly what to do":

> Should you boil or freeze, filter or centrifuge. These are the kinds of crossroads you come to all the time. . . . It's always possible to do four five, or six things, and you have to choose between them. . . . How do you decide?

In this comparative study of one instance of serendipity gained and serendipity lost we have tried to make inferences about some of the factors that led one investigator down the path to a successful and potentially important discovery and another to follow a somewhat different, though eventually perhaps a no less fruitful, trail of research. A large enough series of such case studies could suggest how often and in what ways these factors (and others that might prove relevant) influence the paths that open up to investigators in the course of their research, the choices they make between them, and the experimental findings that result from such choices. Case studies of this kind might also contribute a good deal to the detailed, systematic study of "the ways in which scientists actually . . . think, feel and act," which Robert K. Merton says could perhaps teach us more "in a comparatively few years, about the psychology and sociology of science than in all the years that have gone before."[10]

---

[10] See his Foreword to *Science and the Social Order* by Bernard Barber, p. xxii.

2

Conceptualization

A discussion of the interrelation between research and theory assumes a precise understanding of what is meant by theory. Yet, it has become quite apparent that such an understanding has been lacking or ill-founded. In the literature concepts such as paradigm, model, conceptual framework, ideal type, and theory have been used interchangeably and, it would appear, almost indiscriminately. Only recently have distinctions been explicitly made, and still consensus is lacking.[1]

Whatever one thinks theory is—an elaborate logical system of concepts or a deductively ordered system of empirically verified[2] propositions—it is clear that there are differences between the so-called theories in sociology. Basically they differ in the extent to which there is conceptual clarity and in the extent to which these concepts have explicit and measurable empirical referents.

Dumont and Wilson distinguish between "explicit theories," "theory sketches," and "implicit theories." Picking up on Northrop's notion of the epistemic correlation[3] the authors note that some theories have established the epistemic link which is ultimately necessary; that is, there are rules of correspondence spelling out the link between the conceptual and the operational levels of the theory. These, then, are the explicit theories. Theory sketches lack specific rules of correspondence. Yet, when obliged to, one can work out the empirical referents. The concepts of theory sketches are refined that much at least.

[1] See especially L. Gross, *Symposium on Sociological Theory* (New York: Harper & Row, 1959).

[2] See George Homans' paper in chapter 8.

[3] F. S. C. Northrop, *The Logic of the Sciences and the Humanities* (New York: Meridian Books, Inc., 1959), pp. 119-32.

In addition, in the social sciences there is a body of concepts which are theoretical isolates. That is to say, there are concepts which appear to be of significance, or potentially so, yet which have not been integrated into a system of propositions or laws. These, the authors suggest, should be salvaged. The authors argue for "explication"—the conceptual and empirical clarification of these concepts, with a view to developing them beyond the level of mere "implicit theory."

One need not agree with the manner in which the authors express their distinctions in order to agree that the distinctions which they make are fundamental. Because of the importance which we, as most sociologists, attach to conceptual clarity and to the "epistemic correlation" the suggestions of Dumont and Wilson are recommended for attention.

Peter Blau's paper is a more specific treatment of the general difficulty raised by Dumont and Wilson. Blau's paper is a useful discussion and illustration of how one concept can be explicated and operationalized. And as the author himself notes, his discussion is perhaps also useful as pointing the way toward the translation of the especially abstract theory or model of Talcott Parsons into its operational counterparts—an "explicit theory."

ASPECTS OF CONCEPT FORMATION, EXPLICATION, AND THEORY CONSTRUCTION IN SOCIOLOGY

Richard G. Dumont and William J. Wilson

Philosophers of science have recently raised some challenging and controversial methodological issues concerning "theory" in the social sciences.[1] Their writings apparently have provoked a number of sociologists to re-examine critically the "scientific status" of contemporary sociological "theories."[2] The examination of these theories according to rigorous evaluative criteria (with regard to the structure of explanation, significance of concepts, and the nature of evidence) has cast considerable doubt on their explanatory and predictive import and has thrown their deficiencies into sharp and uncomplimentary relief.[3]

Reprinted with permission of the authors and the publisher, The American Sociological Association, from the *American Sociological Review*, Vol. 32 (1967), 985-95.

The authors would like to thank Richard H. Ogles, John O'Rourke, Peter Park, Nicholas Sofios, Curt Tausky, and David Yaukey for helpful suggestions and criticism of a previous draft of this paper.

[1] Though numerous authors could be cited here, the following serve as examples: Ernest Nagel, *The Structure of Science: Problems in the Logic of Scientific Explanation*, New York: Harcourt, Brace, and World, 1961, Chs. 13 and 14, and *Logic Without Metaphysics*, New York: The Free Press, 1956, pp. 247-283; Carl G. Hempel, "Typological Methods in the Social Sciences," in Maurice Natanson (ed.), *Philosophy of the Social Sciences*, New York: Random House, Inc., 1963, pp. 210-230, and "The Logic of Functional Analysis," in Llewellyn Gross (ed.), *Symposium on Sociological Theory*, New York: Row, Peterson & Co., 1959, pp. 271-307; May Brodbeck, "Methodological Individualisms: Definition and Reduction," *Philosophy of Science*, 25 (1958), pp. 1-22, and "Models, Meaning, and Theories," in Gross, *op. cit.*; Abraham Kaplan, *The Conduct of Inquiry: Methodology for Behavioral Science*, San Francisco: Chandler Publishing Co., 1964; Gustav Bergmann, *Philosophy of Science*, Madison: The University of Wisconsin Press, 1958; and Max Black, "Some Questions about Parsons' Theories," in Max Black (ed.), *The Social Theories of Talcott Parsons*, Englewood Cliffs: Prentice-Hall, Inc., 1962, pp. 268-288.

[2] For example, see Hans Zetterberg, *On Theory and Verification in Sociology*, Totowa: The Bedminster Press, 1965; Clarence Schrag, "Comments on the General Theory of Action," *Alpha Kappa Deltan*, 29 (1959), pp. 46-52, and "Delinquency and Opportunity: Analysis of a Theory," *Journal of Sociology and Social Research*, 46 (1962), pp. 167-175; Llewellyn Gross, "Theory Construction in Sociology: A Methodological Inquiry," in Gross, *op. cit.*; George Homans, "Contemporary Theory in Sociology," in Robert E. L. Faris (ed.), *Handbook of Modern Sociology*, Chicago: Rand McNally & Company, 1964, pp. 915-977; Aaron V. Cicourel, *Method and Measurement in Sociology*, Glencoe: The Free Press, 1964; and William J. Wilson, Nicholas Sofios and Richard Ogles, "Formalization and Stages of Theoretical Development," *Pacific Sociological Review*, 7 (1964), pp. 74-80.

[3] Although there is a lack of consensus among philosophers of science regarding specific explicit criteria for the evaluation of theories, e.g., the thesis of explicit definability of theoretical terms, the following are examples of the general kinds of rigorous criteria that are frequently invoked: explanations may be deductive or probabilistic, but the premises must contain general or statistical laws. Concepts have to be embedded in experimental laws to have empirical significance in the observational language; in the theoretical language,

It is sometimes argued that since the criteria invoked by philosophers of science are based primarily on reconstructions of physical science theories, they are not applicable to the social sciences. Such assertions often stem from a recurrent confusion between *technique and methodology.* Although one may question the extent to which techniques in the natural and social sciences differ, the claim that there is a difference in methodology between the two disciplines is very radical indeed. As Richard Rudner has stated:

"... The methodology of a scientific discipline is not a matter of its transient techniques but of its logic of justification. The method of science *is*, indeed, the rationale on which it bases its acceptance or rejection of hypotheses or theories. Accordingly, to hold that the social sciences are methodologically distinct from the non-social sciences is to hold not merely (or perhaps not at all)) the banal view that the social sciences employ different techniques of inquiry, but rather the startling view that the social sciences require a different logic of inquiry. To hold such a view, moreover, is to deny that all of science is characterized by a common logic of justification in its acceptance or rejection of hypotheses."[4]

The use of rigorous evaluative criteria in the formal examination of sociological theories has two major functions: (1) making explicit their logical and/or empirical status, and (2) helping to evaluate claims made by particular theorists.[5] Both of these functions fall within the *context of justification.* An implicit and less frequently noted function of the use of these criteria falls within the *context of discovery.*[6] Specifically, rigorous evaluations of sociological theories may suggest at least two alternative paths to take in the construction of definitive theories:[7] (1) purging the realm of sociological inquiry of all that does not conform with the standards of rigorous evaluative criteria, or

concepts are given empirical significance if they are embedded in postulate networks, where the postulates and theorems represent theoretical laws, and are connected to terms in experimental laws by rules of correspondence. These latter distinctions are elaborated more specifically below with the introduction of the notions of "epistemic significance" and "constitutive significance."

[4] Richard S. Rudner, *Philosophy of Social Science*, Englewood Cliffs: Prentice-Hall, Inc., 1966, p. 5.

[5] An excellent critique of the claims made by Talcott Parsons with respect to his "general theory of action," for example, is provided by Max Black, *op. cit.*

[6] The terms "context of justification" or "context of validation" and "context of discovery" were originally introduced by Hans Reichenbach. The former refers to the process of rational reconstruction whereby the theorist attempts to justify his findings in presenting them; Reichenbach discussed the latter in terms of thought processes leading to the discovery of theories. We have expanded this notion to include physical steps that the theorist takes in developing or discovering his theory. See Hans Reichenbach, *Experience and Prediction*, Chicago: University of Chicago Press, 1938, and "The Philosophical Significance of the Theory of Relativity," *Readings in the Philosophy of Science*, in Herbert Feigl and May Brodbeck (eds.), New York: Appleton, Century, Crofts, Inc., 1954, pp. 195-211.

[7] Although it is acknowledged that there exist no definitive discovery rules, it is possible that rigorous evaluations of sociological theories might shed some light on the efficacy of current discovery procedures, and that attempts at reconstruction could be suggestive of new directions to be taken. However, the term "suggest" in this context does not mean "logically imply"; what is being asserted is that there may be some empirical connection between rigorous formalizations and steps taken in theory construction.

(2) developing a practical program for selecting or developing those aspects of current sociological theory that show promise for eventual conformity with these criteria.[8]

Though a few of the most extreme advocates of the tradition of logical positivism might find comfort in embracing the first of the two alternatives, such a drastic program is likely to be enshrouded with numerous impracticalities. Even though it is universally agreed that the present "scientific status" of sociological inquiry leaves much to be desired, the discarding of all that does not conform *strictly* with the rigorous evaluative criteria would amount to dismissing nearly all of the accumulated body of the sociological enterprise. Such an approach, in our opinion, would deny recognition to much in the field that shows some merit. In short, the whole-hearted pursuit of any program evolved in conjunction with the adoption of the first alternative might conceivably lead to throwing out the "good" with the "bad" sociology.

It would seem that if one envisions the ultimate emergence of explicit theory in sociology,[9] the adoption of the second alternative provides the most practical approach. This paper elaborates one aspect of the second alternative by suggesting bases for the selection, evaluation, and utilization of "theoretical" concepts that function either within or outside of the context of systematic sociological theories.[10]

THEORY SKETCHES AND CONCEPTS WITH EPISTEMIC AND CONSTITUTIVE CONNECTIONS

In general, theoretical concepts in explicit theories possess both *epistemic* and *constitutive significance*. The former signifies that the concepts are connected, either directly or indirectly, with observables by rules of correspondence that have been empirically justified; i.e., via these rules, confirmed relationships have been established between observable concepts and theoretical concepts.[11] The

---

[8]The decision of whether a concept is to be afforded "promissory status" or "potential significance" is based exclusively on methodological grounds until an empirical association is established between such concepts and the role they subsequently play in scientific theories. This notion is discussed in greater detail below when the "potential significance" of sociological concepts is emphasized.

[9]For a concise account of explicit theory as "an interpreted axiomatic system" see Cicourel, *op. cit.* Briefly, "an interpreted axiomatic system contains descriptive as well as logical terms. Replacing the marks and logical truths of an uninterpreted axiomatic system by descriptive terms and empirical statements leads to an interpreted system. Thus, interpreted axiomatic systems require that a correspondence be demonstrated between the elements, relations, and operations of the mathematical and substantive systems in question. The empirical consequences require that the measurement properties of the theoretical events be specified. Not all theories are axiomatic in nature. When a theory consists of a set of laws and definitions that are deductively interrelated, it is an axiomatic system." *Ibid.*, pp. 8-9.

[10]Corrective suggestions concerning explanation and evidence represent other aspects of the second alternative.

[11]For an excellent elaboration of this point, see Rudolph Carnap, "Methodological Character of Theoretical Concepts," in Herbert Feigl, Michael Scriven and Grover Maxwell (eds.), *Minnesota Studies in the Philosophy of Science*, Vol. 1, Minneapolis: University of Minnesota Press, 1958 and Warren S. Torgerson, *Theory and Methods of Scaling*, New York: John Wiley and Sons, Inc., pp. 3-4.

For a discussion of how rules of correspondence may be variously applied to sociological

latter implies that the concept in question enters into a sufficient number of relations with other terms in the theoretical laws of the postulate network, and contributes to the explanation and prediction of observable events.[12]

Due to the absence of explicit theory, theoretical concepts in sociology lack both epistemic and constitutive significance. Many concepts in sociology, however, function in theories that are more appropriately labeled *"explanation sketches"* (or *"theory sketches"*). An explanation sketch "consists of a more or less vague indication of the laws and initial conditions considered as relevant, and it needs 'filling out' in order to turn into a full-fledged explanation. This filling out requires further empirical research, for which the sketch suggests the direction."[13]

Concepts functioning within these theory sketches have *constitutive connections* in the sense that they are either defined in other "theoretical terms" or are related to other theoretical terms by the propositions in the theory sketch, e.g., the *suicide rate* is inversely related to the degree of *status integration* in society."[14] Yet they lack consititutive significance because they do not function

concepts, see William J. Wilson and Richard G. Dumont, "Rules of Correspondence and Sociological Concepts," *Sociology and Social Research* (forthcoming).

[12]The terms "epistemic significance" and "constructive significance" are used in preference to the general notion of "empirical significance" to convey more precisely the status of theoretical concepts in explicit theories as opposed to theoretical concepts in theory sketches. The separation here is merely a conceptual one, for, in a real sense, a concept must have epistemic significance if it has constitutive significance. That is, if it contributes to the explanation and prediction of an observable event, it must, in some way, be connected with observables. By the same token, a concept has to have constitutive significance if it has epistemic significance, because the constitutive connections provide the rationale for the selection of rules of correspondence; i.e., via the rules of correspondence a confirmed relationship has to be established, according to the assumptions of the theory (constitutive connections), between the observable concepts and the theoretical concepts.

[13]Carl G. Hempel, "The Function of General Laws in History," in Herbert Feigl and Wilfred Sellers (eds.), *Readings in Philosophical Analysis*, New York: Appleton-Century-Crofts, Inc., 1949, p. 465. Since a theory is a type of explanation, the term "theory sketch" (which was suggested by Richard Ogles in private conversations) gives a more precise signification of the kinds of *potential* theories that characterize sociology. Henceforth we shall use the term "theory sketch" to connote the general notion of Hempel's explanation sketch as it relates specifically to theories. Note that the word "potential" was emphasized. Consistent with Hempel's notion, an explanation sketch (theory sketch) must be distinguished from a pseudo explanation. "A scientifically acceptable explanation sketch needs to be filled out by more specific statements; but it points into the direction where these statements are to be found; and concrete research may tend to confirm or to infirm those indications. . . . In the case of non-empirical explanations or explanation sketches, on the other hand . . . the use of empirically meaningless terms makes it impossible even roughly to indicate the type of investigation that would have a bearing upon those formulations and that might lead to evidence either confirming or infirming the suggested explanations." *Ibid.*, pp. 465-466.

For a recent discussion of what might be entailed in "filling out" an explanation sketch, see Fred Newman, "Discussion: Explanation Sketches," *Philosophy of Science*, 32 (1965), pp. 168-172.

[14]There are several scientifically acceptable theory sketches in sociology, as distinguished from pseudo-theory sketches. Homans' theory of elementary social behavior and Gibbs and Martin's theory of status integration are representative examples. George Homans, *Social behavior: Its Elementary Forms*, New York: Harcourt, Brace, and World, 1961; and Jack P. Gibbs and Walter T. Martin, *Status Integration and Suicide: A Sociological Study*, Eugene: University of Oregon Books, 1964. The most important feature of scientifically

within theoretical laws. Such concepts are connected with observables by rules of correspondence, but the theory sketch does not provide a definitive rationale for the use or selection of the rules of correspondence. The connection between the observable concepts and the theoretical concepts is only presumed to represent an empirical relation.[15] The term *"epistemic connections,"* as opposed to *"epistemic significance,"* will be employed to describe this weak connection. The presumed relationship is given added weight as additional research reveals that the observed data agree with the predictions based on the constitutive connections. But it is only after the accumulation of research findings has established the constitutive connections as theoretical laws that we can introduce a definitive rationale for the rules of correspondence.

Although concepts embedded in theory sketches lack epistemic and constitutive significance, they are part of testable propositions, and can be evaluated according to the nature of their constitutive connections with other theoretical terms and their epistemic connections with observable terms. In each instance, they may be accorded "potential significance."

IMPLICIT THEORIES AND ISOLATED ABSTRACT CONCEPTS

Many concepts in sociology cannot be evaluated on this basis, however, because they do not operate within the context of a formal theory, be it a theory sketch or an explicit theory. For those of us concerned not only with evaluation, but also with theory construction, the question is whether or not there is any basis for giving special attention to some of these isolated concepts in sociology. Before attempting to answer this question, it might prove fruitful to review critically the present state of such concepts, which we shall label *isolated abstract concepts.*

The most characteristic feature of such concepts is that they tend to be ambiguous. Even if it is agreed that the specification or definition of theoretical terms never can be complete, i.e., there always remains an *openness of meaning,*

---

acceptable theory sketches is that their propositions are, in principle, testable. Their major weakness lies in the imprecision of definitions and empirical indicators. For example, in Homans theory of elementary social behavior, the value of a unit is vaguely defined as the degree of reinforcement or punishment one receives from that unit. Moreover, Homans states that value is measured by studying the past history of an individual in relation to his present circumstances. Such a measure takes account of the two components of value: amount of past reward and present need. Homans readily admits that these components are not very precise, and that the propositions in which the term functions are necessarily imprecise.

[15] For an example of this weakness with reference to Gibbs and Martin's theory sketch of status integration (cited in footnote 14), see Robert Hagedorn and Sanford Labovitz, "A Note on Status Integration and Suicide," *Social Problems,* 14 (1966), pp. 79-84. Commenting on the theory of status integration, Hagedorn and Labovitz have stated: "A major problem with the theory is the lack of congruence between the theoretical conception of status integration and its operational measurement. As indicated by examples cited, actual occupancy of a status configuration (which is the empirical referent of status integration) does not always reflect incompatibility or role conflict." p. 84.

An interesting exchange on other methodological issues concerning the theory of status integration and suicide was provided by William J. Chambliss and Marion F. Steel, "Status Integration and Suicide: An Assessment," *American Sociological Review,* 31 (1966), pp. 524-532; and Jack P. Gibbs and Walter T. Martin, "On Assessing the Theory of Status Integration and Suicide," *Ibid.,* pp. 533-641.

as Hempel has indicated, the criterion of inter-subjective certifiability requires that "... the terms used in formulating scientific statements have clearly specified meanings and be understood in the same sense by all who use them."[16]

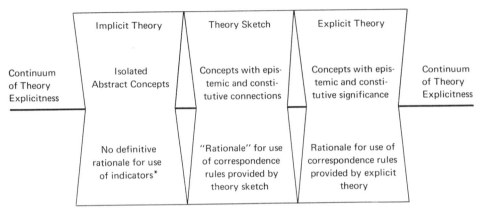

FIGURE 1. *The term 'indicator' is used instead of 'correspondence rules' to signify that isolated abstract concepts are not part of a formal theory.

Though it may be legitimately contended that the criterion of inter-subjective certifiability may be met in each of the contexts in which a specified theoretical term is thought to be applicable, this does not alleviate certain methodological difficulties when the concept is of the isolated abstract variety. The dimensions of this problem become clearer when one considers some of the more fundamental processes involved in concept formation. Concepts, particularly those expressed in theoretical language, represent some degreee of abstraction from the complexities of observable phenomena. Such abstraction is essential if the concept's specific domain of application is extensive. The reason that the sociologist must attribute a variety of meanings to his isolated concepts in the various contexts in which he uses them is primarily a matter of the mode of abstraction. Though abstraction is desirable, it is essential to distinguish between legitimate (scientific or theoretical), and intuitive, or pre-scientific abstractions. Theoretical abstractions occur within the body of a given formal theory (explicit theory or theory sketch). They generally arise as a result of noting, inferring, or deducing certain relationships between or among other established concepts. Intuitive abstractions, on the other hand, afford no clear specification as to how they are derived.

It may be, however, that such abstractions have their bases in some underlying *implicit "theory"* that awaits formal discovery before its form, content, and functions can be made explicit.[17] Both implicit theories and explicit theories

[16]Carl G. Hempel, "Fundamentals of Taxonomy," in Carl G. Hempel, *Aspects of Scientific Explanation: And Other Essays in the Philosophy of Science*, New York: The Free Press, 1965, p. 141.
[17]Cicourel has also used the term "implicit theory" to refer to sociological theories in general. His treatment of the term indicates usage closely related to our notion of the theory sketch. See Cicourel, *op. cit.*

represent polar extremes along a continuum of "theory explicitness," with theory sketches representing intermediate states of explicitness.[18] This process is outlined in Figure 1. The primary difference between an implicit theory and a theory sketch is that the form of the propositions characterizing the latter have been formally spelled out—even though their assertions may not be known to be true. Accordingly, some isolated abstract concepts may be "isolated" and intuitive only in the sense that they are not contained in a theory sketch or explicit theory. However, implicit theories have no systematic usefulness if their form, content, and functions remain hidden.

For example, although there is no explicit theory or theory sketch of social stratification,[19] researchers in the area seem generally agreed as to the importance of the term "social status," and implementations of this concept in actual research situations suggest its candidacy for lower-order theoretical language in any theoretical undertaking.[20] The concept of "social status" represents an abstraction, rather closely bound to common sense usage, that is thought to convey a vague indication of hierarchical ordering among individuals. In general, stratification analysts concur that its value lies in giving meaning to the more directly observable characteristics which it is felt somehow to subsume, and any attempt to operationalize this concept usually requires a mad search for indices that are often only presumed to be related to one another and to the intuitively conceived notion of "social status.[21]

[18] Although the notions of implicit theory, theory sketch, and explicit theory are the only kind of explanations considered here, this should not preclude the possibility of discussing other kinds of explanations as they relate to the above continuum. Hempel has distinguished partial explanations, elliptically formulated explanations, and explanation sketches. However, since Hempel has confessed that any decision as to whether or not a proposed explanation is to be qualified as one of the above kinds is a matter of "judicious interpretation," and further, since it is not our primary purpose to draw such fine distinctions here, we shall not attempt to discuss them further. See Carl G. Hempel, "Explanation in Science and History," in Robert Colodny, (ed.), *Frontiers of Science and Philosophy*, Pittsburgh: University of Pittsburgh Press, 1962, pp. 9-33.

[19] Present so-called "theories" in social stratification can be classified more appropriately as taxonomies or pseudo theory sketches, following Hempel's scheme—see footnote 13. A taxonomy is a schema for the description and classification of social phenomena. Parsons' "A Revised Analytical Approach to the Theory of Social Stratification" and Weber's "Class, Status, and Party" are representative examples. Davis and Moore's theory, "Some Principles of Social Stratification," illustrates our conception of a pseudo theory sketch. More specifically, such notions as "functional importance," "functional necessity," and "need" are treated in a non-empirical manner, that is, there is no clear specification of the objective criteria of their application. Accordingly, sentences containing such terms are not only often used tautologically, but also they do not lend themselves to specific predictions and empirical tests. Consequently, these sentences cannot be said to have potential explanatory import.

[20] It is obvious that the future of this notion in stratification theory in particular, and in sociology in general, is not to be judged *a priori*. Rigorous inquiry alone will determine its significance and empirical import. It is introduced here solely for illustrative purposes.

[21] The concept "social status" will suffice to illustrate the kinds of problems that plague isolated abstract concepts in sociology. For further discussion of the problems associated with these concepts, see, Richard H. Ogles, Marion J. Levy, Jr., and Talcott Parsons, "Culture and Social Systems: An Exchange," *American Sociological Review*, 24 (1959), pp. 246-250; and Reinhard Bendix and Bennett Berger, "Images of Society and Problems of Concept Formation in Sociology," in Gross (ed.), *Symposium on Sociological Theory, op. cit.*, pp. 92-121.

Thus, if we may presume that certain key isolated abstract concepts in sociology suffer from numerous methodological difficulties, what program could be introduced to allow some rigor and consistency of usage so that these concepts can be systematically advanced as candidates for the theoretical language in either a theory sketch or an explicit theory?

EXPLICATION

One answer, we believe, may be found in the general notion of *explication,* the process whereby an initially vague and imprecise concept may be attributed with a more exact meaning, thereby increasing the likelihood of its intersubjective certifiability.

If the present intuitively derived notions which abound in sociology are thought to be essential for the description and explanation of behavioral phenomena, consider how much more useful a clear explication would be. The concept so explicated could then be substituted for its less precise counterpart in propositional statements, thus increasing the explanatory and predictive potential of the proposition in which it is embedded.

Although the notion of explication is itself somewhat vague, it appears to be reducible to a general program that posits two primary tasks, *meaning analysis* and *empirical analysis.*[22] Whereas the former simply requires a validation of the various linguistic expressions of a concept, the latter is concerned with the validation of the assertions stipulating its essential empirical properties. In describing how these modes of analysis function in the process of explication, Hempel has stated:

"An explication of a given set of terms . . . combines essential aspects of meaning analysis and of empirical analysis. Taking its departure from the customary meanings of the terms, explication aims at reducing the limitations, ambiguities, and inconsistencies of their ordinary usage by propounding a reinterpretation intended to enhance the clarity and precision of their meanings as well as their ability to function in hypotheses and theories with explanatory and predictive force.[23]

In order to establish clearly the relevance of the process with respect to concept formation, we shall discuss a procedure of explication that seems appropriate for the present stages of empirical and theoretical development in sociology and that provides criteria for the selection and evaluation of isolated abstract concepts.

Meaning Analysis. The first procedural step of meaning analysis involves a survey of the literature in an attempt to cull out the most basic implicit or explicit assumptions inherent in the various meanings that have been attributed to the concept. We shall illustrate this process by drawing, once again, upon the notion of "social status."

[22]Carl G. Hempel, "Fundamentals of Concept Formation in Empirical Science," *International Encyclopedia of Unified Science*, Vol. 2, Chicago: 1952, pp. 10-12. Rudolph Carnap has also discussed the formal notion of "explication." See Rudolph Carnap, *Logical Foundations of Probability*, Chicago: The University of Chicago Press, 1950.

[23]Hempel, "Fundamentals of Concept Formation in Empirical Science," *op. cit.*, p. 12.

There seems to be general agreement that although social status is thought to be related to such variables as occupational prestige, education, income, etc., it is somehow more than these, taken singly or in combination. It is assumed that they and other variables contribute to status, but how or to what extent invites speculation.[24]

Although it is not necessary to discuss the historical evolution of the concepts of social stratification here, it is essential to note that the Weberian conceptualization has been the most influential in American sociology.[25] Weber conceived of society as being stratified in three basic dimensions: economic class, status, and power. "Social status" was nominally defined as personal honor or prestige. From this and related definitions has resulted the indeterminancy and ambiguity which characterize the usage of "social status" by contemporary stratification analysts.[26]

The difficulties which plague this term are traceable to its defining phrase. As noted previously, whether fully or only partially defined, fruitful scientific concepts are either directly or indirectly connected with observables. For example, the physical property of magnetism is not in itself observable but, its definitions refer to experiential data which are:

If a small iron object is close to 'x' at (time) 't', then 'x' is magnetic at time 't' if and only if that object moves toward 'x' at 't.'[27]

Contrast the above with a grossly similar partial definition of "social status":

Given any two individuals, *a* and *b*, then *a* has higher social status than *b* if and only if *a* has more honor or prestige than *b*.

It is clear that, whereas the former assertion stipulates observable phenomena which are intersubjectively certifiable, the defining terms of the latter, "prestige" and "honor," are not directly observable. Thus "social status," in its most customary usage, may be more appropriately classified as a phenomenological rather than an observational term.[28]

[24] See, for example, Milton M. Gordon, *Social Class in American Sociology*, New York: McGraw-Hill Book Co., Inc., 1950, Ch. 6.
[25] *Ibid.*, Chs. 1 and 2.
[26] See Max Weber, *The Theory of Social and Economic Organization* (translated by A. M. Henderson and Talcott Parsons), New York: Oxford University Press, 1947, and *From Max Weber: Essays in Sociology* (translated and edited by Hans H. Gerth and C. Wright Mills), New York: Oxford University Press, 1946; and Kurt B. Mayer, *Class and Society*, New York: Random House, 1955.
[27] Hempel has employed this particular partial definition of magnetism in an attempt to illustrate the notion of Carnap's "reduction sentences" in Hempel, "Fundamentals of Concept Formation in Empirical Science," *op. cit.*, p. 26.
[28] A solution to this dilemma in sociology has been the tendency of those concerned with "social status" to introduce indicators which are employed to infer its presence and to provide some degree of "objectivity" for its application. Witness the proliferation of social status indices that have been utilized through the years. Social status has been equated with such variables as income, wealth, place of residence, age, sex, religion, ethnicity, living room furnishings, etc. The difficulty with these indices is that their precise relationship to the concept which they are intended to objectify remains unspecified. Though there have been some noteworthy efforts directed toward investigations of the inter-relations among the

The above discussion has been necessarily brief because a thorough documentation of the literature on social status would take us beyond the scope of this paper. For our purposes, however, the following statements of the basic assumptions suggested by the customary usage of the term "social status" seem warranted:[29]

(1) *Social status*, though it may indeed bear a close relationship to objective variables such as education and income, *is basically a phenomenon of human perception*.

(2) Inherent in this conceptualization is the notion that *social status is an orderable attribute*. It is assumed that individuals form some sort of hierarchical status ranking.

There may be numerous other assumptions in the ordinary usage of this concept. In our reconstruction, however, these are the most fundamental.

The discussion thus far illustrates what is implied by culling out the basic assumptions suggested by ordinary usage. We are now in a position to state *the second phase of meaning analysis*, namely, that which *involves certain decisions concerning the syntactical status of the concept's defining phrases*. Questions which might be raised are: is the concept a class of property term, i.e., can it be defined in terms of *genus proximum* and *differentia specifica*, as the logical intersection of two other classes? Or is it customary to conceive of it as a comparative term, i.e., do the defining phrases suggest that the concept is to apply only to those instances where two or more objects in possession of the property may be meaningfully compared and ordered in terms of quantitative representations of the attribute? For example, with respect to "social status", we do not generally make such statements as: "Since John Smith has a high school diploma and earns five thousand dollars per year and is a policeman, John Smith has 'x' units of status." More frequently, statements relative to social status take the form of such assertions as "John Smith is higher (or lower) in social status than Tom Jones." This interpretation is more consistent with "theoretical" writings which suggest that an individual's status is largely a function of the social context of evaluation.

Having thus outlined the essential elements of our proposed program of meaning analysis, we now turn to a consideration of empirical analysis.

Empirical Analysis. The empirical analysis of a concept refers to that process whereby the basic assumptions which have been brought to light as a result of the meaning analysis are submitted to direct empirical test. To illustrate, it will be recalled that the basic assumptions concerning "social status" are that it is a

---

various indices, few attempts have been made to specify clearly the meaning of this term on the basis of the objective data with which it is thought to be related.

[29] Since this form of rational reconstruction is not based on a set of established explicit rules, it is quite possible that alternative conceptualizations and explications may be advanced for the same term. The respective advantages and disadvantages of the alternatives will be decided finally by the extent to which they enable the concept to operate as an efficient instrument in propositional statements. This consideration has led Hempel to state, "Thus understood, an explication cannot be qualified as true or false; but it may be adjudged more or less adequate according to the extent to which it attains its objectives." *Ibid*, p. 12.

phenomenon of human perception, and that it represents an orderable attribute. Further, it was argued that in its customary usage, "social status" is most appropriately classified as a comparative term. Accordingly, an empirical analysis of "social status" should seek to provide at least a tentative answer to the following question: does there exist a measurable attribute, social status, such that a single individual and/or a number of individuals can order others meaningfully in terms of this attribute? This is the crucial question, for the history of science testifies to the superiority of measurable concepts in contributing to the construction of fruitful theories.[30] Thus, if individuals cannot meaningfully order others with respect to their relative statuses, the values of the perception version of this notion as a potentially significant sociological concept may be seriously questioned.

In carrying out this phase of the explication, it is essential that scaling or measurement procedures appropriate to the syntactical status of the concept's defining phrases (as determined by the meaning analysis) be introduced. Since we have tentatively agreed that our illustrative concept, "social status," is most appropriately conceived as a comparative term, we will restrict our discussion to a proposed scaling procedure for such terms.

Scaling (or measurement), in its least rigorous interpretation, consists of the assignment of numerals to objects possessing measurable attributes such that the relationships among the objects maintain a one-to-one or isomorphic relation to the system of numbers of which the numerals are representative. There are several ways by which this isomorphism may be established or demonstrated. We will discuss only two of these: measurement by fiat vs. measurement by fundamental process.

Fundamental measurement, which is sometimes said to reveal the existence of "natural laws," is that which presupposes no other. The first step consists of assigning numerals to represent quantities so that the following postulates of order for a quasi-series hold: given that C=coincidence, P=precedence, and a, b, and c are any three elements which share the attribute in question, then: (1) C is transitive, i.e., whenever aCb and bCc then aCc; (2) C is symmetric, i.e., whenever aCb then bCa; (3) C is reflexive, i.e., aCa, bCb, cCc; (4) P is transitive, i.e., if aPb and bPc then aPc; (5) P is C-irreflexive, if aCb, then it is not the case that aPb; and (6) P is C-connected, if it is not the case that aCb, then either aPb or bPa.[31] The primary difference between measurement by fiat and measurement by fundamental process is that in the former, if these postulates are considered at all, they are merely assumed to be satisfied for the attribute under consideration. Most of the so-called indices of "social status," for example, provide no tests for these postulates and an isomorphism is, at best, "only presumed to exist."[32] What sets fundamental measurement apart is that

[30]For an excellent discussion of this issue, see Kaplan, op. cit., esp. Ch. V.
[31]Adapted from Hempel, "Fundamentals of Concept Formation in Empirical Science," op. cit., p. 59.
[32]Although the North-Hatt-NORC Scale does not represent an attempt to "measure" the social status of individuals per se, but rather focuses upon occupational prestige ranking, it provides an excellent example of a scale which exhibits only a presumptive isomorphism. Of the so-called ranking methods, the authors of a recent replication of the original NORC study have stated:
One indicator of prestige position is the proportion of respondents (among those rating an

whereas some of the postulates are often true by definition, e.g., (2), (3), (5) and (6), others, specifically the transitivity requirements for the relations of precedence and coincidence, have the nature of testable hypotheses. Accordingly, if it can be shown that the attribute being scaled or measured satisfies these requirements, one may conclude that it is fundamentally measurable on an ordinal scale.[33] Although, in the ideal case, ratio measurement is the most desirable, it is essential that whenever the ordinal properties of the particular attribute are in doubt, any ambitions about interval or ratio measurement be preceded by an empirical investigation of the order relations.

In light of these considerations, an empirical analysis of "social status" should concern itself with a direct test of the following basic hypotheses:

(1) The two relations, C and P, determine a comparative concept of perceived social status for a single individual if it can be shown that in that individual's reported perceptions of the social status of other individuals, C is transitive, symmetric, and reflexive, and P is transitive, C-irreflexive, and C-connected.

(2) The two relations, C and P, determine a comparative concept of perceived social status for a number of individuals, if it can be shown that in those individuals' reported perceptions of the social status of other individuals, C is transitive, symmetric, and reflexive, and P is transitive, C-irreflexive, and C-connected.[34]

Hopefully, the preceding discussion conveys what is meant by a direct test of

---

occupation) giving either an 'excellent' or a 'good' response. Another . . . requires weighting the various responses with *arbitrary* numerical values. . . . This latter measure has received rather widespread use despite arbitrariness in the numerical weights. . . . (italics ours)

See Robert W. Hodge, Paul M. Siegel, and Peter H. Rossi, "Occupational Prestige in the United States: 1925-1963," *The American Journal of Sociology*, 70 (1964), pp. 288-289.

[33] See Torgerson, *op. cit.*, Chs. 2-4.

[34] Careful reflection reveals the necessity for both hypotheses (1) and (2), for, clearly, the confirmation of the latter presupposes the validity of the former. That is, if individuals cannot meaningfully order others with respect to their relative statuses, then any order which is uncovered in an investigation of the pooled responses of a number of individuals (employing some form of summary statistics, for example) must be spurious. On the other hand, if a particular study concerns itself solely with hypothesis (2), disconfirming results could foster premature closure, for even if it is found that individuals do not agree in their status rankings of others, it may not be safe to assume *a priori* that "social status" is a useless notion. It may still be meaningful when its perceivers are taken one at a time. Whether or not this is the case depends upon a direct test of hypothesis (1) in the face of negative evidence for (2).

Though we do not wish to undertake an extended discussion of particular scaling techniques, with respect to our illustration, the experimental procedure of paired comparisons seems to offer distinct possibilities because of all the methods appropriate to stimulus or judgment models, paired comparisons is the only one that does not impose transitivity on the data. By the very nature of the procedures, methods of ranking, rating, and sorting require that if *aPb* and *bPc*, then *a* must, as a consequence, *Pc*. In contra-distinction to this, paired comparisons requires that each respondent compares each stimulus to every other stimulus, thus allowing for the possibility of individuals giving the responses *aPb* and *bPc*, but *cPa*. Thus, the method allows for a direct test of the transitivity hypothesis for P. Since no equality judgments are allowed, however, an equivalent test for the relation C is not available, strictly speaking. The equality relation may be inferred by observing the joint proportions. See Torgerson, *op. cit.*, Chs. 8-9. For an alternative example of a scaling technique used to analyze social status ranking data, see Peter Park, "Scale Analysis of Social Status Ranking," *Sociological Inquiry*, 37 (1967), pp. 345-356.

the assumptions which are either implicitly or explicitly suggested by current usage. With respect to our illustration, for example, the meaning analysis dictated the direct test of the postulates of order for a quasi-series. It is not to be concluded that that phase of explication referred to as empirical analysis must always involve attempts at measurement or scaling. Depending on the nature of the concept in question, other approaches might be efficacious. It is likely, however, that the most fruitful explications will be those that involve appropriate measurement procedures.

The relationships between this suggested program of explication for "theoretical" terms and the alternative criteria regarding concepts with epistemic and constitutive connections are apparent. Both provide a methodological rationale for the evaluation of concepts, one on the basis of whether or not the concept is contained within a theory sketch, and the other on the basis of whether or not the concept has been explicated.[35] From the point of view of theory contruction, however, explicated concepts could contribute both to the transformation of an implicit theory into a theory sketch, and of a theory sketch into an explicit theory. Explicated concepts could help transform an implicit theory into a theory sketch by clarifying and validating the assumptions inherent in the vague pre-systematic usage. Or, if the analysis is begun by focusing on the theory sketch, explicated concepts embedded within its propositions may help in "filling out" the sketch, thereby facilitating its transformation into a more explicit theory. As Hempel has stated, "a scientifically acceptable explanation sketch needs to be filled out by more specific statements." In this case, part of the filling out process would involve reducing the ambiguities, inconsistencies, and limitations associated with the unexplicated concepts by introducing reinterpretations that enhance the precision of their meanings. The substitution of an explicated term for a vague one in a propositional statement could very well effect an increase in its explanatory and predictive import. It must be constantly borne in mind, however, that there are presently no definitive rules for exploratory excursions into the "context of discovery," and, in the final analysis, only the ongoing process of rigorous inquiry will reveal the efficacy of any suggestions evoked to improve the "scientific status" of sociologial "theory."

SUMMARY

The purpose of this paper was to suggest bases for the selection, evaluation, and utilization of "theoretical" concepts that function either within or outside

---

[35] It would be unrealistic to assume that all prescientific candidates for the theoretical language are amenable to such explication, but it is most important to realize that vague and intuitively derived notions can be of little use for the realization of the primary goals of the scientific enterprise, sound description and explanation. Although both the explicated concept and the concept with epistemic and constitutive connections in a theory sketch are initially evaluated on methodological grounds, an empirical claim is also being made that such concepts will, in the long run, prove to be more fruitful from the point of view of the systematization of knowledge than concepts that do not possess these characteristics. Accordingly, as we have indicated earlier (see footnote 8), as evidence is gathered to support or refute the empirical claim, the evaluation is based on both methodological and empirical considerations.

of the context of systematic sociological theories. A brief description of the role and status of theoretical concepts in *explicit theories* was provided in order to contrast the role and status of "theoretical" concepts in systematic sociological theories. The term *theory sketch* was used to describe such theories in sociology. It was emphasized that although theoretical concepts functioning within theory sketches lack *epistemic* and *constitutive significance*, they do have *epistemic* and *constitutive* connections. Accordingly, such concepts may be afforded *potential significance* because they satisfy certain minimal criteria of scientific adequacy, e.g., being part of testable propositions.

It is further stipulated, however, that *isolated abstract concepts* in sociology cannot be evaluated on this basis, even though their abstractions may have their bases in some underlying *implicit theory*, because they are not part of a formal theory, i.e., theory sketch or explicit theory. It was suggested that certain isolated abstract concepts could be advanced as candidates for the theoretical language in either a theory sketch or explicit theory via the process of *explication.*

A proposed program of explication, consisting of the interdependent phases of *meaning analysis* and *empirical analysis,* and appropriate to the current stages of theoretical and empirical development in sociology, was advanced. It was argued that whereas the meaning analysis phase is concerned with culling out the most fundamental assumptions which are either implicit or explicit in the customary usage of the term in question, empirical analysis involves a direct test of these assumptions. In addition, the notion of "social status" was employed to illustrate how such a program might be realized. Finally, it was suggested that an explicated concept serves, not only as a basis for evaluating isolated abstract concepts on methodological grounds, but it may also be a useful instrument in theory construction by helping to make implicit theories and theory sketches more explicit.

OPERATIONALIZING A CONCEPTUAL SCHEME:
THE UNIVERSALISM–PARTICULARISM
PATTERN VARIABLE

Peter M. Blau

One of the five distinctions Parsons and Shils draw in their refinement of Toennies' *Gesellschaft-Gemeinschaft* dichotomy is that between universalistic and particularistic standards in the orientations of people.[1] Cognitive evaluation involves discriminating between objects by applying the same standard universalistically to all of them, as in using a yardstick or making scientific judgments. In cathectic evaluation, however, the particular relationship between actor and objects serves as the particularistic standard for discriminating between objects, as in a person's feeling of identification with the symbols of his own culture.[2] This general distinction is applicable to orientations toward all kinds of objects, but of primary interest is its significance for people's orientations to "social objects," that is, to other people.[3] The crucial difference is whether the orientations of people toward one another are governed by standards that are independent of or dependent on the particular relations that exist between them. The former, universalistic standards are illustrated when all candidates for a job are judged solely on the basis of merit; the latter, particularistic standards are exemplified by nepotism in hiring practices or by a mother's love for *her* children.

While such illustrations make the abstract theoretical concepts more vivid and concrete, they are misleading inasmuch as they blur the distinctiveness of the analytical concepts, specifically, the distinction Parsons and Shils make between universalism-particularism and the four other pattern variables. Only one of several relevant differences between judging candidates on the basis of merit and either nepotism or maternal love is that between universalism and particularism. A second difference is that merit judgments are oriented to the other person's performance or achievement, while nepotism entails an orientation to his ascribed qualities—kinship status. A third difference is that the employer who

Reprinted with permission of the author and the publisher, The American Sociological Association, from the *American Sociological Review,* Vol. 27 (1962), 159-69.

I want to acknowledge the helpful comments of James S. Davis, Otis Dudley Duncan, David Gold, Robert W. Hodge, and Elihu Katz, as well as financial assistance from a Ford Foundation grant.

[1] Talcott Parsons and Edward A. Shils, *Toward a General Theory of Action,* Cambridge, Mass.: Harvard University Press, 1951, pp. 76-88.

[2] Talcott Parsons, *The Social System,* Glencoe, Ill.: The Free Press, 1951, p. 62.

[3] When Parsons originally introduced this distinction it clearly referred to people's orientation to other people. See Talcott Parsons, *Essays in Sociological Theory,* Glencoe, Ill.: The Free Press, 1949, pp. 185-99, especially p. 192. This essay was originally published in 1939.

considers only the qualification of candidates does not express personal feeling or affect in evaluating them, whereas the one who gives preference to relatives or friends does express his emotional attachments, and the mother's orientation to her children, too, is affective rather than affectively neutral. A fourth contrast between considering only the candidates' merit and nepotism is that between the specifically circumscribed role relations in the former case and the more diffuse ones in the latter. Finally, the employer who selects the best qualified candidate acts in terms of his self-interest, whereas nepotism indicates that primacy is given to the interest of the kinship collectively in which a person is involved, and so does a mother's treatment of her children. In short, these examples do not really clarify the distinction between universalism and particularism since they confound it with the distinction made by all the other pattern variables—performance-quality, neutrality-affectivity, specificity-diffuseness, and self-collectivity.

There is, then, the danger that the way universalism-particularism and the other pattern variables are actually used in sociological analysis ignores the particular Parsons-Shils contribution: their refinements of the earlier conception of *Gesellschaft and Gemeinschaft*. It is not easy to guard against this danger, because the meaning of these concepts is not unequivocally specified. For example, if employers require candidates for certain jobs to have college degrees, they adopt a universalistic standard. But what standard is manifest in the requirement that candidates be whites? On the one hand, such racial prejudice reflects a cathectic rather than cognitive evaluation, implying a particularlistic standard. On the other hand, however, the requirement that all employees must have a certain skin color does not seem to be any less universal than the requirement that they all must have a certain education, which implies that the former, just as the latter, is a universalistic standard. How do we decide which one it is?

Another problem is posed by the fact that the pattern variables are deliberately formulated so that they can characterize either individual personalities or abstract cultures or social systems. As sociologists, we are primarily interested in the latter, that is, in the actual role relations in social structures rather than in personality dispositions or in cultural symbols. But a definition of universalism-particularism that is based on the orientations expressed by individuals—whether they are guided by objective standards or let their feelings for particular persons influence their judgments—clearly refers to personality differences. To assume that adding or averaging such measures of individual characteristics in a population furnishes an index of a characteristic of the social system surely rests on a naive conception of social system as being merely the sum total of the psychological traits of individuals. And if we substitute for these direct expressions of orientations statements about how people generally *ought* to be oriented to one another under various conditions, we obtain an index that reflects cultural ideals and, again, not the actual structure of role relations in a social system. But what is the distinctive meaning of universalism-particularism in reference to a social system?

The objectives of this paper are to present and discuss an operational definition of universalism-particularism that (1) can be used in systematic research; (2) clearly differentiates this one from the other pattern variables; (3)

refers to social systems rather than personalities or cultures; and (4) clarifies the difference between this and related concepts, such as that of a unique social relationship. In exploring the interrelations between this operationalized pattern variable and the four others, attention will be directed to empirical procedures for testing hypotheses concerning the relationships between pattern variables. In a sense, the paper suggests a framework for research that would help to translate the theoretical scheme and theoretical insights of Parsons and Shils into a substantive, propositional theory of social structure.

OPERATIONAL DEFINITION

Universalistic standards, according to Parsons and Shils, are "defined in completely generalized terms, independent of *the particular relationship of the actor's own statuses* (qualities or performances, classificatory or relational) *to those of the object.*" Particularistic standards, in contrast, "assert the primacy of the values attached to objects by their particular relations to the actor's properties (qualities or performances, classificatory or relational) as over against their general universally applicable class properties."[4] The specific criterion of differentiation, therefore, is whether the standards reflected in people's orientation to one another are or are not independent of the *relationship between the status attributes* of the actors and those of the objects of their orientations. The operational definition suggested focuses upon this fundamental point and infers whether universalistic or particularistic standards govern the orientations in a collectivity from the actual distribution of orientations among its individual members. A hypothetical example will illustrate the procedure involved.

Let us assume that the members of the American Sociological Association had been asked in a survey to name the twenty outstanding living sociologists in the United States. Both the respondents and the persons named are classified by field of specialization into theorists, methodologists, and specialists in a number of substantive fields, and the distribution of nominations among these categories is analyzed. One possible finding would be that sociologists in all fields name a disproportionate number of theorists as their outstanding colleagues. This would show that being a theorist (or its correlates) serves as a universalistic standard in these evaluations. To be sure, it is unlikely that all choices go to theorists; there are idiosyncratic variations. But the *tendency* to select theorists is universal, that is, independent of the respondent's field of specialization. Another possible finding would be that only theorists name other theorists in disproportionate numbers, whereas methodologists overselect other methodologists, and men in each substantive specialty reveal a similar preference for others in their own field. This would indicate that field of specialization serves as a particularistic standard in these evaluations. For it would show that the reputation of sociologists among colleagues is influenced by the particular relationship between the field of the chooser and that of the chosen rather than by a generic characteristic of a field that is universally acknowledged as important.

In sum, the observed distribution of evaluations furnishes a rigorous criterion

[4] Parsons and Shils, *op. cit.*, p. 82 (italics supplied).

for determining whether the independent variable serves as universalistic or particularistic standard for these evaluations (or as neither, which would be manifest in the absence of any distinct pattern).[5] It should be noted that the valence of the evaluations—which ones are predominantly positive or negative— has no bearing upon this discrimination between standards. If sociologists in all fields were found to consider disproportionately few theorists outstanding and to name disproportionately many methodologists or persons in one substantive speciality, or those in several, as outstanding, it would also reflect a universalistic standard. And if for some reasons the sociologists in every field were found to respect colleagues in their own specialty less than those in other specialities, this would also reveal a particularistic standard, albeit an inverse one; that is, complementary needs as well as homophily reflect particularism.

The operational procedure might be further clarified by introducing two empirical illustrations. Caseworkers in a welfare agency were asked which three of their immediate colleagues they considered the best caseworkers.[6] Experience in the agency (or its correlates) served as a universalistic standard in these evaluations: workers with more than one year of seniority were respected in disproportionate numbers by co-workers who had much seniority as well as by those who had little seniority. (See Table 1; the H values presented in alternate columns indicate how much the observed values in a cell exceed or fall short of chance expectation.[7]) Class origin (or its correlates), however, served as a

TABLE 1.   Influence of Seniority on Respect

	Seniority of Chosen					
	Less Than One Year		More Than One Year		*Total*	*Total*
Seniority of Chooser	*N*	*H*	*N*	*H*	*Choices*	*Persons*
Less than one year	11	-.40	41	+.40	52	21
More than one year	23	-.19	58	+.19	81	39
Total choices	34	–	99	–	133	60
Total persons	21	–	39	–	60	–

[5]The assumption is that the characteristics in terms of which the members are classified is the independent variable that influences their evaluations of each other, the dependent variable. Cases where the social evaluations influence people's characteristics will not be considered here.

[6]For a full exposition of these cases and others briefly referred to later in the text, see Peter M. Blau, "Patterns of Choice in Interpersonal Relations," *American Sociological Review,* 27 (February, 1962), pp. 41-55.

[7]See James S. Coleman, "Relational Analysis," *Human Organization,* 17 (Winter, 1958-1959), pp. 28-36. The equations for determining H are: if A is greater than E, H = (A − E)/(M − E); if A is smaller than E, H = (A − E)/E; where A is the number of actual, E the number of expected, and M the maximum number of choices in a cell. Hence, H is the proportion of the maximum possible deviation from the expected frequency that is achieved by the observed deviation from expectation. The maximum possible for a cell is the total number of choices made in a given row (thus, for the upper-right cell in Table 1, M = 52). The expected value in a cell is the product of this number of *choices* in the *row* and the number of *persons* in the *column,* divided by the total number of persons in the sample (for the example, E = 52 x 39/60 = 33.8). Although 60 respondents were asked to make three choices each, the total is only 133, because some made fewer than three choices, and because choices of persons not interviewed are not included.

particularistic standard in these evaluations: caseworkers with fathers in manual occupations tended to overselect colleagues who also came from working-class families, and children of non-manual fathers tended to overselect others who shared their middle-class background (see Table 2). Both universalistic and particularistic standards governed the respect these workers accorded one another.

TABLE 2.   Influence of Father's Occupation on Respect*

| Father's Occupation of Chooser | Father's Occupation of Chosen | | | | | | Total Choices | Total Persons |
| | Manual | | Non-Manual | | Father Deceased | | | |
	N	H	N	H	N	H		
Manual	59	+.17	18	-.06	6	-.28	83	39
Non-manual	17	-.35	20	+.33	3	-.25	40	15
Father deceased	6	-.08	3	+.07	1	.00	10	6
Total choices	82	—	41	—	10	—	133	60
Total persons	39	—	15	—	6	—	60	—

*Respondents were asked to state what their father's occupations were when they were growing up.

In principle, the procedure involves generating a who-to-whom matrix of people's evaluations of each other in which both the respondents and the objects of their evaluations are classified in terms of certain attributes.[8] Any factor by which people can be characterized may be used for this classification, and more than one may be used simultaneously. All relations among persons that meet a given criterion of evaluation or orientation, such as naming another as a respected colleague, are entered into the matrix. The operational criterion of a universalistic standard is that the disproportionately high (or low) frequencies appear in parallel columns; the operational criterion of a particularistic standard is that these frequencies appear in the major diagonal.[9]

IMPLICATIONS

The question that must be raised about an operational definition is: what are the specific parameters of the theoretical concepts presumably measured that are implied by it? In effect, the implications of an operational definition specify—refine or distort, as the case may be—the characteristics of the analytical concept.

The operational criterion suggested does not indicate whether a certain orientation is universalistic or particularistic but whether a factor that influences it does so by acting as a universalistic or particularistic standard for it. An orientation is typically influenced by a number of factors, some of which may

[8] Ideally, enough cases should be available to permit a matrix larger than 2 x 2 and still leave sufficient expected cases in each cell for reliable inference.

[9] If the table is constructed differently from those we have presented, the implications of various visual patterns will, of course, change. Thus, if the headings in Table 2 were "Same as Father" and "Different from Father," particularism would be manifest in a pattern of plusses in parallel columns rather than in the diagonal.

act as universalistic and others as particularistic standards. Moreover, the operational criterion does not show that a given variable, say seniority, constitutes one or the other standard in a collectivity, since it may be a universalistic standard for some orientations and a particularistic one for others (as was, indeed, the case for seniority in the welfare agency). Universalism-particularism is a dimension of the standard that underlies an orientation in a collectivity rather than of the orientation itself, and the same characteristic does not necessarily serve as the same standard for different orientations.

By the very nature of the operational criterion, universalism and particularism so defined necessarily refer to the standards implicit in the role relationships of a social system,[10] not to the standards that guide the motives of individuals, and not to the ideal standards of the culture. The claim that we are dealing here with attributes of social structure, rather than those of culture or personality structure, rests on a certain conception of social structure or system. The study of social systems might be conceived as being concerned with the economic, political, and other basic institutions in a society, and not with the actual orientations and observable patterns of conduct of people. Or it might be conceived as including only the macroscopic analysis of the relations among various groups in a society and not with the microscopic analysis of the social relations between individuals in these groups. In terms of either of these conceptions, it would not be correct to state that universalism-particularism as previously defined is a characteristic of social systems. But a more analytic conception of social system includes under it the interrelationships among all attributes of collectivities that cannot be reduced to attributes of persons, such as suicide rates, status differentiation, the distribution of orientations in a group, or the resulting structure of role relations. In terms of this conception, which views social systems as only analytically distinct from culture or personality systems, the operational criterion clearly pertains to social systems. For the criterion specifically indicates the standard on which the actual distribution of orientations in a collectivity rests. It does not show whether cultural norms legitimate universalistic or particularistic standards under given conditions, nor does it tell us whether the individuals making the evaluations are motivated by universalistic or by particularistic considerations.[11]

The motivational standards that govern the orientations of individuals do not necessarily correspond to the social standards implicit in the distribution of these orientations in a collectivity. Even though individuals make rational judgments on the basis of objective criteria, their collective evaluations might rest on a particularistic standard. Thus, the hypothetical finding that the members of a discipline tend to respect others in their own field of specialization in disproportionate numbers indicates that a particularistic standard underlies these evaluations, but it does not show that the respondents are irrational or biased in their judgments, since we do not know what considerations have motivated their decisions. For example, the tendency to overselect colleagues in

---

[10]The pattern variables are abstract, formal standards underlying role relations, which must be distinguished from the substantive norms to which we usually refer when we talk about roles and role expectations.

[11]But parallel criteria that do refer to cultural norms or to the dispositions of individuals could be developed.

one's own field might be due to the fact that these are the only persons about whose work one knows enough to make intelligent judgments. It is also possible that men in different fields employ different standards in choosing their outstanding colleagues—theorists might judge others by their conceptual sophistication, methodologists, by their statistical acumen—and although the various respondents rationally and impartially employ an objective standard, the end product is a disproportionate number of ingroup selections. The existence of diverse standards of respect, however, is *a fortiori* evidence that there is not one universal standard. And if diverse standards have the result that the pattern of evaluations is contingent on the relationship between the chooser's attribute and that of the chosen, they reflect, in fact, an underlying particularistic standard. Whether the social evaluations in a collectivity rest on universalistic or particularistic standards, and whether individuals make these evaluations on rational grounds or not, are two independent questions.

Another important distinction is that between the standards reflected in the actual social orientations and role relations in a collectivity, on the one hand, and the cultural norms that define what standards ought to govern people's orientations to and treatment of their fellows under various conditions, on the other. In most working relations in modern society, for instance, universalism is culturally approved and particularism is disapproved. Actually, of course, many particularistic standards influence working relations; nepotism and the social significance of ethnic and class background are only the most conspicuous examples. But particularism is culturally prescribed for family relations, since the persistence of families would be threatened if, say, mothers were guided by universalistic standards and thus willing to reject their own children in favor of others that are prettier or more intelligent. The prevailing cultural ideals and the personality traits of the members of a collectivity influences, of course, their orientations toward one another, but the standards implicit in the social pattern of these orientations are distinct from either cultural or personality standards.

According to the operational definition, particularism does not mean that the orientations of two persons toward one another have some unique features. Even such general standards as those manifest in a preference for companionship with persons of one's own sex or in the requirement that civil servants must be citizens of the employing country are defined by the criterion as particularistic. This seems to violate our intuitive conception of particularism as denoting that an individual has a distinctive orientation and unique obligations toward one or a few others, for example, his children. But Parsons explicitly states that particularistic standards "may be formulated in terms of a general rule,"[12] which implies that they are not unique, although the content of what they prescribe may be, and his discussion of particularism as a basis of social solidarity[13] also indicates that in his view this concept referred to a characteristic that is typical for certain role relationships and not to that which makes one role relationship unique. A man's orientation toward his family is considered to be particularistic because it singles out for special attention the members of an ingroup, rather than persons with a certain attribute regardless of

---

[12] Talcott Parsons, *The Social System, op. cit.,* p. 63.
[13] *Ibid.,* p.455, and Talcott Parsons, *et al., Working Papers in the Theory of Action,* Glencoe, Ill.: The Free Press, 1953, p. 229.

whether it makes them part of his ingroup or not. In this respect, a preference for associates of one's own sex, while admittedly an extreme case, differs only in degree from a preference for one's own ethnic group, or social class, or family, but it differs in kind from a general preference for males, or whites, or upper-class people, or the royal British family. The operational procedure quite properly classifies all four former cases as particularistic, and the four latter, as universalistic, since particularism refers to the fact that people's orientations toward the ingroup differ from those toward the outgroup, whatever the definition of group boundaries. Only in the polar case where the boundaries of the ingroup include merely one person, say a spouse, is an individual's particularistic orientation uniquely different from his orientations toward all other people.

The questions raised earlier whether discriminatory employment practices reveal a universalistic or particularistic standard can now be answered. If white employers hire mostly white workers, and Negro employers, Negro workers, the standard is unquestionably particularistic. But if Negro as well as white employers were to prefer white employees, the underlying standard would be defined by the criterion as universalistic. This may appear strange, since anti-Negro prejudice in the second example is even more pervasive than in the first. The issue, however, is not how prejudiced people are. A prejudice shared by all, even the minority in question, reflects a universal standard; only a bias confined to the ingroup reflects a particularistic one.[14]

People's orientations to others find expression not only in answers to essentially sociometric questions but also in many decisions, which can be examined, and in their social interaction, which can be observed. There are many types of data to which the analysis proposed can be applied. To cite a few examples: the decisions of faculty members to give fellowships to students; the decisions of fraternity brothers to pledge new students; the decisions of caseworkers to grant assistance to applicants; the votes of jurors concerning the accused; the sanctions a supervisor administers to subordinates; the frequency with which members of a group initiate social contacts with other members. In each case, the actors and the objects of their action would be classified in terms of some variable to determine whether the distribution of positive (or negative) actions reveals a universalistic or particularistic standard.[15]

[14]Universalism does not imply that people make rational judgments, just as particularism does not imply that they do not. In terms of reference group theory, the difference between the two situations in the illustration is whether Negro employers are oriented toward Negroes as their reference group or whether they as well as white employers are oriented toward whites as their reference group. If the values of one group are the frame of reference for the members of other groups as well as for its own members, the distribution of orientations in the larger collectivity will be governed by universalistic standards, but if most people are oriented toward their own ingroup as their reference group, particularistic standards will prevail. (For the distinction between ingroup and outgroup as reference group, see Robert K. Merton, *Social Theory and Social Structure,* rev. ed., Glencoe, Ill.: Free Press, 1957, pp. 231-33.)

[15]To avoid errors of interpretation in those cases where the respondents who make the evaluations and the persons evaluated are two distinct groups, care must be exercised to take into account possible processes of selection. Let us assume, for example, that most students apply for admission to colleges in their home state. As a result, a disproportionate number of admitted students in most colleges would come from their own states. But this finding would not indicate that state boundaries serve as particularistic standards for admission

62 CONCEPTUALIZATION

There are, however, some measures of social relations that would yield misleading results when used in this type of analysis. Let us assume that most students in a high school, regardless of their academic standing, are attracted to and want to become friends of fellow students whose academic standing is high. This would mean that academic standing is a universalistic standard of attraction. But while the company of outstanding students is much in demand, they themselves do not want to become friends with everybody, nor would they have the time to do so if they did want it. Chances are that under these conditions the best students would primarily associate with equally outstanding students, since here preferences are often reciprocal, and other friendships would also usually involve partners of approximately equal academic standing. From this pattern of ingroup association (with the excessive choices in the diagonal of the matrix) one would conclude that academic standing is a particularistic standard of attraction to associates, but this conclusion is false, since we know it to be a universalistic standard. The actual patterns of association among people— friendships, frequencies of interaction, memberships in voluntary associations— often indicate ingroup choices although the relevant social evaluations are governed by a universalistic standard. For this reason, only measures of social evaluations and not measures of extent of social associations may be used to infer whether particularistic or universalistic standards prevail.

Which standard governs significant social evaluations has important implications for the social structure. Universalistic standards produce social differentiation. If intelligent people, for example, are generally respected, it implies both that intelligence is a universalistic standard for respect and that intelligence helps to create differences in prestige status.[16] Particularistic standards typically produce segregating boundaries in the social structure. Thus, the finding that the members of various religious denominations in a community think more highly of and are more attracted to co-religionists than persons in other denominations would show that religion is a particularistic standard and also that it promotes social divisions among members of the community. This does not contradict Parsons' point that particularism is closely connected with group solidarity.[17] Particularism is, indeed, both an expression and a condition of the solidarity of the subgroup—in the example, the religious denomination—but for this very reason it creates some segregating barriers in the larger collectivity.[18]

-----

policies, since it would largely reflect the actions of the student applicants, not the evaulations of the admission committees. In such cases, a correction for self-selection must be applied. Evidence that these standards are particularistic would require data that show that the proportion of home-state applicants who are admitted is greater than the proportion of admitted out-of-state applicants.

[16] Parsons implies such a nexus between universalism and status of differentiation; see *The Social System, op. cit.,* p. 122.

[17] See references, footnote 13.

[18] A preponderance of negative orientations toward the ingroup and positive ones toward the outgroup, which might be considered inverse particularism, strengthens the solidarity of the larger collectivity at the expense of the subgroup. The strong identification of parents with children and vice versa, for example, strengthens family solidarity by somewhat weakening intragenerational unity.

FRAMEWORK

Universalism-particularism is a dimension of the structure of role relations in a collectivity which can be observed and interpreted only within the framework of other dimensions. An examination of the dimensions that specify, so to speak, the coordinates of universalism-particularism leads to a consideration of the four other pattern variables of Parsons' scheme.

One condition that must be clarified is the nature of the characteristic that serves as a universalistic standard. There are innumerable attributes by which people can be characterized, and these can be classified in many different ways. One possible classification—the one suggested by the scheme of Parsons and Shils—divides variables on the basis of whether they refer to the performance and achievements of a person or to his ascribed qualities—to what he does and can do or to who he is. Is there a consistent relationship between the performance-quality and the universalism-particularism dimension? The data from the welfare agency previously mentioned did not reveal one. They showed, for instance, that some aspects of performance, such as competence, served as universalistic standards of respect, and others, such as how much time and energy caseworkers devoted to checking up on clients, served as particularistic standards of respect. The findings suggest that those differences in performance that reflect differences in values, as many do—for example, whether checking on or furnishing services to clients is more important—constitute particularistic standards of interpersonal evaluations.[19]

A second condition to be specified is the kind of orientations to other people that is under consideration. Are we dealing with answers to sociometric questions, people's decisions concerning others, their actual conduct toward each other, or another form of social evaluation? And how can the orientations indicated by various empirical measures be classified? A fundamental distinction is that between manifestations of respect and expressions of feelings of attraction, and this dichotomy parallels the pattern variable neutrality-affectivity.

The framework presented so far makes it possible to translate the problem of what the interrelations between the dimensions or pattern variables are into a research problem. The basic research questions about the first three dimensions are whether performance or quality characteristics tend to serve as universalistic or particularistic standards for neutral (respect) or affective (attraction) orientations. Evidently, a large number of systematic empirical comparisons under various conditions would be necessary to answer these questions. The research would be guided only by the general hypothesis that the relations between the three dimensions reveal some consistent patterns. It is, of course, possible that even this general hypothesis is not confirmed; indeed, preliminary analysis based on data from two studies and involving several hundred comparisons did not reveal any consistent pattern in these terms. Such a negative finding, if confirmed on a larger scale, would direct attention to needed revisions in the theoretical scheme. How can the classification of characteristics into performances and qualities be refined or altered to encompass the regularities observed? What modifications in the dichotomy of orientations are indicated by the empirical findings? Which further conditions should be specified? In brief,

[19] See Blau, *loc. cit.*

the framework for research suggested would furnish a pragmatic test of the utility of Parsons' theoretical scheme, a procedure for introducing required conceptual refinements, and a method for deriving substantive theoretical propositions from it.

The first three dimensions appear to be the most basic, since every single matrix necessarily involves all three of them—a type of *attribute* that acts as a certain *standard* for a given kind of *orientation*. To analyze the relationships among these dimensions and establish generalizations about them, however, requires comparing many matrices. Once such comparisons are made, two further dimensions must be taken into account.

The significance of attributes of people for their evaluations and treatment of one another varies in scope. It may be specific, confined to one aspect of their orientation to others, or diffuse, extending to most of their orientations. The comparison of the impact of a given attribute on several different orientations to other people provides an index of this dimension of specificity-diffuseness. For example, how often welfare workers came to the office late influenced their choice of consultants but none of their other, broader orientations to each other. Workers tended to prefer consultants who were as punctual or as tardy as they themselves. This measure of strict adherence to official rules, therefore, served as a *specific* particularistic standard. How much time workers spent in the field, on the other hand, apparently reflected differences in values of *diffuse* particularistic significance. Workers who were alike on this measure respected one another, preferred to consult one another, felt attracted to one another, and expressed other positive orientations to one another in disproportionate numbers. Similarly, some variables served as specific, and others, as diffuse universalistic standards.[20]

A final dimension to be considered is the compass or inclusiveness of the social system. Reliable generalizations about the structure of role relations must be based on or tested with data from a representative sample of collectivities. Even if we cannot yet achieve such an ideal research design, however, we must take into consideration that the varying conditions in different social systems in all probability exert a distinct influence on people's orientations to each other. The pattern of role relations among freshmen in a high school, for example, may well differ from that among seniors. These differences and the relationships between the role structures in the various classes of the high school constitute new data that characterize the social system of the high school as distinguished from the social systems of its subgroups. Moreover, the social patterns in the different high schools in a community can be compared, and this comparison yields a description of the social system of the community's high school population. Larger collectivities encompass smaller ones, and while the social system of the latter consists essentially of role relations among individuals, that of the former involves primarily the relationships among these role structures in sub-systems.

---

[20]Specificity-diffuseness as here defined, just as universalism-particularism, refers to the standards that prevail in a collectivity, not to the orientations of individuals. A corresponding measure of specificity-diffuseness in the orientations of individuals could be based on the criterion of whether an individual tends to express only a single one or a variety of positive (or negative) orientations—respect, attraction, and others—to given other persons.

The concept of compass of social systems is akin to the self-collectivity pattern variable not as originally conceived, when it distinguished self-interested from disinterested orientations, but as later redefined, when it came to refer more to the level of system under consideration.[21]

Fictitious research findings will illustrate this dimension. Assume that high schools have been divided on the basis of the average amount of time students spend on academic pursuits outside of school, which may be thought of as an index of academic orientation. Students in all schools are asked which fellow students they would most like to have as friends. In schools with a high academic orientation, the students who devote *most* time to academic pursuits are most popular, that is, they are named in disproportionate numbers not only by others who do equally as much academic work but also by those who do relatively little academic work. This indicates that academic orientation serves as a universalistic standard of attraction. In schools with a low academic orientation, however, the students who devote *least* time to academic pursuits are most popular among fellow students who manifest more interest than they in academic work as well as among those who also have little interest in it. This, too, indicates that academic orientation serves as a universalistic standard of attraction, but here it has a negative rather than a positive valence. In both kinds of schools, then, the prevailing value orientation serves as a universalistic standard for rewarding those individuals who express the dominant value most fully with popularity.

But note what this implies for the larger social system composed of all these high schools. From the perspective of this larger system, academic orientation constitutes a particularistic standard. For a student's popularity in the wider social system does not depend on his having certain academic characteristics that are universally acknowledged as attractive, but it depends on his having the same characteristics that prevail among his fellow students who evaluate him, only in more extreme form.[22] The reason is that diverse and conflicting universalistic standards constitute, in effect, a particularistic standard, as mentioned earlier. Hence, even the influence of a specific attribute on a single orientation to people in a given population cannot be described as either universalistic or particularistic without specifying whether the analysis is concerned with the subsystems into which any larger system can be divided, treating each as a social system, or with the wider social system that encompasses them.

CONCLUSIONS

In the study of the social values and norms that govern role relations in social structures, it is easy to confound traits of personality systems with attributes of social systems. This danger is especially acute for concepts such as universalism-

[21]Parsons, *et al., op. cit.,* pp. 258-63 and especially Talcott Parsons and Robert F. Bales, *Family, Socialization and Interaction Process,* Glencoe, Ill.: The Free Press, 1955, pp. 142-43. Parsons' illustrations, however, tend to revert back to the self-interest meaning.

[22]This type of finding is related to, although not identical with, what I have called a structural effect, which means that the prevalence of an orientation in a collectivity has an effect that is distinct from any effect of the same orientation of individuals. See Peter M. Blau, "Structural Effects," *American Sociological Review,* 25 (April, 1960), pp. 178-193.

particularism and the other pattern variables developed by Parsons and Shils which are explicitly designed to refer either to the role relations in social systems or to the dispositions of individual personalities or to the norms and symbols of a culture. If we ascertain whether the judgments of individuals are governed by objective cognitive standards or dominated by feelings of attachment to particular persons, we are dealing with psychological differences between individuals. If we seek to go beyond such personality differences by determining what kind of orientation is generally considered to be proper and legitimate in various social situations—one guided by objective criteria or one that rests on personal attachments—we are dealing with cultural norms. To be sure, the psychological orientations of people and the prevailing cultural norms are both related to the actual structure of role relations in a social system, but the former two are not identical with the latter. Attempts to characterize social structures in terms of individuals' psychological orientations or normative ideals involves psychological or culturological reductionism in the study of social systems. Moreover, the fine analytical distinctions between universalism-particularism and the other pattern variables, which are essential for the theoretical scheme, can hardly be preserved in measures directly based on the orientations of individuals, since these necessarily reflect admixtures of the analytical concepts.

An operational definition of universalism-particularism has been presented that meets these problems. It unequivocally refers to social systems (if this term is conceived to include interpersonal relations), for it cannot even be used to characterize individuals, or cultural norms, but only to describe the actual structure of role relations in a collectivity. It clearly distinguishes this pair of concepts from the four other pattern variables. Besides, it avoids the frequent confusion between universalism-particularism, on the one hand, and whether an orientation is typical of many social relations or confined to a few, if not unique. The operational criterion is derived from a matrix which shows what influence an attribute of the members of a collectivity has on their orientations to or evaluations of one another. An attribute is defined as a universalistic standard if persons, regardless of their own characteristics, direct a disproportionate number of their positive (or negative) evaluations to others with a certain characteristic. An attribute is defined as a particularistic standard if persons tend to direct their positive (or, in special cases, negative) evaluations to others whose characteristics are like their own.

This paper has, in effect, suggested a framework of research based on Parsons' theoretical scheme. The interrelations between the five dimensions of the structure of role relations defined by the five pattern variables have been delineated. If empirical data analyzed in terms of this framework would yield consistent and meaningful regularities, the adequacy of the scheme as it stands would have been pragmatically demonstrated. But this is undoubtedly too much to expect on the first try. Even if no such regularities are found, however, the framework serves a function by directing attention to the need for conceptual refinements. Preliminary investigations indicate, for example, that the concepts of performance and quality should probably be revised, partly by operational-izing the subtle distinctions Parsons makes in his conceptual analysis, but also partly by introducing further differentiations between various kinds of performances and qualities. Finally research carried out within this framework, particularly after it has been appropriately modified, could test hypotheses concerning the relationships between various concepts and thus help transform Parsons' theoretical scheme into a substantive theory of the structure of role relations. Essential for such a theory is that it be able to range from narrower to ever more encompassing social systems. To achieve a systematic theory of social structure, we must start by investigating the structure of role relations in systems small enough for individuals to interact with one another, proceed to analyze the differences and relationships between the various structures of role relations in the larger system, and go on in similar systematic fashion to more and more encompassing social systems.

3

Measurement

To assert the importance of operationalization is one thing, to do so satisfactorily and consistently is quite another. Enter the problems of measurement.

Many years ago S. S. Stevens specified the four levels of measurement which most of us routinely outline in our introductory methods classes: nominal, ordinal, interval, and ratio. Consistently he has argued for awareness of the extent to which one's statistical operations are dependent upon one's measurements. The more nearly we approximate ratio level measurement, the more sophisticated the mathematical and statistical operations which we are permitted.

We have included in the chapter one of Stevens' earliest papers, published in 1946, where he lucidly distinguishes the four levels of measurement and indicates appropriate statistical procedures. We follow up with his most recent contribution to the measurement argument, where he elaborates this view of the necessary relationships between level of measurement and statistical operations. These papers might well have been included in chapter 7. However, insofar as we accept Stevens' argument of the necessary relationship between measurement and permissable statistical procedure, the papers logically must be considered prior to a consideration of data analysis.

We conclude our chapter on measurement with Richard LaPiere's critical evaluation of one of the discipline's most basic measurement tools: questionnaires. As LaPiere has argued, the assumption that there is a simple relationship between attitude and actual behavior would seem to be demonstrably unfounded. Yet through much of our research we continue to make this assumption, even in the face of contradictory empirical evidence.[1] At the very least, one must be aware that a relationship between attitude and behavior certainly cannot and must not be taken for granted. More than this, we cannot resist the implication that we must begin to pay some attention to measuring behavior more directly if it is in fact behavior that we wish to explain.[2]

[1] See Martin Fishbein, "Attitude and Prediction of Behavior" in M. Fishbein, ed., *Readings in Attitude Theory and Measurement* (New York: John Wiley & Sons, 1967).

[2] See Irwin Deutscher, "Words and Deeds: Social Science and Social Policy," *Social Problems* 13 (1966) 236-54.

ON THE THEORY OF SCALES OF MEASUREMENT

S. S. Stevens

For seven years a committee of the British Association for the Advancement of Science debated the problem of measurement. Appointed in 1932 to represent Section A (Mathematical and Physical Sciences) and Section J (Psychology), the committee was instructed to consider and report upon the possibility of "quantitative estimates of sensory events"—meaning simply: Is it possible to measure human sensations? Deliberation led only to disagreement, mainly about what is meant by the term measurement. An interim report in 1938 found one member complaining that his colleagues "came out by that same door as they went in," and in order to have another try at agreement, the committee begged to be continued for another year.

For its final report (1940) the committee chose a common bone for its contentions, directing its arguments at a concrete example of a sensory scale. This was the Sone scale of loudness (S. S. Stevens and H. Davis. *Hearing.* New York: Wiley, 1938), which purports to measure the subjective magnitude of an auditory sensation against a scale having the formal properties of other basic scales, such as those used to measure length and weight. Again the 19 members of the committee came out by the routes they entered, and their views ranged widely between two extremes. One member submitted "that any law purporting to express a quantitative relation between sensation intensity and stimulus intensity is not merely false but is in fact meaningless unless and until a meaning can be given to the concept of addition as applied to sensation" (Final Report, p. 245).

It is plain from this and from other statements by the committee that the real issue is the meaning of measurement. This, to be sure, is a semantic issue, but one susceptible of orderly discussion. Perhaps agreement can better be achieved if we recognize that measurement exists in a variety of forms and that scales of measurement fall into certain definite classes. These classes are determined both by the empirical operations invoked in the process of "measuring" and by the formal (mathematical) properties of the scales. Furthermore—and this is of great concern to several of the sciences—the statistical manipulations that can legitimately be applied to empirical data depend upon the type of scale against which the data are ordered.

A CLASSIFICATION OF SCALES OF MEASUREMENT

Paraphrasing N. R. Campbell (Final Report, p. 340), we may say that measurement, in the broadest sense, is defined as the assignment of numerals to

Reprinted with permission of the author and the publisher from *Science*, Vol. 684 (June 7, 1946), 677-80.

objects or events according to rules. The fact that numerals can be assigned under different rules leads to different kinds of scales and different kinds of measurement. The problem then becomes that of making explicit (a) the various rules for the assignment of numerals, (b) the mathematical properties (or group structure) of the resulting scales, and (c) the statistical operations applicable to measurements made with each type of scale.

Scales are possible in the first place only because there is a certain isomorphism between what we can do with the aspects of objects and the properties of the numeral series. In dealing with the aspects of objects we invoke empirical operations for determining equality (classifying), for rank-ordering, and for determining when differences and when ratios between the aspects of objects are equal. The conventional series of numerals yields to analogous operations: We can identify the members of a numeral series and classify them. We know their order as given by convention. We can determine equal differences, as 8 - 6 = 4 - 2, and equal ratios, as 8/4 = 6/3. The isomorphism between these properties of the numeral series and certain empirical operations which we perform with objects permits the use of the series as a *model* to represent aspects of the empirical world.

The type of scale achieved depends upon the character of the basic empirical operations performed. These operations are limited ordinarily by the nature of the thing being scaled and by our choice of procedures, but, once selected, the operations determine that there will eventuate one or another of the scales listed in Table 1.[1]

TABLE 1.

Scale	Basic Empirical Operations	Mathematical Group Structure	Permissible Statistics (invariantive)
Nominal	Determination of equality	*Permutation group* $x' = f(x)$ $f(x)$ means any one-to-one substitution	Number of cases Mode Contingency correlation
Ordinal	Determination of greater or less	*Isotonic group* $x' = f(x)$ $f(x)$ means any monotonic increasing function	Median Percentiles
Interval	Determination of equality of intervals or differences	*General linear group* $x' = ax + b$	Mean Standard deviation Rank-order correlation Product-moment correlation
Ratio	Determination of equality of ratios	*Similarity group* $x' = ax$	Coefficient of variation

[1] A classification essentially equivalent to that contained in this table was presented before the International Congress for the Unity of Science, September 1941. The writer is indebted

The decision to discard the scale names commonly encountered in writings on measurement is based on the ambiguity of such terms as "intensive" and "extensive." Both ordinal and interval scales have at times been called intensive, and both interval and ratio scales have sometimes been labeled extensive.

It will be noted that the column listing the basic operations needed to create each type of scale is cumulative: to an operation listed opposite a particular scale must be added all those operations preceding it. Thus, an interval scale can be erected only provided we have an operation for determining equality of intervals, for determining greater or less, and for determining equality (not greater and not less). To these operations must be added a method for ascertaining equality of ratios if a ratio scale is to be achieved.

In the column which records the group structure of each scale are listed the mathematical transformations which leave the scale-form invariant. Thus, any numeral, x, on a scale can be replaced by another numeral, x', where x' is the function of x listed in this column. Each mathematical group in the column is contained in the group immediately above it.

The last column presents examples of the type of statistical operations appropriate to each scale. This column is cumulative in that *all* statistics listed are admissible for data scaled against a ratio scale. The criterion for the appropriateness of a statistic is *invariance* under the transformations in Column 3. Thus, the case that stands at the median (mid-point) of a distribution maintains its position under all transformations which preserve order (isotonic group), but an item located at the mean remains at the mean only under transformations as restricted as those of the linear group. The ratio expressed by the coefficient of variation remains invariant only under the similarity transformation (multiplication by a constant). (The rank-order correlation coefficient is usually deemed appropriate to an ordinal scale, but actually this statistic assumes equal intervals between successive ranks and therefore calls for an interval scale.)

Let us now consider each scale in turn.

NOMINAL SCALE

The *nominal scale* represents the most unrestricted assignment of numerals. The numerals are used only as labels or type numbers, and words or letters would serve as well. Two types of nominal assignments are sometimes distinguished, as illustrated (a) by the 'numbering' of football players for the identification of the individuals, and (b) by the 'numbering' of types or classes, where each member of a class is assigned the same numeral. Actually, the first is a special case of the second, for when we label our football players we are dealing with unit classes of one member each. Since the purpose is just as well served when any two designating numerals are interchanged, this scale form remains invariant under the general substitution or permutation group (sometimes called the symmetric group of transformations). The only statistic relevant to nominal scales of Type A is the number of cases, e.g. the number of

---

to the late Prof. G. D. Birkhoff for a stimulating discussion which led to the completion of the table in essentially its present form.

players assigned numerals. But once classes containing several individuals have been formed (Type B), we can determine the most numerous class (the mode), and under certain conditions we can test, by the contingency methods, hypotheses regarding the distribution of cases among the classes.

The nominal scale is a primitive form, and quite naturally there are many who will urge that it is absurd to attribute to this process of assigning numerals the dignity implied by the term measurement. Certainly there can be no quarrel with this objection, for the naming of things is an arbitrary business. However we christen it, the use of numerals as names for classes is an example of the "assignment of numerals according to rule." The rule is: Do not assign the same numeral to different classes or different numerals to the same class. Beyond that, anything goes with the nominal scale.

ORDINAL SCALE

The *ordinal scale* arises from the operation of rank-ordering. Since any 'order-preserving' transformation will leave the scale form invariant, this scale has the structure of what may be called the isotonic or order-preserving group. A classic example of an ordinal scale is the scale of hardness of minerals. Other instances are found among scales of intelligence, personality traits, grade or quality of leather, etc.

As a matter of fact, most of the scales used widely and effectively by psychologists are ordinal scales. In the strictest propriety the ordinary statistics involving means and standard deviations ought not to be used with these scales, for these statistics imply a knowledge of something more than the relative rank-order of data. On the other hand, for this 'illegal' statisticizing there can be invoked a kind of pragmatic sanction: In numerous instances it leads to fruitful results. While the outlawing of this procedure would probably serve no good purpose, it is proper to point out that means and standard deviations computed on an ordinal scale are in error to the extent that the successive intervals on the scale are unequal in size. When only the rank-order of data is known, we should proceed cautiously with our statistics, and especially with the conclusions we draw from them.

Even in applying those statistics that are normally appropriate for ordinal scales, we sometimes find rigor compromised. Thus, although it is indicated in Table 1 that percentile measures may be applied to rank-ordered data, it should be pointed out that the customary procedure of assigning a value to a percentile by interpolating linearly within a class interval is, in all strictness, wholly out of bounds. Likewise, it is not strictly proper to determine the mid-point of a class interval by linear interpolation, because the linearity of an ordinal scale is precisely the property which is open to question.

INTERVAL SCALE

With the *interval scale* we come to a form that is "quantitative" in the ordinary sense of the word. Almost all the usual statistical measures are applicable here, unless they are the kinds that imply a knowledge of a 'true' zero point. The zero point on an interval scale is a matter of convention or convenience, as is shown by the fact that the scale form remains invariant when a constant is added.

This point is illustrated by our two scales of temperature, Centigrade and Fahrenheit. Equal intervals of temperature are sealed off by noting equal volumes of expansion; an arbitrary zero is agreed upon for each scale; and a numerical value on one of the scales is transformed into a value on the other by means of an equation of the form $x' = ax + b$. Our scales of time offer a similar example. Dates on one calendar are transformed to those on another by way of this same equation. On these scales, of course, it is meaningless to say that one value is twice or some other proportion greater than another.

Periods of time, however, can be measured on ratio scales and one period may be correctly defined as double another. The same is probably true of temperature measured on the so-called Absolute Scale.

Most psychological measurement aspires to create interval scales, and it sometimes succeeds. The problem usually is to devise operations for equalizing the units of the scales—a problem not always easy of solution but one for which there are several possible modes of attack. Only occasionally is there concern for the location of a 'true' zero point, because the human attributes measured by psychologists usually exist in a positive degree that is large compared with the range of its variation. In this respect these attributes are analogous to temperature as it is encountered in everyday life. Intelligence, for example, is usefully assessed on ordinal scales which try to approximate interval scales, and it is not neccessary to define what zero intelligence would mean.

RATIO SCALE

Ratio scales are those most commonly encountered in physics and are possible only when there exist operations for determining all four relations: equality, rank-order, equality of intervals, and equality of ratios. Once such a scale is erected, its numerical values can be transformed (as from inches to feet) only by multiplying each value by a constant. An absolute zero is always implied, even though the zero value on some scales (e.g. Absolute Temperature) may never be produced. All types of statistical measures are applicable to ratio scales, and only with these scales may we properly indulge in logarithmic transformations such as are involved in the use of decibels.

Foremost among the ratio scales is the scale of number itself—cardinal number—the scale we use when we count such things as eggs, pennies, and apples. This scale of the numerosity of aggregates is so basic and so common that it is ordinarily not even mentioned in discussions of measurement.

It is conventional in physics to distinguish between two types of ratio scales: *fundamental* and *derived*. Fundamental scales are represented by length, weight, and electrical resistance, whereas derived scales are represented by density, force, and elasticity.

These latter are *derived* magnitudes in the sense that they are mathematical functions of certain fundamental magnitudes. They are actually more numerous in physics than are the fundamental magnitudes, which are commonly held to be basic because they satisfy the criterion of *additivity*. Weights, lengths, and resistances can be added in the physical sense, but this important empirical fact is generally accorded more prominence in the theory of measurement than it deserves. The so-called fundamental scales are important instances of ratio scales, but they are only instances. As a matter of fact, it can be demonstrated that the fundamental scales could be set up even if the physical operation of addition were ruled out as impossible of performance. Given three balances, for example, each having the proper construction, a set of standard weights could be manufactured without it ever being neccessary to place two weights in the same scale pan at the same time. The procedure is too long to describe in these pages, but its feasibility is mentioned here simply to suggest that physical addition, even though it is sometimes possible, is not neccessarily the basis of all measurement. Too much measuring goes on where resort can never be had to the process of laying things end-to end or of piling them up in a heap.

Ratio scales of psychological magnitudes are rare but not entirely unknown. The Sone scale discussed by the British committee is an example founded on a deliberate attempt to have human observers judge the loudness ratios of pairs of tones. The judgment of equal intervals had long been established as a legitimate method, and with the work on sensory ratios, started independently in several laboratories, the final step was taken to assign numerals to sensations of loudness in such a way that relations among the sensations are reflected by the ordinary arithmetical relations in the numeral series. As in all measurement, there are limits imposed by error and variability, but within these limits the Sone scale ought properly to be classed as a ratio scale.

To the British committee, then, we may venture to suggest by way of conclusion that the most liberal and useful definition of measurement is, as one of its members advised, "the assignment of numerals to things so as to represent facts and conventions about them." The problem as to what is and is not measurement then reduces to the simple question: What are the rules, if any, under which numerals are assigned? If we can point to a consistent set of rules, we are obviously concerned with measurement of some sort, and we can then proceed to the more interesting question as to the kind of measurement it is. In most cases a formulation of the rules of assignment discloses directly the kind of measurement and hence the kind of scale involved. If there remains any ambiguity, we may seek the final and definitive answer in the mathematical group-structure of the scale form: In what ways can we transform its values and still have it serve all the functions previously fulfilled? We know that the values of all scales can be multiplied by a constant, which changes the size of the unit. If, in addition, a constant can be added (or a new zero point chosen), it is proof positive that we are not concerned with a ratio scale. Then, if the purpose of the scale is still served when its values are squared or cubed, it is not even an interval scale. And finally, if any two values may be interchanged at will, the ordinal scale is ruled out and the nominal scale is the sole remaining possibility.

This proposed solution to the semantic problem is not meant to imply that all scales belonging to the same mathematical group are equally precise or accurate or useful or "fundamental." Measurement is never better than the empirical operations by which it is carried out, and operations range from bad to good. Any particular scale, sensory or physical, may be objected to on the grounds of bias, low precision, restricted generality, and other factors, but the objector should remember that these are relative and practical matters and that no scale used by mortals is perfectly free of their taint.

MEASUREMENT, STATISTICS, AND
THE SCHEMAPIRIC VIEW

S. S. Stevens

A curious antagonism has sometimes infected the relations between measurement and statistics. What ought to proceed as a pact of mutual assistance has seemed to some authors to justify a feud that centers on the degree of independence of the two domains. Thus Humphreys (1) dispenses praise to a textbook because its authors "do not follow the Stevens dictum concerning the precise relationships between scales of measurement and permissible statistical operations." Since that dictum, so-called, lurks as the *bête noire* behind many recurrent complaints, there is need to reexamine its burden and to ask how measurement and statistics shape up in the scientific process—the schemapiric endeavor in which we invent schematic models to map empirical domains.

In those disciplines where measurement is noisy, uncertain, and difficult, it is only natural that statistics should flourish. Of course, if there were no measurement at all, there would be no statistics. At the other extreme, if accurate measurement were achieved in every inquiry, many of the needs for statistics would vanish. Somewhere between the two extremes of no measurement and perfect measurement, perhaps near the psychosocial-behavioral center of gravity, the ratio of statisticizing to measuring reaches its maximum. And that is where we find an acute sensitivity to the suggestion that the type of measurement achieved in an experiment may set bounds on the kinds of statistics that will prove appropriate.

After reviewing the issues Anderson (2) concluded that "the statistical test can hardly be cognizant of the empirical meaning of the numbers with which it deals. Consequently," he continued, "the validity of the statistical inference cannot depend on the type of measuring scale used." This sequitur, if we may call it that, demands scrutiny, for it compresses large issues into a few phrases. Here let me observe merely that, however much we may agree that the statistical test cannot be cognizant of the empirical meaning of the numbers, the same privilege of ignorance can scarcely be extended to experimenters.

Speaking as a statistician, Savage (3) said, "I know of no reason to limit statistical procedures to those involving arithmetic operations consistent with the scale properties of the observed quantities." A statistician, like a computer, may perhaps feign indifference to the origin of the numbers that enter into a statistical computation but that indifference is not likely to be shared by the scientist. The man in the laboratory may rather suspect that, if something

Reprinted with permission of the author and publisher from *Science*, Vol. 161 (1968), 849-56. Copyright 1968 by the American Association for the Advancement of Science.

empirically useful is to emerge in the printout, something empirically meaningful must be programed for the input.

Baker, Hardyck, and Petrinovich (4) summed up the distress: "If Stevens' position is correct, it should be emphasized more intensively; if it is incorrect, something should be done to alleviate the lingering feelings of guilt that plague research workers who deliberately use statistics such as *t* on weak measurements." If it is true that guilt must come before repentance, perhaps the age of statistical indifference to the demands of measurement may be drawing to a close. Whatever the outcome, the foregoing samples of opinion suggest that the relation between statistics amd measurement is not a settled issue. Nor is it a simple issue, for it exhibits both theoretical and practical aspects. Moreover, peace is not likely to be restored until both the principles and the pragmatics have been resolved.

THE SCHEMAPIRIC PRINCIPLE

Although measurement began in the empirical mode, with the accent on the counting of moons and paces and warriors, it was destined in modern time to find itself debated in the formal, schematic, syntactical mode, where models can be made to bristle with symbols. Mathematics, which like logic constitutes a formal endeavor, was not always regarded as an arbitrary construction devoid of substantive content, an adventure of postulate and theorem. In early ages mathematics and empirical measurement were as warp and woof, interpenetrating each other so closely that our ancestors thought it proper to prove arithmetic theorems by resort to counting or to some other act of measurement. The divorce took place only in recent times. And mathematics now enjoys full freedom to "play upon symbols," as Gauss phrased it, with no constraints imposed by the demands of empirical measurement.

So also with other formal or schematic systems. The propositions of a formal logic express tautologies that say nothing about the world of tangible stuff. They are analytic statements, so-called, and they stand apart from the synthetic statements that express facts and relations among empirical objects. There is a useful distinction to be made between the analytic, formal, syntactical propositions of logic and the synthetic, empirical statements of substantive discourse.

Sometimes the line may be hard to draw. Quine (5) the logician denies, in fact, that any sharp demarcation can be certified, and debate on the issue between him and Carnap has reached classic if unresolved proportions. For the scientist, meanwhile, the usefulness of the formal-empirical distinction need not be imperiled by the difficulty of making rigorous decisions in borderline cases. It is useful to distinguish between day and night despite the penumbral passage through twilight. So also is it useful to tune ourselves to distinguish between the formally schematic and the empirically substantive.

Probability exhibits the same double aspect, the same schemapiric nature. Mathematical theories of probability inhabit the formal realm as analytic, tautologous, schematic systems, and they say nothing at all about dice, roulette, or lotteries. On the empirical level, however, we count and tabulate events at the gaming table or in the laboratory and note their relative frequencies. Sometimes the relative frequencies stand in isomorphic relation to some property of a mathematical model of probability; at other times the observed frequencies exhibit scant accord with "expectations."

Those features of statistics that invoke a probabilistic schema provide a further instance of a formal-empirical dichotomy: the distinction between the probability model and the statistical data. E. B. Wilson (6), mathematician and statistician, made the point "that one must distinguish critically between probability as a purely mathematical subject of one sort or another, and statistcs which cannot be so regarded." Statistics, of course, is a young discipline—one whose voice changes depending on who speaks for it. Many spokesmen would want to broaden the meaning of statistics to include a formal, mathematical segment.

In another context N. R. Hanson (7) pressed a similar distinction when he said, "Mathematics and physics on this account seem *logically* different disciplines, such that the former can only occasionally solve the latter's problems." Indeed, as Hanson later exclaimed, "Physicists have in unison pronounced, 'Let no man join what nature hath sundered, namely, the *formal creation* of spaces and the physical *description* of bodies.' " Yet it is precisely by way of the proper and judicious joining of the schematic with the empirical that we achieve our beneficial and effective mappings of the universe—the schemapiric mappings known as science. The chronic danger lies in our failure to note the distinction between the map and the terrain, between the simulation and the simulated. The map is an analogue, a schema, a model, a theory. Each of those words has a separate flavor, but they all share a common core of meaning. "Contrary to general belief," wrote Simon and Newell (8), "there is no fundamental, 'in principle,' difference between theories and analogies. All theories are analogies, and all analogies are theories." Indeed, the same can be said for all the other terms that designate the associative binding of schematics to empirics—what I have called the schemapiric bond.

SCALES AND INVARIANCE

Although it could be otherwise if our choice dictated, most measurement involves the assignment of numbers to aspects of objects or events according to one or another rule or convention. The variety of rules invented thus far for the assignment of numbers has already grown enormous, and novel means of measuring continue to emerge. It has proved possible, however, to formulate an invariance criterion for the classification of scales of measurement (9). The resulting systematization of scale types has found uses in contexts ranging from physics (10) to the social sciences (11), but the conception has not enjoyed immunity from criticism (12).

Let me sketch the theory. It can be done very briefly, because details are given in other places (13). The theory proposes that a scale type is defined by the group of transformations under which the scale form remains invariant, as follows.

A *nominal scale* admits any one-to-one substitution of the assigned numbers. Example of a nominal scale: the numbering of football players.

An *ordinal scale* can be transformed by any increasing monotonic function.

Example of an ordinal scale: the hardness scale determined by the ability of one mineral to scratch another.

An *interval scale* can be subjected to a linear transformation. Examples of interval scales: temperature Fahrenheit and Celsius, calendar time, potential energy.

A *ratio scale* admits only multiplication by a constant. Examples of ratio scales: length, weight, density, temperature Kelvin, time intervals, loudness in sones.

The foregoing scales represent the four types in common use. Other types are possible. The permissible transformations defining a scale type are those that keep intact the empirical information depicted by the scale. If the empirical information has been preserved, the scale form is said to remain invariant. The critical isomorphism is maintained. That indeed is the principle of invariance that lies at the heart of the conception. More formal presentations of the foregoing theory have been undertaken by other authors, a recent one, for example, by Lea (*14*).

Unfortunately, those who demand an abstract tidiness that is completely aseptic may demur at the thought that the decision whether a particular scale enjoys the privilege of a particular transformation group depends on something so ill defined as the preservation of empirical information. For one thing, an empirical operation is always attended by error. Thus Lebesgue (*15*) who strove so well to perfect the concept of mathematical measure, took explicit note that, in the assignment of number to a physical magnitude, precision can be pushed, as he said, "in actuality only up to a certain error. It never enables us," he continued, "to discriminate between one number and all the numbers that are extremely close to it."

A second disconcerting feature of the invariance criterion lies in the difficulty of specifying the empirical information that is to be preserved. What can it be other than the information that we think we have captured by creating the scale in the first place? We may, for example, perform operations that allow us simply to identify or discriminate a particular property of an object. Sometimes we want to preserve nothing more than that simple outcome, the identification or nominal classification of the items of interest. Or we may go further, provided our empirical operations permit, and determine rank orders, equal intervals, or equal ratios. If we want our number assignments to reflect one or another accrual in information, we are free to transform the scale numbers only in a way that does not lose or distort the desired information. The choice remains ours.

Although some writers have found it possible to read an element of prescription—even proscription—into the invariance principle, as a systematizing device the principle contains no normative force. It can be read more as a description of the obvious than as a directive. It says that, once an isomorphism has been mapped out between aspects of objects or events, on the one hand, and some one or more features of the number system, on the other hand, the isomorphism can be upset by whatever transformations fail to preserve it. Precisely what is preserved or not preserved in a particular circumstance depends upon the empirical operations. Since the actual day-to-day measurements range from muddled to meticulous, our ability to classify them in terms of scale type must range from hopelessly uncertain to relatively secure.

The group invariance that defines a scale type serves in turn to delimit the statistical procedures that can be said to be appropriate to a given measurement scale (16). Examples of appropriate statistics are tabulated in Table 1. Under the

TABLE 1. Examples of Statistical Measures Appropriate to Measurements Made on Various Types of Scales.

The scale type is defined by the manner in which scale numbers can be transformed without the loss of empirical information. The statistical measures listed are those that remain invariant, as regards either value or reference, under the transformations allowed by the scale type.

Scale Type	Measures of Location	Dispersion	Association or Correlation	Significance Tests
Nominal	Mode	Information H	Information transmitted T	Chi square Fisher's exact test
Ordinal	Median	Percentiles	Rank correlation	Sign test Run test
Interval	Arithmetic mean	Standard deviation Average deviation	Product-moment correlation Correlation ratio	t test F test
Ratio	Geometric mean	Percent variation		
	Harmonic mean	Decilog dispersion		

permissible transformations of a measurement scale, some appropriate statistics remain invariant in value (example: the correlation coefficient r keeps its value under linear transformations). Other statistics change value but refer to the same item or location (example: the median changes its value but continues to refer to mid-distribution under ordinal transformations).

RECONCILIATION AND NEW PROBLEMS

Two developments may serve to ease the apprehension among those who may have felt threatened by a theory of measurement that seems to place bounds on our freedom to calculate. One is a clearer understanding of the bipartite, schemapiric nature of the scientific enterprise. When the issue concerns only the schema—when, for example, critical ratios are calculated for an assumed binomial distribution—then indeed it is purely a matter of relations within a mathematical model. Natural facts stand silent. Empirical considerations impose no constraints. When, however, the text asserts a relation among such things as measured differences or variabilities, we have a right and an obligation to inquire about the operations that underlie the measurements. Those operations determine, in turn, the type of scale achieved.

The two-part schemapiric view was expressed by Hays (17) in a much-praised book: "If the statistical method involves the procedures of arithmetic used on numerical scores, then the numerical answer is formally correct. . . . The difficulty comes with the interpretation of these numbers back into statements about the real world. If nonsense is put into the mathematical system, nonsense is sure to come out."

At the level of the formal model, then, statistical computations may proceed as freely as in any other syntactical exercise, unimpeded by any material outcome of empirical measurement. Nor does measurement have a presumptive voice in the creation of the statistical models themselves. As Hogben (*18*) said in his forthright dissection of statistical theory, "It is entirely defensible to formulate an axiomatic approach to the theory of probability as an internally consistent set of propositions, if one is content to leave to those in closer contact with reality the last word on the usefulness of the outcome." Both Hays and Hogben insist that the user of statistics, the man in the laboratory, the maker of measurements, must decide the meaning of the numbers and their capacity to advance empirical inquiry.

The second road to reconciliation winds through a region only partly explored, a region wherein lies the pragmatic problem of appraising the wages of transgression. What is the degree of risk entailed when use is made of statistics that may be inappropriate in the strict sense that they fail the test of invariance under permissible scale transformations? Specifically, let us assume that a set of items can be set in rank order, but, by the operations thus far invented, distances between the items cannot be determined. We have an ordinal but not an interval scale. What happens then if interval-scale statistics are applied to the ordinally scaled items? Therein lies a question of first-rate substance and one that should be amenable to unemotional investigation. It promises well that a few answers have already been forthcoming.

First there is the oft-heeded counsel of common sense. In the averaging of test scores, says Mosteller (*19*), "It seems sensible to use the statistics appropriate to the type of scale I think I am near. In taking such action we may find the justification vague and fuzzy. One reason for this vagueness is that we have not yet studied enough about classes of scales, classes appropriate to real life measurement, with perhaps real life bias and error variance."

How some of the vagueness of which Mosteller spoke can perhaps be removed is illustrated by the study of Abelson and Tukey (*20*) who showed how bounds may be determined for the risk involved when an interval-scale statistic is used with an ordinal scale. Specifically, they explored the effect on r^2 of a game against nature in which nature does its best (or worst!) to minimize the value of r^2. In this game of regression analysis, many interesting cases were explored, but, as the authors said, their methods need extension to other cases. They noted that we often know more about ordinal data than mere rank order. We may have reason to believe, they said, "that the scale is no worse than mildly curvilinear, that Nature behaves smoothly in some sense." Indeed the continued use of parametric statistics with ordinal data rests on that belief, a belief sustained in large measure by the pragmatic usefulness of the results achieved.

In a more synthetic study than the foregoing analysis, Baker *et al.* (*4*) imposed sets of monotonic transformations on an assumed set of data, and calculated the effect on the *t* distribution. The purpose was to compare distributions of *t* for data drawn from an equal-interval scale with distributions of *t* for several types of assumed distortions of the equal intervals. By and large, the effects on the computed t distributions were not large, and the authors concluded "that strong statistics such as the t test are more than adequate to cope with weak [ordinal] measurements. . . ." It should be noted, however, that the values of t were affected by the nonlinear transformations. As the authors said, "The correspondence between values of t based on the criterion unit interval scores and values of t based on [nonlinear] transformations decreases regularly and dramatically . . . as the departure from linear transformations becomes more extreme."

Whatever the substantive outcome of such investigations may prove to be, they point the way to reconciliation through orderly inquiry. Debate gives way to calculation. The question is thereby made to turn, not on whether the measurement scale determines the choice of a statistical procedure but on how and to what degree an inappropriate statistic may lead to a deviant conclusion. The solution of such problems may help to refurbish the complexion of measurement theory, which has been accused of proscribing those statistics that do not remain invariant under the transformations appropriate to a given scale. By spelling out the costs, we may convert the issue from a seeming proscription to a calculated risk.

The type of measurement achieved is not, of course, the only consideration affecting the applicability of parametric statistics. Bradley is one of many scholars who have sifted the consequences of violating the assumptions that underlie some of the common parametric tests (21). As one outcome of his studies, Bradley concluded, "The contention that, when its assumptions are violated, a parametric test is still to be preferred to a distribution-free test because it is 'more efficient' is therefore a monumental *non sequitur*. The point is not at all academic . . . violations in a test's assumptions may be attended by profound changes in its power." That conclusion is not without relevance to scales of measurement, for when ordinal data are forced into the equal-interval mold, parametric assumptions are apt to be violated. It is then that a so-called distribution-free statistic may prove more efficient than its parametric counterpart.

Although better accommodation among certain of the contending statistical usages may be brought about by computer-aided studies, there remain many statistics that find their use only with specific kinds of scales. A single example may suffice. In a classic text-book, written with a captivating clarity, Peters and Van Voorhis (22) got hung up on a minor point concerning the procedure to be used in comparing variabilities. They noted that Karl Pearson had proposed a measure called the coefficient of variation, which expresses the standard deviation as a percentage of the mean. The authors expressed doubts about its value, however, because it tells "more about the extent to which the scores are padded by a dislocation of the zero point than it does about comparable variabilities." The examples and arguments given by the authors make it plain that the coefficient of variation has little business being used with what I have called interval scales. But since their book antedated my publication in 1946 of the defining invariances for interval and ratio scales, Peters and Van Voorhis did not have a convenient way to state the relationship made explicit in Table 1, namely, that the coefficient of variation, being itself a ratio, calls for a ratio scale.

COMPLEXITIES AND PITFALLS

Concepts like relative variability have the virtue of being uncomplicated and easy for the scientist to grasp. They fit his idiom. But in the current statistics explosion, which showers the investigator with a dense fallout of new statistical models, the scientist is likely to lose the thread on many issues. It is then that the theory of measurement, with an anchor hooked fast in empirical reality, may serve as a sanctuary against the turbulence of specialized abstraction.

"As a mathematical discipline travels far from its empirical source," said von Newmann (23), "there is grave danger that the subject will develop along the line of least resistance, that the stream, so far from its source, will separate into a multitude of insignificant branches, and that the discipline will become a disorganized mass of details and complexities." He went on to say that, "After much 'abstract' inbreeding, a mathematical subject is in danger of degeneration. At the inception the style is usually classical; when it shows signs of becoming baroque, then the danger signal is up."

There is a sense, one suspects, in which statistics needs measurement more than measurement needs statistics. R. A. Fisher alluded to that need in his discourse on the nature of probability (24). "I am quite sure," he said, "it is only personal contact with the business of the improvement of natural knowledge in the natural sciences that is capable to keep straight the thought of mathematically-minded people who have to grope their way through the complex entanglements of error . . . ."

And lest the physical sciences should seem immune to what Schwartz (25) called "the pernicious influence of mathematics," consider his diagnosis: "Thus, in its relations with science, mathematics depends on an intellectual effort outside of mathematics for the crucial specification of the approximation which mathematics is to take literally. Give a mathematician a situation which is the least bit ill-defined—he will first of all make it well defined. Perhaps appropriately, but perhaps also inappropriately . . . . That form of wisdom which is the opposite of single-mindedness, the ability to keep many threads in hand, to draw for an argument from many disparate sources, is quite foreign to mathematics . . . . Quite typically, science leaps ahead and mathematics plods behind."

Progress in statistics often follows a similar road from practice to prescription—from field trials to the formalization of principles. As Kruskal (26) said, "Theoretical study of a statistical procedure often comes after its intuitive proposal and use." Unfortunately for the empirical concerns of the practitioners, however, there is, as Kruskal added, "almost no end to the possible theoretical study of even the simplest procedure." So the discipline wanders far from its empirical source, and form loses sight of substance.

Not only do the forward thrusts of science often precede the mopping-up campaigns of the mathematical schema builders, but measurement itself may often find implementation only after some basic conception has been voiced. Textbooks, those distilled artifices of science, like to picture scientific conceptions as built on measurement, but the working scientist is more apt to devise his measurements to suit his conceptions. As Kuhn (27) said, "The route from theory or law to measurement can almost never be travelled backwards. Numbers gathered without some knowledge of the regularity to be expected almost never speak for themselves. Almost certainly they remain just numbers." Yet who would deny that some ears, more tuned to numbers, may hear them speak in fresh and revealing ways?

The intent here is not, of course, to affront the qualities of a discipline as useful as mathematics. Its virtues and power are too great to need extolling, but in power lies a certain danger. For mathematics, like a computer, obeys commands and asks no questions. It will process any input, however devoid of scientific sense, and it will bedeck in formulas both the meaningful and the absurd. In the behavioral sciences, where the discernment for nonsense is perhaps less sharply honed than in the physical sciences, the vigil must remain especially alert against the intrusion of a defective theory merely because it carries a mathematical visa. An absurdity in full formularized attire may be more seductive than an absurdity undressed.

DISTRIBUTIONS AND DECISIONS

The scientist often scales items, counts them, and plots their frequency distributions. He is sometimes interested in the form of such distributions. If his data have been obtained from measurements made on interval or ratio scales, the shape of the distribution stays put (up to a scale factor) under those transformations that are permissible, namely, those that preserve the empirical information contained in the measurements. The principle seems straight-forward. But what happens when the state of the art can produce no more than a rank ordering, and hence nothing better than an ordinal scale? The abscissa of the frequency distribution then loses its metric meaning and becomes like a rubber band, capable of all sorts of monotonic stretchings. With each nonlinear transformation of the scale, the form of the distribution changes. Thereupon the distribution loses structure, and we find it futile to ask whether the shape approximates a particular form, whether normal, rectangular, or whatever.

Working on the formal level, the statistician may contrive a schematic model by first assuming a frequency function, or a distribution function, of one kind or another. At the abstract level of mathematical creation, there can, of course, be no quarrel with the statistician's approach to his task. The caution light turns on, however, as soon as the model is asked to mirror an empirical domain. We must then invoke a set of semantic rules—coordinating definitions—in order to identify correspondences between model and reality. What shall we say about the frequency function $f(x)$ when the problem before us allows only an ordinal scale? Shall x be subject to a nonlinear transformation after $f(x)$ has been specified? If so, what does the transformation do to the model and to the predictions it forecasts?

The scientist has reason to feel that a statistical model that specifies the form of a canonical distribution becomes uninterpretable when the empirical domain concerns only ordinal data. Yet many consumers of statistics seem to disregard what to others is a rather obvious and critical problem. Thus Burke (28) proposed to draw "two random samples from populations known to be normal" and then "to test the hypothesis that the two populations have the same mean . . . under the assumption that the scale is ordinal at best." How, we must ask, can normality be known when only order can be certified?

The assumption of normality is repeated so blithely and so often that it becomes a kind of incantation. If enough of us sin, perhaps transgression becomes a virtue. But in the instance before us, where the numbers to be fed into the statistical mill result from operations that allow only a rank ordering, maybe we have gone too far. Consider a permissible transformation. Let us cube all the numbers. The rank order would stand as before. But what do we then say about normality? If we can know nothing about the intervals on the scale of a variable, the postulation that a distribution has a particular form would appear to proclaim a hope, not a circumstance.

The assertion that a variable is normally distributed when the variable is amenable only to ordinal measurement may loom as an acute contradiction, but it qualifies as neither the worst nor the most frequent infraction by some of the practitioners of hypothesis testing. Scientific decision by statistical calculation has become the common mode in many behavioral disciplines. In six psychological journals (*29*), for example, the proportion of articles that employed one or another kind of inferential statistic rose steadily from 56 percent in 1948 to 91 percent in 1962. In the *Journal of Educational Psychology* the proportion rose from 36 to 100 percent.

What does it mean? Can no one recognize a decisive result without a significance test? How much can the burgeoning of computation be blamed on fad? How often does inferential computation serve as a premature excuse for going to press? Whether the scholar has discovered something or not, he can sometimes subject his data to an analysis of variance, a *t* test, or some other device that will produce a so-called objective measure of "significance." The illusion of objectivity seems to preserve itself despite the admitted necessity for the investigator to make improbable assumptions, and to pluck off the top of his head a figure for the level of probability that he will consider significant. His argument that convention has already chosen the level that he will use does not quite absolve him.

Lubin (*30*) has a name for those who censure the computational and applaud the experimental in the search for scientific certainty. He calls them stochastophobes. An apt title, if applied to those whose eagerness to lay hold on the natural fact may generate impatience at the gratuitous processing of data. The extreme stochastophobe is likely to ask: What scientific discoveries owe their existence to the techniques of statistical analysis or inference? If exercises in statistical inference have occasioned few instances of a scientific break-through, the stochastophobe may want to ask by what magical view the stochastophile perceives glamour in statistics. The charm may stem in part from the prestige that mathematics, however inapposite, confers on those who display the dexterity of calculation. For some stochastophiles the appeal may have no deeper roots than a preference for the prudent posture at a desk as opposed to the harsher, more venturesome stance in the field or the laboratory.

The aspersions voiced by stochastophobes fall mainly on those scientists who seem, by the surfeit of their statistical chants, to turn data treatment into hierurgy. These are not the statisticians themselves, for they see statistics for what it is, a straightforward discipline designed to amplify the power of common sense in the discernment of order amid complexity. By showing how to amend the mismatch in the impedance between question and evidence, the statistician improves the probability that our experiments will speak with greater clarity. And by weighing the entailments of relevant assumptions, he shows us how to milk the most from some of those fortuitous experiments that nature performs once and may never perform again. The stochastophobe should find no quarrel here. Rather he should turn his despair into a hope that the problem of the relevance of this or that statistical model may lead the research man toward thoughtful inquiry, not to a reflex decision based on a burst of computation.

MEASUREMENT

If the vehemence of the debate that centers on the nature and conditions of statistical inference has hinted at the vulnerability of the conception, what can be said about the other partner in the enterprise? Is the theory of measurement a settled matter? Apparently not, for it remains a topic of trenchant inquiry, not yet ready to rest its case. And debate continues.

The typical scientist pays little attention to the theory of measurement, and with good reason, for the laboratory procedures for most measurements have been well worked out, and the scientist knows how to read his dials. Most of his variables are measured on well-defined, well-instrumented ratio scales.

Among those whose interests center on variables that are not reducible to meter readings, however, the concern with measurement stays acute. How, for example, shall we measure subjective value (what the economist calls utility), or perceived brightness, or the seriousness of crimes? Those are some of the substantive problems that have forced a revision in our approach to measurement. They have entailed a loosening of the restricted view bequeathed us by the tradition of Helmholtz and Campbell—the view that the axioms of additivity must govern what we call measurement (31). As a related development, new axiomatic systems have appeared, including axioms by Luce and Tukey (32) for a novel "conjoint" approach to fundamental measurement. But the purpose here is not to survey the formal, schematic models that have flowered in the various sciences, for the practice and conception of measurement has as yet been little influenced by them.

As with many syntactical developments, measurement models sometimes drift off into the vacuum of abstraction and become decoupled from their concrete reference. Even those authors who freely admit the empirical features as partners in the formulation of measurement may find themselves seeming to downgrade the empirical in favor of the formal. Thus we find Suppes and Zinnes (33) saying, "Some writers . . . appear to define scales in terms of the existence of certain empirical operations . . . In the present formulation of scale type, no mention is made of the kinds of 'direct' observations or empirical relations that exist. . . . Precisely what empirical operations are involved in the empirical system is of no consequence."

How then do we distinguish different types of scales? How, in particular, do we know whether a given scale belongs among the interval scales? Suppes and Zinnes gave what I think is a proper answer: "We ask if all the admissible numerical assignments are related by a linear transformation." That, however, is not a complete answer. There remains a further question: What is it that makes a class of numerical assignments admissible? A full theory of measurement cannot detach itself from the empirical substrate that gives it meaning. But the theorist grows impatient with the empirical lumps that ruffle the fine laminar flow within his models just as the laboratory fellow may disdain the arid swirls of hieroglyphics that pose as paradigms of his measurements.

Although a congenial conciliation between those two polar temperaments, the modeler and the measurer, may lie beyond reasonable expectations, a tempering détente may prove viable. The two components of schemapirics must both be accredited, each in its own imperative role. To the understanding of the world about us, neither the formal model nor the concrete measure is dispensable.

MATCHING AND MAPPING

Instead of starting with origins, many accounts of measurement begin with one or another advanced state of the measuring process, a state in which units and metrics can be taken for granted. At that level, the topic already has the crust of convention upon it, obscuring the deeper problems related to its nature.

If we try to push the problem of measurement back closer to its primordial operations, we find, I think, that the basic operation is always a process of matching. That statement may sound innocent enough, but it contains a useful prescription. It suggests, for example, that if you would understand the essence of a given measuring procedure, you should ask what was matched to what. If the query leads to a pointer reading, do not stop there; ask the same question about the calibration procedure that was applied to the instruments anterior to the pointer: What was matched to what? Diligent pursuit of that question along the chain of measuring operations leads to some of the elemental operations of science.

Or we may start nearer the primordium. The sketchiness of the record forces us to conjecture the earliest history, but quite probably our forefather kept score on the numerosity of his possessions with the aid of piles of pebbles [Latin; *calculi*] or by means of some other tallying device. He paired off items against pebbles by means of a primitive matching operation, and he thereby measured his hoard.

Let us pause at this point to consider the preceding clause. Can the ancestor in question be said to have measured his possessions if he had no number system? Not if we insist on taking literally the definition often given, namely, that measurement is the assignment of numbers to objects or events according to rule. This definition serves a good purpose in many contexts, but it presumes a stage of development beyond the one that we are now seeking to probe. In an elemental sense, the matching or assigning of numbers is a sufficient but not a necessary condition for measurement, for other kinds of matching may give measures.

Numbers presumably arose after our ancestor invented names for the collection of pebbles, or perhaps for the more convenient collections, the fingers. He could then match name to collection, and collection to possessions. That gave him a method of counting, for, by pairing off each item against a finger name in an order decided upon, the name of the collection of items, and hence the numerosity of the items, was specified.

The matching principle leads to the concept of cardinality. Two sets have the same cardinal number if they can be paired off in one-to-one relation to each other. By itself, this cardinal pairing off says nothing about order. (Dictionaries often disagree with the mathematicians on the definition of cardinality, but the mathematical usage recommends itself here.) We find the cardinal principle embodied in the symbols used for the numerals in many forms of writing. Thus the Roman number VI pictures a hand V and a finger I.

Let us return again to our central question. In the early cardinal procedure of matching item to item, fingers to items, or names to items, at what point shall we say that measurement began? Perhaps we had best not seek a line of demarcation between measurement and matching. It may be better to go all the way and propose an unstinted definition as follows: Measurement is the matching of an aspect of one domain to an aspect of another.

The operation of matching eventuates, of course, in one domain's being mapped into another, as regards one or more attributes of the two domains. In the larger sense, then, whenever a feature of one domain is mapped isomorphically in some relation with a feature of another domain, measurement is achieved. The relation is potentially symmetrical. Our hypothetical forefather could measure his collection of fish by means of his pile of pebbles, or his pile of pebbles by means of his collection of fish.

Our contemporary concern lies not, of course, with pebbles and fish, but with a principle. We need to break the hull that confines the custom of our thought about these matters. The concern is more than merely academic, however, especially in the field of psychophysics. One justification for the enlarged view of measurement lies in a development in sensory measurement known as cross-modality matching (34). In a suitable laboratory setup, the subject is asked, for example, to adjust the loudness of a sound applied to his ears in order to make it seem equal to the perceived strength of a vibration applied to his finger. The amplitude of the vibration is then changed and the matching process is repeated. An equal sensation function is thereby mapped out, as illustrated in Fig. 1. Loudness has been matched in that manner to ranges of values on some ten other perceptual continua, always with the result that the matching function approximates a power function (35). In other words, in order to produce equal apparent intensity, the amplitude of the sound p must be a power function of the amplitude of the vibration a, or $p = a^b$, where b is the exponent. Or, more simply, the logarithms of the stimuli are linearly related, which means that ratios of stimuli are proportional.

Experiments suggest that the power function obtains between all pairs of intensive perceptual continua, and that the matchings exhibit a strong degree of transitivity in the sense that the exponents form an interconnected net. If two matching functions have one continuum in common, we can predict fairly well the exponent of the matching function between the other two continua.

Now, once we have mapped out the matching function between loudness and vibration, we can, if we choose, measure the subjective strength of the vibration in terms of its equivalent loudness. Or, more generally, if all pairs of continua have been matched, we can select any one continuum to serve as the reference continuum in terms of which we then measure the subjective magnitude on each of the other continua.

In the description of a measurement system that rests on cross-modality

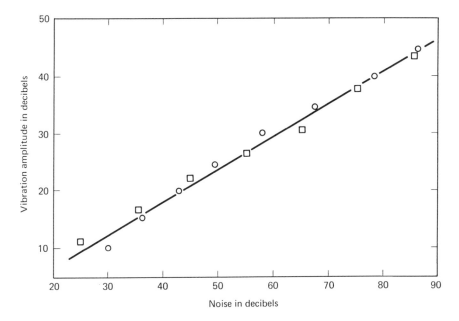

FIGURE 1. Equal-sensation function for cross-modality matching between loudness and vibration. The squares indicate that the observers adjusted the intensity of vibration on the fingertip to match the loudness of a noise delivered by earphones. The circles indicate that the observers adjusted the loudness to match the vibration. Each point is the decibel average of 20 matches, two by each of ten observers. Since the coordinates are logarithmic, the straight line indicates a power function.

matching, no mention has been made of numbers. If we are willing to start from scratch in a measurement of this kind, numbers can in principle be dispensed with. They would, to be sure, have practical uses in the conduct of the experiments, but by using other signs or tokens to identify the stimuli we could presumably eliminate numbers completely. It would be a tour de force, no doubt, but an instructive one.

Instead of dispensing with numbers, the practice in many psychophysical studies has been to treat numbers as one of the perceptual continua in the cross-modality matching experiment. Thus in what has come to be known as the method of magnitude estimation, numbers are matched to loudness, say. In the reverse procedure, called magnitude production, the subject adjusts the loudness to match a series of numbers given by the experimenter (*36*). And as might be expected, despite all the other kinds of cross-modality matches that have been made, it is the number continuum that most authors select as the reference continuum (exponent = 1.0) in terms of which the exponent values for the other perceptual continua are stated. But the point deserves to be stressed: the choice of number as the reference continuum is wholly arbitrary, albeit eminently convenient.

SUMMARY

Back in the days when measurement meant mainly counting, and statistics meant mainly the inventory of the state, the simple descriptive procedures of enumeration and averaging occasioned minimum conflict between measurement and statistics. But as measurement pushed on into novel behavioral domains, and statistics turned to the formalizing of stochastic models, the one-time intimate relation between the two activities dissolved into occasional misunderstanding. Measurement and statistics must live in peace, however, for both must participate in the schemapiric enterprise by which the schematic model is made to map the empirical observation.

Science presents itself as a two-faced, bipartite endeavor looking at once toward the formal, analytic, schematic features of model-building, and toward the concrete, empirical, experiential observations by which we test the usefulness of a particular representation. Schematics and empirics are both essential to science, and full understanding demands that we know which is which.

Measurement provides the numbers that enter the statistical table. But the numbers that issue from measurements have strings attached, for they carry the imprint of the operations by which they were obtained. Some transformations on the numbers will leave intact the information gained by the measurements; other transformations will destroy the desired isomorphism between the measurement scale and the property assessed. Scales of measurement therefore find a useful classification on the basis of a principle of invariance: each of the common scale types (nominal, ordinal, interval, and ratio) is defined by a group of transformations that leaves a particular isomorphism unimpaired.

Since the transformations allowed by a given scale type will alter the numbers that enter into a statistical procedure, the procedure ought properly to be one that can withstand that particular kind of number alteration. Therein lies the primacy of measurement: it sets bounds on the appropriateness of statistical operations. The widespread use on ordinal scales of statistics appropriate only to interval or ratio scales can be said to violate a technical canon, but in many instances the outcome has demonstrable utility. A few workers have begun to assess the degree of risk entailed by the use of statistics that do not remain invariant under the permissible scale transformations.

The view is proposed that measurement can be most liberally construed as the process of matching elements of one domain to those of another domain. In most kinds of measurement we match numbers to objects or events, but other matchings have been found to serve a useful purpose. The cross-modality matching of one sensory continuum to another has shown that sensory intensity increases as the stimulus intensity raised to a power. The generality of that finding supports a psychophysical law expressible as a simple invariance: equal stimulus ratios produce equal sensation ratios.

REFERENCES AND NOTES

1. L. Humphreys, *Contemp. Psychol.* **9**, 76 (1964).
2. N. H. Anderson. *Psychol. Bull.* **58**, 305 (1961).
3. I. R. Savage, *J. Amer. Statist. Ass.* **52**, 331 (1957).

4. B. O. Baker, C. D. Hardyck, L. F. Petrinovich, *Educ. Psychol. Meas.* **26**, 291 (1966).

5. W. V. O. Quine, *The Ways of Paradox and Other Essays* (Random House, New York, 1966), pp. 126–34.

6. E. B. Wilson, *Proc. Natl. Acad. Sci. U.S.* **51**, 539 (1964).

7. N. R. Hanson, *Philos. Sci.* **30**, 107 (1963).

8. H. A. Simon and A. Newell, in *The State of the Social Sciences*, L. D. White, Ed. (Univ. of Chicago Press, Chicago, 1956), pp. 66-83.

9. S. S. Stevens, *Science* **103**, 677 (1946).

10. F. D. Silabee, *J. Wash. Acad. Sci.* **41**, 213 (1951).

11. B. F. Green, in *Handbook of Social Psychology*, G. Lindzey, Ed. (Addison-Wesley, Reading, Mass., 1954), pp. 335-69.

12. Among those who have commented are B. Ellis, *Basic Concepts of Measurement* (University Press, Cambridge, England, 1966); B. Grunstra, "On Distinguishing Types of Measurement," *Boston Studies Phil. Sci.*, vol. 4 (Humanities Press, in press); S. Ross, *Logical Foundations of Psychological Measurement* (Scandinavian University Books, Munksgaard, Copenhagen, 1964); W. W. Rozeboom, *Synthese* **16** 170–233 (1966); W. S. Torgerson, *Theory and Methods of Scaling* (Wiley, New York, 1958).

13. S. S. Stevens in *Handbook of Experimental Psychology*, S. S. Stevens, Ed. (Wiley, New York, 1951), pp. 1–49;____, in *Measurement: Definitions and Theories*, C. W. Churchman and P. Ratoosh, Eds. (Wiley, New York, 1959), pp. 18–64.

14. W. A. Lea, "A Formalization of Measurement Scale Forms" (Technical Memo. KC-T-024, Computer Research Lab., NASA Electronics Res. Ctr., Cambridge, Mass., June 1967).

15. H. Lebesgue, *Measure and the Integral*, K. O. May, Ed. (Holden-Day, San Francisco, 1966).

16. Other summarizing tables are presented by V. Senders, *Measurement and Statistics* (Oxford Univ. Press, New York, 1958). A further analysis of appropriate statistics has been presented by E. W. Adams, R. F. Fagot, R. E. Robinson, *Psychometrika* **30**, 99 (1965).

17. W. L. Hays, *Statistics for Psychologists* (Holt, Rinehart & Winston, New York, 1963).

18. L. Hogben, *Statistical Theory* (Norton, New York, 1958).

19. F. Mosteller, *Psychometrika* **23**, 279 (1958).

20. R. P. Abelson and J. W. Tukey, *Efficient Conversion of Non-Metric Information into Metric Information* (Amer. Statist. Ass., Social Statist. Sec., December 1959), pp. 226–30; see also ____, *Ann. Math. Stat.* **34**, 1347 (1963).

21. J. V. Bradley, "Studies in Research Methodology: II. Consequences of Violating Parametric Assumptions—Facts and Fallacy" (WADC Tech. Rep. 58-574 [II], Aerospace Med. Lab., Wright-Patterson AFB, Ohio, September 1959).

22. C. C. Peters and W. R. Van Voorhis *Statistical Procedures and Their Mathematical Bases* (McGraw-Hill, New York, 1940).

23. J. von Neumann, in *The Works of the Mind*, R. B. Heywood, Ed. (Univ. of Chicago Press, Chicago, 1947), pp. 180−96.

24. R. A. Fisher, *Smoking, the Cancer Controversy* (Oliver and Boyd, Edinburgh, 1959).

25. J. Schwartz, in *Logic, Methodology and Philosophy of Science*, E. Nagel *et al.*, Eds., (Stanford Univ. Press, Stanford, Calif., 1962), pp. 356−60.

26. W. R. Kruskal, in *International Encyclopedia of the Social Sciences* (Macmillan and Free Press, New York, 1968), vol. 15, pp. 206−24.

27. T. S. Kuhn, in *Quantification*, H. Woolf, Ed. (Bobbs-Merrill, Indianapolis, Ind., 1961), pp. 31−63.

28. C. J. Burke, in *Theories in Contemporary Psychology*, M. H. Marx, Ed. (Macmillan, New York, 1963), pp. 147−59.

29. The journals were tabulated by E. S. Edgington, *Amer. Psychologist* **19**, 202 (1964); also personal communication.

30. A. Lubin, in *Annual Review of Psychology* (Annual Reviews, Palo Alto, Calif., 1962), vol. 13, pp. 345−70.

31. H. v. Helmholtz, "Zâhlen und Messen," in *Philosophische Aufsätze* (Fues's Verlag, Leipzig, 1887), pp. 17−52; N. R. Campbell, *Physics: the Elements* [1920] (reissued as *The Philosophy of Theory and Experiment* by Dover, New York, 1957); ____, *Symposium: Measurement and Its Importance for Philosophy*. Aristotelian Soc., suppl., vol. 17 (Harrison and Sons, London, 1938).

32. R. D. Luce and J. W. Tukey, *J. Math. Psychol.* **1**, 1 (1964).

33. P. Suppes and J. L. Zinnes, in *Handbook of Mathematical Psychology*, R. D. Luce *et al.*, Eds. (Wiley, New York, 1963), pp. 1−76.

34. S. S. Stevens, *J. Exp. Psychol.* **57**, 201 (1959); *Amer. Sci.* **54**, 385 (1966).

35. ____, *Percept. Psychophys.* **1**, 5(1966).

36. ____ and H. B. Greenbaum, *ibid.*, p. 439.

37. This article (Laboratory of Psychophysics Rept. PPR-336-118) was prepared with support from NIH grant NB-02974 and NSF grant GB-3211.

ATTITUDES VS. ACTIONS

Richard T. LaPiere

By definition, a social attitude is a behavior pattern, anticipatory set or tendency, predisposition to specific adjustment to designated social situation, or more simply, a conditioned response to social stimuli.[1] Terminological usage differs, but students who have concerned themselves with attitudes apparently agree that they are acquired out of social experience and provide the individual organism with some degree of preparation to adjust, in a well-defined way, to certain types of social situations if and when these situations arise. It would seem, therefore, that the totality of the social attitudes of a single individual would include all his socially acquired personality which is involved in the making of adjustments to other human beings.

But by derivation social attitudes are seldom more than a verbal response to a symbolic situation. For the conventional method of measuring social attitudes is to ask questions (usually in writing) which demand a verbal adjustment to an entirely symbolic situation. Because it is easy, cheap, and mechanical, the attitudinal questionnaire is rapidly becoming a major method of sociological and socio-psychological investigation. The technique is simple. Thus from a hundred or a thousand responses to the question "Would you get up to give an Armenian woman your seat in a street car?" the investigator derives the "attitude" of non-Armenian males towards Armenian females. Now the question may be constructed with elaborate skill and hidden with consummate cunning in a maze of supplementary or even irrelevant questions yet all that has been obtained is a symbolic response to a symbolic situation. The words "Armenian woman" do not constitute an Armenian woman of flesh and blood, who might be tall or squat, fat or thin, old or young, well or poorly dressed—who might, in fact, be a goddess or just another old and dirty hag. And the questionnaire response, whether it be "yes" or "no," is but verbal reaction and this does not involve rising from the seat or stolidly avoiding the hurt eyes of the hypothetical woman and the derogatory stares of other street-car occupants. Yet, ignoring these limitations, the diligent investigator will jump briskly from his factual evidence to the unwarranted conclusion that he has measured the "anticipatory behavior patterns" of non-Armenian males towards Armenian females encountered on street cars. Usually he does not stop here, but proceeds to deduce certain general conclusions regarding the social relationships between Armenians and non-Armenians. Most of us have applied questionnaire technique with greater caution, but not I fear with any greater certainty of success.

Reprinted with the permission of the author and the publisher from *Social Forces*, Vol. 13 (1934), 230-37.

[1] See Daniel D. Droba, "Topical Summaries of Current Literature," *The American Journal of Sociology*, 1934 p. 513.

Some years ago I endeavored to obtain comparative data on the degree of French and English antipathy towards dark-skinned peoples.[2] The informal questionanaire technique was used, but, although the responses so obtained were exceedingly consistent, I supplemented them with what I then considered an index to overt behavior. The hypothesis as then stated *seemed* entirely logical. "Whatever our attitude on the validity of 'verbalization' may be, it must be recognized that any study of attitudes through direct questioning is open to serious objection, both because of the limitations of the sampling method and because in classifying attitudes the inaccuracy of human judgment is an inevitable variable. In this study, however, there is corroborating evidence on these attitudes in the policies adopted by hotel proprietors. Nothing could be used as a more accurate index of color prejudice than the admission or nonadmission of colored people to hotels. For the proprietor must reflect the group attitude in his policy regardless of his own feelings in the matter. Since he determines what the group attitude is towards Negroes through the expression of that attitude in overt behavior and over a long period of actual experience, the results will be exceptionally free from those disturbing factors which inevitably affect the effort to study attitudes by direct questioning."

But at that time I overlooked the fact that what I was obtaining from the hotel proprietors was still a "verbalized" reaction to a symbolic situation. The response to a Negro's request for lodgings might have been an excellent index of the attitude of hotel patrons towards living in the same hotel as a Negro. Yet to ask the proprietor "Do you permit members of the Negro race to stay here?" does not, it appears, measure his potential response to an actual Negro.

All measurement of attitudes by the questionnaire technique proceeds on the assumption that there is a mechanical relationship between symbolic and non-symbolic behavior. It is simple enough to prove that there is no *necessary* correlation between speech and action, between response to words and to the realities they symbolize. A parrot can be taught to swear, a child to sing "Frankie and Johnny" in the Mae West manner. The words will have no meaning to either child or parrot. But to prove that there is no *necessary* relationship does not prove that such a relationship may not exist. There need be no relationship between what the hotel proprietor says he will do and what he actually does when confronted with a colored patron. Yet there may be. Certainly we are justified in assuming that the verbal response of the hotel proprietor would be more likely to indicate what he would actually do than would the verbal response of people whose personal feelings are less subordinated to economic expediency. However, the following study indicates that the reliability of even such responses is very small indeed.

Beginning in 1930 and continuing for two years thereafter I had the good fortune to travel rather extensively with a young Chinese student and his wife.[3] Both were personable, charming, and quick to win the admiration and respect of those they had the opportunity to become intimate with. But they were foreign-born Chinese, a fact that could not be disguised. Knowing the general "attitude" of Americans towards the Chinese as indicated by the "social

[2] "Race Prejudice: France and England," *Social Forces*, September, 1928, pp. 102-111.
[3] The results of this study have been withheld until the present time out of consideration for their feelings.

distance" studies which have been made, it was with considerable trepidation that I first approached a hotel clerk in their company. Perhaps that clerk's eyebrows lifted slightly, but he accommodated us without a show of hesitation. And this in the "best" hotel in a small town noted for its narrow and bigoted "attitude" towards Orientals. Two months later I passed that way again, phoned the hotel and asked if they would accommodate "an important Chinese gentleman." The reply was an unequivocal "No." That aroused my curiosity and led to this study.

In something like ten thousand miles of motor travel, twice across the United States, up and down the Pacific Coast, we met definite rejection from those asked to serve us just once. We were received at 66 hotels, auto camps, and "Tourist Homes," refused at one. We were served in 184 restaurants and cafes scattered throughout the country and treated with what I judged to be more than ordinary consideration in 72 of them. Accurate and detailed records were kept of all these instances. An effort, necessarily subjective, was made to evaluate the overt response of hotel clerks, bell boys, elevator operators, and waitresses to the presence of my Chinese friends. The factors entering into the situations were varied as far and as often as possible. Control was not, of course, as exacting as that required by laboratory experimentation. But it was as rigid as is humanly possible in human situations. For example, I did not take the "test" subjects into my confidence fearing that their behavior might become self-conscious and thus abnormally affect the response of others towards them. Whenever possible I let my Chinese friend negotiate for accommodations (while I concerned myself with the car or luggage) or sent them into a restaurant ahead of me. In this way I attempted to "factor" myself out. We sometimes patronized high-class establishments after a hard and dusty day on the road and stopped at inferior auto camps when in our most presentable condition.

In the end I was forced to conclude that those factors which most influenced the behavior of others towards the Chinese had nothing at all to do with race. Quality and condition of clothing, appearance of baggage (by which, it seems, hotel clerks are prone to base their quick evaluations), cleanliness and neatness were far more significant for person to person reaction in the situations I was studying than skin pigmentation, straight black hair, slanting eyes, and flat noses. And yet an air of self-confidence might entirely offset the "unfavorable" impression made by dusty clothes and the usual disorder to appearance consequent upon some hundred miles of motor travel. A supercilious desk clerk in a hotel of noble aspirations could not refuse his master's hospitality to people who appeared to take their request as a perfectly normal and conventional thing, though they might look like tin-can tourists and two of them belong to the racial category "Oriental." On the other hand, I became rather adept at approaching hotel clerks with that peculiar crabwise manner which is so effective in provoking a somewhat scornful disregard. And then a bland smile would serve to reverse the entire situation. Indeed, it appeared that a genial smile was the most effective password to acceptance. My Chinese friends were skillful smilers, which may account, in part, for the fact that we received but one rebuff in all our experience. Finally, I was impressed with the fact that even where some tension developed due to the strangeness of the Chinese it would evaporate immediately when they spoke in unaccented English.

The one instance in which we were refused accommodations is worth recording here. The place was a small California town, a rather inferior auto-camp into which we drove in a very dilapidated car piled with camp equipment. It was early evening, the light so dim that the proprietor found it somewhat difficult to decide the genus *voyageur* to which we belonged. I left the car and spoke to him. He hesitated, wavered, said he was not sure that he had two cabins, meanwhile edging towards our car. The realization that the two occupants were Orientals turned the balance or, more likely, gave him the excuse he was looking for. "No," he said, "I don't take Japs!" In a more pretentious establishment we secured accommodations, and with an extra flourish of hospitality.

To offset this one flat refusal were the many instances in which the physical peculiarities of the Chinese served to heighten curiosity. With few exceptions this curiosity was considerately hidden behind an exceptional interest in serving us. Of course, outside of the Pacific Coast region, New York, and Chicago, the Chinese physiognomy attracts attention. It is different, hence noticeable. But the principal effect this curiosity has upon the behavior of those who cater to the traveler's needs is to make them more attentive, more responsive, more reliable. A Chinese companion is to be recommended to the white traveling in his native land. Strange features when combined with "human" speech and action seems, at times, to heighten sympathetic response, perhaps on the same principle that makes us uncommonly sympathetic towards the dog that has a "human" expression in his face.

What I am trying to say is that in only one out of 251 instances in which we purchased goods or services necessitating intimate human relationships did the fact that my companions were Chinese adversely affect us. Factors entirely unassociated with race were, in the main, the determinant of significant variations in our reception. It would appear reasonable to conclude that the "attitude" of the American people, as reflected in the behavior of those who are for pecuniary reasons presumably most sensitive to the antipathies of their white clientele, is anything but negative towards the Chinese. In terms of "social distance" we might conclude that native Caucasians are not averse to residing in the same hotels, auto-camps, and "Tourist Homes" as Chinese and will with complacency accept the presence of Chinese at an adjoining table in restaurant or cafe. It does not follow that there is revealed a distinctly "positive" attitude towards the Chinese, that whites prefer the Chinese to other whites. But the facts as gathered certainly preclude the conclusion that there is an intense prejudice towards the Chinese.

Yet the existence of this prejudice, very intense, is proven by a conventional "attitude" study. To provide a comparison of symbolic reaction to symbolic social situations with actual reaction to real social situations, I "questionnaired" the establishments which we patronized during the two year period. Six months were permitted to lapse between the time I obtained the overt reaction and the symbolic. It was hoped that the effects of the actual experience with Chinese guests, adverse or otherwise, would have faded during the intervening time. To the hotel or restaurant a questionnaire was mailed with an accompanying letter purporting to be a special and personal plea for response. The questionnaires all asked the same question, "Will you accept members of the Chinese race as guests in your establishments?" Two types of questionnaire were used. In one this question was inserted among similar queries concerning Germans, French, Japanese, Russians, Armenians, Jews, Negroes, Italians and Indians. In the other the pertinent question was unencumbered. With persistence, completed replies were obtained from 128 of the establishments we had visited; 81 restaurants and cafes and 47 hotels, auto-camps, and "Tourist Homes." In response to the relevant question 92 percent of the former and 91 percent of the latter replied "No." The remainder replied "Uncertain; depend upon circumstances." From the woman proprietor of a small auto-camp I received the only "Yes," accompanied by a chatty letter describing the nice visit she had had with a Chinese gentleman and his sweet wife during the previous summer.

TABLE 1.   **Distribution of Results from Questionnaire Study of Establishment "Policy" Regarding Acceptance of Chinese as Guests.**
Replies are to the question: "Will you accept members of the Chinese race as guests in your establishment?"

		Hotels, etc., Visited		Hotels, etc., Not Visited		Restaurants, etc., Visited		Restaurants, etc., Not Visited	
	Total	47		32		81		96	
		1*	2*	1	2	1	2	1	2
Number replying		22	25	20	12	43	38	51	45
No		20	23	19	11	40	35	37	41
Undecided: depend upon circumstances		1	2	1	1	3	3	4	3
Yes		1	0	0	0	0	0	0	1

*Column (1) indicates in each case those responses to questionnaires which concerned Chinese only. The figures in columns (2) are from the questionnaires in which the above was inserted among questions regarding Germans, French, Japanese, etc.

A rather unflattering interpretation might be put upon the fact that those establishments who had provided for our needs so graciously were, some months later, verbally antagonistic towards hypothetical Chinese. To factor this experience out responses were secured from 32 hotels and 96 restaurants located in approximately the same regions, but uninfluenced by this particular experience with Oriental clients. In this, as in the former case, both types of questionnaires were used. The results indicate that neither the type of questionnaire nor the fact of previous experience had important bearing upon the symbolic response to symbolic social situations. It is impossible to make direct comparison between the reactions secured through questionnaires and from actual experience. On the basis of the above data it would appear foolhardy for a Chinese to attempt to travel in the United States. And yet, as I have shown, actual experience indicated that the American people, as represented by the personnel of hotels, restaurants, etc., are not at all averse to fraternizing with Chinese within the limitations which apply to social relationships between Americans themselves. The evaluations which follow are undoubtedly subject to the criticism which any human judgment must withstand. But the fact is that, although they began their travels in this country with considerable trepidation, my Chinese friends soon lost all fear that they might receive a rebuff. At first somewhat timid and considerably dependent upon me for guidance and support, they came in time to feel fully self-reliant and would approach new social situations without the slightest hesitation.

The conventional questionnaire undoubtedly has significant value for the measurement of "political attitudes." The presidential polls conducted by the *Literary Digest* have proven that. But a "political attitude" is exactly what the questionnaire can be justly held to measure; a verbal response to a symbolic situation. Few citizens are ever faced with the necessity of adjusting themselves to the presence of the political leaders whom, periodically, they must vote for—or against. Especially is this true with regard to the president, and it is in relation to political attitudes towards presidential candidates that we have our best evidence. But while the questionnaire may indicate what the voter will do when he goes to vote, it does not and cannot reveal what he will do when he meets Candidate Jones on the street, in his office, at his club, on the golf course, or wherever two men may meet and adjust in some way one to the other. The questionnaire is probably our only means of determining "religious attitudes." An honest answer to the question "Do you believe in God?" reveals all there is to be measured. "God" is a symbol; "belief" a verbal expression. So here, too, the questionnaire is efficacious. But if we would know the emotional responsiveness of a person to the spoken or written word "God" some other method of investigation must be used. And if we would know the extent to which that responsiveness restrains his behavior it is to his behavior that we must look, not to his questionnaire response. Ethical precepts are, I judge, something more than verbal professions. There would seem little to be gained from asking a man if his religious faith prevents him from committing sin. Of course it does—on paper. But "moral attitudes" must have a significance in the adjustment to actual situations or they are not worth studying. Sitting at my desk in California I can predict with a high degree of certainty what an "average" business man in an average Mid-Western city will reply to the question "Would you engage in sexual intercourse with a prostitute in a Paris brothel?" Yet no one, least of all the man himself, can predict what he would actually do should he by some misfortune find himself face to face with the situation in question. His moral "attitudes" are no doubt already stamped into his personality. But just what those habits are which will be invoked to provide him with some sort of adjustment to this situation is quite indeterminate.

It is highly probable that when the "Southern Gentleman" says he will not permit Negroes to reside in his neighborhood we have a verbal response to a symbolic situation which reflects the "attitudes" which would become operative in an actual situation. But there is no need to ask such a question of the true "Southern Gentleman." We knew it all the time. I am inclined to think that in most instances where the questionnaire does reveal non-symbolic attitudes the case is much the same. It is only when we cannot easily observe what people do in certain types of situations that the questionnaire is resorted to. But it is just

TABLE 2. Distribution of Results Obtained From Actual Experience in the Situation Symbolized in the Questionnaire Study

Conditions	HOTELS, ETC.		RESTAURANTS, ETC.	
	Accompanied by Investigator	*Chinese not so Accompanied at Inception of Situation**	*Accompanied by Investigator*	*Chinese not so Accompanied at Inception of Situation**
Total..............	55	12	165	19
Reception very much better than investigator would expect to have received had he been alone, but under otherwise similar circumstances............	19	6	63	9
Reception different only to extent of heightened curiosity, such as investigator might have incurred were he alone but dressed in manner unconventional to region yet not incongruous..............	22	3	76	6
Reception "normal"...	9	2	21	3
Reception perceptibly hesitant and not to be explained on other than "racial" grounds......	3	1	4	1
Reception definitely, though temporarily, embarrassing..........	1	0	1	0
Not accepted........	1	0	0	0

*When the investigator was not present at the inception of the situation the judgments were based upon what transpired after he joined the Chinese. Since intimately acquainted with them it is probable that errors in judgment were no more frequent under these conditions than when he was able to witness the inception as well as the result of the situation.

here that the danger in the questionnaire technique arises. If Mr. A adjusts himself to Mr. B in a specified way we can deduce from his behavior that he has a certain "attitude" towards Mr. B and, perhaps, all of Mr. B's class. But if no such overt adjustment is made it is impossible to discover what A's adjustment would be should the situation arise. A questionnaire will reveal what Mr. A writes or says when confronted with a certain combination of words. But not what he will do when he meets Mr. B. Mr. B is a great deal more than a series of words. He is a man and he acts. His action is not necessarily what Mr. A. "imagines" it will be when he reacts verbally to the symbol "Mr. B."

No doubt a considerable part of the data which the social scientist deals with can be obtained by the questionnaire method. The census reports are based upon verbal questionnaires and I do not doubt their basic integrity. If we wish to know how many children a man has, his income, the size of his home, his age, and the condition of his parents, we can reasonably ask him. These things he has frequently and conventionally converted into verbal responses. He is competent to report upon them, and will do so accurately, unless indeed he wishes to do otherwise. A careful investigator could no doubt even find out by verbal means whether the man fights with his wife (frequently, infrequently, or not at all), though the neighbors would be a more reliable source. But we should not expect to obtain by the questionnaire method his "anticipatory set or tendency" to action should his wife pack up and go home to Mother, should Elder Son get into trouble with the neighbor's daughter, the President assume the status of a dictator, the Japanese take over the rest of China, or a Chinese gentleman come to pay a social call.

Only a verbal reaction to an entirely symbolic situation can be secured by the questionnaire. It may indicate what the responder would actually do when confronted with the situation symbolized in the question, but there is no assurance that it will. And so to call the response a reflection of a "social attitude" is to entirely disregard the definition commonly given for the phrase "attitude." If social attitudes are to be conceptualized as partially integrated habit sets which will become operative under specific circumstances and lead to a particular pattern of adjustment they must, in the main, be derived from a study of humans behaving in actual social situations. They must not be imputed on the basis of questionnaire data.

The questionnaire is cheap, easy, and mechanical. The study of human behavior is time consuming, intellectually fatiguing, and depends for its success upon the ability of the investigator. The former method gives quantitative results, the latter mainly qualitative. Quantitative measurements are quantitatively accurate; qualitative evaluations are always subject to the errors of human judgment. Yet it would seem far more worthwhile to make a shrewd guess regarding that which is essential than to accurately measure that which is likely to prove quite irrelevant.

4

The Research
Format

There are many types of studies which sociologists can carry out. They range from in-depth studies of a few individuals to extensive surveys of thousands of individuals. Some of these are simply descriptive studies, in that there is no attempt to establish causal relationships between factors. More typical of contemporary sociology, however, are analytical or explanatory studies, which aim explicitly at permitting explanatory statements. The initial three papers in this chapter are related to the general problem of establishing causality. The first two discuss the various research formats available for this task, and, in doing so, describe the relative strengths and weaknesses inherent in each format. The potential researcher is thus given a clear picture of the consequences of choosing each design, and provided a rationale for selecting among them.

Kish classifies studies into three broad categories: experiments, surveys, and what he terms "investigations." This is followed by a discussion of the relative success of each type of study in coping with controlled and uncontrolled variables extraneous to the causal relationship. The discussion of tests of significance and the statistical considerations related to research design anticipate the additional considerations of these topics in Chapter 7. Because we want to emphasize the merits and demerits of alternative research formats rather than the statistical critiques, we present the paper at this time.

Campbell's discussion is more specialized, concerned primarily with experimental and quasi-experimental research designs.[1] He discusses the extraneous factors which affect the validity of experiments, that is, affect the relationships which one has supposedly identified.

Mill's paper deals with an extraneous factor not explicitly covered by either Kish or Campbell—the effect of the observer on the behavior of those being observed. This re-introduces the more general problem discussed previously by Campbell of the "testing" effect, or what Campbell has called a "reactive" factor.[2]

An approach which has long been advocated as a substitute for experimental procedure in the social sciences is comparative research. Comparative investigation can be viewed as a general research format, a step which must characterize any exhaustive consideration of social phenomena. The final two papers in this chapter argue for a research format embodying a comparison between at least two societies. Porter tempers his support for comparative research with some discussion of the general problems typically associated with it, notably problems of data comparability and sampling. Yet, he remains basically optimistic, as does Marsh who, in his paper, emphasizes that the difficulties and annoyances of comparative work are tolerable in view of the contribution of comparative studies to the development of sociological theory.

[1] For further consideration of experimental compromises in social sciences, or "quasi-experimental designs," see Donald T. Campbell and Julian C. Stanley, *Experimental and Quasi-Experimental Designs for Research* (Chicago: Rand McNally & Co., 1966).

[2] Campbell's concern with the "reactive" factor is extensively treated in E. Webb, D. Campbell, R. Schwartz, and L. Sechrest, *Unobtrusive Measures: Non-reactive Research in the Social Sciences* (Chicago: Rand McNally & Co., 1966).

SOME STATISTICAL PROBLEMS
IN RESEARCH DESIGN

Leslie Kish

Statistical inference is an important aspect of scientific inference. The statistical consultant spends much of his time in the borderland between statistics and the other aspects, philosophical and substantive, of the scientific search for explanation. This marginal life is rich both in direct experience and in discussions of fundamentals; these have stimulated my concern with the problems treated here.

I intend to touch on several problems dealing with the interplay of statistics with the more general problems of scientific inference. We can spare elaborate introductions because these problems are well known. Why then discuss then here at all? We do so because, first, they are problems about which there is a great deal of misunderstanding, evident in current research; and, second, they are *statistical* problems on which there is broad agreement among research statisticians—and on which these statisticians generally disagree with much in the current practice of research scientists.[1]

Several problems will be considered briefly, hence incompletely. The aim of this paper is not a profound analysis, but a clear elementary treatment of several related problems. The footnotes contain references to more thorough treatments. Moreover, these are not *all* the problems in this area, nor even necessarily the most important ones; the reader may find that his favorite, his most annoying problem, has been omitted. The problems selected are a group with a common core, they arise frequently, yet they are widely misunderstood.

STATISTICAL TESTS OF SURVEY DATA

That correlation does not prove causation is hardly news. Perhaps the wittiest statements on this point are in George Bernard Shaw's preface to *The Doctor's Dilemma,* in the sections on "Statistical Illusions," "The Surprises of Attention and Neglect," "Stealing Credit from Civilization," and "Biometrika." (These

Reprinted with the permission of the author and the publisher, The American Sociological Association, from the *American Sociological Review*, Vol. 24 (1959), 328-38.

This research has been supported by a grant from the Ford Foundation for Development of the Behavioral Sciences. It has benefited from the suggestions and encouragement of John W. Tukey and others. But the author alone is responsible for any controversial opinions.

[1]*Cf.* R. A. Fisher, *The Design of Experiments*, London: Oliver and Boyd, 6th edition, 1953, pp. 1-2: "The statistician cannot evade the responsibility for understanding the processes he applies or recommends. My immediate point is that the questions involved can be disassociated from all that is strictly technical in the statistician's craft, and *when so detached*, are questions only of the right use of human reasoning powers, with which all intelligent people, who hope to be intelligible, are equally concerned, and on which the statistician, as such, speaks with no special authority. The statistician cannot excuse himself from the duty of getting his head clear on the principles of scientific inference, but equally no other thinking man can avoid a like obligation."

attack, alas, the practice of vaccination.) The excellent introductory textbook by Yule and Kendall[2] deals in three separate chapters with the problems of advancing from correlation to causation. Searching for causal factors among survey data is an old, useful sport; and the attempts to separate true explanatory variables from extraneous and "spurious" correlations have taxed scientists since antiquity and will undoubtedly continue to do so. Neyman and Simon[3] show that beyond common sense, there are some technical skills involved in tracking down spurious correlations. Econometricians and geneticists have developed great interest and skill in the problems of separating the explanatory variables.[4]

The researcher designates the explanatory variables on the basis of substantive scientific theories. He recognizes the evidence of other *sources of variation* and he needs to separate these from the explanatory variables. Sorting all sources of variation into four classes seems to me a useful simplification. Furthermore, no confusion need result from talking about sorting and treating "variables," instead of "sources of variation."

I. The *explanatory* variables, sometimes called the "experimental" variables, are the objects of the research. They are the variables among which the researcher wishes to find and to measure some specified relationships. They include both the "dependent" and the "independent" variables, that is, the "predictand" and "predictor" variables.[5] With respect to the aims of the research all other variables, of which there are three classes, are extraneous.

II. There are extraneous variables which are *controlled*. The control may be exercised in either or both the selection and the estimation procedures.

III. There may exist extraneous uncontrolled variables which are *confounded* with the Class I variables.

IV. There are extraneous uncontrolled variables which are treated as *randomized* errors. In "ideal" experiments (discussed below) they are actually

[2]G. Undy Yule and M. G. Kendall, *An Introduction to the Theory of Statistics*, London: Griffin, 11th edition, 1937, Chapters 4, 15, and 16.

[3]Jerzy Neyman, *Lectures and Conferences on Mathematical Statistics and Probability*, Washington, D. C.: Graduate School of Department of Agriculture, 1952, pp. 143-154. Herbert A. Simon, "Spurious Correlation: A Causal Interpretation," *Journal of the American Statistical Association*, 49 (September, 1954), pp. 467-479; also in his *Models of Man*, New York: Wiley, 1956.

[4]See the excellent and readable article, Herman Wold, "Causal Inference from Observational Data," *Journal of the Royal Statistical Society (A)*, 119 (Part 1, January, 1956), pp. 28-61. Also the two-part technical article, M. G. Kendall "Regression, Structure and Functional Relationship," *Biometrika*, 38 (June, 1951), pp. 12-25; and 39 (June, 1952), pp. 96-108. The interesting methods of "path coefficients" in genetics have been developed by Wright for inferring causal factors from regression coefficients. See, in Oscar Kempthorne *et al., Statistics and Mathematics in Biology*, Ames, Iowa: The Iowa State College Press, 1954; Sewall Wright, "The Interpretation of Multi-Variate Systems," Chapter 2; and John W. Tukey, "Causation, Regression and Path Analysis," Chapter 3. Also C. C. Li, "The Concept of Path Coefficient and Its Impact on Population Genetics," *Biometrics*, 12 (June, 1956), pp. 190-209. I do not know whether these methods can be of wide service in current social science research in the presence of numerous factors, of large unexplained variances, and of doubtful directions of causation.

[5]Kendall points out that these latter terms are preferable. See his paper cited in footnote 4, and M. G. Kendall and W. R. Buckland, *A Dictionary of Statistical Terms*, Prepared for the International Statistical Institute with assistance of UNESCO, London: Oliver and Boyd, 1957. I have also tried to follow in IV below his distinction of "variate" for random variables from "variables" for the usual (nonrandom) variable.

randomized; in surveys and investigations they are only assumed to be randomized. Randomization may be regarded as a substitute for experimental control or as a form of control.

The aim of efficient design both in experiments and in surveys is to place as many of the extraneous variables as is feasible into the second class. The aim of randomization in experiments is to place all of the third class into the fourth class; in the "ideal" experiment there are no variables in the third class. And it is the aim of controls of various kinds in surveys to separate variables of the third class from those of the first class; these controls may involve the use of repeated cross-tabulations, regression, standardization, matching of units, and so on.

The function of statistical "tests of significance" is to test the effects found among the Class I variables against the effects of the variables of Class IV. An "ideal" experiment here denotes an experiment for which this can be done through randomization without any possible confusion with Class III variables. (The difficulties of reaching this "ideal" are discussed below.) In survey results, Class III variables are confounded with those of Class I; the statistical tests actually contrast the effects of the random variables of Class IV against the explanatory variables of Class I confounded with unknown effects of Class III variables. In both the ideal experiment and in surveys the statistical tests serve to separate the effects of the random errors of Class IV from the effects of other variables. These, in surveys, are a mixture of explanatory and confounded variables; their separation poses severe problems for logic and for scientific methods; statistics is only one of the tools in this endeavor. The scientist must make many decisions as to which variables are extraneous to his objectives, which should and can be controlled, and what methods of control he should use. He must decide where and how to introduce statistical tests of hypotheses into the analysis.

As a simple example, suppose that from a probability sample survey of adults of the United States we find that the level of political interest is higher in urban than in rural areas. A test of significance will show whether or not the difference in the "levels" is large enough, compared with the sampling error of the difference, to be considered "significant." Better still, the confidence interval of the difference will disclose the limits within which we can expect the "true" population value of the difference to lie.[6] If families had been sent to urban and rural areas respectively, after the randomization of a true experiment, then the sampling error would measure the effects of Class IV variables against the effects of urban *versus* rural residence on political interest; the difference in levels beyond sampling errors could be ascribed (with specified probability) to the effects of urban *versus* rural residence.

Actually, however, residences are not assigned at random. Hence, in survey results, Class III variables may account for some of the difference. If the test of significance rejects the null hypothesis of no difference, *several* hypotheses remain in addition to that of a simple relationship between urban *versus* rural

---

[6]The sampling error measures the chance fluctuation in the difference of levels due to the sampling operations. The computation of the sampling error must take proper account of the actual sample design, and not blindly follow the standard simple random formulas. See Leslie Kish, "Confidence Intervals for Complex Samples," *American Sociological Review*, 22 (April, 1957), pp. 154-165.

residence and political interest. Could differences in income, in occupation, or in family life cycle account for the difference in the levels? The analyst may try to remove (for example, through cross-tabulation, regression, standardization) the effects due to such variables, which are extraneous to his expressed interest; then he computes the difference, between the urban and rural residents, of the levels of interest now free of several confounding variables. This can be followed by a proper test of significance—or, preferably, by some other form of statistical inference, such as a statement of confidence intervals.

Of course, other variables of Class III may remain to confound the measured relationship between residence and political interest. The separation of Class I from Class III variables should be determined in accord with the nature of the hypothesis with which the researcher is concerned; finding and measuring the effects of confounding variables of Class III tax the ingenuity of research scientists. But this separation is beyond the functions and capacities of the statistical tests, the tests of null hypotheses. Their function is not explanation; they cannot point to causation. Their function is to ask: "Is there anything in the data that *needs* explaining?"—and to answer this question with a certain probability.

Agreement on these ideas can eliminate certain confusion, exemplified by Selvin in a recent article:

> Statistical tests are unsatisfactory in nonexperimental research for two fundamental reasons: it is almost impossible to design studies that meet the conditions for using the tests, and the situations in which the tests are employed make it difficult to draw correct inferences. The basic difficulty in design is that sociologists are unable to randomize their uncontrolled variables, so that the difference between "experimental" and "control" groups (or their analogs in nonexperimental situations) are a mixture of the effects of the variable being studied and the uncontrolled variables or correlated biases. Since there is no way of knowing, in general, the sizes of these correlated biases and their directions, there is no point in asking for the probability that the observed differences could have been produced by random errors. The place for significance tests is after all relevant correlated biases have been controlled. . . . In design and in interpretation, in principle and in practice, tests of statistical significance are inapplicable in nonexperimental research.[7]

Now it is true that in survey results the explanatory variables of Class I are confounded with variables of Class III; but it does not follow that tests of significance should not be used to separate the random variables of Class IV. Insofar as the effects found "are a mixture of the effects of the variable being studied and the uncontrolled variables;" insofar as "there is no way of knowing, in general, the sizes" and directions of these uncontrolled variables, Selvin's logic and advice should lead not only to the rejection of statistical tests; it should lead one to refrain altogether from using survey results for the purposes of finding

---

[7]Hanan C. Selvin, "A Critique of Tests of Significance in Survey Research," *American Sociological Review*, 22 (October, 1957), p. 527. In a criticism of this article, McGinnis shows that the separation of explanatory from extraneous variables depends on the type of hypothesis at which the research is aimed. Robert McGinnis, "Randomization and Inference in Sociological Research," *American Sociological Review*, 23 (August, 1958), pp. 408-414.

explanatory variables. *In this sense*, not only tests of significance but any comparisons, any scientific inquiry based on surveys, any scientific inquiry other than an "ideal" experiment, is "inapplicable." That advice is most unrealistic. In the (unlikely) event of its being followed, it would sterilize social research—and other nonexperimental research as well.

Actually, much research—in the social, biological, and physical sciences—must be based on nonexperimental methods. In such cases the rejection of the null hypothesis leads to several alternate hypotheses that may explain the discovered relationships. It is the duty of scientists to search, with painstaking effort and with ingenuity, for bases on which to decide among these hypotheses.

As for Selvin's advice to refrain from making tests of significance until "after all relevant" uncontrolled variables have been controlled—this seems rather farfetched to scientists engaged in empirical work who consider themselves lucky if they can explain 25 or 50 per cent of the total variance. The control of all relevant variables is a goal seldom even approached in practice. To postpone to that distant goal all statistical tests illustrates that often "the perfect is the enemy of the good."[8]

EXPERIMENTS, SURVEYS, AND OTHER INVESTIGATIONS

Until now, the theory of sample surveys has been developed chiefly to provide descriptive statistics—especially estimates of means, proportions, and totals. On the other hand, experimental designs have been used primarily to find explanatory variables in the analytical search of data. In many fields, however, including the social sciences, survey data must be used frequently as the analytical tools in the search for explanatory variables. Furthermore, in some research situations, neither experiments nor sample surveys are practical, and other investigations are utilized.

By "experiments" I mean here "ideal" experiments in which all the extraneous variables have been randomized. By "surveys" (or "sample surveys"), I mean probability samples in which all members of a defined population have a

[8] Selvin performs a service in pointing to several common mistakes: (a) The mechanical use of "significance tests" can lead to false conclusions. (b) Statistical "significance" should not be confused with substantive importance. (c) The probability levels of the common statistical tests are not appropriate to the practice of "hunting" for a few differences among a mass of results. However, Selvin gives poor advice on what to do about these mistakes; particularly when, in his central thesis, he reiterates that "tests of significance are inapplicable in nonexperimental research," and that "the tests are applicable only when all relevant variables have been controlled." I hope that the benefits of his warnings outweigh the damages of his confusion.

I noticed three misleading references in the article. (a) In the paper which Selvin appears to use as supporting him, Wold (*op. cit.*, p. 39) specifically disagrees with Selvin's central thesis, stating that "The need for testing the statistical inference is no less than when dealing with experimental data, but with observational data other approaches come to the foreground." (b) In discussing problems caused by complex sample designs, Selvin writes that "Such errors are easy enough to discover and remedy" (p. 520), referring to Kish (*op. cit.*). On the contrary, my article pointed out the seriousness of the problem and the difficulties in dealing with it. (c) "Correlated biases" is a poor term for the confounded uncontrolled variables and it is not true that the term is so used in literature. Specifically, the reference to Cochran is misleading, since he is dealing there only with errors of measurement which may be correlated with the "true" value. See William G. Cochran, *Sampling Techniques*, New York: Wiley, 1953, p. 305.

known positive probability of selection into the sample. By "investigations" (or "other investigations"), I mean the collection of data—perhaps with care, and even with considerable control—without either the randomization of experiments or the probability sampling of surveys. The differences among experiments, surveys, and investigations are not the consequences of statistical techniques; they result from different methods for introducing the variables and for selecting the population elements (subjects). These problems are ably treated in recent articles by Wold and Campbell.[9]

In considering the larger ends of any scientific research, only part of the total means required for inference can be brought under objective and firm control; another part must be left to more or less vague and subjective—however skillful—judgment. The scientist seeks to maximize the first part, and thus to minimize the second. In assessing the ends, the costs, and the feasible means, he makes a strategic choice of methods. He is faced with the three basic problems of scientific research: measurement, representation, and control. We ignore here the important but vast problems of measurement and deal with representation and control.

Experiments are strong on control through randomization; but they are weak on representation (and sometimes on the "naturalism" of measurement). Surveys are strong on representation, but they are often weak on control. Investigations are weak on control and often on representation; their use is due frequently to convenience or low cost and sometimes to the need for measurements in "natural settings."

Experiments have three chief advantages: (1) Through randomization of extraneous variables the confounding variables (Class III) are eliminated. (2) Control over the introduction and variation of the "predictor" variables clarifies the *direction* of causation from "predictor" to "predictand" variables. In contrast, in the correlations of many surveys this direction is not clear—for example, between some behaviors and correlated attitudes. (3) The modern design of experiments allows for great flexibility, efficiency, and powerful statistical manipulation, whereas the analytical use of survey data presents special statistical problems.[10]

The advantages of the experimental method are so well known that we need not dwell on them here. It is the scientific method *par excellence*—when feasible. In many situations experiments are not feasible and this is often the case in the social sciences; but it is a mistake to use this situation to separate the social from the physical and biological sciences. Such situations also occur frequently in the physical sciences (in meteorology, astronomy, geology), the biological sciences, medicine, and elsewhere.

The experimental method also has some shortcomings. First, it is often difficult to choose the "control" variables so as to exclude *all* the confounding extraneous variables; that is, it may be difficult or impossible to design an "ideal" experiment. Consider the following examples: The problem of finding a proper control for testing the effects of the Salk polio vaccine led to the use of an adequate "placebo." The Hawthorne experiment demonstrated that the

---

[9]Wold, *op. cit.*; Donald T. Campbell, "Factors Relevant to the Validity of Experiments in Social Settings," *Psychological Bulletin,* 54 (July, 1957, pp. 297-312.
[10]Kish, *op. cit.*

design of a proposed "treatment *versus* control" may turn out to be largely a test of *any* treatment *versus lack* of treatment.[11] Many of the initial successes reported about mental therapy, which later turn into vain hopes, may be due to the hopeful effects of *any* new treatment in contrast with the background of neglect. Shaw, in "The Surprises of Attention and Neglect" writes: "Not until attention has been effectually substituted for neglect as a general rule, will the statistics begin to show the merits of the particular methods of attention adopted."

There is an old joke about the man who drank too much on four different occasions, respectively, of scotch and soda, bourbon and soda, rum and soda, and wine and soda. Because he suffered painful effects on all four occasions, he ascribed, with scientific logic, the common effect to the common cause: "I'll never touch soda again!" Now, to a man (say, from Outer Space) ignorant of the common alcoholic content of the four "treatments" and of the relative physiological effects of alcohol and carbonated water, the subject is not fit for joking, but for further scientific investigation.

Thus, the advantages of experiments over surveys in permitting better control are only relative, not absolute.[12] The design of proper experimental controls is not automatic; it is an art requiring scientific knowledge, foresight in planning the experiment, and hindsight in interpreting the results. Nevertheless, the distinction in control between experiments and surveys is real and considerable; and to emphasize this distinction we refer here to "ideal" experiments in which the control of the random variables is complete.

Second, it is generally difficult to design experiments so as to represent a specified important population. In fact, the questions of sampling, of making the experimental results representative of a specified population, have been largely ignored in experimental design until recently. Both in theory and in practice, experimental research has often neglected the basic truth that causal systems, the distributions of relations—like the distributions of characteristics—exists only within specified universes. The distributions of relationships, as of characteristics, exist only within the framework of specific populations. Probability distributions, like all mathematical models, are abstract systems; their application to the physical world must include the specification of the populations. For example, it is generally accepted that the statement of a value for mean income has meaning only with reference to a specified population; but this is not generally and clearly recognized in the case of regression of assets on income and occupation. Similarly, the *statistical* inferences derived from the experimental testing of several treatments are restricted to the population(s)

[11] F. J. Roethlisberger and W. J. Dickson, *Management and the Worker*, Cambridge: Harvard University Press, 1939. Troubles with experimental controls misled even the great Pavlov into believing *temporarily* that he had proof of the inheritance of an acquired ability to learn: "In an informal statement made at the time of the Thirteenth International Physiological Congress, Boston, August, 1929, Pavlov explained that in checking up these experiments it was found that the apparent improvement in the ability to learn, on the part of successive generations of mice, was really due to an improvement in the ability to teach, on the part of the experimenter." From B. G. Greenberg, *The Story of Evolution*, New York: Garden City, 1929, p. 327.
[12] Jerome Cornfield, "Statistical Relationships and Proof in Medicine," *American Statistician*, 8 (December, 1954), pp. 19-21.

included in the experimental design.[13] The clarification of the population sampling aspects of experiments is now being tackled vigorously by Wilk and Kempthorne and by Cornfield and Tukey.[14]

Third, for many research aims, especially in the social sciences, contriving the desired "natural setting" for the measurements is not feasible in experimental design. Hence, what social experiments give sometimes are clear answers to questions the meanings of which are vague. That is, the artificially contrived experimental variables *may* have but a tenuous relationship to the variables the researcher would like to investigate.

The second and third weaknesses of experiments point to the advantages of surveys. Not only do probability samples permit clear statistical inferences to defined populations, but the measurements can often be made in the "natural settings" of actual populations. Thus in practical research situations the experimental method, like the survey method, has its distinct problems and drawbacks as well as its advantages. In practice one generally cannot solve simultaneously all of the problems of measurement, representation and control; rather, one must choose and compromise. In any specific situation one method may be better or more practical than the other; but there is no over-all superiority in all situations for either method. Understanding the advantages and weaknesses of both methods should lead to better choices.

In social research, in preference to both surveys and experiments, frequently some design of controlled investigation is chosen—for reasons of cost or of feasibility or to preserve the "natural setting" of the measurements. Ingenious adaptations of experimental designs have been contrived for these controlled investigations. The statistical framework and analysis of experimental designs are used, but not the randomization of true experiments. These designs are aimed to provide flexibility, efficiency, and, especially, some control over the extraneous variables. They have often been used to improve considerably research with controlled investigations.

These designs are sometimes called "natural experiments." For the sake of clarity, however, it is important to keep clear the distinctions among the methods and to reserve the word "experiment" for designs in which the uncontrolled variables are randomized. This principle is stated clearly by Fisher,[15] and is accepted often in scientific research. Confusion is caused by the use of terms like "ex post facto experiments" to describe surveys or designs of

[13] McGinnis, *op. cit.*, p. 412, points out that usually "it is not true that one can uncover 'general' relationships by examining some arbitrarily selected population. . . . There is no such thing as a completely general relationship which is independent of population, time, and space. The extent to which a relationship is constant among different populations is an empirical question which can be resolved only by examining different populations at different times in different places."

[14] Martin B. Wilk and Oscar Kempthorne, "Some Aspects of the Analysis of Factorial Experiment in a Completely Randomized Design," *Annals of Mathematical Statistics*, 27 (December, 1956), pp. 950-985; and "Fixed, Mixed and Random Models," *Journal of the American Statistical Association*, 50 (December, 1955), pp. 1144-1167. Jerome Cornfield and John W. Tukey, "Average Values of Mean Squares in Factorials," *Annals of Mathematical Statistics*, 27 (December, 1956), pp. 907-949.

[15] Fisher, *op. cit.*, pp. 17-20. "Controlled investigation" may not be the best term for these designs. "Controlled observations" might do, but "observation" has more fundamental meanings.

controlled investigations. Sample surveys and controlled investigations have their own justifications, their own virtues; they are not just second-class experiments. I deplore the borrowing of the prestige word "experiment," when it cloaks the use of other methods.

Experiments, surveys, and investigations can all be improved by efforts to overcome their weaknesses. Because the chief weakness of surveys is their low degree of control, researchers should be alert to the collection and use of auxiliary information as controls against confounding variables. They also should take greater advantage of changes introduced into their world by measuring the effects of such changes. They should utilize more often efficient and useful statistics instead of making tabular presentation their only tool.

On the other hand, experiments and controlled investigations can often be improved by efforts to specify their populations more clearly and to make the results more representative of the population. Often more should be done to broaden the area of inference to more important populations. Thus, in many situations the deliberate attempts of the researcher to make his sample more "homogeneous" are misplaced; and if common sense will not dispel the error, reading Fisher may.[16] When he understands this, the researcher can view the population base of his research in terms of costs and variances. He can often avoid basing his research on a comparison of one sampling unit for each "treatment." If he cannot obtain a proper sample of the entire population, frequently he can secure, say, four units for each treatment, or a score for each.[17]

Suppose, for example, that thorough research on one city and one rural county, discloses higher levels of political interest in the former. It is presumptuous (although common practice) to present this result as evidence that urban people in *general* show a higher level. (Unfortunately, I am not beating a dead horse; this nag is pawing daily in the garden of social science.) However, very likely there is a great deal of variation in political interest among different

---

[16]*Ibid.*, pp. 99-100. Fisher says: "We have seen that the factorial arrangement possesses two advantages over experiments involving only single factors: (i) Greater *efficiency*, in that these factors are evaluated with the same precision by means of only a quarter of the number of observations that would otherwise be necessary; and (ii) Greater *comprehensiveness* in that, in addition to the 4 effects of single factors, their 11 possible interactions are evaluated. There is a third advantage which, while less obvious than the former two, has an important bearing upon the utility of the experimental results in their practical application. This is that any conclusion, such as that it is advantageous to increase the quantity of a given ingredient, has a wider inductive basis when inferred from an experiment in which the quantities of other ingredients have been varied, than it would have from any amount of experimentation, in which these had been kept strictly constant. The exact standardisation of experimental conditions, which is often thoughtlessly advocated as a panacea, always carries with it the real disadvantage that a highly standardized experiment supplies direct information only in respect of the narrow range of conditions achieved by standardization. Standardization, therefore, weakens rather than strengthens our ground for inferring a like result, when, as is invariably the case in practice, these conditions are somewhat varied."

[17]For simplicity the following illustration is a simple contrast between two values of the "explanatory" variable, but the point is more general; and this aspect is similar whether for true experiments or controlled observations. Incidentally, it is poor strategy to "solve" the problem of representation by obtaining a good sample, or complete census, of some small or artificial population. A poor sample of the United States or of Chicago *usually* has more over-all value than the best sample of freshman English classes at X University.

cities, as well as among rural counties; the results of the research will depend heavily on which city and which county the researcher picked as "typical." The research would have a broader base if a city and a rural county would have been chosen in each of, say, four different situations—as different as possible (as to region, income, industry, for example); or better still in twenty different situations. A further improvement would result if the stratification and selection of sampling units followed a scientific sample design.

Using more sampling units and spreading them over the breadth of variation in the population has several advantages. First, some measure of the variability of the observed effect may be obtained. From a probability sample, statistical inference to the population can be made. Second, the base of the inference is broadened, as the effect is observed over a variety of situations. Beyond this lies the combination of results from researches over several distinct cultures and periods. Finally, with proper design, the effects of several potentially confounding factors can be tested.

These points are brought out by Keyfitz in an excellent example of controlled investigation (which also uses sampling effectively): "Census enumeration data were used to answer for French farm families of the Province of Quebec the question: Are farm families smaller near cities than far from cities, other things being equal? The sample of 1,056 families was arranged in a 2^6 factorial design which not only controlled 15 extraneous variables (income, education, etc.) but incidentally measured the effect of 5 of these on family size. A significant effect of distance from cities was found, from which is inferred a geographical dimension for the currents of social change."[18] The mean numbers of children per family were found to be 9.5 near and 10.8 far from cities; the difference of 1.3 children has a standard error of 0.28.

SOME MISUSES OF STATISTICAL TESTS

Of the many kinds of current misuses this discussion is confined to a few of the most common. There is irony in the circumstance that these are committed usually by the more statistically inclined investigators; they are avoided in research presented in terms of qualitative statements or of simple descriptions.

First, there is "hunting with a shot-gun" for significant differences. Statistical tests are designed for distinguishing results at a predetermined level of improbability (say at P = .05) under a specified null hypothesis of random events. A rigorous theory for dealing with individual experiments has been developed by Fisher, the Pearsons, Neyman, Wold, and others. However, the researcher often faces more complicated situations, especially in the analysis of survey results; he is often searching for interesting relationships among a vast number of data. The keen-eyed researcher hunting through the results of one thousand random tosses of perfect coins would discover and display about fifty "significant" results (at the P = .05 level).[19] Perhaps the problem has become

[18]Nathan Keyfitz, "A Factorial Arrangement of Comparisons of Family Size," *American Journal of Sociology*, 53 (March, 1953), p. 470.
[19]William H. Sewell, "Infant Training and the Personality of the Child," *American Journal of Sociology*, 53 (September, 1952), pp. 150-159. Sewell points to an interesting example: "On the basis of the results of this study, the general null hypothesis that the personality adjustments and traits of children who have undergone varying training

more acute now that high-speed computers allow hundreds of significance tests to be made. There is no easy answer to this problem. We must be constantly aware of the nature of tests of null hypotheses in searching survey data for interesting results. After finding a result improbable under the null hypothesis the researcher must not accept blindly the hypothesis of "significance" due to a presumed cause. Among the several alternative hypotheses is that of having discovered an improbable random event through sheer diligence. Remedy can be found sometimes by a reformulation of the statistical aims of the research so as to fit the available tests. Unfortunately, the classic statistical tests give clear answers only to some simple decision problems; often these bear but faint resemblance to the complex problems faced by the scientist. In response to these needs the mathematical statisticians are beginning to provide some new statistical tests. Among the most useful are the new "multiple comparison" and "multiple range" tests of Tukey, Duncan, Scheffé,[20] and others. With a greater variety of statistical statements available, it will become easier to choose one without doing great violence either to them or to the research aims.

Second, statistical "significance" is often confused with and substituted for substantive significance. There are instances of research results presented in terms of probability values of "statistical significance" alone, without noting the magnitude and importance of the relationships found. These attempts to use the probability levels of significance tests as measures of the strengths of relationships are very common and very mistaken. The function of statistical tests is merely to answer: Is the variation great enough for us to place some confidence in the result; or, contrarily, may the latter be merely a happenstance of the specific sample on which the test was made? This question is interesting, but it is surely *secondary*, auxiliary, to the main question: Does the result show a relationship which is of substantive interest because of its nature and its magnitude? Better still: Is the result consistent with an assumed relationship of substantive interest?

The results of statistical "tests of significance" are functions not only of the magnitude of the relationships studied but also of the numbers of sampling units used (and the efficiency of design). In small samples significant, that is, meaningful, results may fail to appear "statistically significant." But if the sample is large enough the most insignificant relationships will appear "statistically significant."

Significance should stand for meaning and refer to substantive matter. The statistical tests merely answer the question: Is there a big enough relationship here which *needs* explanation (and is not merely chance fluctuation)? The word

---

experiences do not differ significantly cannot be rejected. Of the 460 chi square tests, only 18 were significant at or beyond the 5 per cent level. Of these, 11 were in the expected direction and 7 were in the opposite direction from that expected on the basis of psychoanalytic writings. . . . Certainly, the results of this study cast serious doubts on the validity of the psychoanalytic claims regarding the importance of the infant disciplines and on the efficacy of prescriptions based on them" (pp. 158-159). Note that by chance alone one would expect 23 "significant" differences at the 5 per cent level. A "hunter" would report either the 11 or the 18 and not the hundreds of "misses."

[20]John W. Tukey, "Comparing Individual Means in the Analysis of Variance," *Biometrics*, 5 (June, 1949), pp. 99-114; David B. Duncan, "Multiple Range and Multiple F Tests," *Biometrics*, 11 (March, 1955), pp. 1-42; Henry Scheffé, "A Method for Judging All Contrasts in the Analysis of Variance," *Biometrika*, 40 (June, 1953), pp. 87-104.

significance should be attached to another question, a substantive question: Is there a relationship here *worth* explaining (because it is important and meaningful)? As a remedial step I would recommend that statisticians discard the phrase "test of significance," perhaps in favor of the somewhat longer but proper phrase "test against the null hypothesis" or the abbreviation "TANH."

Yates, after praising Fisher's classic *Statistical Methods,* makes the following observations on the use of "tests of significance":

> Second, and more important, it has caused scientific research workers to pay undue attention to the results of the tests of significance they perform on their data, particularly data derived from experiments, and too little to the estimates of the magnitude of the effects they are investigating.
>
> Nevertheless the occasions, even in research work, in which quantitative data are collected solely with the object of proving or disproving a given hypothesis are relatively rare. Usually quantitative estimates and fiducial limits are required. Tests of significance are preliminary or ancillary.
>
> The emphasis on tests of significance, and the consideration of the results of each experiment in isolation, have had the unfortunate consequence that scientific workers have often regarded the execution of a test of significance on an experiment as the ultimate objective. Results are significant or not significant and this is the end of it.[21]

For presenting research results statistical estimation is more frequently appropriate than tests of significance. The estimates should be provided with some measure of sampling variability. For this purpose confidence intervals are used most widely. In large samples, statements of the standard errors provide useful guides to action. These problems need further development by theoretical statisticians.[22]

The responsibility for the current fashions should be shared by the authors of statistical textbooks and ultimately by the mathematical statisticians. As Tukey puts it:

> *Statistical methods should be tailored to the real needs of the user.* In a number of cases, statisticians have led themselves astray by choosing a problem which they could solve exactly but which was far from the needs of their clients. . . . The broadest class of such cases comes from the choice of significance procedures rather than confidence procedures. It is often much easier to be "exact" about significance procedures than about confidence procedures. By considering only the most null "null hypothesis" many inconvenient possibilities can be avoided.[23]

Third, the tests of null hypotheses of *zero* differences, of no relationships, are frequently weak, perhaps trivial statements of the researcher's aims. In place of

[21]Frank Yates, "The Influence of *Statistical Methods for Research Workers* on the Development of the Science of Statistics," *Journal of the American Statistical Association,* 46 (March, 1951), pp. 32-33.

[22]D. R. Cox, "Some Problems Connected with Statistical Inference," *Annals of Mathematical Statistics,* 29 (June, 1958), pp. 357-372.

[23]John W. Tukey, "Unsolved Problems of Experimental Statistics," *Journal of the American Statistical Association,* 49 (December, 1954), p. 710. See also D. R. Cox, *op. cit.,* and David B. Duncan, *op. cit.*

the test of zero difference (the nullest of null hypotheses), the researcher should often substitute, say, a test for a difference of a specific size based on some specified model. Better still, in many cases, instead of the tests of significance it would be more to the point to measure the magnitudes of the relationships, attaching proper statements of their sampling variation. The magnitudes of relationships cannot be measured in terms of levels of significance; they can be measured in terms of the difference of two means, or of the proportion of the total variance "explained," of coefficients of correlations and of regressions, of measures of association, and so on. These views are shared by many, perhaps most, consulting statisticians—although they have not published full statements of their philosophy. Savage expresses himself forcefully: "Null hypotheses of no difference are usually known to be false before the data are collected; when they are, their rejection or acceptance simply reflects the size of the sample and the power of the test, and is not a contribution to science."[24]

Too much of social research is planned and presented in terms of the mere existence of some relationship, such as: individuals high on variate x are also high on variate y. The *exploratory* stage of research may be well served by statements of this order. But these statements are relatively weak and can serve *only* in the primitive stages of research. Contrary to a common misconception, the more advanced stages of research should be phrased in terms of the quantitative aspects of the relationships. Again, to quote Tukey:

> *There are normal sequences of growth in immediate ends.* One natural sequence of immediate ends follows the sequence: (1) Description, (2) Significance statements, (3) Estimation, (4) Confidence statement, (5) Evaluation. . . . There are, of course, other normal sequences of immediate ends, leading mainly through various decision procedures, which are appropriate to development research and to operations research, just as the sequence we have just discussed is appropriate to basic research.[25]

At one extreme, then, we may find that the contrast between two "treatments" of a labor force results in a difference in productivity of 5 per cent. This difference may appear "statistically significant" in a sample of, say, 1000 cases. It may also mean a difference of millions of dollars to the company. However, it "explains" only about one per cent of the total variance in productivity. At the other extreme is the far-away land of completely determinate behavior where every action and attitude is explainable, with nothing left to chance for explanation.

The aims of most basic research in the social sciences, it seems to me, should be somewhere between the two extremes; but too much of it is presented at the first extreme, at the primitive level. This is a matter of over-all strategy for an entire area of any science. It is difficult to make this judgment off-hand regarding any specific piece of research of this kind: the status of research throughout the entire area should be considered. But the superabundance of research aimed at this primitive level seems to imply that the over-all strategy of research errs in this respect. The construction of scientific theories to cover

[24] Richard J. Savage, "Nonparametric Statistics," *Journal of the American Statistical Association*, 52 (September, 1957), pp. 332-333.
[25] Tukey, *op. cit.*, pp. 712-713.

broader fields—the persistent aim of science—is based on the synthesis of the separate research results in those fields. A coherent synthesis cannot be forged from a collection of relationships of unknown strengths and magnitudes. The necessary conditions for a synthesis include an *evaluation* of the results available in the field, a coherent interrelating of the *magnitudes* found in those results, and the construction of models based on those magnitudes.

FACTORS RELEVANT TO THE VALIDITY OF EXPERIMENTS IN SOCIAL SETTINGS[1]

Donald T. Campbell

What do we seek to control in experimental designs? What extraneous variables which would otherwise confound our interpretation of the experiment do we wish to rule out? The present paper attempts a specification of the major categories of such extraneous variables and employs these categories in evaluating the validity of standard designs for experimentation in the social sciences.

Validity will be evaluated in terms of two major criteria. First, and as a basic minimum, is what can be called *internal validity:* did in fact the experimental stimulus make some significant difference in this specific instance? The second criterion is that of *external validity,* representativeness, or *generalizability:* to what populations, settings, and variables can this effect be generalized? Both criteria are obviously important although it turns out that they are to some extent incompatible, in that the controls required for internal validity often tend to jeopardize representativeness.

The extraneous variables affecting internal validity will be introduced in the process of analyzing three pre-experimental designs. In the subsequent evaluation of the applicability of three true experimental designs, factors leading to external invalidity will be introduced. The effects of these extraneous variables will be considered at two levels: as simple or main effects, they occur independently of or in addition to the effects of the experimental variable; as interactions, the effects appear in conjunction with the experimental variable. The main effects typically turn out to be relevant to internal validity, the interaction effects to external validity or representativeness.

Reprinted with the permission of the author and the publisher from the *Psychological Bulletin,* Vol. 54, No. 4 (1957) 297-311. Copyright 1957 by the American Psychological Association.

[1] A dittoed version of this paper was privately distributed in 1953 under the title "Designs for Social Science Experiments." The author has had the opportunity to benefit from the careful reading and suggestions of L. S. Burwen, J. W. Cotton, C. P. Duncan, D. W. Fiske, C. I. Hovland, L. V. Jones, E. S. Marks, D. C. Pelz, and B. J. Underwood, among others, and wishes to express his appreciation. They have not had the opportunity of seeing the paper in its present form, and bear no responsibility for it. The author also wishes to thank S. A. Stouffer (33) and B. J. Underwood (36) for their public encouragement.

The following designation for experimantal designs will be used: _X_ will represent the exposure of a group to the experimental variable or event, the effects of which are to be measured; _O_ will refer to the process of observation or measurement, which can include watching what people do, listening, recording, interviewing, administering tests, counting lever depressions, etc. The _X_s and _O_s in a given row are applied to the same specific persons. The left to right dimension indicates temporal order. Parallel rows represent equivalent samples of persons unless otherwise specified. The designs will be numbered and named for cross-reference purposes.

THREE PRE-EXPERIMENTAL DESIGNS AND THEIR CONFOUNDED EXTRANEOUS VARIABLES

The One-Shot Case Study. As Stouffer (32) has pointed out, much social science research still uses Design 1, in which a single individual or group is studied in detail only once, and in which the observations are attributed to exposure to some prior situation.

$$X \quad O \qquad \text{1. One-Shot Case Study}$$

This design does not merit the title of experiment, and is introduced only to provide a reference point. The very minimum of useful scientific information involves at least one formal comparison and therefore at least two careful observations (2).

The One-Group Pretest-Posttest Design. This design does provide for one formal comparison of two observations, and is still widely used.

$$O_1 \; X \; O_2 \qquad \text{2. One-Group Pretest-Posttest Design}$$

However, in it there are four or five categories of extraneous variables left uncontrolled which thus become rival explanations of any difference between O_1 and O_2, confounded with the possible effect of X.

The first of these is the main effect of *history*. During the time span between O_1 and O_2 many events have occurred in addition to X, and the results might be attributed to these. Thus in Collier's (8) experiment, while his respondents[2] were reading Nazi propaganda materials, France fell, and the obtained attitude changes seemed more likely a result of this event than of the propaganda.[3] By history is meant the specific event series other than X, i.e., the extra-experimental uncontrolled stimuli. Relevant to this variable is the concept of experimental isolation, the employment of experimental settings in which all extraneous stimuli are eliminated. The approximation of such control in much physical and biological research has permitted the satisfactory employment of Design 2. But in social psychology and the other social sciences, if history is confounded with X the results are generally uninterpretable.

The second class of variables confounded with X in Design 2 is here designated as *maturation*. This covers those effects which are systematic with the passage of time, and not, like history, a function of the specific events involved. Thus

---

[2] In line with the central focus on social psychology and the social sciences, the term *respondent* is employed in place of the terms *subject, patient, or client.*
[3] Collier actually used a more adequate design than this, an approximation to Design 4.

between O_1 and O_2 the respondents may have grown older, hungrier, tireder, etc., and these may have produced the difference between O_1 and O_2, independently of X. While in the typical brief experiment in the psychology laboratory, maturation is unlikely to be a source of change, it has been a problem in research in child development and can be so in extended experiments in social psychology and education. In the form of "spontaneous remission" and the general processes of healing it becomes an important variable to control in medical research, psychotherapy, and social remediation.

(c)   There is a third source of variance that could explain the difference between O_1 and O_2 without a recourse to the effect of X. This is the effect of *testing* itself. It is often true that persons taking a test for the second time make scores systematically different from those taking the test for the first time. This is indeed the case for intelligence tests, where a second mean may be expected to run as much as five IQ points higher than the first one. This possibility makes important a distinction between *reactive* measures and *nonreactive* measures. A reactive measure is one which modifies the phenomenon under study, which changes the very thing that one is trying to measure. In general, any measurement procedure which makes the subject self-conscious or aware of the fact of the experiment can be suspected of being a reactive measurement. Whenever the measurement process is *not* a part of the normal environment it is probably reactive. Whenever measurement exercises the process under study, it is almost certainly reactive. Measurement of a person's height is relatively nonreactive. However, measurement of weight, introduced into an experimental design involving adult American women, would turn out to be reactive in that the process of measuring would stimulate weight reduction. A photograph of a crowd taken in secret from a second story window would be nonreactive, but a news photograph of the same scene might very well be reactive, in that the presence of the photographer would modify the behavior of people seeing themselves being photographed. In a factory, production records introduced for the purpose of an experiment would be reactive, but if such records were a regular part of the operating environment they would be nonreactive. An English anthropologist may be nonreactive as a participant-observer at an English wedding, but might be a highly reactive measuring instrument at a Dobu nuptials. Some measures are so extremely reactive that their use in a pretest-posttest design is not usually considered. In this class would be tests involving surprise, deception, rapid adaptation, or stress. Evidence is amply present that tests of learning and memory are highly reactive (35, 36). In the field of opinion and attitude research our well-developed interview and attitude test techniques must be rated as reactive, as shown, for example, by Crespi's (9) evidence.

Even within the personality and attitude test domain, it may be found that tests differ in the degree to which they are reactive. For some purposes, tests involving voluntary self-description may turn out to be more reactive (especially at the interaction level to be discussed below) than are devices which focus the respondent upon describing the external world, or give him less latitude in describing himself (e.g., 5). It seems likely that, apart from considerations of validity, the Rorschach test is less reactive than the TAT or MMPI. Where the reactive nature of the testing process results from the focusing of attention on the experimental variable, it may be reduced by imbedding the relevant content in a comprehensive array of topics, as has regularly been done in Hovland's attitude change studies (14). It seems likely that with attention to the problem, observational and measurement techniques can be developed which are much less reactive than those now in use.

Instrument decay provides a fourth uncontrolled source of variance which could produce an $O_1 - O_2$ difference that might be mistaken for the effect of X. This variable can be exemplified by the fatiguing of a spring scales, or the condensation of water vapor in a cloud chamber. For psychology and the social sciences it becomes a particularly acute problem when human beings are used as a part of the measuring apparatus, as judges, observers, raters, coders, etc. Thus O_1 and O_2 may differ because the raters have become more experienced, more fatigued, have acquired a different adaptation level, or have learned about the purpose of the experiment, etc. However infelicitously, this term will be used to typify those problems introduced when shifts in measurement conditions are confounded with the effect of X, including such crudities as having a different observer at O_1 and O_2, or using a different interviewer or coder. Where the use of different interviewers, observers, or experimenters is unavoidable, but where they are used in large numbers, a sampling equivalence of interviewers is required, with the relevant N being the N of interviewers, not interviewees, except as refined through cluster sampling considerations (18).

A possible fifth extraneous factor deserves mention. This is *statistical regression*. When, in Design 2, the group under investigation has been selected for its extremity on O_1, $O_1 - O_2$ shifts toward the mean will occur which are due to random imperfections of the measuring instrument or random instability within the population, as reflected in the test-retest reliability. In general, regression operates like maturation in that the effects increase systematically with the $O_1 - O_2$ time interval. McNemar (22) has demonstrated the profound mistakes in interpretation which failure to control this factor can introduce in remedial research.

The Static Group Comparison. The third pre-experimental design is the Static Group Comparison.

$$X - \frac{O_1}{O_2}$$ 3. The Static Group Comparison

In this design, there is a comparison of a group which has experienced X with a group which has not, for the purpose of establishing the effect of X. In contrast with Design 6, there is in this design no means of certifying that the groups were equivalent at some prior time. (The absence of sampling equivalence of groups is symbolized by the row of dashes.) This design has its most typical occurrence in the social sciences, and both its prevalence and its weakness have been well indicated by Stouffer (32). It will be recognized as one form of the correlational study. It is introduced here to complete the list of confounding factors. If the Os

differ, this difference could have come about through biased *selection* or recruitment of the persons making up the groups; i.e., they might have differed anyway without the effect of X. Frequently, exposure to X (e.g., some mass communication) has been voluntary and the two groups have an inevitable systematic difference on the factors determining the choice involved, a difference which no amount of matching can remove.

(b) A second variable confounded with the effect of X in this design can be called experimental *mortality*. Even if the groups were equivalent at some prior time, O_1 and O_2 may differ now not because individual members have changed, but because a biased subset of members have dropped out. This is a typical problem in making inferences from comparisons of the attitudes of college freshmen and college seniors, for example.

TRUE EXPERIMENTAL DESIGNS

(4) *The Pretest-Posttest Control Group Design.* One or another of the above considerations led psychologists between 1900 and 1925 (2. 30) to expand Design 2 by the addition of a control group, resulting in Design 4.

$$O_1 \ X \ O_2 \quad \text{4. Pretest-Posttest Control Group Design}$$
$$O_3 \quad O_4$$

Because this design so neatly controls for the main effects of history, maturation, testing, instrument decay, regression, selection, and mortality, these separate sources of variance are not usually made explicit. It seems well to state briefly the relationship of the design to each of these confounding factors, with particular attention to the application of the design in social settings.

(a) If the differences between O_1 and O_2 were due to intervening historical events, then they should also show up in the $O_3 - O_4$ comparison. Note however several complications in achieving this control. If respondents are run in groups, and if there is only one experimental session and one control session, then there is no control over the unique internal histories of the groups. The $O_1 - O_2$ difference, even if not appearing in $O_3 - O_4$, may be due to a chance distracting factor appearing in one or the other group. Such a design, while controlling for the shared history or event series, still confounds X with the unique session history.

(b) Second, the design implies a simultaneity of O_1 with O_3 and O_2 with O_4 which is usually impossible. If one were to try to achieve simultaneity by using two experimenters, one working with the experimental respondents, the other with the controls, this would confound experimenter differences with X (introducing one type of instrument decay). These considerations make it usually imperative that, for a true experiment, the experimental and control groups be tested and exposed individually or in small subgroups, and that sessions of both types be temporally and spatially intermixed.

As to the other factors: if maturation or testing contributed an $O_1 - O_2$ difference, this should appear equally in the $O_3 - O_4$ comparison, and these variables are thus controlled for their main effects. To make sure the design controls for instrument decay, the same individual or small-session approximation to simultaneity needed for history is required. The occasional practice of running the experimental group and control group at different times is thus ruled out on this ground as well as that of history. Otherwise the observers may have become more experienced, more hurried, more careless, the maze more redolent with irrelevant cues, the lever-tension and friction diminished, etc. Only when groups are effectively simultaneous do these factors affect experimental and control groups alike. Where more than one experimenter or observer is used, counterbalancing experimenter, time, and group is recommended. The balanced Latin square is frequently useful for this purpose (4).

While regression is controlled in the design as a whole, frequently secondary analyses of effects are made for extreme pretest scorers in the experimental group. To provide a control for effects of regression, a parallel analysis of extremes should also be made for the control group.

Selection is of course handled by the sampling equivalence ensured through the randomization employed in assigning persons to groups, perhaps supplemented by, but not supplanted by, matching procedures. Where the experimental and control groups do not have this sort of equivalence, one has a compromise design rather than a true experiment. Furthermore, the O_1-O_3 comparison provides a check on possible sampling differences.

The design also makes possible the examination of experimental mortality, which becomes a real problem for experiments extended over weeks or months. If the experimental and control groups do not differ in the number of lost cases nor in their pretest scores, the experiment can be judged internally valid on this point, although mortality reduces the generalizability of effects to the original population from which the groups were selected.

For these reasons, the Pretest-Posttest Control Group Design has been the ideal in the social sciences for some thirty years. Recently, however, a serious and avoidable imperfection in it has been noted, perhaps first by Schanck and Goodman (29). Solomon (30) has expressed the point as an *interaction* effect of resting. In the terminology of analysis of variance, the effects of history, maturation, and testing, as described so far, are all *main* effects, manifesting themselves in mean differences independently of the presence of other variables. They are effects that could be added on to other effects, including the effect of the experimental variable. In contrast, interaction effects represent a joint effect, specific to the concomitance of two or more conditions, and may occur even when no main effects are present. Applied to the testing variable, the interaction effect might involve not a shift due solely or directly to the measurement process, but rather a sensitization of respondents to the experimental variable so that when X was preceded by O there would be a change, whereas both X and O would be without effect if occurring alone. In terms of the two types of validity, Design 4 is internally valid, offering an adequate basis for generalization to other sampling-equivalent *pretested* groups. But it has a serious and systematic weakness in representativeness in that it offers, strictly speaking, no basis for generalization to the *unpretested* population. And it is usually the *unpretested* larger universe from which these samples were taken to which one wants to generalize.

A concrete example will help make this clearer. In the NORC study of a United Nations information campaign (31), two equivalent samples, of a thousand each, were drawn from the city's population. One of these samples was interviewed, following which the city of Cincinnati was subjected to an intensive publicity campaign using all the mass media of communication. This included special features in the newspapers and on the radio, bus cards, public lectures, etc. At the end of two months, the second sample of 1,000 was interviewed and the results compared with the first 1,000. There were no differences between the two groups except that the second group was somewhat more pessimistic about the likelihood of Russia's cooperating for world peace, a result which was attributed to history rather than to the publicity campaign. The second sample was no better informed about the United Nations nor had it noticed in particular the publicity campaign which had been going on. In connection with a program of research on panels and the reinterview problem, Paul Lazarsfeld and the Bureau of Applied Social Research arranged to have the initial sample reinterviewed at the same time as the second sample was interviewed, after the publicity campaign. This reinterviewed group showed significant attitude changes, a high degree of awareness of the campaign and important increases in information. The inference in this case is unmistakably that the initial interview had sensitized the persons interviewed to the topic of the United Nations, had raised in them a focus of awareness which made the subsequent publicity campaign effective for them but for them only. This study and other studies clearly document the possibility of interaction effects which seriously limit our capacity to generalize from the pretested experimental group to the unpretested general population. Hovland (15) reports a general finding which is of the opposite nature but is, nonetheless, an indication of an interactive effect. In his Army studies the initial pretest served to reduce the effects of the experimental variable, presumably by creating a commitment to a given position. Crespi's (9) findings support this expectation. Solomon (30) reports two studies with school children in which a spelling pretest reduced the effects of a training period. But whatever the direction of the effect, this flaw in the Pretest-Posttest Control Group Design is serious for the purposes of the social scientist.

The Solomon Four-Group Design. It is Solomon's (30) suggestion to control this problem by adding to the traditional two-group experiment two unpretested groups as indicated in Design 5.

$$O_1 \; X \; O_2$$
$$O_3 \qquad O_4 \quad \text{5. Solomon Four-Group Design}$$
$$X \, O_5$$
$$O_6$$

This solomon Four-Group Design enables one both to control and measure both the main and interaction effects of testing and the main effects of a composite of maturation and history. It has become the new ideal design for social scientists. A word needs to be said about the appropriate statistical analysis. In Design 4, an efficient single test embodying the four measurements is achieved through computing for each individual a pretest-posttest difference score which is then used for comparing by t test the experimental and control groups. Extension of this mode of analysis to the Solomon Four-Group Design introduces an inelegant awkwardness to the otherwise elegant procedure. It involves assuming as a pretest score for the unpretested groups the mean value of the pretest from the first two groups. This restricts the effective degrees of freedom, violates assumptions of independence, and leaves one without a legitimate base for testing the significance of main effects and interaction. An alternative analysis is available which avoids the assumed pretest scores. Note that the four posttests form a simple two-by-two analysis of variance design:

	No X	X
Pretested	O_4	O_2
Unpretested	O_6	O_5

The column means represent the main effect of X, the row means the main effect of pretesting, and the interaction term the interaction of pretesting and $\bar{X}$. (By use of a t test the combined main effects of maturation and history can be tested through comparing O_6 with O_1 and O_3.)

The Posttest-Only Control Group Design. While the statistical procedures of analysis of variance introduced by Fisher (10) are dominant in psychology and the other social sciences today, it is little noted in our discussions of experimental arrangements that Fisher's typical agricultural experiment involves no pretest: equivalent plots of ground receive different experimental treatments and the subsequent yields are measured.[4] Applied to a social experiment as in testing the influence of a motion picture upon attitudes, two randomly assigned audiences would be selected, one exposed to the movie, and the attitudes of each measured subsequently for the first time.

$$A \; X \; O_1 \qquad \text{6. Posttest-Only Control Group Design}$$
$$A \quad\;\; O_2$$

In this design the symbol A had been added, to indicate that at a specific time prior to X the groups were made equivalent by a random sampling assignment. A is the point of selection, the point of allocation of individuals to groups. It is the existence of this process that distinguishes Design 6 from Design 3, the Static Group Comparison. Design 6 is not a static cross-sectional comparison, but instead truly involves control and observation extended in time. The sampling procedures employed assure us that a time A the groups were equal, even if not measured. A provides a point of prior equality just as does the pretest. A point A is, of course, involved in all true experiments, and should perhaps be indicated in Designs 4 and 5. It is essential that A be regarded as a specific point in time, for groups change as a function of time since A, through experimental mortality. Thus in a public opinion survey situation employing probability sampling from lists of residents, the longer the time since A, the more the sample underrepresents the transient segments of society, the newer dwelling units, etc. When experimental groups are being drawn from a self-selected extreme population, such as applicants for psychotherapy, time since A introduces maturation (spontaneous remission) and regression factors. In Design 6 these effects would be confounded with the effect of X if the As as well as the Os were not contemporaneous for experimental and control groups.

Like Design 4, this design controls for the effects of maturation and history through the practical simultaneity of both the As and the Os. In superiority over Design 4, no main or interaction effects of pretesting are involved. It is this feature that recommends it in particular. While it controls for the main and interaction effects of pretesting as well as does Design 5, the Solomon Four-Group Design, it does not measure these effects, nor the main effect of history-maturation. It can be noted that Design 6 can be considered as the two

---

[4]This is not to imply that the pretest is totally absent from Fisher's designs. He suggests the use of previous year's yields, etc., in covariance analysis. He notes, however, "with annual agricultural crops, knowledge of yields of the experimental area in a previous year under uniform treatment has not been found sufficiently to increase the precision to warrant the adoption of such uniformity trials as a preliminary to projected experiments" (10, p. 176).

unpretested "control" groups from the Solomon Design, and that Solomon's two traditional pretested groups have in this sense the sole purpose of measuring the effects of pretesting and history-maturation, a purpose irrelevant to the main aim of studying the effect of X (25). However, under normal conditions of not quite perfect sampling control, the four-group design provides in addition greater assurance against mistakenly attributing to X effects which are not due it, inasmuch as the effect of X is documented in three different fashions (O_1 vs. O_2, O_2 vs. O_4, and O_5 vs. O_6). But, short of the four-group design, Design 6 is often to be preferred to Design 4, and is a fully valid experimental design.

Design 6 has indeed been used in the social sciences, perhaps first of all in the classic experiment by Gosnell, *Getting Out the Vote* (11). Schanck and Goodman (29), Hovland (15) and others (1, 12, 23, 24, 27) have also employed it. But, in spite of its manifest advantages of simplicity and control, it is far from being a popular design in social research and indeed is usually relegated to an inferior position in discussions of experimental designs if mentioned at all (e.g., 15, 16, 32). Why is this the case?

In the first place, it is often confused with Design 3. Even where Ss have been carefully assigned to experimental and control groups, one is apt to have an uneasiness about the design because one "doesn't know what the subjects were like before." This objection must be rejected, as our standard tests of significance are designed precisely to evaluate the likelihood of differences occurring by chance in such sample selection. It is true, however, that this design is particularly vulnerable to selection bias and where random assignment is not possible it remains suspect. Where naturally aggregated units, such as classes, are employed intact, these should be used in large numbers and assigned at random to the experimental and control conditions; cluster sampling statistics (18) should be used to determine the error term. If but one or two intact classrooms are available for each experimental treatment, Design 4 should certainly be used in preference.

A second objection to Design 6, in comparison with Design 4, is that it often has less precision. The difference scores of Design 4 are less variable than the posttest scores of Design 6 if there is a pretest-posttest correlation above .50 (15, p. 323), and hence for test-retest correlations above that level a smaller mean difference would be statistically significant for Design 4 than for Design 6, for a constant number of cases. This advantage to Design 4 may often be more than dissipated by the costs and loss in experimental efficiency resulting from the requirement of two testing sessions, over and above the considerations of representativeness.

Design 4 has a particular advantage over Design 6 if experimental mortality is high. In Design 4, one can examine the pretest scores of lost cases in both experimental and control groups and check on their comparability. In the absence of this in Design 6, the possibility is opened for a mean difference resulting from differential mortality rather than from individual change, if there is a substantial loss of cases.

A final objection comes from those who wish to study the relationship of pretest attitudes to kind and amount of change. This is a valid objection, and where this is the interest, Design 4 or 5 should be used, with parallel analysis of experimental and control groups. Another common type of individual difference study involves classifying persons in terms of amount of change and finding associated characteristics such as sex, age, education, etc. While unavailable in this form in Design 6, essentially the same correlational information can be obtained by subdividing both experimental and control groups in terms of the associated characteristics, and examining the experimental-control difference for such subtypes.

For Design 6, the Posttest-Only Control Group Design, there is a class of social settings in which it is optimally feasible, settings which should be more used than they now are. Whenever the social contact represented by X is made to single individuals or to small groups, and where the response to that stimulus can be identified in terms of individuals or type of X, Design 6 can be applied. Direct mail and door-to-door contacts represent such settings. The alternation of several appeals from door-to-door in a fund-raising campaign can be organized as a true experiment without increasing the cost of the solicitation. Experimental variation of persuasive materials in a direct-mail sales campaign can provide a better experimental laboratory for the study of mass communication and persuasion than is available in any university. The well-established, if little-used, split-run technique in comparing alternative magazine ads is a true experiment of this type, usually limited to coupon returns rather than sales because of the problem of identifying response with stimulus type (20). The split-ballot technique (7) long used in public opinion polls to compare different question wordings or question sequences provides an excellent example which can obviously be extended to other topics (e.g., 12). By and large these laboratories have not yet been used to study social science theories, but they are directly relevant to hypotheses about social persuasion.

Multiple X designs. In presenting the above designs, X has been opposed to No-X, as is traditional in discussions of experimental design in psychology. But while this may be a legitimate description of the stimulus-isolated physical science laboratory, it can only be a convenient shorthand in the social sciences, for any No-X period will not be empty of potentially change-inducing stimuli. The experience of the control group might better be categorized as another type of X, a control experience, an X_c instead of No-X. It is also typical of advance in science that we are soon no longer interested in the qualitative fact of effect or no-effect, but want to specify degree of effect for varying degrees of X. These considerations lead into designs in which multiple groups are used, each with a different X_1, X_2, X_3, X_n, or in multiple factorial design, as X_{1a}, X_{1b}, X_{2a}, X_{2b}, etc. Applied to Designs 4 and 6, this introduces one additional group for each additional X. Applied to 5, The Solomon Four-Group Design, two additional groups (one pretested, one not, both receiving X_n) would be added for each variant on X.

In many experiments, X_1, X_2, X_3, and X_n are all given to the same group, differing groups receiving the Xs in different orders. Where the problem under study centers around the effects of order or combination, such counterbalanced multiple X arrangements are, of course, essential. Studies of transfer in learning are a case in point (34). But where one wishes to generalize to the effect of each X as occurring in isolation, such designs are not recommended because of the sizable interactions among Xs, as repeatedly demonstrated in learning studies under such labels as proactive inhibition and learning sets. The use of counterbalanced sets of multiple Xs to achieve experimental equation, where natural groups not randomly assembled have to be used, will be discussed in a subsequent paper on compromise designs.

Testing for effects extended in time. The researches of Hovland and his associates (14, 15) have indicated repeatedly that the longer range effects of persuasive Xs may be qualitatively as well as quantitatively different from immediate effects. These results emphasize the importance of designing experiments to measure the effect of X at extended periods of time. As the misleading early research on reminiscence and on the consolidation of the memory trace indicate (36), repeated measurement of the same persons cannot be trusted to do this if a reactive measurement process is involved. Thus, for Designs 4 and 6, two separate groups must be added for each posttest period. The additional control group cannot be omitted, or the effects of intervening history, maturation, instrument decay, regression, and mortality are confounded with the delayed effects of X. To follow fully the logic of Design 5, four additional groups are required for each posttest period.

True experiments in which O *is not under* E's *control.* It seems well to call the attention of the social scientist to one class of true experiments which are possible without the full experimental control over both the "when" and "to whom" of both X and O. As far as this analysis has been able to go, no such true experiments are possible without the ability to control X, to withhold it from carefully randomly selected respondents while presenting it to others. But control over O does not seem so indispensable. Consider the following design.

$A\ X\ O_1$
$A\qquad O_2$ 6. Posttest Only Design, where O cannot be
$\quad (O)$ withheld from any respondent
$\quad (O)$
$\quad (O)$

The parenthetical Os are inserted to indicate that the studied groups, experimental and control, have been selected from a larger universe all of which will get O anyway. An election provides such an O, and using "whether voted" rather than "how voted," this was Gosnell's design (11). Equated groups were selected at time A, and the experimental group subjected to persuasive materials designed to get out the vote. Using precincts rather than persons as the basic sampling unit, similar studies can be made on the content of the voting (6). Essential to this design is the ability to create specified randomly equated groups, the ability to expose one of these groups to X while withholding it (or providing X_2) from the other group, and the ability to identify the performance of each individual or unit in the subsequent O. Since such measures are natural parts of the environment to which one wishes to generalize, they are not reactive, and Design 4, the Pretest-Posttest Control Group Design, is feasible if O has a predictable periodicity to it. With the precinct as a unit, this was the design of Hartmann's classic study of emotional vs. rational appeals in a public election (13). Note that 5, the Solomon Four-Group Design, is not available, as it requires the ability to withhold O experimentally, as well as X.

FURTHER PROBLEMS OF REPRESENTATIVENESS

The interaction effect of testing, affecting the external validity or representativeness of the experiment, was treated extensively in the previous section, inasmuch as it was involved in the comparison of alternative designs. The present section deals with the effects upon representativeness of other variables which, while equally serious, can apply to any of the experimental designs.

The interaction effects of selection.   Even though the true experiments control selection and mortality for internal validity purposes, these factors have, in addition, an important bearing on representativeness. There is always the possiblity that the obtained effects are specific to the experimental population and do not hold true for the populations to which one wants to generalize. Defining the universe of reference in advance and selecting the experimental and control groups from this at random would guarantee representativeness if it were ever achieved in practice. But inevitably not all those so designated are actually eligible for selection by any contact procedure. Our best survey sampling techniques, for example, can designate for potential contact only those available through residences. And, even of those so designated, up to 19 per cent are not contactable for an interview in their own homes even with five callbacks (37). It seems legitimate to assume that the more effort and time required of the respondent, the larger the loss through nonavailability and noncooperation. If one were to try to assemble experimental groups away from their own homes it seems reasonable to estimate a 50 per cent selection loss. If, still trying to extrapolate to the general public, one further limits oneself to docile preassembled groups, as in schools, military units, studio audiences, etc., the proportion of the universe systematically excluded through the sampling process must approach 90 per cent or more. Many of the selection factors involved are indubitably highly systematic. Under these extreme selection losses, it seems reasonable to suspect that the experimental groups might show reactions not characteristic of the general population. This point seems worth stressing lest we unwarrantedly assume that the selection loss for experiments is comparable to that found for survey interviews in the home at the respondent's convenience. Furthermore, it seems plausible that the greater the cooperation required, the more the respondent has to deviate from the normal course of daily events, the greater will be the possiblity of nonrepresentative reactions. By and large, Design 6 might be expected to require less cooperation than Design 4 or 5, especially in the natural individual contact setting. The interactive effects of experimental mortality are of similar nature. Note that, on these grounds, the longer the experiment is extended in time the more respondents are lost and the less representative are the groups of the original universe.

Reactive arrangements.   In any of the experimental designs, the respondents can become aware that they are participating in an experiment, and this awareness can have an interactive effect, in creating reactions to X which would not occur had X been encountered without this "I'm a guinea pig" attitude. Lazarsfeld (19), Kerr (17), and Rosenthal and Frank (28), all have provided valuable discussions of this problem. Such effects limit generalizations to respondents having this awareness, and preclude generalization to the population encountering X with non-experimental attitudes. The direction of the effect may be one of negativism, such as an unwillingness to admit to any persuasion or change. This would be comparable to the absence of any immediate effect from discredited communicators, as found by Hovland (14). The result is probably more often a cooperative responsiveness, in which the respondent accepts the experimenter's expectations and provides psueudoconfirmation. Particularly is this positive response likely when the respondents are self-selected seekers after the cure that X may offer. The Hawthorne studies (21), illustrate such sympathetic changes due to awareness of experimentation rather than to the specific nature of X. In some settings it is possible to disguise the experimental purpose by providing plausible façades in which X appears as an incidental part of the background (e.g., 26, 27, 29). We can also make more extensive use of experiments taking place in the intact social situation, in which the respondent is not aware of the experimentation at all.

The discussion of the effects of selection on representativeness has argued against employing intact natural preassembled groups, but the issue of conspicuousness of arrangements argues for such use. The machinery of breaking up natural groups such as departments, squads, and classrooms into randomly assigned experimental and control groups is a source of reaction which can often be avoided by the use of preassembled groups, particularly in educational settings. Of course, as has been indicated, this requires the use of large numbers of such groups under both experimental and control conditions.

The problem of reactive arrangements is distributed over all features of the experiment which can draw the attention of the respondent to the fact of experimentation and its purposes. The conspicuous or reactive pretest is particularly vulnerable, inasmuch as it signals the topics and purposes of the experimenter. For communications of obviously persuasive aim, the experimenter's topical intent is signaled by the X itself, if the communication does not seem a part of the natural environment. Even for the posttest-only groups, the occurrence of the posttest may create a reactive effect. The respondent may say to himself, "Aha, now I see why we got that movie." This consideration justifies the practice of disguising the connection between O and X even for Design 6, as through having different experimental personnel involved, using different façades, separating the settings and times, and embedding the X-relevant content of O among a disguising variety of other topics.[5]

Generalizing to other Xs. After the internal validity of an experiment has been established, after a dependable effect of X upon O has been found, the next step is to establish the limits and relevant dimensions of generalization not only in terms of populations and settings but also in terms of categories and aspects of X. The actual X in any one experiment is a specific combination of stimuli, all confounded for interpretative purposes, and only some relevant to the experimenter's intent and theory. Subsequent experimentation should be

---

[5] For purposes of completeness, the interaction of X with history and maturation should be mentioned. Both affect the generalizability of results. The interaction effect of history represents the possible specificity of results to a given historical moment, a possibility which increases as problems are more societal, less biological. The interaction of maturation and X would be represented in the specificity of effects to certain maturational levels, fatigue states, etc.

designed to purify X, to discover that aspect of the original conglomerate X which is responsible for the effect. As Brunswik (3) has emphasized, the representative sampling of Xs is as relevant a problem in linking experiment to theory as is the sampling of respondents. To define a category of Xs along some dimension, and then to sample Xs for experimental purposes from the full range of stimuli meeting the specification while other aspects of each specific stimulus complex are varied, serves to untie or unconfound the defined dimension from specific others, lending assurance of theoretical relevance.

In a sense, the placebo problem can be understood in these terms. The experiment without the placebo has clearly demonstrated that some aspect of the total X stimulus complex has had an effect; the placebo experiment serves to break up the complex X into the suggestive connotation of pill-taking and the specific pharmacological properties of the drug—separating two aspects of the X previously confounded. Subsequent studies may discover with similar logic which chemical fragment of the complex natural herb is most essential. Still more clearly, the sham operation illustrates the process of X purification, ruling out general effects of surgical shock so that the specific effects of loss of glandular or neural tissue may be isolated. As these parallels suggest, once recurrent unwanted aspects of complex Xs have been discovered for a given field, control groups especially designed to eliminate these effects can be regularly employed.

Generalizing to other Os. In parallel form, the scientist in practice uses a complex measurement procedure which needs to be refined in subsequent experimentation. Again, this is best done by employing multiple Os all having in common the theoretically relevant attribute but varying widely in their irrelevant specificities. For Os this process can be introduced into the initial experiment by employing multiple measures. A major practical reason for not doing so is that it is so frequently a frustrating experience, lending hesitancy, indecision, and a feeling of failure to studies that would have been interpreted with confidence had but a single response measure been employed.

Transition experiments. The two previous paragraphs have argued against the *exact* replication of experimental apparatus and measurement procedures on the grounds that this continues the confounding of theory-relevant aspects of X and O with specific artifacts of unknown influence. On the other hand, the confusion in our literature generated by the heterogeneity of results from studies all on what is nominally the "same" problem but varying in implementation, is leading some to call for exact replication of initial procedures in subsequent research on a topic. Certainly no science can emerge without dependably repeatable experiments. A suggested resolution is the *transition experiment,* in which the need for varying the theory-independent aspects of X and O is met in the form of a multiple X, multiple O design, one segment of which is an "exact" replication of the original experiment, exact at least in those major features which are normally reported in experimental writings.

Internal vs. external validity. If one is in a situation where either internal validity or representativeness must be sacrificed, which should it be? The answer is clear. Internal validity is the prior and indispensable consideration. The optimal design is, of course, one having both internal and external validity. Insofar as such settings are available, they should be exploited, without embarrassment from the apparent opportunistic warping of the content of studies by the availability of laboratory techniques. In this sense, a science is as opportunistic as a bacteria culture and grows only where growth is possible. One basic necessity for such growth is the machinery for selecting among alternative hypotheses, no matter how limited those hypotheses may have to be.

SUMMARY

In analyzing the extraneous variables which experimental designs for social settings seek to control, seven categories have been distinguished: history, maturation, testing, instrument decay, regression, selection, and mortality. In general, the simple or main effects of these variables jeopardize the internal validity of the experiment and are adequately controlled in standard experimental designs. The interactive effects of these variables and of experimental arrangements affect the external validity or generalizability of experimental results. Standard experimental designs vary in their susceptibility to these interactive effects. Stress is also placed upon the differences among measuring instruments and arrangements in the extent to which they create unwanted interactions. The value for social science purposes of the Posttest-Only Control Group Design is emphasized.

REFERENCES

1. Annis, A. D., and N. C. Meier. The induction of opinion through suggestion by means of planted content. *J. soc. Psychol.*, 1934, 5, 65-81.
2. Boring, E. G., The nature and history of experimental control. *Amer. J. Psychol.*, 1954, 67, 573-89.
3. Brunswik, E., *Perception and the representative design of psychological experiments*. Berkeley: Univer. of California Press, 1956.
4. Bugelski, B. R., A note on Grant's discussion of the Latin square principle in the design and analysis of psychological experiments. *Psychol. Bull.*, 1949, 46, 49-50.
5. Campbell, D. T., The indirect assessment of social attitudes. *Psychol. Bull.*, 1950, 47, 15-38.
6. Campbell, D. T., On the possibility of experimenting with the "Bandwagon" effect. *Int. J. Opin. Attitude Res.*, 1951, 5, 251-60.
7. Cantril, H., *Gauging public opinion*. Princeton; Princeton Univer. Press, 1944.
8. Collier, R. M., The effect of propaganda upon attitude following a critical examination of the propaganda itself. *J. soc. Psychol.*, 1944, 20, 3-17.
9. Crespi, L. P., The interview effect in polling. *Publ. Opin. Quart.*, 1948, 12, 99-111.
10. Fisher, R. A., *The design of experiments*. Edinburgh: Oliver & Boyd, 1935.
11. Gosnell, H. F., *Getting out the vote: an experiment in the stimulation of voting*. Chicago: Univer. of Chicago Press, 1927.
12. Greenberg, A., Matched samples. *J. Marketing*, 1953-54, 18, 241-45.
13. Hartmann, G. W., A field experiment on the comparative effectiveness of "emotional" and "rational" political leaflets in determining election results. *J. abnorm. soc. Psychol.*, 1936, 31, 99-114.

14. Hovland, C. E., I. L. Janis, and H. H. Kelley, *Communication and persuasion.* New Haven: Yale Univer. Press, 1953.
15. Hovland, C. I., A. A. Lumsdaine, and F. D. Sheffield, *Experiments on mass communication.* Princeton: Princeton Univer. Press, 1949.
16. Jahoda, M., M. Deutsch, and S. W. Cook, *Research methods in social relations.* New York: Dryden Press, 1951.
17. Kerr, W. A., Experiments on the effect of music on factory production. *Appl. Psychol. Monogr.,* 1945, No. 5.
18. Kish, L., Selection of the sample. In L. Festinger and D. Katz (eds.), *Research methods in the behavioral sciences.* New York: Dryden Press, 1953, 175-239.
19. Lazarsfeld, P. F., Training guide on the controlled experiment in social research. Dittoed. Columbia Univer., Bureau of Applied Social Research, 1948.
20. Lucas, D. B., and S. H. Britt, *Advertising psychology and research.* New York: McGraw-Hill, 1950.
21. Mayo, E., *The Human problems of an industrial civilization.* New York: Macmillan, 1933.
22. McNemar, Q., A critical examination of the University of Iowa studies of environmental influences upon the IQ. *Psychol. Bull.,* 1940, 37, 63-92.
23. Menefee, S. C., An experimental study of strike propaganda. *Soc. Forces,* 1938, 16, 574-82.
24. Parrish, J. A., and D. T. Campbell, Measuring propaganda effects with direct and indirect attitude tests. *J. abnorm. soc. Psychol.,* 1953, 48, 3-9.
25. Payne, S. L., The ideal model for controlled experiments. *Publ. Opin. Quart.,* 1951, 15, 557-62.
26. Postman, L. and J. S. Bruner, Perception under stress. *Psychol. Rev.,* 1948, 55, 314-22.
27. Rankin, R. E., and D. T. Campbell, Galvanic skin response to Negro and white experimenters. *J. abnorm. soc. Psychol.,* 1955, 51, 30-33.
28. Rosenthal, D., and J. O. Frank, Psychotherapy and the placebo effect. *Psychol. Bull.,* 1956, 53, 294-302.
29. Schanck, R. L., and C. Goodman, Reactions to propaganda on both sides of a controversial issue. *Publ. Opin. Quart.,* 1939, 3, 107-12.
30. Solomon, R. W., An extension of control group design. *Psychol. Bull.,* 1949, 46, 137-50.
31. Star, S. A., and H. M. Hughes, Report on an educational campaign: the Cincinnati plan for the United Nations. *Amer. J. Sociol.,* 1949-50,55, 389.
32. Stouffer, S. A., Some observations on study design. *Amer. J. Sociol.,* 1949-50, 55, 355-61.
33. Stouffer, S. A., Measurement in sociology. *Amer. sociol. Rev.,* 1953, 18, 591-97.
34. Underwood, B. J., *Experimental psychology.* New York: Appleton-Century-Crofts, 1949.
35. Underwood, B. J., Interference and forgetting. *Psychol. Rev.,* 1957, 64, 49-60.
36. Underwood, B. J., *Psychological research.* New York: Appleton-Century-Crofts, 1957.

37. Williams, R., Probability sampling in the field: a case history. *Publ. Opin. Quart.*, 1950, **14**, 316-30.

THE OBSERVER. THE EXPERIMENTER AND THE GROUP

Theodore M. Mills

Imagine, if you will, the plight of the centipede who suddenly stops to ask: How do I do this? What system do I employ? How am I related to my legs? Which one, or is it several? should I move next? We wonder if he will ever move again. He suffers from the centipede complex.[1]

Stephen Potter applies the concept, you will recall, in his advice to the golfing gamesman: when your opponent is on the green and about to putt, ask him what muscles he brings into play, and from what part of the body the sequence of muscular response begins.[2]

Victims of the complex suffer because while they dread losing what comes naturally to the amateur, they are haunted by the thought of becoming an accomplished professional–a self-conscious, self-governing professional. In this sense I interpret the spirit of this symposium to be professional–an invitation as it were, to inquire professionally into the technical and moral nature of what it is we do when we investigate man or, more accurately, when we study man's relationship *with* man.

Edward Shils, in his epilogue to *Theories of Society,* calls our attention to man's historical quest for *self-awareness* and especially to its dramatic upsurge during the present century.[3] At new depths and over a wider range, persons and peoples are opening themselves to self-inquiry. In being both a product and a propagator of this trend, social science (though Shils wrote specifically of sociology) has emerged with enough talent and energy to alter fundamentally "the relationships of humans to each other and with things they regard as important." One change is the scientist's realization of his affinity with men who make history and another is the realization of his affinity with his subjects as he makes science. "The elaboration of the theory of action," Shils writes,

Reprinted with the permission of the author and the publisher, The Society for the Study of Social Problems, from *Social Problems,* Vol. 14, No. 4 (1967), 373-81.

Written for the symposium on Ethical and Methodological Problems in Social Psychological Experiments under the auspices of the Society for the Psychological Study of Social Issues at the American Psychological Association convention, Chicago, Illinois, September 1965.

[1] Brought to my attention by Robert F. Bales.

[2] Stephen Potter, *The Theory and Practice of Gamesmanship*, New York: Holt, Rinehart and Winston, pp. 102-103.

[3] Talcott Parsons, Edward Shils, Kaspar D. Naegele and Jesse Pitts (Editors), *Theories of Society*, New York: The Free Press of Glencoe, 1961.

"... accepts the human being as an object of sociological study through an act of communion between object and subject. This act of communion is acknowledged through the promulgation of categories of persons, society and culture which are as applicable to the analyst as to the object analyzed, as applicable to the act of analysis as to the actions analyzed."[4] From Karl Deutsch's recent argument in *The Nerves of Government,* we add that to maintain communion with, while being autonomous from, our object of study requires not only constant self-monitoring and self-modification but a capacity to hold the entire system together while it is being monitored and modified.[5] This capacity, he suggests, depends upon a combination of the values of faith and humility—in our case, enough faith to press on with our observation and experimentation (even though we have technical and ethical misgivings) combined with enough humility to be open to new understanding of the significance of what we are doing.

As a sociologist, it is convenient for me to assume a division of labor in our symposium, leaving in other and more experienced hands the investigator's relation with the single subject while I direct my comments to his relation with groups. And since it is germane to later points let me suggest, although in negative terms, what, for purposes of the present discussion, I mean by a group.

A group is more than an *ad hoc* aggregation of persons. If we can extract a person from the aggregation with no one feeling the loss, then it is not a group. If we can inject an outsider into it with no one feeling estranged, then it is not a group. If we can change the rules, reset the beliefs, alter the standards, shift the task, change the purpose, rearrange the power structure, assemble it and disperse it at will—all without anyone caring—then it is not a group. It is instead what we might call a phantom—an apparition with temporal, biological, and ecological features of aggregation but without sociological substance.

By a group I shall mean a collectivity that has emotional, cognitive and moral substance, has a center of judgment and has a seat of government. My purpose is to inquire into the nature of the social relations between such groups and the persons who would investigate them and, in the end, to suggest two major methodological and moral issues. Since the empirical referents of the inquiry are the cumulative experiences over recent years of various persons—students, colleagues, and so on—in our laboratory, I ask you to imagine an apprentice observer just beginning his social science career while I point to highlights in his experience relevant to our problem.

THE OBSERVER AND THE GROUP

The training program may take our apprentice to a number of different settings: the wardroom of a ship, a nursery school, a group therapy session, a training seminar for senior military personnel or to a family conference in the living room. Wherever, one of his first discoveries is that he is in direct and immediate contact with unique, concrete, unrehearsed and largely unpredictable human processes. Events are in disorder and often incoherent, appearing in raw

---

[4]*Ibid.*, p. 1411.
[5]Karl W. Deutsch, *The Nerves of Government*, New York: The Free Press of Glencoe, 1963.

form, unfiltered by anyone else's interpretation of them. Though he may be confused by a lack of pattern, he can see the possiblity for genuinely independent observation and analysis. His discovery, then, is this opportunity to become intuitively familiar with the phenomena—which, L. J. Henderson suggests, is the first requirement in the making of a science.[6]

Soon, and notwithstanding the popular belief, he is surprised by the extent to which people under observation reveal themselves. He finds that they are not always on guard. As a consequence, he inadvertently becomes privy to information that could seriously affect their lives. A military officer's castigation of his commander could ruin his own career; a corporation executive's offhand admission of illegal tax procedures could lead to his imprisonment; wives' intimate talk in group therapy could estrange their husbands; a young psychiatrist's ineptness in a training group could destroy his patient's faith in him. And in the laboratory, an attrative young lady moves over to the mirror, fluffs her hair, strokes her eyebrows, then with her little finger probes deeply into her nose. The apprentice learns, to be sure, that some guards are up, but that many others are down.

This experience, he discovers, affects his personal composure. When he sees more than he expects to, and more than members intend to reveal, and when there are no limits on what he should see or on what he should do with what he sees, he feels uneasy, and embarrassed, as though he had stepped out of bounds, or were a transgressor.[7] His doubts about his right to observe are reflected in the dream of one observer following his first day with a therapy group: dressed in a doctor's white coat, he was in a courtroom being tried as a Peeping Tom before a greatly oversized microphone which later seemed to him to represent the judge. Seeing too much violates childhood taboos and associates oneself with the spy, the snooper or the voyeur—or with lonely persons who are neither entirely inside or outside. Not only the right to observe but one's motivation in observing comes into doubt. One could be a pervert or be construed as a blackmailer. Jokes about observation laboratories and those who frequent them play upon voyeuristic potentials and dangers. At this point some apprentices leave the role of observer altogether.

The ones who stay discover that group members attribute to them super-human powers. In their imagination the observer misses no signals and forgets nothing. He is an all-seeing, all-knowing judge and frequently is thought to be in collusion with the authority figure in the group and aligned with those who have jurisdiction over the group. Members often warn their fellows against the power of the observer, as in the following quotation from a military officer where the ostensible reference to someone at a distant base turns out to be a comment on the observer who was present in the room: "The important thing to remember here is that Sherril is just a spy—no more. He can't do anything—can't produce anything solid. He's just going around getting the dope and sending it over his hot line up above. Everybody should realize that he can make or break anybody on the base. A snooper like that can tear an organization apart." Is not

---

[6]Lawrence J. Henderson, "Procedure in a Science," in Hugh Cabot and Hoseph Kahl, *Human Relations*, Cambridge, Massachusetts: Harvard University Press, 1953, pp. 24-39.
 [7]Erik H. Erikson, "Ontogeny of Ritualization in Man" (mimeographed), read before the Royal Society, London, 1965.

this officer's concern generally shared by those being observed: what is being done with the information about me? Is it being used against me? How safe are we? Who has the observer under control? Until we know, we must close ranks against him before we fall apart.

One interpretation of these disturbances is that observation confuses traditional notions about boundaries. While the observer's exclusion from group activity affirms the existence of a boundary, his access to inside information denies the boundary. While he is an outsider, he wants inside information and wants it without becoming an insider. While privy to the group, he remains outside its jurisdiction. In this sense his presence implies a privileged position with the right to take away information without giving anything in return and to be above the group while it is "subject" to him.

It is a curious fact that groups both define the observer as being above them and feel he takes something away from them. The mechanism is somewhat as follows: if *he* is the observer, then we need not make observations of our own; if he is a superior observer, then we *better not* make our own observations; if he is the judge—a superior judge—then we better not make our own judgments; and, if he can predict our actions, then we better not make our own decisions. They appear to delegate to the outsider their own responsibilities, perhaps in the hope that he will oblige by performing them—for to observe, judge and predict what happens is, indeed, a difficult task. In any case, when, as a well-trained observer, he does not accept these responsibilities, they not only resent him but in the meantime have allowed their own capabilities to atrophy. They have become more watchful but less observant, more critical but less evalutative, more controlled but less committed. They lay their loss of these powers to the presence of the superior, yet nonresponsive, observer. The curious feature is that there is, of course, no technical reason why group and observer cannot make independent observations, judgments and decisions.

The apprentice next discovers that the group wants to observe him. Perhaps, in general, the observed wants to observe the observer. On one occasion a training group in our laboratory stopped abruptly, announced that it would go no further until the several observers were brought out from behind the mirrors, identified and "given the opportunity" of explaining their *real* purposes in being there. This was a first step in "getting to really know the observers." Group members want to contact the observer, have him respond and reveal himself partly, of course, to correct their vague and oversized image of him, partly to find out about themselves and to detect the standards he uses in judging them, but also, I suggest, to bring him into the group and under its jurisdiction.

Should it surprise us that in the meantime the observer discovers an inner tendency to join the group? Increasingly he wants to express his feelings toward members, his warmth toward some, his coolness toward others, his admiration for some, his distaste for others. Increasingly he emphathizes with the leader, wanting to prompt him or advise him or discuss with him the philosophy of leadership. Increasingly his emotional state follows the emotional swings of the group. Like the cowboy who shot the villain, he wants to join the action. In the extreme he may identify with the group to the extent that he comes under all the influences it is under, as for example, in taking the same experimental drugs the group is taking.

The purpose in recounting these experiences is, again, to suggest that the presence of the observer contradicts the traditional notion of the boundary separating insider from outsider: the observer, to repeat, is an outsider wanting inside information without becoming an insider. The group can solidify its boundary against him; whereupon, the observer is excluded. Or, the boundary may be dissolved bilaterally, the group extending its jurisdiction around the observer while he identifies with it. Note, however, that in either case science loses, for in both instances the apprentice vacates the role of independent scientific observer.

In view of this our methodological, ethical and moral problem—for they are bound together—is to imagine, devise and arrange a social relation between observer and group so that the boundaries separating them can be both maintained and transcended: *maintained* through mutual respect for the legitimate and distinct purposes of scientific observation and of group development, and *transcended* in appreciation of the essential kinship between the observer and the observed, in recognition of their affinity as members of the human community.

We might note some progress on the problem under favorable conditions. I refer, first, to the case where the group, under able leadership and through hard work, and in spite of the observer, develops powers of self-observation and an internal center of judgment. As it becomes effective in performing just those functions it thought he took from them, it finds him less important. For the observer's part, as he clarifies group processes to his scientific colleagues, he affirms the legitimacy of his role thereby relieving some anxiety over having transgressed.

The affinity between observer and observed is explicitly acknowledged in one case through setting up a special type of group whose announced purpose is to develop self-conciousness. I refer to the increasing number of self-analytic, learning and training groups—as well as to some therapy groups. The member's role is to observe the here and now, to formulate what is happening and, on occasion, to feed formulations back into the group so that it may act on them. Members combine the functions of observation and participation.

From our viewpoint self-analytic groups are a modern, technical, and, I might say, sociological invention, whereby traditional conceptions of group boundaries are altered and those boundaries are conciously redrawn. The observer's role is incorporated by the group. Members, in addition to acting, observe their own actions. Consequently, detached observation becomes part of the feedback process. At the same time, the newly internalized observer acts on his observations and can, therefore, make immediate empirical tests of their accuracy, relevance and importance. Responses to his formulations become part of the feedback process. In integrating observation and participation within a single role and within the purpose of the single group, the self-analytic group is a significant forward step in transcending the boundary between observer and group. Yet, of course, it is not a panacea: it depends upon persons who are interested in group self-consciousness; and, participation in it is just one step in the career of the apprentice, for although it may enrich his understanding of group process, he can neither generalize from this single experience nor experiment freely on self-analytic groups.

THE EXPERIMENTER AND THE GROUP

Let me shift to a later time and a different place. The scene is the university laboratory; the occasion, the first run of the apprentice's own experiment. Through his acquaintance with groups and for his thesis he has formulated an hypothesis he believes in and considers testable. You are familiar with his previous steps: clear statement of the problem, review of the literature, specification of the independent, intervening and dependent variables, selection of measures, settling on a statistically feasible design and attempting a tie-in with theoretical ideas. You know the types of variables he has taken into account: social class, family background, personality, attitudes, values, intelligence, education, peer group relations, the nature of the task, the number of persons in the group, their age, sex and so on. You are familiar with the difficult logistical problems he has faced: how to contact subjects, how to get them to come into the laboratory, how to obtain enough groups in each cell of the design within the realistic limits of space, time and resources, and so on. And you know that more frequently than not these groups eventuate in a group before him which is *ad hoc*, being comprised of students who do not know each other well, who are present because they are required to participate in experiments for course credit, who will interact in a series of short tasks, fill out questionnaires then depart rarely if ever to meet again as a group.

As he gets the first group underway, the apprentice senses the dramatic nature of experimentation. The laboratory seems a separate theater world; and the first run like opening night. The experimenter knows what it is to be producer, playwright and director, for this is his show: he has screened and selected the actors, composed the groups, constructed the tasks, designed the questionnaires, prescribed the observations to be made and the measures to be taken. He has brought people together and will send them away. From beginning to end he has written the script—except for those few vacancies to be filled in by indicators of the dependent variable. How subjects will respond is part of the drama; but another part arises because it is now *he* who is being judged. It is *he* who is now watchful but less observant, more critical but less evaluative, more controlled but less committed to a broad understanding of man.

If the session goes poorly, he is likely to discard the run, tighten up controls and start over again.

If, on the other hand, the results are clear and positive and other groups follow suit, then he is likely to discover the strangest fact of all. On the intellectual level he will want, naturally, to check against artifacts, sleeper variables, alternative interpretations and so on. But beyond and beneath that he discovers that *success creates a growing doubt about the reality of what has happened.* Is it, he wonders, too good to be true? Are the findings authentic? Or, with the doubt put in a more familiar way, how do the results apply to real groups in the real outside world? Might the whole production be just a play? Are the groups real or artifical? Am I really a scientist or am I something else? Like a sailor when the fog moves in, he must grope for his bearings. And he, like the sailor when told there is fog around, is not in the least helped by empty statements about how obvious it is that laboratory experimentation is irrelevant to real life outside.

The source of his disorientation lies not so much in the laboratory's relation to the outer world as in the experimenter's relation to the group before him. Contrast, if you will, this relation with the earlier one when he observed established groups. Earlier he went to the ship, the hospital or the school; now he brings subjects into his own laboratory—a strange and mysterious place: some call it a hall of mirrors, an electronic showcase, a courtroom, a prison cell, a decompression chamber! Earlier he observed a persistent group; now he deals with one group after the other as they are ushered in and out. Earlier, he observed a group with internal ties of affection and currents of hostility, a group with both a tradition and the power to set its own rules, one with both a purpose and the power to establish its own agenda, one with both boundaries and the power to admit and exclude on its own. In short, an autonomous group—a relatively autonomous group—or at any rate autonomous enough to get along without him.

In contrast, the experimental group is almost wholly dependent upon him for its substance, form and direction. Now, it is *he* who admits and excludes, *he* who assembles and dismisses, *he* who announces the purpose, sets the agenda, prescribes the rules, shifts direction, shields against outside influence, and so on—all in order properly to achieve comparable groups, standard procedures and a reduction in experimental error. The point of the comparison is that while earlier he encountered a group that performed its own executive functions now it is *he* who performs those functions for the group. The group literally does not know what it is until he assembles the members; nor do they know what to do until he tells them.

In these circumstances the experimenter's feeling of unreality is a real response to a real contradiction; while in actuality he performs executive functions *for* the group and is therefore sociologically *inside* the group, according to scientific tradition he conceives himself to be outside, to be detached and disinterested. While in actuality he is the group's creator, goalsetter, programmer, lawmaker, paymaster and judge, he conceives himself as having *no* role at all within it. More than this, he believes he *should not* have a role in it. Consequently, although an insider he must pose as an outsider. He impersonates an outsider. He is in masquerade. As a result he is not sure *where* he is, nor who he is. His disorientation spreads to things around him so that they, too, take on an appearance of artificiality. In this sense, confusion about the sociological boundaries between experimenter and group creates an authentic doubt about realtity.

The use of deception is hardly a departure from this theme. In proclaiming that something is *A* when it is not *A* (and in having this believed), the experimenter injects an existential proposition into the group's culture. His word sets the group's definition of this part of reality—much as in giving task instructions he sets goals and procedures. Closely related, of course, and another elaboration on the theme is the use of role-players or stooges, for to proclaim, or to imply, that these persons are *in* the group when they actually are not is to set a definition of the group's boundary. Parenthetically, it is interesting to note that to have an outsider-stooge pose as a insider may serve as some sort of counterbalance to an insider-experimenter posing as an outsider.

Let us return to the group and learn what has happened to it in the meantime. As already implied, it has become a phantom, compared to what it might have become under more favorable conditions. One could shuffle members from one group to another and it would not matter to the subjects; one could present new tasks, change the rules, proclaim a new purpose and again it would not matter. It has become infinitely responsive, pliable and obedient. It has become this way because when it was formed each person committed himself primarily to the experimenter rather than to his fellow members. It has become this way because experimenters need subjects who are willing to commit themselves primarily to him.

This phantom group is in fact the experimenter's own creation. By being the playwright, the producer and the director and, we might add, by conforming closely to the prevailing practices of journeyman experimental scientists, the apprentice, perhaps inadvertently, usurps for himself just those functions and prerogatives the subjects themselves need if they are to develop into a genuine group. With one hand the experimenter creates the raw potential for a group but with the other he takes away its means for becoming one. Quite precisely, in forming the group he gives it a form. He creates the character of his experimental subject.

This act of creating one's own subject may be peculiar to the group situation. To be sure, in recruiting a single person for an experiment a new social *relation* between him and the experimenter is created, but we would not say a new *person* is created. However, for groups we can say that by bringing people together for the first time the experimenter creates a social unit. A young, indistinct and illusive thing, it is nonetheless a new unit with a potential for developing its character. If this point be granted then we may suggest that the *manner* in which persons are brought together—the way the group is conceived, if you will—makes a difference in what it can and cannot become.

Let me clarify the point by reference to the practice of recruiting subjects from those courses which require participation in experiments. The ultimate decision to enter the laboratory in such cases is not the subject's but the professor's. This fact is known to all. Those who assemble know that they are present through conscription rather than by free choice. As a consequence of the social structure surrounding the laboratory, the act of attending is therefore an act of compliance and one's presence, evidence of having complied. Since the action and its meaning are common for all present, compliance is a demonstrated common ground for group formation. That is to say that at the time of assembly an undeniable reason for the group's existence is collective compliance. At birth, compliance is the group's implicit cultural constitution. Being born through conscription it is, and cannot be other than, a compliant group. There are two points: first, the way a new group is formed determines what it is and influences what it can and cannot become; and, second, our traditional procedures of forming experimental groups tend to produce aggregates devoid of the means for becoming autonomous and self-determining. Instead, these means are simultaneously usurped by, and reliquished to, the experimenter, as though he were the single and the central authority of the group. In spite of this we habitually define these aggregates as *groups*. We call them *groups*, ask them to work as a *group* and to arrive at a *group* decision. I am suggesting that the contradiction between the amorphous and impotent thing we create and the substance and power we attribute to it is a second source of our confusion over authenticity.

To summarize, the first illusion is that the experimenter is outside the group whereas sociologically he functions within it; and, the second is that the assembled aggregate is a group whereas it is actually only a phantom, with its governmental and executive powers having been taken over by the experimenter.

In short, the grand illusion is that experimenter and group are *separate* systems whereas in actuality they are *one*. They are a single system but with functions divided: controlling and being controlled, setting rules and conforming to them, giving directions and obediently following them, being in charge and complying with the one in charge, being the authority and being the subordinate. Though their functions differ, the two parties constitute a single unit. Neither one, let us recognize, can get along without the other. They are a single system masquerading as two. Perhaps the one-way glass in the laboratory and our intellectual preoccupation with how groups make decisions are stage props which support this illusion of separateness and independence.

The methodological and ethical problem is to conceive and to arrange, or shall we say invent, a working relationship between experimenter and group in which they may be both autonomous and interdependent: *autonomous* so that the investigator for his part can experiment for the sake of a science transcending both himself and the immediate group; and, *autonomous* so that groups for their part have the opportunity to develop their capabilities and to achieve their integrity; *interdependent* in the sense that groups become prepared to give up voluntarily part of their autonomy for the sake of knowledge about themselves (as well as about themselves for others); and, *interdependent* in the sense that the experimenter becomes prepared to give up some of his controls for the sake of experimenting with groups that have substance and integrity.

This does not mean, I hasten to say, that in a vain search for reality we close up the laboratory and rush out into the world of natural groups in natural settings. It does mean, however, that we make the laboratory more hospitable, that the groups brought in have a purpose of their own, do meaningful work from which they benefit and have enough freedom and time to work through their emotional and organizational problems. It means a greater investment by the experimenter—more time for each experiment, more money, more resources, more patience. And this in turn means both a clearer distinction among his professional colleagues between exercises in experimentation and experimentation on groups and their accepting the fact that experimentation on groups requires additional time and resources. In addition, of course, it means joint consultation and collaboration between the experimenter and his groups.

The invention of such a working relation would, like the telescope, bring the beholder closer to his object of study. It would be based upon an appreciation of our affinity with those whom we seek to understand, based on the assumption that, unlike the hypothetical centipede, we have the capacity to monitor and modify ourselves and to become professionally self-concious and, finally, based on the notion that exploration of, and experimentation with, the investigator's relation to his object of study *is* social science making.

In summary, the review of the apprentice's experiences in observing established groups and in experimenting on laboratory groups suggests a number of forces which tend, in the first instance, to press him out of the role of independent scientific observer and, in the second, to prevent the group from becoming autonomous and self-governing. The major methodological and moral problems are to conceive and to engineer social relations between investigator and group which honor the integrity of each, reinforce their affinity and permit productve interchange.

SOME OBSERVATIONS ON COMPARATIVE STUDIES

John Porter

I.

In the early years of the present century, when the modern social sciences were beginning to emerge as separate and specialised disciplines, the comparative method was said to be, for some of them, the method par excellence. If the study of human behaviour was to achieve scientific status there had to be some counterpart of the controlled experiment, a method which had enabled the physical sciences to make such great progress. Practical and moral considerations limit the extent to which human beings can be manipulated in the interests of social science. Moreover, when experiments in human behaviour are possible they usually take a long time to work themselves out. One of the most imaginative, and one which greatly changed our views about the relationship between the social environment at work and productivity, was the experiment the Western Electric Company conducted at its Hawthorne plant over a period of nine years.[1] There has been nothing on such a scale since. More recently experimental techniques have been limited to the study of very small, artificially created groups.

Because these efforts to create an experimental technique are so few the social sciences have continued and will continue to rely on the comparative method to produce variations in the conditions under which human behaviour takes place. Both the Hawthorne experiment of the 1930s and the small group research which followed the Second World War were responses to particular social conditions and the particular needs of those who provided the money for research. There is a similar relationship between social needs and the activities of social scientists in the current revival of interest in the comparative method. This relationship can be seen in the need for policies and programmes to assist the advancement of developing societies and, in advanced societies, in the need for full employment, welfare and educational programmes. Thus there has been a shift in emphasis, particularly in sociology, from the study of small groups, or

Reprinted with permission of the author and publisher from International Institute for Labour Studies: *Bulletin*, No. 3, (November, 1967), 82-104.

[1] F. J. Roethlisberger and W. J. Dickson: *Management and the Worker* (Harvard University Press, 1939). These experiments began with changes in the physical conditions of work, that is the relationship between illumination and output.

micro-social systems, to the analysis of macro-social systems, or total societies, including modern complex ones. There are theories about social change and development and about the functioning of macro-social systems, as well as practical considerations of policy, which make the comparative method an important substitute for experimentation.

Human societies are in themselves experiments in different ways of living. Some have long historical continuity, others a brief existence. Some are extraordinarily complex in their internal structure and organisation, others are much more simple or primitive. Genuine primitive societies become much more difficult to find as modern civilisation spreads. Modern societies, as they become increasingly based on science and technology, converge on a path of cultural homogeneity. Despite the gradual obliteration of primitive cultures and increasing similarities of the most advanced societies, human beings still live under a very wide range of conditions and demonstrate a great many forms of adaptation. Thus the reasons for using the comparative method, because it permits the study of the same or similar phenomena, and their fluctuations under a wide variety of conditions, are as strong as they always were.

II.

In the past it was perhaps anthropology which made the best use of the comparative method, in part because, in working with pre-literate societies, anthropologists were more aware of the great variety of forms of social organisation, and were thus able to call into question many of the generalisations of social theories based on the data of European or American history, or a nineteenth century market economy, or a simplistic psychology with its notion that human beings inherited a set of instincts which work themselves out invariably in human behaviour. While economics remained very deductive and abstract with its "Crusoe" models of behaviour, anthropological field workers were finding out at the empirical level something of the processes of primitive value and exchange and the importance of the social and environmental context within which these activities took place. The interrelatedness of such social institutions as property holding, authority, marriage and kinship became apparent from the knowledge of many societies. One early attempt to show the various forms these institutions took in association with each other was made by L. T. Hobhouse, G. C. Wheeler and M. Ginsberg.[1] Something of a lineal descendant of their work has been Yale University's Human Relations Area Files, which record a great deal of data on over 200 cultures, making it possible to apply statistical techniques in comparative analysis of a wide range of human behaviour.[2]

Among other important comparative works were studies by Ruth Benedict[3] and Margaret Mead.[4] Both of these became widely read and did much to destroy

[1] L. T. Hobhouse, G. C. Wheeler and M. Ginsberg: *Material Culture and Social Institutions of the Simpler Peoples* (London, 1913).
[2] See their use in G. F. Murdock: *Social Structure* (New York, Macmillan, 1949).
[3] Ruth Benedict: *Patterns of Culture* (Boston and New York, Houghton Mifflin Co., 1934).
[4] Margaret Mead: *Sex and Temperament in Three Primitive Societies* (New York, New American Library, 1950).

the notion that psychological traits and personality spring from specific instincts or have sex or other biological or genetic links. They were able to establish a relationship between personality and the culture in which it is found. The work of these two gifted anthropologists illustrates one of the important tasks of comparative studies, that is the testing out of general propositions about human behaviour in a variety of cultural contexts. The significant contribution of the comparative studies of the anthropologists was to show the great plasticity of so-called "human nature" evident from the many forms of adaptation human societies make to physical and social habitats.[5]

The other social sciences were slow to move out of the cultures in which they were working. With economics it may have been the requirements of national policy-makers which has resulted in the preoccupation with single system models. On the other hand sociology has been restricted in its comparative work because in the past the development of the discipline in various countries has been very uneven. The pace-setting in the field of sociology has certainly come from the United States. The dominant European tradition of grand theories of social evolution was rejected in favour of fact-collecting studies and manageable middle-range theories to test ideas not about large-scale ill-defined units but about smaller processes and units, such as, for example, the structure of bureaucracy within individual plants or government agencies. The result has been a vast body of empirical materials collected with considerable theoretical sophistication but largely within the cultural context of the United States.

Gradually after the Second World War sociology developed in other countries along the lines on which it was moving so rapidly in the United States, often following the same techniques and theoretical orientations.

In time it was thought that the accumulated data within various countries could be the subject of comparative analysis. The possiblities were further enhanced because of a cadre of well-trained social scientists in several countries who spoke the same technical language and followed the same logic of inquiry. Moreover, this development coincided, as already suggested, with the increasing interdependence of various countries and new obligations of assistance to the underdeveloped world.

III.

Because comparative studies can be viewed as a logical step in the development of the social sciences they have become so fashionable that many studies claiming to be, or thought to be, comparative really are not. An example would be a collection of individual national studies on a particular topic, such as education or political institutions, in the form of papers brought together in one volume. These may be historical and descriptive studies produced with little reference to each other and without a common framework or liaison between the authors. An editor may provide a minimum of analysis in an introductory or concluding chapter, but he must confine himself to taking each one in turn as a

[5]There are varying opinions on the role of the comparative method in anthropology. See I. Schapera: "Some Comments on the Comparative Method in Social Anthropology," in *American Anthropologist,* Vol. 55, No. 3, Aug. 1953; and Fred Eggan: "Social Anthropology and the Method of Controlled Comparison," ibid., Vol., 56, No. 5, Oct. 1954.

distinct thing. There is no comparative analysis, for example, when six scholars produce separate papers on the educational systems of six different countries. Each study may as well have been published separately rather than bound together since they draw nothing from each other.

Such inventories of national data or accounts of procedures in particular countries may be interesting but they are not comparative. At most they might provide a comparative perspective from which hypotheses about cross-systems or cross-cultural variations might be drawn and which a comparative study might test. Often this step is never taken. It is surprising, for all that is said about the value of comparison, that a rigorous comparative methodology has not emerged. The reason for this lack may be the very great difficulties that a rigorous comparative methodology would impose.

One interesting attempt at a comparative analysis which can only in part be criticised on the grounds just indicated is a volume edited by Gabriel Almond and James S. Coleman.[1] One of its aims is ". . . to offer a comparative analysis of the political systems of those areas of the world in which dramatic social and political changes are taking place. . . ."[2] The book includes a long theoretical introduction by Gabriel Almond; five area studies—South-East Asia, South Asia, Sub-Sahara Africa, the Near East and Latin America—in which the political systems of the various countries in these regions are examined by various authors; and a concluding chapter by James S. Coleman. The study has the advantage of some considerable liaison between the co-authors. Thus each of the five area studies employs a common set of categories within which the levels of modernisation and the political systems of the countries within each region are described. Examples of these categories are: "urbanisation", "restratification", "secularisation", "interest groups", "interest articulation", "political social-isation", "rule-making", and so forth. The categories are those developed in the theoretical introduction. Almond's aim in the introduction is to establish a functional approach to political systems rather than a formalistic one which deals only with constitutional and legal aspects of political institutions. The political system" . . . is that system of interactions to be found in all independent societies which performs the functions of integration and adaptation . . . by means of the employment, or threat of employment, of more or less legitimate physical compulsion."[3] Political functions are performed by political structures, such as parties, interest groups, bureaucracies, social movements (called "anomic" structures) and so forth. Some structures are responsible for input functions (political socialisation, interest articulation, interest aggregation, political communication) and others for output functions (rule-making, rule application, rule adjudication). Drawing from a wide knowledge of political institutions Almond presents a masterly exposition of how these functions are performed and their importance for the political system. These functional categories then become the rubrics under which the authors of the five area studies describe, mainly in non-quantitative terms, the countries in their areas. These descriptions vary considerably in their detail because,

[1] Gabriel Almond and James S. Coleman (eds.): *The Politics of the Developing Areas* (Princeton, 1960).
[2] Ibid., foreword by Frederick S. Dunn.
[3] Gabriel Almond and James S. Coleman, op. cit., p. 7.

obviously, there is more knowledge of some than of others, and in some regions there are many more "cases" of political systems than in others. In all, 75 systems are dealt with.

Although some scientists might have chosen or constructed an alternative theoretical scheme there is no doubt that Almond's system of analytical categories designed to examine the data of political systems is an important contribution. It is the comparative aspect of the study which leaves much to be desired. One could at the outset question the scientific wisdom of assembling descriptive material on 75 countries, ranging in their development from Israel to Ethiopia, into a vast but incomplete morphology. It is the absence of statements specifying the interrelationships between the different political functions as they are revealed in the various types of political systems which is disappointing.

In the concluding chapter James S. Coleman sets out ". . . to summarise briefly the modal characteristics of the political systems covered in this survey, to analyse the range of variation among these systems, and where possible to suggest propositions regarding relationships and developmental patterns in the process of modernisation."[4] For these purposes he constructs two typologies, one for the degree of competitiveness in the political system ("competitive", "semi-competitive" and "authoritarian"), and the other for the degree of political modernisation ("modern", "mixed" and "traditional"). Each of the political systems is then classified according to its type (mixed, semi-competitive, for example) and the modal characteristics of the types discussed. This classificatory process is an important scientific activity, but the potential of comparative studies is not utilised until the variations in the characteristics, both within the types and between the types, are specified and measured, or if they are not measured at least presented in some researchable form. At many points in the Coleman text it is possible to pick out hypothesised relationships between variables. For example, ". . . so long as interests are primarily rooted in and find expression through communal groups, they are far less amenable to aggregation in a competitive and bargaining process"[5] (i.e. the system is too fragmented for all the various interests to be mediated by two major political parties). Another example is ". . . the character of the socialisation process varies according to the goals of the governing élite and the nature of the cultural pluralism."[6] Perhaps it is the ambitious attempt to compare so very much all at once that makes it difficult to descend from the most general level and to specify relationships more clearly.

IV.

Typologies are very important in comparative analysis. They are a classification system by which "cases" or "systems" can be grouped by their common elements. Typologies can be broad or narrow, and they can be infinitely refined as more and more distinguishing characteristics are thought to be important, up to the point where there is a type for each case. The construction of typologies is an important analytical exercise and can help alert the investigator to the

---

[4] Gabriel Almond and James S. Coleman, op. cit., p. 532.
[5] Ibid., p. 535.
[6] Ibid., p. 545.

important variables. The arrangement of cases into types is not in itself comparative analysis, but rather a step in determining what cases might be fruitfully compared. There is always the choice of comparison within a type, between similar types or between dissimilar types. Are we likely to get more useful knowledge by comparing systems which might, for example, be typed as "modern-industrial" type systems with "rural-traditional" type systems? Typologies are, of course, gradations along a continuum of differences. It would seem that the farther removed the types are that are being compared the less useful are the results, because the relationships which are expressed are very gross, such as the one established by Coleman in his concluding chapter of a positive relationship between economic development and political competitiveness.

The broader or more inclusive the typologies the less do they help to detect the operation of particular variables. It is fairly easy, but not very helpful, to establish a relationship, for example, between investment in education in "modern" societies and their gross national product, and to compare these factors with those found in societies at a much lower level of development. Much more useful information is likely to emerge from an analysis of systems within the same type, such as a comparative analysis of school retention rates for children of manual workers in three industrial societies. It is the analyses of differences between systems of the same or similar type which come closer to an experimental variation than do gross comparisons, which are, in any case, "detectable to the eye" and require little refinement of instruments to measure. In this sense the comparisons attempted in *The Politics of the Developing Areas* are too numerous and too gross. In the final part of his conclusion Coleman introduces a further typology for the analysis of the Asian and African political systems. He says: "Although many of the Latin American countries could perhaps be fitted into the more detailed typology, the differences between the two major areas are such that the inclusion of those countries in the following analysis of functional profiles would tend to dilute the distinctiveness of the categories."[7]

V.

The important task of comparative studies is the testing of hypotheses about the relationship between variables in more than one society. Because they look at a particular item or items of behaviour beyond the context of a single culture they can contribute to more general theories of human behaviour. Take, for example, the finding of differential fertility between social classes and between urban and rural populations in industrial societies. These facts are interesting enough even within one society, but when the same relationships are found to hold good in several societies, or can be shown to vary under specified conditions, these findings become much more powerful in explaining how this particular phenomenon operates.

The need to clarify concepts and to specify the variables is well illustrated in a scheme, reported by Rokkan[1], for the study of citizenship participation in the

[7]Gabriel Almond and James S. Coleman, op. cit., p. 561.
[1]Stein Rokkan: Introduction to "Citizenship Participation in Political Life," in *International Social Science Journal*, Vol. XII, No. 1, 1960.

political processes, a phenomenon the understanding of which is essential to any theory of political behaviour. Participation may be on the level of running for and holding office, joining and working for parties or—the simplest participation—voting as a citizen. The liberal theory of political behaviour which led to the extension of the franchise in the nineteenth century held that individuals would exercise their political rights on some rational basis such as the calculation of their own self-interest or the public interest. Twentieth century electoral democracies have very much disproved this "intellectualist fallacy."[2] Consequently, twentieth century political theories are largely about oligarchies, élites, dictatorships, authoritarianism and mass apathy. It was not until the Second World War and after that through survey methods it became possible to show on an empirical basis why people voted the way they did and how political attitudes were formed and operated. These methods of investigation quickly spread from the United States to other countries with the result that political behaviour was a subject about which there could be considerable cross-cultural data.

On the basis of these single culture findings Rokkan was able to specify a range of independent and intervening variables making for high and low participation under different systems. He grouped these into life experience variables such as the interest in politics in the family of origin, parents, educational level, closeness to decision-makers through kinship ties, occupational career experience; life situation variables such as occupational status; personality variables; social activity variables such as participation in various types of voluntary associations like trade unions; and political commitment variables such as constancy of attachment of one party and the strength of political convictions held.[3] By specifying relevant variables in advance it then becomes possible to measure in a cross-cultural context the varying intensities by which the variables contribute to high or low participation rates in different social systems. Something of the complex interrelatedness of the variables becomes revealed. It would seem, then, that comparative studies can best be built on the existing knowledge of how processes operate within a single culture, since it is this knowledge which permits the specifications to be made.

VI

It is easy enough to say how important comparative studies are in the development of our knowledge of human behaviour and to advocate a rigorous methodology. It is not easy to maintain these high aims in an actual research programme. There are many technical problems to be solved. To examine some of these problems it is helpful to consider two kinds of comparative research. The first uses already existing data; the second involves a new research design and data collection. Some problems are common to both kinds of projects. Some of the problems associated with the first kind can be corrected by the second.

Undoubtedly the greatest problem associated with the first approach is the comparability of the data. These will have been collected within each country often for quite different purposes and frequently employing different methods and definitions. Almost all countries collect vast quantities of statistics, both

[2] The term is from Graham Wallas: *Human Nature and Politics* (London, 1908).
[3] Rokkan, loc. cit.

official and private. Within countries it is difficult to maintain standards where statistics are gathered by lower levels of government or where the registration of events is made in a large number of different offices. Statistics collected by government agencies or based on official censuses will vary from country to country. Although efforts are being made constantly through international organisations to improve the quality of statistics and to establish standard definitions, it is difficult to find cross-national standards and uniformities in the definitions of such things as "household", "family income", "depreciation", "labour force", "unemployment", "university student", "rural", "delinquency", and so on through almost the entire range of social science ideas and concepts for which statistics record the empirical counterparts. Different countries will have different policy needs and hence different policy-makers will be interested in different kinds of facts. Government agencies may be reluctant to make changes in their statistical series, because what they may gain in cross-national comparability they may lose in comparability over time within their own system. Since it is often possible to make adjustments, this reluctance may reflect inertia in offices where things have been done in a particular way for a long time.

The more countries that are drawn into a comparison the more are these problems confounded. The result is that the investigator tries to adjust the statistics to make them comparable and in doing so makes certain assumptions about their relevance and meaning. An extensive discussion may then be presented of what was desirable but unobtainable, and of the adjustments in the data which consequently had to be made. It takes a certain amount of courage, after having pointed out the deficiencies in the material, to carry on. What is more disconcerting, however, is that the differences which are found could be accounted for by the assumptions relating to and the looseness of the data being compared. If the most fruitful comparisons are between societies of the same or similar type, then the amount of variation is bound to be small, but perhaps crucial, at the level of macroanalysis. If one wants to show, for example, the relationship between the educational level of the labour force and personal income in two countries of a similar social structure, say Canada and the United States, the differences are not likely to be large and when found could quite easily be attributed to the adjustments made in the data in an effort to make them comparable rather than to a real difference. If it is difficult to compare macro-data from the advanced industrial societies, it is much more hazardous to compare those from the developing countries, where minimal standards of enumeration, registration and presentation have yet to be established.

VII

A further source of already existing materials for comparative studies are the sample surveys undertaken in most industrial societies in varying degrees of quantity and quality on many subjects by private, government or university-sponsored research organisations. Family income and expenditure, voting behaviour, political attitudes, occupational prestige, career histories, educational experience and mass media interests are examples of subjects about which surveys have been made. Some time ago it was felt that the materials used in these surveys, the questionnaires, punch cards, code books and so forth, could be saved so that the data could be used a second time, perhaps in relation to some problem that did not interest the original investigator. The Roper Public Opinion Research Center at Williams College in the United States was the first major repository of survey materials from all over the world. There have been efforts to establish similar data repositories in Europe.[1] The mechanical ease with which all these materials can be reproduced and subjected to secondary analysis by any investigator anywhere has led to the neglect of the technical and methodological problems involved.

For comparative studies there seem to be severe limits on the secondary analysis of survey material. Even though the subject matter may be the same, research designs are often not similar; the techniques employed, the field work standards, and the questions asked are different. Since at times the comparison will be across different language groups, the questions may not be the same at all. More important, perhaps, are differences in sample designs. When samples are not the same, or of a high standard, the possibility that differences in findings are from sampling fluctuations rather than from real differences cannot be ruled out. Field work procedures vary a great deal in their standards and techniques. Varying completion rates can skew samples in different directions. Differing methods of dealing with nonresponse can greatly vary the quality of samples, and differences in the training and control of field staff can make differences in the quality of the work which is returned. All these difficulties are obvious, but it is important to remember the limitations which they can impose on comparative studies based on surveys in different countries. Once again it is the small variations of the phenomenon being studied in societies at relatively the same level of development which are likely to be most fruitful, and it is such small differences which could be attributed to sampling fluctuations, or to differences in completion rates or to rules about substitution.

National sample surveys often involve relatively small numbers, thus very much limiting the subgroups into which the sample can be divided, but it is the analysis of subgroups which can be most important in comparative studies. A standard procedure when subgroups have too few cases is to combine them until there are enough cases to make some kind of acceptable statistical statement. When this is done with cross-national comparisons, the collapsing or combining of categories either to overcome the problem of small numbers or to make the categories equivalent can obscure important patterns of differences or can lead to such gross measures as to be not worth the effort.

It may be possible to employ secondary analysis when the questions are simple, such as: "Which party did you vote for in the last election?", and to analyse responses in the light of the more easily obtainable social background characteristics of the respondents. Where, however, more important attitudinal data are compared, where the quality of the data very much depends on interviewers' skill and the categories of analysis, the difficulties which have been reviewed impose great limitations.

---

[1] See the contributions of Philip K. Hastings, Robert E. Mitchell and Stein Rokkan in the collection of papers on "Data in Comparative Research," in *International Social Science Journal*, Vol. XVI, No. 1, 1964. Rokkan's paper on the use of sample surveys in comparative research reviews most of the problems involved.

VIII

Examples of some of the problems which have been reviewed and of attempts to overcome them can be found in international comparisons of social mobility. Social mobility is the interchange between classes, the movement up or down a scale of social status positions, particularly the degree to which adult sons have higher or lower status positions than their fathers. This requires data on the son's (that is usually the respondent's) occupation and his father's occupation. There have been a number of studies of social mobility based on national samples. These have been the subject of secondary analysis for the purpose of cross-national comparisons.

A pioneering effort in this field was made by R. Bendix and S. M. Lipset.[1] Nothing is said of the quality of the samples, completion rates, biases, and so forth, which, if known, would have an important bearing on the conclusions. So that the movement up and down the class structure can be measured, the occupations of fathers and sons have to be classified into hierarchical categories, such as professional, clerical, skilled, semi-skilled, unskilled. Obviously the greater the number of categories used the more mobility will be recorded. In the Lipset and Zetterberg comparisons the occupational categories used in the original studies were so different that in order to make comparisons at all the categories were reduced to two, manual and non-manual.

Thus the comparisons were limited to measuring the movement both up and down across the manual/non-manual line. An important amount of mobility within each of the large categories, say from unskilled to semi-skilled or skilled manual occupations, or from lower white collar to professional occupations, is not counted. Yet much of the mobility that is shown in studies employing, say, six to eight occupational categories takes place between adjacent levels. Thus the degree of mobility measured when the simple dichotomous manual/non-manual categories are used is far from the full amount of mobility, so that the conclusions about cross-national differences measured in this way obscure more than they reveal. The major finding of this study, now much repeated in the sociological literature, is that there is as much social mobility in European industrial societies as there is in the United States, a contradiction of the prevailing mythology that the class structure of European societies is more rigid than that of the United States and that the latter provides greater opportunities to move up. The limitation of this finding of comparative analysis to the broad statement that social mobility is a feature of all industrial societies does not mean that the authors have necessarily wasted their time in arriving at it; rather it shows that the great promise of comparative studies through secondary analysis has scarcely been fulfilled.

Not that the authors are unaware of the limitations of the material with which they are working. After summarising some of the differences they add: "Given the variations in the methods of collecting data, it would be premature to place much reliance on these differences."[2] There have been attempts to improve and refine cross-national comparisons of mobility derived from secondary analysis.

[1] R. Bendix and S. M. Lipset: *Social Mobility in Industrial Society* (Berkeley and Los Angeles, University of California Press, 1959); Chapter II by S. M. Lipset and Hans L. Zetterberg.
[2] R. Bendix and S. M. Lipset, op. cit., p. 26.

But the problems remain as the authors of a later study suggest: "In making comparisons among nations, a leap of courage must be made. Many of the difficulties of individual studies are compounded in comparative perspective. Some national studies are of poor technical quality, but we have no choice of substitutes if we wish to include a particular nation in a comparison. Time periods differ in various studies: occupational titles and ratings are not fully comparable. Consequently it is important to recognise that *any comparisons are at best only approximations.*"[3]

We can see, then, that there are great limitations in comparative analysis based on data collected for other purposes, whether these are the macro-data compiled by government agencies or sample survey data acquired by varying techniques and standards.

IX

Comparative studies based on newly collected data are likely to be much more useful. Here again we can consider two types: the replication study, and studies in which the design is entirely new and specifically planned for comparative purposes. The replication study seeks to repeat in one country as nearly as possible a study already undertaken in another, with the object of determining whether the finding holds in another social or cultural system or, what is more important, the degrees of variations there are in the strengths of the finding. In the replication study it is possible to follow closely the original design. Of course it is not possible to achieve exact replication and there is always a judgment to be made as to whether or not the degree of departure from the original design is so great as to warrant abandoning the effort and turning funds to something else.

An example of this type of comparative research was one undertaken in Canada to replicate a study of occupational prestige in the United States.[1] The data from occupational prestige studies are important in the construction of scales or indices to measure social class position or to construct categories to be used, for example, in studies of social mobility. They also provide useful information to help understand the process of occupational recruitment in that the distribution of prestige through the occupations of the labour force will be related to the flow of recruits into them or into educational programmes appropriate or inappropriate to the occupational structure that exists or is emerging. In addition the study which was to be replicated in Canada sought to find out a range of factors that went into occupational prestige, as well as to secure occupational histories of respondents and other background data. The United States and Canada are sufficiently close in their social structure but yet with sufficient differences to yield, perhaps, some interesting differences in the field of occupational prestige. Since it was possible to establish liaison with those making the United States study, the conditions were almost perfect for a replication study.

The method employed in occupational prestige studies is to have a sample of

[3]Thomas Fox and S. M. Miller: "Intra-Country Variation: Occupational Stratification and Mobility," in R. Bendix and S. M. Lipset: *Class, Status and Power* (revised edition, London, 1967), p. 574. Italics in original.
[1]Peter C. Pineo and John Porter: "Occupational Prestige in Canada," in *The Canadian Review of Sociology and Anthropology* (forthcoming).

the nation's adults (or whatever the population might be) rank a given number of occupations in terms of the social standing which the respondent thinks they have in the community. In this study there were 200 occupational titles to be ranked. Some changes in these titles had to be made so that they would be more representative of the Canadian labour force. At times this meant removing occupations that did not exist in Canada, such as "astronaut", and making slight changes in others, such as "United States Senator", to what could be considered a Canadian counterpart. The number of changes were kept to a minimum, so that there were 172 matching titles, sufficient to allow comparison over a considerable range of the occupational structures.

Drawing a comparable sample for Canada created difficulties. The United States study had used an areal probability sample with household listings in the sampling units. No commercial survey firm in Canada maintained such a high quality sample. It seems to be normal practice in commercial surveys in Canada to allow, under controls, interviewer substitution for refusals and people not at home. In the United States study the method used required frequent call backs to designated households within sampling units. In the Canadian study it was possible to modify the sampling procedures of one firm and to introduce a call back system to help minimise the difference between the two samples. It is one thing to draw a good sample but quite another to maintain uniform standards of field work. The University of Chicago's National Opinion Research Center has a highly trained and experienced field staff which is able to achieve high completion rates and properly completed interview schedules. The Canadian study could only hope to approximate these standards. Very detailed instructions to interviewers, compiled on the basis of the instructions given to the United States interviewers, were prepared. As it turned out, it was the field work stage of the project which proved to be the most disappointing. The final completion rate after great efforts to improve it was 63.4 per cent., compared to most United States studies where completion rates are well over 80 per cent. Thus the differences in the completion rates could well preclude the analysis of certain kinds of differences between the two countries.

This attempt at a Canada-United States comparative study had to deal with another problem very often found in cross-national studies, that is the translation of all the field materials including instructions to interviewers into a second language, in this case French. An interview schedule or a card handed to a respondent during an interview is a stimulus the character of which can change according to the words used. That is why in social research these instruments are prepared and pre-tested with great care. In translation the main problem is to maintain an equivalence of the stimulus. Even such things as occupational titles give difficulties in translation because often the word by which the occupation is described, "grease monkey" for example, will effect its prestige. More complicated questions aimed at eliciting attitudes require even greater care to maintain equivalence. One technique, the one employed in the occupations study, is to have a panel of bilingual judges rank translations for their adequacy. Where there is a high degree of agreement it can be assumed that some equivalence has been achieved. Where there is disagreement it is necessary to do more work on the translations.

As a method of comparing the operation of variables cross-culturally the replication study has great advantages over attempts to find comparable data derived from unrelated studies.

X

Comparative research is likely to be most fruitful when it is comparative from the beginning, and designed specifically to test hypotheses cross-culturally. It is also the most expensive type of study, particularly when it involves interviewing operations. Many of the problems already referred to, particularly that of achieving equivalence of the research instruments used in more than one culture, do not disappear, but they are easier to control. Cultures will vary greatly in the extent to which invasions of privacy (without which social research could not possibly proceed) will be accepted. Investigators must be sensitive to the different ways in which cultures will define the roles of interviewer and interviewee. Furthermore, cultures will give different emphasis to different social groups and institutions such as the family, the wider kin group, the work group, the government agency, the authority system, religion and so forth. The nuances of social relationships will be different.[1] Consequently a thorough knowledge of the cultures to be compared is necessary. It would be unusual for any one investigator to have such knowledge and, therefore, it is almost essential for the research to be collaborative between scientists in different countries. One of the main problems here is to find a group of qualified people in two or more countries who can be persuaded of the value of comparative analysis. This problem is greater the less the countries considered for comparison have a developed social science.

Assuming that a group of interested researchers can be brought together (international agencies can play an important entrepreneurial role in this respect), it is then possible for the group to work together on the research design, adapting it to the cultural differences of which they are aware. Sampling problems, the selection of regions and social units, such as tribes, schools, firms, families, etc., can be carefully selected to maximise comparability. Specific plans to minimise non-response and to control faulty interviewing can be made, and the uniform training of interviewers (with the proper allowances for the cultural differences in the interviewer's role) can be attempted. The researchers can also agree on the coding and tabulation of data and the subsequent analysis.

XI

In these observations the difficulties of comparative research have been emphasised because an awareness of them is essential for coping with them in a reasonable way. It may appear, too, that the remarks about comparative studies already undertaken are overly critical considering the obstacles to be overcome. It is important to recognise that it is because some have been bold enough to tackle comparative studies that the difficulties have become apparent. We are, therefore, much indebted to these pioneers. Anyone planning a comparative

---

[1] The *International Social Science Bulletin*, Vol. VII, No. 4, 1955, is devoted almost entirely to the matter of cross-national research. For an excellent review of the problem of comparative research on the family see Reuben Hill: "Cross-National Family Research: Attempts and Prospects," in *International Social Science Journal*, Vol. XIV, No. 3, 1962.

project should be familiar with the work of others who have undertaken them. In addition to those already referred to there are a number of others worthy of note.[1]

The present state of comparative studies may be summarised by the following quotation from McClelland[2]: "Those who might be discouraged by such complexities, as we have often been, can only take comfort in the thought that for the most part error is fairly random and operates to reduce relationships, rather than to create them where they do not exist. So whatever relationships are found may be taken the more seriously because they have somehow managed to 'shine through' the many sources of error and confusion that undoubtedly exist in the data to be presented; nevertheless, many may in the end be more persuaded, as we have been, by the over-all direction of the evidence rather than by any particular study." If the rigorous comparative method that is desirable has not yet been arrived at we are at least beginning to get some comparative perspectives and some idea about "the over-all directions" of relationships.

[1] Daniel Lerner: *The Passing of Traditional Society* (Glencoe, The Free Press, 1962); David C. McClelland: *The Achieving Society* (Princeton, D. Van Nostrand, 1961); S. M. Lipset: *The First New Nation* (New York, Basic Books, 1963); Gabriel Almond and Sidney Verba: *The Civic Culture: Political Attitudes and Democracy in Five Nations* (Princeton University Press, 1963).
[2] *The Achieving Society*, op. cit., p. 61.

THE BEARING OF COMPARATIVE ANALYSIS ON SOCIOLOGICAL THEORY

Robert M. Marsh

I

"Comparative analysis," as used in the literature, often refers to either (1) intra-societal comparisons, as between middle and working class delinquency or between types of complex organization in American society,[1] or some other individual society; or, (2) studies of a *single* society other than one's own. Thus, studies of French or Japanese social structure are called "comparative" when reviewed by American sociologists for American readers. But in such studies, the comparisons between French or Japanese data and American data tend to be implicit rather than explicit; the real burden of systematic cross-societal comparisons is often left to the reader.

Reprinted with permission of the author and publisher from *Social Forces*, Vol. 43 (1964), 188-96.

[1] Amitai Etzioni, *A Comparative Analysis of Complex Organizations* (New York: The Free Press of Glencoe, 1961), exemplifies this practice.

The present conception of comparative analysis is distinct from the above two. Comparative analysis is here restricted to the systematic and explicit comparison of data from two or more societies. These comparisons include a variety of methodological strategies—"holistic," descriptive analyses as well as studies which rigorously test theoretically-derived, or at least theoretically-relevant, propositions and hypotheses. Comparisons may be of total societies, though more usually they are of sub-systems of different societies, such as socialization practices of polity.

Several hundred such comparative studies have been published since 1950.[2] A fairly extensive bibliographical search in both sociological and social anthropological publications has revealed that there are now in the literature a number of comparative analyses in each of the major sub-fields of these two disciplines. Having attained some bibliographical control over the literature of recent comparative analysis, my next step has been to attempt to *codify* it. This is done by asking and attempting to answer the following questions for each piece of comparative analysis codified: (1) What societies, cultural areas, and types of data are being used? (2) What hypotheses, if any, are being tested? (3) What methodological problems are encountered, and what innovations, if any, are made in methodology and research techniques? (4) Are existing theory and substantive knowledge confirmed, generalized, refined or refuted? (5) What, if any, are the peculiar virtues and limitations of comparative analysis as against analysis limited to one society? Underlying all these questions is a more basic question which has prompted the codification: to what extent will sociological theory, based upon or tested with data from only modern Western industrial societies, show itself able to account for patterns in non-Western and pre-industrial societies? It is my assumption that the progress of sociology in the coming years must confront this question as one of its greatest challenges.

I set out to codify comparative analysis with much the same attitude in which Merton undertook to codify functional analysis[3]. In neither instance is codification a vehicle for glossing over the deficiencies in the work codified. At the same time, each attempt at codification springs from the same motive: just as Merton believed that functional analysis, with all its shortcomings, was the most promising mode of analysis at our present state of development as a science, so now it is my judgment that sociology will do well to adopt cross-societal comparative analysis as its customary procedure.

The present paper provides only a progress report on the results of codification in relation to questions four and five above; a much fuller treatment will appear in a forthcoming book.[4]

---

[2] The bibliographical search has covered all articles published and books reviewed in the following journals: *American Sociological Review* (1950-April 1963); *American Journal of Sociology* (1950-May 1963); *Sociological Abstracts* (January 1954-February-March 1963); *American Anthropologist* (1950-1961); *Social Forces* (1950-1961); *Sociological Inquiry* (1959-1962); *British Journal of Sociology* (1950-March 1963); *Journal of Social Issues* (1950-1961). Comparative analyses by earlier sociologists, such as Weber, Durkheim and others, are well known and are not codified here.

[3] Robert K. Merton, *Social Theory and Social Structure* (Glencoe, Illinois: The Free Press, 1957), pp. 12-16 and chap. 1.

[4] Robert M. Marsh, *Comparative Sociology: Toward the Codification of Cross-Societal Analysis*.

Codification has revealed the following ways in which cross-societal comparative analysis fruitfully bears upon sociological theory.

1. Comparative analysis broadens the range of variation in variables, thereby
   requiring theory to explain more than it has heretofore.
2. Comparative analysis replicates studies originally done in one society, or in a
   small number of societies, in other, similar societies.
3. Comparative analysis generalizes propositions, originally verified only in one
   type of society, in other types of societies.
4. Comparative analysis specifies apparently discrepant findings from different
   societies by developing new propositions which account for the originally
   discrepant findings.

This paper attempts no more than to present selected examples of each of
these four points. My concern here is more to call attention to these four ways
in which comparative analysis bears on theory than to exhaustively cover the
findings of comparative research.

II

*1. Comparative analysis broadens the range of variation in variables, thereby
requiring theory to explain more than it has heretofore.* Rosen compared data
on Achievement Motivation by social class for samples from the United States
and Brazil.[5] Analysis of variance reveals that there is greater variance in mean
achievement motivation scores by nationality than by social class. Mean scores
by class do not even overlap: the lowest score for the U.S. sample (4.7) is higher
than the highest score in the Brazilian sample (3.9).[6] If the scores by class from
the two societies are now treated as one continuum, the range of variation has
thereby been extended from 1.9 (Brazilian class IV) to 7.3 (U.S. classes II and
III)–a range much greater than was possible within either society.

Murdock[7] has shown effectively that sociology, because of its concentration
on modern Western industrial societies, has typically explained too little.
Murdock randomly selected ten societies each from Asia, Africa, Oceania, and
native North and South America. He then made a judgmental selection of ten
European societies of common derivation, but widely heterogeneous in regard to
time, space, language and cultural diversity (for example, ancient Athenians,
English of the Elizabethan period, Hungarians immediately prior to World War
II, etc.). Each of these 60 societies was classified with respect to 30 distinct
cultural categories: such as, type of economy, division of labor, kinship and
marriage, social stratification and government. Murdock found that the cultural
characteristics of the contemporary United States were identical to those of the
ten European societies in 61 percent of the cultural items compared, and variant
in 39 percent of the items. When the comparison was made between the United

[5] Bernard Rosen, "Socialization and Achievement Motivation in Brazil," *American
Sociological Review,* 27 (October 1962), p. 623, Table 3.
[6] It is possible, of course, that TAT achievement imagery is culture-bound and that
Brazilian achievement scores are not really so low. But until this is demonstrated we shall
assume that these are real differences.
[7] George P. Murdock, "Anthropology as a Comparative Science," *Behavioral Science, 2*
(1957), pp. 249-254.

States and the other 50 non-European societies, however, the similarities declined to 26 percent of the cultural characteristics. Murdock also found that almost 50 percent of the items listed in the randomly selected non-European societies belong in cultural categories which were completely unrepresented in any of the European societies.

Enough has been said perhaps to persuade of the value of cross-societal data. A sociologist may, of course, want to explain the social phenomena of only one society; in this case my strictures will be less relevant. On the other hand, insofar as one's problems are conceived of in comparative terms—as is, I think, increasingly the case—then one must confront this stricture.

2. *Comparative analysis replicates studies originally done in one society, or in a small number of societies, in other, similar societies.* The proposition that voting rates are highest where involvement in government policies is greatest, and that therefore government employees should have the highest rate of electoral participation, was originally supported with U.S. data.[8] Subsequently, the findings have been successfully replicated in Germany,[9] France,[10] and Switzerland and Sweden.[11]

Again, U.S. studies of electoral participation have shown that while, in general, voting varies directly with socioeconomic status, among blue collar workers, union members have higher voting rates than non-union members. Lipset, *et al.*,[12] cite European data which replicate this finding. In Vienna, Berlin and other European cities, the socialist labor movement creates in working class districts an even tighter working class network than is created by U.S. unions. As would be predicted, workers in these districts have an even higher voting rate than do U.S. union members. In both the U.S. and European cities, then, voting rates among workers vary positively with: (1) tightness of network of working class oriented norms; (2) isolation from middle class norms; (3) amount of working class conformity pressures.

These two examples of replication will suffice to illustrate the second contribution comparative analysis can make to sociological theory; namely, to demonstrate that relationships which hold in one society also hold in other, similar societies. Our examples were drawn from Western industrialized societies; they could just as well have been drawn from studies which have been replicated within other types of societies, e.g., primitive societies.

3. *Comparative analysis generalizes propositions, originally verified only in one*

[8] Ben A. Arneson, "Non-Voting in a Typical Ohio Community," *American Political Science Review*, 19 (November 1925), pp. 821, 825; Roscoe C. Martin, "The Municipal Electorate: A Case Study," *Southwestern Social Science Quarterly*, 14 (December 1933), pp. 213-214; Dewey Anderson and Percy E. Davidson, *Ballots and the Democratic Class Struggle* (Stanford: Stanford University Press, 1943), pp. 157-158.

[9] Herbert Tingsten, *Political Behaviour: Studies in Election Statistics* (London: P. S. King & Son, 1937), pp. 137-138.

[10] George Dupeux, "Le problem des abstentions dans le département du Loir-et-Cher au début de la troisième republique," *Revue Française de la Science Politique*, 3 (1952), pp. 71-86 at 74. Tingsten, *op. cit.*, pp. 126, 128, 132; 161-62, 174.

[11] Robert Girod, "Facteurs de l'abstentionisme en Suisse," *Revue Française de la Science Politique*, 3 (1953), pp. 349-376 at 369.

[12] S. M. Lipset *et al*, "The Psychology of Voting: an Analysis of Political Behavior," in Gardner Lindzey, (ed.) *Handbook of Social Psychology* (Cambridge: Addison Wesley Press, 1954), chap. 30, pp. 1124-1175.

type of society, in other types of societies. When an original relationship is found to "hold up," not in another society of the same type (as in 2, above), but in a different type of society, we can say that the original relationship has been *generalized.* Thus, Hyman[13] summarized American findings on class differences in levels of aspiration and in values relevant to social mobility. Baker[14] generalized Hyman's propositions on the basis of Japanese public opinion data. In both societies, working class people are more likely than middle class people to have low aspirations, and values which are dysfunctional with respect to successful mobility striving. For example, in both societies the working class puts less emphasis on getting a college education than does the middle class. Baker is also able to generalize Knupfer's "portrait of the underdog" from the U.S. to Japan.

A major obstacle to the codification of studies done within or between types of societies is that despite the relatively large number of societal typologies which have been constructed,[15] there is at present no generally accepted operational typology of societies, either in sociology or social anthropology. In the examples given, Baker's data are said to generalize Hyman's and Knupfer's because Japan is less industrialized than the U.S. as well as culturally different. Our attempts to distinguish between replication and generalization would be greatly facilitated were there general agreement on which societies are of the same type and which of different types.

Whatever the eventual solution of the problem of societal typology, the important point at present is that societies do differ, more or less systematically, on a number of dimensions. Therefore, studies which show that the same propositions can account for the observed relationships among variables in societies otherwise markedly different have made a distinct contribution to sociological theory: they have demonstrated that the range of application of given propositions and theories is not limited to societies which are generally similar to one another, but can be successfully extended to other societies, generally dissimilar, as well.

4. Comparative analysis specifies and otherwise refines apparently discreptant findings from different societies by developing new propositions which account for the originally discrepant findings. Up to now, we have dealt only with findings which "held up" in a number of (similar or different) societies. When, however, relationships observed in one society (or a small number of societies) are found not to take the same form in other societies, comparative analysis faces what is perhaps its greatest challenge—and therefore a situation which offers the greatest potentiality for making a contribution to theory. Unfortunately, all too few comparative studies follow through, from the finding that the original proposition is not supported in the new societies tested, to the crucial next step: accounting for the differences in terms of meaningful concommitant variations among the societies being compared. When this latter step *is* taken and successfully completed, we have what can be called *specification.*

[13] Herbert H. Hyman, "The Value Systems of Different Classes," in Reinhard Bendix and Seymour M. Lipset, *Class, Status and Power* (Glencoe, Illinois: The Free Press, 1953), pp. 426-442.
[14] Wendell D. Baker, *A Study of Selected Aspects of Japanese Social Stratification: Class Differences in Values and Levels of Aspiration,* unpublished Ph.D. dissertation, Columbia University, 1956.
[15] Such as those of Marx, Spencer, Durkheim, Toennies, Redfield, Becker, Parsons, etc.

As a first example of specification consider studies of the relationship between business cycles and suicide. Several studies in the U.S.[16] show a negative correlation between business cycles and male suicide rates. But Wood[17] found that in Ceylon the suicide rate for males between 1928 and 1954 has a correlation of +.20 with the business cycle. Faced with a discrepant set of findings, Wood was able to reformulate the original hypothesis by *specifying* an intervening or contextual variable: *the relative importance of economic vs. non-economic aspects of status in relation to the maintenance of self-esteem.* For Ceylonese, non-economic aspects of status, such as failure of marriage expectations or failure in the examination system, are more important than economic failure. The new, specified hypothesis would now be: to the extent that economic aspects of status and self-esteem are more important than non-economic aspects, there will be a negative relationship between the male suicide rate and business cycles. When noneconomic aspects are more important, there will be no relationship or a positive relationship, between suicide and business cycles.

A second example of specification appears in comparative studies of extended versus independent family systems. In traditional "Chicago" sociological analyses the relation between societal development and family organization was held to be an essentially linear one: traditional agricultural societies were characterized as having one or another type of extended family; the extended family then "declined" and gave way to the simpler nuclear independent family type.[18] Anthropologists such as Forde,[19] on the other hand, have for some time been arguing that, in effect, the overall relationship between societal development and family organization is a *curvilinear* rather than a linear one. Comparative ethnographic data show that clan organization, indicative of highly developed unilinear kinship systems, tends to be absent from the least developed, simplest societies, as well as from the most developed societies. Forde states this curvilinear relationship in the following way:

(1) Limiting conditions of habitat and techniques for essential production make for low stability, low density and high mobility of population, and a community made up of only an unformalized aggregate of nuclear families. Systems of this type—e.g., Andamanese, Eskimo, the Basin Shoshoneans, and other aborigines of the Great Basin of Western North America—have solidary nuclear families, but lack stable, formalized unilinear kin groups. (2) When the above environmental and technological conditions are less limiting, we find corporate unilineal kin groups, e.g., segmentary lineages, with inherited rights and possessions. (3) Still more favorable conditions of environment and ecology make possible the development of wider unilineal organizations, e.g., clans including several lineages. Here, the greater scale and degree of autonomy of the territorial

[16] William F. Ogburn and Dorothy S. Thomas, "The Influence of the Business Cycle on Certain Social Conditions," *Journal of the American Statistical Association*, 18 (1922), pp. 305-350; Dorothy S. Thomas, *Social Aspects of the Business Cycle* (New York: E. P. Dutton & Co., 1925).

[17] Arthur L. Wood, *Crime and Aggression in Changing Ceylon, A Sociological Analysis of Homocide, Suicide and Economic Crime* (Philadelphia: The American Philosophical Society, 1961).

[18] See for example, Ernest W. Burgess and Harvey J. Locke, *The Family: From Institution to Companionship* (2 ed; New York: American Book Company, 1953), chap 1 and *passim.*

[19] C. Daryll Forde, "The Anthropological Approach in Social Science," *The Advancement of Science*, 4 (1947), pp. 213-224.

groups or local communities, the more extensive the clanship. (4) But the scale and degree of autonomy begins to decrease as political centralization increases, and the latter, along with the development of economic specialization begin to inhibit the continued proliferation of widely extended unilineal kin groups. Political centralization organizes status and power vertically; status comes to depend on economic specialization, rather than on membership in kin groups; solidarity with remote kin declines.

By presenting this overall relationship as *curvilinear* rather than linear, as in the traditional "Chicago" or Burgess and Ogburn theory, a host of significant new theoretic problems emerges, two of which may be mentioned here: (1) What in fact are the structural and functional similarities and differences between the "independent" family system in hunting and gathering societies as compared with industrial societies? Is the "democratic, equalitarian, companionship family" of Burgess found in any sense in hunting and gathering societies? (2) Spatial mobility is ascribed a large role in American sociologists' "explanation" of the nuclear-neolocal middle class U.S. family. But Nimkoff and Middleton point out that, as far as hunting and gathering, animal husbandry and agricultural societies are concerned,

> ... mobility patterns do not constitute an independent variable; rather they tend to be an integral part of the general pattern of subsistence. There are relatively few agricultural societies which are nomadic or semi-nomadic, and few societies in which animal husbandry or hunting and gathering are dominant that are sedentary. Thus, when general subsistence patterns are partialled out in the analysis, there is no significant relationship between mobility and family type.[20]

In the field of racial-cultural-ethnic relations, Park's "race relations cycle"[21] has occupied a prominent position. Park posited a unidirectional sequence of contact, competition-conflict, accommodation and eventual assimilation in the contact between different groups. One particular proposition was: "What are popularly referred to as race relations ordinarily involve some sort of conflict."[22] Lieberson has attempted to specify Park's proposition: "In societies where the indigenous population at their initial contact is subordinate, warfare and nationalism often—though not always—develop later in the cycle of relations. By contrast, relations between migrants and indigenous populations that are subordinate and superordinate, respectively, are generally without long-term conflict."[23] In other words, the situations to which Park was generalizing turn out, following more comparative analysis, to be only one type of race relations situation, namely, those where the migrants are superordinate with respect to the "natives." In this situation—such as the white invasion of the

[20]Meyer F. Nimkoff and Russell Middleton, "Types of Family and Types of Economy," *American Journal of Sociology*, 67 (November 1960), pp. 215-225.
[21]Robert E. Park, "Our Racial Frontier in the Pacific," *Survey Graphic*, 9 (May 1926), pp. 192-196.
[22]Robert E. Park, *Race and Culture* (Glencoe, Illinois: The Free Press, 1950), p. 194.
[23]Stanley Lieberson, "A Societal Theory of Race and Ethnic Relations," *American Sociological Review*, 26 (December 1961), pp. 902-910 at 908.

New World, of Australia and New Zealand, etc.,–early warfare and violent, sometimes revolutionary "nationalism" on the part of the subordinate native population are the results. On the other hand, there was much less warfare, nationalism or long-term conflict in a second type of situation, found in the migration of Orientals and groups from southern and western Europe to the United States. In the latter situation, migrant groups more or less freely seek assimilation to the superordinate culture, instead of resisting it; disadvantaged though their lot may be at first with respect to the superordinate population, the migrant group is likely to define its position as better off than in the Old World. These facts help account for the different histories of race relations in the two types of situations. The specified proposition now reads: The presence or absence of prolonged and extreme conflict and resistance in a "race relation cycle" is a function of the relative position of the migrant and native groups during the history of contact.

Elkins[24] has utilized a comparative socialization framework in the explanation of the "Sambo" personality syndrome of the American plantation Negro slave. The key element in the syndrome was *childlike dependence or infantilism.* Explanations of this personality syndrome in terms of either racial inheritance or African "cultural survivals" in the New World are, of course, defective for the reason that West African natives in Africa do not exhibit any "Sambo" syndrome. The effect of Myrdal's work was to virtually explain away the "Sambo" syndrome by conceiving of it as "only" a sterotype. But Elkins, an historian, takes the evidence on the "Sambo" personality seriously. Two bodies of comparative data—Latin American slavery and Nazi concentration camps— support Elkins' thesis that it is a specific type of social system which predictably gives rise to the "Sambo" pattern. In contrast to the looseness and openness of the legal and social structure of Latin American slavery, both the American plantation and the Nazi concentration camp institutionalized absolute power within a closed system. And, correlatively, a high incidence of infantilism was observed in both the latter systems, but not in the Latin American case. There were similarities in the American slave experience and the Nazi prisoner experience: (1) the shock of capture; (2) the shock of being herded and transported to a new destination—the Middle Passage to the New World, and the shipment in cattle cars to the concentration camp; (3) the severing of all past connections and the total dependence upon new masters; (4) loss of individuality; (5) development of the view that the only "real" life was that *within* the plantation, or the camp, since there was no forseeable termination of the slave or prisoner status; (6) finally, the development of a high degree of identification with the masters, i.e., the slaveowner or SS guard.

In both the American plantation and the Nazi concentration camp, then, the highly limited range of choice open to the "inmates" elicited childlike conformity and dependence as adaptations. The sheer closedness of the systems is more significant than the cruelty per se, in accounting for the development of the "Sambo" role in both situations. Where the system was more "open," as in Latin America. ". . . one finds no social tradition in which slaves were defined by virtually complete concensus, as children incapable of being trusted with the full

---

[24] Stanley Elkins, "Slavery and Personality," in Bert Kaplan (ed). *Studying Personality Cross-Culturally* (Evanston, Illinois: Row, Peterson & Co., 1961), pp. 243-267.

privileges of freedom and adulthood." The Negro in Latin America ". . . could take initiative, . . . could give as well as receive protection. . . ."[25] His situation provided more latitude; the lines of authority over him, instead of all converging on one man, were somewhat dispersed among: the priest, the confessor, the local magistrate, with his eye on the king's official protector of slaves, the king's informer. And the slave in Latin America could more often look forward to becoming an artisan, peddler, petty merchant, truck gardener, independent farmer, priest, military officer, even a *rebel*. The plantation's childlike dependence is further illustrated by the fact that slave revolts were *more* serious in South than in North America, and that even those which did occur in North America tended to be planned not by plantation laborers but by Negroes who had more or less escaped the closed plantation system.

Thus, Elkins' general proposition—the more diverse the symbols of authority are, and the greater the range of permissible adjustment to them, the wider the margin of individuality and the less the infantile dependence—helps to account for personality variations in three structures, the Nazi concentration camp, the North American plantation, and Latin American slavery.

The sociology of law has also profited from comparative research. As long as sociologists limit their attention to the role of law in only the modern West or in primitive societies, many elements are taken for granted, treated as givens. Rabinowitz's[26] comparison of American and Japanese societies suggest new, specified hypotheses for the study of the sociology of law. Rabinowitz's study can be seen as a test of the hypothesis that the role of lawyers and the structure of the legal profession vary with the degree of industrialization and social differentiation. He shows that the lawyer role is much less professionalized and less integrated into the total society in Japan than in the U.S. The following can be posited as preconditions for a high development of professionalism and integration in the lawyer role: (1) The lawyer role has continuity with the old social order. This is less true in Japan than in the U.S. Early Meiji roles such as that of *bengokan, deigennin* and *kujishi* were nothing like the role of the modern lawyer. (2) Lawyers participated significantly in the major formative events of the nation. The Japanese "lawyer" did not so participate in the formative events of the Meiji modernization, because his role was not understood and his status was low. This is in contrast to the important role American lawyers played in the American Revolution. (3) The lawyer's role is limited to advocacy, and advocacy is a role fulfilled exclusively by lawyers. Japanese lawyers typically had inadequate education, both academically and practically, prior to practicing law. Law faculties in universities train men for government and business bureaucracies, not for the legal profession as such. (The recent Judicial Research and Training Institute is an exception). (4) Professional associations should be strong. Again, less true in Japan than in the West.

On each of these variables, Japan is "below" the U.S., and we should predict, therefore, that the legal profession in Japan would accordingly be less professionalized and less integrated into the society than the American legal system. The prediction, as we have seen, holds.

[25] *Ibid.,* p. 262.
[26] R. W. Rabinowitz, *The Japanese Lawyer: A Study in the Sociology of the Legal Profession*, unpublished Ph.D. dissertation. Harvard University, 1955.

A second difference between Japan and the U.S. noted by Rabinowitz, is that the density of lawyers and the volume of litigation per capita are less in Japan than in the U.S. Even in Tokyo, which has the greatest density of lawyers, there are only 53 lawyers per 100,000 population. In contrast, South Carolina, the state with the lowest density of lawyers, has 66/100,000, and for the U.S. as a whole the figure is 118 lawyers in private practice per 100,000 population. American lawyers are 20 times more numerous per capita than are Japanese lawyers (118 vs. 5.4/100,000). Even if judges, notaries, procurators, and judicial scriveners are added to the Japanese total, the figure is only 24/100,000 (as of 1950).

The specified propositions would read: the volume of litigation is a function of: (1) Mode of dispute resolution. There has long been pressure in Japan to seek dispute resolution through means of social control other than law and the courts. Tokugawa society elaborated many elements of *group* responsibility which devolved upon families (the "House"), quasi-families and fictitious families rather than upon the legal individual; these groups functioned to prevent deviance and thereby to prevent litigation. In *mura hachibu,* the offending family would be ritually excluded from the rural community, as a means of dispute-resolution. Even courts and officials often preferred the litigants themselves to work out solutions, so that courts need not involve themselves in intricate personal complexities. (2) Degree of emphasis on compromise. When litigation did occur in Japan, there was great emphasis on compromise, conciliation and dispute resolution by heads of the houses, by powerful families of the community, by *oyabun* for their *kobun,* and the like. (3) Degree of simplicity of divorce, marriage and adoption. Divorce, marriage and adoption were simple in Japan; divorce required litigation only when there was no mutual consent.

These specified propositions based upon Rabinowitz's research are, of course, ex post facto explanations of the particular cases of American and Japanese legal development. As such, they need to be tested in other societies.

Another case of specification may be drawn from the field of demography-ecology. Students of the early "Chicago" school of urban research, implicitly at least, tended to discuss "the City" in isolation from the question of the degree of industrialization.[27] Their concerns were with cities in relatively highly industrialized societies; more recent, comparative research has begun to focus on cities in less industrialized societies. Wilkinson's[28] cross-national study begins by noting that previous studies (based almost exclusively on U.S. and Western European data) have established the existence of a high positive association between urbanization, as measured by the proportion of total population in administratively defined cities, and industrialization, or economic development. With data from forty-nine nations on the proportion of urban population living in metropolitan areas, drawn from International Urban Research, University of California, Berkeley, Wilkinson then proceeds to show that there is close association (+.776) between metropolitanization (ratio of metropolitan popula-

[27]Louis Worth, "Urbanism as a Way of Life," *American Journal of Sociology*, 44 (July 1938), pp. 1-24.
[28]Thomas O. Wilkinson, "Urban Structure and Industrialization," *American Sociological Review*, 25 (June 1960), pp. 356-363.

tion to total urban population) and industrialization, but not so close as the relationship between urbanization and industrialization. Comparative analysis enables Wilkinson to specify earlier theory: the association of metropolitaniza- tion and economic development becomes closer as the extent of urbanization increases. "This is to say that as the proportion of population in administratively defined cities increases, the concentration of urban population in metropolitan areas reflects more clearly the level of industrial development."[29] Thus, the development of metropolitan population concentrations is *not* invariably linked to a high degree of urbanization and industrialization. Metropolitanization may "run ahead" of the other two processes. In particular, three distinct patterns emerge on a regional basis:

	Western Europe and Anglo-America	Latin America	Asia-Africa
Industrialization	High	Moderate/ Low	Moderate/ Low
Urbanization	High	High	Low
Metropolitanization	High	Low	High

Wilkinson's contribution to theory centers on his explanation of why metropolitanization is not as closely correlated with industrialization as is urbanization. His explanation is that metropolitan growth is heavily influenced by the *structure* of the industrialization process, not by industrialization as such alone. Japan provides a test case of the proposition: Japanese urban growth has meant an increase of populations in central cities (metropolitanization), rather than the suburbanization or fringe growth experienced by the Western nations. This is explained by the distinct character of Japanese industrialization.

One final instance of specification may be drawn from the writer's own work in comparative social mobility.[30] It would seem to be a fact that industrial societies have a higher rate of social mobility than pre-industrial societies. What accounts for this fact? One explanation which has been offered is that industrial societies institutionalize universalistic-achievement values within mobility channels to a greater extent than do pre-industrial societies. Another explanation, following Rogoff's work for the U.S., is that industrial societies have a greater occupational demand at the middle and elite levels, which in turn necessitates more upward mobility than in pre-industrial societies. One way of testing these competing explanations is to hold constant occupational demand as between more and less industrialized societies, and see if industrial societies still exhibit more mobility. If values and norms are the key, this should be the case, even after demand differences have been controlled. Comparative data from a number of societies revealed, however, that this is not the case. The new, specified proposition now states that the greater rate of mobility in industrial societies is due almost wholly to sheer quantitative occupational demand, rather than to values and norms of a universalistic-achievement sort.

[29]*Ibid.*, p. 359.
[30]Robert M. Marsh, "Values, Demand and Social Mobility," *American Sociological Review,* 28 (August 1963), pp. 565-575.

Finally, a few remarks about specification in general are in order. Where replication and generalization demonstrate that societies of similar or different types all exhibit the patterns or relationships stated in the original proposition, specification seeks to reformulate the original proposition in such a way that comparative variations between societies or sub-systems thereof are incorporated into the proposition as control factors or intervening variables. When the critical variation in the social contexts which account for the observed differences between the original findings and subsequent comparative findings have been identified, the original proposition can then be reformulated as a specified universal proposition.

When specified propositions are retested in still other (types of) societies it is to be expected that further specification will result. In the examples we have reviewed, we have seen that when we move from the study of one society to even a few societies, one additional variable is introduced into the specification. Therefore, when we attempt to account for a large number of societies—say 100 or more—we should be prepared to increasingly specify our original proposition, i.e., to incorporate more and more contextual or intervening variables into the proposition. However, it is here assumed: (1) the process of developing increasingly specified propositions constitutes scientific progress; and (2) the number of new, "specifying" variables will *not* continue indefinitely to increase linearly with the addition of more and more societies in the comparison. That is, as more and more societies are added, the specified proposition will need to take into account only a relatively small number of variables in order to account for the observed cross-societal variations. The continued addition of new variables would account for a smaller and smaller proportion of the total variance.

III

Codification has shown four ways[31] in which cross-societal (including both "cross-cultural" and "cross-national") comparative analysis has already contributed to sociological theory. Comparative studies in voting behavior, social stratification and mobility, suicide, family, racial-ethnic relations, socialization and personality, law, and metropolitanization have been reviewed, as a partial demonstration of the fact that the contributions of comparative analysis to sociological theory are not limited to only certain sub-fields.

Any science strives to formulate universal propositions. Once a proposition has been tentatively formulated, the task of research becomes that of replicating it, attempting to state limiting conditions and intervening variables, and analyzing apparently "exceptional" cases. In this process, *cross*-societal comparative analysis is but a necessary extension of *intra*-societal comparative analysis. It is a necessary step, but a step which most sociologists and social anthropologists have heretofore abrogated. By attempting to codify the experience of those who have taken this necessary step, we have meant to encourage others to commit

---

[31] As codification proceeds, other contributions of comparative analysis to theory are being identified. Space limitations prevent further discussion here; a full treatment will be found in Marsh, *Comparative Sociology, op. cit.,* forthcoming.

themselves to comparative analysis. The anthropologist Nadel has argued this case eloquently:

> Even if we are initially concerned only with a single society and with the appearance in it of a particular social fact (which we wish to 'explain'), our search for co-variations capable of illuminating our problem will often lead us beyond that society to others, similar or diverse, since the given society may not offer an adequate range of variations. Also, the regularities which we can extract from narrow-range comparisons are themselves of narrow applicability, they would exhibit specific phenomena present only in a limited number of societies . . . while in the far-flung comparisons we deal with the ubiquitous classes of social facts, which are features of human society writ large.[32]

[32] Siegfried F. Nadel, *The Foundations of Social Anthropology* (Glencoe, Illinois: The Free Press, 1951), p. 227.

5

Sampling

Once you have decided *what* is to be studied, the next relevant problem is *who* should be studied. The solution to this problem will depend on the kinds of statements you want to emerge from the study. If you do not wish to generalize to a wider population, choosing your respondents is not much of a problem. In case study research, for example, you are often interested in describing in depth the functioning of a particular organization, or perhaps a particular friendship group. Here one generally talks to, questions, or observes all the members of these "collectivities" in order to derive a complete picture of what is going on. But in no way are you justified in generalizing this picture to other groups or organizations, no matter how similar they may appear to the one with which you are concerned.

As soon as you wish to go beyond the particular set of individuals you are studying, and argue that they are somehow "typical" of a more inclusive group, you must adhere to certain rules of selecting your set of individuals. A general discussion of these rules and the main notions of sampling appear in the first paper by Cochran, Mosteller, and Tukey. Here some of the samples typically drawn by researchers are discussed, notably simple random samples, cluster samples, and stratified samples.[1] The second paper, by Grebnik and Moser, sets the problem of sampling in a specifically sociological context—that of the statistical survey of individuals. In addition to a discussion of sampling in regard to surveys, the authors present a brief discussion of interviews and questionnaires, thereby introducing our consideration of these data collection tools in chapter 6.

[1] For further reading, see Freda Conway, *Sampling: An Introduction for Social Scientists* (London: George Allen & Unwin Ltd., 1967).

PRINCIPLES OF SAMPLING

William G. Cochran, Frederick Mosteller and John W. Tukey.

I. SAMPLES AND THEIR ANALYSES

1. Introduction

Whether by biologists, sociologists, engineers, or chemists, sampling is all too often taken far too lightly. In the early years of the present century it was not uncommon to measure the claws and carapaces of 1000 crabs, or to count the number of veins in each of 1000 leaves, and then to attach to the results the "probable error" which would have been appropriate had the 1000 crabs or the 1000 leaves been drawn at random from the population of interest. Such actions were unwarranted shotgun marriages between the quantitatively unsophisticated idea of sample as "what you get by grabbing a handful" and the mathematical precise notion of a "simple random sample." In the years between we have learned caution by bitter experience. We insist on some semblance of mechanical (dice, coins, random number tables, etc.) randomization before we treat a sample from an existent population as if it were random. We realize that if someone just "grabs a handful," the individuals in the handful almost always resemble one another (on the average) more than do the members of a simple random sample. Even if the "grabs" are randomly spread around so that every individual has an equal chance of entering the sample, there are difficulties. Since the individuals of grab samples resemble one another *more* than do individuals of random samples, it follows (by a simple mathematical argument) that the means of grab samples resemble one another *less* than the means of random samples of the same size. From a grab sample, therefore, we tend to *under*estimate the variability in the population, although we should have to *over*estimate it in order to obtain valid estimates of variability of grab sample means by substituting such an estimate into the formula for the variability of means of simple random samples. Thus using simple random sample formulas for grab sample means introduces a double bias, both parts of which lead to an unwarranted appearance of higher stability.

Returning to the crabs, we may suppose that the crabs in which we are interested are all the individuals of a wide-ranging species, spread along a few hundred miles of coast. It is obviously impractical to seek to take a simple random sample from the species—no one knows how to give each crab in the species an equal chance of being drawn into the sample (to say nothing of trying to make these chances independent). But this does not bar us from honestly assessing the likely range of fluctuation of the result. Much effort has been applied in recent years, particularly in sampling human populations, to the development of sampling plans which *simultaneously,*

Reprinted with the permission of the authors and the publishers from the *Journal of American Statistical Association*, Vol. 49 (March, 1954), 13-35.

(1) are economically feasible
(2) give reasonably precise results, and
(3) show within themselves an honest measure of fluctuation on their results.

Any excuse for the dangerous practice of treating non-random sample as random ones is now entirely tenuous. Wider knowledge of the principles involved is needed if scientific investigations involving samples (and what such investigation does not?) are to be solidly based. Additional knowledge of techniques is not so vitally important, though it can lead to substantial economic gains.

A botanist who gathered 10 oak leaves from each of 100 oak trees might feel that he had a fine sample of 1000, and that, if 500 were infected with a certain species of parasites, he had shown that the percentage infection was close to 50%. If he had studied the binomial distribution he might calculate a standard error according to the usual formula for random samples, $p \pm \sqrt{pq/n}$, which in this case yields $50 \pm 1.6\%$ (since $p = q = .5$ and $n = 1000$). In this doing he would neglect three things:

(1) Probable selectivity in selecting trees (favoring large trees, perhaps?),
(2) Probable selectivity in choosing leaves from a selected tree (favoring well-colored or, alternatively, visibly infected leaves perhaps), and
(3) the necessary allowance, in the formula used to compute the standard error, for the fact that he has not selected his leaves individually at random, as the mathematical model for a simple random sample prescribes.

Most scientists are keenly aware of the analogs of (i) and (ii) in their own fields of work, at least as soon as they are pointed out to them. Far fewer seem to realize that, even if the trees were selected at random from the forest and the leaves were chosen at random from each selected tree, (iii) must still be considered. But if, as might indeed be the case, each tree were either wholly infected or wholly free of infection, then the 1000 leaves tell us *no more* than 100 leaves, one from each tree. (Each group of 10 leaves will be all infected or all free of infection.) In this case we should take $n = 100$ and find an infection rate of $50 \pm 5\%$.

Such an extreme case of increased fluctuation due to sampling in clusters would be detected by almost all scientists, and is not a serious danger. But less extreme cases easily escape detection and may therefore be very dangerous. This is one example of the reasons why the principles of sampling need wider understanding.

We have just described an example of *cluster sampling,* where the individuals or sampling units are not drawn into the sample independently, but are drawn in clusters, and have tried to make it clear that "individually at random" formulas do not apply. It was not our intention to oppose, by this example, the use of cluster sampling, which is often desirable, but only to speak for proper analysis of its results.

2. Self-Weighting probability samples

There are many ways to draw samples such that each individual or sampling unit in the population has an equal chance of appearing in the sample. Given such a sample, and desiring to estimate the population average of some characteristic, the appropriate procedure is to calculate the (unweighted) mean of all the individual values of that characteristic in the sample. Because weights are equal and require no obvious action, such a sample is *self-weighting*. Because the relative chances of *different* individuals entering the sample are known and compensated for (are, in this case, equal), it is a *probability sample*. (In fact, it would be enough if we knew somewhat less, as is explained in Section 5.)

Such a sample need not be a simple random sample, such as one would obtain by numbering all the individuals in the population, and then using a table of random numbers to select the sample on the basis: one random number, one individual. We illustrate this by giving various examples, some practical and others impractical.

Consider the sample of oak leaves; it might in principle be drawn in the following way. First we list all trees in the forest of interest, recording for each tree its location and the number of leaves it bears. Then we draw a sample of 100 trees, arranging that the probability of a tree's being selected is proportional to the number of leaves which it bears. Then on each selected tree we choose 10 leaves at random. It is easy to verify that each leaf in the forest has an equal chance of being selected. (This is a kind of two-stage sampling with probability proportional to size at the first stage.)

We must emphasize that such terms as "select at random," "choose at random," and the like, always mean that some mechanical device such as coins, cards, dice, or tables of random numbers, is used.

A more practical way to sample the oak leaves might be to list only the locations of the trees (in some parts of the country this could be done from a single aerial photograph), and then to draw 100 trees in such a way that each tree has an equal chance of being selected. The number of leaves on each tree is now counted and the sample of 1000 is prorated over the 100 trees in proportion to their numbers of leaves. It is again easy to verify that each leaf has an equal chance of appearing in the sample. (This is a kind of two-stage sampling with probability proportional to size at the second stage.)

If the forest is large, and each tree has many leaves, either of these procedures would probably be impractical. A more practical method might involve a four-stage process in which:

(a) the forest is divided into small tracts,
(b) each tract is divided into trees,
(c) each tree is divided into recognizable parts, perhaps limbs, and
(d) each part is divided into leaves.

In drawing a sample, we would begin by drawing a number of tracts, then a number of trees in each tract, then a part or number of parts from each tree, then a number of leaves from each part. This can be done in many ways so that each leaf has an equal chance of appearing in the sample.

A different sort of self-weighting probability sample arises when we draw a sample of names from the Manhattan telephone directory, taking, say, every 17,387th name in alphabetic order starting with one of the first 17,387 names selected at random with equal probability. It is again easy to verify that every name in the book has an equal chance of appearing in the sample (this is a systematic sample with a random start, sometimes referred to as a systematic random sample).

As a final example of this sort, we may consider a national sample of 480 people divided among the 48 states. We cannot divide the 480 cases among the individual states in proportion to population very well, since Nevada would then receive about one-half of a case. If we group the small states into blocks, however, we can arrange for each state or block of states to be large enough so that on a pro rata basis it will have at least 10 cases. Then we can draw samples within each state or block of states in various ways. It is easy to verify that the chances of any two persons entering such a sample (assuming adequate randomness within each state or block of states) are approximately the same, where the approximation arises solely because a whole number of cases has to be assigned to each state or block of states. (This is a rudimentary sort of stratified sample.)

All of these examples were (at least approximately) self-weighting probability samples, and all yield honest estimates of population characteristics. *Each one* requires a *different* formula for assessing the stability of its results! Even if the population characteristic studied is a fraction, almost never will

$$p \pm \sqrt{\frac{pq}{n}}$$

be a proper expression for "estimate ± standard error." In every case, a proper formula will require more information from the sample than merely the overall percentage. (Thus, for instance, in the first oak leaf example, the variability from tree to tree of the number infested out of 10 would be needed.)

3. Representativeness

Another principle which ought not to need recalling is this: By sampling we can learn only about collective properties of populations, not about properties of individuals. We can study the average height, the percentage who wear hats, or the variability in weight of college juniors, or of University of Indiana juniors, or of the juniors belonging to a certain fraternity or club at a certain institution. The population we study may be small or large, but there must be a population—and what we are studying must be a population characteristic. By sampling, we cannot study individuals as particular entities with unique idiosyncrasies; we can study regularities (including typical variabilities as well as typical levels) in a population as exemplified by the individuals in the sample.

Let us return to the self-weighted national sample of 480. Notice that about half of the times that such a sample is drawn, there will be no one in it from Nevada, while almost never will there be anyone from Esmeralda County in that state. Local pride might argue that "this proves that the sample was unrepresentative," but the correct position seems to be this:

(1) The particular persons in the sample are there by accident, and this is appropriate, so far as population characteristics are concerned,
(2) the sampling plan is representative since each person in the U.S. had *an equal chance* of entering the sample, whether he came from Esmeralda County or Manhattan.

That which can be and should be representative in the *sampling plan,* which includes the manner in which the sample was drawn (essentially a specification of what other samples might have been drawn and what the relative chances of selection were for any two possible samples) *and* how it is to be analyzed.

However great their local pride, the citizens of Esmeralda County, Nevada, are entitled to representation in a national sampling plan only as individual members of the U.S. population. They are *not* entitled to representation as a group, or as particular individuals—only as individual *members* of the U.S. population. The same is true of the citizens of Nevada, who are represented in only half of the actual samples. The citizens of Nevada, as a group, are no more and no less entitled to representation than *any* other group of equal size in the U.S. whether geographical, racial, marital, criminal, selected at random, or selected from those not in a particular national sample.

It is clear that many such groups fail to be represented in any particular sample, yet this is not a criticism of that sample. Representation is not, and should not be, by groups. It is, and should be, by individuals as *members* of the sampled population. Representation is not, and should not be, in any particular sample. It is, and should be, in the sampling *plan.*

4. One method of assessing stability

Because representativeness is inherent in the sampling plan and not in the particular sample at hand, we can never make adequate use of sample results without some measure of how well the results of this particular sample are likely to agree with the results of other samples which the same sampling plan might have provided. The ability to assess stability fairly is as important as the ability to represent the population fairly. Modern sampling plans concentrate on both.

Such assessment must basically be in terms of sample results, since these are usually our most reliable source of information about the population. There is no reason, however, why assessment should depend only on the sample size and the overall (weighted) sample mean for the characteristic considered. These two suffice when measuring percentages with a simple random sample, but in almost all other cases the situation is more complex.

It would be too bad if, every time such samples were used, the user had to consult a complicated table of alternative formulas, one for each plan, before calculating his standard errors. (These formulas do need to be considered whenever we are trying to do a really good job of maximum stability for minimum cost—considered very carefully in selecting one complex design in preference to another.) Fortunately, however, this complication can often be circumvented.

One of the simplest ways is to build up the sample from a number of independent subsamples, each of which is self-sufficient, though small, and to tabulate the results of interest separately for each subsample. Then variation among separate results gives a simple and honest yardstick for the variability of the result or results obtained by throwing all the samples together. Such a sampling plan involves *interpenetrating replicate subsamples.*

All of us can visualize interpenetrating replicate subsamples when the individuals or sampling units are drawn individually at random. Some examples in more complex cases may be helpful. In the first oak leaf example, we might select randomly, not one sample of 100 trees, but 10 subsamples of 10 trees each. If we then pick 10 leaves at random from each tree, placing them in 10 bags, one for each subsample, and tabulate the results separately, bag by bag, we will have 10 interpenetrating replicate subsamples. Similarly, if we were to pick 10 subsamples out of the Manhattan phone book, with each subsample consisting of every 173,870th name (in alphabetical order) and with the 10 lead names of the 10 subsamples selected at random from the first 173,870 names we would again have 10 interpenetrating replicate subsamples.

We can always analyze 10 results from 10 independent interpenetrating replicate subsamples just as if they were 10 random selected individual measurements and proceed similarly with other numbers of replicate subsamples.

5. General Probability Samples

The types of sample described in the last section are not the only kinds from which we can confidently make inferences from the sample to the population of interest. Besides the trivial cases where the sample amounts to 90% or even 95% of the population, there is a broad class of cases, including those of the last section as special cases. This is the class of *probability samples,* where:

(1) There is a population, the *sampled population,* from which the sample is drawn, and each element of which has some chance of entering the sample.
(2) For each pair of individuals or sampling units which are in the actual sample, the relative chances of their entering the sample are known. (This implies that the sample was selected by a process involving one or more steps of mechanical randomization.)
(3) In the analysis of the actual sample, these relative chances have been compensated for by using relative weights such that (relative chance) *times* (relative weight) equals a constant.
(4) For any two possible samples, the sum of the reciprocals of the relative weights of all the individuals in the sample is the same.

(Conditions (3) and (4) can be generalized still further.) In practice of course, we ask only that these four conditions shall hold with a sufficiently high degree of approximation.

We have made the sampling plan representative, not by giving each individual an equal chance to enter the sample and then weighting them equally, but by a more noticeable process of compensation, where those individuals very likely to enter the sample are weighted less, while those unlikely to enter are weighted more when they do appear. The net result is to give each individual an equal chance of affecting the (weighted) sample mean.

Such general probability samples are just as honest and legitimate as the self-weighting probability samples. They often offer substantial advantages in terms of higher stability for lower cost.

We can alter our previous examples, so as to make them examples of general, and not of self-weighting, probability samples. Take first the oak leaf example. We might proceed as follows:

(1) locate all the trees in the forest of interest,

(2) select a sample of trees at random,

(3) for each sampled tree, choose 10 leaves at random and count (or estimate) the total number of leaves,

(4) form the weighted mean by summing the products (fraction of 10 leaves infested) *times* (number of leaves on the tree) and then divide by the total number of leaves on the 100 trees in the sample.

When we selected trees at random, each tree had an equal probability of selection. When we chose 10 leaves from a tree at random, the chance of getting a particular leaf was

$$\frac{10}{\text{(number of leaves on the tree)}} \, .$$

Thus the chance of selecting any one leaf was a constant multiple of this and was proportional to the *reciprocal* of the number of leaves of the tree. Hence the correct relative weight is proportional to the number of leaves on the tree, and it is simplest to take it as $1/10$ of that number. After all, summing the products

(fraction of 10 infected) *times* (leaves on tree)

or

$(1/10)$ *times* (number out of 10 infected) *times* (leaves on tree)

over all trees in the sample gives the same answer. One-tenth of this answer is given by summing

$(1/10)$ *times* (number out of 1 infected) *times* (leaves on tree)

or

$$\text{(number out of 1 infected)} \, \frac{\text{(leaves on tree)}}{10}$$

which shows that the weighted mean prescribed above is just what would have been obtained with relative weights of (number of leaves on tree)/10.

If in sampling the names in the Manhattan telephone directory, we desired to sample initial letters from P through Z more heavily, we might proceed as follows:

(1) Select one of the first 17,387 names at random with equal probability as the lead name.

(2) Take the lead name, and every 17,387th name in alphabetic order following it, into the sample.

(3) Take every name which begins with *P, Q, R, S, . . . , Z and* is the 103rd or 207th name after a name selected in step 2 of the sample.

Each name beginning with *A, B, . . . , N, O* has a chance of $1/17,387$ of entering the sample. Each name beginning with *P, Q, . . . , Y, Z* has a chance of $3/17,387$ of entering the sample (it enters if any one of *three* names among the first 17,387 is selected as the lead name). Thus the relative weight in the sample of a name beginning with *A, B, . . . , N, O* is 3 times that of a name beginning with *P, Q, . . . , Y, Z*. The weighted mean is found simply as:

$$\frac{3(\text{sum for } A, B, \cdots, N, O\text{'s}) + (\text{sum for } P, Q, \cdots, Y, Z\text{'s})}{3(A, B, \cdots, N, O\text{'s in sample}) + (P, Q, \cdots, Y, Z\text{'s in sample})}.$$

Finally we may wish to distribute our national sample of 480 with 10 in each state. The analysis exactly parallels the oak leaf case, and we have to form the sum of

(mean for state sample) *times* (population of state)

and then to divide by the population of the U.S.

6. Nature and properties of general probability samples

We can carry over the use of independent interpenetrating replicates to the general case without difficulty. We need only remember that the replicates must be independent. In the oak leaf example, the replicates must come from groups of independently selected trees. In the Manhattan telephone book example, the replicates must be based on independently chosen lead names; in the national sample, the replicates must have members in every state. In every case they must interpenetrate, and do this independently.

It is clear from discussion and examples that general probability samples are inferior to self-weighting probability samples in two ways, for both simplicity of exposition and ease of analysis are decreased! If it were not for compensating advantages, general probability samples would not be used. The main advantages are:

(1) better quality for less cost due to reduction in administrative costs or prelisting cost,
(2) better quality for less cost because of better allocation of effort over strata,
(3) greater possibility of making estimates for individual strata.

All three of these advantages can be illustrated on our examples. In the general oak leaf example, in contrast to the first oak leaf example in Section 2, there is no need to determine the size (number of leaves) of all trees. This is a clear cost reduction, whether in money or time. Suppose that, in the Manhattan telephone book sample, one aim was an opinion study restricted to those of Polish descent. Such persons' names tend to be concentrated in the second part of the alphabet, so that the general sample will bring out more persons of Polish descent and the interviewing effort will be better allocated. In the case of the national sample of 480, the general sample, although probably giving a less stable national result, does permit (rather poor) state-by-state estimates where the self-weighting sample would skip Nevada about half the time.

It is perhaps worth mentioning at this point that, if cost is proportional to the total number of individuals without regard to number of strata or the distribution of interviews among strata, the optimum allocation of interviews is proportional to the product

(size of stratum) *times* (standard deviation within stratum).

In particular, optimum allocation calls for sample strata not in proportion to population strata. If we weight appropriately, disproportionate samples will be better than proportionate ones—if we choose the disproportions wisely.

In specifying the characteristics of a probability sampling at the beginning of this paper, we required that there be a *sampled population,* a population from which the sample comes and each member of which has a chance of entering the sample. We have not said whether or not this is exactly the same population as the population in which we are interested, the *target population.* In practice they are rarely the same, though the difference is frequently small. In human sampling, for example, some persons cannot be found and others refuse to answer. The issues involved in this difference between sampled population and target population are discussed at some length in Part II, and in chapter III-D of Appendix D in our complete report.

7. Stratification and adjustment

In many cases general probability samples can be thought of in terms of

(1) a subdivision of the population into strata,
(2) a self-weighting probability sample in each stratum, and
(3) combination of the stratum sample means weighted by the size of the stratum.

The general Manhattan telephone book sample can be so regarded. There are two strata, one made up of names beginning in $A, B, \ldots, N, O,$ and the other made up of names beginning in $P, Q, \ldots, Y, Z.$ Similarly the general national sample may be thought of as made up of 48 strata, one for each state.

This manner of looking at general probability samples is neat, often helpful, and makes the entire legitimacy of unequal weighting clear in many cases. But it is not general. For in the general oak leaf example, if there were any strata they would be whole trees or parts of trees. And not all trees were sampled. (Still every leaf was fairly represented by its equal chance of affecting the weighted sample mean.) We cannot treat this case as one of simple stratification.

The stratified picture is helpful, but not basic. It must fail as soon as there are more potential strata than sample elements, or as soon as the number of elements entering the sample from a certain stratum is not a constant of the sampling plan. It usually fails sooner. There is no substitute for the relative chances that different individuals or sampling units have of entering the sample. This is the basic thing to consider.

There is another relation of stratification to probability sampling. When sizes of strata are known, there is a possibility of *adjustment.* Consider taking a simple random sample of 100 adults in a tribe where exactly 50% of the adults were known to be males and 50% females. Suppose the sample had 60 males and 40 females. If we followed the pure probability sampling philosophy so far expounded, we should take the equally weighted sample mean as our estimate of the population average. Yet if 59 of the 60 men had herded sheep at some time in their lives, and none of the 40 women, we should be unwise in estimating that 59% of the tribe had herded sheep at some time in their lives. The adjusted mean is a far better indicator of what we have learned.

$$.50 \left(\frac{59}{60} \right) + .50 \left(\frac{0}{40} \right) = 49^{+}\%$$

How can adjustment fail? Under some conditions the variability of the adjusted mean is enough greater than that of the unadjusted mean to offset the decrease in bias. It may be a hard choice between adjustment and nonadjustment.

The last example was extreme, and the unwise choice would be made by few. But, again, less extreme cases exist, and the unwise choice, whether it be to adjust or not to adjust, may be made rather easily (and probably has been made many times). A quantitative rule is needed. One is given in chapter V-C of the complete report. In the preceding example the relative sizes of the strata were known exactly. It turns out that inexact knowledge can be included in the computation without great increase in complexity.

An example in Kinsey's area is cited by one critic of the Kinsey report:

> These weighted estimates do not, of course, reflect any population changes since 1940, which introduces some error into the statistics for the present total population. Moreover, on some of the very factors that Kinsey demonstrates to be correlated with sexual behavior, there are no Census data available. For example, religious membership is shown to be a factor affecting sexual behavior, but Census data are lacking and no weights are assigned. While the investigators interviewed members of various religious groups, there is no assurance that each group is proportionately represented, because of the lack of systematic sampling controls. Thus, the proportion of Jews in Kinsey's sample would seem to be at least 13 per cent whereas their true proportion in the population is of the order of 4 per cent.[1]

Do we know the percentage of Jews well enough to make an adjustment for it? If we can assess the stability of the "4%" figure, the procedure of Chapter V-C will answer this question. Failing this technique, we could translate the question into more direct terms as follows: "In considering Kinsey's results, do we want to have 13 per cent Jews or 4 per cent Jews in the sampled population?" and try to answer with the aid of general knowledge and intuition.

We have discussed the adjustment of a simple random sample. The same considerations apply to the possibility of adjusting any self-weighting or general probability sample. No new complications arise when adjustment is superposed on weighting. The presence of a complication might be suspected in the case where not all segments appear in the sample, and we attempt to use these segments as strata. Careful analysis shows the absence of the complication, as may be illustrated by carrying our example further.

Suppose that the sheep-herding tribe in question contains a known, very small percentage of adults of indeterminate sex, and that none have appeared in our sample. To be sure, their existence affected, albeit slightly, the chances of males and females entering the sample, but it does not affect the thinking which urged us to take the adjusted mean. We still want to adjust, and have only the question "Adjust for what?" to answer.

If the fraction of indeterminate sex is 0.000002, and the remainder are half

[1]Hyman, H. H. and Sheatsley, P. B. "The Kinsey report and survey methodology," *International Journal of Opinion and Attitude Research*, Vol. 2 (1948), 184-85.

males and half females, and if our anthropological expert feels that about 1 in 7 of the indeterminate ones has herded sheep, we have a choice between

$$.499999 \left(\frac{59}{60}\right) \ + \ .499999 \left(\frac{0}{40}\right) \ + \ .000002 \left(\frac{1}{7}\right)$$

which represents adjustment for three strata, one measured subjectively, and

$$.500000 \left(\frac{59}{60}\right) \ + \ .500000 \left(\frac{0}{40}\right)$$

which represents adjustment for the two observed strata.

Clearly, in this extreme example, the choice is immaterial. Clearly, also, the estimated accuracy of the anthropologist's judgment must enter. We can again use the methods of Chapter V-C.

8. Upper semiprobability sampling

Let us be a little more realistic about our botanist and his sample of oak leaves. He might have an aerial photograph, and be willing to select 100 trees at random. But any ladder he takes into the field is likely to be short, and he may not be willing to trust himself in the very top of the tree with lineman's climbing irons. So the sample of 10 leaves that he chooses from each selected tree will not be chosen at random. The lower leaves on the tree are more likely to be chosen than the highest ones.

In the two-stage process of sampling, the first stage has been a probability sample, but the second has not (and may even be entirely un-planned!). These are the characteristic features of an *upper semiprobability sample.* As a consequence, the sampled population agrees with the target population in certain large-scale characteristics, but not in small-scale ones and, usually, not in other large-scale characteristics.

Thus, if in the oak leaf example we use the weights appropriate to different sizes of tree, as we should, the sampled population of leaves will:

(1) have the correct relative number of leaves for each tree, but
(2) will have far too many lower leaves and far too few upper leaves.

The large-scale characteristic of being on a particular tree is a matter of agreement between sampled and target populations. The large-scale characteristic of height in the tree (and many small-scale characteristics that the reader can easily set up for himself), is a matter of serious disagreement between sampled and target populations.

The sampled population differs from the target population within each segment, here a tree, although sampled population segments and target population segments are in exact proportion.

If infestation varies between the bottoms and the tops of the trees this type of sampling will be biased, and, while the inferences from sample to sampled population will be correct, they may be useless or misleading because of the great difference between sampled population and target population.

Such dangers always exist with any kind of nonprobability sampling. Upper semiprobability sampling is no exception. By selecting the trees at random we have stultified biases due to probable selectivity between trees, and this is good. But we have done nothing about almost certain selectivity between leaves on a particular tree—this may be all right, or very bad. It would be nice to always have probability samples, and avoid these difficulties. But this may be impractical. (The conditions under which a nonprobability sample may reasonably be taken are discussed in Part II.)

There is one point which needs to be stressed. The change from probability sampling within segments (in the example, within trees) to some other type of sampling, perhaps even unplanned sampling, shifts a large and sometimes difficult part of the inference from sample to target population—shifts it by moving the sampled population away from the target population toward the sample—shifts it from the shoulders of the statistician to the shoulders of the subject matter "expert." Those who use upper semiprobability samples, or other nonprobability samples, take a heavier load on themselves thereby.

Upper semiprobability samples may be either self-weighting or general. The "quota samples" of the opinion pollers, where interviewers are supposed to meet certain quotas by age, sex, and socioeconomic status, are rather crude forms of upper semiprobability samples, and are often self-weighting. Bias within segments arises, some contribution being due, for example, to the different availability of different 42 year old women of the middle class. The sampled population may contain sexes, ages, and socioeconomic classes in the right ratios, but retiring persons are under-represented (and hermits are almost entirely absent) in comparison with the target population.

Election samples of opinion, although following the same quota pattern, will ordinarily only be self-weighting within states (if we ignore the "who will vote" problem). Predictions are desired for individual states. If Nevada had a mere 100 cases in a self-weighting sample, the total size of a national sample would have to be about 100,000. When national percentages are to be compiled, it would be foolish not to weight each state mean in accordance with the size of the state. No one would favor, we believe, weighting each state equally just because there may be (and probably are) biases within each state.

Disproportionate samples and unequal weights are just as natural and wise a part of upper semiprobability sampling as they are of probability sampling. The difficulties of upper semiprobability sampling do not lie here; instead they lie in the secret and insidious biases due to selectivity within segments.

Our sampling of names from the Manhattan telephone directory might conceivably be drawn by listing the numbers called by subscribers on a certain exchange during a certain time, and then taking into the sample names from each exchange in proportion to the names listed for the exchange. The result would be an upper semiprobability sample with substantial selectivity within the segments, which here are exchanges. The nature of this selectivity would depend on the time of day at which the listing was made.

Whether all segments are represented in an upper semiprobability sample or not, the segments may be used as strata for adjustment. The situation is exactly similar to that for probability sampling. The only difficulty worthy of note is the difficulty of assessing the stability of the various segment means.

Independent interpenetrating replicate subsamples can be used to estimate stabilities of over-all or segment means in upper semiprobability samples without difficulty, if we can obtain a reasonable facsimile of independence in taking the different subsamples. They provide, if really independent, respectable bases for inference from sample to sampled population. We still have a nonprobability sample, however, and there is no reason for the sampled population to agree with the target population. The problem is just reduced to "What was the sampled population?"

What finally is the situation with regard to bias in an upper semiprobability sample? We shall have a weighted mean or an adjusted one. In either case, any bias originally contributed by selectivity between segments will have been substantially removed. *But,* in either case, the contribution to bias due to selectivity within segments will *remain unchanged*. This is an unknown and hence additionally dangerous, sort of bias.

The great danger in weighting or adjusting such samples is not so much that that weighting or adjusting may make the results worse (as it will from time to time) but rather that its use may cause the user to feel that his values are excellent because they are "weighted" or "adjusted" and hence to neglect possible or likely biases within segments. Like all other nonprobability sample results, weighted means from upper semiprobability samples should be *presented and interpreted with caution.*

9. Salvage of unplanned samples

What can we do for such samples? We can either try to improve the results of their analysis, or try to inquire how good they are anyway. We may try to improve either actual quality, or our belief in that quality. The first has to be by way of manner of weighting or adjustment, the second must involve checking sample characteristics against population characteristics.

Weighting is impossible, since we cannot construct a sampling plan and hence cannot estimate chances of entering the sample in any other manner than by observing the sample itself. So all that we can do under this head is to adjust. We recall the salient points about adjustment, which are the same in a complete salvage operation as they are in any other situation:

(1) The population is divided into segments.
(2) Each individual in the sample can be uniquely assigned to a segment.
(3) The population fraction is either known with inappreciable error or estimated with known stability.
(4) The procedures of Chapter V-C of Appendix C of the complete report are applied to determine whether, or how much, to adjust.

After adjustment, what is the situation as to bias? Even worse than with upper semiprobability sampling, because if we do not adjust, we cannot escape bias by turning to weighting. In summary

(1) whether adjusted or not, the result contains all the effects of all the selectivity exercised *within* segments, while
(2) if adjustment is refused by the methods of Chapter V-C, we face additional

biases resulting from selectivity *between* segments of a magnitude comparable with the difference between unadjusted and adjusted mean.

This is, to put it mildly, not a good situation.

Clearly even more caution is needed in presenting and interpreting the results of a salvage operation on an unplanned sample than for any of the other types of sample discussed previously. (If it were not for the psychological danger that adjustment might be regarded as cure, the caution required for results based on the original, unadjusted, unplanned sample would, however, be considerably greater.)

Having adjusted or not as seems best, what else can we do? Only something to make ourselves feel better about the sample. Some other characteristic than that under study can sometimes be compared in the adjusted sample and in the population. A large difference is evidence of substantial bias within segments. Good agreement is comforting, and strengthens the believability of the adjusted mean for the characteristic of interest. The amount of this strengthening depends very much on the *a priori* relation between the two characteristics.

Some would say that an unplanned sample does not deserve adjustment, but the discussion in Part II indicates that if any sort of a summary is to be made, it might as well, in principle, be an adjusted mean.

II. SYSTEMATIC ERRORS

In order to understand how systematic errors in sampling should be treated, it seems both necessary and desirable to fall back on the analogy with the treatment of systematic errors in measurement. No clear account of the situation for sampling seems to be available in the literature, although understanding of the issues is a prerequisite to the critical assessment of nonprobability samples. On the other hand, one of physical science's greatest and more recurrent problems is the treatment of systematic errors.

10. The presence of systematic errors

Almost any sort of inquiry that is general and not particular involves both sampling and measurement, whether its aim is to measure the heat conductivity of copper, the uranium content of a hill, the visual acuity of high school boys, the social significance of television or the sexual behavior of the (white) human (U.S.) male. Further, *both* the measurement *and* the sampling will be imperfect in almost every case. We can define away either imperfection in certain cases. But the resulting appearance of perfection is usually only an illusion.

We can define the thermal conductivity of a metal as the average value of the measurements made with a particular sort of apparatus, calibrated and operated in a specified way. If the average is properly specified, then there is no "systematic" error of measurement. Yet even the most operational of physicists would give up this definition when presented with a new type of apparatus, which standard physical theory demonstrated to be less susceptible to error.

We can relate the result of a sampling operation to "the result that would have been obtained if the same persons had applied the same methods to the whole population." But we want to know about the population and not about what we would find by certain methods. In almost all cases, applying the method to the "whole" population would miss certain persons and units.

Recognizing the inevitability of (systematic) error in both measurement and sampling, what are we to do? Clearly, attempt to hold the combined effect of the systematic errors down to a reasonable value. What is reasonable? This must depend on the cost of further reduction and the value of accurate results. How do we *know* that our systematic errors have been reduced sufficiently? We don't! (And neither does the physicist!) We use all the subject-matter knowledge, information and semi-information that we have—we combine it with whatever internal evidence of consistency it seems worthwhile to arrange for the observations to provide. The result is not foolproof. We may learn new things and do better later, but who expects the last words on any subject?

In 1905, a physicist measuring the thermal conductivity of copper would have faced, unknowingly, a very small systematic error due to the heating of his equipment and sample by the absorption of cosmic rays, then unknown to physics. In early 1946, an opinion poller, studying Japanese opinion as to who won the war, would have faced a very small systematic error due to the neglect of the 17 Japanese holdouts, who were discovered later north of Saipan. These cases are entirely parallel. Social, biological and physical scientists all need to remember that they have the same problems, the main difference being the decimal place in which they appear.

If we admit the presence of systematic errors in essentially every case, what then distinguishes good inquiry from bad? Some reasonable criteria would seem to be:

(1) Reduction of exposure to systematic errors from *either* measurement *or* sampling to a level of unimportance, *if possible and economically feasible,* otherwise

(1+) Balancing the assignment of available resources to reduction in systematic or variable errors in either measurement or sampling reasonably well, in order to obtain a reasonable amount of information for the "money."

(2) Careful consideration of possible sources of error and careful examination of the numerical results.

(3) Presentation of results and inferences in a manner which adequately points out both observed variability and conjectured exposure to systematic error.

In many situations it is easy, and relatively inexpensive, to reduce the systematic errors in sampling to practical unimportance. This is done by using a probability sampling plan, where the chance that any individual or other primary unit shall enter the sample is known, and allowed for, and where adequate randomness is ensured by some scheme of (mechanical) randomization. The systematic errors of such a sample are minimal, and frequently consist of such items as:

(a) failure of individuals or primary units to appear on the "list" from which selection has been made,

(b) persons perennially "not at home" or samples "lost,"

(c) refusals to answer or breakdowns in the measuring device.

These are the hard core of causes of systematic error in sampling. Fortunately, in many situations their effect is small—there a probability sample will remove almost all the systematic error due to sampling.

11. Should a probability sample be taken?

But this does not mean that it is always good policy to take probability samples. The inquirer may not be able to "afford" the cost in time or money for a probability sample. The opinion pollers do not usually afford a probability sample (instead of designating individuals to be interviewed by a random, mechanical process, they allow their interviewers to select respondents to fill "quotas") and many have criticized them for this. Yet the behavior of the few probability samples in the 1948 election (see pp. 110-112 of *The Pre-election Polls of 1948,* Social Science Research Council Report No. 60) does not make it clear that the opinion pollers should spend their limited resources on probability samples for best results. (Shifts *toward* a probability sample have been promised, and seem likely to be wise.)

The statement "he didn't use a probability sample" is thus *not* a criticism which should end further discussion and doom the inquiry to the cellar. It is always necessary to ask two questions:

(a) Could the inquirer afford a probability sample?
(b) Is the exposure to systematic error from a non-probability sample small enough to be borne?

If the answer is "no" to both, then the inquiry should not be, or have been, made—just as would be the case with a physical inquiry if the systematic errors of all the forms of measurement which the physicist could afford were unbearably large.

If the answer is "yes" to the first question and "no" to the second, then the failure to use a probability sample is very serious, indeed.

If the answer is "yes" to both, then careful consideration of the economic balance is required—however it should be incumbent on the inquirer using a nonprobability sample to show why it gave more information per dollar or per year. (As statisticians, we feel that the onus is on the user of the *non*probability sample. Offhand we know of no expert group who would wish to lift it from his shoulders.)

If the answer is "no" to the first question, and "yes" to the second, then the appropriate reaction would seem to be "lucky man."

Having admitted that the sampling, as well as the measurement, will have some systematic errors, how then do we do our best to make good inferences about the subject of inquiry? Sampling and measurement being on the same footing, we have only to copy, for the sampling area, the procedure which is well established and relatively well understood for measurement. This procedure runs about as follows:

We admit the existence of systematic error—of a difference between the quantity measured (the measured quantity) and the quantity of interest (the target quantity). We ask the observations about the measured quantity. We ask our subject matter knowledge, intuition, and general information about the relation between the measured quantity and the target quantity.

We can repeat this nearly verbatim for sampling:

We admit the existence of systematic error—of a difference between the population sampled (the sampled population) and the population of interest (the target population). We ask the observations about the sampled population. We ask our subject matter knowledge, intuition, and general information about the relation between sampled population and target population.

Notice that the measured quantity is not the raw readings, which usually define a *different* measured quantity, but rather the adjusted values resulting from all the standard corrections appropriate to the method of measurement. (Not the actual gas volume, but the gas volume at standard conditions!) Similarly, the result for the sampled population is not the raw mean of the observations, which usually defines a *different* sampled population, but rather the adjusted or weighted mean, all corrections, weightings and the like appropriate to the method of sampling having been applied. Weighting a sample appropriately is no more fudging the data than is correcting a gas volume for barometric pressure.

The third great virtue of probability sampling is the relative definiteness of the sampled population. It is usually possible to point the finger at most of the groups in the target population who have no chance to enter the sample, who therefore were not in the sampled population; and to point the finger at many of the groups whose chance of entering the sample was less than or more than the chance allotted to them in the computation, who therefore were fractionally or multiply represented in the sampled population. When a nonprobability sample is adjusted and weighted to the best of an expert's ability, on the other hand, it may still be very difficult to say what the sampled population really is. (Selectivity *within* segments cannot be allowed for by weights or adjustments, but it arises to some extent in every nonprobability sample and alters the sampled population.)

12. The value and conditions of adjustment

Some would say that correcting, adjusting and weighting most nonprobability samples is a waste of time, since you do not *know*, when this process has been completed, to what sampled population the adjusted result refers. This is entirely equivalent to saying that it does not pay to adjust the result of a physical measurement for a known systematic error because there are, undoubtedly, other systematic errors and some of them are likely to be in the other direction. Let us inquire into good practice in the measurement situation, and see what guidance it gives us for the sampling situation.

When will the physicist adjust the principle for the known systematic error? When (i) he has the necessary information and (ii) the adjustment is likely to help. The necessary information includes a theory or empirical formula, and the necessary observations. Empirical formulas and observations are subject to fluctuations, so that adjustment will usually change the magnitude of fluctuations as well as altering the systematic error. The adjustment is likely to help unless the supposed reduction of systematic error coincides with a substantial increase in fluctuations.

If the known systematic error is so small as not to

(1) affect the result by a meaningful amount, or

(2) affect the result by an amount likely to be as large as, or a substantial fraction of, the unknown systematic errors,

then the physicist will report either the adjusted or the unadjusted value. If he reports the unadjusted value, he should state that the adjustment has been examined, and is less than such-and-so. To do this, either he must have calculated the adjustment or he must have had generally applicable and strong evidence that it is small.

In any event, his main care, which he will not always take, must be to warn the reader about the dangers of further systematic errors, perhaps, in some cases, even by saying bluntly that "the adjusted value isn't much better than the raw value," and then provide raw values for those who wish to adjust their own.

If the physicist is aware of systematic errors of serious magnitude and has no basis for adjustment, his practice is to name the measured quantity something, like Brinnell hardness, Charpy impact strength, or if he is a chemist—iodine value, heavy metals as Pb, etc. By analogy, those who feel that the combination of recall and interview technique make Kinsey's results subject to great systematic error might well define "KPM sexual behavior" as a standard term,[2] and work with this.

By analogy then, when should a nonprobability sample be adjusted in principle? (Most probability samples are made to be weighted anyway—this is part of the design and must be carried out.) When (i) we have the necessary information and (ii) when the adjustment is likely to help. The necessary information will usually consist of facts or estimates of the true fractions in the population of the various segments.

When is the adjustment likely to help? This problem has usually been a ticklish point requiring technical knowledge and intuition. A quantitative solution is now given in Chapter V–C of Appendix C in the complete report. With this as a guide, it should be possible to make reasonable decisions about the helpfulness of adjustment.

If the decision is to adjust, we should accept the sampled population corresponding to the adjusted mean, and calculate the adjustment. We then report the adjusted value, unless the adjustment is small, when we may report the unadjusted value with the statement that the adjustment alters it by less than such-and-so.

Our main care, which we may not always take, must be to warn the reader about the dangers of further lack of representativeness, perhaps, in some cases, even by saying bluntly that "the adjusted mean isn't much better than the raw mean, even if we took 20 pages to tell you how we did it and six months to do it," and to provide raw means for those who wish to adjust their own.

If we were prepared to report an unadjusted mean, we were clearly inviting inference to some sampled population. Adjustment will give us a sampled population that is usually nearer to the target population. Hence we should adjust.

If we cannot adjust, and must present raw data which we feel *badly* needs

[2]The letters KPM stand for Kinsey, Pomeroy and Martin, the authors of *Sexual Behavior in the Human Male*.

adjustment, we may say that this is what we found in these cases—take 'em or leave 'em. Except from the point of view of protecting the reader from over-belief in the results, this would seem to be a counsel of despair. By analogy with the physicist, it seems better to introduce "KPM sexual behavior" and its analogs in such situations.

STATISTICAL SURVEYS

E. Grebenik and C. A. Moser

Any attempt to study society must begin with observation—the collection and gathering of facts and their interpretation. When these facts concern social groups, and sometimes even when they concern individuals, this process inevitably entails the use of the statistical method. Indeed, the beginning of sociology as an empirical discipline is closely linked with the development of statistics; the political arithmeticians of the seventeenth century used statistical methods to obtain the simple elementary facts about the society in which they lived, such as the number of individuals of each sex, the number of houses, and the density of crowding, a knowledge of which is today taken for granted in civilized society. Graunt and Petty, the earliest writers of this school, were closely associated with the 'invisible college', the forerunner of the Royal Society, and it seemed natural to them that the method of observation which had yielded such valuable results in the natural sciences could be applied to the study of society. Indeed, it was only when some of the elementary social facts became available that it was possible for even a theoretical sociology to become more than a branch of speculative social philosophy.

The period between 1662, when Graunt's *Natural and Political Observations on the Bills of Mortality*[25] were first published, and the end of the nineteenth century, when Charles Booth conducted the first modern social survey on the *Life and Labour of the People of London*[9], saw a gradual but slow extension of the empirical investigation of social problems. In Britain Gregory King, John Howard, Patrick Colquhoun, C. T. Thackrah, and Bisset Hawkins—to name but a few—used the numerical method in their descriptions of the problems with which they were concerned, though not all their work was primarily statistical in character.[a] But the power of the method for the elucidation of information was sufficiently recognized in the nineteenth century to lead to the foundation of

Reprinted with the permission of the authors and publishers from A. T. Welford et al (eds.), *Society: Problems and Methods of Study*, London: Routledge and Kegan Paul and New York: Philosophical Library, 1962, pp. 5-24.

[a]For Gregory King's work see [23]; see also [34],[14] (Colquhoun used statistics collected by others to illustrate his points, rather than collect data himself);[56],[28].

statistical societies in many countries; in England, Manchester led the way in 1833, and London followed in the succeeding year, on the motion of the Rev. T. R. Malthus that "... it is advisable to take immediate steps to establish a Statistical Society in London, the object of which shall be the collection and classification of all facts illustrative of the present condition and prospects of Society. . ."[2] In the early years of its existence the Society set up committees which were to carry out investigations themselves, such as a survey of the condition of the poor in St. George's in the East, which was carried out in the 1840s.[3] But, on the whole, private surveys were few in number, and most of the statistical information we have about nineteenth-century England derives from the labours of official statisticians, or Royal Commissions and similar inquiries.

It has already been mentioned that the first social survey which is considered modern was Booth's monumental work on London. It was the problem of poverty in the midst of an increasingly affluent middle class which led Booth to undertake his inquiry. The lack of information about the problem, and an unwillingness to accept theories which attributed poverty to personal inadequacies or fecklessness, stimulated him to undertake a factual investigation, using the method which Beatrice Webb has called "wholesale interviewing". As Professor and Mrs. Simey have shown in their recent appreciation of his work,[53] he took considerable trouble to eliminate any personal bias on the part of his colleagues and collaborators and was at pains to devise methods which could be repeated in other circumstances so that a cumulative body of knowledge could be built up. His invention of the poverty line, later to be refined by Seebohm Rowntree,[49],[50] was one of the first operational definitions used in social investigation, and Rowntree's and Bowley's successive investigations were sufficient to end argument about the extent of poverty. When Bowley added the sampling method in his Five Town Surveys,[10],[11] thus bringing social investigation within the reach of the researcher with limited funds, the local social survey, that distinctive British contribution to the study of society, had arrived.

Although poverty surveys—the main subject matter of the chapter on *Social Surveys* in the previous edition of this book[61]—are now the exception rather than the rule, the technique and rationale of the methods used by social scientists, government departments, and market and opinion researchers, owes a heavy debt to the early pioneers.[b] Their aim was to fill gaps in our information about society and social conditions, and this information had to be accurate and reliable (in the sense that it was to be independent of the individual investigator collecting it). Whenever possible, the facts were to be given in quantitative form, and one does not have to go all the way with Lord Kelvin's view of measurement,[c] to prefer such facts to personal impressions. To say this is not to belittle the non-statistical form of investigation: the Lynds' books on Middletown,[40],[41] or F. Zweig's investigations in Britain[65],[66],[67] for example, have been very fruitful in suggesting hypotheses and providing an insight into social phenomena. But statistical surveys are essential for the testing and

[b]For an idea of applications in varied fields see [1],[19],[45],[63].

[c]'When you can measure what you are speaking about and express it in numbers you know something about it; but when you cannot measure it, when you cannot express it in numbers, your knowledge is of a meager and unsatisfactory kind.'

validation of these hypotheses. The 'sociological imagination' may be a necessary, but is not a sufficient, condition for social investigation; it needs to be supplemented by the disciplined testing of its products, and it is in this testing that surveys are vital.

It is rare nowadays for a survey to be purely descriptive. Occasionally in market research, commercial organizations may be satisfied with simply ascertaining the consumption pattern for their products; newspapers and advertising agencies may wish to estimate numbers of readers, viewers, or listeners, but even here the numbers are generally subdivided in a way which implies the existence of certain presuppositions. Indeed, when a survey is completely descriptive, it is generally of limited value. The limitation of purely factual reports can be seen in Kinsey's surveys of sexual behaviour:[37] Kinsey and his colleagues were so concerned with providing estimates of the frequency of "outlets" of different kinds that anyone unfamiliar with the facts of life might remain ignorant of the connexion between sexual "outlets" and reproduction (though it must be stated in fairness that Kinsey and his associates were studying aspects of human behaviour about which there was little systematic knowledge). Such single-minded devotion to factual description is mercifully rare; much of more recent survey work has been more sophisticated, and attempts have been made to use surveys to test previously formulated hypotheses about certain areas of social life. Thus, the Indianapolis survey on social and psychological factors affecting fertility[62] was designed to test a number of hypotheses on reproductive behaviour, and to link fertility with other socio-psychological variables. Mrs. Floud and her associates in their work on social class and educational opportunity[21] attempted amongst other problems to elucidate the extent to which equality of opportunity followed changes in educational legislation. Douglas and his colleagues investigated factors showing the importance of the social environment on child growth and development.[17] Doll and Hill attempted to study the link between carcinoma of the lung and smoking.[d] Himmelweit and her colleagues studied the effect of exposure to television on the subsequent behaviour of children.[30]

These surveys differ from the early poverty surveys in many respects, but most fundamentally in that they were designed to test theories which were explicitly formulated. In fact, it is broadly true to say that, whereas the earlier surveys provided data to inform discussion of social problems or for people to theorize upon, to-day social scientists more often use surveys to test theories already formulated, almost to serve as a substitute for social experimentation.

An experiment is normally used to test the consequences of a theoretical prediction. If the consequences are not in accord with the theory, the theory is discarded; if there is no difference, then, provisionally at any rate, the theory stands. The formulation of the theory or hypothesis to be tested is thus of prime importance, and the survey will have to be designed with this in mind. Thus, in the Indianapolis survey on social and psychological factors affecting fertility, some twenty-three hypotheses were set up, suggesting associations between different variables to be tested, and the results added considerably to our understanding of behaviour in this field.

[d]See [16] for a discussion of these investigations, and for a list of references.

The demonstration of associations between different variables is, of course, important, and in a properly designed survey may contribute to the understanding of the phenomenon studied. But it is a big step from this to the assertion of causal connexions. The surveys on the relation between cigarette smoking and lung cancer may be taken as an example: although it seems clear that heavy smokers are considerably more likely to contract cancer of the lung than others, little is known as yet about the mechanism by which this association works, and it is at least logically possible that the association is due to a third variable, itself associated both with proneness to cancer and the liability to smoke heavily. In a survey one can never be certain that some relevant variable has not been missed from the analysis, and may be confounding the picture. This is the fundamental difficulty in trying to unravel relationships between variables through surveys. By a judicious use of matching, control groups, and ingenious analysis the surveyor can often minimize the problems, but he can never achieve the security of causal interpretation that a randomized experiment can provide.[e]

SAMPLING

Principles of Design

What is the particular merit of statistical surveys as a way of contributing to our knowledge? The most important aspect is that the design of surveys can be based on statistical theory, and that from a properly designed sample survey it is possible to draw valid generalizations with a known margin of sampling error. This possibility depends upon the use of probability theory in survey design, for nowadays most surveys are taken by sample. Occasionally, the population studied may be so small that it is feasible and desirable to study every member, but such situations are exceptional. Normally, we are interested in large populations, and the additional expense and trouble of a full inquiry are rarely repaid in terms of increased accuracy; indeed the reverse may be the case, for the study of a selected sample may be easier to control, and more money may be available to obtain and process the information for each unit studied, whilst yielding considerable economies in total expenditure.

But if inferences about a population (which must be precisely defined) are to be drawn, it is essential that some form of random sampling should be used. Only this method leads to results that are statistically unbiased, and enables us to calculate sampling errors. To say this, is not to deny the value of case studies. A research worker may, for practical reasons, confine his work to a particular district, or to a particular section of the population. The studies of Young and Willmott in East London are a case in point.[64] Such studies yield valuable information about the areas studied, provide an insight into problems, and suggest hypotheses for testing; but they apply only to the areas investigated, and cannot be generalized to a wider population. Thus, we cannot know whether Young and Willmott's results relating to the relationship between mothers and

[e]For discussions of the problems of explanatory surveys see [32], [36], [38].

daughters are specific to London, or whether they apply throughout English urban society. In order to establish their general applicability a national sampling scheme of some kind would have to be used.

The essential point is that the researcher must be clear about the kind of generalization he wants. If he is content not to generalize beyond the cases actually studied, no selection problem need arise. But as soon as he aims at drawing inferences from these cases to a wider population, he needs to avail himself of the apparatus of random sample design.

The basic principles of sampling design are not hard to grasp.[f] The first essential is randomness, i.e. every member of the population to be surveyed must have a calculable, non-zero chance of being selected. There is no need for this chance actually to be calculated, but it must be calculable. Nor is it essential that the chances of selection should be the same for every member of the population; sampling with varying probabilities is more common than sampling with equal probabilities, and often carries distinct advantages.

A simple type of random sample might involve taking some complete record of the population—say, a list, map, card-index or hat full of numbers corresponding to the population members—and picking out the number required for the sample. The actual mechanism depends on the type of record or, to use the technical term, 'sampling frame'. But whatever the frame, randomness requires a rigorous and impersonal method of selection.[g]

Randomness in fact characterizes the method of selection rather than the sample selected. One cannot recognize a sample as random by looking at it; a perfectly random method of selection may produce a sample which looks markedly 'untypical or unrepresentative'. This is not particularly important; what matters is that the method of choosing the sample has not been biased for or against any section of the population, and has given each population member a calculable (and non-zero) chance of selection. The results of such a method—and of no other—can be investigated mathematically in ways which notably include the calculation of sampling errors attending the survey results.

So far only the simplest kind of random sample has been mentioned. In practice, designs tend to be complex. One almost universal refinement is to divide the population into strata according to factors relevant to the survey topic (and convenient with the sampling frame used), and then to take a random sample from each stratum. The gain, apart from practical convenience, is to make the sample more safely representative of the population, by ensuring that, in certain important respects, it is not left to chance whether the sample is right or not; this rightness is built into the sample by the stratification itself, and the results are almost invariably made more precise.

There are many other refinements. Samples are often designed in stages; thus a sample of the population of a town may be confined to certain parts of the

---

[f]For textbooks on sampling, see [13, 63]. For a more elementary presentation see [45], and for an illustration of sample designs used by the government Social Survey see [26].

[g]A method much favoured in market and opinion research is quota sampling. Here interviewers are given interview quotas (e.g. according to age, sex, social class) to fill, and are, broadly speaking, left to choose individuals to fit these quotas. This human element in the selection cuts across the basic requirement of random sampling and is the reason why quota sampling—in spite of its ease and cheapness—is not favoured by most statisticians.[46]

town, perhaps to one or two polling districts. With this in mind, one might first select a sample of wards, then a sample of polling districts in the wards selected at the first stage, and finally a sample of households in the selected polling districts. Such multi-stage designs clearly reduce costs and labour, but they also, less obviously, increase sampling errors; they are almost invariably used when a widely dispersed population needs to be covered.

We may also mention multi-phase sampling, where some of the information in a questionnaire is asked of all sample units, while additional questions are confined to sub-samples. This procedure is appropriate, for example, when different accuracy is needed for different items of information, so that smaller samples are adequate for some parts of the survey than for others. The 1961 Population Census in Great Britain is an example.[7]

The sample designer's task may be summarized as follows. First, he must know the precise nature of the information to be obtained, and the way it is to be analysed. Secondly, he must know what precision is required for the overall and the sub-group results; in other words, what margins of sampling error can be tolerated. With this information, and with knowledge of the resources available, he can decide the sample size needed, and design a sample to provide optimum precision for given resources, or given precision at minimum cost. The central feature of this design will be randomness, with such use of stratification, distribution between stages and phases, and other refinements, as may be appropriate.

Non-response

It is sometimes argued that much of the now customary sophistication in sample design is misplaced, first because the remaining phases of a survey tend to be far less rigorous, and secondly because the beauty of a sample design may in any case be marred by non-response. The first argument hardly needs discussion, since it is an unsound principle not to use reliable methods at one stage just because this is not yet possible in others. As regards non-response, improvements in survey techniques have in fact considerably improved levels of response. Response rates of 70-90 per cent are customary in well-administered surveys, and rates over 90 per cent are not uncommon. Even in mail surveys, non-response is often reduced to small proportions.[51] Certainly one cannot dismiss the problem of non-response, in the sense that the respondents *may* be sufficiently numerous and different from the rest of the population to cause bias. But enough is known about ways of increasing response and follow-up methods for the problem not to dominate survey design.[h] On no account is the likelihood of non-response to be regarded as an argument against rigorous sample design.

Inferences from Samples

It now becomes necessary to deal in general terms with the kind of inference that may be drawn from a sample. Fundamentally, there are two problems which are dealt with: the testing of significance, and the problem of estimation.

[h]See discussion in [13]: and [15, 18].

In the former case, we wish to establish whether certain populations or sections of a population differ from one another in particular characteristics; in the second we attempt to estimate the value of a hitherto unknown quantity from our information on the sample. The two procedures use essentially different analytical techniques.

Take the question of significance testing first. A typical problem in this field is that investigated by Bowley in his two surveys in the Five Towns: *Livelihood and Poverty* and *Has Poverty Diminished*? He surveyed the towns by sample twice; once before and once after the First World War, and obtained in each case the proportion falling below a well-defined poverty line. The problem he had to investigate was, whether the differences shown by these proportions indicated real differences between the two populations, or whether they could be accounted for by sampling fluctuations.

The procedure is as follows:[i] A hypothesis—the so-called null hypothesis—is formulated which postulates that there is no difference in poverty between the two populations. It should be noted that this hypothesis asserts nothing about the actual level of poverty, either before or after the First World War. It is possible by mathematical argument to deduce from this hypothesis the probability that if there were no difference in the level of poverty in the populations, two samples taken from that population would show proportions in poverty differing from one another by more than a given amount. Obviously, the larger the difference between the sample proportions, the smaller this probability would be. If it is sufficiently small (in practice the values taken are usually 5 per cent, 1 per cent or even 0.1 per cent), this difference is said to be *statistically significant*, and the null hypothesis is rejected at that level of significance. Thus, if a difference between two proportions or averages is said to be significant at the 5 per cent level, this means that the probability of a difference of this magnitude, or larger, arising by chance would be 5 per cent or less, and we could conclude that there is a *prima facie* case for believing that the two populations really do differ.

A number of points need to be made in this connexion. First, certainty can never be achieved. Improbable events do happen. A difference may be found to be statistically significant, when there is no real difference between the populations. But we know that if we use a 5 per cent level of significance, this will happen in the long run only on one occasion out of twenty, and the probability can be made lower still, by using a different significance level. Secondly, significance depends on sample size, and a difference which turns out to be not significant may well prove to be significant when a larger sample is taken. Often the magnitude and direction of a difference are of greater intrinsic interest than the mere determination of statistical significance. Yet the sociological literature is full of the results of significance tests, and there is a tendency to confuse statistical significance with substantive importance. The establishment of significant differences is not the end of survey research, but the beginning (cf,[8],[38]).

Estimation is a different process altogether. Whereas in significance testing the argument is deductive, proceeding from a hypothesis about the population to the behaviour of samples, in estimation we attempt to infer something about the

[i]See, e.g.,[22],[42],[60].

population as a whole from our knowledge of the sample. Thus, we might wish to estimate the extent of poverty in the population of one of the five towns from the poverty level found in the sample. Now at the time that the survey was taken there must have been a determinate proportion of persons living below the poverty line in that town. It is not, therefore, possible to make a statement about the probability of such and such a proportion of people living in poverty. The statistician overcomes this difficulty by computing a so-called 'confidence interval'. This procedure designates an interval within which the true population value will lie in a determinate proportion of cases. This proportion is often 95 per cent but may be as high as 99 per cent, or even 99.9 per cent. If it were stated, for instance, with 95 per cent confidence that poverty in one of the five towns lay between 12 and 15 per cent of the population, this would imply that a procedure had been used for estimating the interval which was known to contain the correct population value 95 per cent of the time.

The two procedures which have been described in general terms depend upon the use of the random sampling method, and the application of rigorous sample design. It is this design which makes possible generalizations about large populations, on the basis of the study of smaller groups, and the estimation of the margin of uncertainty associated with these generalizations. This process plays a vital role in the study of contemporary society; without sampling, accurate knowledge of social processes could take place only by aggregating successive case studies, a much less satisfactory procedure.

OBTAINING THE DATA

The most striking aspect of the survey phases discussed so far is their mathematical basis. Sampling is a branch of theoretical statistics, so that in this part of a survey more than in any other the researcher can be on safe scientific ground. When we turn to the task of data collection we find no such security. Psychology offers some help, but it must be admitted that many of the decisions on question wording, choice of approach, and the like are heavily determined by past experience, trial and error, and hunches. Clearly this is a serious weakness, since the compilation of correct data is after all the purpose of the whole operation; everything else, including the sampling, is merely a means towards this end.

The difficulties start at the beginning, in deciding what topics to include in the survey. It is necessary to confine investigations to items which are, in principle at least, measurable or orderable. The questions or definitions used are therefore often only operational approximations to the matters it is desired to investigate. An example is the use of occupational groups as an indication of social class differentials. These are used, not because it is believed that occupation is identical with social class, but merely in order to make the latter concept 'countable' or 'measurable' for survey purposes. It is up to the sociologist to decide which indicator or combination of indicators approximates most closely to what he means by 'social class'. It is sometimes objected that reliance on such indicators leads to the loss of something essential in the study of these phenomena. On the other hand, the gain in the comparability of the results of different investigators is undeniable, and it is an accepted procedure of science to study phenomena which are not directly observable through indices which can be used in experimental testing.

Documentary Sources

This is not the place to discuss in detail the different ways of data collection open to the research worker,[j] since so much must depend on the resources available, the subject matter, the accuracy demanded and the depth and degree of quantification required in the individual survey. But a few general remarks are in order.

First of all there are the many documentary and statistical sources which can give background data about the populations, institutions, or groups covered by a survey. But our interest here is with ways of getting information about individual units, and in this documentary sources are of limited use. Perhaps the most interesting possibilities are personal documents, such as diaries, essays, and the like. If unsolicited, personal documents often provide a fuller, less self-conscious picture than can be reached by formal methods, but then unsolicited documents are of little help as a systematic form of inquiry. If solicited, personal records at once lose some of their advantages. Even so, they can provide illuminating data, as was demonstrated, to take only two examples, in the study of evacuation by Isaacs[34] and the survey of the effects of television by Himmelweit and others.[30] In both cases the essay-writers were children, and this form of approach is of particular attraction in such cases. But by and large personal documents are of only marginal importance as a source of survey data.

The same must, one supposes, apply to case records collected by social workers, such as almoners, probation officers, and psychiatric social workers. There is no doubt that such records often throw searching light on the persons concerned, but they are difficult to harness to a systematic social survey. Such difficulties may, however, be overcome by systematic attempts to make the information collected comparable and to eliminate personal bias on the part of the compiler. If this were done such records could be more widely used in throwing light on the particular populations they cover.

Mail Questionnaires

The attraction of using a postal questionnaire in collecting survey data is that it is cheap, quick, and suitable for reaching widely dispersed populations, and that it avoids interviewer bias. What is more, when the questions are few and simple, there seems little need to have recourse to personal interviews. When, on the other hand, one is dealing with a complicated survey topic, with unavoidably lengthy questionnaires, with issues where prior consideration or consultation is undesirable, or with questions which might require probing, the postal approach is ruled out.

For many years mail questionnaires were considered a very inferior mode of approach even when the subject matter seemed suitable. The reason was the problem of getting an adequate response. The literature was full of response

---

[j]See, e.g. [20], [32], [52]. For a useful reference source see [5].

rates of 20-30 per cent or even lower in which case it was difficult to take the results seriously. Mail questionnaires were regarded as suitable for surveys of special populations—e.g. members of a profession—but not for general populations. A trend in the opposite direction is now discernible. Research by the Social Survey has aimed at discovering ways of designing schedules and covering letters so as to improve response rates to mail questionnaires, and rates of 90 per cent or more have been achieved even for general population surveys, though always on simple questionnaires. A particularly useful application is in surveys of special populations for which no convenient sampling frame exists. An example might be a survey of all those in the population with university degrees. A form could be sent to a large sample of the entire working population, with enough questions to identify the graduates; these would then be used for the main survey, probably by interview. This is a form of multi-phase sampling where the first phase, by mail, is used to produce a sampling frame for the second.

There naturally remain many types of inquiries for which a personal approach is essential, but the recent work of the Social Survey, which seems to be supported in other organizations, suggests that the mail questionnaire deserves more sympathetic consideration than it has been receiving. A comprehensive discussion on this subject has been given by Scott.[51]

Interviewing

The most prominent and obviously the most valuable method of survey inquiry is personal interviewing. For the overwhelming majority of survey topics, the information can be obtained only by direct inquiry, rather than from documents or by observation, and this nearly always means a personal interview. Once this is decided, however, there is a wide range of interviewing techniques to choose from. The type that comes most readily to mind pictures the interviewer on the doorstep, asking a housewife a number of pre-set questions in a supposedly uniform manner, both the order and the wording of the questions corresponding to precise instructions. And in fact this is probably the predominant approach in official inquiries, in commercial surveys and perhaps even in social research. But it is by no means the only one. Often the interviewer is given scope to choose the precise form and order of the questions, though within a well-defined framework of points to be covered. In some surveys, the interviewer may be allowed even more latitude. Interviewing of the 'depth' type, often used to discover people's attitudes and motivations, demands that the interviewer has a clear idea of the level of information to be reached, and is given great latitude in achieving it (cf.[29]).

This is not the place to discuss the technical features of interviewing,[k] but it must be stressed that the choice between alternative approaches to interviewing involves important issues of methodology. Though any classification is bound to over-simplify, one can conceive of these approaches as ranged along a continuum of formality. At one extreme is the completely formalized interview: the interviewer behaves as much like a machine as is humanly possible. The more

[k]On interviewing see [20, 33, 35, 52].

closely she is able to keep to the question form and order laid down, the more alike different interviewers are in their approach, in their accents and so forth, the more exactly comparable will be the final answers obtained from different respondents to the same interviewer, and by different interviewers. In other words, the aim underlying formal interviewing is to maximize the *reliability*[1] of the results. But reliability is not everything. The correct answers may lie at different levels with different respondents, and it may require quite differently orientated and worded questions to elicit them. From this viewpoint, it might be better for the interviewers not to behave like machines, but to adjust their approach to the individual respondent, in an effort to penetrate to the valid (i.e. correct) reply. This sort of approach aims at maximizing the *validity* of the responses. The more straightforward and simple the subject matter, the more one inclines to the formal approach; the more complex, the more desirable does it seem to use a flexible, informal mode of attack. Survey practitioners differ in their preferences. Some believe that even the most complex problem—say a survey seeking views on homosexuality—is best handled formally, so that at least comparable pieces of information are obtained from all respondents. Certainly the results are then easy to aggregate and to quantify. But there remains the doubt whether pre-set questions, and an inflexible approach, are right for a delicate situation, with the respondent perhaps hesitant to disclose his true inclinations, or unsure where he stands. In such a case, an informal approach has much to commend it, giving full rein to the respondent's own way of thinking about and answering the questions. But then the real problem comes in the analysis; the very comparability of the answers given by different respondents must be open to question, and there is the severe difficulty of coding and aggregating the qualitative kind of material which such an approach produces.

Questionnaire design

This discussion may suffice to show that it is necessary to decide whether to go mainly for comparability, reliability, and easy quantification, or for depth, detail, and validity. We will not take the subject further here, nor embark on the matter of questionnaire design.[m] It has to be recognized that question framing is one of the hardest tasks in a survey, especially when—as is increasingly the case—the questions relate to attitudes and opinions. Sometimes these relate to future behaviour, such as in investigating voting intentions in pre-election surveys, and here the record of the pollsters has in recent elections been creditable.[12, 47] On the other hand, it is not always easy to know how much importance to attach to expressions of opinions, which can vary so radically in 'informedness' and intensity. Furthermore, it has been shown that interaction between interviewer and respondent, the exact framing of the question, the order in which questions appear, and other factors may affect the response

---

[1]The term 'reliability' is here used in a technical sense, to denote the extent to which repeated interviews on the same respondents by the same interviewers get the same results; by a slight extension, the word may be taken to cover *different* interviewers working under comparable conditions.

[m]On questionnaire design see [20, 32, 45, 52] for a summary of problems and for references; and also [48].

elicited from the questionnaire. A great deal of research on the measurement of attitudes is proceeding but it is doubtful whether the problems have yet been satisfactorily resolved. (See[20], [39], [57]). In any case, the subject of question design is hard to deal with in general terms, and will not be further pursued here.

Response errors

Whatever method of obtaining the survey data is adopted, we can be sure that some errors will enter the results at the various stages of the survey.[n] Those due to sampling, mentioned earlier, are the least worrying, since they are subject to scientific treatment. Errors of a non-sampling type—many of which are as likely to occur in complete as in sample surveys—are much more elusive. Respondents may give inaccurate answers because they are disinclined to tell the truth—perhaps actuated by prestige feelings or by the personality of the interviewer, or perhaps because they do not recall the correct answer, or have misunderstood the question. Interviewers, though provided with the right answer, may misunderstand it, misinterpret and therefore wrongly classify it, and may make purely clerical errors. Numerous other types of error may occur in the interview situation. Postal questionnaires are subject to some of these errors and to others, and so are observational techniques. And to all these must be added errors occurring in the editing, coding, and analysis of the results.

This is a list of some *potential* sources of error. Not every survey is beset by errors of every kind, for the quality of performance may be so high as to reduce some of them to negligible proportions. And even when a particular type of error is met with, different types of error may partially cancel out. There is in fact an essential distinction between gross errors and net errors.

Some of the possibilities of detection and measurement can be mentioned briefly. *External checks* of the survey results against known facts are of less value than the layman might suppose. For one thing, the check data have to be of high comparability if they are to serve as a yardstick for assessing the survey aggregates, and such situations are rare. Secondly, the check data are themselves probably subject to error, and one may well have less faith in them than in the survey results. Thirdly, even where the survey results can be checked in certain particulars, these will not include the main topic of the survey, for otherwise why was the survey necessary? Fourthly, external checks on survey aggregates only disclose net errors, yet it is the gross errors that have to be tackled if survey procedures are to be improved. Sometimes individual records, e.g. birth certificates, can be used for checking individual responses and therefore for assessing gross errors, but these situations are rare indeed. In sum, though external checks should be used wherever possible, they rarely take one much of the way towards measuring response errors.

Certain *internal checks* are worth considering. Kinsey and his colleagues in some cases checked accuracy by collecting information from both husband and wife.[37] Sometimes the same piece of information can be sought in more than one way in the same interview, such as by asking a respondent not only how old he is but what his date of birth was. But consistency checks are one-sided: if

---

[n]See the references in chap. 13 of [45].

both results agree one gains in confidence, though it is possible that both are wrong. When the two results do not agree, one does not—without additional information—know which is correct.

What is wanted is a check measurement which is known to be at a higher level of accuracy than the original one. In this lies the attraction of quality checks or *post-enumeration surveys,* which are now customary in census work in the United States and elsewhere.[6, 7, 59] This involves re-surveying a sub-sample of the original sample, but with procedures at an assumedly higher level than used on the first occasion. Various steps are taken to ensure this. Only the very best interviewers (usually supervisors) are employed; several questions are asked, in place of one on the original occasion, in order to ensure that the question intent has been correctly understood and the answer properly interpreted; efforts are made to get the information from the person most likely to give it accurately (and not just from anyone in the household); and so forth. In these ways, it is hoped that the second measurement is more accurate than the first, and information is obtained not only on the accuracy achieved in the main survey but on the ways in which errors entered. For it is an essential part of quality checks to track down how a particular error came to be made. So far, quality checks have been used mainly as a way of detecting sources of error and thus of improving future procedures. Whether they can be used for adjusting the survey estimates is another matter; there remain problems in the conduct of these check surveys that need to be settled, and the number of recalls would have to be larger than has been customary.

In any event, quality checks are the most hopeful method yet developed for dealing with response errors, but it remains to be seen whether they can be as useful for *ad hoc* surveys of modest scale as they have proved to be for large-scale censuses on the one hand, and for regular inquiries (like the labour force surveys in Canada and the United States) on the other.

There are many other ways of tracking down errors, and given sufficiently careful survey design, some components of total response error can even be treated in a theoretically precise manner (see e.g. [27]). The subject of response errors has been discussed at relative length because the improvement in the accuracy achieved in surveys constitutes the main challenge in this field. Inaccurate measurements remain inaccurate, however sound the sample design or sophisticated the statistical analysis. Research workers in the social sciences should be much more demanding in the standards of accuracy they ask of their evidence.

ANALYSIS

This is not the place to discuss the practical survey operations, such as editing, coding, and tabulating, which intervene between the return of the raw survey material and the presentation of the data, or the specific statistical techniques which may be used in their analysis.[o] What is necessary is a general comment on the argument often advanced by critics of quantitative sociology, namely that elaborate statistical techniques are out of place in dealing with the approximate, vague, and highly involved data the sociologist often produces.

[o]See [22, 42, 60, 63].

While it is unfortunately true that some of the concepts used in sociology are vague and approximate, this is no argument against the use of statistical methods, but should rather be a challenge to the sociologist to revise his concepts so that their vagueness disappears. It is usually considered to be an essential part of a scientific discipline that its result should be capable of being empirically tested; and it is surely essential that sociological information should be capable of objective classification. The methods that are used are often exceedingly simple, little more than counting and categorization is involved, and this is hardly likely to 'stretch' the data. The computation of ratios, percentages, averages, and measures of dispersion, where applicable, is standard descriptive technique in statistics and is normally well understood.

Objection is frequently taken to the application of more elaborate mathematical techniques. It has already been shown that the use of probability methods follows logically, if sampling procedures are used. Their employment is a function of the method of conducting the survey, rather than of the kind of data studied. In the attempt to unravel relationships between variables, however, it is often necessary to combine series of measurements into indices, or to assess the influence of one or more variables upon others. Statistical methods have been devised in the field of multivariate analysis, which have proved very powerful in social research.[p] The complexity of the relationships studied makes it more rather than less necessary for the appropriate statistical methods to be used. At the same time, however, it is necessary for the research worker to understand the rationale of the methods which he employs. Multivariate analysis is based upon models which are subject to certain assumptions, and it is essential that these assumptions should be clearly understood. This is particularly important, as a number of the techniques that are commonly used in statistics have been devised with the needs of the agricultural or biological sciences in mind, and may have to be modified before they can be applied in social research.

This is not to say that statistical techniques should replace all other kinds of survey analysis. No one familiar with the writings of Mayhew and Charles Booth or, in our own day, with some of the work of the Institute of Community Studies (cf. [58,64]) can deny that verbal descriptions of individual cases, institutions, and the like can often give a more vivid, richer and, in a sense, deeper picture of life than the statistical tables to be found in conventional survey reports. The two ways of presenting data are complementary; the statistical tables are essential for conveying the characteristics of aggregates, for testing relationships and the like, whilst the qualitative description can be brought in to give a fuller account of parts of the picture. But, as regards the latter, infinite care needs to be taken not to present the case studies with a greater implication of 'typicality' than they merit.[4]

In recent years more use has been made of the so-called 'longitudinal' surveys. This rather unfortunate term is used to describe surveys in which a specific group of individuals is observed and surveyed over a relatively lengthy period of time. Thus, in the National Survey of the Health and Development of Children, a group of children born in 1946 has now been kept under observation for fifteen years,[17] and a group of children tested in the Scottish Mental Survey of 1947

---

[p]See e.g. [24,43,44,54,55]. For discussion of relevant problems see also [32,36,38]

has been kept under observation in order to relate their test performance to subsequent development. Such surveys present difficulties of their own, particularly in connexion with the wastage of respondents due to removals etc., and also tend to be expensive. Nevertheless it is possible to obtain from them information which it would be very difficult to obtain in any other way.

Our discussion of statistical surveys has necessarily been somewhat selective and limited. It will, however, have shown the importance of the survey as an instrument of sociological research, and a perusal of sociological journals will demonstrate its increasing frequency. Some will welcome this trend as a confirmation of their belief that sociology is at last becoming 'scientific'; others will see in it a substitution of facile techniques for hard thinking. There is some truth in both views. A well-conducted survey can produce data of better quality and greater significance (in the non-statistical sense) than most other research methods. But it is also true that it is not very difficult to collect facts or compile tables, though it must be added that even this is not quite as easy as would appear at first sight. Some surveys, as a result, are more distinguished for technical virtuosity than for the contribution they make to sociological knowledge. This is often due to the fact that there exists a gulf between the sociologist, who is frequently trained on the Arts side, and who will know little about statistical techniques, and the statistician, whose knowledge of the subject-matter of the survey is often limited. The design and execution of a survey is thus left to the specialist statistician, who is an expert in techniques. It is to be hoped that in the future there will be more sociologists whose training will include the necessary mathematics and statistics useful in survey analysis.

The main fields in which research is necessary in surveys, however, lies outside statistics proper. It is in the control of response errors, and in the improvement of the quality of data collection, that one hopes for advances in the future.

REFERENCES

1. Abrams, M., *Social Surveys and Social Action* (London, 1951).
2. *Annals of the Royal Statistical Society, 1834-1934,* p. 10
3. *ibid.,* p. 49.
4. Barton, A. H. & P. F. Lazarsfeld, 'Some Functions of Qualitative Analysis in Social Research.' In *Sociologica,* Frankfurter Beiträge zur Soziologie, I, 1955.
5. Belson, W. & C. R. Bell, *A Bibliography of Papers Bearing on the Adequacy of Techniques Used in Survey Research.* London, 1960.
6. Benjamin, B., "Quality of Response in Census Taking," *Popul. Stud.,* 1955.
7. Benjamin, B., "Statistical Problems Connected with the 1961 Population Census," *J. R. statist. Soc.,* A, 1960.
8. Blalock, H. M., *Social Statistics.* New York, 1960, chap 10.
9. Booth, Charles. *Labour and Life of the People of London.* London, 1889-91, 2 vols. *Life and Labour of the People in London* (2nd ed.). 9 Vols., London 1892-7. 3rd edn., 17 Vols. London, 1902-3.
10. Bowley, A. L. & A. R. Burnett-Hurst, *Livelihood and Poverty.* London, 1915.
11. Bowley, A. L. & M. H. Hogg, *Has Poverty Diminished?* London, 1925.
12. Butler, D. E. & R. Rose, *The British General Election of 1959.* London, 1960, chap. 8.

13. Cochran, W. G., *Sampling Techniques.* New York, 1953.

14. Colquhoun, P., *A Treatise on the Police of the Metropolis,* etc. (2nd ed.) London, 1800.

15. Deming, W. E., "On a Probability Mechanism to Attain an Economic Balance Between the Resultant Error of Response and the Bias of Non-response," *J. Amer. Statist. Assoc.* (1953).

16. Doll, R., "Retrospective and Prospective Studies," chap. 4, in Witts, L. J. (ed.) *Medical Surveys and Clinical Trials.* London, 1959.

17. Douglas, J. W. B. & M. Blomfield, *Children Under Five.* London, 1958.

18. Durbin, J. & A. Stuart, "Callbacks and Clustering in Sample Surveys: An Experimental Study," *J. R. statist. Soc.,* A, 1954.

19. Edwards, F. (ed.), *Readings in Market Research.* London, 1956.

20. Festinger, L. & D. Katz, (eds.), *Research Methods in the Behavioral Sciences.* London, 1954.

21. Floud, J. E., A. H. Halsey, & F. M. Martin, *Social Class and Educational Opportunity.* London, 1957.

22. Freund, J. E. & F. J. Williams, *Modern Business Statistics.* London, 1959.

23. Glass, D. V., "Gregory King and the Population of England and Wales at the End of the Seventeenth Century," *Eugen. Rev.,* 1946.

24. Glass, D. V. (ed.), *Social Mobility in Britain.* London, 1953.

25. Graunt, John., *Natural and Political Observations Mentioned in a Following Index and Made upon the Bills of Mortality.* London, 1662.

26. Gray, P. G. & T. Corlett, "Sampling for the Social Survey." *J. R. statist. Soc.,* A, 1950.

27. Hansen, M. H., W. N. Hurwitz, & W. G. Madow, *Sample Survey Methods and Theory.* New York, 1953 (2 vols.).

28. Hawkins, F. Bisset, *Elements of Medical Statistics.* London, 1829.

29. Henry, H., *Motivation Analysis.* London, 1958.

30. Himmelweit, H., *et al., Television and the Child.* London, 1958.

31. Howard, John, *The State of the Prisons in England and Wales, with Preliminary Observations and an Account of Some Foreign Prisons and Hospitals,* (2nd ed.). Warrington, 1780.

32. Hyman, H. H., *Survey Design and Analysis: Principles, Cases, and Procedures.* (Urbana, Ill., 1955.

33. Hyman, H. H., *et al., Interviewing in Social Research. Chicago,* 1955.

34. Isaacs, S., *et al., The Cambridge Evacuation Survey: A Wartime Study in Social Welfare and Education.* London, 1941.

35. Kahn, R. L., & C. F. Carnell, *The Dynamics of Interviewing: Theory, Techniques and Cases.* New York, 1957.

36. Kendall, P. L., & P. F. Lazarsfeld, "Problems of Survey Analysis," in R. K. Merton and P. F. Lazarsfeld (eds.), *Continuities in Social Research.* Urbana, Ill., 1950.

37. Kinsey, A. C., W. B. Pomeroy, & C. E. Martin, *Sexual Behaviour in the Human Female.* Philadelphia, 1953.

38. Kish, L., "Some Statistical Problems in Research Design," *Amer. Sociol. Rev.,* 1959.

39. Lindzey, G., *Handbook of Social Psychology* (chapters on attitude measurement).

40. Lynd, R. S. & H. Lynd, *Middletown.* New York and London, 1929.
41. Lynd, R. S., & H. Lynd, *Middletown in Transition.* New York, 1937.
42. McCarthy, P. J., *Introduction to Statistical Reasoning.* New York, 1957.
43. Mannheim, H. & L. T. Wilkins, *Prediction Methods in Relation to Borstal Training.* London, 1955.
44. Martin, J. P., *Social Aspects of Prescribing.* London, 1957.
45. Moser, C. A. *Survey Methods in Social Investigation.* London, 1958, chap 2.
46. Moser, C. A. & A. Stuart, "An Experimental Study of Quota Sampling." *J. R. statist. Soc.,* A, 1953.
47. Mosteller, F. *et al., The Pre-Election Polls of 1948.* New York, 1949.
48. Payne, S. L., *The Art of Asking Questions.* Princeton, 1951.
49. Rowntree, B. Seebohm, *Poverty: A Study of Town Life.* London, 1899.
50. Rowntree, B. Seebohm, *Poverty and Progress: A Second Social Survey of York.* London, 1941.
51. Scott, C., "Research on Mail Surveys," *J. R. statist. Soc.,* A, 1961.
52. Selltiz, C. *et al.* (eds.), *Research Methods in Social Relations.* London, 1954.
53. Simey, T. S. & M. B. Simey, *Charles Booth: Social Scientist.* London, 1961.
54. Stouffer, S. A. *et al., The American Soldier.* Princeton, 1949, 2 vols.
55. Stouffer, S. A. *et al., Measurement and Prediction.* Princeton, 1950.
56. Thackrah, C. T., *The Effects of Arts, Trades and Professions . . . on Health and Longevity.* London, 1832.
57. Torgerson, W., *Theory and Methods of Scaling.* London, 1958.
58. Townsend, P., *The Family Life of Old People.* London, 1957.
59. United States Bureau of the Census, *The Post-Enumeration Survey,* 1950. Technical Papers, No. 4, Washington, 1960.
60. Wallis, W. A. & H. V. Roberts, *Statistics: A New Approach.* Urbana, Ill., 1956.
61. Wells, A. F., "Social Surveys," chap. 18 in F. C. Bartlett, *et al.* (ed.), *The Study of Society: Methods and Problems.* London, 1939.
62. Whelpton, P. K. & C. V. Kiser, *Social and Psychological Factors Affecting Fertility,* 5 vols. New York, 1946-58. Cf. also the resumé of the study by these authors in *Popul. Stud.,* 1954.
63. Yates, F., *Sampling Methods for Censuses and Surveys* (3rd ed.). London, 1960
64. Young, M. & P. Willmott, *Family and Kinship in East London.* London, 1957.
65. Zweig, F., *Labour, Life, and Poverty.* London, 1948.
66. Zweig, F., *Women's Life and Labour.* London, 1952.
67. Zweig, F., *The British Worker.* Harmondsworth, 1952.

6

Data
Collection

With problems of study format and sampling considered, the task of data collection arises. Here there are several options, the major types being observation (either as a participant in the groups or as a detached observer), interviews, and use of questionnaires. The first paper, by Becker, discusses the problems unique to participant observation, as well as possible solutions. Of major concern are the problems of statistical precision and the reliability of data gathered.

The Bales paper is at the other end of the continuum from the participant approach, in that the situation maximizes control over the subjects involved. They appear in a laboratory setting and the observer codes their behavior according to a preconceived set of categories. The paper presents these categories and includes as well some clues as to their applicability.

Williams' paper on interviewing suggests that objectivity and rapport can both work to minimize possible bias due to social differences and a feeling of "threat" between interviewer and respondent. Finally, the generally high level of interview reliability and validity is confirmed by John Ball, who compares the responses of drug addicts obtained in an interview situation with information drawn from FBI and hospital records of independent chemical analyses of drug use.

The two papers on questionnaires concern the central problem of validity. Hagburg carries out essentially the same kind of comparison that Ball did on interviews—that between reported and actual information. His results, however, are not as comforting for sociologists as Ball's findings. To combat this very real problem in survey research, Schuman suggests the use of "random probes," a relatively inexpensive way of enhancing validity.

The concluding paper by Zelditch emphasizes that these various data gathering techniques are by no means mutually exclusive. In fact, he indicates clearly how observation, interviewing, and sample surveys, far from being incompatible, can fruitfully complement one another in one and the same study.

PROBLEMS OF INFERENCE AND PROOF IN
PARTICIPANT OBSERVATION

Howard S. Becker

The participant observer gathers data by participating in the daily life of the group or organization he studies.[1] He watches the people he is studying to see what situations they ordinarily meet and how they behave in them. He enters into conversation with some or all of the participants in these situations and discovers their interpretations of the events he has observed.

Let me describe, as one specific instance of observational technique, what my colleagues and I have done in studying a medical school. We went to lectures with students taking their first two years of basic science and frequented the laboratories in which they spend most of their time, watching them and engaging in casual conversation as they dissected cadavers or examined pathology specimens. We followed these students to their fraternity houses and sat around while they discussed their school experiences. We accompanied students in the clinical years on rounds with attending physicians, watched them examine patients on the wards and in the clinics, sat in on discussion groups and oral exams. We ate with the students and took night call with them. We pursued internes and residents through their crowded schedules of teaching and medical work. We stayed with one small group of students on each service for periods ranging from a week to two months, spending many full days with them. The observational situations allowed time for conversation and we took advantage of this to interview students about things that had happened and were about to happen, and about their own backgrounds and aspirations.

Sociologists usually use this method when they are especially interested in understanding a particular organization or substantive problem rather than

Reprinted with the permission of the author and the publisher, The American Sociological Association, from the *American Sociological Review*, Vol. 23 (1958), 652-60.

This paper developed out of problems of analysis arising in a study of a state medical school. The study is sponsored by Community Studies, Inc., of Kansas City, Missouri. It is directed by Everett C. Hughes; Anselm Strauss is also a member of the research team. Most of the material presented here has been worked out with the help of Blanche Geer, who has been my partner in field work and analysis in this study. I am grateful to Alvin W. Gouldner for a thorough critique of an earlier draft.

Substantive papers on the study, whose findings are made use of throughout, include: Howard S. Becker and Blanche Geer, "The Fate of Idealism in Medical School," *American Sociological Review*, 23 (February, 1958), pp. 50-56, and "Student Culture in Medical School," *Harvard Educational Review*, 28 (Winter, 1958), pp. 70-80. Another paper on participant observation by the same authors is "Participant Observation and Interviewing: A Comparison," *Human Organization*, 16 (Fall, 1957), pp. 28-32.

[1] There is little agreement on the specific referent of the term *participant observation*. See Raymond L. Gold, "Roles in Sociological Field Observations," *Social Forces*, 36 (March, 1958), pp. 217-223, for a useful classification of the various procedures that go by this name. Our own research, from which we have drawn our illustrations, falls under Gold's type, "participant-as-observer." The basic methods discussed here, however, would appear to be similar in other kinds of field situations.

demonstrating relations between abstractly defined variables. They attempt to make their research theoretically meaningful, but they assume that they do not know enough about the organization *a priori* to identify relevant problems and hypotheses and that they must discover these in the course of the research. Though participant observation can be used to test *a priori* hypotheses, and therefore need not be as unstructed as the example I have given above, this is typically not the case. My discussion refers to the kind of participant observation study which seeks to discover hypotheses as well as to test them.

Observational research produces an immense amount of detailed description; our files contain approximately five thousand single-spaced pages of such material. Faced with such a quantity of "rich" but varied data, the researcher faces the problem of how to analyze it systematically and then to present his conclusions so as to convince other scientists of their validity. Participant observation (indeed, qualitative analysis generally) has not done well with this problem, and the full weight of evidence for conclusions and the processes by which they were reached are usually not presented, so that the reader finds it difficult to make his own assessment of them and must rely on his faith in the researcher.

In what follows I try to pull out and describe *the basic analytic operations carried on in participant observation,* for three reasons: to make these operations clear to those unfamiliar with the method; by attempting a more explicit and systematic description, to aid those working with the method in organizing their own research; and, most importantly, in order to propose some changes in analytic procedures and particularly in reporting results which will make the processes by which conclusions are reached and substantiated more accessible to the reader.

The first thing we note about participant observation research is that analysis is carried on *sequentially,* [2] important parts of the analysis being made while the researcher is still gathering his data. This has two obvious consequences: further data gathering takes its direction from provisional analyses; and the amount and kind of provisional analysis carried on is limited by the exigencies of the field work situation, so that final comprehensive analyses may not be possible until the field work is completed.

We can distinguish three distinct stages of analysis conducted in the field itself, and a fourth stage, carried on after completion of the field work. These stages are differentiated, first, by their logical sequence: each succeeding stage depends on some analysis in the preceding stage. They are further differentiated by the fact that different kinds of conclusions are arrived at in each stage and that these conclusions are put to different uses in the continuing research. Finally, they are differentiated by the different criteria that are used to assess evidence and to reach conclusions in each stage. The three stages of field analysis are: the selection and definition of problems, concepts, and indices; the check on the frequency and distribution of phenomena; and the incorporation of individual

[2] In this respect, the analytic methods I discuss bear a family resemblance to the technique of *analytic induction.* Cf. Alfred Lindesmith, *Opiate Addiction* (Bloomington: Principia Press, 1947), especially pp. 5-20, and the subsequent literature cited in Ralph H. Turner, "The Quest for Universals in Sociological Research," *American Sociological Review,* 18 (December, 1953), pp. 604-611.

findings into a model of the organization under study.[3] The fourth stage of final analysis involves problems of presentation of evidence and proof.

SELECTION AND DEFINITION OF PROBLEMS, CONCEPTS, AND INDICES

In this stage, the observer looks for problems and concepts that give promise of yielding the greatest understanding of the organization he is studying, and for items which may serve as useful indicators of facts which are harder to observe. The typical conclusion that his data yield is the simple one that a given phenomenon exists, that a certain event occurred once, or that two phenomena were observed to be related in one instance; the conclusion says nothing about the frequency or distribution of the observed phenomenon.

By placing such an observation in the context of a sociological theory, the observer selects concepts and defines problems for further investigation. He constructs a theoretical model to account for that one case, intending to refine it in the light of subsequent findings. For instance, he might find the following: "Medical student X referred to one of his patients as a 'crock' today."[4] He may then connect this finding with a sociological theory suggesting that occupants of one social category in an institution classify members of other categories by criteria derived from the kinds of problems these other persons raise in the relationship. This combination of observed fact and theory directs him to look for the problems in student-patient interaction indicated by the term "crock." By discovering specifically what students have in mind in using the term, through questioning and continued observation, he may develop specific hypotheses about the nature of these interactional problems.

Conclusions about a single event also lead the observer to decide on specific items which might be used as indicators[5] of less easily observed phenomena. Noting that in at least one instance a given item is closely related to something less easily observable, the researcher discovers possible shortcuts easily enabling him to observe abstractly defined variables. For example, he may decide to investigate the hypothesis that medical freshmen feel they have more work to do than can possibly be managed in the time allowed them. One student, in discussing this problem, says he faces so much work that, in contrast to his undergraduate days, he is forced to study many hours over the weekend and

---

[3] My discussion of these stages is abstract and simplified and does not attempt to deal with practical and technical problems of participant observation study. The reader should keep in mind that in practice the research will involve all these operations simultaneously with reference to different particular problems.

[4] The examples of which our hypothetical observer makes use are drawn from our own current work with medical students.

[5] The problem of indicators is discussed by Paul F. Lazarsfeld and Allen Barton, "Qualitative Measurement in the Social Sciences: Classification, Typologies, and Indices," in Daniel Lerner and Harold D. Lasswell, editors, *The Policy Sciences: Recent Developments in Scope and Method*, Stanford: Stanford University Press, 1951, pp. 155-192; "Some Functions of Qualitative Analysis in Sociological Research," *Sociologica*, 1 (1955), pp. 324-361 (this important paper parallels the present discussion in many places); and Patricia L. Kendall and Paul F. Lazarsfeld, "Problems of Survey Analysis," in R. K. Merton and P. F. Lazarsfeld, editors, *Continuities in Social Research*, Glencoe: Free Press, 1950, pp. 183-186.

finds that even this is insufficient. The observer decides, on the basis of this one instance, that he may be able to use complaints about weekend work as an indicator of student perspectives on the amount of work they have to do. The selection of indicators for more abstract variables occurs in two ways: the observer may become aware of some very specific phenomenon first and later see that it may be used as an indicator of some larger class of phenomena; or he may have the larger problem in mind and search for specific indicators to use in studying it.

Whether he is defining problems or selecting concepts and indicators, the researcher at this stage is using his data only to speculate about possibilities. Further operations at later stages may force him to discard most of the provisional hypotheses. Nevertheless, problems of evidence arise even at this point, for the researcher must assess the individual items on which his speculations are based in order not to waste time tracking down false leads. We shall eventually need a systematic statement of canons to be applied to individual items of evidence. Lacking such a statement, let us consider some commonly used tests. (The observer typically applies these tests as seems reasonable to him during this and the succeeding stage in the field. In the final stage, they are used more systematically in an overall assessment of the total evidence for a given conclusion.)

The Credibility of Informants. Many items of evidence consist of statements by members of the group under study about some event which has occurred or is in process. Thus, medical students make statements about faculty behavior which form part of the basis for conclusions about faculty-student realtions. These cannot be taken at face value; nor can they be dismissed as valueless. In the first place, the observer can use the statement as evidence *about the event,* if he takes care to evaluate it by the criteria an historian uses in examining a personal document.[6] Does the informant have reason to lie or conceal some of what he sees as the truth? Does vanity or expediency lead him to mis-state his own role in an event or his attitude toward it? Did he actually have an opportunity to witness the occurrence he describes or is hearsay the source of his knowledge? Do his feelings about the issues or persons under discussion lead him to alter his story in some way?

Secondly, even when a statement examined in this way proves to be seriously defective as an accurate report of an event, it may still provide useful evidence for a different kind of conclusion. Accepting the sociological proposition that an individual's statements and descriptions of events are made from a perspective which is a function of his position in the group, the observer can interpret such statements and descriptions as indications of the individual's perspective on the point involved.

Volunteered or Directed Statements. Many items of evidence consist of informants' remarks to the observer about themselves or others or about something which has happened to them; these statements range from those which are a part of the running casual conversation of the group to those arising in a long intimate tete-a-tete between observer and informant. The researcher

[6]Cf. Louis Gottschalk, Clyde Kluckhohn, and Robert Angell, *The Use of Personal Documents in History, Anthropology, and Sociology*, New York: Social Science Research Council, 1945, pp. 15-27, 38-47.

assesses the evidential value of such statements quite differently, depending on whether they have been made independently of the observer (volunteered) or have been directed by a question from the observer. A freshman medical student might remark to the observer or to another student that he has more material to study than he has time to master; or the observer might ask, "Do you think you are being given more work than you can handle?", and receive an affirmative answer.

This raises an important question: to what degree is the informant's statement the same one he might give, either spontaneously or in answer to a question, in the absence of the observer? The volunteered statement seems likely to reflect the observer's preoccupations and possible biases less than one which is made in response to some action of the observer, for the observer's very question may direct the informant into giving an answer which might never occur to him otherwise. Thus, in the example above, we are more sure that the students are concerned about the amount of work given them when they mention this of their own accord than we are when the idea may have been stimulated by the observer asking the question.

The Observer-Informant-Group Equation. Let us take two extremes to set the problem. A person may say or do something when alone with the observer or when other members of the group are also present. The evidential value of an observation of this behavior depends on the observer's judgment as to whether the behavior is equally likely to occur in both situations. On the one hand, an informant may say and do things when alone with the observer that accurately reflect his perspective but which would be inhibited by the presence of the group. On the other hand, the presence of others may call forth behavior which reveals more accurately the person's perspective but would not be enacted in the presence of the observer alone. Thus, students in their clinical years may express deeply "idealistic" sentiments about medicine when alone with the observer, but behave and talk in a very "cynical" way when surrounded by fellow students. An alternative to judging one or the other of these situations as more reliable is to view each datum as valuable in itself, but with respect to different conclusions. In the example above, we might conclude that students have "idealistic" sentiments but that group norms may not sanction their expression.[7]

In assessing the value of items of evidence, we must also take into account the observer's role in the group. For the way the subjects of his study define that role affects what they will tell him or let him see. If the observer carries on his research incognito, participating as a full-fledged member of the group, he will be privy to knowledge that would normally be shared by such a member and might be hidden from an outsider. He could properly interpret his own experience as that of a hypothetical "typical" group member. On the other hand, if he is known to be a researcher, he must learn how group members define him and in particular whether or not they believe that certain kinds of information and events should be kept hidden from him. He can interpret evidence more accurately when the answers to these questions are known.

[7] See further, Howard S. Becker, "Interviewing Medical Students," *American Journal of Sociology*, 62 (September, 1956), pp. 199-201.

CHECKING THE FREQUENCY AND DISTRIBU-
TION OF PHENOMENA

The observer, possessing many provisional problems, concepts, and indicators, now wishes to know which of these are worth pursuing as major foci of his study. He does this, in part, by discovering if the events that prompted their development are typical and widespread, and by seeing how these events are distributed among categories of people and organizational sub-units. He reaches conclusions that are essentially quantitative, using them to describe the organization he is studying.

Participant observations have occasionally been gathered in standardized form capable of being transformed into legitimate statistical data.[8] But the exigencies of the field usually prevent the collection of data in such a form as to meet the assumptions of statistical tests, so that the observer deals in what have been called "quasi-statistics."[9] His conclusions, while implicitly numerical, do not require precise quantification. For instance, he may conclude that members of freshmen medical fraternities typically sit together during lectures while other students sit in less stable smaller groupings. His observations may indicate such a wide disparity between the two groups in this respect that the inference is warranted without a standardized counting operation. Occasionally, the field situation may permit him to make similar observations or ask similar questions of many people, systematically searching for quasi-statistical support for a conclusion about frequency or distribution.

In assessing the evidence for such a conclusion the observer takes a cue from his statistical colleagues. Instead of arguing that a conclusion is either totally true or false, he decides, if possible, how *likely* it is that his conclusion about the frequency or distribution of some phenomenon is an accurate quasi-statistic, just as the statistician decides, on the basis of the varying values of a correlation coefficient or a significance figure, that his conclusion is more or less likely to be accurate. The kind of evidence may vary considerably and the degree of the observer's confidence in the conclusion will vary accordingly. In arriving at this assessment, he makes use of some of the criteria described above, as well as those adopted from quantitative techniques.

Suppose, for example, that the observer concludes that medical students share the perspective that their school should provide them with the clinical experience and the practice in techniques necessary for a general practitioner. His confidence in the conclusion would vary according to the nature of the evidence, which might take any of the following forms: (1) *Every* member of the group said, *in response to a direct question,* that this was the way he looked at the matter. (2) *Every* member of the group *volunteered* to an observer that this was how he viewed the matter. (3) *Some given proportion* of the group's members either *answered* a direct question or *volunteered* the information that he shared this perspective, but none of the others was asked or volunteered information on the subject. (4) Every member of the group was asked or

---

[8] See Peter M. Blau, "Co-operation and Competition in a Bureaucracy," *American Journal of Sociology*, 59 (May, 1954), pp. 530-535.

[9] See the discussion of quasi-statistics in Lazarsfeld and Barton, "Some Functions of Qualitative Analysis . . .," *op. cit.*, pp. 346-348.

volunteered information, but *some given proportion said* they viewed the matter from the differing perspective of a prospective specialist. (5) No one was asked questions or volunteered information on the subject, but *all members were observed to engage in behavior* or to make other statements from which the analyst *inferred* that the general practitioner perspective was being used by them as a basic, though unstated, premise. For example, all students might have been observed to complain that the University Hospital received too many cases of rare diseases that general practitioners rarely see. (6) *Some given proportion* of the group *was observed* using the general practitioner perspective as a basic premise in their activities, but *the rest of the group* was not observed engaging in such activities. (7) *Some proportion of the group was observed* engaged in activities implying the general practitioner perspective while *the remainder* of the group was observed engaged in activities implying the perspective of the prospective specialist.

The researcher also takes account of the possibility that his observations may give him evidence of different kinds on the point under consideration. Just as he is more convinced if he has many items of evidence than if he has a few, so he is more convinced of a conclusion's validity if he has *many kinds* of evidence.[10] For instance, he may be especially persuaded that a particular norm exists and affects group behavior if the norm is not only described by group members but also if he observes events in which the norm can be "seen" to operate—if, for example, students tell him that they are thinking of becoming general practitioners and he also observes their complaints about the lack of cases of common diseases in University Hospital.

The conclusiveness which comes from the convergence of several kinds of evidence reflects the fact that separate varieties of evidence can be reconceptualized as deductions from a basic proposition which have now been verified in the field. In the above case, the observer might have deduced the desire to have experience with cases like those the general practitioner treats from the desire to practice that style of medicine. Even though the deduction is made after the fact, confirmation of it buttresses the argument that the general practitioner perspective is a group norm.

It should be remembered that these operations, when carried out in the field, may be so interrupted because of imperatives of the field situation that they are not carried on as systematically as they might be. Where this is the case, the overall assessment can be postponed until the final stage of postfield work analysis.

CONSTRUCTION OF SOCIAL SYSTEM MODELS

The final stage of analysis in the field consists of incorporating individual findings into a generalized model of the social system or organization under study or some part of the organization.[11] The concept of social system is a basic

---

[10] See Alvin W. Gouldner, *Patterns of Industrial Bureaucracy*, Glencoe, Ill.: Free Press, 1954, pp. 247-269.

[11] The relation between theories based on the concept of social system and participant observation was pointed out to me by Alvin W. Gouldner. See his "Some Observations on Systematic Theory, 1945-55," in Hans L. Zetterberg, editor, *Sociology in the United States*

intellectual tool of modern sociology. The kind of participant observation discussed here is related directly to this concept, explaining particular social facts by explicit reference to their involvement in a complex of interconnected variables that the observer constructs as a theoretical model of the organization. In this final stage, the observer designs a descriptive model which best explains the data he has assembled.

The typical conclusion of this stage of the research is a statement about a set of complicated interrelations among many variables. Although some progress is being made in formalizing this operation through use of factor analysis and the relational analysis of survey data,[12] observers usually view currently available statistical techniques as inadequate to express their conceptions and find it necessary to use words. The most common kinds of conclusions at this level include:

1. Complex statements of the necessary and sufficient conditions for the existence of some phenomenon. The observer may conclude, for example, that medical students develop consensus about limiting the amount of work they will do because (a) they are faced with a large amount of work, (b) they engage in activities which create communication channels between all members of the class, and (c) they face immediate dangers in the form of examinations set by the faculty.

2. Statements that some phenomenon is an "important" or "basic" element in the organization. Such conclusions, when elaborated, usually point to the fact that this phenomenon exercises a persistent and continuing influence on diverse events. The observer might conclude that the ambition to become a general practitioner is "important" in the medical school under study, meaning that many particular judgments and choices are made by students in terms of this ambition and many features of the school's organization are arranged to take account of it.

3. Statements identifying a situation as an instance of some process or phenomenon described more abstractly in sociological theory. Theories posit relations between many abstractly defined phenomena, and conclusions of this kind imply that relationships posited in generalized form hold in this particular instance. The observer, for example, may state that a cultural norm of the medical students is to express a desire to become a general practitioner; in so doing, he in effect asserts that the sociological theory about the functions of norms and the processes by which they are maintained which he holds to be true in general is true in this case.

In reaching such types of conclusions, the observer characteristically begins by constructing models of parts of the organization as he comes in contact with them, discovers concepts and problems, and the frequency and distribution of the phenomena these call to his attention. After constructing a model specifying the relationships among various elements of this part of the organization, the observer seeks greater accuracy by successively refining the model to take

───────────
of America, Paris: UNESCO, 1956, pp. 34-42; and "Theoretical Requirements of the Applied Social Sciences," *American Sociological Review,* 22 (February, 1957), pp. 92-102.
    [12] See Alvin W. Gouldner, "Cosmopolitans and Locals: Toward an Analysis of Latent Social Roles," *Administrative Science Quarterly,* 2 (December, 1957), pp. 281-306, and 3 (March, 1958), pp. 444-480; and James Coleman, "Relational Analysis: The Study of Social Structure with Survey Methods," mimeographed.

account of evidence which does not fit his previous formulation;[13] by searching for negative cases (items of evidence which run counter to the relationships hypothesized in the model) which might force such revision; and by searching intensively for the interconnections *in vivo* of the various elements he has conceptualized from his data. While a provisional model may be shown to be defective by a negative instance which crops up unexpectedly in the course of the field work, the observer may infer what kinds of evidence would be likely to support or to refute his model and may make an intensive search for such evidence.[14]

After the observer has accumulated several partial-models of this kind, he seeks connections between them and thus begins to construct an overall model of the entire organization. An example from our study shows how this operation is carried on during the period of field work. (The reader will note, in this example, how use is made of findings typical of earlier stages of analysis.)

When we first heard medical students apply the term "crock" to patients we made an effort to learn precisely what they meant by it. We found, through interviewing students about cases both they and the observer had seen, that the term referred in a derogatory way to patients with many subjective symptoms but no discernible physical pathology. Subsequent observations indicated that this usage was a regular feature of student behavior and thus that we should attempt to incorporate this fact into our model of student-patient behavior. The derogatory character of the term suggested in particular that we investigate the reasons students disliked these patients. We found that this dislike was related to what we discovered to be the students' perspective on medical school: the view that they were in school to get experience in recognizing and treating those common diseases most likely to be encountered in general practice. "Crocks," presumably having no disease, could furnish no such experience. We were thus led to specify connections between the student-patient relationship and the student's view of the purpose of his professional education. Questions concerning the genesis of this perspective led to discoveries about the organization of the student body and communication among students, phenomena which we had been assigning to another part-model. Since "crocks" were also disliked because they gave the students no opportunity to assume medical responsibility, we were able to connect this aspect of the student-patient relationship with still another tentative model of the value system and hierarchical organization of the school, in which medical responsibility plays an important role.

Again, it should be noted that analysis of this kind is carried on in the field as time permits. Since the construction of a model is the analytic operation most closely related to the observer's techniques and interests he usually spends a great deal of time thinking about these problems. But he is usually unable to be as systematic as he would like until he reaches the final stage of analysis.

FINAL ANALYSIS AND THE PRESENTATION OF RESULTS

The final systematic analysis, carried on after the field work is completed,

[13] Note again the resemblance to analytic induction.
[14] See Alfred Lindesmith's discussion of this principle in "Comment on W. S. Robinson's

consists of rechecking and rebuilding models as carefully and with as many safeguards as the data will allow. For instance, in checking the accuracy of statements about the frequency and distribution of events, the researcher can index and arrange his material so that every item of information is accessible and taken account of in assessing the accuracy of any given conclusion. He can profit from the observation of Lazarsfeld and Barton that the "analysis of 'quasi-statistical data' can probably be made more systematic than it has been in the past, if the logical structure of quantitative research at least is kept in mind to give general warnings and directions to the qualitative observer."[15]

An additional criterion for the assessment of this kind of evidence is the state of the observer's conceptualization of the problem at the time the item of evidence was gathered. The observer may have his problem well worked out and be actively looking for evidence to test an hypothesis, or he may not be as yet aware of the problem. The evidential value of items in his field notes will vary accordingly, the basis of consideration being the likelihood of discovering negative cases of the proposition he eventually uses the material to establish. The best evidence may be that gathered in the most unthinking fashion, when the observer has simply recorded the item although it has no place in the system of concepts and hypotheses he is working with at the time, for there might be less bias produced by the wish to substantiate or repudiate a particular idea. On the other hand, a well-formulated hypothesis makes possible a deliberate search for negative cases, particularly when other knowledge suggests likely areas in which to look for such evidence. This kind of search requires advanced conceptualization of the problem, and evidence gathered in this way might carry greater weight for certain kinds of conclusions. Both procedures are relevant at different stages of the research.

In the post field work stage of analysis, the observer carries on the model building operation more systematically. He considers the character of his conclusions and decides on the kind of evidence that might cause their rejection, deriving further tests by deducing logical consequences and ascertaining whether or not the data support the deductions. He considers reasonable alternative hypotheses and whether or not the evidence refutes them.[16] Finally, he completes the job of establishing interconnections between partial models so as to achieve an overall synthesis incorporating all conclusions.

After completing the analysis, the observer faces the knotty problem of how to present his conclusions and the evidence for them. Readers of qualitative research reports commonly and justifiably complain that they are told little or nothing about the evidence for conclusions or the operations by which the evidence has been assessed. A more adequate presentation of the data, of the

---

'The Logical Structure of Analytic Induction,' " *American Sociological Review*, 17 (August, 1952), pp. 492-493.

[15]"Some Functions of Qualitative Analysis . . .," *op. cit.*, p. 348.

[16]One method of doing this, particularly adapted to testing discrete hypotheses about change in individuals or small social units (though not in principle limited to this application), is "The Technique of Discerning," described by Mirra Komarovsky in Paul F. Lazarsfeld and Morris Rosenberg, editors, *The Language of Social Research*, Glencoe, Ill.: Free Press, 1955, pp. 449-457. See also the careful discussion of alternative hypotheses and the use of deduced consequences as further proof in Lindesmith, *Opiate Addiction, passim.*

research operations, and of the researcher's inferences may help to meet this problem.

But qualitative data and analytic procedures, in contrast to quantitative ones, are difficult to present adequately. Statistical data can be summarized in tables, and descriptive measures of various kinds and the methods by which they are handled can often be accurately reported in the space required to print a formula. This is so in part because the methods have been systematized so that they can be referred to in this shorthand fashion and in part because the data have been collected for a fixed, usually small, number of categories—the presentation of data need be nothing more than a report of the number of cases to be found in each category.

The data of participant observation do not lend themselves to such ready summary. They frequently consist of many different kinds of observations which cannot be simply categorized and counted without losing some of their value as evidence—for, as we have seen, many points need to be taken into account in putting each datum to use. Yet it is clearly out of the question to publish all the evidence. Nor is it any solution, as Kluckhohn has suggested for the similar problem of presenting life history materials,[17] to publish a short version and to make available the entire set of materials on microfilm or in some other inexpensive way; this ignores the problem of how to present *proof.*

In working over the material on the medical school study a possible solution to this problem, with which we are experimenting, is a description of the natural history of our conclusions, presenting the evidence as it came to the attention of the observer during the successive stages of his conceptualization of the problem. The term "natural history" implies not the presentation of every datum, but only the characteristic forms data took at each stage of the research. This involves description of the form that data took and any significant exceptions, taking account of the canons discussed above, in presenting the various statements of findings and the inferences and conclusions drawn from them. In this way, evidence is assessed as the substantive analysis is presented. The reader would be able, if this method were used, to follow the details of the analysis and to see how and on what basis any conclusion was reached. This would give the reader, as do present modes of statistical presentation, opportunity to make his own judgment as to the adequacy of the proof and the degree of confidence to be assigned to conclusion.

CONCLUSION

I have tried to describe the analytic field work characteristic of participant observation, first, in order to bring out the fact that the technique consists of something more than merely immersing oneself in data and "having insights". The discussion may also serve to stimulate those who work with this and similar techniques to attempt greater formalization and systematization of the various operations they use, in order that qualitative research may become more a "scientific" and less an "artistic" kind of endeavor. Finally, I have proposed that new modes of reporting results be introduced, so that the reader is given greater access to the data and procedures on which conclusions are based.

[17]Gottschalk, Kluckhohn, and Angell, *op. cit.*, pp. 150-156.

A SET OF CATEGORIES FOR THE ANALYSIS OF
SMALL GROUP INTERACTION

Robert F. Bales

In a recent review of the state of research in the field of small groups, Edward Shils makes some remarks which aptly point up the problem to which this paper is addressed:

"Because problems are dimly 'felt,' because they are neither related to a general theory of behavior on the one side, nor rigorously connected with the categories and indices to be chosen for observation on the other, the results of the research can very seldom become part of the cumulative movement of truth which constitutes the growth of scientific knowledge. When concrete indices (and classifications) are not clearly related to the variables of a general theory of human behavior in society, they tend to be *ad hoc*. Under these conditions they are only with difficulty, applicable, i.e., translatable into another concrete situation by an investigator who seeks to confirm, revise, or disconfirm the previously 'established' proposition."[1]

Probably most of us have some difficulty in thinking of a session between a psychiatrist and patient, a corner boy's gang in a political huddle, and a staff conference of business executives as comparable within a single frame of reference. It is probably more difficult, for example, than thinking of the social systems of China, of Bali, and the United States as legitimate objects for comparative analysis. At least the latter three constitute full scale, and in some sense, complete social systems.

What do the former three groups have in common? They are small face-to-face groups. If we call them social systems, we shall have to say that they are partial, as well as microscopic social systems. To place a slightly different emphasis, it can be said that they are systems of human interaction. At this degree of abstraction there is no necessary incongruity in comparing them with each other, or with full-scale social systems. Both small groups and complete societies can be viewed as types of interaction systems, even though one is tremendously more inclusive than the other. If this point of view turns out to be excessively formal or abstract, we may have to retreat to less generalized frames of reference.

To take the more hopeful view, it may very well be that one of the main contributions of the study of small groups will be an expanding of the range of available empirical data in such a way as to force our theory of social systems to

Reprinted with permission of the author and the publisher, The American Sociological Association, from the *American Sociological Review*, Vol. 15 (1950), 257-63.

Paper read at the annual meeting of the American Sociological Society held in New York, December 28-30, 1949.

The development of the method reported here has been made possible through the support of the Laboratory of Social Relations, Harvard University.

[1] Edward Shils, *The Present State of American Sociology*, Glencoe, Illinois: The Free Press, 1948, p. 45.

a more general and powerful level of abstraction. If the theory of social systems has been generalized and strengthened by the necessity of making it applicable to a range of full-scale social systems, non-literate as well as literate, Eastern as well as Western, then there is at least the possibility that it will be further strengthened by the necessity of making it applicable up and down the scale from large to small.

However this may be, the present set of categories was developed with this hope, and took its initial point of departure from a body of theory about the structure and dynamics of full-scale social systems. This will not be immediately apparent in viewing the set of categories, nor can it be spelled out to any satisfactory degree in this article. A manual dealing with both the theoretical and practical aspects of the method for those who may wish to apply it in their own research has recently been published.[2] The present paper will give only a simplified introductory description of the method and some of its possible uses.

DESCRIPTION OF THE METHOD

The method is called interaction process analysis. It is a type of content analysis in the basic sense, but the type of content which it attempts to abstract from the raw material of observation is the type of problem-solving revelance of each act for the total on-going process. Hence it has seemed less confusing to refer to what we are doing as "process analysis" rather than as "content analysis."

The heart of the method is a way of classifying behavior act by act, as it occurs in small face-to-face groups, and a series of ways of analyzing the data to obtain indices descriptive of group process, and derivatively, of factors influencing that process. The set of categories as it actually appears on the observation form is shown under the twelve numbers in Chart I. The outer brackets and labels do not appear on the observation form, but constitute a part of the mental set of the observer. The twelve observation categories are numbered from the top down, but are arranged in a series of complementary pairs proceeding from the center pair, 6 and 7, outward. The phrases and terms within the numbered categories are only catch-phrases designed to be concretely descriptive of the implied theoretical content of the categories in their usual forms. Actually there are extended definitions of each of the categories, and the central meaning of each is given by its position in the frames of reference to which they are all related as indicated by the labeled brackets on the Chart.

The set of twelve categories (and the actual behavior which is classified under them) are brought into working relation to other bodies of theory[3] in terms of the frame of reference. The key assumption which provides this articulation is the notion that all organized and at least partially cooperative systems of human interaction, from the smallest to the most inclusive, and of whatever concrete

[2] Robert F. Bales, *Interaction Process Analysis: A Method for the Study of Small Groups.* Cambridge, Massachusetts: Addison-Wesley Press, 1950.

[3] More specifically, theory applying to larger social systems, and perhaps also theory applying to personality. There seems to be no particular incongruity in thinking of the personality as an interaction system, if we understand by this, not a system of "persons," but a system of interdependent acts or potential acts. This, in fact, seems to me to be the character of much of contemporary personality theory.

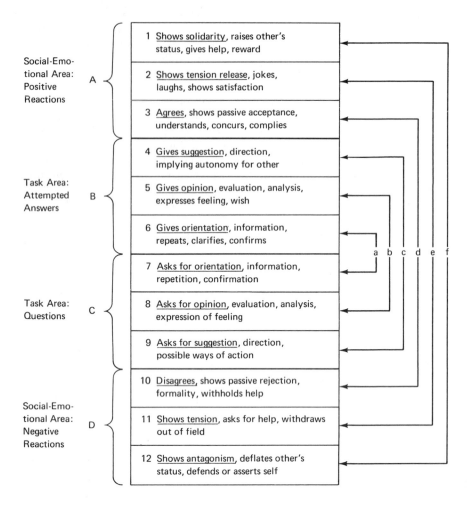

CHART. I. The System of Categories Used in Observation and Their Relation to Major Frames of Reference.

Key:

a. Problems of orientation   c. Problems of control   e. Problems of tension-management
b. Problems of evaluation   d. Problems of decision   f. Problems of integration

variety, may be approached for scientific analysis by abstracting from the events which go on within them in such a way as to relate the consequences of these events to a set of concepts formulating what are hypothetically called "functional problems of interaction systems."

For purposes of the present set of categories we postulate six interlocking functional problems which are logically applicable to any concrete type of interaction system. As indicated in Chart I, these are in one-word terms: problems of orientation, evaluation, control, decision, tension-management, and integration. These terms are all related to a hypothetical conception of an over-arching problem-solving sequence of interaction between two or more persons. As a concrete first approximation we may find it helpful to think of the functional problems as related in an order of "stages" or "steps" in a problem-solving sequence, as their order suggests. Actually this is an over-simplified view. However, in order to illustrate the notion of stages as they may appear under certain conditions, let us take a short description of a fictional group meeting. The same example will serve to illustrate the method of scoring with the categories.

HOW THE SCORING IS DONE

Let us imagine we are observing a group of five persons who are meeting together to come to a decision about a point of policy in a project they are doing together. Three or four of the members have arrived, and while they wait they are laughing and joking together, exchanging pleasantries and "small talk" before getting down to business. The missing members arrive, and after a little more scattered conversation the chairman calls the meeting to order. Usually, though not necessarily, this is where the observer begins his scoring.

Stage 1. Emphasis on problems of orientation: (deciding what the situation is like). The chairman brings the meeting up to date with a few informal remarks. He says, "At the end of our last meeting we decided that we would have to consider our budget before laying out plans in greater detail." The observer, sitting with the observation form in front of him, looks over the list of twelve categories and decides that this remark is most relevant to the problem of orientation, and specifically that it takes the form of an "attempted answer" to this problem, and so he classifies it in Category 6, "Gives orientation, information, repeats, clarifies, confirms." The observer has already decided that he will designate the chairman by the number 1, and each person around the table in turn by the numbers 2, 3, 4, and 5. The group as a whole will be designated by the symbol 0. This remark was made by the chairman and was apparently addressed to the group as a whole, so the observer writes down the symbols 1-0 in one of the spaces following Category 6 on the observation form.

In this one operation, the observer has thus isolated a unit of speech or process which he considers a proper unit for classification, has classified it, identified the member who performed the act, and the person or persons to whom it was directed. If he were writing on a moving tape instead of a paper form, as we do for some purposes,[4] he would also have identified the exact position of the act in sequence with all others. In practice we find that we obtain from 10 to 20 scores per minute in keeping up with most interaction, and that this speed is not excessive for a trained observer.

As the chairman finishes his remark, Member 2 asks the chairman, "Has anybody gone over our expenditures to date?" The observer decides that this is a "question" indicating that a problem of orientation exists, and so should be classified in Category 7, "Asks for orientation, information, repetition, confirmation." He so records it by placing the symbols 2-1 in a box following this category. The chairman replies, "I have here a report prepared by Miss Smith on

[4]Robert F. Bales and Henry Gerbrands, "The Interaction Recorder; An Apparatus and Check List for Sequential Content Analysis of Social Interaction," *Human Relations*, Vol. I, No. 4, 1948.

the expenditures to date." The observer marks down the symbols I-2 under Category 6, as an "attempted answer" to the indicated problem of orientation. As the chairman goes over the report the observer continues to score, getting a good many scores in Categories 6 and 7, but also occasional scores in other categories.

Stage 2. Emphasis on problems of evaluation: (deciding what attitudes should be taken toward the situation). As the chairman finishes reviewing the items on the report he may ask, "Have we been within bounds on our expenditures so far?" The observer puts down a score under Category 8, "Asks for opinion, evaluation, analysis, expression of feeling." Member 3 says, "It seems to me that we have gone in pretty heavily for secretarial help." The observer puts down a score in Category 5, "Gives opinion, evaluation, analysis, expresses feeling." Member 4 comes in with the remark, "Well I don't know. It seems to me ..." The observer puts down the symbols 4-3 in Category 10, "Disagrees, shows passive rejection, formality, witholds help," and continues with scores in Category 5 as Member 4 makes his argument. The discussion continues to revolve around the analysis of expenditures, with a good many scores falling in Category 5, but also in others, particularly Categories 10 and 3, and interspersed with a number in Categories 6 and 7 as opinions are explained and supported.

Stage 3. Emphasis on problems of control: (deciding what to do about it). Finally the chairman says, "Well a little more than half our time is gone." The observer scores 1-0 in Category 6. "Do you want to go ahead and decide whether we should buy that piece of equipment or ..." The observer scores 1-0 in Category 9, "Asks for suggestion, direction, possible ways of action." Member 2 says, "I think we should get it." The observer scores 2-0 in Category 4, "Gives suggestion, direction, implying autonomy for other." As Member 2 begins to support his suggestion, Member 3 breaks in with a counter argument, and the discussion begins to grow more heated.

The observer begins to have trouble in keeping up as the members are talking more rapidly and some remarks are left unfinished. He does not forget to keep scanning the group, however, and presently he notices that Member 5, who has said little up to this point, sighs heavily and begins to examine his fingernails. The observer puts down a score under Category 11, "Shows tension, asks for help, withdraws out of field." He enters this score as 5-y, since he has decided ahead of time to use the symbol y to stand for "self," and to use it when activity is directed toward the self, or is expressive and non-focal, that is, not directed toward other members.

Meantime, Member 3, the chronic objector, comes through with a remark directed at Member 2, "Well, I never did agree about hiring that deadhead secretary. All she's got is looks, but I guess that's enough for Joe." The others laugh at this. The observer scores the first and second remarks under Category 12, "Shows antagonism, deflates other's status, defends or asserts self." The laugh which follows is scored in Category 2, "Shows tension release, jokes, laughs, shows satisfaction." In this case the score is written 0-3, all to Member 3.

At this point Member 5 comes in quietly to sum up the argument, and by the time he finishes several heads are nodding. The observer scores both the nods and the audible agreements in Category 3, "Agrees, shows passive acceptance, understands, concurs, complies." The chairman says, "Then it looks like we are in agreement." The observer scores in Category 6, and scores the answering nods in Category 3. Member 3, the chronic objector, who is also the chronic joker, comes in with a joke at this point, and the joking and laughing continue for a minute or two, each member extending the joke a little. The observer continues to score in Category 2 as long as this activity continues. As the members pick up their things one of them says, "Well, I think we got through that in good shape. Old Bill certainly puts in the right word at the right time, doesn't he." The observer marks down two scores under Category 1, "Shows solidarity, raises other's status, gives help, reward," and after a few more similar remarks the meeting breaks up.

THE POSSIBILITY OF EMPIRICAL NORMS

The foregoing is a fictional example, designed to illustrate the nature of the scoring operation, as well as a kind of hypothetical sequence of stages which may occur under certain conditions. To summarize, we might say that during the course of this meeting there were a series of "phases" portrayed, during which one or more of the functional problems included in our conceptual framework received more than its usual share of attention. The temporal order of these phases in this fictional example follows in a rough way the logical order in which we arrange the categories on the observation form in pairs from the center line outward, that is, as dealing with problems of orientation, evaluation, control, and then in rapid order, a special emphasis on final decision, tension reduction, and reintegration. Each of the major functional problems has been made into an implicit "agenda topic."

The categories of activity as classified by the present system are assumed to bear a functional relation to each other similar to the relation of the phases in the meeting just portrayed. The example has been constructed so that in its phases the relations of the categories to each other are "written large," to borrow an idea from Plato. Hence it is relevant to ask what degree the notion of phases on the larger scale is actually to be taken as an empirical description rather than as a logical model. It is important to emphasize in answer to this question that we do not assume nor believe that all group meetings actually proceed in just this way. One of the thorniest problems in the history of thinking about the process of small groups is whether or not, or in what sense there may be a series of "steps" or "stages" in group problem solving. Data will later be published which indicate that under *certain conditions,* which must be carefully specified, a group problem-solving process essentially like that sketched above, does tend to appear. The data indicate that the sequence described is a kind of average sequence for problem-solving groups, that is, an empirical norm. It further appears that departures from the average picture can be used as diagnostic indicators of the nature of the conditions under which interaction takes place.

Similarly, it appears that there are empirical uniformities in the way activities are distributed between persons. We have some data which indicate that, on the average, if we rank order participants according to the total number of acts they originate, they will then also stand in rank order as to (1) the number of acts they originate to the group as a whole (to 0), (2) the number of acts they originate to specific other members of the group, and (3) the number of acts they receive from all other members of the group. In addition, (4) each person in the rank order series addresses a slightly larger amount of activity to the person just above him in the series than the person above addresses to him, with the top person addressing the group as a whole to a disproportionate degree. It seems likely that these uniformities can be tied together in a more comprehensive theory, and that departures from this average picture can be used as a diagnostic indicator of the nature of the conditions under which interaction takes place. Data on this problem will be published later.

Similarly, ignoring time sequence and the specific persons who initiate or receive acts, empirical uniformities appear in the gross frequency with which each category of activity tends to occur. Preliminary data on these uniformities are given below.

FREQUENCY OF OCCURRENCE OF EACH TYPE OF ACTIVITY

We have available for this tabulation some 23,000 scores in terms of the present twelve categories, from observations of groups of different sizes and kinds, ranging through nursery school children, high school and college students, married couples, college faculty discussions, etc., on tasks of widely different kinds. We do not know how badly biased this collection of scores may be as a

TABLE I. Raw Scores Obtained on All Interaction Observed to Date, Percentage Rates, and Suggested Limits, by Categories

| Category | Raw Scores | Percentage | Suggested Limits for Inspection of Profiles* | |
			Lower	Upper
1	246	1.0	0.0	5.0
2	1675	7.3	3.0	14.0
3	2798	12.2	6.0	20.0
4	1187	5.2	2.0	11.0
5	6897	30.0	21.0	40.0
6	4881	21.2	14.0	30.0
7	1229	5.4	2.0	11.0
8	809	3.5	1.0	9.0
9	172	.8	0.0	5.0
10	1509	6.6	3.0	13.0
11	1009	4.4	1.0	10.0
12	558	2.4	0.0	7.0

*Suggested limits shown have been established for each category by use of binomial confidence limits given in Snedecor, *Statistical Methods,* 1946, p. 4, with p equal "Percentage of total" and n equal 100. This provides relatively wider ranges for the smaller values and although such conventions do not properly reflect the multinomial character of the variation, they provide a first approximation for present purposes.

sample of something larger. They are simply all of the raw scores we have to date on all of the groups and tasks we happen to have observed for a variety of reasons. The scorings were made by the present author. The general problems of reliability are treated in the manual mentioned above.[5] Very briefly it may be said that satisfactory reliability has been obtained between observers, but requires intensive training which should be regarded as an integral part of the method.

Table 1 shows the raw scores and their percentage distribution (or rates) in the twelve categories. In order to have certain conventional limits for inspection of the variability of particular profiles we have employed an external criterion rather than utilize the variance of our samples, which are known to be quite heterogeneous. Our experience indicates that when the rate for a given category on a particular profile is outside the range suggested in Table 1, we are usually able to connect the deviation with some more or less obvious source of variation in the conditions under which the interaction took place. For example, we find that a profile of nursery school children at free play is over the suggested limits on showing solidarity and showing antagonism, on giving direct suggestions and on disagreement, and is under the limits on asking for opinion, giving orientation, and giving opinion. A group of high school boys in group discussion is over the limits on laughing and joking, and under the limits on giving orientation. A group of faculty members planning a thesis problem with a graduate student is within the limits on all categories. Pending the development of a satisfactory typology of groups, tasks, and other sources of variation, and the accumulation of more experience, this arbitrary procedure for detecting "significant variations" may serve a useful purpose.

APPLICABILITY OF THE METHOD

Verbal interaction accounts for the largest part of the scores, but the categories apply to non-verbal interaction as well. Groups of manageable size for the method fall in the range between two and perhaps twenty, but there is no definitely established top limit—the top manageable size depends upon the character of the interaction. The method is most easily applied in groups where the attention of the members tends to focus in turn on single speakers or members, as in most discussion groups. Hence it might be said to apply to groups small enough so that each member potentially takes into account the reactions of each of the others.

In concrete terms, the groups which one might be able to study with the method are very diverse. They would include a series of groups concerned primarily with substantive problems external to their own process, such as discussion groups, planning groups, policy forming and executive committees, boards and panels, diagnostic councils in clinical work, seminars and classroom groups, teams and work groups, certain kinds of problem-solving groups in experimental social psychology and sociology, etc. In addition, there are certain groups with a primary focus on their own procedure in an impersonal way, for training purposes, such as those formed for training in basic human relations

[5] See footnote 2, above.

skills, now an important branch of small group research. In a less impersonal way, there are large numbers of small groups which have the interaction or interpersonal relations of the members as a primary focus, whatever their concern with substantive external problems. These would include family and household groups, children's play groups, adolescent gangs, adult cliques, social and recreational clubs, and small associations of a great many kinds. Finally there are groups which might be said to have a primary focus on problems of personal content or experience of members, such as therapy or confessional groups of various kinds, and groups of two, such as therapist and patient, counselor and client, interviewer and interviewee, and a number of others in the general class of professional specialist and client.

Some of these types of groups have been studied with the present method or others similar to it. Some of them are unexplored as yet. Taken together, however, the total range of possible types of groups constitutes a challenging array. If interaction in groups of the diverse sorts mentioned can be brought within the range of a single frame of reference, and can be made to yield data by the same method of analysis, we should be some distance along toward meeting the difficulties which Shils indicates in the comments at the beginning of this paper.

INTERVIEWER ROLE PERFORMANCE: A FURTHER NOTE ON BIAS IN THE INFORMATION INTERVIEW

J. Allen Williams, Jr.

There is some evidence that bias is likely to occur in the interview when there is social distance between interviewer and respondent.[1] Status distance and

Reprinted with the permission of the author and the publisher from *The Public Opinion Quarterly*, Vol. 32 (1968), 287-94.

The research reported in this paper was made possible by grants from the National Institute of Mental Health (MPW-15, 132) and Rockefeller Foundation. This research was done as part of a larger project being conducted by the Institute for Research in Social Science of the University of North Carolina on The Changing Position of the Negro in the United States. The author wishes to express his gratitude to Daniel O. Price, Ruth Searles, Harry J. Crockett, Richard L. Simpson, and Charles Gordon for their help throughout the study. He also wishes to express appreciation to S. Dale McLemore and Charles M. Bonjean for their helpful comments on earlier drafts of this paper. Any errors in analysis or interpretation are the author's responsibility.

J. Allen Williams, Jr., is an Assistant Professor of Sociology at The University of Texas at Austin.

[1] In a previous paper the author reported findings from a study of bias in the information interview (J. Allen Williams, Jr., "Interviewer-Respondent Interaction: A Study of Bias in the Information Interview," *Sociometry*, Vol. 27, September 1964, pp. 338-352). On the basis of responses from 840 Negroes, race of interviewer was shown to be consistently associated with bias only when status distance between interviewer and respondent is great and when an interview question has high threat potential. Specifically, it was shown that middle-class white interviewers obtained significantly greater percentages of conservative

threatening questions may create a situation in which the respondent feels pressure to answer in the direction he believes will conform to the opinions or expectations of the interviewer.[2] This encourages the respondent to avoid the possible negative consequences of answering a question the "wrong" way.[3]

It seems likely that the role performance of the interviewer could either enhance or mitigate the biasing effects of status characteristics and potentially threatening questions. It has been suggested, for example, that the interviewer may be able to "alter the respondent's perception of the situation."[4] Two major role-performance characteristics have received extensive discussion in this respect.[5] First, it has been suggested that the interviewer should be able to establish good rapport.[6] By doing so he will be able to minimize or dispel the respondent's fears of the possible negative consequences of his answers. On the other hand, rapport may also produce a strain toward consensus on the subject matter of the interview schedule.[7] If the respondent is attracted to the interviewer, he may attempt to answer questions in agreement with his perception of the interviewer's opinion in order to maintain or even increase the reward value of the interaction.[8] In this case, then, the respondent is not so much attempting to avoid possible costs of the situation as he is attempting to maximize the rewards produced through the interaction. This source of bias may be reduced if the interviewer does not allow the respondent to perceive his own opinions toward the subject matter.[9] This does not prevent the respondent from guessing

responses from lower-status Negroes than did middle-class Negro interviewers. This occurred only for questions judged as highly threatening. A threatening question in this context is one for which a particular response would be either a behavioral or attitudinal violation of the norms prevailing in a racially segregated social system.

[2] That the interviewer's own opinions or expectations affect responses is not, of course, a new proposition. For example, see H. L. Smith and H. Hyman, "The Biasing Effect of Interviewer Expectations on Survey Results," *Public Opinion Quarterly*, Vol. 14, 1950, pp. 491-506, and D. F. Wyatt and D. T. Campbell, "A Study of Interviewer Bias as Related to Interviewer's Expectations and Own Opinions," *International Journal of Opinion and Attitude Research*, Vol. 4, 1950, pp. 77-83.

[3] Acquiescence of this sort was suggested by G. E. Lenski and J. C. Leggett, "Caste, Class, and Deference in the Research Interview," *American Journal of Sociology*, Vol. 65, March 1960, pp. 463-467.

[4] A. Kornhauser and P. Sheatsley, "Questionnaire Construction and Interview Procedure," in C. Selltiz, M. Jahoda, M. Deutsch, and S. Cook, *Research Methods in Social Relations*, New York, Holt, 1959, pp. 546-587.

[5] This, of course, does not mean that other behavioral characteristics are less important. There are such attributes as ability to obtain usable information, ability to obtain complete information, emotional stability, efficiency, etc. However, the two characteristics discussed below appear to be among the more important in relation to interviewer bias.

[6] The notion of rapport is discussed in almost all books and articles dealing with the interview. For extensive discussion, see S. A. Richardson, B. S. Dohrenwend, and D. Klein, *Interviewing: Its Forms and Functions*, New York, Basic Books, 1965, and R. L. Kahn and C. F. Cannell, *The Dynamics of Interviewing*, New York, Wiley, 1958.

[7] This notion has been empirically demonstrated in a number of other contexts. For example, see T. M. Newcomb, *The Acquaintance Process*, New York, Holt, Rinehart and Winston, 1961, and F. E. Emery, O. A. Oeser, and J. Tully, *Information, Decision and Action*, Melbourne, Australia, Melbourne University Press, 1957.

[8] Recent discussion of this notion, along with the idea of avoiding negative consequences, may be found in J. W. Thibaut and H. H. Kelley, *The Social Psychology of Groups*, New York, Wiley, 1959.

[9] Neutrality, or objectivity, has received extensive discussion in the literature. See the references listed in footnote 6 for discussion on this subject also.

the interviewer's opinions, but at least he will not be influenced by behavioral or verbal cues from him. The interviewer's ability to avoid giving cues to the respondent may be called "objectivity." Taking these two role-performance characteristics together, the general proposition is that the good interviewer should be able to establish rapport and also maintain objectivity.[10]

METHOD

An attempt was made to examine the effects of ability to establish rapport and objectivity, holding the threat potential of interview questions and the status distance between interviewer and respondent constant. Although the research design, including the measurement of status distance, threat potential of interview schedule questions, sampling procedures, and a complete listing of the interview schedule items used in this analysis, is presented in the author's previous report,[11] some points concerning the research design deserve mention here. The sample of Negro respondents was drawn from two predominantly rural areas and two urban areas in North Carolina. Both samples were area samples of Negro residential districts. Interviewers were randomly assigned to these areas. An adult member of each household in the selected area was interviewed. Each interviewer conducted half his interviews in an urban area and half in a rural area. Since there were not enough male interviewers for comparison of the possible sex effect on respondents, the male interviewers were dropped for this analysis. The interviewers were recruited from several sources, including wives of graduate students, schoolteachers, and graduate students. All interviewers received a five-day training course.

The two role-performance characteristics were measured by the Guilford-Zimmerman Temperament Survey.[12] The measure of objectivity was achieved by combining the measures of "objectivity" and "thoughtfulness."[13] The most appropriate measure of ability to establish rapport is called "personal relations." These measures of role performance are, of course, only presumptive evidence of actual behavior. However, this measuring instrument has been demonstrated to have high predictive validity in other settings.[14] Among the 9 white interviewers, 4 were classified as low and 5 as high on objectivity. On personal relations, 4 of the whites were classified as high and 5 as low. Among the 12 Negro interviewers, 4 were low and 8 were high on objectivity. Five of the Negroes were high on personal relations and 7 were low.

Given the notion that an interviewer who is low on objectivity will be more

[10]There have been criticisms of this proposition. See, for example, L. A. Dexter, "Role Relationships and Conceptions of Neutrality in Interviewing," *American Journal of Sociology*, Vol. 62, September 1956, pp. 153-164.

[11]Williams, *op. cit.*

[12]J. P. Guilford and W. S. Zimmerman, *The Guilford-Zimmerman Temperament Survey*, Beverly Hills, Calif., Sheridan Supply Company, 1949.

[13]Guilford and Zimmerman suggest that a very high   score on objectivity may mean that the person is totally insensitive. It is proposed that a high objectivity score should be balanced with a high score on thoughtfulness. One Negro interviewer who was very high on objectivity and quite low on thoughtfulness was not used for this portion of the study.

[14]For a listing of studies dealing with the Guilford-Zimmerman Temperament Survey see O. K. Buros, ed., *The Fifth Mental Measurements Yearbook*, Highland Park, N. J., Gryphon Press, 1959, pp. 65-66.

likely to give cues to the respondent, it was necessary to measure the opinions of the interviewers. Each completed the interview schedule as a questionnaire during the training period. All the interviewers expressed liberal orientations toward the questions concerned with race and race-related material.

Thus study provides no data that permit the direct measurement of the validity of responses. With equivalent subsamples, however, there is no reason to expect differences in responses (beyond sampling error) between respondents interviewed by different interviewers, if the responses are valid.[15] Thus, if differences in responses are found by role performance, they are believed to indicate interview bias.

FINDINGS[16]

Interviewers' objectivity and response bias. Interviewers were classified as being high or low on objectivity, and the percentages of responses in a conservative direction were computed for low-, medium-, and high-threat potential questions for each of five social-rank categories.[17]

No large or consistent differences by objectivity were found for any of the three highest social ranks of Negro respondents. Further, no large or consistent differences by objectivity were found for any of the low- or moderate-threat-potential questions for any of the five social ranks. However, consistent—and in some cases quite large—differences in percentages of respondents answering in a conservative direction were found by objectivity under conditions of high status distance (the two lowest ranks of respondents) for high-threat-potential questions.[18] Since no important differences in response patterns were found between the two lower ranks, these two groups were combined. As can be seen in Table 1, interviewers who are high on objectivity obtain larger percentages of conservative responses for all items but one with race of interviewer held constant. White interviewers who are high on objectivity obtain larger percentages of conservative responses than high-objectivity Negro

[15] There is very reasonable assurance that the subsamples interviewed by white and Negro interviewers are equivalent. An attempt was made to obtain equivalent subsamples for each interviewer. Several interviewers were eliminated from the analysis because they did not obtain sufficient numbers of respondents from the different social-rank categories. Among the remaining interviewers, the subsamples are roughly equivalent by rural-urban residence of respondents and sex ratio. Further, the social rank of the respondents is held constant.

[16] All the percentages reported in the findings are adjusted. Interviewers obtained different numbers of interviews, so that, for example, the percentage of respondents answering a question in a conservative direction for all interviewers high on objectivity would give some interviewers greater weight than others. The adjusted percentage is the arithmetic mean of the percentages of respondents answering in a conservative direction for the interviewers. This procedure gives each interviewer an equal weighting.

[17] One of the high-threat-potential items was eliminated for this part of the analysis because two of the interviewers did not obtain a sufficient number of responses for this item (a very arbitrary ten or more responses for the two lower social ranks).

[18] In reference to these comparisons and all following comparisons, the following point should be made. Some of the differences are quite small while others are quite large. There is no real way to determine how large a difference in percentages must be in order to consider it an important bias. This would doubtless depend on the purposes of the researcher. The demonstrated existence of bias does suggest, however, that errors in interpretation of data could have been made in some studies.

TABLE 1. Per Cent Conservative Responses by Negro Respondents of Low Social Rank to High-Threat-Potential Items, by Objectivity of Interviewers[a] (in adjusted per cents)

| | Objectivity of White Interviewers | | | Objectivity of Negro Interviewers | | |
Item	High	Low	Dif-ference	High	Low	Dif-ference
1. Disapprove of sit-ins	43.6	23.2	20.4	30.9	11.7	19.2
2. State that a Negro mother should send her daughter to a Negro school	74.0	56.0	18.0	67.0	52.2	14.8
3. State that it is not a good idea to make changes in the way our country is run	35.4	15.7	19.7	17.0	12.0	5.0
4. State that they do not read a Negro newspaper	76.6	85.5	-8.9	69.3	53.5	15.8
5. State that they do not read a daily newspaper	71.4	68.5	2.9	60.3	38.3	22.0
6. Want less than a college degree for son	54.6	38.2	16.4	39.4	30.0	9.4

[a]There were 9 white interviewers and approximately 137 respondents. There were 12 Negro interviewers and approximately 315 respondents.

interviewers. The same pattern can be seen among white and Negro interviewers who are low on objectivity and Negroes who are high on objectivity shows that for four of the six items the latter obtain larger percentages of responses in a *conservative* direction. This suggests that objectivity is not only related to interview bias but may be as significant as race of interviewer.

Interviewers' personal relations and response bias. Interviewers were classified as being high or low on personal relations, and the percentages of responses in a conservative direction were computed for low-, moderate-, and high-threat-potential questions for each of five social-rank categories. No large or consistent differences were found by personal relations for any of the questions for any of the social-rank categories.

Interviewers' objectivity, personal relations, and response bias. Table 2 shows the effect of personal relations with objectivity held constant. Among the Negro interviewers, for eleven of the twelve comparisons, those who are low on personal relations obtain the largest percentages of conservative responses. These data support the expectation discussed above. In a situation of good rapport the respondent attempts to answer questions in agreement with the interviewer. In this study the interviewers were liberal. Among white interviewers, however, the expectation is not supported. Indeed, for ten of the twelve comparisons, white interviewers who are high on personal relations obtain the larger percentages of conservative responses. Perhaps lower-status Negroes are suspicious of whites

TABLE 2.   Per Cent Conservative Responses by Negro Respondents of Low Social Rank to High-Threat-Potential Items, by Objectivity and Personal Relations of Interviewers[a] (in adjusted per cents)

Item[b]	Objectivity of White Interviewers		Objectivity of Negro Interviewers	
	High	Low	High	Low
Sit-ins:				
High personal relations	51.5	31.0	28.5	4.0
Low personal relations	38.3	15.5	33.3	14.3
School:				
High personal relations	75.5	58.5	58.5	50.0
Low personal relations	73.0	53.5	75.5	53.5
Changes:				
High personal relations	35.5	11.0	10.5	10.0
Low personal relations	33.3	19.0	23.5	12.6
Negro paper:				
High personal relations	77.5	95.5	65.7	52.0
Low personal relations	76.0	75.5	72.8	54.0
Education:				
High personal relations	44.5	50.0	34.0	17.0
Low personal relations	61.3	26.5	44.7	34.3
Daily paper:				
High personal relations	77.0	80.5	62.3	26.0
Low personal relations	67.7	56.5	58.3	42.3

[a]There were 9 white interviewers and approximately 137 respondents. There were 12 Negro interviewers and approximately 315 respondents. There is a slight variation in the number of respondents per interview-schedule item. Four Negro and 2 white interviewers were high on objectivity and personal relations, 4 Negroes and 3 whites were high on objectivity and low on personal relations, 1 Negro and 2 whites were low on objectivity and high on personal relations, and 3 Negroes and 2 whites were low on objectivity and personal relations.

[b]A more specific wording of each interview-schedule item is given in Table 1.

who are friendly in the interview situation. A friendly white person who enters a Negro's home and asks questions about race relations may be even more threatening than behavior following more conventional caste roles.

With the exception of white interviewers' personal relations, the expectations suggested at the outset of this note are fairly consistently supported. However, the combined effect of these role-performance characteristics is also of interest. Combining the two characteristics and using only a high-low categorization for each yields a fourfold classification. Although the number of interviewers for each category is very small, some speculation concerning these combinations is possible. It was suggested that low-objectivity interviewers will give cues as to their own attitudes. In this study, these cues should be liberal ones. If these interviewers also are able to create good rapport, then respondents will attempt to maximize the possible rewards from the interaction by answering in agreement with the interviewer. Thus, in this study, respondents should answer in a liberal direction. Hence, the expectation is that interviewers who are low on objectivity and high on personal relations will obtain the smallest percentages of conservative responses. Interviewers who are high on objectivity will presumably give few cues to their own attitudes. If these interviewers also are unable to establish good rapport, then the respondent's primary motivation will be to answer questions in the direction he believes will have the least likelihood of negative consequences. Generally, the safest response to a white interviewer is a conservative one. This is probably also true for the Negro interviewer. A respondent receiving no cues to the contrary may perceive a Negro interviewer as a representative of whites or as a person holding conservative views.[19] Since no liberal cues are forthcoming and since the interviewer also is inept at establishing good rapport, this may be taken as evidence of a conservative attitude. Hence, the expectation is that interviewers who are high on objectivity and low on personal relations will obtain the largest percentages of conservative responses.

Table 2 shows that among Negro interviewers the expectations are supported. Negro interviewers who are low on objectivity and high on personal relations have the smallest percentages of conservative responses for all high-threat-potential questions. Negro interviewers who are high on objectivity and low on personal relations have the largest percentages of conservative responses for five of the six questions. Among the white interviewers these expectations are not supported. Those who are low on both objectivity and personal relations obtain the smallest percentages for five of the six questions and the second smallest percentage for the other. No combination of the role-performance characteristics consistently obtains the largest percentages of conservative responses. However, interviewers who are high on objectivity and personal relations have the largest percentages for three of the questions and the second largest for two others.

Although it is purely speculative, some explanation for these unexpected findings may be offered. It was suggested above that a friendly white (high personal relations) may threaten a lower-status Negro by seeming out of character. The friendly white interviewer may be perceived as attempting to initiate interaction on an equalitarian basis, thus arousing the suspicions of the Negro. Consequently, whites who give no cues as to their own attitudes (high objectivity) and who are acting friendly may produce a situation in which the respondent feels threatened and perceives the safest response to be a conservative one. On the other hand, whites who are supplying liberal cues and who are acting friendly may create a confusing situation for the respondent. At any rate, larger proportions of respondents answer in a conservative direction to these interviewers than to those who are supplying liberal cues but are not as sociable.

---

[19] A plausible case could be made that lower-status Negroes would perceive middle-class Negroes as holding liberal attitudes. Consequently, they would choose a liberal answer if attempting either to obtain rewards from the interviewer or to avoid costs. However, if the Negro interviewer gave no cues about his own opinions, the respondent would have to guess. Since the interviewers were known by the respondents to be representing a predominantly white university and since the respondents did not know exactly what use their answers would be put to, it seems more likely that they would see a conservative answer as the safest response.

CONCLUSION

It was suggested at the outset of this note that the role performance of an interviewer could affect the influence of factors over which he has little or no direct control—status distance and the threat potential of interview questions. Although they are not always consistent with theoretical expectations, the findings from this study clearly demonstrate that the interviewer's role performance affects responses when these other factors are held constant. The crucial question that remains unanswered is which combination of factors minimizes bias. It is hoped that the findings presented in this note and the previous report will stimulate research attempting to answer this important question.

THE RELIABILITY AND VALIDITY OF INTERVIEW DATA OBTAINED FROM 59 NARCOTIC DRUG ADDICTS

John C. Ball

The question of the reliability and validity of interview data obtained from various deviant populations has been an issue of recurrent interest in the social sciences. Two contrary positions have been advanced: (*a*) Deviant groups, and especially those engaged in illegal behavior, are motivated to—and do—conceal or deny their proscribed behavior,[1] and (*b*) deviant subjects will, under appropriate research procedures, report their deviant actions.[2] The present report is restricted to an analysis of interview data obtained from a single deviant population, narcotic drug addicts.

The sample consists of fifty-nine Puerto Rican addicts who were formerly incarcerated at the U.S. Public Health Service Hospital at Lexington, Kentucky. This sample was drawn from a larger study population of the 242 patients admitted to the hospital from Puerto Rico between 1935 and 1962. Although considerable field, clinical, and institutional data were available with respect to the 242 follow-up subjects, the 59 addicts consisted of all those interviewed who had also been federal prisoners at the Lexington or Fort Worth hospitals. The remaining 183 subjects had either been voluntary patients at the hospital (*N* = 98) on whom FBI records could not be obtained or they were not interviewed (*N* = 85). One purpose of the follow-up study was to ascertain the post-hospital history of the former addict, including whether or not he had relapsed to drug use.

Reprinted with the permission of the author and the publisher, The University of Chicago Press, from the *American Journal of Sociology*, Vol. 72 (1967), 650-54.

[1] Howard Becker, *Outsiders* (New York: Free Press, 1963), pp. 168-70; William Butler Eldridge, *Narcotics and the Law* (New York: American Bar Association, 1962), p. 26.
[2] Alfred C. Kinsey *et al., Sexual Behavior in the Human Male* (Philadelphia: W. B. Saunders Co., 1948), chaps. i-iv; Meyer H. Diskind and George Klonsky, *Recent Developments in the Treatment of Paroled Offenders Addicted to Narcotic Drugs* (Albany: New York State Division of Parole, 1964), pp. 29-30, 108.

The procedure employed in ascertaining the reliability and validity of the interview data consisted of a comparison of interview items with: (a) clinical and administrative records of the hospital, (b) FBI arrest records, and (c) urine samples obtained from the patient. A brief description of each of these sources of information is pertinent.

The interview schedule consisted of six pages of questions pertaining to the addiction, employment, and criminal history of the former patient. Most of these interviews were obtained in Puerto Rico by an experienced interviewer;[3] in the case that the addict returned to the Lexington hospital after 1962, he was interviewed upon re-admission. The clinical and administrative records of the Lexington hospital contain quite voluminous, but often non-comparable, information. Commonly included in these patients' records were the following: the physician's examination, including drug diagnosis; psychiatric diagnosis; criminal history and pre-sentence report; family and employment data; and treatment progress while hospitalized.

The FBI record enumerates arrests reported for the subject anywhere in the United States or Puerto Rico during his lifetime. The urine specimen was secured from each subject immediately after the interview; these were analyzed for the presence of opiates and barbiturates at the Addiction Research Center laboratory in Lexington.

Five items from the interview were selected for comparison with the other sources of data. These were: (1) age of the subject, (2) age at onset of drug use, (3) type and place of first arrest, (4) total number of arrests, and (5) drug use at time of interview. The first two items were compared with the prior hospital records to ascertain whether the patients were reliably reporting their age and onset of drug use.[4] The last three items were validity checks of the interview data.[5] Offenses reported by the subject were compared with his arrest record; his admission or denial of drug use at the time of interview was contrasted with the urinalysis.

THE RESEARCH FINDINGS

Age. A comparison of the age of each of the fifty-nine subjects reported at the time of interview with the age obtained from his prior Lexington hospitalization revealed that there was agreement as to the year of birth among 82.8 per cent of the subjects.[6] In the ten instances wherein there were response errors, eight of these differed by only one or two years. Of the two remaining cases, one female admitted to being uncertain of her age, but there was no evident expla-

---

[3] See John C. Ball and Delia O. Pabon, "Locating and Interviewing Narcotic Addicts in Puerto Rico," *Sociology and Social Research,* XLIX (July, 1965), 401-11.

[4] Following Festinger and Katz, reliability was operationally defined as the consistency or agreement of information given by the subject at different times (Leon Festinger and Daniel Katz, *Research Methods in the Behavioral Sciences* [New York: Dryden Press, 1953], p. 42).

[5] Validity herein refers to comparison of the interview data with "an outside criterion," after Festinger and Katz, *ibid.,* p. 46. The outside criterion in the case of arrest information was the FBI record for the individual; in the case of drug use, the criterion was laboratory analysis of the subject's urine.

[6] Among the fifty-two males, 90.2 per cent were in agreement as to year of birth.

nation for the age difference recorded for the male subject. The females were significantly less reliable than the males in reporting their age, as five of the seven females in the sample were responsible for half of the response error. No other response bias was noted.[7]

Onset. In the field interview in Puerto Rico, the subject was asked the age at which drug use was started. Similar information was usually available from the clinical records of the Lexington hospital; the mean years between first Lexington admission and time of interview was 9.2 years. A comparison of these two sources of data showed that there was agreement as to the year of onset among thirty-six of the fifty-five subjects (65.5 per cent).[8] Another fifteen records differed by only one to three years (27.3 per cent). Four cases (7.3 per cent) differed by five or more years.

In analyzing the nineteen cases in which age at onset was not reliably reported, no response bias was found. Eleven persons reported an earlier age of onset at time of interview, while eight reported a later onset; the mean difference was 3.4 years for the former group and 3.3 years for the latter.

First arrest. The interview schedule contained a full page of questions pertaining to the addict's (or former addict's) criminal history. Type, place, and age at first arrest were part of the information asked. This first event was compared with each subject's FBI record. In thirty-one of the fifty-seven comparisons, there was agreement between the two sources of data (54.4 per cent). In another fifteen instances, the subject recounted an earlier arrest than that shown (26.3 per cent); these were mostly minor or juvenile offenses.[9] Thus, in 80.7 per cent of the interviews, the subject either reported his first arrest correctly or admitted an earlier offense.

Of the eleven cases in which the FBI record showed an arrest prior to the one reported as his first arrest in the interview, nine did not mention this first arrest, but did recount others. For example, Case No. 49 did not mention an arrest for assault and battery in 1945 (the first arrest shown), but did mention his arrest in 1946 for possession of narcotics (the second arrest shown on his FBI record). Similarly, Case No. 138 did not mention his first four arrests, but described his fifth which was for homicide. Two subjects did not fit this response pattern. One subject—No. 15—admitted various arrests, but could not give details of a first arrest. A second, who was a physician, denied any arrest, but admitted being "committed" to both the Lexington and Fort Worth hospitals (in fact he was a federal prisoner in both instances, although these were his only arrests).

Number of arrests. A comparison of the total arrests stated in the interview with those recorded by the FBI is more complex, and somewhat less valid, than a single item comparison because of the difficulties in defining what is and what is not an arrest, and because of the considerable time period and number of arrests or events involved. Thus, the mean years between first arrest and interview for the males was 14.2 years; for the females it was 11.0 years. Although the mean number of arrests recorded by the FBI for the fifty-nine former addicts

---

[7]The terms "response error" and "response bias" follow Moser's usage (C. A. Moser, *Survey Methods in Social Investigation* [New York: Macmillan Co., 1958], chap.xiii).

[8]No data for such a comparison were available for four subjects.

[9]Juvenile offenses are not commonly reported to the Identification Division of the FBI.

was only 3.5, some subjects reported twenty or more arrests in the field interview.[10] These difficulties, or limitations, in effecting a comparison of verbal reports in an interview situation with official records based on fingerprint documentation are not mentioned to negate the validity of such a comparison, but to describe the practical problems involved.

Of fifty-eight former addicts, nineteen gave valid reports of the exact number of arrests recorded; twenty-two reported more arrests and seventeen fewer arrests than their respective FBI records enumerated. Thus, 70.7 per cent gave valid reports of their criminal history in the strict sense that they reported those events recorded by the FBI. Among the seventeen subjects who under-enumerated their arrests, it was primarily minor offenses that were omitted; they recounted their felonies and often stressed the circumstances of the more serious offenses and the sentence received.

Current drug use. The chemical analysis of a urine specimen is the most valid physical means devised of ascertaining current opiate use.[11] Following each interview, the subject was asked to provide such a specimen. Of the fifty-nine subjects, three refused to provide a urine specimen, five were readmissions to the Lexington hospital, twenty-two were interviewed in jail or while hospitalized in Puerto Rico, and twenty-nine were living at home. The most meaningful validity measure concerned this last group; an accurate comparison of the verbal report of addiction and urinalysis was feasible for twenty-five of these twenty-nine subjects.

Of these twenty-five subjects "on the street" in Puerto Rico at the time of interview and urinalysis, eighteen reported they were not using heroin and their urinalysis was negative for opiates; five admitted drug use and their specimen was positive; and two denied drug use, but the laboratory report was positive. On this basis, it may be said that 92 per cent of the subjects' reports of current drug use were valid, employing the criterion of chemical analysis. A more cautious and perhaps preferable statement is that 71 per cent of those using heroin admitted such use to the interviewer (five of seven addicts).

INTERPRETATION OF RESULTS

The reliability and validity of the subjects' verbal reports pertaining to their illicit actions have been analyzed. The former addict patients did enumerate and describe their addiction and criminal histories during a focused interview in Puerto Rico. The research results indicate a rather surprising veracity on the part

---

[10] All fifty-nine subjects admitted one or more arrests, with the possible exception of Case No. 15 already referred to. The mean number of arrests admitted by fifty-four subjects (excluding five subjects who admitted numerous arrests for breach of peace and drunkenness) was 3.8; the same fifty-four subjects had 3.5 mean arrests on their FBI records.

[11] Henry W. Elliott, Norman Nomof, Kenneth Parker, Marjorie L. Dewey, and E. Leong Way, "Comparison of the Nalorphine Test and Urinary Analysis in the Detection of Narcotic Use," *Clinical Pharmacology and Therapeutics,* V (July-August, 1964), 405-13; Ronald Serwer Poze, "Opiate Addiction: I. The Nalorphine Test, II. Current Concepts of Treatment," *Stanford Medical Bulletin,* XX (February, 1962), 1-4. For a discussion of the broader question of ascertaining abstinence or relapse in field studies, see: John A. O'Donnell, "The Relapse Rate in Narcotic Addiction: A Critique of Follow-Up Studies," in Daniel M. Wilner and Gene G. Kassebaum (eds.), *Narcotics* (New York: McGraw-Hill Book Co., 1965), pp. 236-40.

of the former addicts, especially when the various procedures employed in data collection are considered. Thus, age at onset of drug use was consistently asked in the field interview, but this precise question was not asked at time of hospital admission some ten years earlier. Therefore, it was often not possible to ascertain whether the clinical report referred to age at first use or age at which addicted. In addition to differences in the question asked, there were problems of recall, language, definition, and interpretation. For example, subjects sometimes initially forgot arrests which did not result in a sentence or thought we were only interested in drug offenses. Considering the varied sources of response error, the interview data were quite reliable and valid.

It seems likely that the completeness and validity of the interview data were related to a number of factors. The principal interviewer was extremely competent and familiar with interviewing procedures in Puerto Rican slums.[12] The use of an interview schedule which focused upon specific topics (such as the group situation at time of first drug use) usually precluded vague or offhand replies. Of considerable importance was the fact that our project staff was not associated with police authorities and that our study was exclusively a research undertaking. In this respect and others, the prior Lexington hospitalization of the subject seemed significant: We were outsiders from Lexington who had come to ask about his post-hospital adjustment. And it soon became known in the San Juan addict community that we were not reporting to any police authority. Further, we felt it was often efficacious to have knowledge of the local community in questioning a subject: He might say he had only been in prison once in the States, but when asked about La Princessa jail, he would say, "Oh sure, but I didn't know you meant that also."

The results of the present analysis indicate that former narcotic addicts can and will recount their illicit personal behavior valid under specified research conditions. This is not to suggest that the rather voluminous source material collected in the Puerto Rico Follow-Up Project was without numerous minor discrepancies or that conflicting reports were always easily or confidently resolved. But the data do support the interpretation that the addicts were motivated to describe their past and present deviant behavior and that they could recall events of ten to twenty years ago with surprising accuracy. It appears that the first shot of heroin or the first felony arrest were dramatic events in the addict's life.

The question arises as to whether the fifty-nine addicts would have admitted their illicit behavior in the absence of corroborative data from the FBI and other official sources. Would the addict admit proscribed behavior to the field interviewer if later corroboration were not available to the research staff? A partial answer to the question is afforded by an analysis of interviews obtained from the sixty-one addicts in the follow-up study who had previously been voluntary patients at the Lexington hospital. It was found that the former voluntary addict patients (whose hospitalization at Lexington was legally confidential and for whom FBI records were not obtainable) also recounted their illicit behavior to the interviewer.[13]

[12] One indication of the competency of the interviewer was the low refusal rate in Puerto Rico—only 3 of 112 subjects refused to be interviewed; Ball and Pabon, *op. cit.*, p. 407.
[13] Of the sixty-one former voluntary patients, forty-nine admitted one or more arrests,

The results of the present analysis and the findings of relevant other studies[14] suggest that the social situation and auspices under which interviews are obtained affect the deviant subject's motivation to be either candid, equivocal, or deceitful. Thus, it would be as unwarranted to maintain that addicts' responses are invariably valid as it would be to assume that they are invalid when appropriate research procedures are employed. The research procedures in the present study which appeared to be particularly relevant to securing valid interviews were: prior institutional contact (their Lexington hospitalization), the interviewer's knowledge of the addict subculture and familiarity with lower-class slum neighborhoods, past field experience and competency of the interviewer, absence of a service or police function, and the use of a structured personal interview which enabled probing questions to be asked.

---

and twelve denied any arrest. These twelve included a physician, a nurse, two housewives, three dependent males living with their parents, three youths aged twenty-one to twenty-four (one of whom was a student), an office clerk, and an accountant. The mean number of arrests enumerated by the forty-nine former voluntary patients was 3.9.

[14] See Isidor Chein, Donald L. Gerard, Robert S. Lee, and Eva Rosenfeld, *The Road to H* (New York: Basic Books, 1964), pp. 112-13, 209; Richard Blum and Associates, *Utopiates* (New York: Atherton Press, 1964), chap. ii; P. D. Scott and D. R. C. Willcox, "Delinquency and the Amphetamines," *British Journal of Psychiatry*, III, No. 478 (September, 1965), 865-75; Hunter Gillies, "Murder in the West of Scotland," *British Journal of Psychiatry*, III, No. 480 (November, 1965), 1087-94; John P. Clark and Larry L. Tifft, "Polygraph and Interview Validation of Self-Reported Deviant Behavior," *American Sociological Review*, XXXI, No. 4 (August, 1966), 516-23.

VALIDITY OF QUESTIONNAIRE DATA: REPORTED AND OBSERVED ATTENDANCE IN AN ADULT EDUCATION PROGRAM

Eugene C. Hagburg

The validity of questionnaire responses continues to be a central concern in social science research,[1] and periodic efforts are made to remind the researcher

Reprinted with the permission of the author and publisher, from *The Public Opinion Quarterly*, Vol. 32 (1968), 453-56.

An earlier version of this paper was presented at the Annual Meeting of the Ohio Valley Sociological Society at the University of Notre Dame in April 1967. This research note is part of a larger research project sponsored by the Labor Education and Research Service of The Ohio State University, which is being conducted under the direction of Professor Harry R. Blaine.

Dr. Hagburg, an industrial sociologist, is a Division Chief in the U. S. Post Office Department's Postal Service Institute.

[1] See for example, Herbert Hyman, "Do They Tell the Truth?" *Public Opinion Quarterly*,

of the need for caution in viewing questionnaire data. One sociologist suggests that "sociologists and anthropologists have tended to assume that a statement about a simple objective fact by a responsible person, who is in a position to know the facts, is a reliable piece of information," when, in fact, tests of the accuracy of such factual information "are so low as to be distressing to the social researcher."[2]

This particular research note addresses itself to this general question of data validity and, more specifically, to the accuracy of responses dealing with attendance in an adult education program. The primary purpose is to show how inaccurate such data can be and to encourage more sophistication in the data-collection process.

THE DATA

The data for this research note were provided by 227 local union leaders participating in a long-term Union Leadership Program conducted by The Ohio State University. Questionnaires were distributed to these participants during a regular class period to collect general information relating to adult participation in such a program. In addition to these data, special attention was given to the accuracy of answers to a factual question on class attendance, for the purpose of reinforcing other studies in this area.[3]

Each respondent was presented with the questions: "How many Union Leadership Program classes did you attend the first eight weeks of this year? How many the second eight weeks?" The questionnaires were administered immediately following the second eight-week period. These responses were then compared to the official attendance records, which were obtained from each instructor.

Table 1 reveals a significant difference between the reported behavior and observed attendance. Only 36 per cent accurately reported their attendance during the sixteen classes of the adult education program. Differences were

Vol 8, No. 4, 1944, pp. 557-559; Hugh J. Parry and Helen M. Crossley, "Validity of Responses to Survey Questions," *Public Opinion Quarterly*, Vol. 14, No. 1, 1950, pp. 61-80; and Ernest B. Gurman and Bernard M. Bass, "Objective Compared with Subjective Measures of the Same Behavior in Groups," *Journal of Abnormal and Social Psychology*, Vol. 63, September 1961, pp. 360-374.

Also see Eleanor E. Maccoby and Nathan Maccoby, "The Interview: A Tool of Social Science," in Gardner Lindzey, ed., *Handbook of Social Psychology*, Vol. 1, Reading, Mass., Addison-Wesley, 1954; F. Ivan Nye and James F. Short, "Scaling Delinquent Behavior," *American Sociological Review*, Vol. 22, June 1957, pp. 326-331; James Walters, "Relation between Reliability of Responses in Family Life: Research and Method of Data Collection," *Marriage and Family Living*, Vol. 22, August 1960, pp. 232-237; and Julius A. Roth, "Hired Hand Research," *American Sociologist*, Vol. 1, August 1966, pp. 190-196.

For a related problem, see Leo Crespi, "The Cheater Problem in Polling," *Public Opinion Quarterly*, Vol. 9, No. 4, 1945, pp. 431-445. See also Arnold M. Rose, "Generalizations in the Social Sciences," *American Journal of Sociology*, Vol. 59, July 1953, pp. 49-58.

[2] See Arnold M. Rose, "Reliability of Answers to Factual Questions," *Ohio Valley Sociologist*, June 1966, p. 14. For another illustration, see Peter M. Blau, *The Dynamics of Bureaucracy*, Chicago, University of Chicago F ss, 1955, p. 125. In his study of a Federal enforcement agency, Blau reports a high proportion of discrepancies—39 per cent—in comparing statements by pairs of workers as to whether or not they had ever lunched together.

[3] The questionnaires were coded to permit identification of each respondent, so that responses could be compared with the observations of the instructor.

TABLE 1.   Respondents Reporting Attendance in Class Sessions (in per cent)

No. of Class Sessions	Accurate Reporting	Over- reporting	Under- reporting
First period: 8 classes	53	41	6
Second period: 8 classes	48	38	15
Total, both periods: 16 classes	36	52	12

x^2 for both periods = 52.9 ($p < .001$).

similar for each eight-week period, although in twenty cases respondents under-reported in one period and overreported in the other. Such responses explain the differences between the total percentages shown in Table 1 and the percentages for each period.

An interesting finding, which is also revealed in Table 1, relates to the effect of the temporal proximity of the event on the subjects' accuracy in reporting about it. It appears that the time factor exerts little influence on the amount of accurate reporting and of overreporting, but it does have some influence on the amount of underreporting. This influence, however, appears to be exerted in the unexpected direction. One would expect more underreporting for the earlier period because of the time lapse, and yet only 6 per cent underreported in the first period, compared with 15 per cent in the second. The reason for this is not clear and further research is needed to provide an adequate explanation.

Table 2 provides additional insight on the extent of inaccurate reporting. Although a substantial proportion of the respondents incorrectly reported their attendance at classes, the inaccuracies cluster around the true answer. For example, for the first-period classes, 53 per cent answered correctly; 28 per cent erred by only one class and another 10 per cent were in error by only two classes. In other words, 91 per cent of the respondents either answered correctly or were in error by one or two class periods. The corresponding figure for the

TABLE 2.   Respondents Reporting Attendance in Class Sessions by Amount Error (in per cent)

No. of Class Sessions	Accurate Reporting	Overreporting – No. of Classes					Underreporting – No. of Classes				
		1	2	3	4	5 or More	1	2	3	4	5 or More
First period: 8 classes	53	24	9	7	1	1	4	1			
Second period: 8 classes	48	22	10	5	1		12	1			
Total, both periods: 16 classes	36	21	16	6	4	5	9	1	1		

second period is 93 per cent. This finding suggests, at least in part, that, when in doubt, respondents tended to exaggerate in the direction of the ideal.

The data as presented in Table 3 also provided an opportunity to compare

TABLE 3.   Selected Characteristics of Respondents, by Reporting Categories Attendance

Selected Characteristics	Accurate Reporting	Over- reporting	Under- reporting	Average for Total Sample
Mean age	41	39	41	40
Mean monthly family income	$606	$663	$579	$630
Religion (per cent):				
Protestant	70	67	87	71
Catholic	30	33	13	29
Distance of residence from class (per cent):				
a. 10 miles or less	56	53	74	57
b. More than 10 miles	44	47	26	43
Community of orientation (per cent):				
a. Rural or small town	60	51	61	56
b. Urban	40	49	39	44

accurate reporters with those who erred, on several social and demographic variables. For example, the mean age of overreporters was slightly less than that of both the accurate and the underreporters. Overreporters indicated a higher monthly family income than did the other comparison groups. Other interesting differences are revealed but not readily explicable.

The data, in general, suggest that responses are in the direction of ideal norms, i.e. high attendance in an educational program in accordance with explicit expectations. The respondents were advised upon enrollment that attendance was required to qualify for a certificate of completion and encouraged to do so in order to contribute to the maintenance of such an adult education program. This explains, at least in part, the extensive overreporting and supports other findings of validity studies, particularly that of Maccoby and Maccoby.[4]

---

[4]Maccoby and Maccoby, *op. cit.*, p. 482.

THE RANDOM PROBE: A TECHNIQUE FOR EVALUATING THE VALIDITY OF CLOSED QUESTIONS

Howard Schuman

Important sociological analysis is often based on a small number of "closed" survey questions.[1] To the survey analyst, and perhaps even more to the non-survey-oriented sociologist, doubts sometimes arise about whether a question carries the same meaning for respondents as for the social scientist who constructed it. This is particularly true when the respondents differ greatly from the investigator in education, cultural characteristics, or life chances. True, the process of analysis itself is intended to elucidate the sense of data, yet there is often a need on the part of both investigator and reader to hear the respondent's own voice, and this is doubtless an important reason why surveys make use of open-ended questions and why free responses often make up a significant part of survey reports.

As surveys are increasingly undertaken in non-Western countries the problem becomes both more salient and more important. Questions framed in English by middle-class American professors are translated into Bengali and put in formal fashion by educated and urbanized Pakistani students to illiterate peasants in East Pakistan. Is this a reasonable endeavor? The survey researcher, accustomed to being told "it can't be done," plunges ahead boldly, but even he at times must wonder whether his tables really mean what he thinks they mean. If he himself has wrestled with problems of translation, and realized the ease with which unwanted connotations are added and wanted connotations lost, he cannot help but be aware that wording can be equally meaningful to both parties without that meaning being shared.

One solution is to work largely with open-ended questions. But in addition to immense problems of translation and coding when large-scale surveys are involved, it is difficult to obtain sufficiently rich responses from individuals who are both uneducated and unused to expressing opinions. Moreover, the very variety of frames of reference produced by open-ended questions changes from asset to liability when one is attempting to classify all respondents in terms of

Reprinted with permission of the author and the publisher, The American Sociological Association, from the *American Sociological Review*, Vol. 31 (1966), 218-22.

The writer is indebted for advice and encouragement to Alex Inkeles, Director of the comparative project of which the Pakistan study was one part, and to David H. Smith, an Associate of the project. The project is an aspect of research on development undertaken by the Center for International Affairs, Harvard University.

[1]One among many examples is the use of a single question on aspirations in Alan B. Wilson, "Class Segregation and Aspirations of Youth," *American Sociological Review*, 24 (December, 1959), pp. 836-845. One solution to the problem discussed here leads of course toward scaling, but few exploratory cross-cultural surveys develop unidimensional or even adequately reliable Likert scales. More often the focus is on individual questions or on small sets of very modestly intercorrelated items. There are few "scales" in the sociological literature for which the problem raised here would not be relevant.

single variables. Because of these difficulties, surveys continue to rely heavily on closed multiple-choice questions even in settings very different from the United States.[2]

In this paper I would like to suggest a simple technique for obtaining on a routine basis both qualitative and quantitative information on the meaningfulness and meaning of responses to closed survey questions. The approach is an obvious extension of interviewer probing, traditionally used in surveys to encourage more detailed answers to *open*-ended questions. Such probing has undoubtedly been used in pre-testing closed questions and perhaps has been tried in regular surveys; but it seems never to have been developed and applied systematically. The technique is direct and simple: each interviewer is required to carry out follow-up probes for a set of closed items *randomly* selected from the interview schedule for *each* of his respondents. The probe does not replace the regular closed question in any way, but follows immediately after the respondent's choice of an alternative. Using non-directive phrases, the interviewer simply asks the respondent to "explain a little" of what he had in mind in making his choice.[3] The recorded comments (or occasionally lack of comments) are used by the investigator to compare the intended purpose of the question and chosen alternative with its meaning as perceived and acted on by the respondent.

Both the randomization method and its usefulness will be illustrated by describing its application in a complex attitude survey of 1000 factory workers and cultivators in East Pakistan in 1964. In addition to background and open-ended questions, the schedule consisted of 200 closed and quasi-closed items, mostly in the form of two to four forced alternatives.[4] Each interviewer was given a list of these 200 questions and shown how to select by a chance method ten items from the list prior to each interview. He was to probe these ten questions *regardless* of the respondent's general or specific level of understanding. (Interviewers were also instructed to probe under certain other circumstances, but different symbols distinguished random from other probes.) The essence of the method is to obtain probe material on a *random* sample of the 200,000 closed responses expected in the survey.

The selection of ten questions per interview results in a sample of ten expla-

---

[2]Cf., Gabriel A. Almond and S. Verba, *The Civic Culture*, Princeton University Press, 1963, p. 46, where approximately 90 per cent of the questions are closed. For a full discussion of the advantages of both open and closed questions, see P. F. Lazarsfeld, "The Controversy over Detailed Interviews—An Offer for Negotiations," reprinted in Daniel Katz, et al., *Public Opinion and Propaganda*, The Dryden Press, 1954.

[3]Phrases used by the interviewer are: "Would you give me an example of what you mean?"; "I see—why do you say that?"; "Could you tell me a little more about that?" As with most probes, the exact wording is less important than the manner in which it is made. It is particularly important that the respondent's closed choice not seem challenged.

[4]Not all of the questions probed were completely closed. Some required brief free replies which were highly constrained by the form of the question (e.g., "Generally, how often during a day do you pray?"). Still others involved quite free responses (e.g., ten sentence completion items). In these latter it also seemed desirable to obtain probe material on a random basis to clarify the sometimes cryptic patterns of answers. Such open and quasi-closed questions are involved in the random selection procedure but are generally excluded from the quantitative scoring to be discussed here. Scoring was applied to 175 questions.

nations by *each respondent,* and these can be evaluated to provide a measure of his ability to understand the questionnaire as a whole. From exactly the same item evaluations, we simultaneously obtain on the average fifty randomly proved responses for *each question;* working with these across individuals gives us an evaluation for each of the two hundred items, indicative of how well *they* are understood.[5]

EVALUATING THE RANDOM PROBES QUANTITATIVELY

The Pakistan random probe material has been evaluated question by question on a five-point scale by regular coders who first read the follow-up material blind, then used it to predict the respondent's original closed alternative, and finally evaluated the total "fit" between probe explanation and chosen alternative. The evaluation code, explanations, and point equivalents are shown below.

Code	Interpretation	Points
A	Explanation is quite clear and leads to accurate prediction or closed choice.	1
B	Explanation of marginal clarity and leads to accurate prediction of closed choice.	2
C	Explanation very unclear; cannot make any prediction about closed choice.	4
D	(a) Explanation seems clear, but leads to wrong prediction of closed choice;	
	(b) Respondent was unable to give any explanation of his closed choice ("don't know");	5
	(c) Respondent in course of explanation shifted his closed choice away from original.	
(R)	(Explanation is simply literal repetition of closed choice; cannot judge respondent's understanding of question.)	(omit)

The point gap between "B" and "C" reflects the fact that "B" is close to "A" in meaning and implication, while "C" points to an essentially unsatisfactory explanation. The symbol "R" really indicates inadequate probing by the interviewer, since rote repetition of a chosen alternative by the respondent does not allow us to judge his understanding one way or the other. Such repetitions are excluded from score computations, but a separate count of them can be kept for both individuals and questions. In general, the evaluation scheme is conservative: some of the responses coded "C" may be due to inadequate probing or translation, and some proportion of the responses coded "D" for incorrect prediction may actually have involved mis-check during the interview.[6]

---

[5] To obtain similar follow-up qualitative information, Almond and Verba, *op. cit.,* reinterviewed in depth a ten per cent sub-sample of their original survey respondents. Their method has the advantage of allowing construction of a stratified rather than simple random sample, thus insuring better representation for infrequent responses. On the other hand, it is very costly in time and money, and it may also lead to over-probing and to "second-thought" explanations rather different from those a respondent might have given in the original interview. Our method involves only slight additional costs in interviewing time and provides a more natural inflow of information for all questions and for all individuals.

[6] The major limitation of the quantitative evaluation scheme is its inapplicability to subtle

To obtain quantitative indices, the numerical scores for separate responses are summed separately for each individual and for each question, and the sums are divided by the number of scorable probes available in each case. The resulting averages constitute 1000 individual probe scores and 200 question probe scores.[7] For the Pakistan survey, the reliability of the scoring was estimated by having the necessary responses reevaluated independently for a random sample of 30 individuals and a random sample of 30 questions. Product moment correlations of 0.75 and 0.92, respectively, were obtained, indicating satisfactory scoring reliabilities for both types of scores. The higher question reliability is due to the larger number of responses on which question scores are based.

Both individual and question scores can be interpreted directly in terms of the meanings used in the original evaluation procedure. For example, a mean score of 3, whether for an individual or for a question, indicates understanding half way between the "B" and "C" levels. If an individual score, it becomes a signal that the respondent probably had a generally low understanding. This supplements interviewer comments and ratings with a more objective measure of comprehension. But the more important warning is a high *question* probe score, for it suggests ambiguity, lack of clarity, or unintended meaning for the question over the entire sample. This provides information not ordinarily obtained from interviewers, especially newly-trained interviewers in developing countries.

In the Pakistan study the median question probe score is 1.4; 87 per cent of the closed questions have mean scores between 1.0 ("A" understanding) and 2.0 ("B" understanding). Thus most but not all of the questions fall within what would appear to be an acceptable range. On an individual basis, the median score is 1.4 and 87 per cent of the respondents average between 1.0 and 2.0. A small but significant minority of respondents thus seem to have real difficulties with the questions—not surprising for a sample with generally low education—although it should also be noted that within the sample the correlation between individual probe scores and schooling is trivial (−0.10), and between the same scores and a verbal aptitude measure the relation is not much greater (−0.23). There are a few individuals with such low scores as to suggest that they contribute mostly random error to the study (22 persons score 3.0 or greater), but to a considerable extent error seems to be concentrated in a few questions. Questions and individuals are inextricably related, of course, because the unit of analysis is the single response to a single question, but it is of some significance that more than half the responses rated "C" or "D" are concentrated in only one-fifth of the questions.

---

grades of intensity. In general, on items that ask a person not only to select among qualitatively different alternatives but also to indicate his strength of feeling, only the former can be evaluated readily from probe material. Thus a response is evaluated as "A" if it is spontaneously worded, clear in meaning, and correctly predicts the respondent's basic closed choice among two or more possibilities—even though his intensity of feeling cannot be predicted.

[7]Since only ten out of two hundred responses were probed in each interview, there is sampling error in the sense that a given individual may have been probed by chance on a particularly easy or difficult set of items. Sampling error by question is less, since 50 respondents were probed on each question. The number of questions probed is limited not only by cost of evaluation (the present ratio produced $(10 \times 1000 = 10,000$ free responses) but also by the need to avoid questioning too frequently a respondent's choices.

QUALITATIVE USE OF RANDOM PROBES

Formal numerical scoring provides only a rough index of the general value of an item. The qualitative understanding gained by reading 50 responses to a question offers a much richer source of information on the way the question was perceived and the meaning of the closed responses it evoked.[8] The kinds of elucidation provided will be illustrated by several examples from a set of questions on religion.

In the Pakistan study two questions were included to determine whether Islamic religious obligations are interpreted by various sample groups to include achievement-related effort as an end in itself. The answers to these questions show excellent variation, intercorrelate well, are significantly related to a number of background variables, and are relevant to an important hypothesis. But the random probes suggest that the questions were reasonably well understood by less than half the sample. Most respondents reinterpreted them in ways that had little to do with their original purpose. This question, with a mean probe score of 2.3, is an example:

"Do you think that whether a man works diligently every day is:
1. An absolutely essential part of religion,
2. An important but not essential part of religion, or
3. Of little importance to religion."

A common interpretation is represented by the following probe response from a man who had chosen the first alternative: "My family depends on me. If there is no food and empty stomachs [because of laziness], then I cannot give attention to prayer." Respondents who chose the third alternative tended to give even more distant explanations, for example: "It is not good to work hard everyday. It will ruin the health."

The minority of probed respondents (about two-fifths) who did appear to understand the question in the intended frame of reference (e.g., "Allah has written in the Koran that men should work hard each day") were more educated than average, as would be expected. For them the question can certainly be used. For the less educated in the sample, however, the question must at the very least be treated with caution, and empirical relationships discoverable with it should be subjected to special scrutiny before final interpretation is made. Indeed, some researchers may prefer to drop such a question altogether.

Quite the opposite type of case is provided by the following yes-or-no question, intended to determine whether ethical actions and religious actions are conceived as separable by certain of the groups studied:

"Do you think a man can be truly good who has no religion at all?"

When this question was first presented to local translators and interviewers, their

---

[8]In the Pakistan analysis, coders not only provided a score for each individual response but also wrote a brief holistic evaluation of each question on the basis of having read all fifty responses to it.

reaction was unanimously negative. No ordinary man would understand the point of the question, they felt. Whatever might be the case among Westerners or among the University-educated, the average Pakistani Muslim would certainly see a non-religious man as by definition devoid of goodness. All agreed that the question could not lead to meaningful responses and should not be included.

It was included, however, and in fact produced about one third "yes" and two-thirds "no" choices. But was the question perhaps misinterpreted in some way? The random probes indicate that understanding was very good indeed (mean score 1.1). A typical probe explanation for a "yes" response was: "He may not believe any religion, yet he can render good offices to the people of the land." Another man said: "He may be good and his heart may be very pure, and he can help people anyway." The "no" responses were also to the point: "The man who has no faith has no idea of good and bad, so he cannot be good." "The person who has no religion, what good thing may be in him? He is wretched." More generally, of the 52 probes to this question, only one was coded as confused. It therefore seems quite reasonable to interpret Pakistani response patterns for the question much as one would for ordinary Americans.

The two questions discussed thus far have shown the usefulness of random probe material in reaching decisions about the inclusion or exclusion of questions for analysis. But probably the greatest value of this additional material comes from making the analyst aware of subtle changes in meaning that have occurred between question formulation and tabular analysis. Usually it is not a case of rejecting a question, but rather of bringing into clearer focus the impact the wording had upon respondents and thus interpreting response patterns in a more accurate way.

The following forced-choice question, for example, was intended to contrast material striving with concern for more spiritual ideals:

"Some people say that the more things a man possesses—like new clothes, furniture, and conveniences—the happier he is.

Others say that whatever material things a man may possess, his happiness depends upon something else beyond those.

What is your opinion?"

This question produced a wide distribution of responses and was understood without difficulty. However, the Bengali phrase for "something else beyond those" was interpreted in a broader way than the limited religious idea conceived in constructing the question and attempted in translation. Those who chose the second alternative sometimes gave religious justification ("It depends upon God's blessing"), but even more frequently they gave other sensible non-material explanations for their responses:

"Suppose a man has no child, whereas he has all other things; then he is not happy."

"It depends on one's wife. If she is not good, one is not happy."

"I may have much wealth but there are many enemies against me."

Clearly the question was well understood. But just as clearly it would be incorrect to use the question as a direct indicator of religious *vs.* secular orientation. The probe material here helps the analyst to understand more precisely what it is he has measured—which is, after all, the final goal of "validity."

This last illustration also indicates why the quantitative evaluation described earlier must remain a relatively crude index. For each question that was not understood exactly as originally intended, it becomes a matter first of judgment and then of convention whether the question is being "misinterpreted" or simply differently interpreted. In practice the decision is seldom difficult, but occasionally a set of scores would be considerably altered had a different convention been established.

CONCLUSION

Through qualitative and quantitative review of random probe responses the survey researcher has an opportunity to increase his own sensitivity to what his questions mean to actual respondents, and thereby improve his comprehension of the resulting data. At the same time, quotations become available that can offer emotional insight into a table representing answers from people he and his readers are attempting to understand.

Of course, the addition of random probes to a survey is no panacea. It does not reduce the need for careful pre-testing, or solve the problems of survey analysis, but it is a simple, inexpensive, and natural way of obtaining valuable free response material on a systematic basis. In research in other cultures—and under some conditions in one's own culture—it forms a useful supplement to standard attitude survey methods.

SOME METHODOLOGICAL PROBLEMS OF FIELD STUDIES[1]

Morris Zelditch, Jr.

The original occasion for this paper was a reflection on the use of sample survey methods in the field: that is, the use of structured interview schedules, probability samples, etc., in what is usually thought of as a participant-observation study. There has been a spirited controversy between, on the one hand, those who have sharply criticized field workers for slipshod sampling, for failing to document assertions quantitatively, and for apparently accepting

Reprinted with the permission of the author and the publisher, The University of Chicago Press, from the *American Journal of Sociology*, Vol. 67 (1962), 566-76.

[1]This paper reports part of a more extensive investigation of problems of field method in which Dr. Renée Fox is a collaborator. The author gratefully acknowledges the partial support given this investigation by funds from Columbia University's Documentation Project for Advanced Training in Social Research.

impressionistic accounts—or accounts that the quantitatively minded could not distinguish from purely impressionistic accounts;[2] and, on the other hand, those who have, sometimes bitterly, been opposed to numbers, to samples, to questionnaires, often on the ground that they destroy the field workers' conception of a social system as an organic whole.[3]

Although there is a tendency among many younger field workers to accent criticisms made from the quantitative point of view,[4] there is reason to believe that the issue itself has been stated falsely. In most cases field methods are discussed as if they were "all of a piece,"[5] There is, in fact, a tendency to be either *for* or *against* quantification, as if it were an either/or issue. To some extent the battle lines correlate with a relative concern for "hardness" versus "depth and reality" of data. Quantitative data are often thought of as "hard," and qualitative as "real and deep"; thus if you prefer "hard" data you are for quantification and if you prefer "real, deep" data you are for qualitative participant observation. What to do if you prefer data that are real, deep, *and* hard is not immediately apparent.

A more fruitful approach to the issue must certainly recognize that a field

[2]See, e.g., Harry Alpert, "Some Observations on the Sociology of Sampling," *Social Forces*, XXXI (1952), 30-31; Robert C. Hanson, "Evidence and Procedure Characteristics of 'Reliable' Propositions in Social Science," *American Journal of Sociology*, LXIII (1958), 357-63.

[3]See W. L. Warner and P. Lunt, *Social Life of a Modern Community* (New Haven, Conn.: Yale University Press, 1941), p. 55; Conrad Arensberg, "The Community Study Method," *American Journal of Sociology*, LX (1952), 109-24; Howard Becker, "Field Work among Scottish Shepherds and German Peasants," *Social Forces*, XXXV (1956), 10-15; Howard S. Becker and Blanche Geer, "Participant Observation and Interviewing: A Comparison," *Human Organization*, XVI (1957), 28-34; Solon Kimball, "Problems of Studying American Culture," *American Anthropologist*, LVII (1955), 1131-42; and A. Viditch and J. Bensman, "The Validity of Field Data," *Human Organization*, XIII (1954), 20-27.

[4]See particularly Oscar Lewis, "Controls and Experiments in Field Work," in *Anthropology Today* (Chicago: University of Chicago Press, 1953), p. 455 n.; also cf. Howard S. Becker, "Problems of Inference and Proof in Participant Observation," *American Sociological Review*, XXIII (1958), 652-60; Elizabeth Colson, "The Intensive Study of Small Sample Communities," in R. F. Spencer (ed.), *Method and Perspective in Anthropology* (Minneapolis: University of Minnesota Press, 1954), pp. 43-59; Fred Eggan, "Social Anthropology and the Method of Controlled Comparison," *American Anthropologist*, LVI (1954), 743-60; Harold E. Driver, "Statistics in Anthropology," *American Anthropologist*, LV (1953), 42-59; Melville J. Herskovitz, "Some Problems of Method in Ethnography," in R. F. Spencer (ed.), *op. cit.*, pp. 3-24; George Spindler and Walter Goldschmidt, "Experimental Design in the Study of Culture Change," *Southwestern Journal of Anthropology*, VIII (1952), 68-83. And see the section "Field Methods and Techniques" in *Human Organization*, esp. in its early years and its early editorials. Some quantification has been characteristic of "field" monographs for a very long time; cf. Kroeber's *Zuni Kin and Clan* (1916). Such classics as *Middletown* and the *Yankee City* series are studded with tables.

[5]A significant exception is a comment by M. Trow directed at Becker and Geer. Becker and Geer, comparing interviewing to participant observation, find participant observation the superior method and seem to imply that it is superior for all purposes. Trow insists that the issue is not correctly formulated, and that one might better ask: "What kinds of problems are best studied through what kinds of methods; . . . how can the various methods at our disposal complement one another?" In their reply, Becker and Geer are more or less compelled to agree. See Becker and Geer, "Participant Observation and Interviewing: A Comparison," *op. cit.*, Trow's "Comment" (*Human Organization*, XVI [1957], 33-35), and Becker and Geer's "Rejoinder" (*Human Organization*, XVII [1958], 39-40).

study is not a single method gathering a single kind of information. This approach suggests several crucial questions: *What* kinds of methods and *what* kinds of information are relevant? How can the "goodness" of different methods for different purposes be evaluated? Even incomplete and imperfect answers—which are all that we offer here—should be useful, at least in helping to restate the issue. They also pose, order, and to some extent resolve other issues of field method so that in pursuing their implications this paper encompasses a good deal more than its original problem.

THREE TYPES OF INFORMATION

The simplest events are customarily described in statements predicating a single property of a single object at a particular time and in a particular place. From these descriptions one may build up more complex events in at least two ways. The first is by forming a configuration of many properties of the same object at the same time in the same place. This may be called an "incident." A more complex configuration but of the same type would be a sequence of incidents, that is, a "history."

A second way to build up more complex events is by repeating observations of a property over a number of units. Units here can be defined formally, requiring only a way of identifying events as identical. They can be members of a social system or repetitions of the same type of incident at different times or in different places (e.g., descriptions of five funerals). The result is a frequency distribution of some property.

From such information it is possible to deduce certain underlying properties of the system observed, some of which may be summarized as consequences of the "culture" of S (S stands here for a social system under investigation). But at least some portion of this culture can be discovered not only by inference from what is observed but also from verbal reports by members of S—for example, accounts of its principal institutionalized norms and statuses. The rules reported, of course, are to some extent independent of the events actually observed; the norms actually followed may not be correctly reported, and deviance may be concealed. Nevertheless, information difficult to infer can be readily and accurately obtained from verbal reports. For example, it may take some time to infer that a member occupies a given status but this may readily be discovered by asking either him or other members of S.

We thus combine various types of information into three broad classes.

Type I: Incidents and Histories. A log of events during a given period, a record of conversations heard, descriptions of a wedding, a funeral, an election, etc. Not only the actions observed, but the "meanings," the explanations, etc., reported by the participants can be regarded as part of the "incident" insofar as they are thought of as data rather than actual explanations.

Type II: Distributions and Frequencies. Possessions of each member of S, number of members who have a given belief, number of times member m is observed talking to member n, etc.

Type III: Generally Known Rules and Statuses. Lists of statuses, lists of persons occupying them, informants' accounts of how rules of exogamy apply, how incest or descent are defined, how political leaders are supposed to be chosen, how political decisions are supposed to be made, etc.

This classification has nothing to do with what is *inferred* from data, despite the way the notion of reported rules and statuses was introduced. In particular, more complex configurations of norms, statuses, events which are "explained" by inferring underlying themes or structures involve a level of inference outside the scope of this paper: the classification covers only information *directly* obtained from reports and observations. Moreover, this classification cuts across the distinction between what is observed by the investigator and what is reported to him. Although Type III consists only of reports, Types I and II include both observations by the investigator himself *and* reports of members of *S*, insofar as they are treated as data. Later we talk of an event as seen through the eyes of an informant, where the investigator trusts the informant as an accurate observer and thinks of the report as if it were his own observation. Now, however, interest is focused not on the facts of the report but rather on what the report reveals of the perceptions, the motivations, the world of meaning of the informant himself. The report, in this case, does not transmit observational data; it is, itself, the datum and so long as it tells what the person reporting thinks, the factual correctness of what he thinks is irrelevant. (This is sometimes phrased as making a distinction between *informants* and *respondents,* in the survey research sense.) Thus Type I includes both observations (what we see going on) and the statements of members telling what they understand the observed events to mean, which is regarded as part of the event. In a somewhat different way, Type II also includes both reports (e.g., an opinion poll) and observations (e.g., systematically repeated observations with constant coding categories).

THREE TYPES OF METHOD

It is possible to make a pure, logically clear classification of methods of obtaining information in the field, but for the present purpose this would be less useful than one that is, though less precise, rather closer to what a field worker actually does.

Two methods are usually thought of as characteristic of the investigator in the field. He invariably keeps a daily log of events and of relatively casual, informal continuous interviews, both of which go into his field notes. Almost invariably he also develops informants, that is, selected members of *S* who are willing and able to give him information about practices and rules in *S* and events he does not directly observe. (They may also supply him with diaries, autobiographies, and their own personal feelings; i.e., they may also function as respondents.) Contrary to popular opinion, almost any well-trained field worker also keeps various forms of census materials, records of systematic observations, etc., including a basic listing of members of *S,* face-sheet data on them, and systematically repeated observations of certain recurrent events. Many field workers also collect documents; however, we will classify field methods into only three broad classes which we conceive of as primary. These are:

Type I. Participant-observation. The field worker directly observes and also participates in the sense that he has durable social relations in *S*. He may or may not play an active part in events, or he may interview participants in events which may be considered part of the process of observation.

Type II. Informant-interviewing. We prefer a more restricted definition of the informant than most field workers use, namely that he be called an "informant" only where he is reporting information presumed factually correct about others rather than about himself; and his information about events is about events in their absence. Interviewing during the event itself is considered part of participant-observation.

Type III. Enumerations and samples. This includes both surveys and direct, repeated, countable observations. Observation in this sense may entail minimal participation as compared with that implied in Type I.

This classification excludes documents on the ground that they represent resultants or combinations of primary methods. Many documents, for example, are essentially informant's accounts and are treated exactly as an informant's account is treated: subjected to the same kinds of internal and external comparisons, treated with the same suspicions, and often in the end, taken as evidence of what occurred at some time and place from which the investigator was absent. The fact that the account is written is hardly important. Many other documents are essentially enumerations; for example, personnel and cost-accounting records of a factory, membership rolls of a union, tax rolls of a community.

TWO CRITERIA OF "GOODNESS"

Criteria according to which the "goodness" of a procedure may be defined are:

1. *Informational adequacy,* meaning accuracy, precision, and completeness of data.
2. *Efficiency,* meaning cost per added input of information.

It may appear arbitrary to exclude validity and reliability. Validity is excluded because it is, in a technical sense, a relation between an indicator and a concept, and similar problems arise whether one obtains information from an informant, a sample, or from direct observation. Construed loosely, validity is often taken to mean "response validity," accuracy of report, and this is caught up in the definition of informational adequacy. Construed more loosely yet, validity is sometimes taken as equivalent to "real," "deep" data, but this seems merely to beg the question. Reliability is relevant only tangentially; it is a separate problem that cuts across the issues of this paper.

FUNDAMENTAL STRATEGIES

Certain combinations of method and type of information may be regarded as formal prototypes, in the sense that other combinations may be logically reduced to them. For example: Instead of a sample survey or enumeration, an informant is employed to list dwelling units, or to estimate incomes, or to tell who associates with whom or what each person believes with respect to some issue. The information is obtained from a single informant, but he is treated *as if he himself* had conducted a census or poll. More generally, in every case in which the information obtained is logically reducible to a distribution of the members of *S* with respect to the property *a*, the implied method of obtaining the information is also logically reducible to an enumeration. The enumeration may be either through direct observation (estimating the number of sheep each Navaho has by actually counting them: establishing the sociometric structure of the community by watching who interacts with whom), or through a questionnaire survey (determining household composition by questioning a member of each household, or administering a sociometric survey to a sample of the community). If an informant is used, it is presumed that he has himself performed the enumeration. We are not at the moment concerned with the validity of this assumption in specific instances but rather in observing that regardless of the actual way in which the information was obtained, the logical and formal character of the procedure is that of a census or survey.

Suppose an informant is asked to describe what went on at a community meeting which the observer is unable to attend; or a sample of respondents is asked to describe a sequence of events which occurred before the observer entered *S*. In either case his reports are used as substitutes for direct observation. Such evidence may, in fact, be examined critically to establish its accuracy—we begin by assuming the bias of the reports—but it is presumed that, having "passed" the statements they become an objective account of what has occurred in the same sense that the investigator's own reports are treated as objective, once his biases have been taken into account. The informant, one usually says in this case, is the observer's observer; he differs in no way from the investigator himself. It follows that the prototype is direct observation by the observer himself.

The prototype so far is not only a formal model; it is also a "best" method, efficiently yielding the most adequate information. In learning institutionalized rules and statuses it is doubtful that there is a formal prototype and all three methods yield adequate information. Here we may choose the *most efficient* method as defining our standard of procedure. To illustrate: We wish to study the political structure of the United States. We are told that the principal national political figure is called a "president," and we wish to know who he is. We do not ordinarily think of sampling the population of the United States to obtain the answer; we regard it as sufficient to ask one well-informed member. This question is typical of a large class of questions asked by a field worker in the course of his research.

A second example: Any monograph on the Navaho reports that they are matrilineal and matrilocal. This statement may mean either of two things:

1. All Navaho are socially identified as members of a descent group defined through the mother's line, and all Navaho males move to the camp of their wife's family at marriage.
2. There exists a set of established rules according to which all Navaho are supposed to become socially identified as members of a descent group defined through the mother's line, and to move to the camp of their wife's family at marriage.

The truth of the first interpretation can be established only by an enumeration of the Navaho, or a sample sufficiently representative and sufficiently precise. It is readily falsified by exceptions, and in fact there *are* exceptions to both principles. But suppose among thirty Navaho informants at least one says that the Navaho are patrilineal and patrilocal. If this is intended to describe institutionalized norms as in (2) above, we are more likely to stop using the informant than we are to state that there are "exceptions" in the sense of (1) above. We might sample a population to discover the motivation to conform to a rule, or the actual degree of conformity, but are less likely to do so to establish that the rule *exists,* if we confront institutionalized phenomena. This also constitutes a very large class of questions asked by the field worker.

ADEQUACY OF INFORMANTS FOR VARIOUS PROBLEMS IN THE FIELD

It does not follow from the definition of a prototype method that no other form of obtaining information can suffice; all we intend is that it *does* suffice, and any other method is logically reducible to it. Further, comparison with the prototype is a criterion by which other forms can be evaluated. In considering the adequacy in some given instance of the use of an informant as the field worker's surrogate census, for example, we are interested primarily in whether he is likely to know enough, to recall enough, and to report sufficiently precisely to yield the census that we ourselves would make. Comments below, incidentally, are to be taken as always prefixed with the phrase, "by and large." It is not possible to establish, at least yet, a firm rule which will cover every case.

The informant as a surrogate census-taker. A distinction must again be made between *what* information is obtained and how it is obtained. It is one thing to criticize a field worker for not obtaining a frequency distribution where it is required—for instance, for not sampling mothers who are weaning children in order to determine age at weaning—and another to criticize him for not obtaining it *directly* from the mothers. If the field worker reports that the average age at weaning is two years and the grounds for this is that he asked an informant, "About when do they wean children around here?" it is not the fact that he asked an informant but that he asked the wrong question that should be criticized. He should have asked, "How many mothers do you know who are now weaning children? How old are their children?"

The critical issue, therefore, is whether or not the informant can be assumed to have the information that the field worker requires, granting that he asks the proper questions. In many instances he does. In some cases he is an even better source than an enumerator; he either knows better or is less likely to falsify. Dean, for example, reports that workers who are ideologically pro-union, but also have mobility aspirations and are not well-integrated into their factory or local unions, are likely to report attending union meetings which they do not in fact attend.[6] She also shows that, when *respondent-reported* attendance is used as a measure of attendance, this tends spuriously to increase correlations of attendance at union meetings with attitudes toward unions in general, and to reduce correlations of attendance at union meetings with attitudes more specifically directed at the local union. The list of those actually attending was

[6] L. R. Dean, "Interaction, Reported and Observed: The Case of One Local Union," *Human Organization*, XVII (1958), 36-44.

obtained by an observer, who, however, had sufficient rapport with officers of the local to obtain it from them.[7] Attendance, largely by "regulars," was stable from meeting to meeting so that the officers could have reproduced it quite accurately.[8]

On the other hand, there are many instances in which an informant is *prima facie* unlikely to be adequate, although no general rule seems to identify these clearly for the investigator. The nature of the information—private versus public, more or less objective, more or less approved—is obviously relevant, yet is often no guide at all. Some private information, for example, is better obtained from informants, some from respondents. The social structure of *S*, particularly its degree of differentiation and complexity, is also obviously relevant. An informant must be in a position to know the information desired, and if *S* is highly differentiated and the informant confined to one part of it, he can hardly enumerate it. Probably to discover attitudes and opinions that are relatively private and heterogeneous in a structure that is relatively differentiated, direct enumeration or sampling should be used.

The informant as a "representative respondent." An "average" of a distribution is sometimes obtained not by asking for an enumeration by the informant, nor even by asking a general question concerning what people typically do; sometimes it is obtained by treating the informant as if he were a "representative respondent." The informant's reports about himself—perhaps deeper, more detailed, "richer," but nevertheless like those of a respondent in a survey rather than an informant in the technical sense—stand in place of a sample. Where a multivariate distribution is thought of, this person is treated as a "quintessential" subject, "typical" in many dimensions. Some field workers speak favorably of using informants in this way, and it is likely that even more of them actually do so.

Since, as yet, we have no really hard and fast rules to follow, it is possible that in some cases this is legitimate; but, by and large, it is the most suspect of ways of using informants. It is simply a bad way of sampling. The legitimate cases are probably of three types: first, as suggestive of leads to follow up; second, as illustration of a point to be made in a report that is verifiable on other grounds. But in this second case the proviso ought to be thought of as rather strict; it is not sufficient to "have a feeling" that the point is true, to assume that it is verifiable on other grounds. The third case is perhaps the most legitimate, but is really a case of using informants to provide information about generally known rules: for example, using informants to collect "typical" genealogies or kinship terms, the assumption being that his kin terms are much like those of others (which is not always true, of course) and his genealogy sufficiently "rich"—this being the basis on which he was chosen—to exhibit a wide range of possibilities.

The informant as the observer's observer. The third common use of the informant is to report events not directly observed by the field worker. Here the investigator substitutes the observations of a member for his own observation. It is not simply interviewing that is involved here, because participant-observation was defined earlier as including interviewing on the spot, in conjunction with direct observation. Thus, some of the most important uses of the informant—to

[7]*Ibid.*, p. 37, n. 4
[8]*Ibid.*

provide the meaning and context of that which we are observing, to provide a running check on variability, etc.—are actually part of participant observation. It is the use of informants as if they were colleagues that we must now consider.

Such a procedure is not only legitimate but absolutely necessary to adequate investigation of any complex structure. In studying a social structure by participant observation there are two problems of bias that override all others, even the much belabored "personal equation." One results from the fact that a single observer cannot be everywhere at the same time, nor can he be "everywhere" in time, for that matter—he has not been in S forever, and will not be there indefinitely—so that, inevitably, something happens that he has not seen, cannot see, or will not see. The second results from the fact that there exist parts of the social structure into which he has not penetrated and probably will not, by virtue of the way he has defined himself to its members, because of limitations on the movement of those who sponsor him. etc. There has never been a participant-observer study in which the observer acquired full knowledge of all roles and statuses through his own direct observation, and for that matter there never will be such a study by a single observer. To have a team of observers in one possible solution; to have informants who stand in the relation of team members to the investigator is another. The virtue of the informant used in this way, is to increase the accessibility of S to the investigator.

EFFICIENCY OF SAMPLING FOR VARIOUS PROBLEMS IN THE FIELD

Sampling to obtain information about institutionalized norms and statuses.
It has already been argued that a properly obtained probability sample gives adequate information about institutionalized norms and statuses but is not very efficient. Two things are implied: that such information is *general* information so that any member of S has the same information as any other; and that the truth of such information does not depend solely on the opinions of the respondents—the information is in some sense objective.

The first of these implications is equivalent to assuming that S is homogeneous with respect to the property a, so that a sample of one suffices to classify S with respect to it. It then becomes inefficient to continue sampling. The principal defect in such an argument is a practical one: By what criterion can one decide S is homogeneous with respect to a without sampling S? There are two such criteria, neither of which is wholly satisfactory. The first is to use substantive knowledge. We would expect in general that certain norms are invariably institutionalized, such as incest and exogamy, descent, inheritance, marriage procedures, patterns of exchange of goods, formal structure of labor markets, etc. We may assume a priori, for example, that a sample of two hundred Navaho is not required to discover that marriage in one's own clan is incestuous. But the pitfall for the unwary investigator is that he may stray beyond his substantive knowledge or apply it at the wrong time in the wrong place.

A second is to employ a loose form of sequential sampling. Suppose, for example, that we ask an informed male in S whom he may marry, or whom any male may marry. He answers, "All who are A, but no who is B." We ask a second informant and discover again that he may marry all who are A, but no one who is B. We ask a third, a fourth, a fifth , and each tells us the same rule. We do not need to presume that the rule is actually obeyed; that is quite a different question. But we may certainly begin to believe that we have found an institutionalized norm. Conversely, the more variability we encounter, the more we must investigate further. The pitfall here is that we may be deceived by a homogeneous "pocket" within which all members agree but which does not necessarily represent all structural parts of S. For this reason we try to choose representative informants, each from a different status group. This implies, however, that we are working outward from earlier applications of this dangerous principle; we have used some informants to tell us what statuses there are, thereafter choosing additional informants from the new statuses we have discovered.

The second implication—that in some sense the truth of the information obtained depends not on the opinions of respondents but on something else that is "objective" in nature—simply paraphrases Durkheim: institutions are "external" to given individuals, even though they exist only "in" individuals; they have a life of their own, are *sui generis*. Illustrating with an extreme case: a "belief" of S's religion can be described by an informant even where neither he nor any living member of S actually believes it, although if no member ever did believe it we might regard the information as trivial. In other words, this type of information does not refer to individuals living at a given time, but rather to culture as a distinct object of abstraction. It is this type of information that we mean by "institutionalized norms and statuses." It bears repeating at this point that if one Navaho informant told us the Navaho were patrilineal and patrilocal, we would be more likely to assume he was wrong than we would be to assume that the Navaho had, for the moment, changed their institutions.

Sampling to obtain information about incidents and histories. If we had the good fortune to have a report from every member of S about what happened in region R at time T, would it really be good fortune? Would we not distinguish between those in a position to observe the event and those not? Among those who had been in the region R itself, would we not also distinguish subregions which provided different vantage points from which to view the event? Among those viewing it from the same vantage point, would we not distinguish more and less credible witnesses? Enumeration or not, we would apply stringent internal and external comparisons to each report in order to establish what truly occurred. Formally, of course, this describes a complex technique of stratification which, if carried out properly, would withstand any quantitative criticism. But if all the elements of a decision as to what is "truth" in such a case are considered, it is a moot point how important enumeration or random sampling is in the process.[9]

Informants with special information. Some things happen that relatively few people know about. A random sample is not a sensible way in which to obtain information about these events, although it is technically possible to define a universe U containing only those who do know and sample from U. A parallel case is the repetitive event in inaccessible parts of a social structure. A social

---

[9]None of this applies to *repeated* events. If we are interested in comparing several repetitions of the same event, generalizing as to the course that is typical, care must be taken in sampling the events.

structure is an organized system of relationships, one property of which is that certain parts of it are not readily observed by members located in other parts. There is a considerable amount of relatively esoteric information about S. It may be satisfactory from a formal point of view to regard S as consisting in many universes U_i, each of which is to be sampled for a different piece of information, but again the usefulness of such a conception is questionable, particularly if most U_i contain very few members.

EFFICIENCY AND ADEQUACY OF PARTICIPANT OBSERVATION FOR VARIOUS PROBLEMS IN THE FIELD

Ex post facto quantitative documentation. Because certain things are observed repeatedly, it sometimes occurs to the field worker to count these repetitions in his log as quantitative documentation of an assertion. In such cases, the information obtained should be subjected to any of the canons by which other quantitative data are evaluated; the care with which the universe is defined and the sense in which the sample is representative are particularly critical. With few exceptions, frequency statements made from field logs will *not* withstand such careful examination.

This sharp stricture applies only to ex post facto enumeration or sampling of field logs, and it is because it is ex post facto that the principal dangers arise. Events and persons represented in field logs will generally be sampled according to convenience rather than rules of probability sampling. The sample is unplanned, contains unknown biases. It is not so much random as haphazard, a distinction which is critical. When, after the fact, the observer attempts to correlate two classes of events in these notes very misleading results will be obtained. If we wish to correlate a and b it is characteristic of such samples that *"a"* will be more frequently recorded than *"not-a,"* and *"a and b"* more frequently than *"not-a and b"* or *"a and not-b."* As a general rule, only those data which the observer actually intended to enumerate should be treated as enumerable.

There are, of course, some valid enumerations contained in field notes. For example, a verbatim account kept of all meetings of some organization is a valid enumeration; a record kept, in some small rural community, of all members of it who come to the crossroads hamlet during a year is a valid enumeration. These will tend, however, to be intentional enumerations and not subject to the strictures applicable to ex post facto quantification. A much rarer exception will occur when, looking back through one's notes, one discovers that, without particularly intending it, every member of the community studied has been enumerated with respect to the property a, or that almost all of them have. This is likely to be rare because field notes tend not to record those who do *not* have the property a, and, of all those omitted in the notes, one does not know how many are *not-a* and how many simply were not observed. If everyone, or almost everyone, can be accounted for as either a or *not-a*, then a frequency statement is validly made.[10] But, if such information were desired in the first place,

[10]We may make a less stringent requirement of our notes, using what might be called "incomplete" indicator spaces. Briefly, if we wish to classify all members of S with respect

participant observation would clearly be a most inefficient means of obtaining it.

Readily verbalized norms and statuses. It is not efficient to use participant observation to obtain generally known norms and statuses so long as these can be readily stated. It may take a good deal of observation to infer that which an informant can quickly tell you. Participant observation would in such cases be primarily to check what informants say, to get clues to further questions, etc. It is, of course, true that the concurrent interviewing involved in participant observation will provide the information—it is necessary to make sense out of the observations—but it comes in bits and pieces and is less readily checked for accuracy, completeness, consistency, etc.

METHODS OF OBTAINING INFORMATION

INFORMATION TYPES	Enumerations and Samples	Participant Observation	Interviewing Informants
Frequency distributions	Prototype and best form	Usually inadequate and inefficient	Often, but not always, inadequate; if adequate it is efficient
Incidents, histories	Not adequate by itself; not efficient	Prototype and best form	Adequate with precautions, and efficient
Institutionalized norms and statuses	Adequate but inefficient	Adequate, but inefficient, except for unverbalized norms	Most efficient and hence best form

FIGURE 1. Methods of Obtaining Information

Latent phenomena. Not all norms and statuses can be verbalized. Consequently, there remains a special province to which participant observation lays well-justified claims. But certain misleading implications should be avoided in admitting them. Because such phenomena may be described as "latent"—as known to the observer but not to the members of S—it may be concluded that *all* latent phenomena are the province of participant observation. This does not follow. The term "latent" is ambiguous; it has several distinct usages, some of which do not even share the core meaning of "known to the observer, unknown to members." Lazarsfeld, for example, refers to a dimension underlying a series of manifest items as a "latent" attribute; it cannot be observed by anyone, and is inferred by the investigator from intercorrelations of observables. But the members of S may also make these inferences. (They infer that a series of statements classify the speaker as "liberal," for example.) The most advanced

---

to the underlying property A, and behaviors $a, b, c, d \ldots$, all indicate A, then it is sufficient for our purpose to have information on *at least one* of these indicators for each member of S. For some we might have only a, for some only b, etc., but we might have one among the indicators for all members, even though not the same one for all members; and thus be able to enumerate S adequately.

techniques for searching out such latent phenomena are found in survey research and psychometrics, not in participant observation.

These are matters of inference, not of how data are directly obtained. The same is true of the discovery of "latent functions." Often the observer is aware of connections between events when the members of S are not, even though they are aware of the events themselves. But again, relations among events are not the special province of any one method; we look for such connections in *all* our data. In fact, owing to the paucity and non-comparability of units that often plague the analysis of field notes, it might be argued that participant observation is often incapable of detecting such connections. The great value of participant observation in detecting latent phenomena, then, is in those cases in which members of S are unaware of actually observable events, of some of the things they do, or some of the things that happen around them, which can be directly apprehended by the observer. Any other case requires inference and such inference should be made from *all* available data.

SUMMARY AND CONCLUSION

Figure 1 offers a general summary.

With respect to the problem with which this paper originated the following conclusion may be drawn: Because we often treat different methods as concretely different types of study rather than as analytically different aspects of the same study, it is possible to attack a field study on the ground that it ought to be an enumeration and fails if it is not; and to defend it on the ground that it ought to be something *else* and succeeds only if it is. But, however we classify types of information in the future—and the classification suggested here is only tentative—they are not all of one type. True, a field report is unreliable if it gives us, after consulting a haphazard selection of informants or even a carefully planned "representative" selection, a statement such as, "All members of S believe that . . ." or "The average member of S believes that . . ." *and* (1) there is variance in the characteristic reported, (2) this variance is relevant to the problem reported, *and* (3) the informants cannot be seriously thought of as equivalent to a team of pollsters, *or* (4) the investigator has reported what is, essentially, the "average" beliefs of his *informants,* as if *they* were a representative, probability sample of respondents. But to demand that every piece of information be obtained by a probability sample is to commit the researcher to grossly inefficient procedure and to ignore fundamental differences among various kinds of information. The result is that we create false methodological issues, often suggest quite inappropriate research strategies to novices, and sometimes conceal real methodological issues which deserve more discussion in the literature—such as how to establish institutionalized norms given only questionnaire data. It should be no more satisfactorily rigorous to hear that everything is in some way a sample, and hence must be sampled, than to hear that everything is in some sense "whole" and hence cannot be sampled.

7

Data
Analysis

There are two distinct kinds of analysis generally carried out by sociologists. The first one might be called "descriptive," where the primary goal is to describe a particular population in terms of selected characteristics. Measures such as the mean or mode, as well as visual tools like the histogram or polygon are the stuff of which such description is generally made. Because these are considered in virtually all statistics texts, they will not be discussed here. Instead, the emphasis in this section will be on "explanatory" analysis, where the prime concern is establishing causality between two factors. It should be pointed out however, that any explanatory analysis is typically preceded by a description of the population, so that these two types of analysis are by no means independent enterprises.

Rosenberg's paper represents the basic logical process underlying explanatory analysis in sociology. Rosenberg is interested in what happens to a supposed two variable causal relationship when a third variable is introduced.[1] He argues that an examination of partial correlations or of percentages is inadequate in that it is difficult to discern a meaningful trend among several partial correlations or numerous cells in a frequency distribution. As an alternative, Rosenberg suggests "standardization," that is, a process of standardizing on some factor which one wishes to control in order to permit pure comparisons between sub-groups. One of the virtues of Rosenberg's paper is that it attempts to deal with the problem of small cell size, an occurrence constantly plaguing percentage

[1] See also H. Hyman, "The Introduction of Additional Variables and the Elaboration of the Analysis" in *Survey Design and Analysis* (New York: Free Press, 1955), pp. 275-329.

difference analysis. As an extension of this discussion, Labovitz addresses himself exclusively to this problem, suggesting the techniques of index-formation, and cell ordering and combination as possible solutions.

The next three papers are concerned with what some would call "true" sociological analysis. This is the situation where one's major independent or causal factor is a group characteristic, rather than an individual characteristic. Blau begins by presenting his seminal statement on such analyses, which he terms the consideration of "structural effects."[2] Tannenbaum and Bachman then introduce a cautious note, showing clearly the dangers of failing to control rigidly enough individual level variables, a procedure which is crucial to establishing a true structural effect.[3] Finally, Campbell and Alexander present a refinement of Blau's statement, postulating a two-step model of structural effects where the intervening variable of interpersonal relationships is emphasized.

The next paper centers on the argument of statistical significance. Taking up where Kish left off in chapter 4, Labovitz outlines several criteria for selecting significance levels.

The last paper in this chapter is a not ungentle reminder by Selvin and Stuart that our approach to analysis in sociology is often contrary to our formal ideology of what analysis should be. We are collectively chastised for such tactics as "fishing," "snooping," or "hunting" for worthwhile tidbits in our data, while discarding that which is less presentable.

---

[2] For additional discussion, see J. Davis, J. Spaeth, and C. Hudson, "Analyzing Effects of Group Composition," *American Sociological Review*, 26 (1961), 215-25.

[3] See also J. Bachman, C. Smith, and J. Slesinger, "Control, Performance, and Satisfaction: An Analysis of Structural and Individual Effects," *Journal of Personality and Social Psychology*, 4 (1966), 127-36. For a recent paper challenging the utility of structural analysis, see R. Hauser, "Context and Consex: A Cautionary Tale," *American Journal of Sociology*, 75 (1970), 645-64.

TEST FACTOR STANDARDIZATION AS A METHOD
OF INTERPRETATION

Morris Rosenberg

One of the major analytic tools in survey research is the operation which Kendall and Lazarsfeld have labelled "interpretation." As an analytic model, interpretation is the explanation of a relationship between two variables by means of an intervening variable called a "test factor."[1] The criterion for determining whether an interpretation has been effected is whether, when one stratifies by (holds constant) the test factor, the partial associations disappear or are reduced.

For reasons to be discussed later, the complete disappearance of the original relationship in all of the partial associations is so rare as to be an oddity, a triviality, or a tautology. In practice, then, the survey researcher usually examines the data to see whether the partial associations have been reduced;[2] if such a reduction occurs, then he may conclude that the control variable is a "contributory factor."

One problem in the use of this method is that, since it is based entirely on the inspection of each of the partial relationships,[3] it is often difficult to make a clear statement about whether the relationship has been reduced, and it is virtually impossible to stipulate the degree to which it has been reduced. This problem is particularly acute when the test factor or factors introduced have a large number of categories, since each category yields a separate partial relationship. Let us say that we wish to examine a relationship between two variables, controlling simultaneously on three others, each of which is trichotomized. This procedure yields 27 partial associations. For both statistical and theoretical reasons, the likelihood that a uniform reduction will appear in all 27 partial associations is so slight as to be negligible. Most frequently there is considerable variation among these partial associations. Under these circumstances, it is sometimes difficult to provide a clear answer to the question of

Reprinted with the permission of the author and the publisher from *Social Forces*, Vol. 41 (1962), 53-61.

[1] If the third variable is antecedent, the analytic procedure is called "explanation"; such relationships have typically been called "spurious." If the third variable is "intervening," the operation is called "interpretation." See P. L. Kendall and P. F. Lazarsfeld, "Problems of Survey Analysis," in R. K. Merton and P. F. Lazarsfeld, eds., *Continuities in Social Research: Studies in the Scope and Method of "The American Soldier"* (Glencoe, Ill.: The Free Press, 1950), p. 157. Discussions of interpretation also appear in Morris Zelditch, Jr., *A Basic Course in Sociological Statistics* (New York: Holt, 1959), Chap. 8; in Herbert Hyman, *Survey Design and Analysis* (Glencoe, Ill.: The Free Press, 1955), Chap. 7; and in Hans Zeisel, *Say It With Figures* (New York: Harper, 1947), Chap. IX.

[2] Both explanation and interpretation are examples of the "M" type of elaboration in which, according to Hyman, *ibid.*, p. 287, "one is interested in noting whether the partial relationships become smaller than the original relationships."

[3] "Partial relationships are those observed within particular subgroups of the total sample. They are obtained when other variables, in this case what we have called the test factor or factors, are held constant." *Ibid.*, p. 278, fn. 5.

whether the original association has or has not been reduced as a result of controlling on these test factors.

Dependence upon the inspection of the partial associations to determine whether an interpretation has been effected may thus produce ambiguous and imprecise conclusions. Where such ambiguity exists, it would often be helpful to have a simple summary measure which would indicate the effect of controlling on the test factor or factors. Ideally, one would want a single table which would indicate the relationship between the original two variables when the test factor or factors are controlled, and which could readily be compared with the original table.

One method which does enable us to obtain a single table showing the relationship between two variables when one or more test factors are "controlled" or "held constant" is *standardization.*[4] This method, which has long been widely used in demographic and public health research, has apparently not been employed in opinion and attitude studies. Both demographic studies and attitude studies are largely concerned with "controlling on" or "holding constant" certain population or sample characteristics for purposes of clarification or analysis. But while attitude studies control on test factors by inspecting the association within each of the test factor categories, standardization provides a summary measure of what population rates would be if certain population characteristics were held constant. Thus, standardization provides a simpler summary measure of the effect of the control variable.

A concrete example may help to demonstrate this point. In a recent survey of high school students, we undertook to examine the relationship between religious affiliation and self-esteem, controlling simultaneously on three variables—father's education, social class identification, and high school grades. Since each of these control variables had four categories, the basic table yielded 64 partial associations between religion and self-esteem. Inspection of these 64 tables revealed rather confusing and ambiguous results: there was considerable variation among the partial associations. It was difficult to determine whether these partial associations revealed a trend and, if such a trend existed, how one might express it precisely. This made it particularly difficult to provide a clear and simple answer to the question: If we control on these three factors, is the relationship between religious affiliation and self-esteem reduced?

By introducing the method of test factor standardization, however, it was possible to produce a simple standardized table which could easily be compared with the original table. For example, Table 1-A shows the original relationship between religion and self-esteem and Table 1-B the standardized relationship.[5] Let us compare Jewish and Catholic students in these two tables. In the original relationship, Jewish students are 7.2 percent[6] more likely than Catholics to have

[4]A clear exposition of the logic and method of standardization is presented in Margaret J. Hagood, *Statistics for Sociologists* (New York: Reynal and Hitchcock, 1941), Chap. 27.

[5]In demographic standardization we emerge with theoretic rates. In applying standardization to opinion and attitude studies, we are interested in obtaining the entire table that would appear if the test factor or factors were controlled. A method of doing this is suggested later in this paper.

[6]The measure of association employed here will be simply the percentage difference between two groups. This measure, which Kendall and Lazarsfeld, *op. cit.*, p. 163, designate as "f" and Morris Zelditch, *op. cit.*, p. 164, calls epsilon is commonly used in opinion and attitude surveys.

TABLE 1. Religion and Self-Esteem: (A) Original Relationship and (B) Relationship Standardized on Three Test Factors

Self-Esteem	A Original Relationship			Self-Esteem	B Standardized Relationship		
	Catholic	Jewish	Protestant		Catholic	Jewish	Protestant
High	70.6	77.8	70.0	High	71.3	75.0	69.3
Medium	24.5	19.1	25.9	Medium	24.3	21.0	26.1
Low	4.9	3.1	4.1	Low	4.4	4.0	4.6
Total percent	100.0	100.0	100.0	Total percent	100.0	100.0	100.0
Number	(1413)	(517)	(1315)	Number	(1413)	(517)	(1315)

high self-esteem, whereas in the standardized relationship this difference is 3.6 percent; in other words, half of the original difference between these two groups vanishes. While the control factors do not account for the relationship completely, this result suggests that they do contribute to it.

Just as standardization can deal with any number of control variables (so long as there are sufficient cases available), so it can be applied to any substantive area. We have, for example, applied it to the following kinds of tables: self-esteem by psychosomatic symptoms, controlling simultaneously on indicators of isolation, psychological vulnerability, and stability of self-image; social class and self-esteem, controlling on school grades; self-esteem and participation in discussions of public affairs, controlling on indicators of "interpersonal sensitivity"; and many more. In each case, standardization enabled us to obtain a much clearer picture of the relevance of the interpretive variable or variables. In several cases standardization produced reductions of the order of 15 to 18 percent from the original difference. Generally speaking, the larger the original difference, the greater the size of the reduction.

As noted above, the usefulness of standardization is most apparent when the test factor(s) yield a large number of partial associations, for the results are then particularly difficult to encompass by inspection. Even when the number of categories is fairly small, however, it is often not easy to provide a clear answer to the research question. The author encountered this recent example. He wished to determine whether the introduction of a test factor would reduce the relationship between two variables. The original difference between the two groups was 10 percent. Stratification of the sample by the test factor produced four partial associations. The difference in the first partial was 20 percent, in the second 5 percent, in the third 6 percent, and in the fourth 10 percent. Even in this case, it was hard to provide an unequivocal answer to the question of whether the relationship had been reduced. By standardizing on the test factor, however, it was possible to obtain a picture of what the relationship between the two variables would be if they were equalized in terms of the test factor.

The general point, then, is that if one is interested in learning whether a relationship is reduced when one controls on a test factor (or factors), and if, as is often the case, the results yielded by inspection are unclear and ambiguous, then standardization may be a useful method for providing a clearer answer to the question of whether, and to what extent, the relationship has been reduced.

In demographic standardization, the population groups to be compared are typically standardized on some standard population. For example, if one wished to compare the death rates of New York State and Florida, one would probably standardize both states on the age distribution of the United States (the standard population). This would insure that the differences in death rates in the two states were not simply a reflection of the unusual number of aged people in Florida. In attitude surveys, of course, there is seldom a standard population available; hence, it is necessary to use the total sample as the standard population.

For some purposes, however, demographers will standardize one population on another. For example, if one standardized Florida on New York State, one would determine the "theoretic" death rate of Florida if the age distribution of its population were the same as that of New York State; or one might standardize a county on the total state in order to determine whether its rate were unusual. When the procedure of standardizing one group on another is applied to attitude survey data, certain interesting results may appear which cannot be obtained by the usual method of inspecting partial associations.

For example, if we hypothesize that one reason Jewish students have higher self-esteem than Catholics is that their fathers are more highly educated, then we might ask: Were the Jewish fathers not more highly educated—were their educational levels the same as those of the Catholics—would their self-esteem level be less? To answer this question, we would standardize the Jewish group not on the total sample but on the Catholic subgroup. When we perform this operation, we find that the proportion of Jewish students with high self-esteem is reduced by 3.1 percent. In other words, if the Jewish fathers had the same educational level as the Catholic fathers, the difference in self-esteem level between the two groups would be reduced from 7.8 percent to 4.7 percent, a reduction of about two-fifths in the size of the difference.

Or we might ask: Is the lower self-esteem level of the Catholics partly due to the fact that their fathers are more poorly educated? Otherwise expressed, would their self-esteem levels be higher if their fathers were as well educated as the Jewish fathers? In this case we standardize the Catholics on the Jewish subgroup. We find that the self-esteem of the Catholics shows a scarcely perceptible increase of 0.3 percent. Thus, if the Catholic fathers had the same educational level as the Jewish fathers, their children would still have about the same self-esteem level.

Such standardization enhances our understanding by enabling us to specify the relevance of the control variable. In the example cited earlier, we standardized both religious groups on the total sample. In the present case, we have standardized each subgroup on the other. This procedure yields the interesting finding that the difference in self-esteem level between Jews and Catholics *is more due to the fact that the Jewish fathers are relatively well-educated than that the Catholic fathers are relatively poorly educated.*

The application of the method of standardization to opinion and attitude studies may thus make it possible to answer certain questions which are more difficult to answer by the usual method of inspection. It should be emphasized that the method of standardization is mainly useful when one is attempting to "interpret" a relationship by observing whether the relationship is reduced when one controls on a test factor or factors. It does not eliminate the usefulness of specification,[7] *i.e.*, the analysis of the differential relationships in the various partial associations. In this sense it is not considered a substitute for any method currently in use but rather an additional method which can help to answer certain relevant questions.

Standardization is, of course, an established procedure, and it shares with much of survey research an interest in attributes although it is somewhat less likely to be concerned with ordinal measurement. In recommending the application of standardization to survey research, however, certain new problems arise. When we apply standardization to demographic problems, we are usually

[7]Specification, called by Kendall and Lazarsfeld the *P type* of elaboration, "is focussed on the relative size of the partial relationships in order to specify the circumstances under which the original relation is more or less pronounced." Hyman, *op. cit.*, p. 287.

TABLE 2. Religion by Self-Esteem, Controlling on Father's Education

Self-Esteem	8th Grade or Less (Partial Association I)			Self-Esteem	Some High School (Partial Association II)			Self-Esteem	High School Graduate (Partial Association III)		
	Catholic	Jewish	Protestant		Catholic	Jewish	Protestant		Catholic	Jewish	Protestant
High	A.681 .1075	B.718 .1134	C.648 .1023	High	A.685 .1704	B.706 .1757	C.720 .1791	High	A.717 .2073	B.745 .2154	C.574 .1659
Medium	D.258 .0407	E.256 .0404	F.290 .0458	Medium	D.261 .0649	E.262 .0652	F.252 .0627	Medium	D.235 .0679	E.197 .0570	F.355 .1026
Low	G.061 .0096	H.026 .0041	I.062 .0098	Low	G.054 .0134	H.032 .0080	I.028 .0070	Low	G.048 .0139	H.058 .0168	I.071 .0205
N =	(360)	(39)	(193)	N =	(482)	(126)	(325)	N =	(541)	(137)	(406)
	Proportion in test factor category .1579				Proportion in test factor category .2488				Proportion in test factor category .2891		

266

TABLE 2. (Continued)

Self-Esteem	Some College (Partial Association IV)			Self-Esteem	College Graduate (Partial Association V)			Self-Esteem	Post-Graduate (Partial Association VI)		
	Catholic	Jewish	Protestant		Catholic	Jewish	Protestant		Catholic	Jewish	Protestant
High	A .709 .0722	B .788 .0803	C .699 .0712	High	A .675 .0886	B .879 .1153	C .706 .0926	High	A .729 .0519	B .827 .0589	C .738 .0525
Medium	D .241 .0246	E .176 .0179	F .269 .0274	Medium	D .298 .0391	E .111 .0146	F .265 .0348	Medium	D .257 .0183	E .147 .0105	F .205 .0146
Low	G .050 .0051	H .035 .0036	I .032 .0033	Low	G .026 .0034	H .010 .0013	I .029 .0038	Low	G .014 .0010	H .027 .0019	I .057 .0041
N =	(141)	(85)	(156)	N =	(114)	(99)	(279)	N =	(70)	(75)	(122)
	Proportion in test factor category .1019				Proportion in test factor category .1312				Proportion in test factor category .0712		

267

interested in determining theoretic *rates;* each rate represents a single figure. In survey research, however, we are interested in *total distributions.* Thus, if we examine the association between X and Y standardizing on Z, we must emerge with a standardized table which contains all the cells of the original table. Hence, if the original table contains 16 cells, we must perform 16 standardizations. Such a procedure may become quite laborious. In order to deal with this problem, we wish to suggest a somewhat simplified standardization procedure which appears to reduce the computations involved and which may therefore make the method more generally useful.

STANDARDIZATION COMPUTATIONS

In the example cited above, we found that Jewish adolescents were more likely than Catholic adolescents to have high self-esteem scores, and we hypothesized that this might be due in part to the fact they came from more highly educated families. How do we proceed to test this hypothesis by standardizing on the total sample? The first step is to set up the control table as one would in the usual survey procedure. This table would be religion by self-esteem controlling on father's education: the data are percentaged in the usual fashion. (We will use proportions rather than percentages, since this simplifies the computations somewhat.) Table 2 illustrates this procedure. The top figure in each cell represents the proportion of the total in each column. Looking at these figures, we see that irrespective of father's education, Jewish students are more likely than Catholic students to have high self-esteem. For example, among those whose fathers did not go beyond grade school, 71.8 percent of the Jews, but 68.1 percent of the Catholics, had high self-esteem. This is exactly the table we would set up in the usual procedure of interpretation in survey research.

The second step is to compute the proportion in each test factor category. How many fathers did not go beyond elementary school, how many had some high school, how many were high school graduates, etc.? This can be determined by adding the marginal totals in each partial association and dividing by the sample total. Thus, the number of fathers who did not go beyond elementary school is 360 + 39 + 193 = 592, which is 15.79 percent of the total sample. The same computations are made for each of the partial associations. All the proportions, when added, equal 100 percent or 1.0000.

The third step is to multiply the calculated proportion in each test factor category by the proportion in each cell. The same "test factor proportion" is applied to each cell in each partial association. Thus, for those whose fathers did not go beyond elementary school (Partial Association I), we multiply .1579 by .681, .1579 by .718, .1579 by .648, .1579 by .258, and so on for all cells labelled A to I. We then move on to Partial Association II, where we multiply .2488 (the test factor proportion) by .685, .2488 by .706, .2488 by .720, and so on for all the cells labelled A to I. These figures are entered on the second line of each cell; we will call them the standardized figures. Thus, for Catholics with high self-esteeem whose fathers have not gone beyond grade school (Cell A in Partial Association I), we enter the figure .1075, which is the test factor proportion, .1579, times the column proportion, .681. For Jews with high self-esteem whose fathers have not gone beyond grade school (Cell B in Partial

Association I), we enter the figure .1134, which is the test factor proportion, .1579, times the column proportion, .718; and so on for all the cells in the table.

The lower figure in each cell (*i.e.*, the standardized figure) is thus the product of the test factor proportion and the column proportion. The final step is to add up these standardized figures in the corresponding cells of all six of the Partial Associations and enter them into a new table. This new result gives us the relationship between religion and self-esteem, standardized on father's education. For example, we would add the standardized figures in the cells labelled B in all six Partial Associations. Specifically, we would add .1134 + .1757 + .2154 + .0803 + .1153 + .0589 = .7590. This means that standardizing on father's education, 75.8 percent of the Jewish students would have high self-esteem whereas, in actual fact, 77.5 percent of them have high self-esteem. In other words, if the educational level of the Jewish fathers were the same as the average, the self-esteem levels of the Jewish students would be slightly lower.

The same procedure is followed in adding up the figures for all the other corresponding cells. All six D's are added together, all six C's are added together, all six B's are added together, *etc.*, and the totals are entered in the corresponding cells of the standardized table. Table 3-A shows the original relationship between religion and self-esteem and Table 3-B shows this relationship standardized on father's education. It will be seen that in Table 3-A, the difference in self-esteem between Jews and Catholics is 7.8 percent whereas in Table 3-B it is 6.0 percent.

The main advantage of this computational format over that usually employed in demographic standardization is that it enables us to perform certain repetitive operations and thus reduces the computational effort involved. There are, however, certain other advantages in the use of this format. First, it enables us to work directly from the original control table, thus enabling us to keep in mind which is the independent variable, which the dependent variable, and which the test factor. Second, this procedure contains several built-in checks which enable us to determine whether computational errors have been made and provides a simple guide to locating such errors. The first check is that in the final table, as in the original table, each column must total 100 percent. In addition, the column total of the standardized figures (the lower figures) in each cell is equal to the test factor proportion for that Partial Association. For example, in Partial Association I (Table 2), the test factor proportion is .1579. Among the Catholics (cells A, D, and G) the standardized figures are .1075 + .0407 + .0096 = .1578. Similarly, in Partial Association IV, the test factor proportion is .1019. For the Jewish students in this group (cells B, E, and H) the total of the standardized figures is .0803 + .0179 + .0036 = .1018. Some slight discrepancies will appear due to rounding, but all column totals should be close to the test factor proportion in each partial association. Finally, the standardized figures for all corresponding columns combined (*e.g.*, the standardized figures for cells A, D, and G for all six partial associations) must equal 100 percent. Checks can thus be introduced at several stages of the calculations.

The only condition under which these results will not appear is one in which there is a column in the control table which does not have at least one case. In using this procedure, then, it is necessary to make such combinations as to insure that every column total in the control table includes one or more cases.

TABLE 3. Religion and Self-Esteem: (A) Original Relationship and (B) Relationship Standardized on Father's Education

Self-Esteem	A Original Relationship			B Relationship Standardized on Father's Education		
	Catholic	Jewish	Protestant	Catholic	Jewish	Protestant
High	69.7	77.5	66.7	69.8	75.8	66.3
Medium	25.3	19.1	28.6	25.6	20.6	28.8
Low	5.0	3.4	4.7	4.6	3.6	4.9
Total percent	100.0	100.0	100.0	100.0	100.0	100.0
Number	(1708)	(561)	(1481)	(1708)	(561)	(1481)

There is one statistical advantage of standardization over the inspection of partial associations which in certain cases may be of importance, *viz.*, that standardization tends to minimize the effect of random fluctuations arising from small numbers of cases. The reason is this: In the usual survey research procedure, a test factor is introduced; this creates a number of partial associations, each of which is examined separately. This method thus treats each partial association as equivalent to every other, even though one partial association is based on 5 percent of the cases (and is therefore unstable) and another partial association is based upon 50 percent of the cases (and is therefore stable). The method of standardization does not eliminate the problem of instability based on small numbers of cases, but it does minimize its effect. For example, assume that the partial is based on 5 percent of the cases and, because of small numbers, the percentage differences between groups in this partial association are large. We then standardize one group on another in this partial. Since the proportion in this test factor category is small, the standardized figures will also be small; hence, their contributions to the final standardized total will be small. On the other hand, if the partial contained 50 percent of the cases, then its contribution to the total would be large. The method of standardization thus gives less weight to partial relationships with smaller numbers of cases, *i.e.*, it gives less weight precisely to those partial relationships which are most unstable, most subject to random fluctuation. In this sense it has an advantage over the usual procedure, which, in interpreting the data, accords equal weight to all partial relationships.

This does not, of course, eliminate the danger of random fluctuations of partial relationships with small totals, but it does tend to minimize the effect of such errors. The main danger occurs under the following conditions: If we are comparing two groups in a partial association, and if the number of cases in one group is quite large and the other very small, then random fluctuations in the small group may exercise a considerable influence upon the total result because it is standardized on the large group. Under such conditions it is best to recombine in such a manner as to have sufficient cases in the small group for reasonable stable results.

THE USEFULNESS OF INTERPRETATION

It may not be extravagant to suggest that the operation called "interpretation" is the central "tool of causal analysis"[8] in attitude survey research. There is reason to believe, however, that reports of its use appear infrequently in research literature. For example, in an outstanding critique of problems of survey analysis in *The American Soldier*, Kendall and Lazarsfeld present a detailed discussion of the elements involved in the interpretation of survey data with a view to abstracting out those analytic methods employed by the researchers in this work. After presenting the analytic model, they make the following revealing statement: "... there is one further point which merits our attention. *The American Soldier* does not present any example in which the full scheme of interpretation, as outlined above is utilized."[9] In other words, *The American*

---

[8] Zeisel, *op. cit.*, Part III.
[9] *Op. cit.*, p. 158.

Soldier, which probably represents the largest and most sophisticated concentration of survey research talent and resources ever brought to bear upon a single sociological study, does not report a single case of a relationship cancelling out when a third variable is controlled.

It may further be noted that Kendall and Lazarsfeld, on the basis of their extensive experience, state that: "In actual practice it is rare to find pure P or M types" (*i.e.,* interpretation, explanation, and specification). They do not "represent common empirical situations."[10] In fact, *The People's Choice,* whose authors were keenly alert to examples of this method, provides only one example of a relationship disappearing almost completely; and even in this one example, we find, the original difference between the two groups was only 7 percent.[11]

Since the logic of interpretation is sound and since it appears to be of central importance to the analysis of survey data, it is important to consider why it appears so rarely.

Interpretation is said to be accomplished when stratification by the intervening test factor results in the disappearance or the reduction of the relationship in each of the partial associations. Let us treat the *disappearance* of the relationship as one issue and the *reduction* of the relationship as another.

Probably the main reason that a relationship so rarely disappears when one controls on a test factor is simply that a large number of factors are implicated in most relationships. This is the most elementary principle of multiple causation in social life. Hence, it may be as difficult completely to explain a relationship between two variables by means of a third as it is completely to explain a dependent variable by means of an independent one. If we operate on the principle of multiple causation, we are driven to abandon almost all hope that a single variable will completely explain the relationship between two others, unless we are dealing with a virtual tautology.

But this does not explain why we so rarely find reports of the relationship being reduced. There does not seem to be anything in the nature of social reality which should make it so difficult to specify factors which *contribute* to the relationship, even if we cannot explain the relationship completely. One reason may be that the attempt to interpret a relationship by inspecting a number of partial associations often leads to ambiguous and imprecise conclusions. If this is so, then the method of standardization, which can provide a simpler and clearer summary picture of the effect of a test factor or factors, may increase our ability to indicate whether a test factor has contributed in part to the observed relationship.

SUMMARY

The operation called interpretation has long been considered one of the central tools of causal analysis in opinion and attitude research. The procedure

[10] *Ibid.,* p. 155. As a matter of fact, we have found that P types (conditional relationships) are by no means rare in our work; it is the M types—where the partial relationships disappear—that are rare.

[11] P. F. Lazarsfeld, B. Berelson, and H. Gaudet, *The People's Choice* (New York: Columbia University Press, 1948), p. 47.

involves the stratification of the sample by an intervening test factor and the inspection of the partial associations to determine whether the relationship has vanished or been reduced. In many cases, particularly when a large number of partial associations are involved, it is difficult to determine by inspection whether the relationship has been reduced and it is not possible to specify the degree to which it has been reduced. The method of standardization, which has a long tradition in demographic and public health research, can help to deal with these problems by indicating the relationship which would exist if the test factor or factors were controlled. A simplified method of computing standardizations, which makes it more easily adaptable to attitude survey research, has been presented. It is suggested that the application of standardization may help to produce a wider use of interpretation in attitude research.

METHODS FOR CONTROL WITH
SMALL SAMPLE SIZE

Sanford I. Labovitz

A small sample size often does not permit the use of standard procedures for controlling two or more variables, for partialling decreases the ratio between the number of cases and the number of cells. Consider the association between storks and babies. To demonstrate whether the relationship is due to a third variable, urbanization, the correlation between the number of storks and the number of babies must be computed for rural areas, and again for urban areas. But the very act of partialling, even with a dichotomy, requires an N large enough to be split and still yield a fruitful cross-classification. In the illustration, the number of cells increases from four to eight. If only 15 rural and urban areas had been analyzed, partialling would have led to non-interpretable results. The problem increases geometrically when two or more controls are considered simultaneously. Even when all control classifications are dichotomies, six define 64 cells, and nine define 512. The problem is to distribute a constant number of cases over an increasing number of cells; for 64 cells, one is likely to need at least 500 to 1,000 cases.

Three possible solutions, when N is relatively small, are selection, index formation, and cellordering and combination.[1]

Reprinted with the permission of the author and the publisher, The American Sociological Association, from the *American Sociological Review*, Vol. 30 (1965). 243-49.

This paper grew out of a special seminar in statistics at Stanford University supported by the Social Science Research Council, in 1963. The major ideas in the paper are from John W. Tukey, *Data Analysis and Behavioral Science*, unpublished manuscript, 1963, ch. H. I have found Tukey's ideas both extremely useful and widely applicable and feel they should be accessible to other sociologists. I wish to thank Lincoln Moses for his initial help on some of the ideas presented in the paper, and Santo F. Camilleri for his valuable criticism and advice.

[1] These methods are discussed briefly by Tukey, *op. cit.*

SELECTION

The simplest solution is to select from a number of variables the one or two deemed most important. Selection may be based on the relations between the control classifications and the dependent variable, those most highly correlated being selected for control. This approach may lead to difficulty when one of the candidates is strongly related to the independent variable;[2] it also forces one to use only a few of the potential control variables, though one may want to allow for the effects of most of them.

Another method of selection is to consider the relations among all the control variables. If two or more are highly correlated, one can perhaps be chosen to represent the others; and if two or three highly interrelated clusters occur, a few variables may adequately represent all. But this solution is not applicable when the variables are not highly correlated. Furthermore, two variables may be highly related, yet have different effects on a third, so that both variables must be controlled.

Finally, of course, selection can be based on the nature of the problem, theoretical considerations, or previous research findings.

INDEX FORMATION

The method of index formation is based on the relation of each control classification to the dependent variable.[3] On the basis of these relationships, weights are assigned to each category in a control classification and each individual in a category receives the designated weight. These weights are summed for each individual to yield an index based on all of the controls. Finally, the index is used as a control classification in the usual sense, i.e., the individuals are grouped by similarity of composite weighting values.

In general, "to control" or "controlling for" a variable or classification[4] means to take out (almost always only in part) the effects of a factor, and thus make visible a more nearly "pure" relation between the variables under consideration. For example, to take out the effects of urbanization, the relation between storks and babies is computed separately for urban and rural areas. Urbanization is controlled by being held broadly constant with regard to the variables in question.[5]

Index formation is a method of control in this sense, because it takes out the effects of selected classifications. The weighting system is based on the relations between the control classifications and the dependent variable. The sum of these weights yields a measure, or index, which is a plausible predictor of the dependent variable, at least by contrast with many other choices. By grouping all individuals with similar indices, certain effects (hopefully important ones) of the

---

[1] These methods are discussed briefly by Tukey, *op. cit.*

[2] *Ibid.*, p. H45.

[3] *Ibid.*

[4] For a discussion of certain theoretical aspects of control, see Paul F. Lazarfeld, "Interpretation of Statistical Relations as a Research Operation," in Paul F. Lazarsfeld and Morris Rosenberg (eds.), *The Language of Social Research*, Glencoe, Ill.: The Free Press, 1957, pp. 115-125.

[5] This, of course, is not perfect control, for urban and rural areas are of different sizes. More precise control would involve a finer classification. Perfect control is never possible.

control classifications (considered simultaneously but not concurrently) are taken out. This type of control may not be as desirable as conventional partialling, e.g., female Protestants may end up with the same index value as male Catholics. But note that if female Protestants and male Catholics report a similar mean value of the dependent variable—in the example below, number of organizational memberships—the two groups are homogeneous in this respect. By grouping these apparently different aggregates, the effects of religion and sex are simultaneously controlled.

As an illustration of the method of index formation, consider the hypothetical data in Table 1. The problem is to find the relation between education and number of organizational memberships for 64 individuals, holding constant, social class, age, religion, income, sex and city size. Even controlling for sex alone greatly reduces the ratio of the number of individuals to the number of cells: the relationship for females is based on 31 cases. If religion were partialled, the relationship among Jews would be based on only 14 cases. Controlling on two variables with an N of 64, let alone all six, is virtually impossible by conventional partialling methods, but index formation does permit such control.

TABLE 1. Hypothetical Data for 64 Individuals on Education, Number of Organizational Memberships, Social Class, Age, Religion, Income, Sex and City Size

	Education[a]	Memberships	Social Class[b]	Age	Religion[c]	Income	Sex	City Size
1	10	8	M	42	J	$ 7,500	M	35,000
2	4	1	L	57	P	4,000	M	20,000
3	8	3	L	49	C	4,000	F	2,500
4	6	3	M	35	C	2,500	F	4,000
5	8	4	M	50	P	3,500	M	75,000
6	12	6	U	29	P	6,000	F	100,000
7	16	10	U	26	J	12,000	M	100,000
8	5	1	L	63	C	8,500	F	30,000
9	6	1	L	59	P	3,000	M	4,000
10	8	0	L	42	P	3,000	M	8,000
11	12	5	M	39	P	5,500	F	100,000
12	7	4	L	47	P	4,500	F	50,000
13	13	9	M	33	C	9,000	M	75,000
14	14	7	U	25	P	8,500	M	100,000
15	2	0	L	72	P	2,000	M	2,500
16	7	3	L	54	C	2,500	F	1,000
17	4	1	M	59	J	3,000	F	1,000
18	11	5	M	38	P	4,500	F	45,000
19	9	5	M	42	P	4,500	F	50,000
20	8	6	M	41	C	3,500	M	30,000
21	4	2	L	58	C	2,000	M	100,000
22	15	8	U	28	J	14,000	M	50,000
23	8	7	M	38	P	7,500	F	35,000
24	9	9	M	45	P	6,000	M	15,000
25	12	8	U	36	P	8,500	M	25,000
26	7	6	M	58	C	4,000	F	20,000
27	11	5	M	41	J	6,500	F	100,000

TABLE 1. (Continued)

	Educa-tion[a]	Member-ships	Social Class[b]	Age	Religion[c]	Income	Sex	City Size
28	9	4	L	47	J	6,000	M	50,000
29	15	9	U	35	P	11,000	M	60,000
30	6	2	L	66	C	4,000	M	15,000
31	10	7	M	46	P	6,800	M	50,000
32	12	6	U	54	J	7,500	M	65,000
33	8	6	M	50	C	6,500	M	75,000
34	7	5	M	62	P	10,000	M	60,000
35	8	6	M	46	P	7,000	M	20,000
36	6	4	L	58	P	7,200	M	15,000
37	7	2	L	50	C	12,000	M	18,000
38	7	4	M	52	P	6,500	M	25,000
39	10	5	M	41	J	9,000	M	35,000
40	6	5	L	55	J	7,000	F	45,000
41	8	5	L	65	C	7,200	F	75,000
42	4	0	M	51	P	8,000	F	50,000
43	7	2	M	48	P	8,500	F	100,000
44	9	15	U	28	P	9,000	F	52,000
45	6	7	M	41	J	7,000	F	55,000
46	6	5	L	33	P	7,200	F	80,000
47	6	2	M	65	J	8,000	F	20,000
48	3	1	L	74	C	9,500	F	10,000
49	5	0	M	52	P	7,000	F	30,000
50	6	3	M	32	P	7,200	F	1,500
51	4	1	M	38	C	7,100	F	5,000
52	7	3	L	60	P	3,500	M	50,000
53	4	0	M	35	J	4,500	M	55,000
54	15	10	U	40	J	6,000	M	65,000
55	10	7	M	38	P	5,500	M	100,000
56	8	3	M	29	P	4,200	M	50,000
57	8	6	M	35	P	5,000	M	30,000
58	3	0	L	38	C	3,500	M	1,500
59	9	3	M	66	C	3,000	F	54,000
60	2	1	L	48	P	3,800	F	100,000
61	5	2	M	54	P	5,200	F	58,000
62	3	1	L	27	P	2,500	F	1,500
63	5	0	M	35	J	3,200	F	20,000
64	2	0	L	33	P	2,800	F	35,000

[a]Number of years of formal education.
[b]U = Upper class; M = Middle class; L = Lower class.
[c]P = Protestant; C = Catholic; J = Jew.

Table 2 illustrates a simple method—not the only one, nor necessarily the best one—of assigning a weight to each category of the control classifications.[6] Each

[6]Ideally, the rationale for weighting combines theoretical and empirical considerations. Theoretical explanations of phenomena necessarily "weight" variables by including some and excluding others; in addition, theory may assign differential weights to the independent variables in question. The empirical techniques include the general methods of multivariate

control is divided into a number of categories, and the mean number of organizational memberships for each category is determined and used as its weight. For example, the age group 65-74 has a mean and hence a weight of 2.2. Every individual in this age group receives a weight of 2.2 on age.

TABLE 2.   Mean Number of Organizational Memberships for Each Category of Six Control Classifications

Control Classification	Mean Number of Organizational Memberships
Social Class:	
Upper	7.7
Middle	4.3
Lower	2.2
Age:	
65-74	2.2
55-64	2.9
45-54	3.7
35-44	4.9
25-34	5.2
Religion:	
Protestant	4.3
Catholic	3.3
Jew	5.1
Income:	
0-2,499	1.0
2,500-4,999	2.4
5,000-7,499	5.1
7,500-9,999	4.7
10,000+	6.8
Sex:	
Male	4.9
Female	3.1
City Size:	
0- 4,999	1.7
5,000-19,999	2.7
20,000-49,999	4.1
50,000-99,999	5.0
100,000+	5.0

analysis (beta weights), factor analysis (factor loadings), and scaling. For a discussion of empirical techniques, see William J. Goode and Paul K. Hatt, *Methods in Social Research*, New York: McGraw-Hill, 1952, pp. 232-296; Clyde H. Coombs, "Theory and Methods of Social Measurement," in Leon Festinger and Daniel Katz (eds.), *Research Methods in the Behavioral Sciences*, New York: Holt, Rinehart and Winston, 1953, pp. 471-536; Quinn McNemar, *Psychological Statistics*, New York: John Wiley, 3rd ed., 1963, pp. 169-188; Hubert M. Blalock, *Social Statistics*, New York: McGraw-Hill, 1960, pp. 326-359; and Paul Horst, *The Prediction of Personal Adjustment*, New York: Social Science Research Council, Bulletin 48, 1941, pp. 349-365.

Table 3 lists the weights assigned to each individual on the basis of the six control classifications. Each individual is given a total index (shown in the last column) equal to the sum of these weights. The indices range from 16.3 to 34.7. These scores may now be used for simultaneous control of social class, age, religion, income, sex, and city size. With 64 cases it is feasible only to dichotomize or trichotomize the index; further divisions would yield too few cases in some of the control groups. For illustrative purposes, the index has been divided into three groups: (a) 20 cases with scores ranging from 16.8 to 21.4, (b) 28 cases with scores ranging from 21.5 to 27.4 and (c) 16 cases with scores ranging from 27.5 to 34.7. The relation between education and number of memberships within each of the three control groups may now be evaluated by computing correlation coefficients.[7]

TABLE 3.   Weights Assigned to Individuals on the Basis of Six Control Classifications*

Subject	Social Class	Age	Religion	Income	Sex	City Size	Index
1	4.3	4.9	5.1	4.7	4.9	4.1	28.0
2	2.2	2.9	4.3	2.4	4.9	4.1	20.8
3	2.2	3.7	3.3	2.4	3.1	1.7	16.4
4	4.3	4.9	3.3	2.4	3.1	1.7	19.7
5	4.3	3.7	4.3	2.4	4.9	5.0	24.6
6	7.7	5.2	4.3	5.1	3.1	5.0	30.4
7	7.7	5.2	5.1	6.8	4.9	5.0	34.7
8	2.2	2.9	3.3	4.7	3.1	4.1	20.3
9	2.2	2.9	4.3	2.4	4.9	1.7	18.4
10	2.2	4.9	4.3	2.4	4.9	2.7	21.4
11	4.3	4.9	4.3	5.1	3.1	5.0	26.7
12	2.2	3.7	4.3	2.4	3.1	5.0	20.7
13	4.3	5.2	3.3	4.7	4.9	5.0	27.4
14	7.7	5.2	4.3	4.7	4.9	5.0	31.8
15	2.2	2.2	4.3	1.0	4.9	1.7	16.3
16	2.2	3.7	3.3	2.4	3.1	1.7	16.4
17	4.3	2.9	5.1	2.4	3.1	1.7	19.5
18	4.3	4.9	4.3	2.4	3.1	4.1	23.1
19	4.3	4.9	4.3	2.4	3.1	5.0	24.0
20	4.3	4.9	3.3	2.4	4.9	4.1	23.9
21	2.2	2.9	3.3	1.0	4.9	5.0	19.3
22	7.7	5.2	5.1	6.8	4.9	5.0	34.7
23	4.3	4.9	4.3	4.7	3.1	4.1	25.4
24	4.3	3.7	4.3	5.1	4.9	2.7	25.0
25	7.7	4.9	4.3	4.7	4.9	4.1	30.6
26	4.3	2.9	3.3	2.4	3.1	4.1	20.1
27	4.3	4.9	5.1	5.1	3.1	5.0	27.5
28	2.2	3.7	5.1	5.1	4.9	5.0	26.0
29	7.7	4.9	4.3	6.8	4.9	5.0	33.6

[7]The index may not always be highly correlated with the dependent variable, because of the highest and lowest scores. The correlation between the index and the dependent variable should be assessed *before* the control is introduced.

TABLE 3. (Continued)

Subject	Social Class	Age	Religion	Income	Sex	City Size	Index
30	2.2	2.2	3.3	2.4	4.9	2.7	17.7
31	4.3	3.7	4.3	5.1	4.9	5.0	27.3
32	7.7	3.7	5.1	4.7	4.9	5.0	31.1
33	4.3	3.7	3.3	5.1	4.9	5.0	26.3
34	4.3	2.9	4.3	6.8	4.9	5.0	28.2
35	4.3	3.7	4.3	5.1	4.9	4.1	26.4
36	2.2	2.9	4.3	5.1	4.9	2.7	22.1
37	2.2	3.7	3.3	6.8	4.9	2.7	23.6
38	4.3	3.7	4.3	5.1	4.9	4.1	26.4
39	4.3	4.9	5.1	4.7	4.9	4.1	28.0
40	2.2	2.9	5.1	5.1	3.1	4.1	22.5
41	2.2	2.2	3.3	5.1	3.1	5.0	20.9
42	4.3	3.7	4.3	4.7	3.1	5.0	25.1
43	4.3	3.7	4.3	4.7	3.1	5.0	25.1
44	7.7	5.2	4.3	4.7	3.1	5.0	30.0
45	4.3	4.9	5.1	5.1	3.1	5.0	27.5
46	2.2	5.2	4.3	5.1	3.1	5.0	24.9
47	4.3	2.2	5.1	4.7	3.1	4.1	23.5
48	2.2	2.2	3.3	4.7	3.1	2.7	18.2
49	4.3	3.7	4.3	5.1	3.1	4.1	24.6
50	4.3	5.2	4.3	5.1	3.1	1.7	23.7
51	4.3	4.9	3.3	5.1	3.1	2.7	23.4
52	2.2	2.9	4.3	2.4	4.9	5.0	21.7
53	4.3	4.9	5.1	2.4	4.9	5.0	26.6
54	7.7	4.9	5.1	5.1	4.9	5.0	32.7
55	4.3	4.9	4.3	5.1	4.9	5.0	28.5
56	4.3	5.2	4.3	2.4	4.9	5.0	26.1
57	4.3	4.9	4.3	5.1	4.9	4.1	27.6
58	2.2	4.9	3.3	2.4	4.9	1.7	19.4
59	4.3	2.2	3.3	2.4	3.1	5.0	20.3
60	2.2	3.7	4.3	2.4	3.1	5.0	20.7
61	4.3	3.7	4.3	5.1	3.1	5.0	25.5
62	2.2	5.2	4.3	2.4	3.1	1.7	18.9
63	4.3	4.9	5.1	2.4	3.1	4.1	23.9
64	2.2	5.2	4.3	2.4	3.1	4.1	21.3

*Derived from Tables 1 and 2.

The zero-order correlation between education and number of memberships is .84. Even when the correlation is as high as this, other variables could be responsible for the relation between these two. That is, once the six control classifications have been partialled out, the relationship may be reduced. The correlation coefficients for the three control groups are: (a) .66 for the group with the lowest indices, (b) .77 for the middle group and (c) .69 for the group with the highest index values. Thus, in this instance, controlling for the six variables still leaves a substantial relation between education and number of memberships although r^2, representing the proportion of variation accounted for, was reduced to about 70 per cent of its zero-order value. Considered simultaneously, the six control classifications have a small but positive influence on the relation between education and number of organizational memberships. Index formation does not obviate the use of standard partialling procedures for each control classification separately, if there are theoretical reasons for determining the independent effects of each one. Or, an index could be formed using only two, three, four, or five of the controls, rather than all six: this would help determine which of the controls, considered simultaneously, has the greatest influence on the relationship in question.

CELL-ORDERING AND COMBINATION

In the procedure designated as cell-ordering and combination *(COAC)* the independent variable is "neglected," just as it was in index formation, that is, its effects are not considered. Three steps are required. First, cells are determined by the cross-classification of all control variables. A representative value of the dependent variable is assigned to each cell, e.g., the average number of organizational memberships.[8] Finally, the cells are ordered into broad classes which are subsequently used for control (in the same fashion as index values in the preceding method).

The *COAC* procedure is not as widely applicable as index formation, because it can be used only when the number of cases is *just barely too small* adequately to assess the original relationship. To illustrate the method, four control classifications—income, age, city size, and sex—have been dichotomized, yielding 16 cells when cross-tabulated. The mean number of memberships in each cell is given in Table 4.

To obtain control classes the 16 cells are ranked according to mean number of organizational memberships, which varies from a high of 8.6 for young male high-income, large-city residents to a low of 1.0 for young female low-income, small-city residents and older female high-income, small-city residents. Once ranked, cells are combined to form classes; in this example, all cells with a mean of 5.3 or more memberships are combined into one control class (Control I), those with a mean between 3.3 and 5.0 are combined into a second control class (Control II), and finally, cells with a mean of 3.0 or less are combined into a third control class (Control III). This method, like the index-formation method, controls simultaneously (but not concurrently) for more than one variable. In the example, four variables are controlled simultaneously because, when considered in selected combinations, they yield similar values of the dependent variable.

The zero-order correlation coefficient between education and number of memberships is .84. The three first-order correlations are .63 for Control I, .81

---

[8] The dependent variable in the example (memberships) is measured on an interval scale; a necessary condition for the interpretation of mean scores. Note that interval measurement is not required for the *COAC* method, because the mode and the median (which may be computed with nominal and ordinal scales) may be used as the representative value for each cell. On the other hand, the method of index formation combines scores and therefore requires at least an interval scale. The mode and the median are inadequate for this purpose because they cannot be manipulated algebraically.

TABLE 4.   Mean Number of Organizational Member-
            ships,[a] by Income,[b] Age,[c] City Size,[d] and
            Sex

| | | High Income | | Low Income | |
		Young	Old	Young	Old
Male	Large City	8.6	6.0	5.0	3.3
	Small City	7.0	4.0	4.0	2.6
Female	Large City	5.4	3.0	5.3	2.5
	Small City	3.7	1.0	1.0	3.3

[a]Derived from the data in Table 1.
[b]Income: High = $6,500+
               Low = less than $6,500
[c]Age: Old = 45+
               Young = less than 45
[d]City Size: Large = 40,000+
               Small = less than 40,000

for Control II and .74 for Control III. Thus, the zero-order correlation is not substantially reduced by controlling (incompletely, as usual) for income, age, city size, and sex, On the other hand, these four control classifications do have a positive though somewhat small influence on the original relationship.

The *COAC* method is similar to standardization, a technique used extensively in demographic and public health research.[9] Standardization provides a single summary measure of an observed distribution by adjusting the data to one or more characteristics of a constant (i.e., standard) distribution. For example, one way to compare the death rates for New York and Florida (which has a large number of aged people) is by standardizing both states on the age distribution of the United States,[10] thereby controlling for the effects of age on the death rates. In terms of the present example, one may compare individuals with a high education (10 years or more) to those with a low education (nine years or less) with regard to organizational memberships, standardizing both groups on the income, age, city size and sex distributions for the total sample.

Standardization, like the *COAC* method, controls simultaneously for more than one variable. Note, however, that standardization does not help solve the problem of controlling for a large number of variables with a small sample size, for it requires as many cases as conventional partialling.[11] The utility of

[9]For a discussion of some of the applications and interpretations of standardization to partial analysis, see Morris Rosenberg, "Test Factor Standardization as a Method of Interpretation," *Social Forces*, 41 (October, 1962), pp. 53-61.

[10]*Ibid.*, p. 56.

[11]For example, when a column of the control table has no cases, the results of the method are noninterpretable. See *ibid.*, p. 59.

standardization is in assessing the effects of one or more control classifications, when the partial correlations are highly variable in size.[12] Since one seldom finds a uniform reduction in the partial correlations, one can seldom claim unequivocally that the zero-order correlation has been reduced (let alone determine the degree of reduction). Standardization helps solve the problem by providing a single summary measure, utilizing all of the controls.

The *COAC* method does not provide a summary measure, but it may be used to reduce the number of partial correlations (three in the above example). While a summary measure is useful for an overall picture of the effects of all controls, a few partial correlations may indicate interaction effects (as well as the effect of the controls on the relation in question).

SUMMARY

The primary concern of this paper has been to present three solutions to the problem of controlling for a large number of variables with a small sample size. The first method is to choose a few of the potential controls, basing the selection on the size of correlations between control and dependent variables or among the control variables, on substantive considerations, or on previous research findings.

The second method is to form an index based on all of the control classifications. This is a widely applicable and useful method, because it can be used with an extremely small N and a large number of control classifications, but each control must be weighted so that an index can be derived for each individual. The third method presented, cell-ordering and combination, involves grouping the cells into broad classes to be used for control purposes. This method is not as widely applicable as index formation, for it requires a larger number of cases.

[12]This is the problem Rosenberg considers. *Ibid.*, p. 54.

STRUCTURAL EFFECTS

Peter M. Blau

Two basic types of social fact can be distinguished: the common values and norms embodied in a culture or subculture; and the networks of social relations in which processes of social interaction become organized and through which social positions of individuals and subgroups become differentiated.[1] Kroeber

Reprinted with the permission of the author and the publisher, The American Sociological Association, from the *American Sociological Review*, Vol. 25 (1960), 178-93.

[1]See, e.g., Robin M. Williams, Jr., *American Society*, New York: Knopf, 1951, pp. 443-448.

and Parsons have recently re-emphasized the importance of this analytical distinction.[2] Many theoretical concepts illustrate the distinction: Weber's Protestant ethic and Sumner's mores exemplify social values and norms, while Marx's investigation of the class structure and Simmel's study of coalitions in triads deal with networks of social relationships.

These concepts refer to attributes of social collectivities, not to those of individuals, but they have counterparts that do refer to characteristics of individuals. Individuals can be described in terms of their orientations and dispositions, just as groups or entire societies can be described in terms of the prevailing social values and norms; and individuals can be distinguished on the basis of their social status, just as communities can be distinguished on the basis of the status distribution in them.[3] These parallels tend to conceal the fundamental difference between the implications of group structure and those of the individual's own characteristics for his conduct. Even socially acquired or socially defined attributes of individuals are clearly distinct in their effects from attributes of social structures.

Systematic social research has often been criticized for distorting, if not entirely ignoring, crucial characteristics of social structure.[4] Interviewing surveys have provided much information about the influences of attitudes of individuals and their social status on human behavior, but they have contributed little to our knowledge of the structural constraints exerted by common values and status distributions in groups or communities, because sampling procedures tend to make isolated individuals the focus of the analysis. And while ecological studies have examined social units, with a few exceptions,[5] they have not separated the consequences of social conditions from those of the individual's own characteristics for his behavior, because ecological data do not furnish information about individuals except in the aggregate. But the systematic analysis of structural constraints requires, as Merton and Kitt have pointed out, the simultaneous use of indices of social structure and of individual behavior.[6] This paper suggests and illustrates a method for isolating the effects of social structure.[7]

[2] A. L. Kroeber and Talcott Parsons, "The Concepts of Culture and of Social System," *American Sociological Review*, 23 (October, 1958), pp. 582-583.

[3] The relationships between measures of individual attributes and of group attributes are discussed by Patricia L. Kendall and Paul F. Lazarsfeld, "Problems of Survey Analysis," in Robert K. Merton and Paul F. Lazarsfeld, editors, *Continuities in Social Research*, Glencoe, Ill.: Free Press, 1950, pp. 187-196.

[4] See, e.g., Herbert Blumer, "Public Opinion and Public Opinion Polling," *American Sociological Review* 13 (October, 1948), pp. 542-549.

[5] For example: Robert E. L. Faris and H. Warren Dunham, *Mental Disorders in Urban Areas*, Chicago: University of Chicago Press, 1939.

[6] Robert K. Merton and Alice S. Kitt, "Contributions to the Theory of Reference Group Behavior," in Merton and Lazarsfeld, *op. cit.*, pp. 82-83; see also pp. 70-81. Cf. Samuel A. Stouffer *et al.*, *The American Soldier*, Princeton: Princeton University Press, 1949, Vol. II, pp. 242-272, for a notable exception to the tendency of ignoring effects of social structure in survey research.

[7] I have briefly discussed this method in "Formal Organization," *American Journal of Sociology*, 63 (July, 1957), pp. 63-65. Structural effects are a special type of the "contextual propositions" discussed by Paul F. Lazarsfeld in "Problems in Methodology," in Robert K. Merton *et al.*, editors, *Sociology Today*, New York: Basic Books, 1959, pp. 69-73.

SOCIAL VALUES AND NORMS

Social values and norms are common orientations toward social conduct that prevail in a society or group. Social values govern the choice of objectives that are experienced as worth striving for, and social norms differentiate between proper and improper conduct.

Since social values and norms are shared, internalized orientations, the most plausible procedure for ascertaining them in empirical research would seem to be to determine, first, what values the members of a number of communities hold and, then, which ones of these are shared by members of any given community. For example, one could administer the F-Scale to a sample of the American population[8] and divide communities on the basis of whether authoritarian values are more or less prevalent. Let us assume that such a study finds that the relative prevalence of authoritarian values in a community is associated with a high degree of discrimination against minorities. (We shall also assume that other relevant conditions have been controlled and that we have evidence that authoritarianism is the antecedent variable and discrimination the dependent one.) Two conclusions could be drawn from this finding: first, if a community has an authoritarian subculture, discriminatory practices will prevail in it; second, if an individual has an authoritarian personality, he will tend to discriminate against minorities.

There is a fundamental difference between these two interpretations: the former implies that social processes external to individual personalities are responsible for the differences in discrimination; the latter that internal psychological processes are responsible. To be sure, the prevalence of authoritarian dispositions in some communities and not in others may well be largely due to differences in their social structures. What the determinants of prevailing values are, however, has no direct bearing on what their consequences are or on how these consequences are effected. These are the issues under consideration here. The individual's orientation undoubtedly influences his behavior; the question is whether the prevalence of social values in a community also exerts social constraints upon patterns of conduct that are independent of the influences exerted by the internalized orientations.

The sociologist assumes that this is the case. But how can one demonstrate that social values and norms exert *external* constraints upon the acting and thinking of individuals if they only exist in the minds of individuals? Durkheim, who is concerned with various aspects of this problem in most of his writings, suggests a specific answer in *Suicide.* After admitting, notwithstanding his social realism, that "social consciousness" exists only in individual minds, he states that the social force it exerts, nevertheless, is *"external to each average individual taken singly."*[9]

The common values and norms in a group have two distinct kinds of effect upon the conduct of its members. Ego's conduct is influenced by his own normative orientation for fear of his conscience, and ego's conduct is also influenced by alters' normative orientation for fear of social sanctions. In other words, people conform to prevailing norms partly because they would feel guilty

---

[8]T. W. Adorno *et al.*, *The Authoritarian Personality*, New York: Harper, 1950.
[9]Emile Durkheim, *Suicide*, Glencoe, Ill.: Free Press, 1951, p. 316 (italics in original); see also pp. 309-320 for what may be Durkheim's most perceptive discussion of the problem.

if they did not and partly because they gain social approval and avoid disapproval by doing so. This conception is somewhat oversimplified. It ignores, for example, the fact that the strength of ego's normative orientation itself is in part due to the reinforcement it receives from the social sanctions of alters. Despite its oversimplification, however, this analytical distinction makes it possible to demonstrate empirically the external constraints exerted by social values and norms by differentiating them from the influences of the internalized orientations of individuals.

The structural effects of a social value can be isolated by showing that the association between its prevalence in a community or group and certain patterns of conduct is independent of whether an individual holds this value or not. To return to our illustration: if we should find that, regardless of whether or not an individual has an authoritarian disposition, he is more apt to discriminate against minorities if he lives in a community where authoritarian values prevail than if he lives in one where they do not, we would have evidence that this social value exerts external constraints upon the tendency to discriminate—structural effects that are independent of the internalized value orientation of individuals.

DIRECT EFFECTS

To illustrate the method of analysis suggested above and the distinguishable types of structural effects, data from a pilot study of a public assistance agency will be used.[10] The clients who came to the agency as applicants for general public assistance constituted the poorest stratum in a large American city. The primary job of the caseworker was to determine whether new applicants are eligible for public assistance and to check recurrently whether old recipients continue to be eligible. This involved visiting the clients in their homes and a considerable amount of paper work in the office. Many workers tried to provide some casework service as well, although their ability to do so was limited by their heavy work loads—the average number of cases per worker was over 120—and by their lack of training—the majority of workers had only a college degree and no professional training in social work.

Caseworkers were organized into units of five or six under a supervisor. After a period of observation in the agency, the members of twelve supervisory units were interviewed. The analysis presented below is based on these interview responses of 60 caseworkers who were members of twelve work groups. Not quite half of these workers were women; one-third of them were Negroes; and one-third had been with the agency less than one year, which indicates the high rate of turnover of personnel characteristic of public assistance agencies.

When caseworkers were asked whether the amount of public assistance should be increased, remain the same, or be decreased, one-half stated unequivocally that it should be increased; the majority of the rest felt that an increase is needed only for certain special cases, for example, clients who must pay high rent; and a few thought that no increase is necessary. Nobody suggested that the amount should be decreased. The number of correlations between this item and

[10]Philip M. Marcus was of great help in the collection and analysis of these data. I am also indebted to the Social Science Research Committee of the University of Chicago, which provided the funds for this study.

other measures of orientation to clients is larger than that of any other, which suggests that it is indicative of a fairly basic aspect of orientation to clients.

Does the prevalence of pro-client values in a group affect the performance of duties of its members independently of the individual's own attitude to clients? The description by workers of what they did when visiting clients provides a measure of their orientation in the performance of duties. It indicates that some largely confined their work to checking on eligibility, whereas others were also concerned with furnishing casework service. To isolate the structural effects of pro-client values, groups are divided on the basis of whether or not a majority of group members favors raising the assistance budget for all clients, and within each type of group, individuals are divided into those that favor an increase in assistance for all clients and those that do not. The first item in Table 1 shows that individuals with pro-client attitudes were more often service oriented in their work than others (compare adjacent columns). It also shows, and this is the pertinent finding, that regardless of their own attitudes, members of groups in which pro-client values prevailed were more apt to be oriented toward casework service than members of groups with other values (compare alternate columns). Of the pro-client individuals, 60 per cent in pro-client groups and 44 per cent in other groups were service-oriented; of the other workers, 44 per cent in pro-client groups and 27 per cent in other groups were service-oriented.

Although the differences in the proportion of service-oriented workers associated with contrasting group values are not large, they are just as large as those associated with contrasting individual attitudes. (The combination of group value and individual attitude made a considerable difference for orientation toward work: only about one-quarter of the workers who neither had pro-client attitudes nor were in groups where pro-client values prevailed were service-oriented, compared to three-fifths of those with pro-client attitudes most of whose co-workers shared these pro-client values.) Moreover, other measures of performance reveal the same pattern of relationships with group values. For example, making relatively few field visits generally implied the provision of more intensive services. Individuals with pro-client attitudes tended to make slightly fewer visits to recipients than other workers, and whatever the individual's attitudes were, he was more prone to make fewer visits if he was a member of a group in which pro-client values prevailed than of a group with different values (see Table 1, # 2). Although all these relationships are small, their consistency makes it unlikely that they are entirely due to chance.[11]

These findings suggest that the social values that prevail in a work group do exert external constraints upon the thinking and acting of its members. If pro-client values prevail in a group, merely checking on the eligibility of clients meets with social disapproval while providing casework services gains a worker

[11] Structural effects cannot be expected to account for most of the variance in dependent variables, but since there are a mere 60 cases divided into four unequal columns, only large differences would be statistically significant. It was necessary, therefore, to include in the illustrations findings that are not significant at the .05 level. (But it should be noted that each type of structural effect was observed repeatedly.) Since the respondents are not a representative sample, the applicability of tests of significance is questionable in any case. For a recent criticism of the indiscriminate use of statistical tests of significance, see Hanan C. Selvin, "A Critique of Tests of Significance in Survey Research," *American Sociological Review* 22, (October, 1957), pp. 519-527.

TABLE 1. Effects of Value Orientation Toward Clients

	Group's Prevailing Value Orientation toward Clients			
	Positive		Not Positive	
	Individual's Orientation		Individual's Orientation	
	Positive	Not Positive	Positive	Not Positive
1. Orientation to Work				
Checking eligibility	30%	56%	56%	55%
Intermediate	10	0	0	18
Casework service	60	44	44	27
Total	100	100	100	100
2. Visits to Recipients*				
Forty or less per month	59	50	44	31
Over 40 per month	41	50	56	69
Total	100	100	100	100
3. Delegating Responsibility to Clients				
Unwilling to delegate	45	22	67	50
Willing to delegate	55	78	33	50
Total	100	100	100	100
4. Involvement with Work				
High (worrying much)	75	44	89	68
Low (worry little)	25	56	11	32
Total	100	100	100	100
Number of cases	20	9	9	22

*This information is taken from performance records; since insufficient information was available for the newer workers the totals for this item in the four columns, reading from left to right, are: 17, 6, 9, 13.

approval and respect. But this is not the case if pro-client values do not prevail; indeed, the opposite may be the case. In other words, the pro-client values of the members of a group motivate them not only to furnish more intensive service to their own clients but also to express social approval of colleagues who are service-oriented and social disapproval of those who are not. In response to those sanctioning patterns, individuals tend to modify their approach to clients.

The conclusion that pro-client group values have structural effects on the performance of duties rests on the assumptions that the relationships observed are not spurious and that pro-client values are the independent variable in these relationships. Differences in supervision might constitute a correlated bias that accounts for the relationships, but examination of the data reveals that this is not the case. Of course, this does not exclude the possibility of other influential correlated biases, and neither can the possibility be excluded that pro-client values are actually consequence rather than antecedent in these relationships. But this is a limitation of cross-sectional studies, not of the method of isolating structural effects. Given more adequate data than those used here for illustrative purposes, this method makes it possible to demonstrate structural effects as firmly as the effects of a characteristic of individuals can be demonstrated.

INVERSE EFFECTS

The structural effects of the prevailing values in a group are not necessarily parallel to the effects of the individual's value orientation. In some respects pro-client group values and the individual's own pro-client attitudes have opposite implications for his conduct.

In this agency, clients received money to buy clothing when needed; the caseworker and his supervisor exercised considerable discretion in establishing this need. In some other public assistance agencies, recipients receive a regular clothing allowance, which they spend at their own discretion. Respondents were asked whether they would favor giving such a regular allowance to clients. This change would save the caseworker some tedious and time-consuming work, but it would also deprive him of discretionary power over clients and their welfare.

Individuals with pro-client attitudes were *less* willing than others to delegate this responsibility to clients, but the prevalence of pro-client values in a group *increased* the willingness to delegate it (see Table 1, # 3)—from one-third to 55 per cent for pro-client workers, and from one-half to 78 per cent for others. Pro-client values had the same kind of inverse structural effect on the extent to which workers worried about their cases after working hours: individuals with pro-client attitudes worried *more* than others, but the members of groups in which pro-client values prevailed worried *less* than the members of other groups (see Table 1, #4).

The fact that an individual is favorably disposed toward clients would be expected to increase his concern for their welfare and the gratification he receives from helping them, and thus to make him eager to exercise responsibilities that permit him to furnish more help to them and that make them grateful to him. If most members of a group share pro-client values, their common interest in the welfare of clients will induce them to develop at least implicit normative standards that promote the interest of clients. They are likely to react with social disapproval toward a colleague whose involvement leads him to lose his temper when talking to a client or toward one who uses his discretion not to help clients more but to withhold help from them or to hold a club over their heads. Discussion of such experiences by pro-client members of a group may lead to an agreement that the interest of clients is best served by encouraging detachment and the delegation of responsibilities to them. Or these group members may adopt explicit professional standards of social work, according to which a worker should remain detached toward his clients and foster their independence by letting them make their own decisions. The members of groups where pro-client standards do not prevail are less apt to adopt professional casework standards.

Such inverse structural effects of social values call attention to the importance of social norms. Since the emotional reaction to pro-client dispositions is greater involvement and an unwillingness to delegate responsibility, whereas the welfare of clients is best served by detachment and delegation of responsibility, the workers most interested in the welfare of clients are psychologically least able to provide effective service to them. But the prevalence of positive values in a group promotes the development of casework standards, which curb the psychological consequences of pro-client feelings that impede effective service. Professional training in social work probably leads to the internalization of these casework standards, but the untrained workers in this agency had not fully internalized them; if they had, no inverse structural effects would have been observed.

CONTINGENCY EFFECTS

The influence of the prevalence of social values in a group may be more indirect than in the examples discussed above. Instead of having an effect on a third variable that is independent of the individual's value orientation, it may determine whether the individual's value orientation and a third variable are related or how they are related. In technical terms, the group values and the individual's orientation may have an interaction effect on a third variable. Conceptually, this implies that the relationship between the individual's orientation and another variable is contingent on the prevalence of this value orientation in his group.

All assistance budgets made out by caseworkers were reviewed by an audit section. Caseworkers tended to accuse auditors of being too rigid about eligibility procedures and too little concerned with the welfare of clients, and conflicts with them were frequent. In groups most of whose members were service-oriented, the individual's orientation had no bearing upon his conflicts with auditors; seven out of every ten workers, whatever their orientation, reported such conflicts. In groups where an eligibility orientation prevailed, however, the individual's orientation made a pronounced difference; all five of the service-oriented workers reported conflicts with auditors, in contrast to less than half of the 24 workers oriented toward eligibility (see Table 2). It seems that the chances of conflict with auditors decline only if neither the individual's own orientation nor that of the other members in his group demand that he place serving the interests of clients above strict conformity with eligibility procedures.

The extreme case of contingency effect is the one where the relationship between the individual's orientation and another factor becomes reversed,

TABLE 2. Effects of Orientation Toward Work

	Group's Prevailing Orientation			
	Casework Service		Checking Eligibility	
	Individual's Orientation		Individual's Orientation	
	Service	Eligibility	Service	Eligibility
Reported Conflicts with Auditors				
None	29%	30%	0%	54%
Some	71	70	100	46
Total	100	100	100	100
Number of cases	21	10	5	24

dependent on the prevalence of the orientation in the group. The extent of involvement with the work had such contingency effects. Respondents were asked how often they worry about their work after working hours, which is the measure of involvement used; then they were asked to exemplify what they worry about. The illustrations of the majority reveal worries about clients: "If they'd have enough to eat over the weekend," "Problems the people have—I hope that a deserted family can manage—I remember the expressions on their faces." But some workers worried about their own performance: "If you mean their personal problems, then the answer is, no; but I worry about the record which is open to the supervisor's checking."

If involvement—that is, extensive worrying—prevailed in a group, there was an inverse relationship between the individual's involvement and whether he worried about clients rather than his own performance, but if involvement did not prevail in a group, these two factors were directly related. The implications of this interaction effect can be clearly seen when percentages are computed horizontally (for each half-row) instead of vertically, as in Table 3, #1. If all the members within any given group were alike in their involvement, 100 per cent of those in groups with much involvement would be highly involved, but none of those in groups with little involvement. In other words, the two central columns (marked by a single asterisk) of the table represent the deviants—the lows in groups with much involvement and the highs in groups with little involvement. It is evident that workers mostly concerned with their clients' welfare were deviants in disproportionate numbers in both kinds of groups. They were *more* apt than workers primarily concerned with their own performance to be involved in groups where involvement was rare, but they were *less* apt than the others to be involved in groups where involvement was common.[12] Indeed, they apparently were not at all influenced by the prevailing group climate; whether they were in groups where the majority was involved or in groups where the majority was not, about half of these client-identified workers were highly involved. In contrast to only two of the 16 workers who were concerned about their performance, 17 of the 32 who were concerned with their clients' welfare deviated from the group climate. This suggests that identification with clients is a source of strength which makes a worker somewhat independent of peer group pressures.

This finding has a general methodological implication. Whenever the distribution of value orientations in a group and the individual's value orientation show such an interaction effect on a third variable, the latter differentiates members who tend to deviate from the standards of their own group from those who tend to conform to them, regardless of what these standards are. For this pattern of findings inevitably indicates that the X's have orientation Y *more* often than the non-X's in groups where this orientation is rare but *less* often than the non-X's in groups where it is common, which means that the X's tend to be the deviants whatever the prevailing orientation of the group.

Several studies have investigated the relationship between an individual's social integration among peers or his informal status and his conformity or resistance

[12]Contrary to what this finding seems to imply, differences in supervisory practices were not associated with amount of worrying.

TABLE 3. Patterns of Deviancy in Respect to Involvement with Work

	Group's Dominant Climate							
	Much Involvement				Little Involvement			
	Individual's Involvement				Individual's Involvement			
	High	Low*	Total	N**	High*	Low	Total	N**
1. Source of Worries								
Client's welfare	47%	53%	100%	19	54%	46%	100%	13
Own performance	89	11	100	9	14	86	100	7
Not asked ***				3				9
2. Status in Work Group								
Integrated	50	50	100	18	50	50	100	16
Not integrated	62	38	100	13	0	100	100	13
3. Self-Confidence								
High	50	50	100	8	50	50	100	10
Low	57	43	100	23	16	84	100	19

*These two columns represent the deviants—the lows in much-involved groups and the highs in little-involved groups.

**The number of cases on which the percentages, computed horizontally for each half-row, are based.

***Respondents who said they never worried, and thus are classified among those with low involvement, could not be asked what they worried about; they are, therefore, not considered in this comparison.

to group pressure.[13] An important problem is whether social integration increases, or decreases, resistance to group pressure independent of the kind of pressure involved. The procedure outlined above facilitates the study of the relationship between social position and response to *opposite* kinds of group pressure.

Individuals who were integrated in their work group were more prone than those who were not to deviate from the prevailing group climate in respect to involvement. (Whether a worker was called by his first name by some of the other members of this group, as reported by the others, is the measure of social integration used.) In groups where the majority was involved with their work, integrated workers were slightly less likely to be involved than others, but in groups where the majority was not involved, integrated workers were more likely to be involved than others (see Table 3, #2). In other words, whether much or little involvement characterized the group climate, the integrated workers were more apt than the rest to deviate from it. Their resistance to group pressure is indicated by the fact that their involvement was quite independent of the group climate; the proportion of integrated workers who were involved in their work was the same in groups with much involvement as in groups with little involvement. One-half of the 34 integrated workers deviated from the prevailing group climate, as contrasted with only one-fifth of the 26 unintegrated workers.

The finding seems to be typical. If other measures of orientation toward work and clients are substituted for involvement, and if other aspects of informal status are used instead of integration, one also finds superior status among peers associated with the tendency to deviate from the prevailing orientation in a group regardless of the particular content of this orientation.[14] Since it is improbable that deviation creates more liking and respect than conformity, the opposite direction of influence is the plausible inference. The acceptance and respect of his colleagues provides a worker with social support. His consequent feelings of security apparently permit him to resist group pressures and depart from group norms more readily than can the worker whose insecure position provides strong incentives to improve his standing and to court social approval through strict conformity. This interpretation implies that self-confident workers are more prone to deviate from the prevailing group pattern than those lacking in self-confidence. Indeed, this seems to have been the case (see Table 3, #3).[15]

SOCIAL COHESION

An important aspect of the network of social relations in a group is the strength of the bonds that unite its members—the group's social cohesion. One

[13]See, e.g., George C. Homans, *The Human Group*, New York: Harcourt, Brace, 1950, pp. 140-144; and Harold H. Kelley and M. M. Shapiro, "An Experiment on Conformity to Group Norms," *American Sociological Review*, 19 (December, 1954), pp. 667-677.

[14]But informal status was differently related to orientation to the supervisor. For a discussion of the implications of these and similar findings, see my paper, "Patterns of Deviation in Work Groups," *Sociometry*, forthcoming.

[15]The measure used is the respondent's confidence in his ability to work without supervision. Several indices of informal status, such as popularity, were directly related to self-confidence, but the index of integration used here was not.

possible procedure for measuring group cohesion is to ascertain how strongly each member is identified with the group and compute some average. The objection that such an index is purely phenomenological and does not pertain to the group structure could be met by isolating the structural effects of group identification, using the method suggested in this paper.

Another measure of group cohesion, which Festinger and his colleagues have made popular, is based on ingroup sociometric choices, for example, the proportion of friendship choices made by the members of a group.[16] The conception of cohesion underlying this measure has been criticized by Gross and Martin because it emphasizes "individual perceptions and minimizes the importance of the relational bonds between and among group members."[17] Sociometric measures, however, are indicative of relational bonds, since they are based on reports of choices made by one individual and received by another. Moreover, the alternative the authors propose is not likely to bring us closer to a structural definition of cohesion. They suggest that it should be measured by subjecting groups to disruptive forces of varying degrees and observing when they "begin to disintegrate."[18] But the sign of beginning disintegration would undoubtedly be that some members quit the group, or that some stop attending meetings, and an index based on such signs of disintegration relies as much on the strength of the group ties of individual members as does Festinger's sociometric index.[19]

Nevertheless, Gross and Martin's criticism should not be summarily dismissed. It draws attention to the important distinction between group structure and interpersonal relations. To be sure, interpersonal relationships (and relationships between subgroups, if they exist) are the very core of group structure. But atomizing group structure into its component interpersonal relations is as little justified as reducing groups to the individual personalities who compose them. Group structure refers to the distribution or network of social relationships, which may have a significance that is quite distinct from that of the social relationships in which specific individuals are involved. Thus, it cannot be assumed that the influence of the network of cohesive bonds in a group is the same as that of the interpersonal bonds of individual group members. The method of isolating structural effects makes it possible to distinguish between these two kinds of influence—those exerted by the prevalence of cohesive ties in a group and those exerted by the integrative ties of the individual members.

EFFECTS OF SOCIAL COHESION

Group cohesion is operationally defined in terms of ingroup sociometric choices. Respondents were asked to name the five persons in the agency with whom they were most friendly. The median proportion of ingroup choices is used to divide groups into cohesive and non-cohesive ones. Within each type of group, individuals are divided on the basis of whether or not they received

[16]Leon Festinger *et al.*, *Social Pressures in Informal Groups*, New York: Harper, 1950.
[17]Neal Gross and William E. Martin, "On Group Cohesiveness," *American Journal of Sociology*, 57 (May, 1952), p. 554.
[18]*Loc. cit.*
[19]See also Lazarsfeld's discussion of this controversy, *op. cit.*, pp. 55-59.

ingroup choices. (An alternative procedure would have been to divide individuals by the ingroup choices they *made*. But if we accept the notion that cohesion is related to group attractiveness, and wish to hold constant the aspect of the individual's interpersonal relations that is most parallel, received choices, which indicate attractiveness, are preferable to choices made.)

Cohesion in these work groups had structural effects on the approach of caseworkers to clients, that is, effects that were independent of the individual's interpersonal bonds in the group. Respondents were asked, "What are the things clients do that are particularly trying?" The answers of some reveal behavior of clients they considered a personal affront—"Demands get under my skin, or a client's trying to tell me my job," "If they cheat on me it makes me awfully mad"—whereas those of others refer to behavior that is improper or harmful to the client and his family—". . . they were winos, constantly drunk and beating each other up," ". . . she hadn't even gotten her children the routine inoculations." Thus, some workers reacted in personal terms and objected to behavior of clients when they felt offended, while others reacted in accordance with generally accepted rules of conduct and objected to behavior of clients not primarily because it was discourteous to them but because it was morally wrong.[20]

The members of cohesive groups were less apt to take personal affront at the behavior of clients than those of less cohesive groups, and this difference persists if the individual's sociometric position is held constant (see Table 4, #1). Only about one-third of the former, in contrast to over two-thirds of the latter reacted in personal terms. The prevalence of supportive ties in cohesive groups is a source of emotional strength for their members. The absence of extensive ego support in less cohesive groups throws their members upon other social resources for this support, such as their relations with clients. If an individual defines an interpersonal relationship as a potential source of ego support, he is apt to react in personal terms, feeling insulted or more or less appreciated, but if he does not, it is easier for him to take the view of an outsider and judge the behavior of others in accordance with impersonal criteria. Apparently, it is the general extensive support of group cohesion rather than the specific intensive support of the individual's own interpersonal ties that promotes an impersonal approach in social interaction with clients. Only group cohesion was associated with this approach; the individual's sociometric position was not.

Performance, too, was influenced by social cohesion. Data taken from production records show that the members of cohesive groups, whether or not they personally received sociometric choices, tended to make more field visits than those of other groups (see Table 4, #2). Since numerous field visits indicate both that much work has been accomplished and, probably, that less intensive service has been furnished, one may deduce from the finding either that cohesion fosters the fulfillment of tasks or that it lessens concern with the provision of much service to clients. Two factors, however, make the first inference the more probable: cohesion is not inversely related to a service

---

[20] This distinction is related to Parsons' distinction between particularism and universalism.

TABLE 4.   Effects of Group Cohesion

	Group Cohesion			
	High		Low	
	Individual's Attractiveness		Individual's Attractiveness	
	High	Low	High	Low
1. Reaction to Clients*				
Personal	38%	34%	70%	80%
Impersonal	62	66	30	20
Total	100	100	100	100
2. Total Field Visits**				
Sixty or less per month	60	67	77	82
Over 60 per month	40	33	23	18
Total	100	100	100	100
3. High Respect for Own Supervisor				
Present	76	58	50	41
Absent	24	42	50	59
Total	100	100	100	100
4. Orientation to Work				
Checking eligibility	29	59	50	53
Intermediate	18	8	7	6
Casework Service	53	33	43	41
Total	100	100	100	100
Number of cases	17	12	14	17

*Since some clients were not asked this question, the column totals for this item, reading from left to right, are: 13, 6, 10, 15.

**This information is taken from performance records; insufficient information for newer workers reduces the column totals for this item to: 15, 6, 13, 11. The total number of visits rather than only visits with recipients are used here, where concern is with productivity.

orientation, as the second interpretation implies; and a number of other studies suggests that cohesion promotes high productivity.[21]

When asked to choose the best supervisors in the organization, members of cohesive groups were more prone to name their own supervisor than members of less cohesive groups (see Table 4, #3). Independent of this relationship, individuals who received sociometric choices from the ingroup were also

[21] A pioneering study, of course, is F. J. Roethlisberger and William J. Dickson, *Management and the Worker*, Cambridge: Harvard University Press, 1951, pp. 1-186. For a more recent study, see Daniel Katz and Robert L. Kahn, "Some Recent Findings in Human Relations Research in Industry," in Guy E. Swanson *et al.*, editors, *Readings in Social Psychology*, New York: Holt, 1952, pp. 650-665. Neither these investigations nor the findings reported here can exclude the alternative interpretation that low productivity impedes cohesion.

somewhat more likely to name their own supervisor than others. Perhaps the fact that a supervisor commands the respect of his workers increases the chances that cohesive ties will develop among them. But it is also possible that the absence of strong ingroup bonds produces strains and tensions which find expression in more critical attitudes toward the supervisor.

A contingency effect is illustrated by the implications of ingroup choices for the caseworker's orientation to his work; that is, group cohesion and its individual counterpart had an interaction effect upon whether a worker was oriented primarily toward checking eligibility or toward casework service. In groups with low cohesion, whether or not an individual received ingroup choices did not influence his orientation, but in groups with high cohesion, individuals who received choices from their peers were less apt than others to confine themselves to checking on the eligibility of clients (see Table 4, #4). Social support from prevailing cohesive bonds and from specific interpersonal bonds both seem to be necessary to reduce the chances that workers will confine their work to rigid enforcement of eligibility procedures. The group and the individual measure of ingroup choices also had interaction effects on other indications of strict adherence to established procedures, such as ritualistic punctuality and opposition to change in the rules defining responsibilities.

EFFECTS OF COMMUNICATION STRUCTURE

Instrumental as well as socio-emotional patterns of social interaction form into networks of social relationships which characterize group structures. The pattern of friendly associations among workers is one aspect of the social structure of the work group, the pattern of communication assumed by their consultations and discussions of problems is another. The two are not unrelated, but neither are they identical.

The procedure used to define the communication structure is a familiar one. Respondents were asked with which colleagues they usually discuss their problems; they were free to name any number of colleagues, either members of their own group or outsiders. On the basis of the ingroup choices, groups are divided into those with relatively dense and those with sparse internal communication networks, and within each type of group, individuals are divided according to whether or not they were named as regular consultants by two or more colleagues.

In several instances, the structural effects of this consultation network were quite similar to those of social cohesion. Both aspects of group structure, for example, had closely parallel consequences for the respect workers accorded to their supervisor. In other cases, however, their impact was different. Thus, the consultation structure did not influence a worker's reaction to the behavior of clients in personal or impersonal terms. In still other respects, the degree of reciprocity in the consultations of a group rather, than their frequency had effects that paralleled those of cohesion. For instance, reciprocity in consultation, like cohesion, was associated with high productivity (many field visits). Further research with a larger number of groups is needed to derive generalizations about the different implications of various aspects of group structure.

TABLE 5.   Effects of Communication Network

	Extent of Communication in Group			
	Much Consultation		Little Consultation	
	Individual's Position		Individual's Position	
	Consultant	Not	Consultant	Not
Attitudes to Clients				
Negative	25%	36%	8%	9%
Qualified	17	36	42	36
Positive	58	28	50	55
Total	100	100	100	100
Number of cases	12	14	12	22

The density of the group's communication network had an interesting double effect on attitudes toward clients, as indicated by attitudes toward increasing the amount of assistance. Negative attitudes were more common in groups where consultation was frequent than in those where it was rare (see Table 5). Whether a worker was regularly consulted or not, he was three times as likely to oppose any increase in the assistance allowance if he was a member of a group in which consultation was prevalent than one in which it was rare. This does not mean, however, that the individual's social status—how often he was consulted—was entirely unrelated to his attitude toward clients. But whether or not these two factors were related was contingent on the group structure. In groups whose members consulted little the attitude of consultants toward increasing public assistance did not differ from that of others, but in groups whose members consulted much consultants were more likely to advocate an increase than non-consultants. Hence, the group's communication network had two effects on the attitudes toward clients: first, frequent communication fostered more negative attitudes; and second, such communication partly determined whether or not the individual's position in the communication network influenced his attitudes toward clients. Furthermore, while the frequency of consultation in a group was associated with *negative* attitudes toward clients, the fact that an individual member of a group where consultation prevailed was often consulted was associated with *positive* attitudes.[22]

To interpret this finding, it is necessary to examine briefly the strained relations between caseworkers and clients in this agency. There were many reasons for conflict. Most clients were in dire need and had strong incentive to conceal any slim resources they might have had or otherwise to try to increase the amount of assistance they would get even if this required some dishonesty. Caseworkers, many of whom came to the agency directly from college with idealistic views about helping people, tended to experience what Everett Hughes has called a "reality shock" when they encountered clients who, instead of appreciating their help, lied to them and broke their promises, and whose values

---

[22] An earlier study makes the parallel finding that a competitive work group was less productive than a cooperative one, but in the former group competitive individuals were more productive than others; see Peter M. Blau, *The Dynamics of Bureaucracy*, Chicago: University of Chicago Press, 1955, pp. 49-67.

were so different from their own. Even when a worker tried to help clients he sometimes found that they blamed him for limitations the agency's procedure imposed on him. Caseworkers protected themselves against such frustrating experiences by developing and publicly flaunting a hardened attitude toward clients. Their discussions among themselves were dominated by aggressive remarks and jokes about clients. Many workers were undoubtedly much more favorably disposed toward recipients than their statements to colleagues indicated. Even those who clearly had positive attitudes toward clients seemed to feel compelled to present a hardened front by making aggressive remarks about them when talking to colleagues. This pattern of relieving tension appears to be typical of work groups whose members experience conflicts with clients.[23] Most members of this agency did not have a callous attitude toward clients, but expressing anti-client sentiments was the prevailing norm.

The enforcement of social norms requires an effective network of communication in a group. Hence, a group with a strong communication network will be more effective in enforcing the prevailing anti-client norms than one with a weak network. To be sure, the anti-client norms in this organization were not so severe as to include opposition to any increase in the assistance allowance; after all, only a minority of respondents expressed such opposition. However, the more effective the enforcement of general anti-client norms in a group, the greater the chances that some of its members will take an extreme position—one more extreme than that called for by the norms—and this is what the finding shows. Informal status in a group, as data presented earlier suggest, is inversely associated with conformity to the normative orientation toward clients. In groups with communications networks that permit effective enforcement of anti-client norms, non-consultants, whose low status makes them subject to the full impact of group pressures, therefore have more negative attitudes toward clients than consultants, whose high status removes them somewhat from group control. But in groups where consultation is rare, the status of consultant has less significance, and since, moreover, the prevailing anti-client norms are not effectively enforced in these groups, whether or not an individual is regularly consulted does not influence his attitudes toward clients. These considerations also explain the seeming paradox: the fact that there is much consultation in a group and the fact that a member of such a group is much consulted have opposite consequences for attitudes toward clients. An effective network of communication increases the group's power to enforce prevailing anti-client norms, but the superior status of consultant reduces the individual's conformity to these group norms.

CONCLUSIONS: TYPES OF STRUCTURAL
EFFECTS AND THEIR STUDY

Robinson has criticized research based on ecological correlations for implicitly assuming that these indicate relationships between the characteristics of individuals, and he has demonstrated that an ecological correlation between, say, the proportion of Negroes and the proportion of illiterates in an area does not

---

[23] For another illustration of this pattern, see *ibid.*, pp. 82-96.

prove that more Negroes than whites are illiterate.[24] Menzel has pointed out, however, that ecological studies may well be concerned with relationships between aspects of social structures without making any assumptions about relationships between attributes of individuals.[25] But Robinson's strictures apply also to Menzel's sociological conception. If the psychologically oriented investigator assumes that ecological correlations *are* due to correlations between traits of individuals, the sociologically oriented analyst assumes that they *are not,* and neither assumption is warranted. A correlation between divorce rates and suicide rates, for example, might be sociologically interpreted to indicate that anomie in the marital institutions of a society, operationally defined by a high divorce rate, increases suicide rates. This theory clearly implies that the ecological correlation is *not* entirely due to the fact that divorced persons are more apt to commit suicide than married ones; for if it were, a much simpler explanation would suffice. To demonstrate that it is anomie, as measured by divorce rates, rather than the psychological state or personality of the divorced individual that is responsible for high suicide rates, it is necessary to show that married as well as divorced persons have higher suicide rates in countries where divorce is frequent than in those where it is rare. This, of course, is precisely how Durkheim tested his theory of anomic suicide.[26]

Durkheim, then, some sixty years ago, illustrated the method of isolating structural effects. The essential principle is that the relationship between the distribution of a given characteristic in various collectivities and an effect criterion is ascertained, while this characteristic is held constant for individuals. This procedure differentiates the effects of social structures upon patterns of action from the influences exerted by the characteristics of the acting individuals or their interpersonal relationships. If a structural effect is observed, it invariably constitutes evidence that social processes originating outside the individual personality are responsible for the differences in the dependent variable, since the influences of psychological processes have been controlled in the analysis. The futile arguments of whether or not a certain concept or empirical measure is *really* a social factor can be dismissed if this method of analysis is employed, since its results demonstrate whether social forces or psychological ones produce given effects regardless of the empirical index used to define the independent variable. Take such an individualistic characteristic as intelligence. If it were found that the average IQ scores in fraternities are associated with the scholastic records of their members when the individual's score is held constant, there could be no doubt, provided other relevant conditions are controlled, that the level of intelligence in a fraternity influences performance on examinations through *social* processes (although, of course, the finding would not show whether these processes involve social stimulation of learning or collaboration on examinations).

A tentative typology of structural effects can be derived by classifying them

[24]W. S. Robinson, "Ecological Correlations and the Behavior of Individuals," *American Sociological Review,* 15 (June, 1950), pp. 351-357.

[25]Herbert Menzel, "Comment on Robinson's 'Ecological Correlations and the Behavior of Individuals,'" *American Sociological Review*, 15 (October, 1950), p. 674.

[26]Durkheim, *op. cit.,* pp. 259-276. The hypothesis is confirmed only for men; Durkheim advanced another though related interpretation to account for the suicide rates of women.

along two dimensions. The first distinguishes between the consequences of the common values or shared norms of a collectivity and those of its networks of social relationships or distribution of social positions. Second, either of these two basic aspects of the social structure can have direct effects, inverse effects, and contingency effects. (Still another type is that where the variance of a characteristic in a group, rather than its frequency, exerts an influence upon social conduct. But such an association between the variance and an effect criterion usually indicates the impact of a social force even when the characteristic is not held constant for individuals,[27] and therefore this type, which generally requires no special method of analysis, is not discussed in this paper.)

These two dimensions differentiate six types of structural effects:

1. *Direct structural effects of common values* indicate that the individual's conduct is influenced not only by the motivating force of his own value orientation but also by the social pressure resulting from the shared values of the other members of the group. In a public assistance agency, for example, a worker's positive orientation toward clients seemed to increase his tendency to provide casework services, and quite independently of the individual's orientation, the prevalence of a positive orientation in a group also made it more likely that casework services were provided.

2. *Inverse structural effects of common values* suggest that group values give rise to normative constraints that counteract the individual's psychological reaction to his own value orientation. Thus, the individual's positive attitude to clients tended to *increase* his involvement with his work and his unwillingness to delegate responsibility to recipients, but the prevalence of positive attitudes in a group tended to *decrease* involvement and unwillingness to delegate responsibility.

3. *Contingency effects of common values* are those in which the distribution of a value in a group influences the correlation between the individual's value orientation and a third variable. In the extreme case, the prevalence of the value in a group determines whether this correlation is positive or negative, and this pattern of findings identifies the deviants. It shows that individuals with a certain characteristic in terms of the third variable are more prone than others to resist group pressures and deviate from group norms regardless of the specific content of these norms. Whether most members of a group were much involved with their work or only little involved, those with an integrated status among peers, for instance, were more apt than others to deviate from the prevailing group climate, and so were workers identified with clients.

4. *Direct structural effects of relational networks* abstract the supportive or constraining force exerted by the social *organization* of the relationships between individuals and subgroups in a collectivity from the influences of each member's interpersonal relationships or social status. This is illustrated by the findings that group cohesiveness, defined by the extent of ingroup ties, apparently promoted a more impersonal approach to clients and high productivity, and that these effects were independent of the ingroup ties particular individuals had established.

[27]Only if the distribution of the characteristic is not normal is there a need to control it for individuals when ascertaining the structural effects of its variance.

5. *Inverse structural effects of relational networks* are indicative of the fact that the status distribution or network of social relations in a collectivity has an impact which is the very opposite of that of the individual's social status or his social relationships. A perfect case is the well-known finding reported by Stouffer that a soldier's rank was *directly* associated with favorable attitudes toward the army's promotion system, but the proportion of high-ranking enlisted men in a military unit was *inversely* associated with favorable attitudes.[28] A more complex instance of this type has been observed in the public assitance agency: in work groups where consultation was frequent, *negative* attitudes toward clients were more prevalent than in other groups, but individuals who were often consulted had more *positive* attitudes than those who were not; however, this difference between individuals existed only in groups where consultation was common and not in those where it was rare.

6. *Contingency effects of relational networks* are those in which the association between the individual's social position or relations and another factor depends on the distribution of social positions or relations in the collectivity. This pattern of findings demonstrates that individuals whose social status differs from that of the majority in their group, regardless of the nature of this difference, also tend to have different characteristics in another respect. Contingency effects of status variables identify the implications of minority status as such, just as contingency effects of normative variables identify the correlates of deviancy as such. For example, Zena S. Blau finds that the proportion of widowed in an age-sex category determined the influence widowhood had on the friendships of older people. Among men in their sixties, only a small minority of whom were widowed, the widowed had much less extensive friendships than the married; but among women over seventy, three-quarters of whom were widowed, the widows had slightly more extensive friendships than the married women. Older people whose marital status places them in a minority position among age-sex peers seem to have less chance to maintain friendship ties than others.[29]

This list of effects of social structures is tentative and incomplete. Further refinements are needed, for example, with respect to differences in the nature of the dependent variable, and with respect to the distinction between large societies and small groups. Omitted from the enumeration are influences of those aspects of social structures that are not manifestations of frequency distributions, such as the form of government in a community, because in these cases there are no corresponding individual characteristics to be held constant. However, even if the empirical measure of social structure is not based on a frequency distribution but the theoretical conception implies one, corresponding characteristics of individuals should be controlled. Thus, if we are concerned with the differential impact on social conduct of democratic and authoritarian cultures, rather than with that of political institutions, and use the form of government in a country merely as an inexpensive and indirect index of its culture, we implicitly refer to differences in prevailing value orientations and should control the individual's value orientation in order to distinguish the

---

[28]Stouffer *et al., op. cit.*, Vol. I, pp. 250-254.
[29]Zena S. Blau, "Structural Constraints on Friendships in Old Age," forthcoming.

external constraints of culture patterns from the influences of internalized values.

The method of isolating structural effects presented above underestimates the social constraints of structural differences, since the prevalence of certain shared values or social relationships in some collectivities and not in others, which is taken as given, is also often due to social forces, specifically, processes of socialization. It cannot be simply assumed, however, that any observed group pattern is the result of socialization. Other processes, such as differential selection, might be responsible. Moreover, whatever its plausibility, the claim that the common values of communities are social in origin and the product of processes of socialization is a hypothesis that requires empirical confirmation, and testing this hypothesis involves the use of procedures essentially similar to those discussed in this paper. To demonstrate its validity requires evidence that individuals who do not have a certain orientation but live in communities where this orientation prevails are more apt to develop such an orientation over time than those in other communities. Thus, Lazarsfeld and Thielens use this procedure to show that members of conservative university faculties are more apt to become increasingly conservative as they grow older than members of less conservative faculties.[30] In diachronic as well as synchronic investigations where social structures are defined, explicitly or implicitly, in terms of frequency distributions, structural effects on patterns of conduct must be analytically separated from the influences of the individuals' own characteristics or interpersonal relations.

[30]Paul F. Lazarsfeld and Wagner Thielens, Jr., *The Academic Mind*, Glencoe, Ill.: Free Press, 1958, pp. 247-250.

STRUCTURAL VERSUS INDIVIDUAL EFFECTS

Arnold S. Tannenbaum and Jerald G. Bachman

One may define structural constructs as opposed to purely individual variables for purposes of group or organization theory. However, the frequent reliance, in empirical studies, on measures based on individual member responses often creates some operational ambiguity. Do the relationships observed when employing measures based on individual responses truly represent the effects of structural variables, or are they simply reflections of individual-level relationships?

Reprinted with the permission of the authors and the publisher, The University of Chicago Press, from *The American Journal of Sociology*, Vol. 69 (May, 1964), 585-95.

This article is written as part of a program of research on organizations under a grant from the Carnegie Corporation of New York to the Survey Research Center, Institute for Social Research, University of Michigan. We are indebted to the following friends and colleagues who kindly read an earlier draft and offered suggestions: David Bowers, Bruce Hill, Leslie Kish, Bernard Indik, John Kirscht, Philip Marcus, James Morgan, Frank Neff, Donald Pelz, Clagett Smith, and John Sonquist.

Blau has suggested one approach to this problem. He proposes an analytic technique which provides, in effect, an operational definition of structure.[1] Davis, Spaeth, and Huson also provide an approach through the measurement of what they refer to as "compositional" effects.[2] These approaches overlap in several essential respects, and both represent significant contributions toward the solution of a difficult problem of sociological analysis. It is our intention to explore further the meaning of these methods, to consider some of their assumptions which appear to impose limitations on their applicability as presently formulated, and to suggest several means which may be helpful in reducing (if not overcoming) the effects of these limitations. Since Blau's approach is simpler in format, it will be easier to introduce the issues of the present paper primarily through reference to that approach. We shall then indicate their relevance to the method of Davis, Spaeth, and Huson.

Blau's strategy for determining structural effects may be summarized in three steps:[3]

1. An empirical measure, Z, is obtained that pertains to some characteristic of individual group members that has direct or indirect bearing upon the members' relations to each other (e.g., group identification, sociometric choices, initiation of interaction, rate of communication, or promotions).

2. The scores for measure Z, which describes individuals, are combined into one index for each group, and this index no longer refers to any characteristic of individuals but to a characteristic of the group. The value of this index is presumed to vary across groups; we will define this variable as Z_{gp}. Thus any individual may now be characterized in terms of his *own* score along variable Z and his *group's* score along variable Z_{gp}.[4]

3. To isolate a structural effect, the relationship between the group attribute (Z_{gp}) and some dependent variable, W, is determined while the corresponding characteristic of individuals (Z) is held constant. The structural effect thus refers to the effect of Z_{gp} on W.

This method is illustrated by Blau through the hypothetical data of Table 1 in which five hundred persons are assumed to be arranged in fifty groups of about ten members each. We have numbered the cells for convenience from 1 to 4. Blau suggests that a structural effect is demonstrated by the differences in average performance scores between the two columns in Table 1. "This finding would show that, even when the effect of the individual's discussion rate of his problems on his performance is eliminated, just to be in a group where

[1] Peter M. Blau, "Formal Organization: Dimensions of Analysis," *American Journal of Sociology*, LXIII (1957), 58-69, and his "Structural Effects," *American Sociological Review*, XXV (1960), 178-93.

[2] James A. Davis, Joe L. Spaeth, and Carolyn Huson, "A Technique for Analyzing the Effects of Group Composition," *American Sociological Review*, XXVI (1961), 215-25.

[3] The following section closely paraphrases Blau, "Formal Organization . . . ," *op. cit.*, p. 63.

[4] Lazarsfeld and Menzel would define the Z_{gp} variable in this usage as a "contextual property" of individuals, i.e., a property which stems from the individual's membership in a group (Paul F. Lazarsfeld and Herbert Menzel, "On the Relation between Individual and Collective Properties" in Amitai Etzioni [ed.], *Complex Organizations* [New York: Holt, Rinehart & Winston, 1961], pp. 422-40; see also Hannan C. Selvin and Warren O. Hagstrom, "The Empirical Classification of Formal Groups," *American Sociological Review*, XXVIII [1963], 399-411).

communication flows freely improves performance—other things being equal."[5] This statement, however, is based on an assumption which we must question.

TABLE 1.* Performance Scores by Rate and Frequency of Discussion (Hypothetical Example)

Individuals Who Discuss Their Problems	Groups Most of Whose Members Discuss Their Problems	
	Rarely	*Often*
Often	0.65 (1)	0.85 (2)
Rarely	0.40 (4)	0.70 (3)

*Adapted from Blau, "Formal Organization. . .," *op. cit.,* p. 64.

The assumption of constancy within rows is asserted frequently by social researchers in relation to the type of analysis represented in Table 1. It can, however, lead to serious misinterpretations of data. It is important to recognize first of all that continuums underlie each of the axes in Table 1, even though dichotomous categories are employed. Individuals (and groups) are not simply "often" or "rarely" communicators, but are likely to differ along a broad continuum of frequency of discussion. With this in mind, let us assume that all distributions within groups are normal (although almost any type of continuous distribution would lead to the same conclusion). The effects of this assumption can be seen in Figure 1. The points $Z_1 - Z_4$ represent the average individual discussion scores of individuals in cells 1-4 of Table 1. Several facts of importance are apparent from Figure 1:

1. In comparing individuals in cell 1 of Table 1 with those in cell 2, we are comparing individuals who have relatively low (Z_1) discussion scores with those having higher (Z_2) scores. We are not, in other words, holding the individual independent variable (Z) constant, and cannot say that the difference between the two cells on the dependent variable represents the effects of social structure. The same problem applies to the comparison of the remaining two cells.

2. The failure to hold Z strictly constant within rows has its counterpart in the failure to hold Z_{gp} constant within columns when more than two groups are being analyzed. The reader can see for himself how this unfortunate state of affairs develops by adding two normal frequency distributions, representing two additional groups, to the curves drawn in Figure 1. The pair of curves on the right would be labeled "High Discussion Groups." However, the one furthest to the right would contribute more members toward the computation of the mean in cell 2 than would the second group in that pair, while it would contribute fewer to the computation of the mean in cell 3 than would the second group. We would therefore be contaminating the individual-level (i.e., within-column) comparison with group effects.

Figure 1 implies a positive correlation between the Z scores of individuals and

[5] Blau, "Formal Organization . . . " *op. cit.,* p. 64.

Z_1 = Average discussion score for individuals high on frequency of discussion in low-discussion group

Z_3 = Average for low individuals in high group

Z_2 = Average for high-discussion individuals in high group

Z_4 = Average for low individuals in low group

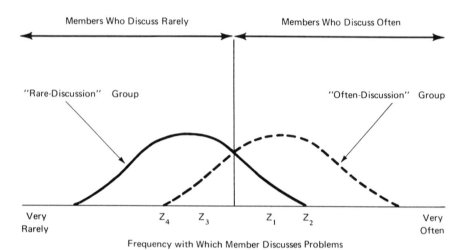

FIGURE 1. Hypothetical frequency distributions of members within two groups on a scale of frequency with which member discusses problems

the Z_{gp} scores assigned these individuals according to the groups in which they are located. A more detailed and concrete illustration of this relationship and of the problems it creates can be seen from data which we have obtained employing Monte Carlo (random) techniques as follows: (*a*) A random sample of 150 individuals was drawn from a population which is normally distributed on individual variable Z. (*b*) This sample was randomly divided into fifty groups of three members each, and a Z_{gp} score (equal to the mean Z for the three members) was derived for each group. Figure 2 presents the data obtained in this way. Each of the 150 "statistical individuals" is located in the matrix according to his own Z score and the Z_{gp} score assigned to his group.

Let us define for these data a perfect linear relationship between the individual variable Z and the dependent variable W.[6] Table 2 analyzes these data by the Blau method. According to this method the results would be interpreted as showing a strong individual-level effect coupled with a moderate (but quite

[6]For the sake of clarity we have assumed a linear correlation of 1.00 between Z and W. It is important to note, however, that the general observations which we will illustrate with these data apply equally well when there is *any* direct positive relationship between Z and W. The use of a perfect correlation in our illustration simply serves to rule out random variation or "noise." Individual-level, curvilinear relationships between Z and W might lead spuriously to "contingency" or "inverse" type structural relationships described by Blau, depending upon the shape of the individual-level relationships. We are illustrating here a spurious "direct" type structural effect (see *ibid.*).

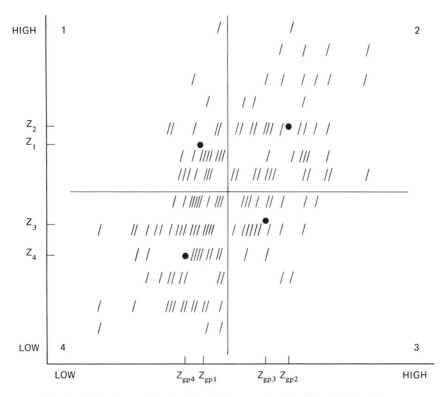

FIGURE 2. Scatter diagram showing Z and Zgp scores based on Monte Carlo data

definite) direct structural effect. However, we have defined dependent variable W as being perfectly related to individual variable Z and have assigned members randomly to groups, thus effectively ruling out any possibility of a genuine structural effect. The spurious structural effect indicated in Table 2 reflects the failure to hold the individual characteristic strictly constant within rows.

The processes underlying the problems noted above can be seen more clearly by returning to Figure 2. The intersecting lines in the diagram correspond to the dichotomies employed in deriving Table 2, and the four quadrants match the four cells in that table. The solid black circle in each cell indicates the mean Z and Z_{gp} for those cases falling within the cell. It is apparent that the level of Z for individuals in cell 1 is, on the average, lower than that for individuals in cell 2. In other words, individual effects are not held strictly constant across the "high Z" individuals. And, of course, the same problem appears for the "low Z" individuals in cells 3 and 4.

The failure to hold group effects constant within columns can also be seen readily from this figure. "Low Z_{gp}" individuals in cell 4 come, on the average, from groups with *lower* Z_{gp} scores than do individuals in cell 1; and Z_{gp} scores are lower for "high Z_{gp}" individuals in cell 3 than for those in cell 2.

The strategy used by Davis, Spaeth, and Huson is similar in several respects to

TABLE 2.*   Dependent Variable W as Related to Individual Variable Z and Group Variable Z_{gp} (Hypothetical Example—Blau Technique)

	Groups	
Individuals	*Low Z_{gp}*	*High Z_{gp}*
High Z	93.3	100.4
	(1)	(2)
Low Z	49.5	61.4
	(4)	(3)

*Cell entries indicate mean W (for all individuals in the cell).

that proposed by Blau. However, the former dichotomizes only on the Z variable and not the Z_{gp}. The groups are spread out along the horizontal axis according to their Z_{gp} scores. This eliminates the problem of contaminating within-column differences with group effects. However, the problem of eliminating individual effects in the intergroup comparisons remains. A limited solution to this problem, implicit in the Davis, Spaeth, and Huson method, is its restriction to individual characteristics that are dichotomous: "Within each population, individuals may be characterized by the presence or absence of a given *independent* attribute (A or $\bar{A}$)."[7] To the extent that the individual variables involved are truly dichotomous, neither the Blau method nor that of Davis, Spaeth, and Huson need be concerned about the problem of controlling for individual effects. However, most variables of interest to social scientists (including some of those discussed by Davis *et al.*) are continuous, and the problem remains for these. In Figure 3 we apply the method of Davis, Spaeth, and Huson to our Monte Carlo data and see demonstrated (spuriously) a "Type IIIA" compositional effect: "a constant individual difference, along with a linear effect of group composition."[8]

STRATEGIES FOR HOLDING CONSTANT INDIVIDUAL AND GROUP CHARACTERISTICS

The problems we have discussed stem from the assumptions that individual variables are held constant within rows and that group variables are held constant within columns. It is possible to reduce, if not to overcome, these problems through several modifications of the Blau or the Davis *et al.* methods. However, it is worth noting that the two problems may not be equally important in all situations. For example, a researcher who is interested primarily in determining the presence of a structural effect may not be especially interested in whether a spurious individual-level effect appears as a result of his failure to hold group characteristics strictly constant. He will, on the other hand, be

[7]Davis *et al., op. cit.*, p. 216 (italics as in original).
[8] *Ibid.*, p. 220.

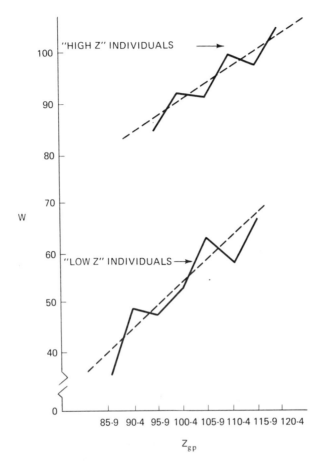

FIGURE 3. Dependent variable W as related to individual variable Z and group variable Zgp (hypothetical example—Davis *et al.* technique)

seriously concerned as to whether the structural effect he isolates is a spurious one caused by failure to hold individual characteristics constant. The techniques outlined below are not exhaustive, nor are they spelled out in fine detail. Our purpose is to open a number of avenues which may be useful in dealing with the problems raised above.

More precise matching of the individual variable.—The need for holding individual effects constant when comparing "high Z_{gp}" and "low Z_{gp}" groups suggests that individuals be matched more closely on the individual independent variable (Z). It should be noted that the fairly crude matching achieved when Z is dichotomized represents a very great improvement over the situation which would exist if no attempt whatever were made to match individuals according to Z. However, as we have demonstrated, the dichotomy may not be sufficient. The larger the number of categories, of course, the greater the accuracy in matching;

however, a "point of diminishing returns" is soon reached as the matching becomes more precise and as the number of cases falling within each category is reduced. The optimum number of categories to be used in any particular situation must be determined by the researcher.

Once the researcher has determined the number of categories into which to divide variable Z, he can proceed as in the Blau technique; he will, however, use an $N \times 2$ rather than Blau's 2×2 table. Certain of the cells in such a table might be empty; these, as well as their counterparts in the opposite column, would have to be abandoned. The remaining cells will provide an estimate of structural effects with individual effects held (more or less) strictly constant. Returning to our random data, the application of this modification (using a 7×2 table rather than a 2×2 one) completely eliminates the spurious structural effect shown in Table 2. It may not, however, eliminate spurious individual effects.

The modified technique described above can be extended further so as to cover a broader range of scale points along the horizontal azis (Z_{gp}) in a manner suggested by Davis *et al.* This is preferable to the dichotomous analysis for several reasons. First, the dichotomy is usually inefficient statistically. Second, the use of a sufficient number of categories along the horizontal (Z_{gp}) dimension would hold group characteristics strictly constant and thus avoid the problem of spurious individual effects. Finally, the broader range of cases along the horizontal axis may lead to richer possibilities of analysis, increasing the likelihood of detecting the direct, inverse, and contingency effects discussed by Blau, or the various relationships in the typology outlined by Davis *et al.* Returning once again to our random data, the use of a 7×8 table rather than a 2×8 table would convert Figure 3 into a series of seven essentially horizontal lines, correctly indicating the presence of an individual, but not a structural effect. However, the use of such a large number of cells drastically reduces the number of cases within each cell, so this variation will be appropriate only when the over-all number of cases is quite large.

Correlational methods.—Given a breakdown into N levels of the individual variable (Z) as described in the preceding section, it would be possible to determine the presence of structural effects by correlating Z_{gp} and W at each of the N levels of Z. This requires that each individual be assigned a Z_{gp} score according to the group in which he is located as well as his own individual W score. In the case of our Monte Carlo data, we would have seven separate correlation coefficients (corresponding to the seven levels of individual variable Z). These correlations would not provide information about individual-level effects. Such effects might be detected through the use of intragroup correlations, that is, by correlating Z and W separately within each group (thereby holding group effects constant).

Each of the above correlational procedures involves holding one variable constant while measuring the relationship between two others. If the particular data to be analyzed meet the necessary statistical requirements, the technique of partial correlation might achieve the same result. This could have the advantage of simplicity and precision. A structural effect could be measured in terms of the correlation between Z_{gp} and W with Z partialed out. An individual effect would be determined by the correlation of Z and W with Z_{gp} partialed out.[9]

[9]Thanks are due to Peter Blau for suggesting this possibility. Hubert M. Blalock, Jr.,

A more thorough analysis of the dependent variable W using Z and Z_{gp} as the independent variables could be carried out through multiple-regression techniques. In such an approach, the change in W expected with a unit change in Z_{gp} provides a measure of the structural effect, and the change in W expected with a unit change in Z provides a measure of the individual effect. It is very important in applying either this technique or that of partial correlation to remember the assumption of linearity upon which they are based. Unless the relationships between Z, Z_{gp}, and W are linear, the results of these analyses can be very misleading. However, it may sometimes be possible when the relationships are curvilinear to employ transformations, such as Z^2, log W, $(Z_{gp})^2$, and the like, to achieve the necessary linearity.[10]

The correlational techniques described thus far are all concerned with predicting the dependent variable (W) at the individual level. Another approach to detecting structural effects makes use of aggregate data such as those in the N × M table described in the preceding section. Given such a table, the correlations between Z_{gp} and *mean* W can be determined at each of the N levels of Z. In the case of the 7 × 8 table derived from our Monte Carlo data, we would have seven correlation coefficients (corresponding to the seven levels of individual variable Z). Each correlation would be based upon eight cells, with each cell referring to a certain level of Z_{gp} and the *mean* of the dependent variable W for all individuals located in that cell.

Several cautions should be borne in mind in applying this method. First, while correlations based upon *mean* data can provide information about the over-all presence or absence of a structural effect, they cannot be used to estimate how much of the variance in *individual-level* W can be related to Z_{gp}. Second, correlations based upon aggregate data are not directly comparable to intragroup correlations since different N's and different groupings of the data are used; accordingly, their relative magnitudes do not indicate a relative strength of structural as compared to individual effects. Third, a correlation based upon a small number of data points (eight in our illustration) is subject to a great deal of variation due to chance, although this may be somewhat reduced when each of the points is based upon averages. Accordingly, any conclusion concerning the presence or absence of a structural effect should probably be based upon the over-all pattern of correlations.[11] On the positive side, the use of aggregative

---

explains that "the partial correlation coefficient can be interpreted as a *weighted average* of the correlation coefficients that would have been obtained had the control variable been divided into very small intervals and separate correlations computed within each of these categories" (*Social Statistics* [New York: McGraw-Hill Book Co., 1960], p. 332).

[10]The multiple regression approach is somewhat related to L. A. Goodman's "Some Alternatives to Ecological Correlation," *American Journal of Sociology*, LXIV (1959), 610-25 (see esp. pp. 623-25); and Dean Harper's Ph.D. dissertation ("Some New Applications of Dichotomous Algebra to Survey Analysis and Latent Structure Analysis" [Columbia University, 1961]).

[11]A weighted average correlation combining all of the correlations for each Z level may sometimes be justified as a summary measure. In some cases it may be reasonable to derive a weighted average regression curve from the 7 (or N) curves, and a single, more stable correlation may be computed from this (see, e.g., A. S. Tannenbaum and C. G. Smith, "The Effects of Member Influence in an Organization: Phenomenology versus Organization Structure," *Journal of Abnormal and Social Psychology*, 1964 [in press]). While a single

instead of individual data may provide a more stable and accurate estimate of the true effect across groups, since each data point represents the observation of a number of individuals, thus eliminating a large portion of the random variance which occurs at the individual level.[12]

SOME FURTHER CONSIDERATIONS

A number of problems remain which apply to the original methods of Blau and of Davis et al. as well as to the modifications outlined in the preceding section.

The problem of overlap.—It can be seen through examination of Figure 1 and Table 1 that the N's in the four cells of the table are likely to be unequal, depending upon the extent to which the distributions of individual scores within the respective groups overlap. The N's in the four cells approach equality as the two distributions approach each other. But as this statistically desirable condition is approached, the data become meaningless as a basis for demonstrating structural effects; that is, structurally the groups are the same (on the independent variable) when the distributions coincide exactly. On the other hand, as the groups become more and more distinct, it is less and less possible to tell whether or not group effects are present. The N's in cells 1 and 3 become zero when the two distributions do not overlap at all. This implies, in terms of the scatter diagram of Figure 2, a correlation between Z and Z_{gp} approaching 1.00. It is ironic that this situation, which seems conceptually most felicitous for the discovery of structural effects, precludes their detection by the methods under consideration.

Deviants.—A further qualification can be seen from Figure 1 and Table 1. Individuals in cells 1 and 3 are deviants within their respective groups (at least with respect to their scores on the independent variable), and their responses may be influenced by that fact alone. Thus, when we compare individuals in cell 2 with those in cell 1 we may be comparing "average" members in one group with "deviant" members in another. The same problem applies in the comparison of cells 3 and 4. The importance of this problem cannot be ascertained easily. One can hope that it is not a serious source of contamination in most cases, although we know that deviants are likely to be affected differently by group experiences than are average members. The researcher would probably do well to consider its possible effects in terms of the particular variables being analyzed.

Selection.—The manner in which members are selected into groups may influence the relationship between Z_{gp} and W and may create in this way a spurious structural effect. For example, members of fraternities with high average intelligence (Z_{gp}) may have higher grade-point averages (W) than members of low average intelligence fraternities, even when individual intelligence (Z) is held strictly constant. This finding might be interpreted as indicating that being in a group of intelligent students creates better performance. Suppose, however, that certain fraternities maintain a policy of

correlation obscures distinctions between the types of group compositional effects suggested by Davis et al. (*op cit.*, p. 219), it can indicate a general overriding trend of the data.
[12] Selvin and Hagstrom, *op. cit.*

stressing high academic standing. Such a policy could lead to the selection of members directly on the basis of grades. Since intelligence and grades tend to be related, fraternities with such policies would be relatively high in average intelligence, thus producing the spurious structural relationship between average intelligence (Z_{gp}) and grade-point average (W), while holding individual intelligence (Z) constant.

It is probably worth keeping this problem in mind when interpreting group effects, since selection is a common phenomenon in social life. It is not unusual for individuals to join groups whose members are like themselves. Furthermore, even if selection *into* a group is random, selection *out* may be systematic, leaving a non-random selection behind. The various bases for selection may differ from case to case, and the corresponding interpretation of group effects would have to differ accordingly. Obviously, the problem can be completely eliminated in laboratory studies where groups are constructed by random procedures. Many field situations too would seem reasonably safe. The selection processes employed in creating formal work groups in industry, for example, are in many cases irrelevant to the particular variables under study, and these groups can be considered reasonably free of the problem. Certain informal and voluntary groups, however, may be more problematic, but this would depend again upon the variables under investigation.

Structural effects, operations versus concepts.—There is some conceptual haziness about variables which somehow are characterizations of both the organization and the individual. Research in group or organization functioning would do well to distinguish effects which are uniquely structural. While it may be easy enough to denote *conceptually* some variables that apply uniquely to structure and have no meaningful counterparts on the individual level, the fact that much social research must fall back upon measures based on individual responses creates a difficulty. While the concepts may be structural, the measures may be contaminated by individual effects. It is for this reason that the Blau method and that of Davis *et al.* are important approaches to the discovery of structural effects.

It is interesting to note, however, that Blau's original method, which is an operational approach to the definition of structural effects (and consequently structural characteristics), precludes from consideration, according to Blau, "those aspects of social structure which are not manifestations of frequency distributions, such as the form of government in the community."[13] This type of variable, however, is obviously of great interest to the social researcher. Furthermore, the Blau method *can* be helpful in approaching this type of variable if it is employed not simply as a means of operationally defining structural variables and effects, but as a means of helping to ascertain whether the instrument chosen to measure a structural variable is in fact measuring such a characteristic.

We would like, therefore, to maintain the important distinction between a structural concept and a structural measure. While the concept, for example, may refer to aspects of the organization such as "chain of command," "flexibility," or "distribution of control," which are not manifestations of frequency distributions, the measures may very well be based on distributions,

[13] Blau, "Structural Effects," *op cit.,* p. 192.

that is, on the responses of individual members.[14] Measures of these structural concepts would be subsumed under Kendall and Lazarsfeld's unit datum of Type V where "the unit item characterized the group only" and where "no information is introduced about a single individual."[15] We add simply that, while no information may be introduced about a single individual, information may be introduced *by* individuals. It is for this reason that the Blau method and that of Davis *et al.* can prove helpful.

Structural variables should be chosen first on the basis of their theoretical meaningfulness. Measurement is a second step, and tests of relationships between these variables and others are a third. Measurement of a pure structural effect in this sense might then be gauged by the occurrence of a difference between groups according to one of the above methods and a zero difference within groups. This is, with some modification, the Type II effect described by Davis *et al.* Conceptually, we would attempt to approach in this way the effect of a structural variable which has no meaningful counterpart on the individual level—although all of our measures are obtained at that level.

SUMMARY AND CONCLUSIONS

Since measures of group and organization variables are often based on responses of individuals, it is sometimes difficult to know whether the effects observed are due to structure or due simply to individual characteristics. Blau has suggested a useful approach to this difficulty, but one that appears to contain two problems: (1) it fails to hold individual characteristics strictly constant and thereby makes it possible to obtain spurious structural effects; (2) it fails to hold group characteristics strictly constant, making possible the occurrence of spurious individual-level effects. A technique similar in some respects to Blau's has been developed by Davis *et al.*; this method is susceptible only to problem (1).

We have proposed several modifications of the Blau and the Davis *et al.* methods, making use of more precise matching and correlational techniques. Each of these modified methods involves certain advantages and limitations, and the researcher may want to employ them in combination or modify them further to suit his particular purposes.

Several additional problems have been considered including the effect of

---

[14] See, e.g., Ellis L. Scott, who is concerned with the causes of error in the perception of the "chain of command" (*Leadership and Perceptions of Organizations* [Research Monograph No. 82 (Ohio State University, Columbus: Bureau of Business Research, Ohio State University, 1956)]). Basil Georgopolous and Arnold S. Tannenbaum measure organizational flexibility by averaging responses of organization members to questions designed to provide estimates of this variable ("A Study of Organizational Effectiveness," *American Sociological Review*, XXII [October, 1957], 534–40). Martin Patchen is concerned with the validity of measures, based on member responses, of distribution of control in organizations ("Alternative Questionnaire Approaches to the Measurement of Influences in Organizations," *American Journal of Sociology*, LXIX [July, 1963], 41-52).

[15] Patricia L. Kendall and Paul F. Lazarsfeld, "Problems of Survey Analysis," in Robert K. Merton and Paul F. Lazarsfeld (eds.), *Continuities in Social Research* (Glencoe, Ill.: Free Press, 1950), pp. 133-96. See also Selvin and Hagstrom's discussion (*op. cit.*) of aggregative and integral properties of groups and their distinction between members as respondents and as informants.

deviants, overlap of distributions among groups, and selection. We were also concerned about the purpose of the original methods discussed here, namely, defining structural or compositional effects (and, by implication, structural variables) *operationally.* In the authors' opinion this is not an adequate substitute for the conceptual definition of structural variables; conceptualization should come first. The application of the above techniques could then serve the very useful function of determining whether or not the operations employed can be justified as measures of structural characteristics and effects.

STRUCTURAL EFFECTS AND
INTERPERSONAL RELATIONSHIPS

Ernest Q. Campbell and C. Norman Alexander

Ever since Durkheim pointed out the importance of social facts, sociologists have generally felt justified in asserting that the social climate exerts influence upon the behaviors of individuals. Frequently, however, problems that arise with the attribution of causal influence to these structural and contextual variables have been ignored or dealt with casually. Just as we oppose a reductionist tendency to make inferential leaps from the traits or characteristics of individuals to the behavior of larger groups, and even whole societies, so must we take care to avoid any simplistic notions of direct, unmediated "structural effects."

The value systems and normative milieus of the larger social structure typically influence the behaviors of individuals through transmission and enforcement by certain *specific* others for any given individual. In Inkeles' cogent comment. "All institutional arrangements are ultimately mediated through individual human action."[1] In short, it is necessary to consider the position of the individual within the social structure—defined in terms of his specific relationships to other members of the collectivity—before attributing causal relevance to characteristics of the total collectivity. While this general statement may appear rather obvious, the implications that follow from it are sometimes overlooked.

Reprinted with the permission of the authors and the publisher, The University of Chicago Press, from the *American Journal of Sociology,* Vol. 73 (1968), 284-89.

Based on data secured during conduct of Grants M-04302 and MH-08489, National Institute of Mental Health, Ernest Q. Campbell, Principal Investigator. The Graduate Fellowship Program, National Science Foundation, freed the time of the second author for work on this paper, an assistance gratefully acknowledged. We are indebted to Charles Federspiel for statistical consultation.

[1] Alex Inkeles, "Personality and Social Structure," in R. K. Merton, Leonard Broom, and L. S. Cottrell, Jr. (eds.), *Sociology Today: Problems and Prospects* (New York: Basic Books, 1959), p. 251.

Rather than proceed directly from characteristics of the larger system to the behavioral responses of individuals, it is more appropriate to apply a two-step model for the purposes of causal inference. This involves, first, social-psychological theory, which deals with the individual's response to a *given* social situation, and, second, theory at the structural level, which deals with the determination of that given social situation by characteristics of the larger social system. We must keep in mind the fact that the actor responds to that segment of the total system which, for him, is perceptually important and salient; rarely does he (inter-) act with reference to the system as a whole.

Thus, more sophisticated analyses of "structural effects" must take into account *both* steps in this causal chain—moving from the characteristics of the total system to the situation faced by the individual due to the effects of these characteristics and then from the social situation confronting the individual to his responses to it. In this manner we hope to achieve greater theoretical understanding of the causal processes involved and, perhaps, contribute to the integration of social-psychological and structural theory. It is the purpose of this paper, then, to interpret the nature of certain structural effects by linking them to a systematic social psychological theory.

SOCIAL-PSYCHOLOGICAL AND STRUCTURAL LEVELS

A number of theorists have developed relatively similar and systematic theories to account for interpersonal influences among the members of a collectivity and to explain how consensus emerges through interpersonal attractions.[2] Since the basic propositions are common to the theories of Festinger, Heider, Homans, and Newcomb,[3] we shall assume a sufficient familiarity with them to justify the following statement of only those hypotheses specific to our immediate purposes: (1) The greater the attraction of a person, *P,* to another, *O,* the more likely he is to come to be similar to *O* with regard to *X*—where *X* represents those values, behaviors, and attitudes that are perceived to be of importance and common relevance. (2) The greater the similarity of a person, *P,* to another, *O,* with regard to *X,* the more likely he is to come to be highly attracted to *O.*

Blau, on the other hand, has dealt with structural effects, demonstrating that an individual with attribute *X* may manifest different behaviors—in behavioral areas related to *X*—as a function of the distribution of *X* in the collectivity.[4] However, Blau shows only that this analytic variable, the distribution of *X, may* influence the behaviors of the individual independently of his own value on *X;*

[2] C. Norman Alexander, Jr., and Richard L. Simpson, "Balance Theory and Distributive Justice," *Sociological Inquiry,* XXXIV (Spring, 1964), 182-92.

[3] Leon Festinger, *Theory of Cognitive Dissonance* (Chicago: Row Peterson & Co., 1957); Fritz Heider, *The Psychology of Interpersonal Relations* (New York: John Wiley & Sons, 1958); George Homans, *Social Behavior: Its Elementary Forms* (New York: Harcourt, Brace, & Co., 1961); Theodore M. Newcomb, *The Acquaintance Process* (New York: Holt, Rinehart & Winston, 1961).

[4] Peter M. Blau, "Structural Effects," *American Sociological Review,* XXV April, 1960), 178-93.

he does not provide a rationale for predicting the direction or nature of differences nor specify when and under what conditions these effects are likely to occur. The question of how it comes about that structural characteristics lead to an accurate prediction of personal response inconsistent with predictions based on personal attributes is unexplored.

Two recent studies by Simpson and Wilson[5] find interpersonal and structural influences on the aspirations of high-school students. Simpson shows that the higher the reported socioeconomic status of an individual's best friends, the higher his own aspirations are likely to be, holding parental influence constant. Wilson finds that the larger the proportion of middle-class students in a high school, the greater the likelihood that students of a given socioeconomic stratum have high educational aspirations.

Although Wilson's emphasis is structural and Simpson's interpersonal, both of these studies may be interpreted in terms of balance-theory predictions based on interpersonal influences. At the social-psychological level, it has been shown that the educational aspirations and attainments of an individual's friends influence his own aspirations and achievement apart from the status of his parents.[6] Since mobility and educational aspirations are directly related to the socioeconomic status of a student, we should observe that the educational aspirations of an individual are directly related to the status of his friendship choices, holding his own status constant. This is precisely the relationship found by Simpson.

In order to explain Wilson's findings at the structural level in these terms, it is necessary to assume only that friendship choices are randomly distributed in the system. As the average socioeconomic status in a school rises, the more often will individuals at each status level choose friends of high status—simply because there are proportionately more of them available to be chosen. We can then explain the observed association between the average status of a school and the educational aspirations of its students in terms of the intervening variable of interpersonal influence by an individual's friends. Whether we regard the relationship between average school status and student aspirations as spurious will depend, of course, on the theoretical assumptions we make about the nature of these relationships. Before discussing these possibilities, however, we will present certain data relevant to the points being raised.

DATA ANALYSIS

In connection with a larger study,[7] questionnaires were administered to 1,410 male seniors in thirty high schools in the eastern and Piedmont sections of North

[5]Richard L. Simpson, "Parental Influence, Anticipatory Socialization, and Social Mobility," *American Sociological Review,* XXVII (August, 1962), 517-22; Alan B. Wilson, "Residential Segregation of Social Classes and Aspirations of High School Boys," *American Sociological Review,* XXIV (December, 1959), 836-45.

[6]C. Norman Alexander, Jr., and Ernest Q. Campbell, "Peer Influences on Adolescent Aspirations and Attainments," *American Sociological Review,* XXIX (August, 1964), 568-75.

[7]Normative Controls and the Social Use of Alcohol," National Institute of Mental Health Grants M-4302 and MH-08489. Questionnaires were administered to 5,115 seniors of both sexes in sixty-two high schools. The sample in this paper includes only males in the thirty high schools that met the following criteria: (1) more than 15 males responded; (2) more than 95 per cent of the males gave their names; (3) more than 90 per cent of the males

Carolina. Each respondent was asked the following question: "What students here in school of your own sex do you go around with most often?" Up to two choices were coded for each case, a choice being considered codable if directed to another member of the high-school senior class who returned a signed questionnaire.[8]

Students were divided into five status levels according to the educational attainment of their parents.[9] Next, each of the thirty schools in the sample was assigned the average status of its students, that is, we arbitrarily assigned weights (from 1 to 5) to the five status levels and, treating this as an interval scale, computed a mean value for each school. For convenience, we shall refer to this measure as "school status." Finally, the average (mean) status of friends was determined for each respondent by this same arbitrary weighting of parental educational levels. Thus, we have three measures for each respondent: his personal status, his friends' status, and the status of his school. In addition, his college plans were determined by his response to the question: "Realistically, do you expect to go to college this coming fall?"

First, we shall examine the correlation between the status of the school and the proportion of individuals at each status level who plan to attend college. A positive value will be consistent with the structural effect reported by Wilson. Second, we shall examine the association between the status of an individual's friends at each personal-status level and the percentage who plan to go to college. A positive relationship will support Simpson's findings. When both of these expectations are confirmed, we shall determine whether there is a direct association between the average status of a school and the tendency of individuals at each status level to choose friends of high status. Confirmation of this hypothesis would suggest that the influence of friends may be an intervening variable that mediates the association between average school status and college expectations. Then we will examine at each of the five personal-status levels the partial correlations between (*a*) friends' status and college plans with school status controlled and (*b*) college plans and school status with friends' status controlled. We expect the relationship between school status and college plans to disappear in this analysis; but the relationship between college plans and friends' status should remain strong despite controls on school status. If this is the case, we shall argue that a two-step model is required for proper interpretation of structural effects phenomena, and we shall present this model.

The correlation coefficients pertaining to these expectations are presented in Table 1. It is apparent from inspection of column (1) of this table that, following the conceptions of Blau and Wilson, there *is* a structural effect: at each of five personal-status levels, the association between average school status and

---

completed the questionnaire; (4) more than one-third of the males planned to go to college. The fourth criterion resulted in the elimination of only one school which would otherwise not have been eliminated. The criterion was included because there are certain data available only for those adolescents who plan to attend college.

[8]We coded only two choices per case in order to maximize information about the respondent's interpersonal relationships and to minimize the loss of cases who selected a limited number of friends.

[9]The status levels and their arbitrary weights were as follows: (5) both parents went to college; (4) only one parent went to college; (3) neither parent went to college, but both graduated from high school; (2) neither parent went to college, and only one graduated from high school; (1) neither parent graduated from high school.

TABLE 1.   Correlations Among School Status, Friends' Status, and College Plans of High-School Seniors—by Parental Educational Level

	Zero-Order Correlations			Partial Correlations		
Parental Educational Level	School Status with College Plans (1)	Friends' Status with College Plans (2)	School Status with Friends' Plans (3)	* (4)	† (5)	N (6)
Both parents college	.10	.15	.49	.03	.12	172
One parent college	.16	.29	.36	.06	.26	183
Both parents high-school graduates	.15	.28	.50	.01	.24	147
One parent high-school graduate	.07	.19	.34	.01	.18	178
Neither parent high-school graduate	.14	.31	.40	.02	.28	295

*School status with college plans, holding friends' status constant.
†Friends' status with college plans, holding school status constant.

college plans is positive. Similarly, column (2) supports Simpson's findings: within each personal-status level there is a positive association between college plans and the status level of friendship choices. And in column (3) we see that persons at every status level are more likely to choose high-status friends when there are relatively large numbers of high-status persons in the system. Thus, school status is related to the individual's college plans; so is the status of his friends; and the status of friends chosen by those at each status level is related to the status of the school.

We come now to the basic question of interest: Is there a relationship between school status and the college plans of individuals at each status level apart from the effects of interpersonal influence that are indicated by the status of friends? The answer to this question should be negative if our hypothesized two-step model is correct. In other words, we expect only negligible variation to be explained by school status when friendship status is held constant. The partial correlations presented in column (4) of the table show that this is precisely what occurs. By contrast, when school status is held constant, the relationship between college plans and friends' status remains strong, as revealed in the partial correlations in column (5) of table 1. These two sets of partial-correlation coefficients support the inference that the structural effects of school status are best conceived of as due to the interpersonal influences of an individual's significant others.

DISCUSSION

Given knowledge of an individual's immediate interpersonal influences, the characteristics of the total collectivity provide no additional contribution to the prediction of his behaviors in these data. Thus we have no indication that an important structural effect exists independently of interpersonal influences. So little additional variation is explained by school status that we could easily regard the remainder as due to our inability to involve in the analysis *all* of the relevant interpersonal influences (e.g., the individual's additional friends of the same sex, his friends of the opposite sex, his "ideal" referents in the system, etc.).

On the other hand, we would support as reasonable the expectation that there are structural factors that determine the orientations of individuals to others having particular characteristics. This is why we want to stress the use of a two-step analytical model. Social-psychological theories specify the conditions under which individuals respond to *given* characteristics of their social environments. But research on "structural effects" is required to permit a specification of the conditions under which certain structural variables produce these relevant characteristics of an individual's social environment, the characteristics that furnish the "givens" in social-psychological theories. Then, with knowledge of structural variables, we should be able to specify when individuals will orient themselves toward specific types of others, and then use the characteristics of their significant others to predict their behaviors.

It is well established that the values and attitudes of individuals are shaped by and emerge from their continued interaction in social situations and that significant others are particularly influential in these processes. We are also convinced that there are certain regularities in the frequency with which particular types of individuals are chosen as focuses of interaction in certain social situations; and we believe that these regularities could be predicted from knowledge of relevant characteristics of the collectivity as a whole. However, until there is specification of the correspondence between structural variables and the proclivity to relate to particular types of persons in the collectivity, it is not possible to speak in causally relevant terms of structural effects on individual behaviors—inasmuch as these seem due to intervening interpersonal influences.

We must raise also the possibility of a direct causal link between individual behaviors and characteristics of the total collectivity. Here we are asking whether it may be that values of the total collectivity constitute behaviorally relevant expectations toward which the individual orients himself. The crucial question, but one to which our data cannot provide an answer, is this: Is there a school-wide value system toward which the individual is oriented and upon which he bases his behaviors apart from the immediate influences of his particular significant others? That is, measures of the values held by individuals in a given system neither confirm nor deny the independent existence of a collective value system. In order to say that X is an influential system value, we have to know that people in the system perceive it as such and act accordingly. Lacking evidence that participants perceive the existence of system-wide values and norms, researchers cannot draw firm conclusions about their effects; and we do not establish the existence of such perceived value systems with analytic structural variables. We therefore are not prepared to deny the potential influence of collectivity value systems, though we do assert the necessity for their independent measurement.

SUMMARY

We have worked toward the integration of social-psychological and structural theory, and we believe that this has important implications for research dealing with structural effects. We have argued that the normative influences of the distribution of an attribute within a collectivity are best explained by a two-step model. This perspective suggests a research strategy that first employs structural variables to account for the psychologically relevant characteristics of an individual's social environment and then explains his behaviors in terms of a social-psychological theory whose predictions are based on given conditions of the social environment. It also argues that the norms and value systems of collectivities are not appropriately assessed by analytic measures.

CRITERIA FOR SELECTING A SIGNIFICANCE LEVEL: A NOTE ON THE SACREDNESS OF .05

Sanford Labovitz

Sociologists have now been formally warned that not only is .05 not sacred, but the selection of a significance level is a complex process. One major suggestion by Skipper, *et al.* (1967) is that the researcher should no longer choose a standard level, but report the obtained level, e.g., .40 or .003. On the one hand, this suggestion seems to involve less thinking than choosing the conventional .05 or .01. At least here there are two or three conventions on which to base a selection. On the other hand, reporting the obtained level and letting the reader figure out the significance is not entirely a new suggestion. Some authors already have been reporting the obtained level, and they do not appear to give more consideration to the dynamics of a significance level any more than their more conventional colleagues. However, the article by Skipper and his associates may prove to be important, if it can sensitize sociologists to some of the serious problems involved with tests of significance.

The authors give three suggestions pertaining to significance levels and how to report them: (1) think and reflect on the arbitrary nature of conventional levels of significance, (2) report the actual level obtained, and (3) regardless of the level obtained, give an opinion on whether or not it supports the hypothesis. If these suggestions are followed extensively in research reporting, some of the problems of interpreting significance tests should diminish. However, the authors do not adequately spell out the guide lines (criteria) leading to the selection of a significance level.[1] The following section specifies eleven criteria applicable to this problem.

SOME CRITERIA TO CONSIDER IN CHOOSING A SIGNIFICANCE LEVEL

The following is neither an exhaustive nor all inclusive classification scheme of

Reprinted with the permission of the author and the publisher, The American Sociological Association, from the *American Sociologist,* Vol. 3 (1968), 220-22.

[1] Besides the problem of criteria for significance levels, there are three general points that are not handled adequately by the authors. First, the authors do not place the arbitrariness of a significance level within the perspective of the general state of theory, knowledge and evidence. Instead, they emphasize the single test. Actually a single test, *whether or not* it reaches a predetermined significance level leads to no major decision. Few, if any, researchers would accept or reject any statement on the basis of a single test. Second, Skipper, *et al.* ignore cross-classification versus tests of significance arguments. While this is not their concern, their whole article is essentially meaningless if tests of significance are not applicable. Finally, the authors emphasize applied research and the lay, statistically unsophisticated, audience. If statistically adroit colleagues are the prospective audience, perhaps their suggestions are less useful.

criteria on which to select a significance level. However, it appears to represent the major dimensions that should be either explicitly or implicitly considered by researchers. There is no attempt to integrate the entire list, nor to rank order the criteria in terms of importance. To do either seems premature. Note that none of the criteria should be considered in isolation—each should constitute just one of several guide lines in selecting a significance level.

Eleven more or less independent criteria are delimited.

1. *Practical consequences.* The practicality of the problem refers to the gravity of available kinds of error on the basis of value orientations. Testing whether prefrontal lobotomy or sedation is the better method for curing patients is a grave choice if we value vitality and recognize the long lasting and extreme effects of lobotomy. In this example, a small error rate (level of significance) of perhaps .001 or less would be chosen so that it would be extremely difficult to reject the null hypothesis of no difference and accept lobotomy over sedation. On the other hand, if we were testing the difference between two types of sedation, perhaps a larger error rate would be chosen (.05), if there were few drastic or long range effects for either one.

2. *Plausibility of alternatives.* A test of hypothesis should not be considered in isolation. Unless the inquiry is in an area where virtually nothing is known, the available rationales and empirical evidence (from other studies) should be considered in interpreting a significance test. Suppose the results are directly opposed to existing theory and empirical evidence, or even "common sense." That is, the evidence against the conclusion is large, and there is no theoretical or empirical support for the finding. Under these conditions, it would probably be best to choose a small error rate (.01 or .001), because in all the studies opposing the conclusion we are bound to find a few negative results on the basis of chance alone. We would hesitate to so easily reject the null hypothesis, when rejection is such a deviant result. On the other hand, if the evidence supports the conclusion, a larger significance level would be more appropriate, since now we are usually more willing to reject the null hypothesis of no difference.

3. *Power of the test—sample size.* The power of a test varies directly with sample size, that is, as N increases there is a greater probability of correctly rejecting the null hypothesis (in comparison to a specific alternative hypothesis). Moreover, the standard error varies inversely with sample size. Consequently, with a large N a small difference is likely to be statistically significant, while with a small N even large differences may not reach the predetermined level. Therefore, small error rates (.01 or .001) should usually accompany large N's and large error rates (.10 or .05) should be used for small N's.

4. *Power of the test—size of true difference.* The power of a test not only varies with sample size (and level of significance), but also with the size of the "true" difference, e.g., the magnitude of the difference between means. Therefore when the true difference is large, the probability of correctly rejecting the null hypothesis is also large, except if the sample size is small enough to offset this condition. A small error rate probably should be used when the difference is expected to be substantial. This conclusion is based on the rationale that if a large difference is expected and only a small difference is obtained, the null hypothesis of no difference should not be rejected.

5. *Type I vs. type II error.* As pointed out by Skipper, *et al.,* most textbooks

emphasize the criterion of minimizing the probability of errors described as type I (rejecting a true null) and type II (failing to reject a false null). These errors, to some extent, vary inversely with one another. Consequently, minimizing one type of error tends to increase the other. To illustrate, a .05 significance level yields fewer type II errors than the .01.

To digress on tests of hypotheses, a large significance level (.05) makes it easier to reject the null hypothesis and accept the original hypothesis set up by the researcher. The original hypothesis usually states a difference (and perhaps specifies the direction), while the null usually is stated in terms of no difference. Therefore, a large error rate increases the probability of accepting the researcher's hypothesis, but it also increases the probability of doing so incorrectly (type I error). However, with a large error rate, there is a low probability that the original hypothesis is both correct and we failed to accept it. If we feel that the original hypothesis should not be accepted until a high level of certainty is certainty is reached, then many true original hypotheses are likely to be lying around that are not accepted (type II error). Which error is best? Aside from our personal feelings on how a science should develop, at this point, the other alternatives listed should help solve the apparent dilemma.

6. *Convention.* Skipper, *et al.*, strongly argue against using conventional levels of significance such as .05 and .01. For the most part their conclusion seems justified, and the other criteria listed further indicate the limitations of using a conventional level. It is listed as a separate criterion primarily because (1) these conventions are used in sociology, and (2) they may be positively evaluated as yielding some consistency among research results. If most results are applied to a similar standard, readers have some idea of the comparability of results from one study to another. However, the disadvantages of a conventional level (such as not considering available evidence or the nature of the problem) well outweigh this factor. As a final remark, the selection of a conventional level may not rest on any sound rationale, but on such incidental factors as the particular field of social science, where an individual received his degree, or the journal under consideration.

7. *Degree of control in design.* It is well known that R. A. Fisher generally selected the .05 level in his agricultural experiments. These experiments were based on complex (e.g., latin square or factorial) designs that offered a high degree of control over the effects of extraneous factors. The effects of "other factors" were handled by randomizing plots of ground, rows and columns of products, etc. Under such highly controlled conditions Fisher seemed justified in using the larger error rate of .05 instead of .01 or lower. If other factors are controlled, the results of the experiment are likely to be due to the experimental variable or chance differences and not due to extraneous factors. Stated otherwise, a large amount of control in an experiment reduces alternative interpretations so that a larger level of significance can be tolerated. In designs of low control, perhaps a more stringent error rate should be selected (.01) since the alternative to chance differences could be due to extraneous factors as well as to the independent variable. Consequently, under low control conditions we should make it more difficult to reject the null hypotheses of no difference.

8. *Robustness of test.* Robustness is the ability of a statistical test to maintain its logically deduced conclusion when one or more assumptions have

been violated. For example, Student's *t* and analysis of variance have been demonstrated to be robust under the conditions of nonnormality and heterogeneity. However, under these conditions the actual .02 level of significance may be met at the .01 level and the .10 at the .05. Consequently, depending on the statistical test in question, when the data do not meet all the assumptions, a small error rate should be chosen and interpreted as a larger one, e.g., .01 is interpreted as .02 or .05. On the other hand, if the data reasonably meet the assumptions, then a large error rate can be used with confidence.

9. *One-tail vs. two-tail tests.* As stated in most introductory statistics books, it is easier to reject the null hypothesis in a directional (one-tail test) as opposed to a nondirectional (two-tail test) hypothesis. The z-score equivalents for a one-tail test are lower than those for two tail (e.g., 1.65 as compared to 1.96 at the .05 level). It is reasoned that knowledge of the direction of the hypothesis should give the researcher the advantage of more easily rejecting the null and accepting the original hypothesis.

However, the notion of one-tail vs. two-tail is largely a myth, because it is based on the rationale that we either have absolutely no idea of the direction of the hypothesis or we have absolute knowledge of the direction. Either extreme alternative is an unlikely occurrence. It is most probable that we have some idea of the direction of the hypothesis, but there is a small to large amount of uncertainty in our reasoning. Consequently, we should neither accept the z-score equivalent of the one-tail or two-tail test, e.g., 1.96 or 1.65, but an intermediate score between the two values. At the .05 level if we are largely certain of the direction (that is, it is supported by previous research or sound rationale), then we should select a z-score closer to 1.65. If, on the other hand, there is a large degree of uncertainty, a z-score nearer to 1.96 would be more appropriate. This is the equivalent of saying that we should choose a larger or smaller error rate depending upon our degree of confidence in the direction of our hypothesis.

10. *Confidence interval.* A confidence interval not only provides a probability band containing some statistical measure or difference, but actually provides tests of hypotheses. Therefore, the difference between a test and an interval is not clearcut. The importance of considering the confidence interval as a criterion is selecting a level of significance depends on whether or not the problem requires a small or large interval. For a smaller interval a larger error rate is necessary (.05), while for larger intervals (in which there is more confidence that they contain the parameters) a smaller error rate is necessary (.01).

11. *Testing vs. developing hypotheses.* If testing a well reasoned and developed hypothesis that will distinguish between two theories, it seems logical to select a small level of significance. This is based on the notion that we want to be fairly sure if one theory is to be selected over another. On the other hand, if we are just exploring a set of interrelations for the purpose of developing hypotheses to be tested in another study, a larger error rate will tend to yield more hypotheses—any of which may be subsequently validated. Therefore, in this exploration stage perhaps the .10 or .20 level would be sufficient.

Caution should be used not to fall into the trap of thinking that the few "significant" relations out of many possible ones have truly reached the designated level. Out of twenty interrelations we are likely to find one significant at the .05 level on the basis of chance alone. However, we do not fall into this trap if the "significant" relations are subsequently tested.

CONCLUSION

In conclusion, Skipper, *et al.* have performed a definite service to sociology if more of us probe deeper into the rationales behind significance levels and stop using an absolute standard as proof of a hypothesis. To buttress this position, eleven criteria are presented that hopefully will aid researchers in selecting an appropriate level. These criteria should not be viewed as definitive in any sense, and some undoubtedly are more important than others. I welcome any response on other possible criteria, and any thoughts on the evaluation of those presented above.

REFERENCE

Skipper, J. K., Jr., *et al.* "The sacredness of .05; a note concerning the uses of significance in social sciences," *American Sociologist*, 2 (February, 1967), 16-19.

DATA-DREDGING PROCEDURES IN SURVEY ANALYSIS

Hanan C. Selvin and Alan Stuart

INTRODUCTION AND SUMMARY

1. It is a commonplace of the statistical design of experiments that the hypotheses to be tested should be formulated before examining the data that are to be used to test them. Even in experimental situations, this is sometimes not possible, and in the last decade or so some progress has been made toward the development of more flexible testing procedures which allow the data to be dredged for hypotheses in certain ways. In survey analysis, which is commonly exploratory, it is rare for precise hypotheses to be formulable independently of the data. It follows that normally no precise probabilistic interpretations can validly be given to relationships found among the survey variables. In practice, this has not prevented survey practitioners from reporting probability levels as if

Reprinted with the permission of the authors and the publisher from the *American Statistician* (June, 1966), pp. 20-23.

The work leading to this paper was begun when Selvin was at the London School of Economics in the fall of 1963, as a Senior Postdoctoral Fellow of the National Science Foundation.

they were precisely meaningful. Most investigators are so accustomed to making probability statements that a survey report looks naked without them, but we fear that many survey reports are wearing the Emperor's clothes. This paper offers a classification of data-dredging procedures and some comments on their use.

SURVEY ANALYSIS

2. The survey analyses we consider here are *explanatory* or *theoretical;* such a survey aims, not primarily to describe some population by estimating one or more of its parameters (although this may be one of its aims) but, by invoking more general substantive propositions, to explain why certain phenomena in that population behave as they do. One may want to learn how people make up their minds in an election, why the rates of mental illness vary from one social class to another, or how new farm practices diffuse through a rural community. Even when the problem derives from practical concerns, the theoretically-oriented survey always involves such nonstatistical tasks as the "operationalization" of the variables (what does it mean to say that an instructor at an American university was "frightened" by the investigations of the McCarthy era?) and the interpretation of the statistical findings, often by reference to variables on which data were not gathered (to what extent is the observed relation between social class and arrests for juvenile delinquency a manifestation of differential treatment by the police?).

Most surveys of this kind are based on long questionnaires and large samples. A typical academic survey may ask 100 questions of 1,000 people, and market surveys, if they usually ask fewer questions, may have 10,000 cases or more. Gathering and processing the data take a long time—several months in most cases—and analysing the data for their theoretical implications may take even longer. With such a long and expensive procedure, the survey analyst wants to maximize the intellectual returns on his investment. Rarely, if ever, does he undertake a study with a single specific hypothesis in mind. He usually has many diffuse and ill-formulated hypotheses in mind; and the marginal cost of an additional question is so low that many different problems can be investigated in the same survey without raising its cost very much. Indeed, the vein of data in most surveys is so rich and the amount of information extracted by the original analyst so little that libraries of survey data have been established to facilitate "secondary analysis", the re-study of surveys for purposes that may not have been intended by the original investigator.

In the sense that relatively few of the possible and meaningful hypotheses are specified in advance of gathering the data, the typical survey is exploratory, and the analyst alternates between examining the data and formulating hypotheses. In an experiment the form of the analysis is specified in the design, but the form of survey analysis typically evolves as the data are examined. In the present state of the art there is seldom only a single viable path at any stage of the analysis, so that the analyst has a great deal of freedom, regardless of the configurations of the data.

To make the survey analyst's problem more vivid, we may liken him to a hunter stalking an unknown quarry through an unfamiliar landscape with an arsenal of complex weapons. This metaphor suggests the names we have given to some practices of survey analysts: snooping, fishing, and hunting.

ORDERED AND UNORDERED OBSERVATIONS: SNOOPING

3. The effect of knowledge of the data upon the performance of statistical tests has long been known. Perhaps its best-known manifestation is in the case when a single random sample of $n(>2)$ observations is available from a known distribution, say the normal with zero mean, unit variance for convenience. The difference between any predesignated pair of observations (say, the 4th and 17th in order of drawing) is self normal, with zero mean, variance two; so is the difference between any pair of observations chosen at random. But if the pair to be compared is chosen in any way related to the values observed, their difference is not normally distributed. In particular, if we choose the *largest* observed difference between pairs (which is, of course, the sample range) its distribution depends critically on n and is never normal.

We may put the point more generally, without reference to normality: the set of n observations on a variable y may either be labelled $y_1, y_2, \ldots, y_n$ where the subscript refers to the order of drawing, or $y_{(1)}, y_{(2)}, \ldots y_{(n)}$ where $y_{(1)} \leqslant y_{(2)} \leqslant \ldots \leqslant y_{(n-1)} \leqslant y_{(n)}$ are the ordered sample values. The distribution of the differences between any pair of y's defined by their places in the ordering, $y_{(r)} \ y_{(s)}$, is obtainable if r and s are fixed. Thus, we can calculate the distribution of the range (the case $r = n, \ s = 1$) for any n; we can also calculate the distribution of the difference between any other *predesignated* pair of ordered observations.

Similarly, so long as we follow a precisely predesignated procedure, we can use test procedures involving a sequence of pairwise comparisons. Such are the *multiple comparisons* tests in the analysis of variance. In the extreme case, we may even be able to predesignate an infinite class of comparisons to be made on the data—this is what is equivalently done in the "all contrasts" procedures of Tukey and Scheffé (see Scheffé, 1959), where every linear function (with coefficients summing to zero) of a set of variables may validly be tested simultaneously with a known probability level. In conformity with the term "data-snooping", which has sometimes been used in connection with these procedures, we define the first category in our classification of data-dredging procedures: SNOOPING is the process of testing from the data all of a *predesignated* (though possibly infinite) set of hypotheses. It will be seen from the discussion above that snooping is a rigorous and valid statistic procedure. It is, however, rather limited in scope because of the difficulty of solving the mathematical problems involved when large numbers of correlated tests are to be made. We believe that the two applications we have mentioned (range and all-contrasts procedures) are the only important snooping procedures in practice.

SEARCHING FOR A MODEL: FISHING

4. Snooping procedures, or at least such as have so far been developed, are of little practical use to the survey practitioner as opposed to the experimentalist. Pre-data hypotheses are commonly imprecise or even non-existent, and often

one of the principal motives for undertaking a survey is to provide material from which some rather precise hypothesis may be dredged. One may, for example, wish to decide which independent variables to include in a relationship explaining one or more other variables.

In studies with a single important dependent variable—for example, of voting behavior—analysts frequently examine all possible two-variable relations between the dependent variable and independent variables, but only a few of these relations will appear in the published report, the others not being considered "useful". A more elaborate form of fishing appears in many computer programs for regression, in which the independent variables are screened by the program to see if they account for a worthwhile (possibly predetermined) proportion of the variation in the dependent variable; those that fail to meet this test do not appear in the final regression equation.

We therefore define our second category: FISHING is the process of using the data to choose which of a number of candidate variables to include in an explanatory model.

Here we come upon another aspect of the conditioning of statistical tests by knowledge of the data. If we decide, on the basis of the data, to discard one or more variables from an explanatory relation, we cannot validly apply standard statistical procedures to the retained variables in the relation as though nothing had happened. In the nature of the case, the retained variables have had to pass some kind of preliminary test (possibly an imprecise intuitive one) that the discarded variables failed. In our picturesque terminology the fish which don't fall through the net are bound to be bigger than those which do, and it is quite fruitless to test whether they are of average size. Not only will this alter the performance of all subsequent tests on the retained explanatory model—it may destroy unbiasedness and alter mean-square-error in estimation (see Larson and Bancroft, 1963, a, b, and their references). Some of these fishing effects have been investigated for regression models with predesignated candidate variables, and for a number of preliminary tests leading to pooling procedures in the analysis of variance and elsewhere. Box and Cox (1964) consider general methods of fishing for the appropriate scale on which to analyze experimental data.

Although the results of these investigations throw light on the nature of the conditioning imposed by preliminary search procedures, this conditioning is not of a simple or clearcut kind, and many of the important questions for survey analysts have not yet been examined. In general, we can only say that any preliminary search of data for a model, even when the alternatives are predesignated, affects the probability levels of all subsequent tests based on that model on the same data, and in no very simple way, and also affects the characteristics of subsequent estimation procedures. The only valid course for the survey analyst is to use different data for testing the model he has dredged from his first set of data. This need not involve a new sample since the initial sample may be divided (by carefully randomised methods which take account of all the complexities of the sample structure) into two parts for just this purpose.

But even if such segregation is not carried out (because the sample is too small or for other reasons), we do not suggest that fishing is a reprehensible procedure; indeed it is often the only way to produce the food needed for the survey analyst's thought. We are arguing only that the survey analyst should admit that he *has* been fishing, rather than pretend that the model fell upon him as manna from heaven, and take the consequences, which are that the apparent probability levels of tests may have little relation to their true probability levels, and that the properties of estimates may be radically different from what is supposed.

Computers make it possible for fishing trips to be completely systematic. Thus Morgan and Sonquist (1963 a, b; see also Sonquist and Morgan, 1964) have developed a program that fishes for the most important independent variables and the most important successive dichotomizations of these variables. In other words, it isolates the successive splits of the sample that account for as large a proportion of the variation in the dependent variable as possible, with a specified minimum level of variation, usually 0.5 per cent, for each split. They write (1963 a, p. 433):

> Most statistical estimates carry with them procedures for estimating their sampling variability. Sampling stability with the proposed program would mean that using a different sample, one would end up with the same complex groups segregated. No simple quantitative measure of similarity seems possible, nor any way of deriving its sampling properties. The only practical solution would seem to be to try the program out on some properly designed half-samples, taking account of the original sample stratification and controls, and to describe the extent of similarity of the pedigrees of the groups so isolated. Since the program "tries" an almost unlimited number of things, no significance tests are appropriate, and in any case the concern is with discovering a limited number of "indexes" or complex constructs which will explain more than other possible sets.

Fishing for the variables to go into a model, though often a complex procedure, is essentially a variant of the ordering of observations discussed in section 3: the candidate variables are ordered into two classes, "useful" and "not useful." To ignore this fact in subsequent analysis is the same kind of error as to ignore the fact that the range of a normal sample is not normally distributed. Its effects on a survey analysis may be devastating.

NON-PREDESIGNATED PARAMETERS: HUNTING AND THE CHI-SQUARE TEST

5. Whereas snooping predesignates all tests to be made, and fishing uses a predesignated set of candidate variables, HUNTING involves no predesignation: the data are simply dredged for information in the area of interest. Hunting is distinguished from snooping and fishing in that it is impossible, *in principle,* for rigorous statistical tests to be devised to cover the procedure, since the procedure itself is necessarily ill-defined and consequently impossible to express in the precise language of a computer program. It has an analog, often not recognized as such, in general statistical practice. Consider the ordinary "curve-fitting" procedure—we have a sample distribution of observations in k groups and fit a theoretical distribution (with p parameters estimated quite properly by efficient methods from the grouped data) which we then test by chi-square with $k-p-1$ degrees of freedom. But how was the *form* of the

theoretical distribution chosen? In most cases known to us, it is hunted for by eye-examination of the histogram. This imposes an unknown (but presumably large) number of constraints[1] upon the agreement between observed and theoretical distributions, and destroys the probability level of the subsequent chi-square test, which is only valid if the form of the theoretical distribution is given by pre-data knowledge. It is a somewhat startling fact that most P-values reported in routine curve-fitting chi-square tests are meaningless, but it underlines our main point in this section, that hunting, by its very nature, precludes subsequent probability statements.

Hunting can take many forms. As defined here, it involves searching through a body of data and examining many relations in order to find some worth testing. Or one may examine a single hypothesis in several different bodies of data—as in parapsychology experiments, when the probability of a run of successful guesses is computed only after a subject gets "hot". Sterling (1959) has pointed out that fallacious test results may appear when different investigators examine the same false hypothesis. Here the failure to replicate published studies and the practice of publishing only "significant" results mean that a procedure intended to guard against the acceptance of "chance" outcomes actually promotes their acceptance. Tullock (1959) has remarked that this is even more likely to happen when a single investigator does a series of studies and reports only those hypotheses that turn out to be "significant".

Because hunting offers maximum scope for the data-dredger, since there are no rules at all, it must always be acknowledged, at the cost of subsequent probability statements. What is more, there is no possibility that hunting can ever be made to lead to precise probability statements. Hunting is essential to many survey analysts. As with fishing, the only criticism to be made is of the delusion that one has to pay no price for the sport.

It is worth remarking that in general hunting cannot be made probabilistically respectable by splitting the sample in advance. When one is fishing for a single model, or carrying out a single chi-square test, one essentially wishes to test a single hypothesis, and segregation of one part of the data for this purpose will make this possible as indicated above. But hunting typically throws up a group of interrelated hypotheses, and we do not know in advance how many these will be so there is no possibility of separating off a part of the data for each hypothesis to be tested independently. (It would be pleasant to imagine the survey analyst with a large stock of reserve sub-samples to test the hypotheses he hunts up, but this is unrealistic.)[2] If hunting on one sub-sample produces a number of related hypotheses, the results of the tests of them carried out on a second sub-sample will be correlated in unknown ways unless we follow a strictly predesignated testing procedure whose statistical properties are known. Nevertheless it must presumably be better in general to use a reserve sub-sample for this purpose than to have no such sub-sample at all.

---

[1] Moreover, these constraints are not linear functions of the group frequencies, so there is no possible way of adjusting degrees of freedom for them.

[2] For a discussion of ways in which libraries of survey data might be used to test hypotheses derived from hunting, see Selvin (1965).

REFERENCES

Box, G. E. P. and E. R. Cox "An analysis of transformations," *Journal of the Royal Statistical Society*, B, 26, 1964, pp. 211-52.

Larson, H. J. and T. A. Bancroft, "Sequential model building for prediction in regression analysis I," *Annals of Mathematical Statistics*, 1963a, pp. 462-79.

Larson, H. J. and T. A. Bancroft, "Biases in prediction by regression for certain incompletely specified models," *Biometrika*, 50, 1963b, pp. 391-402.

Morgan, J. N. and J. A. Sonquist, "Problems in the analysis of survey data and a proposal," *JASA*, 58, 1963a, pp. 415-34.

Morgan, J. N. and J. A. Sonquist, "Some results of a non-symmetrical branching process that looks for interaction effects," *Proceedings of the Social Statistics Section, American Statistical Association, 1963*, 1963b, pp. 40-53.

Scheffé, H., *The Analysis of Variance*. New York: John Wiley and Sons, 1959.

Selvin, H. C., "Durkheim's *Suicide:* further thoughts on a methodological classic," in Robert A. Nisbet (ed.) *Emile Durkheim*. Englewood Cliffs, N.J.: Prentice-Hall, 1965, pp. 113-36.

Sonquist, J. A. and J. N. Morgan, *The Detection of Interaction Effects*. Ann Arbor: Survey Research Center, The University of Michigan, 1964.

Sterling, T. D., "Publication decisions and their possible effects on inferences drawn from tests of significance—or vice-versa," *JASA*, 54, 1959, pp. 30-34.

Tullock, G., "Publication decisions and tests of significance—a comment," *JASA*, 54, 1959, p. 593.

8

Data
Interpretation

Perhaps the most conspicuous controversy in sociology has been that between those advocating causal interpretative models and those advocating functionalist interpretative models. The first three papers in this chapter discuss causal interpretations. Hirschi and Selvin indicate some "false criteria of causality" evident in the delinquency literature, and go on to suggest some general rules for determining a "real" causal relationship.[1]

Carey, in his paper, is critical of the famous Hawthorne studies. His critique illustrates a style of logical argument central to any science—the successive elimination of alternative hypotheses as a prerequisite to causal argument. Carey suggests that a failure on the part of the Hawthorne researchers to examine and eliminate alternative hypotheses renders their interpretations very questionable.

The Forbes and Tufte paper brings a more precise technique to the problem of causal inference. They provide a discussion of causal modelling which is oriented about a critical evaluation of two works from political science. They make perfectly clear that causal modelling, despite its utility in delimiting the number of possible explanations, provides no ultimate solutions. One must still employ one's knowledge of a particular substantive area, of the "real world", in order to argue persuasively for one model rather than another. They further note the problems of interaction effects in causal analysis, as well as the problem of two or more highly related independent variables.

[1] For additional discussion, see Travis Hirschi and Hanan Selvin, *Delinquency Research: An Appraisal of Analytic Methods* (New York: Free Press, 1967).

In a controversial paper, Homans argues that functionalist models fail to provide true explanations of behavior. His view is that the functionalists lack the general propositions which would permit adequate deduction. Thus, functionalists fail to provide explanations and fail to build theory.

Stinchcombe, taking a different stance, indicates that functionalist and causal interpretations alike depend upon criteria of scientific inference, and that deductions are, in fact, possible from a functionalist position.

In this chapter we have, in a sense, come full circle. We began with a discussion of the nature of science and the nature of scientific theory. We here debate the nature of sociological explanation and sociological theory.

FALSE CRITERIA OF CAUSALITY
IN DELINQUENCY RESEARCH

Travis Hirschi and Hanan C. Selvin

Smoking per se is not a cause of lung cancer. Evidence for this statement comes from the thousands of people who smoke and yet live normal, healthy lives. Lung cancer is simply unknown to the vast majority of smokers, even among those who smoke two or more packs a day. Whether smoking is a cause of lung cancer, then, depends upon the reaction of the lung tissues to the smoke inhaled. The important thing is not whether a person smokes, but how his lungs react to the smoke inhaled. These facts point to the danger of imputing causal significance to superficial variables. In essence, it is not smoking as such, but the carcinogenic elements in tobacco smoke that are the real causes of lung cancer.[1]

The task of determining whether such variables as broken homes, gang membership, or anomie are "causes" of delinquency benefits from a comparison with the more familiar problem of deciding whether cigarette smoking "causes" cancer. In both fields many statistical studies have shown strong relations between these presumed causes and the observed effects, but the critics of these studies often attack them as "merely statistical." This phrase has two meanings. To some critics it stands for the belief that only with experimental manipulation of the independent variables is a satisfactory causal inference possible. To others it is a brief way of saying that observing a statistical association between two phenomena is only the first step in plausibly inferring causality. Since no one proposes trying to give people cancer or to make them delinquent, the fruitful way toward better causal analyses in these two fields is to concentrate on improving the statistical approach.

In setting this task for ourselves we can begin with one area of agreement: all statistical analyses of causal relations in delinquency rest on observed associations between the independent and dependent variables. Beyond this there is less agreement. Following Hyman's reasoning,[2] we believe that these two

Reprinted with the permission of the authors and the publisher, The Society for the Study of Social Problems, from *Social Problems,* Vol. 13 (1966), 254-68.

This is publication A-56 of the Survey Research Center, University of California, Berkeley. We are grateful to the Ford Foundation for financial support of the larger study from which this paper is drawn. An early account of this study, which does not include the present paper, is *The Methodological Adequacy of Delinquency Research,* Berkeley: Survey Research Center, 1962. Ian Currie, John Lofland, Alan B. Wilson, and Herbert L. Costner made useful criticisms of previous versions of this paper.

[1] This is a manufactured "quotation"; its source will become obvious shortly.

[2] Herbert H. Hyman, *Survey Design and Analysis.* Glencoe, Illinois: The Free Press, 1955, chs. 5-7.

additional criteria are the minimum requirements for an adequate causal analysis: 1) the independent variable is causally prior to the dependent variable (we shall refer to this as the criterion of "causal order"), and 2) the original association does not disappear when the influences of other variables causally prior to both of the original variables are removed ("lack of spuriousness").[3]

The investigator who tries to meet these criteria does not have an easy time of it.[4] Our examination of statistical research on the causes of delinquency shows, however, that many investigators do not try to meet these criteria but instead invent one or another new criterion of causality—or, more often, of noncausality, perhaps because noncausality is easier to demonstrate. To establish causality one must forge a chain of three links (association, causal order, and lack of spuriousness), and the possibility that an antecedent variable not yet considered may account for the observed relation makes the third link inherently weak. To establish noncausality, one has only to break any one of these links.[5]

Despite the greater ease with which noncausality may be demonstrated, many assertions of noncausality in the delinquency literature turn out to be invalid. Some are invalid because the authors misuse statistical tools or misinterpret their findings. But many more are invalid because the authors invoke one or another false criterion of noncausality. Perhaps because assertions of noncausaility are so easy to demonstrate, these invalid assertions have received a great deal of attention.

A clear assertion that certain variables long considered causes of delinquency are not really causes comes from a 1960 *Report to The Congress:*

> Many factors frequently cited as causes of delinquency are really only concomitants. They are not causes in the sense that if they were removed delinquency would decline. Among these factors are:
> Broken homes.
> Poverty.
> Poor housing.
> Lack of recreational facilities.
> Poor physical health.
> Race.
> Working mothers.[6]

[3] Hyman appears to advocate another criterion as well: that a chain of intervening variables must link the independent and dependent variables of the original relation. We regard this as psychologically or theoretical desirable but not as part of the minimum methodological requirements for demonstrating causality in nonexperimental research.

[4] Hirschi and Selvin, *op. cit.*

[5] Popper calls this the asymmetry of verifiability and falsifiability. Karl R. Popper, *The Logic of Scientific Discovery,* New York: Basic Books, 1959, esp. pp. 27-48. For a fresh view of the verification-falsification controversy, see Thomas S. Kuhn, *The Structure of Scientific Revolutions,* Chicago: University of Chicago Press, 1962. Kuhn discusses Popper's views on pp. 145-146. Actually, it is harder to establish non-causality than our statement suggests, because of the possibility of "spurious independence." This problem is discussed in Hirschi and Selvin, *op. cit.,* pp. 38-45, as "elaboration of a zero relation."

[6] U.S. Department of Health, Education, and Welfare, *Report to The Congress on Juvenile Delinquency,* United States Government Printing Office, 1960, p. 21. The conclusion that "poor housing" is not a cause of delinquency is based on Mildred Hartsough, *The Relation Between Housing and Delinquency,* Federal Emergency Administration of Public Works, Housing Division, 1936. The conclusion that "poor physical health" is not a cause is based

According to this report, all of these variables are statistically associated with delinquency, i.e., they are all "concomitants." To prove that they are not causes of delinquency it is necessary either to show that their relations with delinquency are spurious or that they are effects of delinquency rather than causes. Since all of these presumptive causes appear to precede delinquency, the only legitimate way to prove noncausality is to find an antecedent variable that accounts for the observed relations. None of the studies cited in the *Report* does this.[7] Instead, the assertion that broken homes, poverty, lack of recreational facilities, race, and working mothers are not causes of delinquency appears to be based on one or more of the following false "criteria":[8]

1. Insofar as a relation between two variables is not *perfect,* the relation is not causal.
    a. Insofar as a factor is not a *necessary condition* for delinquency, it is not a cause of delinquency.
    b. Insofar as a factor is not a *sufficient condition* for delinquency, it is not a cause of delinquency.
2. Insofar as a factor is not *"characteristic"* of delinquents, it is not a cause of delinquency.
3. If a relation between an independent variable and delinquency is found for a *single value of a situational or contextual factor,* then the situational or contextual factor cannot be a cause of delinquency.[9]
4. If a relation is observed between an independent variable and delinquency and if a psychological variable is suggested as *intervening* between these two variables, then the original relation is not causal.
5. *Measurable* variables are not causes.
6. If a relation between an independent variable and delinquency is *conditional*

---

on Edward Piper's "unpublished Children's Bureau manuscript summarizing the findings of numerous investigators on this subject." Since we have not examined these two works, the following conclusions do not apply to them.

[7] The works cited are: broken homes, Negly K. Teeters and John Otto Reinemann, *The Challenge of Delinquency,* New York: Prentice-Hall, 1950, pp. 149-154; poverty, Bernard Lander, *Toward an Understanding of Juvenile Delinquency,* New York: Columbia University Press, 1954; recreational facilities, Ethel Shanas and Catherine E. Dunning, *Recreation and Delinquency,* Chicago: Chicago Recreation Commission, 1942; race, Lander, *op. cit.;* working mothers, Eleanor E. Maccoby, "Children and Working Mothers," *Children,* 5 (May-June, 1958), pp. 83-89.

[8] It is not clear in every case that the researcher himself reached the conclusion of noncausality or, if he did, that this conclusion was based on the false criteria discussed below. Maccoby's article, for example, contains a "conjectural explanation" of the relation between mother's employment and delinquency (i.e., without presenting any statistical evidence she suggests that the original relation came about through some antecedent variable), but it appears that the conclusion of noncausality in the *Report* is based on other statements in her work.

[9] All of the foregoing criteria are related to the "perfect relation" criterion in that they all require variation in delinquency that is unexplained by the "noncausal" variable. A more general statement of criterion 3 would be: "if variable X is related to delinquency when there is no variation in variable T, then variable T is not a cause of delinquency." In order for this criterion to be applicable, there must be some residual variation in delinquency after T has had its effect.

Although both forms of this criterion fairly represent the reasoning involved in some claims of non-causality, and although both are false, the less explicit version in the text is superficially more plausible. This inverse relation between explicitness and plausibility is one reason for the kind of methodological explication presented here.

upon the value of other variables, the independent variable is not a cause of delinquency.

In our opinion, all of these criteria of noncausality are illegitimate. If they were systematically applied to any field of research, no relation would survive the test. Some of them however, have a superficial plausibility, both as stated or implied in the original works and as reformulated here. It will therefore be useful to consider in some detail just why these criteria are illegitimate and to see how they appear in delinquency research.

False Criterion 1. Insofar as a relation between two variables is not perfect, the relation is not causal.

> Despite the preponderance of Negro delinquency, one must beware of imputing any causal significance to race per se. There is no *necessary* concomitance between the presence of Negroes and delinquency. In Census Tracts 9-1 and 20-2, with populations of 124 and 75 Negro juveniles, there were no recorded cases of delinquency during the study period. The rates of Negro delinquency also vary as widely as do the white rates indicating large differences in behavior patterns that are not a function or effect of race per se. It is also of interest to note that in at least 10% of the districts with substantial Negro juvenile populations, the Negro delinquency rate is lower than the corresponding white rate.[10]

There are three facts here: (1) not all Negroes are delinquents; (2) the rates of Negro delinquency vary from place to place; (3) in some circumstances, Negroes are less likely than whites to be delinquent. These facts lead Lander to conclude that race has no causal significance in delinquency.

In each case the reasoning is the same: each fact is another way of saying that the statistical relation between race and delinquency is not perfect, and this apparently is enough to disqualify race as a cause. To see why this reasoning is invalid one has only to ask for the conditions under which race *could be* a cause of delinquency if this criterion were accepted. Suppose that the contrary of the first fact above were true, that *all* Negroes are delinquent. It would then follow necessarily that Negro delinquency rates would not vary from place to place (fact 2) and that the white rate would never be greater than the Negro rate (fact 3). Thus in order for race to have "any" causal significance, all Negroes must be delinquents (or all whites non-delinquents). In short, race must be perfectly related to delinquency.[11]

[10]Bernard Lander, *Towards an Understanding of Juvenile Delinquency*, New York: Columbia University Press, 1954, p. 32. Italics in original. An alternative interpretation of the assumptions implicit in this quotation is presented in the discussion of criterion 6, below.

[11]Strictly speaking, in this quotation Lander does not demand that race be perfectly related to delinquency, but only that all Negroes be delinquents (the sufficient conditions of criterion 1-b). Precedent for the "perfect relation" criterion of causality appears in a generally excellent critique of crime and delinquency research by Jerome Michael and Mortimer J. Adler published in 1933: "There is still another way of saying that none of the statistical findings derived from the quantitative data yields answers to etiological questions. The findings themselves show that every factor which can be seen to be in some way

Now if an independent variable and a dependent variable are perfectly associated,[12] no other independent variable is needed: that is, perfect association implies single causation, and less-than-perfect association implies multiple causation. Rejecting as causes of delinquency those variables whose association with delinquency is less than perfect thus implies rejecting the principle of multiple causation. Although there is nothing sacred about this principle, at least at the level of empirical research it is more viable than the principle of single causation. All studies show that more than one independent variable is needed to account for delinquency. In this field, as in others, perfect relations are virtually unknown. The researcher who finds a less-than-perfect relation between variable X and delinquency should not conclude that X is not a cause of delinquency, but merely that it is not the *only* cause.[13]

For example, suppose that tables like the following have been found for variables A, B, C, and D as well as for X:

Delinquency by X, where X is neither
a necessary nor a sufficient condition
for delinquency, but may
be one of several causes.

	X	Not X
Delinquent	40	20
Nondelinquent	60	80

The researcher using the perfect relation criterion would have to conclude that none of the causes of delinquency has yet been discovered. Indeed, this criterion would force him to conclude that there are *no causes* of delinquency except *the* cause. The far-from-perfect relation between variable X and delinquency in the table above leads him to reject variable X as a cause of delinquency. Since variables A, B, C, and D are also far from perfectly related to delinquency, he must likewise reject them. Since it is unlikely that *the* cause of delinquency will ever be discovered by quantitative research, the researcher who accepts the perfect relation criterion should come to believe that such research is useless: all it can show is that there are *no* causes of delinquency.

---

associated with criminality is also associated with non-criminality, and also that criminality is found in the absence of every factor with which it is also seen to be associated. In other words, what has been found is merely additional evidence of what we either knew or could have suspected, namely, that there is a plurality of related factors in this field." *Crime, Law and Social Science,* New York: Harcourt Brace, p. 53.

[12] "Perfect association" here means that all of the cases fall into the main diagonal of the table, that (in the 2 X 2 table) the independent variable is both a necessary and a sufficient cause of the dependent variable. Less stringent definitions of perfect association are considered in the following paragraphs. Since Lander deals with ecological correlations, he could reject race as a cause of delinquency even if it were perfectly related to delinquency at the census tract level, since the ecological and the individual correlations are not identical.

[13] We are assuming that the causal order and lack of spuriousness criteria are satisfied.

False Criterion 1-a. Insofar as a factor is not a necessary condition for delinquency, it is not a cause of delinquency.

The "not necessary" (and of course the "not sufficient") argument against causation is a variant of the "perfect relation" criterion. A factor is a necessary condition for delinquency if it must be present for delinquency to occur—e.g., knowledge of the operation of an automobile is a necessary condition for auto theft (although all individuals charged with auto theft need not know how to drive a car). In the following table the independent variable X is a necessary (but not sufficient[14]) condition for delinquency.

Delinquency by X, where X is a necessary
but not sufficient condition
for delinquency.

	X	Not X
Delinquent	67	0
Nondelinquent	33	100

The strongest-statement we can find in the work cited by the Children's Bureau in support of the contention that the broken home is not a cause of delinquency is the following:

> We can leave this phase of the subject by stating that the phenomenon of the physically broken home is a cause of delinquent behavior is, in itself, not so important as was once believed. In essence, it is not that the home is broken but rather that the home is inadequate, that really matters.[15]

This statement suggests that the broken home is not a necessary condition for delinquency (delinquents may come from intact but "inadequate" homes). The variable with which the broken home is compared, inadequacy, has all the attributes of a necessary condition for delinquency: a home that is "adequate" with respect to the prevention of delinquency will obviously produce no delinquent children. If, as appears to be the case, the relation between inadequacy and delinquency is a matter of definition, the comparison of this relation with the relation between the broken home and delinquency is simply an application of the illegitimate "necessary conditions" criterion. Compared to a necessary condition, the broken home is "not so important." Compared to some (or some *other*) *measure* of inadequacy, however, the broken home may be very important. For that matter, once "inadequacy" is empirically

[14]To say that X is a necessary condition for delinquency means that all delinquents are X (i.e., that the cell in the upper right of this table is zero); to say that X is a sufficient condition for delinquency implies that all X's are delinquent (i.e., that the cell in the lower left is zero); to say that X is a necessary and sufficient condition for delinquency means that all X's and no other persons are delinquent (i.e., that both cells in the minor diagonal of this table are zero).

[15]Teeters and Reinemann, *op. cit.*, p. 154.

defined, the broken home may turn out to be one of its important causes. Thus the fact that the broken home is not a necessary condition for delinquency does not justify the statement that the broken home is "not [a cause of delinquency] in the sense that if [it] were removed delinquency would decline."[16]

False Criterion 1-b. Insofar as a factor is not a sufficient condition for delinquency, it is not a cause of delinquency.

A factor is a sufficient condition for delinquency if its presence is invariably followed by delinquency. Examples of sufficient conditions are hard to find in empirical research.[17] The nearest one comes to such conditions in delinquency research is in the use of predictive devices in which several factors taken together are virtually sufficient for delinquency.[18] (The fact that several variables are required even to approach sufficiency is of course one of the strongest arguments in favor of multiple causation.) Since sufficient conditions are rare, this unrealistic standard can be used against almost any imputation of causality.

First, however, let us make our position clear on the question. Poverty per se is not a cause of delinquency or criminal behavior; this statement is evidenced by the courage, fortitude, honesty, and moral stamina of thousands of parents who would rather starve than steal and who inculcate this attitude in their children. Even in the blighted neighborhoods of poverty and wretched housing conditions, crime and delinquency are simply non-existent among most residents.[19]

Many mothers, and some fathers, who have lost their mates through separation, divorce, or death, are doing a splendid job of rearing their children.[20]

Our point of view is that the structure of the family *itself* does not cause delinquency. For example, the fact that a home is broken does not cause delinquency, but it is more difficult for a single parent to provide material needs, direct controls, and other important elements of family life.[21]

---

[16]*Report to The Congress,* p. 21. Two additional illegitimate criteria of causality listed above are implicit in the quotation from Teeters and Reinemann. Inadequacy of the home" could be treated as an intervening variable which interprets the relation between the broken home and delinquency (criterion 4) or as a theoretical variable of which the broken home is an indicator (criterion 5). These criteria are discussed below.

[17]In his *Theory of Collective Behavior* (New York: The Free Press of Glencoe, 1963) Neil J. Smelser suggests sets of necessary conditions for riots, panics, and other forms of collective behavior; in this theory the entire set of necessary conditons for any one form of behavior is a sufficient condition for that form to occur.

[18]In the Gluecks' prediction table, those with scores of 400 or more have a 98.1% chance of delinquency. However, as Reiss has pointed out, the Gluecks *start* with a sample that is 50% delinquent. Had they started with a sample in which only 10% were delinquent, it would obviously have been more difficult to approach sufficiency. Sheldon Glueck and Eleanor Glueck, *Unraveling Juvenile Delinquency,* Cambridge: Harvard University Press, 1950, pp. 260-262; Albert J. Reiss, Jr., "Unraveling Juvenile Delinquency. II. An Appraisal of the Research Methods," *American Journal of Sociology,* 57:2, 1951, pp. 115-120.

[19]Teeters and Reinemann, *op. cit.,* p. 127.

[20]*Ibid.,* p. 154.

[21]F. Ivan Nye, *Family Relationships and Delinquent Behavior,* New York: John Wiley, 1958, p. 34. Italics in original.

The error here lies in equating "not sufficient" with "not *a* cause." Even if every delinquent child were from an impoverished (or broken) home—that is, even if this factor were a necessary condition for delinquency—it would still be possible to show that poverty is not a sufficient condition for delinquency.

In order for the researcher to conclude that poverty is a cause of delinquency, it is not necessary that all or most of those who are poor become delinquent.[22] If it were, causal variables would be virtually impossible to find. From the standpoint of social action, this criterion can be particularly unfortunate. Suppose that poverty were a necessary but not sufficient condition for delinquency, as in the table on page 258. Advocates of the "non sufficient" criterion would be forced to conclude that, if poverty were removed, delinquency would not decline. As the table clearly shows, however, removal of poverty under these hypothetical conditions would *eliminate* delinquency!

To take another example, Wootton reports Carr-Saunders as finding that 28% of his delinquents and 16% of his controls came from broken homes and that this difference held in both London and the provinces. She quotes Carr-Saunders' "cautious" conclusion:

> We can only point out that the broken home may have some influence on delinquency, though since we get control cases coming from broken homes, we cannot assert that there is a direct link between this factor and delinquency.[23]

Carr-Saunders' caution apparently stems from the "not sufficient" criterion, for unless the broken home is a sufficient condition for delinquency, there must be control cases (nondelinquents) from broken homes.

In each of these examples the attack on causality rests on the numbers in a single table. Since all of these tables show a non-zero relation, it seems to us that these researchers have misinterpreted the platitude "correlation is not causation." To us, this platitude means that one must go beyond the observed fact of association in order to demonstrate causality. To those who employ one or another variant of the perfect relation criterion, it appears to mean that there is something suspect in any numerical demonstration of association. Instead of being the first evidence for causality, an observed association becomes evidence against causality.

False Criterion 2. Insofar as a factor is not "characteristic" of delinquents, it is not a cause of delinquency.

> Many correlation studies in delinquency may conquer all these hurdles and still fail to satisfy the vigorous demands of scientific causation. Frequently a group of delinquents is found to differ in a statistically significant way from a nondelinquent control group with which it is compared. Nevertheless, the differentiating trait may not be at all characteristic of the delinquent group. Suppose, for example, that a researcher compares 100

[22]We are of course assuming throughout this discussion that the variables in question meet what we consider to be legitimate criteria of causality.

[23]Barbara Wootton, *Social Science and Social Pathology*, New York: Macmillan, 1959, p. 118.

delinquent girls with 100 nondelinquent girls with respect to broken homes. He finds, let us say, that 10% of the nondelinquents come from broken homes, whereas this is true of 30% of the delinquent girls. Although the difference between the two groups is significant, the researcher has not demonstrated that the broken home is characteristic of delinquents. The fact is that 70% of them come from unbroken homes. Again, ecological studies showing a high correlation between residence in interstitial areas and delinquency, as compared with lower rates of delinquency in other areas, overlook the fact that even in the most marked interstitial area nine tenths of the children do not become delinquent.[24]

This argument is superficially plausible. If a factor is not characteristic, then it is apparently not important. But does "characteristic" mean "important"? No. Importance refers to the variation accounted for, to the size of the association, while "being characteristic" refers to only one of the conditional distributions (rows or columns) in the table (in the table on page 258, X is characteristic of delinquents because more than half of the delinquents are X). This is not enough to infer association, any more than the statement that 95% of the Negroes in some sample are illiterate can be taken to say anything about the association between race and illiteracy in that sample without a corresponding statement about the whites. In the following table, although Negroes are predominantly ("characteristically") illiterate, race has no effect on literacy, for the whites are equally likely to be illiterate.

	Race	
	Negro	*White*
Literate	5	5
Illiterate	95	95

More generally, even if a trait characterizes a large proportion of delinquents and also characterizes a large proportion of nondelinquents, it may be less important as a cause of delinquency than a trait that characterizes a much smaller proportion of delinquents. The strength of the relation is what matters—that is, the *difference* between delinquents and nondelinquents in the proportion having the trait (in other words, the difference between the conditional distributions of the dependent variable). In the quotation from Barron at the beginning of this section, would it make any difference for the inputation of causality if the proportions coming from broken homes had been 40% for the nondelinquents and 60% for the delinquents, instead of 10 and 30%? Although broken homes would now be "characteristic" of delinquents, the percentage difference is the same as before. And the percentage difference would still be the same if the figures were 60 and 80%, but now broken homes would be characteristic of *both* nondelinquents and delinquents!

The "characteristic" criterion is thus statistically irrevelant to the task of assessing causality. It also appears to be inconsistent with the principle of

[24]Milton L. Barron, *The Juvenile in Delinquent Society*, New York: Knopf, 1954, pp. 86-87.

multiple causation, to which Barron elsewhere subscribes.[25] If delinquency is really traceable to a plurality of causes," then some of these causes may well "characterize" a minority of delinquents. Furthermore, this "inconsistency" is empirical as well as logical: in survey data taken from ordinary populations it is rare to find that any group defined by more than three traits includes a majority of the cases.[26]

False Criterion 3. If a relation between an independent variable and delinquency is found for a single value of a situational or contextual factor, that situational or contextual factor cannot be a cause of delinquency.

No investigation can establish the causal importance of variables that do not vary. This obvious fact should be even more obvious when the design of the study restricts it to single values of certain variables. Thus the researcher who restricts his sample to white Mormon boys cannot use his data to determine the importance of race, religious affiliation, or sex as causes of delinquency. Nevertheless, students of delinquency who discover either from research or logical analysis that an independent variable is related to delinquency in certain situations or contexts often conclude that these situational or contextual variables are not important causes of delinquency. Since personality or perceptual variables are related to delinquency in most kinds of social situations, social variables have suffered most from the application of this criterion:

> Let the reader assume that a boy is returning home from school and sees an unexpected group of people at his doorstep, including a policeman, several neighbors, and some strangers. He may suppose that they have gathered to welcome him and congratulate him as the winner of a nationwide contest he entered several months ago. On the other hand, his supposition may be that they have discovered that he was one of several boys who broke some windows in the neighborhood on Halloween. If his interpretation is that they are a welcoming group he will respond one way; but if he feels that they have come to "get" him, his response is likely to be quite different. In either case he may be entirely wrong in his interpretation. *The important point, however, is that the external situation is relatively unimportant.* Rather, what the boy himself thinks of them [it] and how he interprets them [it] is the crucial factor in his response.[27]

There are a least three independent "variables" in this illustration: (1) the

---

[25]*Ibid.*, pp. 81-83.

[26]There are two reasons for this: the less-than-perfect association between individual traits and the fact that few traits are simple dichotomies. Of course, it is always possible to take the logical complement of a set of traits describing a minority and thus arrive at a set of traits that does "characterize" a group, but such artificial combinations have too much internal heterogeneity to be meaningful. What, for example, can one say of the delinquents who share the following set of traits: not Catholic, not middle class, not of average intelligence?

The problem of "characteristic" traits arises only when the dependent variable is inherently categorical (Democratic; member of a gang, an athletic club, or neither) or is treated as one (performs none, a few, or many delinquent acts). In other words, this criterion arises only in tabular analysis, not where some summary measure is used to describe the association between variables.

[27]Barron, *op. cit.*, pp. 87-88. Italics added.

external situation–the group at the doorstep; (2) the boy's past behavior–entering a contest, breaking windows, etc.; (3) the boy's interpretation of the group's purpose. As Barron notes, variable (3) is obviously important in determining the boy's response. It does not follow from this, however, that variables (1) and (2) are unimportant. As a matter of fact, it is easy to see how variable (2), the boy's past behavior, could influence his interpretation of the group's purpose and thus affect his response. If he had not broken any windows in the neighborhood, for example, it is less likely that he would think that the group had come to "get" him, and it is therefore less likely that his response would be one of fear. Since Barron does not examine the relation between this situational variable and the response, he cannot make a legitimate statement about its causal importance.

Within the context of this illustration it is impossible to relate variable (1), the group at the doorstep, to the response. The reason for this is simple: this "variable" does not vary–it is fixed, given, constant. In order to assess the influence of a group at the doorstep (the external situation) on the response, it would be necessary to compare the effects of groups varying in size or composition. Suppose that there was no group at the doorstep. Presumably, if this were the case, the boy would feel neither fear nor joy. Barron restricts his examination of the relation between interpretation and response to a single situation, and on this basis concludes that what appears to be a necessary condition for the response is *relatively unimportant!*

In our opinion, it is sometimes better to say nothing about the effects of a variable whose range is restricted than to attempt to reach some idea of its importance with inadequate data. The first paragraph of the following statement suggests that its authors are completely aware of this problem. Nevertheless, the concluding paragraphs are misleading:

> We recognized that the Cambridge-Somerville area represented a fairly restricted socio-economic region. Although the bitter wave of the depression had passed, it had left in its wake large numbers of unemployed. Ten years after its onset, Cambridge and Somerville still showed the effects of the depression. Even the best neighborhoods in this study were lower middle class. Consequently, our results represent only a section of the class structure.
>
> In our sample, however [*therefore*], there is not a *highly* significant relation between "delinquency areas," or subcultures, and crime. If we had predicted that every child who lived in the poorer Cambridge-Somerville areas would have committed a crime, we would have been more often wrong than right. Thus, current sociological theory, by itself, cannot explain why the majority of children, even those from the "worst" areas, never became delinquent.
>
> *Social factors,* in our sample, were not strongly related to criminality. The fact that a child's neighborhood did not, by itself, exert an independently important influence may [*should not*] surprise social scientists. Undeniably, a slum neighborhood can mold a child's personality–but apparently only if other factors in his background make him susceptible to the sub-culture that surrounds him.[28]

[28]William McCord and Joan McCord, *Origins of Crime,* New York: Columbia University Press, 1959, pp. 71 and 167.

False Criterion 4. If a relation is observed between an independent variable and delinquency and if a psychological variable is suggested as intervening between these two variables, then the original relation is not causal.

There appear to be two elements in this causal reasoning. One is the procedure of *conjectural interpretation.*[29] The other is the confusion between *explanation,* in which an antecedent variable "explains away" an observed relation, and *interpretation,* in which an intervening variable links more tightly the two variables of the original relation. In short, the vanishing of the partial relations is assumed, not demonstrated, and this assumed statistical configuration is misconstrued.

This criterion is often encountered in subtle form suggestive of social psychological theory:

> The appropriate inference from the available data, on the basis of our present understanding of the nature of cause, is that whether poverty, broken homes, or working mothers are factors which cause delinquency depends upon the meaning the situation has for the child.[30]

> It now appears that neither of these factors [the broken home and parental discipline] is so important in itself as is the child's reaction to them.[31]

> A factor, whether personal or situational, does not become a cause unless and until it first becomes a motive.[32]

The appropriate inference about whether some factor is a cause of delinquency depends on the relation between that factor and delinquency (and possibly on other factors causally prior to both of these). All that can be determined about meanings, motives, or reactions that *follow from* the factor and *precede* delinquency can only strengthen the conclusion that the factor is a cause of delinquency, not weaken it.

A different example may make our argument clearer. *Given* the bombing of Pearl Harbor, the crucial factor in America's response to this situation was its interpretation of the meaning of this event. Is one to conclude, therefore, that

---

In a study restricted to "known *offenders*" in which the dependent variable is the *seriousness* of the *first offense* Richard S. Sterne concludes: "Delinquency cannot be fruitfully controlled through broad programs to prevent divorce or other breaks in family life. The prevention of these would certainly decrease unhappiness, but it would not help to relieve the problem of delinquency." Since the range of the dependent variable, delinquency, is seriously reduced in a study restricted to *offenders,* such conclusions can not follow from the data. *Delinquent Conduct and Broken Homes,* New Haven: College and University Press, 1964, p. 96.

[29] Like conjectural explanation, this is an argument, unsupported by statistical data, that the relation between two variables would vanish if the effects of a third variable were removed; here, however, the third variable "intervenes" causally between the original independent and dependent variables.

[30] Sophia Robison, *Juvenile Delinquency,* New York: Holt, Rinehart and Winston, 1961, p. 116.

[31] Paul W. Tappan, *Juvenile Delinquency,* New York: McGraw-Hill, 1949, p. 135.

[32] Sheldon and Eleanor Glueck, *Family Environment and Delinquency,* Boston: Houghton-Mifflin, 1962, p. 153. This statement is attributed to Bernard Glueck. No specific reference is provided.

the bombing of Pearl Harbor was relatively unimportant as a cause of America's entry into World War II? Intervening variables of this type are no less important than variables further removed from the dependent variable, but to limit analysis to them, to deny the importance of objective conditions, is to distort reality much as do those who ignore intervening subjective states.[33]

This kind of mistaken causal inference can occur long after the original analysis of the data. A case in point is the inference in the *Report to The Congress*[34] that irregular employment of the mother does not cause delinquency. This inference appears to come from misreading Maccoby's reanalysis of the Gluecks' results.

Maccoby begins by noting that "the association between irregular employment and delinquency suggests at the outset that it may not be the mother's absence from home per se which creates adjustment problems for the children. Rather, the cause may be found in the conditions of the mother's employment or the family characteristics leading a mother to undertake outside employment."[35] She then lists several characteristics of the sporadically working mothers that might account for the greater likelihood of their children becoming delinquent. For example, many had a history of delinquency themselves. In our opinion, such conjectural "explanations" are legitimate guides to further study but, as Maccoby says, they leave the causal problem unsettled:

It is a moot question, therefore, whether it is the mother's sporadic employment as such which conduced to delinquency in the sons; equally tenable is the interpretation that the emotionally disturbed and antisocial characteristics of the parents produced both a sporadic work pattern on the part of the mother and delinquent tendencies in the son.[36]

Maccoby's final step, and the one of greatest interest here, is to examine simultaneously the effects of mother's employment and mother's supervision on delinquency. From this examination she concludes:

It can be seen that, whether the mother is working or not, the quality of the supervision her child receives is paramount. If the mother remains at home but does not keep track of where her child is and what he is doing, he is far more likely to become a delinquent (within this highly selected sample), than if he is closely watched. Furthermore, if a mother who works does arrange adequate care for the child in her absence, he is no more likely to be delinquent . . . than the adequately supervised child of a mother who does not work. But there is one more lesson to be learned

[33] "Write your own life history, showing the factors *really* operative in you coming to college, contrasted with the external social and cultural factors of your situation." Barron, *op. cit.*, p. 89.

[34] *Op. cit.*, p. 21.

[35] Eleanor E. Maccoby, "Effects upon Children of Their Mothers' Outside Employment," in Norman W. Bell and Ezra F. Vogel (eds), *A Modern Introduction to The Family*, Glencoe, Illinois: The Free Press. 1960, p. 523. In fairness to the Children's Bureau report, it should be mentioned that Maccoby's argument against the causality of the relation between mother's employment and delinquency has a stronger tone in the article cited there (see footnote 7) than in the version we have used as a source of quotations.

[36] *Ibid.*

from the data: among the working mothers, a majority did not in fact arrange adequate supervision for their children in their absence.[37]

It is clear, then, that regardless of the mother.s employment status, supervision is related to delinquency. According to criterion 3, employment status is therefore not a cause of delinquency. It is also clear that when supervision is held relatively constant, the relation between employment status and delinquency disappears. According to criterion 4, employment status is therefore *not* a cause of delinquency. This appears to be the reasoning by which the authors of the *Report to The Congress* reject mother's employment as a cause of delinquency. But criterion 3 ignores the association between employment status and delinquency and is thus irrelevant. And criterion 4 treats what is probably best seen as an intervening variable as an antecedent variable and is thus a misconstruction of a legitimate criterion. Actually, the evidence that allows the user of criterion 4 to reach a conclusion of noncausality is, at least psychologically, evidence of *causality*. The disappearance of the relation between mother's employment and delinquency when supervision is held relatively constant makes the "How?" of the original relation clear: working mothers are less likely to provide adequate supervision for their children, and inadequately supervised children are more likely to become delinquent.

False Criterion 5. Measurable variables are not causes.

> In tract 11-1, and to a lesser extent in tract 11-2, the actual rate [of delinquency] is lower than the predicted rate. We suggest that these deviations [of the actual delinquency rate from the rate predicted from home ownership] point up the danger of imputing a causal significance to an index, per se, despite its statistical significance in a prediction formula. It is fallacious to impute causal significance to home ownership as such. In the present study, the author hypothesizes that the extent of home-ownership is probably highly correlated with, and hence constitutes a measure of community anomie.[38]

> As a preventive, "keeping youth busy," whether through compulsory education, drafting for service in the armed forces, providing fun through recreation, or early employment, can, at best, only temporarily postpone behavior that is symptomatic of more deep-seated or culturally oriented factors. . . . Merely "keeping idle hands occupied" touches only surface symptoms and overlooks underlying factors known to generate norm-violating behavior patterns.[39]

The criterion of causation that, in effect, denies causal status to measurable variables occurs frequently in delinquency research. In the passages above, home ownership, compulsory education, military service, recreation, and early employment are all called into question as causes of delinquency. In their stead one finds as causes anomie and "deepseated or culturally oriented factors." The appeal to abstract as opposed to more directly measurable variables appears to

[37]*Ibid.* p. 524.

[38]Lander, *op. cit.,* p. 71.

[39]William C. Kvaraceus and Walter B. Miller, *Delinquent Behavior: Culture and the Individual,* National Education Association, 1959, p. 39.

be especially persuasive. Broad general concepts embrace such a variety of directly measurable variables that their causal efficacy becomes almost self evident. The broken home, for example, is no match for the "inadequate" home:

> [T]he physically broken home as a cause of delinquent behavior is, in itself, not so important as was once believed. In essence, it is not that the home is broken, but rather that the home is inadequate, that really matters.[40]

The persuasiveness of these arguments against the causal efficacy of measurable variables has two additional sources: (1) their logical form resembles that of the legitimate criterion "lack of spuriousness"; (2) they are based on the seemingly obvious fact that "operational indices" (measures) do not *cause* the variations in other operational indices. Both of the following arguments can thus be brought against the assertion that, for example, home ownership causes delinquency.

Anomie causes delinquency. Home ownership is a measure of anomie. Anomie is thus the "source of variation" in both home ownership and delinquency. If the effects of anomie were removed, the observed relation between home ownership and delinquency would disappear. This observed relation is thus causally spurious.

Home ownership is used as an indicator of anomie, just as responses to questionnaire items are used as indicators of such things as "authoritarianism," "achievement motivation," and "religiosity." No one will argue that the responses to items on a questionnaire *cause* race hatred, long years of self-denial, or attendance at religious services. For the same reason, it is erroneous to think that home ownership "causes" delinquency.

Both of these arguments beg the question. As mentioned earlier, conjectural explanations, although legitimate guides to further study, leave the causal problem unsettled. The proposed "antecedent variable" may or *may not* actually account for the observed relation.

Our argument assumes that the proposed antecedent variable is directly measurable. In the cases cited here it is not. If the antecedent variable logic is accepted as appropriate in these cases, all relations between measurable variables and delinquency may be said to be causally spurious. If anomie can "explain away" the relation between *one* of its indicators and delinquency, it can explain away the relations between *all* of its indicators and delinquency.[41] No matter how closely a given indicator measures anomie, the indicator is not anomie, and thus not a cause of delinquency. The difficulty with these conjectural explanations is thus not that they may be false, but that they are *non-falsifiable.*[42]

---

[40]Teeters and Reinemann, *op. cit.,* p. 154.

[41]As would be expected, Lander succeeds in disposing of all the variables in his study as causes of delinquency—even those he says at some points are "*fundamentally* related to delinquency."

[42]While Lander throws out his measurable independent variables in favor of anomie, Kvaraceus and Miller throw out their measurable dependent variable in favor of "something else." "Series of norm-violating behaviors, which run counter to legal codes and which are

The second argument against the causality of measurable variables overlooks the following point: it is one thing to use a measurable variable as an indicator of another, not directly measurable, variable; it is something else again to assume that the measurable variable is *only* an indicator. Not owning one's home may indeed be a useful indicator of anomie; it may, at the same time, be a potent cause of delinquency in its own right.

The user of the "measurable variables are not causes" criterion treats measurable variables as epiphenomena. He strips these variables of all their causal efficacy (and of all their meaning) by treating them merely as indexes, and by using such words as *per se, as such,* and *in itself.*[43] In so doing, he begs rather than answers the important question: Are these measurable variables causes of delinquency?

False Criterion 6. If the relation between an independent variable and delinquency is conditional upon the value of other variables, the independent variable is not a cause of delinquency.

> The rates of Negro delinquency also vary as widely as do the white rates indicating large differences in behavior patterns that are not a function or effect of race per se. It is also of interest to note that in at least 10 percent of the districts with substantial Negro juvenile populations, the Negro delinquency rate is lower than the corresponding white rate.[44]

> The appropriate inference from the available data, on the basis of our present understanding of the nature of cause, is that whether poverty, broken homes, or working mothers are factors which cause delinquency depends upon the meaning the situation has for the child.[45]

Both of these quotations make the same point: the association between an independent variable and delinquency depends on the value of a third variable. The original two-variable relation thus becomes a three-variable conditional relation. In the first quotation, the relation between race and delinquency is shown to depend on some (unspecified) property of census tracts. In the second quotation, each of three variables is said to "interact" with "the meaning of the situation" to cause delinquency.

One consequence of showing that certain variables are only conditionally related to delinquency is to invalidate what Albert K. Cohen has aptly named "the assumption of intrinsic pathogenic qualities"—the assumption that the causal efficacy of a variable is, or can be, independent of the value of other causal variables.[46] Invalidating this assumption, which Cohen shows to be widespread in the literature on delinquency, is a step in the right direction. As

---

engaged in by youngsters [delinquency], are [is] only symptomatic of something else in the personal make-up of the individual, in his home and family, or in his cultural milieu." *Op. cit.,* p. 34. The result is the same, as the quotations suggest.

[43] The appearance of these terms in the literature on delinquency almost invariably signals a logical difficulty.

[44] Lander, *op. cit.,* p. 32. This statement is quoted more fully above (see footnote 10).

[45] See footnote 30.

[46] "Multiple Factor Approaches," in Marvin E. Wolfgang *et al.* (eds.), *The Sociology of Crime and Delinquency,* New York: John Wiley, 1962, pp. 78-79.

many of the quotations in this paper suggest, however, the discovery that a variable has no *intrinsic* pathogenic qualities has often led to the conclusion that it has no pathogenic qualities at all. The consequences of accepting this conclusion can be shown for delinquency research and theory.

Cloward and Ohlin's theory that delinquency is the product of lack of access to legitimate means *and* the availability of illegitimate means assumes, as Palmore and Hammond have shown,[47] that each of these states is a necessary condition for the other—i.e., that lack of access to legitimate and access to illegitimate means "interact" to produce delinquency. Now, if "conditional relations" are non-causal, neither lack of access to legitimate nor the availability of illegitimate means is a cause of delinquency, and one could manipulate either without affecting the delinquency rate.

Similarly absurd conclusions could be drawn from the results of empirical research in delinquency, since all relations between independent variables and delinquency are at least conceivably conditional (the paucity of empirical generalizations produced by delinquency research as a whole shows that most of these relations have already actually been found to be conditional).[48]

Although conditional relations may be conceptually or statistically complicated and therefore psychologically unsatisfying, their discovery does not justify the conclusion that the variables involved are not causes of delinquency. In fact, the researcher who would grant causal status only to unconditional relations will end by granting it to none.

Any one of the criteria of causality discussed in this paper makes it possible to question the causality of most of the relations that have been or could be revealed by quantitative research. Some of these criteria stem from perfectionistic interpretations of legitimate criteria, others from misapplication of these legitimate criteria. Still others, especially the argument that a cause must be "characteristic" of delinquents, appear to result from practical considerations. (It would indeed be valuable to the practitioner if he could point to some easily identifiable trait as the "hallmark" of the delinquent.) Finally, one of these criteria is based on a mistaken notion of the relation between abstract concepts and measurable variables—a notion that only the former can be the causes of anything.

The implications of these standards of causality for practical efforts to reduce delinquency are devastating. Since nothing that can be pointed to in the practical world is a cause of delinquency (e.g., poverty, broken homes, lack of recreational facilities, working mothers), the practitioner is left with the task of combatting a nebulous "anomie" or an unmeasured "inadequacy of the home"; or else he must change the adolescent's interpretation of the "meaning" of events without at the same time changing the events themselves or the context in which they occur.

Mills has suggested that accepting the principle of multiple causation implies

[47]Erdman B. Palmore and Philip E. Hammond, "Interacting Factors in Juvenile Delinquency," *American Sociological Review,* 29 (December, 1964), pp. 848-854.

[48]After reviewing the findings of twenty-one studies as they bear on the relations between twelve commonly used independent variables and delinquency, Barbara Wootton concludes: "All in all, therefore, this collection of studies, although chosen for its comparative methodological merit, produces only the most meager, and dubiously supported generalizations." *Op. cit.,* p. 134.

denying the possibility of radical change in the social structure.[49] Our analysis suggests that rejecting the principle of multiple causation implies denying the possibility of *any* change in the social structure—since, in this view, nothing causes anything.

THE HAWTHORNE STUDIES: A RADICAL CRITICISM

Alex Carey

There can be few scientific disciplines or fields of research in which a single set of studies or a single researcher and writer has exercised so great an influence as was exercised for a quarter of a century by Mayo and the Hawthorne studies. Although this influence has declined in the last ten years as a result of the widespread failure of later studies to reveal any reliable relation between the social satisfactions of industrial workers and their work performance, reputable textbooks still refer almost reverentially to the Hawthorne studies as a classic in the history of social science in industry.

One might have expected therefore that the Hawthorne studies would have been subjected to the most searching and skeptical scrutiny; that before the remarkable claims of these studies, especially about the relative unimportance of financial rewards compared with purely social rewards, became so widely influential, the quality of the evidence produced and the validity of the inferences from it would have been meticulously examined and assessed. There have been broad criticisms of Mayo's approach and assumptions, many of them cogent. They include charges of pro-management bias, clinical bias, and scientific naiveté[1] But no one has applied systematically and in detail the method of critical doubt to the claim that there is scientific worth in the original reports of the Hawthorne investigators.

BACKGROUND

The Hawthorne studies comprise a long series of investigations into the importance for work behavior and attitudes of a variety of physical, economic, and social variables. The principal investigations were carried out between 1927

---

[49]C. Wright Mills, "The Professional Ideology of Social Patholgists," *American Journal of Sociology*, 44 (September, 1942), pp. 165- 180, esp. pp. 171-172.

Reprinted with the permission of the author and the publisher, The American Sociological Association, from the *American Sociological Review*, Vol. 32 (1967), 403-16.

[1]For a review of these charges and criticisms see Delbert Miller and William Form, *Industrial Sociology*, New York: Harper, 1951, pp. 74-83. For a defense see Henry A. Landsberger, *Hawthorne Revisited*, New York: Cornell, 1958. Landsberger's defense is restricted to the report of the Hawthorne studies by Fritz J. Roethlisberger and William Dickson, *Management and the Worker*, Cambridge, Harvard Univ. Press, 1939. Even this

and 1932, whereafter economic depression caused their suspension. The component studies may be distinguished as five stages:

Stage I: The Relay Assembly Test Room Study. (New incentive system and new supervision).
Stage II: The Second Relay Assembly Group Study. (New incentive system only).
State III: The Mica Splitting Test Room Study. (New supervision only).
Stage IV: The Interviewing Program.
Stage V: The Bank-Wiring Observation Room Study.

Stages I to III constitute a series of partially controlled studies which were initially intended to explore the effects on work behavior of variations in physical conditions of work, especially variations in rest pauses and in hours of work, but also in payment system, temperature, humidity, etc.

However, after the studies had been in progress for at least twelve months the investigators came to the entirely unanticipated conclusion that social satisfactions arising out of human association in work were more important determinants of work behavior in general and output in particular than were any of the physical and economic aspects of the work situation to which their attention had originally been limited.[2] This conclusion came as "the great *éclaircissement* . . . an illumination quite different from what they had expected from the illumination studies."[3] It is the central and distinctive finding from which the fame and influence of the Hawthorne studies derive.

This "éclaircissement" about the predominant importance of social satisfactions at work occurred during Stage I of the studies. In consequence, all the later studies are in important ways subordinate to Stage I: "It was the origin from which all the subsequent phases sprang. It was also their main focal point. It gave to these other phases their significance in relation to the whole enquiry."[4]

Stages II and III were "designed to check on" (and were taken to supplement and confirm) the Stage I conclusion "that the observed production increase was a result of a change in the *social situation* . . . (and) not primarily because of wage incentives, reduced fatigue or similar factors."[5] *Stage IV* was an interviewing program undertaken to explore worker attitudes. *Stage V* was a study of informal group organization in the work situation.

The two later studies (IV and V) resulted directly from conclusions based on Stages I-III about the superior influence of social needs. Observations made in both were interpreted in the light of such prior conclusions. Hence it is clear that, as maintained by Urwick, Stage I was the key study, with Stages II and III

report, in Landsberger's view, has "done the field of human relations in industry an amount of harm which, in retrospect, appears to be almost irreparable." Landsberger, *op. cit.*, p. 64.

[2] George A. Pennock, "Industrial Research at Hawthorne," *Personnel Journal*, 8 (February, 1930), pp. 296-313; Mark L. Putman, "Improving Employee Relations," *Personnel Journal*, 8 (February, 1930), pp. 314-325.
[3] Fritz J. Roethlisberger, *Management and Morale*, Cambridge: Harvard University Press, 1941, p. 15.
[4] Lyndall Urwick and Edward Brech, *The Making of Scientific Management*, vol. III, London: Management Publications Trust, 1948, p. 27. See also Roethlisberger and Dickson, *op. cit.*, p. 29.
[5] Morris S. Viteles, *Motivation and Morale in Industry*, London: Staples, 1954, p. 185.

adding more or less substantial support to it. The present paper will therefore be limited to a consideration of the evidence produced in Stages I-III for the famous Hawthorne conclusions about the superior importance for work behavior of social needs and satisfactions.

THE PREFERRED INCENTIVE SYSTEM AND OUTPUT

Stage I: Relay Assembly Test Room (new incentive and new supervision). In Stage I of the Hawthorne studies, five girls who were employed assembling telephone relays were transferred from the factory floor to a special test room. Here their output of relays was recorded for over two years during which a large number of alterations were made in their working conditions. These alterations included a much less variable assembly task,[6] shorter hours, rest pauses, freer and more friendly supervision, and a preferred incentive system.[7] These changes were introduced cumulatively and no control group was established. Nonetheless, it was originally expected that the study would yield information about the influence of one or another physical condition of work.[8]

At the end of two years, the girls' output had increased by about 30 percent.[9] By this time, the investigators were confident that the physical changes in work conditions had been of little importance, and that the observed increase was due primarily to a change in "mental attitude" of the employees resulting from changed methods of supervision.[10] This change in mental attitude was chiefly characterized by a more relaxed "relationship of confidence and friendliness ... such ... that practically no supervision is required."[11]

However, the standard report of the study recognizes that any of several changes introduced concurrently could, hypothetically, have caused both the observed change in mental outlook and the associated increase in output. The authors of the report list the following as providing possible "hypotheses to explain major changes" in work behavior:[12] (i) changes in the character and physical context of the work task; (ii) reduction of fatigue and monotony consequent upon introduction of rest pauses and reduced hours of work;[13] (iii) change in the payment system; and (iv) changes in supervision with consequent social changes in group relations.

The remainder of this paper will critically examine the evidence and arguments from which the investigators reached conclusions favorable to the last of these alternative hypotheses.

First hypothesis: changes in work task and physical context. The investigators allow that "the fact that most of the girls in the test room had to assemble fewer types of relays could not be entirely ignored. Operator 5's

---

[6] Roethlisberger and Dickson, *op. cit.,* pp. 21, 26.

[7] *Ibid.,* pp. 22, 30-73.

[8] *Ibid.,* p. 129; Pennock, *op. cit., p. 299.*

[9] Roethlisberger and Dickson, *op. cit.,* p. 160.

[10] *Ibid.,* pp. 189-190; Pennock, *op. cit.,* pp. 297-309.

[11] Pennock, *op. cit.,* p. 309.

[12] Roethlisberger and Dickson, *op. cit.,* pp. 86-89.

[13] The investigators list fatigue and monotony as separate hypotheses. For brevity, these have been combined as one hypothesis. The same sort of critical objections are relevant to the arguments and evidence advanced by the investigators with respect to both.

performance offered a convincing example. Of all the girls in the room she had had more different types of relays to assemble and of all the girls her output rate had shown the least improvement."[14] Whitehead reports that "later (1930-31) her (Operator 5's) working conditions were in line with the rest of the group and her comparative standing in the group definitely improved."[15]

However, it was subsequently found that statistical analysis of the relevant data (i.e., the varying output of five girls who were subjected to numerous cumulatively introduced experimental changes) did not show "any *conclusive* evidence in favor of the first hypothesis." On this ground the investigators "concluded that the change from one type of relay to another familiar type did not sufficiently slow up output to explain the increased output of the relay test room assemblers as compared with the assemblers in the regular department."[16] This conclusion leads the investigators to dismiss from further consideration the possibility that changes in task and conditions played any part at all in the observed increase in output.[17]

Second hypothesis: reduced fatigue due to rest pauses and shorter hours. The investigators recognize that "the rest pauses and shorter hours (may have) provided a relief from cumulative fatigue" resulting in higher output. They acknowledge that the fact that the rate of output of all but the slowest worker declined once the girls were returned to standard hours is "rather convincing evidence in favor of this argument."[18] Yet the investigators eventually dismiss these factors on the grounds that under the new conditions of work neither work curves not medical examinations provided evidence that fatigue effects were present. Viteles has commented bluntly in this connection: "It is interesting to note that (these grounds) are exactly the same used by other investigators in illustrating the effectiveness of rest pauses *by reason of reduced fatigue.*"[19]

By these arguments, the investigators eliminated the first two of the four hypotheses originally proposed as alternative explanations of the 30 percent increase in output observed in Stage I. This left two contending "explanations," the new incentive system, and the new kind of supervision and related social factors. The problem of choosing between these explanations led directly to the next two major experiments.

Stage II: Second Relay Assembly Group (new incentive system only). "The aim of (this experiment) was to reproduce the testroom situation (i.e., Stage I) only in respect to the one factor of method of payment, using another group of

[14] *Ibid.,* p. 87.

[15] T. North Whitehead, *The Industrial Worker,* London: Oxford Univ. Press, 1938, Vol. I, p. 65.

[16] Roethlisberger and Dickson, *op. cit.,* p. 89. (Italics added.)

[17] The scientifically illiterate procedure of dismissing non-preferred explanations on the grounds that (i) the experimenters had found no *conclusive* evidence in favor of them and/or (ii) there was no evidence that any *one* of these explanations, considered by itself, accounted for *all* the effect observed, recurs throughout Roethlisberger and Dickson's report of the Hawthorne studies. This procedure is never applied to preferred hypotheses, which are assumed to be well-founded provided only that the evidence *against* them is less than conclusive. See, e.g., Roethlisberger and Dickson, *op. cit.,* p. 160 and pp. 96, 108, 127.

[18] *Ibid.,* p. 87.

[19] Morris S. Viteles, *Industrial Psychology,* New York: Norton, 1932, p. 476. Italics in original.

operators. Since method of payment was to be the only alteration from the usual situation, it was thought that any marked changes in output could be reasonably related to this factor."[20]

Five girls who were employed on the same sort of task as the girls in Stage I under normal conditions on the factory floor were given the preferred incentive system which had been used throughout Stage I. Under this system, the earnings of each girl were based on the average output of the five. Under the regular payment system, the earnings of each girl were based on the average output of the whole department (i.e., about 100 girls).

Almost at once the Stage II girls' output increased by 12.6 percent.[21] But the experiment caused so much discontent among the rest of the girls in the department, who wanted the same payment conditions,[22] that it was discontinued after only nine weeks. The output of the five girls promptly dropped by 16 percent.[23]

As Viteles comments, " the increase in output during the period when the wage incentive was in effect, followed by a production decrease with the elimination of the wage incentive, represents evidence ordinarily interpreted as indicative of the direct and favorable influence of financial incentives upon output."[24] However, the investigators reject this interpretation and, without producing supporting evidence of any substance, conclude firmly[25] that the increase was due to inter-group rivalry resulting from the setting up of this second small group.

The change in payment system alone (Stage II) produced as much increase in output in nine weeks (possibly five weeks[26]) as was produced in about nine months by change in payment system together with a change to genial supervision (Stage I).[27] Yet this comparison appears not to have made any impression on the investigators' confidence about the superior importance of social factors.[28]

Stage III: Mica Splitting Test Room (new supervision but no change in payment system). In *Stage I,* numerous changes had been introduced, resulting in a 30 percent increase in output. In *Stage II,* only one of these changes (the preferred incentive system) was introduced and a rapid 12 percent increase in output resulted. In *Stage III,* "the test-room situation was to be duplicated in all respects except for the change in pay incentive. If . . . output showed a trend similar to that noted in (Stage I), it would suggest that the wage incentive was not the dominant factor in the situation."[29] Stage III, then, sought to test the combined effect on output of change to a separate room, change in hours, and

[20] Roethlisberger and Dickson, *op. cit.,* p. 129.

[21] *Ibid.,* pp. 131-132, 577; Pennock, *op. cit.,* p. 307.

[22] *Ibid.,* p. 133.

[23] According to an earlier report (Pennock, *op. cit.,* p. 307), the increase in output was 13.8 percent, the experiment was discontinued after five weeks, and output then fell by 19-24 percent.

[24] Viteles, Motivation . . . , *op. cit.,* p. 187.

[25] Roethlisberger and Dickson, *op. cit.,* pp. 133-134, 158, 577.

[26] Pennock, *op. cit.,* p. 307.

[27] That is, by the end of Experimental Period 7 in Roethlisberger and Dickson's output chart, *op. cit.,* p. 78.

[28] Roethlisberger and Dickson, *op. cit.,* pp. 160, 577.

[29] *Ibid.,* p. 129.

the introduction of rest pauses and friendly supervision. Again a selected group of five girls was closely studied and an increase in output was recorded—15.6 percent in fourteen months[30] or, if one follows Pennock, 20 percent in twelve months.[31]

A comparison between Stage III and Stage I has little prospect of scientific usefulness since in Stage III (i) the incentive system was different from both the disliked system used at the beginning of Stage I and the preferred system introduced shortly afterwards, (ii) the type of work was quite different from Stage I, and (iii) the experimental changes were quite different.[32] However, it is this comparison which has been taken by reporters of the studies[33] and by textbook authors[34] to provide the principal experimental evidence about the relative importance of financial and social motives as influences on output. Assuming with Roethlisberger and Dickson that Stage I and Stage III have some minimum comparability, it is important to examine precisely how the investigators dealt with the evidence from these stages for the purpose of the comparison.

Comparison Between Results in Stages I, II, and III. (i) Stage III produced a claimed 15 percent increase in rate of output over fourteen months. Thereafter the group's average rate of output declined for twelve months before the study was terminated due to the depression and lay-offs. The investigators attribute this decline *entirely* to anxieties induced by the depression,[35] ignoring the possibility that the preceding increase might also have been influenced by changing general economic and employment conditions. They do this despite evidence that output among a group of 5,500 Hawthorne workers rose by 7 percent in the two years preceding the experiment.[36]

(ii) In Stage III, the output rate for each girl shows continuous and marked fluctuations over the whole two years of the study.[37] To obtain the percentage increase to be attributed to each girl the investigators chose, for each girl, a "peak" output period within the study period and measured her increase as the difference between this peak and her output rate at the outset of the study.[38] These peaks occur at different dates for different girls. To secure the 15 percent

[30]*Ibid.*, p. 148.
[31]Pennock, *op. cit.*, p. 307.
[32]Roethlisberger and Dickson, *op. cit.*, pp. 156, 159.
[33]*Ibid.*, pp. 146-149, 159-160; Pennock, *op. cit.*, p. 307.
[34]For example, "we cannot avoid being impressed by the fact that a wage incentive alone (Stage II) increased production 12%, a change in the social situation raised output 15%, (Stage III) and a combination of the two gave an increase of 30%. This looks surprisingly like an additive effect, with the social rewards being somewhat more potent in influencing behaviour than the monetary reward." Ross Stagner, *Psychology of Industrial Conflict*, New York: Wiley, 1956, pp. 131-132. See also Milton Blum, *Industrial Psychology and Its Social Foundations*, New York: Harper, 1949, p. 26.
[35]Viteles comments on this period of declining output: "Both 'the investigators and the operators were of the opinion that the rates on the new piece parts were not high enough in comparison with the old.' Nevertheless scant consideration is given to the possibility that . . . a reduced appeal to economic motives could readily account in large part for the very severe drop in output observed during this final phase of the *Mica Splitting Room experiment*." Viteles, Motivation . . . , *op. cit.*, p. 191.
[36]Whitehead, *op. cit.*, vol. II, Chart J-53.
[37]Roethlisberger and Dickson, *op. cit.*, p. 147.
[38]*Ibid.*, p. 148.

increase that is claimed, the study is, in effect, terminated at different conveniently selected dates for different girls. There is *no one period* over which the group achieved the 15 percent average increase claimed.[39]

(iii) In Stage I, two measures of the workers' performance are used: total output per week,[40] and hourly rate of output by weeks.[41] It is not clear from Roethlisberger and Dickson's report of Stage I whether the increase is in *total output* or *rate of output*. It is described only as "increase in output," and "output rose . . . roughly 30%,"[42] which would ordinarily be taken to mean an increase in *total output*. But the investigators make it clear in passing[43] that throughout the studies they used rate of output per hour as "the most common arrangement of output data" by which to "portray the general trend in efficiency of each operator and of the group." Whitehead, who produced a two-volume statistical study of Stage I as companion volumes to Roethlisberger and Dickson's standard report, is very clear on this point: "All output will be expressed in the form of a *rate* . . . as so many relays per hour."[44]

However, Whitehead employs throughout his study the description *"weekly rate of output"* when he means *rate of output per hour by weeks.*[45] This practice, coupled with his habit of not labelling the ordinates of his charts dealing with changes in output, and added to by Roethlisberger and Dickson's use of phrases such as "increase in output" to mean both *increase in rate of output per hour* and *increase in total output,* has led to widespread misinterpretation of the Hawthorne results, and textbook accounts which are seriously in error.[46]

Several points are of present importance. For Stage I, it is not clear whether the 30 percent increase in output claimed refers to *rate of output* or *total output.* It does not matter which measure is used to calculate percent increase in output in Stage I since the total hours worked per week at the end of the study period is only 4.7 percent less than at the beginning.[47] Thus, an increase of the order of 30 percent would result from either method of calculation. In Stage III, however, it makes a great deal of difference which method is used, and hourly rate of output is the only measure used. Thus, the 15 percent "increase in output"[48] claimed for Stage III is an increase in *rate of output per hour worked,* not in *total output.* Indeed, it is only by this measure that any increase *at all* in output can be shown.

[39]*Ibid.,* pp. 146-148, 159-160.
[40]*Ibid.,* p. 78.
[41]*Ibid.,* p. 76.
[42]*Ibid.,* p. 160
[43]*Ibid.,* pp. 55, 77.
[44]Whitehead, *op. cit.,* vol. I, p. 34.
[45]*Ibid.,* vol. II, Chart B4.
[46]For example, Edwin Ghiselli and Clarence Brown, *Personnel and Industrial Psychology,* New York: McGraw Hill, 1948, pp. 435-437; and James A. C. Brown, *Social Psychology of Industry,* Harmondsworth: Penguin, 1954, pp. 71-72. These authors incorrectly report on almost continuous increase in total weekly output over the first nine months of State I. In fact, there was no increase except in the period of eight weeks immediately following the introduction of the preferred incentive system. There was no improvement in weekly output in either the preceding period or the four experimental periods extending over six months which followed it.
[47]Roethlisberger and Dickson, *op. cit.,* pp. 76-77.

If *total output per week* is used to measure performance in Stage III, the 15 percent increase claimed for Stage III reduces to less than zero because although output per hour increased by 15 percent, the weekly hours decreased by 17 percent, from 55½ to 46 1/6.[49]

From Evidence to Conclusions. By subtracting the 15 percent increase in Stage III (which is an increase in *rate* of output) from the 30 percent increase in output in Stage I (which is all, or nearly all, an increase in *total* output), the investigators conclude that 15 percent remains as "the maximum amount (of increase in output) to be attributed to the change in wage incentive" introduced in Stage I. The investigators acknowledge the wholly speculative nature of this calculation, yet go on to assert in a summary of events to date that the conclusion "seemed to be warranted from the test room studies so far . . . that it was impossible to consider (a wage incentive system) as a thing in itself having an independent effect on the individual."[50]

It is important to appreciate just how invalid are the inferences made. In Stage I, friendly supervision and a change to a preferred incentive system led to an increase in total output of about 30 percent. In Stage III, friendly supervision without a change in payment system led to no increase in total output, but to a less than compensating increase in output per hour over a period during which working hours were reduced from 55 1/2 to 46 1/6. This could be interpreted to mean that when working hours exceed about 48 per week such extra working-time may bring little or no increase in total output—a finding which had been well-established many years before.[51] This interpretation would have left the way clear to attribute the 30 percent increase in Stage I entirely to the preferred incentive system. Instead, by the rather special method of analysis and argument that has been outlined, the investigators reached the conclusion that the effect of a wage incentive system is so greatly influenced by social considerations that it is impossible to consider it capable of independent effect.

A similar situation holds with regard to Stage II. As Stage II was planned, the "method of payment was to be the only alteration from the usual situation" with the express intention that "any marked changes in output" could then be "related to this factor."[52] There *was* a marked change in output—an immediate 12 percent increase. There *was* an immediate change in behavior—the other girls in the department demanded the same conditions. This would seem to require a conclusion in favor of the importance of a preferred incentive system, but no such conclusion was reached.

As a first step in the interpretation of the Stage II results, Roethlisberger and Dickson noticed, *post hoc*, that somewhere in the "daily history record" of the

---

[48]*Ibid.*, pp. 159-160.

[49]*Ibid.*, pp. 136-139.

[50]*Ibid.*, p. 160. Viteles bluntly rejects this inference as invalid, but textbook treatments of the Hawthorne studies generally accept it without demur. Viteles, *Motivation . . . ,op. cit.*, p. 193.

[51]Horace M. Vernon, *Industrial Fatigue and Efficiency*, London: Dutton, 1921. Ghiselli and Brown have summarized Vernon's findings as follows: "In a munitions plant, when the working week was reduced from 66 to 48.6 hours (a reduction of 26%) hourly output was increased by 68% and total output for the week by 15%. This instance could be multiplied many times." Ghiselli and Brown, *op. cit.*, p. 242.

[52]Roethlisberger and Dickson, *op. cit.*, p. 129.

Stage I group was a reference to a comment by one member of that group that a "lively interest" was being taken in their output by members of the new Stage II group.[53] At this point, the investigators simply note this and hint at significance to come. Twenty-four pages later we are told that "although output had risen an average of 12% in (Stage II) it was *quite apparent* that factors other than the change in wage incentive contributed to that increase ... *There was some evidence* to indicate that the operators in (Stage II) had seized upon this test as an opportunity to prove to everyone that they could do as well as the (Stage I) operators. They were out to equal the latters' record. In view of this, even the most liberal estimate would put the increase in output due to the change in payment alone at somewhat less than 12%." (Italics added). Since no additional evidence had been produced, this judgment lacks any serious foundation.

Much later (p. 577) the matter is returned to and, with no additional evidence, we are given to understand that the increase in output in Stage II was due to certain "social consequences" of the "basic social situation." This situation is simply asserted to have been one in which "rivalry (with the Stage I group) was brought to a focus" by setting up the Stage II group whose "output rose rapidly" in consequence.

Stage II was "designed to test the effect of a (change in) wage incentive" on output.[54] The preferred incentive system was introduced and output immediately rose 12 percent. It was withdrawn and output immediately dropped 17 percent. Not encouraging results for anyone who believed that wage incentives were relatively unimportant and incapable of "independent effects." Yet these awkward results were not only explained away but converted to positive support for just such conclusions, all on the basis of a single hearsay comment by one girl.

The investigators carry the day for the hypothesis that "social factors were the major circumstances limiting output." They conclude that "none of the results (in Stages I, II and III) gave the slightest substantiation to the theory that the worker is primarily motivated by economic interest. The evidence indicated that the efficacy of a wage incentive is so dependent on its relation to other factors that it is impossible to separate it out as a thing in itself having an independent effect."[55] This conclusion is a striking contrast to the objective results obtained in Stages I, II and III as these bear on incentive systems: (i) when a preferred wage incentive system was introduced, total weekly output per worker rose (Stage I and Stage II); (ii) when the preferred incentive system was withdrawn, output promptly dropped (Stage II); (iii) when changes in supervision, hours, etc. were introduced but with *no change in incentive system,* no increase in weekly output per worker resulted (Stage III).

Viteles, an unusually perceptive critic of the Hawthorne studies, has commented caustically on Stage III: "This increase in output, representing an average rise of 15% in the first 14 months of the experiment, would ordinarily be accepted as evidence that the introduction of rest pauses and the shortening of the work day can in themselves result in increased output, even in the absence of changes in the way of enhancing the wage incentive."[56] Yet Viteles misses

---

[53]*Ibid.,* p. 134.
[54]*Ibid.,* p. 576.
[55]*Ibid.,* pp. 575-576.
[56]Viteles, *op. cit., Motivation* ... , p. 190.

the important point that there was no overall increase in total weekly output in Stage III—only a less than compensating increase in output per hour when shorter hours were worked. It is clear that he supposes the 15 percent increase to be an increase in total output.[57] Viteles' patience is great, and his criticism of the Hawthorne studies restrained. But they eventually draw from him a testy general protest about "the more 'subtle'—certainly more subjective—form of analysis and interpretation which has generally characterized interpretation of the Hawthorne data by the Harvard group."[58]

It remains to consider more closely the complementary Hawthorne claim that it was friendly supervision and social factors which were the principal influences leading to the large rise in output in Stage I.

A CLOSER LOOK AT FRIENDLY SUPERVISION IN ACTION

The *whole* of the Hawthorne claim that friendly supervision and resulting work-group social relations and satisfactions are overwhelmingly important for work behavior rests on whatever evidence can be extracted from Stage I, since that is the only study in the series which exhibits even a surface association between the introduction of such factors and increased output.

Stage I began with five girls specially selected[59] for being both "thoroughly experienced" and "willing and cooperative,"[60] so there was reason to expect this group to be more than ordinarily cooperative and competent. Yet from very early in the study "the amount of talking indulged in by all the operators" had constituted a "problem," because it "involved a lack of attention to work and a preference for conversing together for considerable periods of time."[61] The first indication in the report that this might be a serious matter occurs on August 2nd, 1927, twelve weeks after the girls' installation in the test-room, when four of the five operators were brought before the foreman[62] and reprimanded for talking too much.[63] Until November, however, "no attempt had been made to do away with this privilege, although several attempts had been made by the foreman to diminish what seemed to him an excessive amount of talking." But Operators 1A and 2A in particular continued to fail to display "that 'wholehearted cooperation' desired by the investigators." "Any effort to reprimand them would bring the reply 'We thought you wanted us to work as we feel',"[64] since that was what the supervisors had told them at the beginning of the study.[65]

---

[57]*Ibid.*, p. 5.

[58]*Ibid.*, p. 256.

[59]Note, however, that while the five girls were "all chosen from among those with a considerable experience in the assembly of this kind of relay" . . . "the actual method of selection was quite informal and somewhat obscure; it appears to have been determined by the girls themselves in conjunction with their shop foreman." Whitehead, *op. cit.*, vol. I, p. 14.

[60]Roethlisberger and Dickson, *op. cit.*, p. 21.

[61]*Ibid.*, p. 53.

[62]Foremen were on a par with departmental chiefs and four ranks above operatives. *Ibid.*, p. 11.

[63]*Ibid.*, p. 38.

[64]*Ibid.*, p. 53.

[65]*Ibid.*, p. 21; Whitehead, *op. cit.*, vol. I, p. 26.

By November 17th, 1927, the situation had not improved and disciplinary rules were resorted to. All of the operators were required to call out whenever they made mistakes in assembly, and they were prevented from talking. By December, "the lack of cooperation on the part of some of the operators was seriously alarming a few of the executives concerned." Supervisors were asked to give the girls a "hint" by telling them that they were not doing as well as expected of them and that if they didn't improve they would lose their free lunches.[66]

From now on the girls, but especially 1A and 2A, were "threatened with disciplinary action" and subjected to "continual reprimands." "Almost daily" 2A was "reproved" for her "low output and behavior" (sic).[67] The investigators decided 1A and 2A did not have "the 'right' mental attitude." 2A was called up before the test-room authorities "and told of her offenses of being moody and inattentive and not cooperative." She was called up again before the superintendent.[68] Throughout this period output for all five girls remained static or falling.[69] After eleven weeks of serious but ineffective disciplinary measures and eight months after the beginning of the study, 1A and 2A were dismissed from the test room for "gross insubordination" and declining or static output.[70] Or, as Whitehead puts it, they "were removed for a lack of cooperation, which would have otherwise necessitated greatly increased disciplinary measures."[71]

1A and 2A were replaced by two girls chosen by the foreman[72] "who were experienced relay assemblers and desirous of participating in the test." These two girls (designated Operators 1 and 2) were transferred to the test room on January 25th, 1928.[73] They *both* immediately produced an output much greater (in total and in rate per hour) than that achieved by *any* of the original five girls on their transfer to the test room and much above the performance *at any time* of the two girls they replaced.[74]

---

[66]Whitehead, *op. cit.,* vol. I, p. 16.

[67]*Ibid.,* pp. 116-118.

[68]Roethlisberger and Dickson, *op. cit.,* p. 55. Superintendents controlled a branch of the works and were seven ranks above operators. *Ibid.,* p. 11.

[69]*Ibid.,* p. 78. See Experimental Period 7 in Figure 7.

[70]*Ibid.,* pp. 53-57.

[71]Whitehead, *op. cit.,* vol. I, p. 118. In Mayo's accounts it is first said that these two operators "dropped out" (Elton Mayo, *The Human Problems of an Industrial Civilization,* Boston: Harvard Business School, 1946, p. 56) and later that they "retired." (Elton Mayo, *The Social Problems of an Industrial Civilization,* London: Routledge and Kegan Paul, 1949, p. 62.) It is also interesting to compare the above account of events in the test room and drawn from the standard reports with Mayo's picture of the test room. According to Mayo's account, success was achieved "largely because the experimental room was in charge of an interested and sympathetic chief observer. He understood clearly from the first that any hint of the 'supervisor' in his methods might be fatal to the interests of the inquiry . . . He helped the group to feel that its duty was to set its own conditions of work, he helped the workers to find the 'freedom' of which they so frequently speak . . . At no time in the (whole period of the study) did the girls feel that they were working under pressure." (Mayo, *The Human Problems . . . op. cit.,* pp. 68-69).

[72]Roethlisberger and Dickson, *op. cit.,* p. 60.

[73]*Ibid.,* pp. 55, 56, 60.

[74]*Ibid.,* Figure 6, p. 76 and Figure 7, p. 78. Compare output curves during the first seven Experimental Periods with output from the second week of Experimental Period 8.

Operators 1 and 2 had been friends in the main shop. Operator 2 was the only Italian in the group; she was young (twenty-one) and her mother died shortly after she joined the test room;[75] after this "Operator 2 earned the larger part of the family income." "(F)rom now on the history of the test room revolves around the personality of Operator 2."[76] Operator 2 rapidly (i.e., without any delay during which she might have been affected by the new supervision) adopted and maintained a strong and effective disciplinary role with respect to the rest of the group,[77] and led the way in increased output in *every* period from her arrival till the end of the study. In this she was closely followed by the other new girl, Operator 1.[78]

At the time that Operators 1 and 2 were brought into the test room, daily hours of work were shortened by half an hour but it was decided to *pay the operators the day rate for the half hour of working time lost.* A little later, the working day was reduced by a further half hour, and again the girls were paid for the time (one hour per day) they didn't work.[79] Later still, the girls were given Saturday mornings off and again they were paid for the time not worked.[80]

Summing up experience in the test room up to *exactly* the time when the two operators were dismissed,[81] the investigators claim that "it is clear" that over this period there was "a gradual change in social interrelations among the operators themselves, which displayed itself in the form of new group loyalties and solidarities . . . (and) . . . a change in the relations between the operators and their supervisors. The test room authorities had taken steps to obtain the girls' cooperation and loyalty and to relieve them of anxieties and apprehensions. From this . . . arose . . . a change in human relations which came to be of great significance in the next stage of the experiment, when it became necessary to seek a new hypothesis to explain certain unexpected results of the inquiry."[82] In view of the evidence reviewed here this would seem to be a somewhat sanguine assessment of developments in the test room up to this point. It is, therefore, necessary to examine more systematically the way in which the behavior of the supervisors on the one hand and of the operators on the other (including their changing output) varied during the period under consideration.

It is already clear that whatever part satisfying social relations at work—resulting from free and friendly supervision—may have played in

---

[75]*Ibid.,* pp. 61-62.

[76]Whitehead, *op. cit.,* vol. I, p. 120.

[77]*Ibid.,* pp. 120-129; Roethlisberger and Dickson, *op. cit.,* pp. 63, 74, 86, 156, 167.

[78]Roethlisberger and Dickson, *op. cit.,* p. 162.

[79]Whitehead, *op. cit.,* vol. I, pp. 121-122. Roethlisberger and Dickson (*op. cit.,* pp. 60, 62) give no indication that the operators were paid for these hours not worked. Indeed, their account clearly implies that they were not so paid (*ibid.,* pp. 63-64). But Whitehead is quite explicit on this point.

[80]Roethlisberger and Dickson do report (*op. cit.,* p. 68) that the girls were paid for the half day on Saturdays which was not worked. They acknowledge that this "added a new factor to the situation which cannot be disregarded and which has to be taken into account in comparing this period with any other" (*ibid.,* p. 69). They take no further account of it, however, just as they take no further account of the unworked hours paid for on the occasions when the work day was shortened.

[81]That is, up to the end of Experimental Period 7 in Roethlisberger and Dickson's terminology.

[82]Roethlisberger and Dickson, *op. cit.,* pp. 58-59.

producing the increase in output, there were other influences likely to have been important, e.g., a period of fairly stern discipline, the dismissal of two workers, and their replacement by people of rather special personality and motivation. In order to assess these various influences on output it is necessary to consider how work performance varied during the periods when these changes were introduced. This is difficult because none of the reports of the Hawthorne studies provides actual figures covering the way in which output changed throughout Stage I. Consequently, one must work with such estimates as can be derived from the various graphs and charts of output-change that are supplied, and supplemented by occasional statements in the texts which give additional quantitative information.

AN EXAMINATION OF THE EVIDENCE: VARIATIONS IN SUPERVISORY PRACTICE AND VARIATIONS IN OUTPUT

For present purposes, Stage I may be divided into three phases: Phase I: the first three and a half months in the test room during which supervision seems to have been fairly consistently friendly, casual, and at low pressure; Phase II: a further interval of about seven months during which supervision became increasingly stern and close. This phase culminates in the dismissal of two of the five operators and their replacement by workers of rather special character and motivation. Phase III: a final long period during which output rose rapidly and there was a return to free and friendly supervision.

Supervision during Phase I. "Besides the girls who composed the group under study there was a person in the experimental room who was immediately in charge of the test." This was the test room observer whose twofold function was "to keep accurate records . . . and to create and maintain a friendly atmosphere in the test room." He "assume(d) responsibility for most of the day to day supervision" while in other matters such as accounting, rate revision, and promotion, responsibility rested with the foreman.[83]

It is quite clear from Roethlisberger and Dickson's account that during Phase I the supervisors did everything in their power to promote a free, cooperative, and noncoercive relationship.[84] At the outset of the study the girls "were asked to work along at a comfortable pace" and were assured "that no attempt would be made to force up production." They were led to expect changes in working conditions which might be "beneficial and desirable from the employees' point of view," and were told that there was no reason why "any (such) change resulting in greater satisfaction of employees" should not be maintained, and this "regardless of any change in production rate."[85] "The test room observer was chiefly concerned with creating a friendly relation with the operators which would ensure their cooperation. He was anxious to dispel any apprehensions they might have about the test and, in order to do this, he began to converse informally with them each day."[86] Some weeks after the study began, there was a friendly talk with the doctor about the physical examinations and ice cream

[83]*Ibid.*, pp. 22, 37.
[84]*Ibid.*, pp. 32-39.
[85]*Ibid.*, p. 33.
[86]*Ibid.*, p. 37.

was provided and a party planned. Also, the girls were "invited to the office of the superintendent who had talked to them, and in various other ways they had been made the object of considerable attention."[87] Although there had been from almost the beginning a good deal of talking among the girls, a fairly permissive attitude had been taken about this.[88]

Output during Phase 1. There was "no appreciable change in output" on transfer to the test room,[89] but there was a "downward tendency" during the first five weeks thereafter,[90] despite facilities which "made the work slightly easier."[91]

At the end of five weeks, the new wage incentive system was introduced and output increased.[92] From the output chart[93] this increase may be estimated at 4 or 5 percent. However, this increase must be accepted with some caution, for the investigators report that the "change in method of payment necessitated a change in piece-rates."[94] It was apparently judged that under the new conditions of work, (which did not include all of the types of relay assembled on the shop floor, and where there was one layout operator to five assemblers instead of one to six or seven as on the shop floor) new rates were necessary. We are told that "the chief consideration in setting the new piece rates was to determine a rate for each relay type which would pay the operators the same amount of money they had received in the regular department for an equivalent amount of work."[95] But it is well-established that the unreliability of time-study ratings can be expected to yield errors of at least 5 percent between different ratings of similar tasks.[96] So no great reliance can be placed on the observed 4 or 5 percent increase in output following the introduction of the new incentive system and the associated new piece-rates. Indeed, there is perhaps some recognition of this in Roethlisberger and Dickson's introductory comment that early in the study "a change in wage payment was introduced, a necessary step before the *experiment proper* could begin."[97] Phase I ends after fifteen weeks of friendly supervision with a somewhat doubtful increase of 5 percent which occurred with the introduction of a preferred incentive system.

Supervision during Phase II. "The second phase . . . covering an interval of approximately seven months was concerned with the effects of various kinds of rest pauses."[98] The investigators emphasize that by the *beginning* of this phase not only was supervision friendly, but the relation between workers and supervisors was "free and easy."[99] Their account of actual supervisory behavior during succeeding months supports these claims. (i) On each of the

---

[87]*Ibid.*, pp. 34, 39.
[88]*Ibid.*, p. 53.
[89]Pennock, *op. cit.*, pp. 301, 304.
[90]Roethlisberger and Dickson, *op. cit.*, p. 58.
[91]*Ibid.*, pp. 33-34, 39.
[92]*Ibid.*, p. 58.
[93]*Ibid.*, p. 56.
[94]*Ibid.*, p. 34.
[95]*Ibid.*, p. 35.
[96]Viteles, *Motivation . . .* , *op. cit.*, pp. 30-38.
[97]Roethlisberger and Dickson, *op. cit.*, p. 29, italics added.
[98]*Ibid.*, p. 40. This phase actually extends from Aug. 8, 1927 to January 21, 1928, a period of twenty-four weeks.
[99]*Ibid.*, pp. 45-46.

occasions when rest pauses were varied, the girls were consulted in advance, and on all but one occasion their expressed preferences were accepted. (ii) The investigators decided to pay the girls their bonuses monthly instead of weekly, but when the girls were told about this decision they objected and the plan was dropped. That the girls "felt free to express their attitudes" and that the investigators altered their plans out of regard for these attitudes is said to be "typical of the supervisory technique employed" which "proved to be a factor of utmost importance in interpreting the results of the study." (iii) Later the girls were given free lunches and were consulted about what should be served.[100]

However, the problem of excessive talking among the girls worsened. No attempt had been made to prohibit talking, although four of the girls had been "given a talk regarding their behavior."[101] Now this "lack of attention to work and preference for conversing together for considerable periods" was judged to be reaching such proportions that the "experiment was being jeopardized and something had to be done."[102] A variety of disciplinary procedures of increasing severity were applied, but with little effect. Finally, the leaders in talking (operators 1A and 2A) were dismissed from the test room "for lack of cooperation which would have otherwise necessitated greatly increased disciplinary measures."

Output during Phase II. There was no change in weekly output during this six-month period. "Total weekly output does not decline when rest pauses are introduced, but remains practically the same during all the rest period experiments."[103]

Supervision during Phase III. At the beginning of Phase III,[104] the two dismissed girls were replaced by two girls chosen by the foreman. Something has already been said about the way in which these girls at once took and maintained the lead in output and about how one of them, who had a special need for more money took over the general leadership and discipline of the rest of the group. These points will bear underlining by direct quotation:

> "When Operator 2 joined the group, her home was largely dependent upon her earnings, and within a few weeks her father lost his job and became temporarily unemployed. Thus, to her natural sense of responsibility was added the factor of poverty; and Operator 2 began to urge the remainder of the group to increase their output."[105]

> "Operators 1 and 2 were very definitely the fastest workers of the group in 1928, and this was freely recognized by the others."[106]

> "On the whole, from January to November 1928, the Relay Test Group showed no very marked developments apart from a growing tendency for

[100]*Ibid.*, pp. 48-9, 51.
[101]*Ibid.*, p. 38.
[102]*Ibid.*, pp. 53-54.
[103]*Ibid.*, p. 79.
[104]Actually on January 25, 1928, two days after the beginning of Phase III. Thus, the resulting sharp rise in output does not show fully on Roethlisberger and Dickson's weekly output charts (*op. cit.*, pp. 76, 78) until the second week of their Experimental Period 8.
[105]Whitehead, *op. cit.*, vol. I, pp. 122-123.
[106]*Ibid.*, p. 126.

the discipline to pass from the hands of the supervisor to those of the group itself, largely as represented in the person of Operator 2."[107]

Operator 2 became recognized as the leader of the group, both by the operators themselves and by the supervisor. It is doubtful whether any operator could have secured this position unless she had been the fastest worker, but the other qualifications possessed by Operator 2 were a high sense of the importance of the work for the group and a forceful personality."[108]

"Op. 2. 'Oh! what's the matter with those other girls. I'll kill them.' "[109] (This expostulation was provoked by the output curves showing operators 3, 4, and 5 on a downward trend.)

From then on supervision again became increasingly friendly and relaxed. This friendliness of supervision often had a very tangible character. From the arrival of the new workers in the test room, the observer "granted them (all) more and more privileges." The preferred incentive system, the rest pauses, the free lunches, and the "parties" following the regular physical examinations all continued.[110] In addition, within the next eight months the girls were first paid for half an hour per day not worked, and then for an hour a day not worked, and finally for Saturday mornings not worked. Approximately eight months after the arrival of the new girls, all these privileges except the preferred incentive system and the parties were withdrawn. The girls were warned in advance about this withdrawal of privileges and were assured that the new and heartily disliked conditions "would terminate after approximately three months." Despite this promise, the girls' work deteriorated immediately: they wasted time in various ways such as reading newspapers, eating candy, and going for drinks and the observer shortly "discovered that the girls were attempting to keep the output rate low . . . so as to make sure that rest pauses would be reinstated." The observer "again tried to stop the excessive talking" by "reprimand and threat." He told the girls that "unless excessive talking ceased it might become necessary to continue the experiment without rest pauses for a longer period."[111]

At this point, the girls had been in the test room eighteen months and had achieved nearly all the eventual 30 percent increase in output. Yet it would seem that Operator 2, the incentive system, and the other privileges, as well as "reprimand and threat" played a significant part in determining the work behavior and output of the group. It is also clear from Roethlisberger and Dickson's account that for a great part of the time following the arrival of Operators 1 and 2, the girls worked very well and happily and that while they did so, supervision was relaxed and friendly and relations continued to be satisfactory. But there would seem to be good grounds for supposing that supervision became more friendly and relaxed because output increased rather than vice versa.

Output during Phase III. Output for the whole group rose markedly during

---

[107]*Ibid.*, p. 124.
[108]*Ibid.*, p. 129.
[109]*Ibid.*, p. 127.
[110]Roethlisberger and Dickson, *op. cit.*, pp. 71, 72, 77.
[111]*Ibid.*, pp. 70-72.

the several months after the dismissal of 1A and 2A, owing chiefly to the contributions from the new operators.[112] Thereafter, the group's total output rose more slowly for a further year (with a temporary drop when the Saturday morning shift was discontinued for a time).

SUMMARY OF EVIDENCE ABOUT
SUPERVISION AND OUTPUT

(i) Apart from a doubtful 4–5 percent increase following the introduction of a preferred incentive system, there was no increase in weekly output during the first nine months in the test room, despite a great deal of preoccupation on the part of the supervisors with friendliness towards the workers, with consultation, and the provision of a variety of privileges not enjoyed on the factory floor.

(ii) From the beginning of what Roethlisberger and Dickson describe as the "experiment proper," that is, after the period in which the new incentive system was introduced, there was no increase in weekly output during the next six months. When it became apparent that free and friendly supervision was not getting results, discipline was tightened, culminating in the dismissal of two of the five girls.

(iii) The dismissed girls were replaced by two girls of a special motivation and character who *immediately* led the rest in a sustained acceleration of output. One of these girls who had a special need for extra money rapidly adopted and maintained a strong disciplinary role with respect to the rest of the group. The two new girls led the way in increased output from their arrival til the end of the study.

(iv) Total output per week showed a significant and sustained increase only after the two girls who had the lowest output[113] were dismissed and replaced by selected output leaders who account for the major part of the groups' increase, both in output rate and in total output, over the next seventeen months of the study.

(v) After the arrival of the new girls and the associated increase in output, *official* supervision became friendly and relaxed once more. The investigators, however, provide no evidence that output increased because supervision became more friendly rather than vice versa. In any case, friendly supervision took a very tangible turn by paying the girls for time not worked the piece-rate was in effect increased.

DISCUSSION AND CONCLUSIONS

The critical examination attempted here by no means exhausts the gross error and the incompetence in the understanding and use of the scientific method which permeate the Hawthorne studies from beginning to end. Three further studies were conducted: the Bank Wiring Observation Room Study; the Interviewing Program; and the Counselling Program. These studies cannot be discussed here, but I believe them to be nearly as worthless scientifically as the

[112]*Ibid.*, Figure 7, p. 78.
[113]*Ibid.*, p. 162.

studies which have been discussed.[114] This should not be surprising, for they arose out of "evidence" found and conclusions reached in the earlier studies and were guided by and interpreted in the light of the strongest preconceptions based on the conclusions of the earlier studies.

There are major deficiencies in Stages I, II and III which have hardly been touched on: (i) There was no attempt to establish sample groups representative of any larger population than the groups themselves. Therefore, no generalization is legitimate. (ii) There was no attempt to employ control data from the output records of the girls who were *not* put under special experimental conditions. (iii) Even if both of these points had been met, the experiments would still have been of only minor scientific value since a group of five subjects is too small to yield statistically reliable results. Waiving all these points, it is clear that the objective evidence obtained from Stages I, II, and III does not support any of the conclusions derived by the Hawthorne investigators. The results of these studies, far from supporting the various components of the "human relations approach," are surprisingly consistent with a rather old-world view about the value of monetary incentives, driving leadership, and discipline. It is only by massive and relentless reinterpretation that the evidence is made to yield contrary conclusions. To make these points is not to claim that the Hawthorne studies can provide serious support for any such old-world view. The limitations of the Hawthorne studies clearly render them incapable of yielding serious support for any sort of generalization whatever.

If the assessment of the Hawthorne studies offered here is cogent, it raises some questions of importance for university teachers, especially for teachers concerned with courses on industrial organization and management. How is it that nearly all authors of textbooks who have drawn material from the Hawthorne studies have failed to recognize the vast discrepancy between evidence and conclusions in those studies, have frequently misdescribed the actual observations and occurrences in a way that brings the evidence into line with the conclusions, and have done this even when such authors based their whole outlook and orientation on the conclusions reached by the Hawthorne investigators? Exploration of these questions would provide salutary insight into aspects of the sociology of social scientists.

---

[114]For substantiation of this judgment with respect to the Bank Wiring Observation Room Study see A. J. Sykes, "Economic Interest and the Hawthorne Researches: A Comment," *Human Relations*, 18 (August, 1965), pp. 253-263.

A NOTE OF CAUTION IN CAUSAL MODELLING

Hugh Donald Forbes
and
Edward R. Tufte

Many empirical investigations in the behavioral sciences today aim at tracing the causes of variations in some key dependent variable. The search for satisfying causal explanations is difficult because of the complexity of social phenomena, the crudeness of the measures of many important variables, and the prevalence of simultaneous cause and effect relations among variables. Although these difficulties remain, a number of important methodological contributions have clarified the conditions under which causal inferences can be made from non-experimental data.[1] In particular the Simon-Blalock technique has recently gained considerable attention, and has been profitably used by a number of political scientists in their research.[2] Examination of some of these applications does, however, reveal the need for a better understanding of the purposes and limitations of the technique. This paper reviews two studies: (1) the reanalysis of the Miller-Stokes data by Cnudde and McCrone,[3] and (2) the analysis of the determinants of Negro political participation in the South by Matthews and Prothro.[4] We shall argue that both these applications have two faults: (1) a

Reprinted with the permission of the authors and the publisher from the *American Political Science Review*, Vol. 62 (1968), 1258-64.

[1] See Herbert A. Simon, "Causal Ordering and Identifiability," and "Spurious Correlation: A Causal Interpretation," reprinted in *Models of Man* (New York: Wiley, 1957), chs. 1-2; and Paul F. Lazarsfeld, "Evidence and Inference in Social Research," *Daedalus*, 87 (Fall, 1958), 99-130. Blalock's work is reported in Hubert M. Blalock, Jr., *Causal Inferences in Nonexperimental Research* (Chapel Hill: University of North Carolina Press, 1964).

[2] Political science applications of causal modeling approaches include Warren E. Miller and Donald E. Stokes, "Constituency Influence in Congress," this Review, 57 (March, 1963), 45-56; Hayward R. Alker, Jr., "Causal Inferences and Political Analysis," in Joseph Bernd (ed.), *Mathematical Applications in Political Science* (Dallas: Southern Methodist University Press, 1966); and Arthur S. Goldberg, "Discerning a Causal Pattern Among Data on Voting Behavior," this Review, 60 (December, 1966), 913-922. Causal modelling ideas have also been used to clarify the study of power; for example, Herbert A. Simon, "Notes on the Observation and Measurement of Political Power," *op. cit.,* ch. 4; and Robert A. Dahl, "Power," *International Encyclopedia of the Social Sciences* (Macmillan, 1968), vol. 12, pp. 405-415.

[3] Charles F. Cnudde and Donald J. McCrone, "The Linkage Between Constituency Attitudes and Congressional Voting Behavior: A Causal Model," this Review, 60 (March, 1966), 66-72. More recently the same authors have published an analysis of the causes of democratic political development that suffers from the same faults as their earlier paper. See Donald J. McCrone and Charles F. Cnudde, "Toward a Communications Theory of Democratic Political Development: A Causal Model," this Review, 61 (March, 1967), 72-79.

[4] Donald R. Matthews and James W. Prothro, *Negroes and the New Southern Politics* (New York: Harcourt, Brace and World, 1966), ch. 11.

failure to distinguish conclusions from assumptions, and (2) an inadequate correspondence between the assumptions made in constructing the mathematical models and our prior knowledge about the phenomena being studied. In addition, we shall use the first study to illustrate a principle of general importance in causal analysis: the investigator should check the possibility that different causal mechanisms occur in different subgroups of his data. And we shall use the second study to illustrate the difficulty of separating the effects of two highly correlated independent variables.

The purpose of these criticisms is not to suggest that causal modelling is an inherently misleading technique. On the contrary, this note should be seen as a defense of the technique against some of its proponents. Causal modelling formalizes and extends the common practice of social scientists in much of their work. Potentially, by making the logic of causal inference clearer and by introducing more powerful procedures, causal modelling can lead to great improvements in data analysis. Misguided applications of the technique, however, not only lend a spurious air of certainty to false conclusions; such misapplications can also lead to an unwarranted distrust of the methods which seem to have produced the conclusions.

1. ASSUMPTIONS AND CONCLUSIONS

In any kind of statistical analysis, conclusions about the nature of the world are the result of both the investigator's data and his prior assumptions. A change in assumptions in data analysis may lead to a change in conclusions. For example, a given collection of data may be used to estimate the parameters of many different causal models—models that incorporate different assumptions about the nature of the causal mechanisms that produced the data. The Simon-Blalock technique uses correlations and regression coefficients to test hypotheses about the presence or absence of particular causal links in a given hierarchical model (Hierarchical models are those in which it is assumed that there is only one-way causation within the whole set of variables being analyzed; simultaneous cause and effect relationships are assumed not to exist, as are feedback loops around several variables.[5]) The structure of the hierarchical model—including the *direction* of all possible causal links between variables—must be decided before a test of the existence or nonexistence of any particular link is possible. Given a fair number of variables, a great many different initial assumptions are logically possible, and a large number may often be equally plausible. To choose any one of these possible hierarchical orderings is, in effect, to decide the directions of causal impact among all of the variables. If several initial assumptions about the ordering of the variables are equally plausible, then the Simon-Blalock technique provides no means for deciding between them.[6]

[5]These models are called "hierarchical" because they assume that all the variables in the analysis can be ordered *a priori* in a hierarchy of causes and effects. Variables in a model are said to form a causal hierarchy if they can be ranked so that those "higher" in the ranking appear in the equations of the model only as causes, and never as effects, of those variables which are "lower" in the ranking.

[6]Moreover it is not true, in general, that we can "infer the most likely [model]" if we "resort to the use of regression coefficients": Cnudde and McCrone, *op. cit.,* p. 68. A given set of data may be used to estimate the parameters of many different models. The basic

Both the applications of causal mòdelling examined in this paper ignore this important fact.

In their reanalysis of the Miller-Stokes data Cnudde and McCrone fit a hierarchical causal model to a pattern of six correlations and then make a number of inferences about the relationship between Congressmen and their constituents. Their most important conclusions, seemingly disconfirming the results of other research on Congressmen, are (for civil rights issues): "1. The lack of a direct link between Congressmen's attitudes and district attitudes indicates that elite recruitment is not the basis for constituency control. 2. Unlike the private citizen, the Congressman does not distort his perceptions to coincide with his own attitudes. Because the costs of misperceiving are so high for an elected official, his perceptions are likely to cause him to modify his attitudes to fit his reasonably accurate perceptions.[7]" Their report suggests that these conclusions are empirical findings in the ordinary sense: the Miller-Stokes data imply these conclusions and no others (they are said to "emerge" from the analysis of the data). Using the Simon-Blalock technique, however, the second conclusion—about the direction of causation between Congressmen's attitudes and their perceptions of district opinion—can never be more than a (perhaps justified) prior assumption. The first conclusion—about the existence of a causal link between constituency attitudes and Congressmen's attitudes—is contingent upon the assumption that they present as their second conclusion; change the assumption and the opposite conclusion results. In neither case do their manipulations of correlation coefficients constitute empirical tests of their conclusions.

To illustrate this argument, we shall examine three causal models connecting district attitudes with Congressmen's roll call votes. All three models fit the

---

logic of model building and testing is especially clearly set out in Stefan Valavanis, *Econometrics: An Introduction to Maximum Likelihood Methods* (New York: McGraw-Hill, 1959), ch. 1.

[7]*Ibid.*, pp. 71-72. Compare the second proposition with Lewis Anthony Dexter's description of the representative: "A congressman's conception of his district confirms itself, to a considerable extent, and may constitute a sort of self-fulfilling prophecy. . . . A congressman hears most often from those who agree with him. . . . Some men automatically interpret what they hear to support their own viewpoints." See "The Representative and His District," in Robert L. Peabody and Nelson W. Polsby (eds), *New Perspectives on the House of Representatives* (Chicago: Rand McNally, 1963), pp. 9f. See also Raymond A. Bauer, Ithiel de Sola Pool, and Lewis Anthony Dexter, *American Business and Public Policy* (New York: Atherton, 1963), part V. Donald R. Matthews makes the same point with reference to Senators: "Without the most stubborn and conscientious efforts, a senator is almost certain to see and talk mostly with friends and supporters on such a trip [to his constituency]. Since both categories are likely to be in general agreement with him, the image of constituency opinion he brings back to Washington is usually distorted in favor of his own views": Donald R. Matthews, *U.S. Senators and Their World* (New York: Vintage Books, 1960), p. 229.

The first proposition seems inconsistent with the frequent emphasis on the "localism" of Congressmen; see Samuel P. Huntington, "Congressional Responses to the Twentieth Century," in David B. Truman (ed.), *The Congress and America's Future* (Englewood Cliffs, N.J.: Prentice-Hall, 1965), pp. 5-31, especially Table II, p. 13; also David B. Truman, "Federalism and the Party System," in Arthur W. Macmahon (ed.), *Federalism: Mature and Emergent* (Garden City, N.Y.: Doubleday, 1955), pp. 115-136. Even though restricted to the civil rights issue area (in 1958), Cnudde and McCrone's findings, if valid, would be of considerable substantive importance in view of the above literature.

pattern of correlations. Moreover all three models satisfy two additional restrictions: they treat district attitudes as purely an independent variable and they do not require any direct link between district attitudes and roll call votes. Figure 1 shows the basic pattern of correlations used in this analysis.

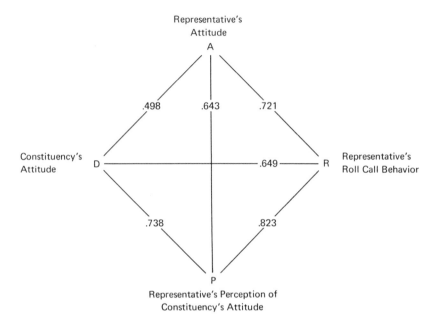

Note: Data are Miller-Stokes correlations reported in Cnudde and McCrone, *op. cit.*, p. 67.
FIGURE 1. Intercorrelations of variables pertaining to civil rights—whole district.

Figure 2 shows three different causal models linking district opinion and the votes of Congressmen. Cnudde and McCrone have shown that Model 2(a) fits the

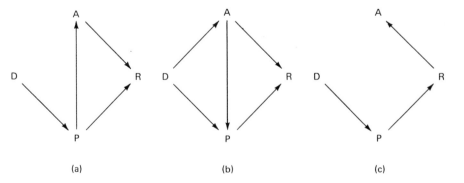

FIGURE 2. Three causal models that fit the intercorrelations of variables pertaining to civil rights.

data. Model 2(b) also fits: the addition of the link between district opinion and Congressmen's attitudes generates no new prediction equations that distinguish model 2(b) from 2(a). And model 2(c) also fits as Table 1 shows.

TABLE 1.   Prediction Equations and Degree of Fit for Model 2(c) of Constituency Influence[a]

Prediction Equations	Predicted	Actual	Difference
$^rDP^rPR^rRA = {^r}DA$	$(.738)(.823)(.721) = .438$	.498	.060
$^rDP^rPR = {^r}DR$	$(.738)(.823) = .607$	.649	.042
$^rPR^rRA = {^r}PA$	$(.823)(.721) = .493$	.543	.050

[a]Data are Miller-Stokes correlations reported in Cnudde and McCrone, *op. cit.*, p. 67.

How do we choose between these three different models, each of which suggests a different conclusion about the relationship between attitudes and perceptions? It should be apparent that the choice between them must rest (in the absence of additional data) on the investigator's hunch (or assumption) about what causal mechanisms are likely to exist in the real world. The only other imaginable basis for choice is the criterion of parsimony: the fewer the links (or causal paths) in a model, the better. Model 2(a), suggesting that perceptions cause attitudes, might be accepted over 2(b) (which suggests the opposite) since the former contains one less causal link.[8] But if we were to take parsimony seriously, then Model 2(c) would seem most acceptable: it has the minimum number of links possible between four variables. Thus this criterion of parsimony leads to the surprising conclusion that there is a correspondence between Congressmen's own attitudes and their perceptions of their district's attitudes only because of their participation in roll call voting.[9] One need not accept this conclusion; the criterion of parsimony that leads to it is really irrelevant. There is no reason to believe that parsimony in this sense (a relatively small number of unidirectional causal linkages) is a distinguishing characteristic of valid models of social phenomena.

In this case, then, the choice between the three models is, in itself, a decision about the relationship between the attitudes, perceptions, and votes of Congressmen; it is a decision that is logically prior to looking at the data, and one for which the prescription of parsimony provides no guidance. Similarly it is clear that the first proposition (which suggests that elite recruitment is not relevant to district control of Congressmen) rests on the postulated relationship between attitudes and perceptions.[10] Neither of the assertions made by Cnudde and McCrone are "findings."[11]

[8]This seems to be the approach of Cnudde and McCrone; see the reasoning leading to their model III (p. 69) and the comment about parsimony (p. 72).

[9]Model 2(c) is actually somewhat plausible; it implies that the representative's perceptions of constituent attitudes have an impact only when mediated by voting in accordance with district opinion, that is, playing the role of agent of the constituency.

[10]In addition, the absence of a direct link between district opinion and Congressmen's attitudes *in a single issue area* would not seem to be an adequate basis for inferences about "elite recruitment."

[11]The three models just discussed are *hierarchical* models; they force the investigator to

II. INTERACTION EFFECTS

Applying a single causal model to all the data that an investigator has collected is not always the best way of revealing the structure of the data. To fit a single causal model to a collection of data means, in effect, to assume that the data have been generated by an underlying causal mechanism that is roughly the same for all the units being studied. The structure of the mechanism is represented by the mathematical model, and the data are used to estimate its parameters. But different units can have different causal processes.[12] In any case, the validity of the mechanism hypothesized for all units in the population is not established by using all the data at once for a single estimation. Rather the general validity of the model is established by showing that the hypothesized set of relationships holds for various relevant subgroups within the population. This is the familiar notion of controlling for a variable applied to causal modelling; a model ought to be tested within different subgroups of the sample. This method may, indeed, yield interesting results even if a single causal model is inappropriate, since it may be possible to show that different causal processes are operating in different parts of the population. The importance of examining subgroups of the data to establish the wider validity of a causal model is not merely a methodologist's maxim; in this section we shall show the consequences of the failure to test a model among relevant subgroups of the study population.

Miller, in a paper using the Miller-Stokes data on Congressmen, shows that the correlation patterns between district opinion and Congressmen's perceptions, attitudes, and votes vary widely across different types of districts (competitive and noncompetitive) and across three issue areas (social welfare, civil rights, and foreign policy).[13] There are, in short, many different types of representation. The model proposed by Cnudde and McCrone would have been more plausible if it had been tested among various subgroups of Congressmen, and in different

---

decide at the outset, for example, whether attitudes cause perceptions or the other way around. Yet both these alternatives seem excessively strong in the light of research revealing the significant interaction between attitudes and perceptions. Miller and Stokes (*op. cit.*, p. 51) observe: "Out of respect for the processes by which the human actor achieves cognitive congruence we have also drawn arrows between the two intervening factors, since the Congressman probably tends to see his district as having the same opinion as his own and also tends, over time, to bring his own opinion into line with the district's." Lacking adequate theory to justify temporal or psychological priority of one variable over another, one will be unable to select between a number of hierarchical models that fit the data.

The assumptions made in a *reciprocal* model, in contrast to a hierarchical model, allow some variables to be both the cause and effect of each other. Such a model would, in theory at least, help disentangle attitudes and perceptions. Estimation of links in such models is a difficult empirical matter, however. On the problems and requirements in estimating the parameters of reciprocal models, see Valavanis, *op. cit.*, chs. 4 and 6; and J. Johnston, *Econometric Methods* (New York: McGraw Hill, 1963), ch. 9.

[12] Alker has drawn attention to the importance of this point in inter-nation comparisons. See Hayward R. Alker, Jr., "Regionalism Versus Universalism in Comparing Nations," in Bruce Russett *et al., World Handbook of Political and Social Indicators* (New Haven: Yale University Press, 1964), pp. 322-340; and also Hubert M. Blalock, Jr., "Theory Building and the Statistical Concept of Interaction," *American Sociological Review*, 30 (June, 1965), 374-380. In many cases it may be useful to transform the variables to eliminate nonadditive effects. See Joseph B. Kruskal, "Transformations of Data," *International Encyclopedia of the Social Sciences* (Macmillan, 1968), vol. 16, pp. 182-193.

issue areas—if they had, in effect, controlled for some of the prominent variables suggested by other studies of Congress.

Additional analysis of the Miller-Stokes data sharply illustrates the dangers of accepting a causal model tested only by reference to correlations across the entire sample. Using the data in Miller's paper, we tested the two major propositions for Congressmen from competitive and noncompetitive districts in the civil rights issue area. The basic Cnudde-McCrone model under consideration holds that there is no relationship between district opinion and the attitudes of the Congressmen when preceptions of district opinion by the Congressman are held constant: " . . .perceptions are likely to cause him [the Congressman] to modify his attitudes to fit his reasonably accurate perceptions."[14]

Analysis of the data shows that the model fits for one-party districts but does not fit for competitive districts (Table 2). Furthermore, as we saw earlier, there

TABLE 2.   Test of the District Opinion—Perceptions—
            Attitudes Model for Competitive and Non-
            competitive Districts[a]

Civil Rights	Predicted Correlation	Fit Model?[b]
One-party districts	$\dfrac{.54}{.78} = .69$	yes
Competitive districts	$\dfrac{-.16}{.23} = -.70$	no

[a]Data are for majority district opinion from Miller, *op. cit.*, pp. 362-363.

[b]The Cnudde-McCrone model implies that $^rDA = {^rDP}{^rPA}$. This in turn implies that the ratio $^rDA/^rDP$ is positive.

are many other possible models which would fit the data from one-party districts.[15]

III. MULTICOLLINEARITY

In *Negroes and the New Southern Politics,* Matthews and Prothro propose a causal model to account for variations in Negro political participation. Figure 3 shows the model which leads to the conclusion that:

[13]Warren E. Miller, "Majority Rule and the Representative System of Government," in Erik Allardt and Yrjo Littunen (eds.), *Cleavages, Ideologies, and Party Systems: Contributions to Comparative Political Sociology* (Helsinki: Proceedings of the Westermarck Society, 1964), pp. 343-376.

[14]Cnudde and McCrone, *op. cit.,* p. 72.

[15]Although Cnudde and McCrone restrict themselves to the civil rights issue area, their hypotheses would, if true, have more general significance. We tested their model for welfare and foreign policy issues in competitive and noncompetitive districts (based on the data in Miller, *op. cit.*). The model failed to fit in all four of these tests.

Community structure ... is thus seen to have *direct* effects on social and economic attributes of individual southern Negroes and on the community political system, but *not* on Negro attitudes and cognitions *or* on Negro political participation. Individual socio-economic attributes and the political system have direct effects *only* on attitudes and cognitions. *All effects on political participation are interpreted by Negro attitudes and cognitions.*[16]

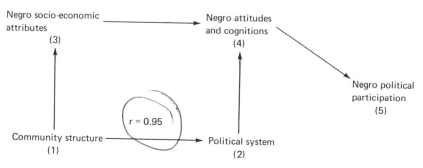

FIGURE 3. **Causal model of negro political participation.**
Source: Matthews and Prothro, *op. cit.*, pp. 322-323.

There are two major difficulties in this use of causal modelling that point to more general problems in multivariate analysis. First is a difficulty we have already discussed: the reporting of assumptions as conclusions. The causal model of Negro political participation makes dubious assumptions about the relationships between the variables in the model (a good example is the one-way relationship postulated between characteristics of the political system and political participation by individuals), and, in the end, these assumptions are presented as if they were findings based on the analysis of the data.[17]

The second problem, deserving the attention of political scientists using multivariate models, is that of separating out the independent effects of highly correlated independent variables. In the study of Negro political participation for example, the correlation between the "community structure" variable and the "political system" variable is 0.95. The extremely high correlation immediately raises the question of whether it is possible to disentangle the effects of these two variables, as the model requires, since they are virtually identical. It is, in fact, impossible to assess the independent effects of the "community structure" and the "political system" on Negro political participation in any reliable fashion.[18] This is the problem of "multicollinearity": when two or more independent variables are highly correlated, it is difficult to make reliable inferences about their relative contribution to the determination of the dependent variable. As the correlation between two independent variables approaches unity, it becomes literally impossible to tell one variable from the other. As Blalock puts it:

[16] Matthews and Prothro, *op. cit.*, pp. 323-324, emphasis in the original.
[17] See the reasoning about "direction of causation," *ibid.*, pp. 321-323.
[18] The beta weights included in the analysis (*ibid.*, p. 321) also run contrary to the model.

Stated in most simple terms, whenever the correlation between two or more independent variables is high, the sampling error of the partial slopes and partial correlations will be quite large. As a result there will be a number of different combinations of regression coefficients, and hence partial correlations, which give almost equally good fittings to the empirical data. In any given case the method of least squares will usually yield unique solutions, but with slight modifications of the magnitude that could easily be due to sampling or measurement error, one might obtain estimates which differ considerably from the original set.[19]

Finally, as a matter of general interest, it should be noted that the difficulties arising from multicollinearity persist regardless of the method of data anaysis. In short, multicollinearity not only affects estimates in multiple regression procedures; it also weakens inferences based on cross-tabulations. While occasionally the use of additional information may alleviate the problem, it often happens that when the social scientist must rely on "experiments" performed by nature, he will be unable to obtain the independent variation necessary to assess the independent effects of his explanatory variables.

IV. CONCLUSIONS

This review of two recent applications of causal models to political data suggests the need to stress certain elementary principles of data analysis. As models grow more complex, basic principles may often be lost in the maze of elaborate analyses. We can suggest a number of specific points growing out of the preceding discussion:

1. In complicated multivariate models, there are a number of inherent problems of estimation. These often arise in attempts to distinguish the relative impact of different variables that are themselves highly intercorrelated. The accuracy of the estimates degenerates as the intercorrelation between independent variables approaches unity. Indeed, in the case of perfect correlation between two variables, the variance of the estimates of the relative impact is infinite!

2. Any investigator, and especially those aiming to give a causal interpretation of their findings, should consider the possibility that different causal processes operate in different subgroups of their data. This may be formally incorporated into the model by using statistical procedures that take interaction effects into account.

3. Complex multivariate models require a good many assumptions in order to estimate the parameters of the model. These assumptions are often not testable and they do not, of course, "emerge" from the analysis of the data, and should not be reported as empirically grounded conclusions.

The Simon-Blalock technique does not eliminate these problems. The

[19]Hubert M. Blalock, Jr., "Correlated Independent Variables: The Problem of Multicollinearity," *Social Forces,* 42 (December, 1963), p. 233. For more detailed discussions of the problem, see Donald E. Farrar and Robert R. Glauber, "Multicollinearity in Regression Analysis: The Problem Revisited," *Review of Economics and Statistics,* 49 (February, 1967), 92-107; and Johnston, *op. cit.,* pp. 201-207.

investigator, regardless of his particular data analysis strategy, must face them and avoid the unthinking manipulation of correlation coefficients in an attempt to "eliminate" causal links.

BRINGING MEN BACK IN

George C. Homans

I am going to talk about an issue we have worried over many times. I have worried over it myself. But I make no excuses for taking it up again. Although it is an old issue, it is still not a settled one, and I think it is the most general intellectual issue in sociology. If I have only one chance to speak *ex cathedra*, I cannot afford to say something innocuous. On the contrary, now if ever is the time to be nocuous.

In the early 'thirties a distinct school of sociological thought was beginning to form. Its chief, though certainly not its only, intellectual parents were Durkheim and Radcliffe-Brown. I call it a school, though not all its adherents accepted just the same tenets; and many sociologists went ahead and made great progress without giving a thought to it. The school is usually called that of structural-functionalism, or functionalism for short. For a whole generation it has been the dominant, indeed the only distinct, school of sociological thought. I think it has run its course, done its work, and now positively gets in the way of our understanding social phenomena. And I propose to ask, Why?

THE INTERESTS OF FUNCTIONALISM

I begin by reminding you of the chief interests and assumptions of functionalism, especially as contrasted with what it was not interested in and took for granted, for the questions it did not ask have returned to plague it. If what I say seems a caricature, remember that a caricature emphasizes a person's most characteristic features.

First, the school took its start from the study of norms, the statements the members of a group make about how they ought to behave, and indeed often do behave, in various circumstances. It was especially interested in the cluster of norms called a role and in the cluster of roles called an institution. It never tired of asserting that its concern was with institutionalized behavior, and that the unit of social analysis was not the acting individual but the role. The school did not ask why there should be roles at all.

Reprinted with the permission of the author and the publisher, The American Sociological Association, from the *American Sociological Review*, Vol. 29 (1964), 809-18.

Presidential Address delivered at the annual meeting of the American Sociological Association in Montreal, September 2, 1964.

Second, the school was empirically interested in the interrelations of roles, the interrelations of institutions: this was the structural side of its work. It was the sort of thing the social anthropologists had been doing, showing how the institutions of a primitive society fitted together; and the sociologists extended the effort to advanced societies. They would point out, for instance, that the nuclear family rather than some form of extended kinship was characteristic of industrialized societies. But they were more interested in establishing *what* the interrelations of institutions were than in *why* they were so. In the beginning the analyses tended to be static, as it is more convincing to speak of a social structure in a society conceived to be stable than in one undergoing rapid change. Recently the school has turned to the study of social change, but in so doing it has had to take up the question it disregarded earlier. If an institution is changing, one can hardly avoid asking why it is changing in one direction rather than another.

Third, the school was, to put it crudely, more interested in the consequences than in the causes of an institution, particularly in the consequences for a social system considered as a whole. These consequences were the *functions* of the institution. Thus the members of the school never tired of pointing out the functions and dysfunctions of a status system, without asking why a status system should exist in the first place, why it was there to have functions. They were especially interested in showing how its institutions helped maintain a society in equilibrium, as a going concern. The model for research was Durkheim's effort to show, in *The Elementary Forms of the Religious Life,* how the religion of a primitive tribe helped hold the tribe together.

Such were the empirical interests of functionalism. As empirically I have been a functionalist myself, I shall be the last to quarrel with them. It is certainly one of the jobs of a sociologist to discover what the norms of a society are. Though a role is not actual behavior, it is for some purposes a useful simplification. Institutions *are* interrelated, and it is certainly one of the jobs of a sociologist to show what the interrelations are. Institutions do have consequences, in the sense that, if one institution may be taken as given, the other kinds of institution that may exist in the society are probably not infinite in number. It is certainly one of the jobs of a sociologist to search out these consequences and even, though this is more difficult, to determine whether their consequences are good or bad for the society as a whole. At any rate, the empirical interests of functionalism have led to an enormous amount of good work. Think only of the studies made by Murdock[1] and others on the cross-cultural interrelations of institutions.

As it began to crystallize, the functional school developed theoretical interests as well as empirical ones. There was no necessity for the two to go together, and the British social anthropologists remained relatively untheoretical. Not so the American sociologists, particularly Talcott Parsons, who claimed that they were not only theorists but something called general theorists, and strongly emphasized the importance of theory.

Theirs was to be, moreover, a certain kind of theory. They were students of Durkheim and took seriously his famous definition of *social facts:* "Since their essential characteristic consists in the power they possess of exerting, from

---

[1]George P. Murdock, *Social Structure,* New York: Macmillan, 1949.

outside, a pressure on individual consciousnesses, they do not derive from individual consciousnesses, and in consequence sociology is not a corollary of psychology."[2] Since Durkheim was a great man, one can find statements in his writings that have quite other implications, but this caricature of himself was the one that made the difference. If not in what they said, then surely in what they did, the functionalists took Durkheim seriously. Their fundamental unit, the role, was a social fact in Durkheim's sense. And their theoretical program assumed, as he did, that sociology should be an independent science, in the sense that its propositions should not be derivable from some other social science, such as psychology. This meant, in effect, that the general propositions of sociology were not to be propositions about the behavior of "individual consciousnesses"—or, as I should say, about men—but propositions about the characteristics of societies or other social groups as such.

Where functionalism failed was not in its empirical interests but, curiously, in what it most prided itself on, its general theory. Let me be very careful here. In a recent Presidential Address, Kingsley Davis asserted that we are all functionalists now,[3] and there is a sense in which he was quite right. But note that he was talking about functional *analysis*. One carries out functional analysis when, starting from the existence of a particular institution, one tries to find out what difference the institution makes to the other aspects of social structure. That is, one carries out the empirical program of functionalism. Since we have all learned to carry out functional analyses, we are in this sense all functionalists now. But functional analysis, as a method, is not the same thing as functional theory. And if we are all functional analysts, we are certainly not all functional theorists. Count me out, for one.

The only inescapable office of theory is to explain. The theory of evolution is an explanation why and how evolution occurs. To look for the consequences of institutions, to show the interrelationships of institutions is not the same thing as explaining why the interrelationships are what they are. The question is a practical and not a philosophical one—not whether it is legitimate to take the role as the fundamental unit, nor whether institutions are really real, but whether the theoretical program of functionalism has in fact led to explanations of social phenomena, including the findings of functional analysis itself. Nor is the question whether functionalism might not do so, but whether it has done so as of today. I think it has not.

THE NATURE OF THEORY

With all their talk about theory, the functionalists never—and I speak advisedly—succeeded in making clear what a theory was. It must be allowed in their excuse that, in the early days, the philosophers of science had not given as clear an answer to the question as they have now.[4] But even then, the

---

[2] Émile Durkheim, *Les régles de la méthode sociologique* (8th ed.) Paris: Alcan, 1927, pp. 124-125.

[3] "The Myth of Functional Analysis as a Special Method in Sociology and Anthropology," *American Sociological Review*, 24 (December, 1959), pp. 757-773.

[4] See especially R. B. Braithwaite, *Scientific Explanation*, Cambridge: Cambridge University Press, 1953.

functionalists could have done better than they did, and certainly the excuse is valid no longer. Today we should stop talking to our students about sociological theory until we have taught them what a theory is.

A theory of a phenomenon consists of a series of propositions, each stating a relationship between properties of nature. But not every kind of sentence qualifies as such a proposition. The propositions do not consist of definitions of the properties: the construction of a conceptual scheme is an indispensable part of theoretical work but is not itself theory. Nor may a proposition simply say that there is some relationship between the properties. Instead, if there is some change in one of the properties, it must at least begin to specify what the change in the other property will be. If one of the properties is absent, the other will also be absent; or if one of the properties increases in value, the other will too. The properties, the variables, may be probabilities.

Accordingly, to take a famous example, Marx's statement that the economic organization of a society determines the nature of its other institutions is an immensely useful guide to research. For it says: "Look for the social consequences of economic change, and if you look, you will surely find them!" But it is not the sort of proposition that can enter a theory. For by itself it says only that, if the economic infrastructure changes, there will be some change in the social superstructure, withoug beginning to suggest what the latter change will be. Most of the sentences of sociology, alleged to be theoretical, resemble this one of Marx's, yet few of our theorists realize it. And while we are always asking that theory guide research, we forget that many statements like Marx's are good guides to research without being good theory.

To constitute a theory, the propositions must take the form of a deductive system. One of them, usually called the lowest-order proposition, is the proposition to be explained, for example, the proposition that the more thoroughly a society is industrialized, the more fully its kinship organization tends towards the nuclear family. The other propositions are either general propositions or statements of particular given conditions. The general propositions are so called because they enter into other, perhaps many other, deductive systems besides the one in question. Indeed, what we often call a theory is a cluster of deductive systems, sharing the same general propositions but having different *explicanda*. The crucial requirement is that each system shall be deductive. That is, the lowest-order proposition follows as a logical conclusion from the general propositions under the specified given conditions. The reason why statements like Marx's may not enter theories is that no definite conclusions may in logic be drawn from them. When the lowest-order proposition does follow logically, it is said to be explained. The explanation of a phenomenon is the theory of the phenomenon. A theory is nothing—it is not a theory—unless it is an explanation.

One may define properties and categories, and one still has no theory. One may state that there *are* relations between the properties, and one still has no theory. One may state that a change in one property will produce a definite change in another property, and one still has no theory. Not until one has properties, and propositions stating the relations between them, and the propositions form a deductive system—not until one has all three does one have a theory. Most of our arguments about theory would fall to the ground, if we first asked whether we had a theory to argue about.

FUNCTIONAL THEORIES

As a theoretical effort, functionalism never came near meeting these conditions. Even if the functionalists had seriously tried to meet them, which they did not, I think they would still have failed. The difficulty lay in the characteristic general propositions of functionalism. A proposition is not functional just because it uses the word *function*. To say that a certain institution is functional for individual men in the sense of meeting their needs is not a characteristic proposition of functionalism. Instead it belongs to the class of psychological propositions. Nor is the statement that one institution is a function of another, in the quasi-mathematical sense of function, characteristic. Though many functional theorists make such statements, non-functionalists like myself may also make them without a qualm. The characteristic general propositions of functional theory in sociology take the form: "If it is to survive, or remain in equilibrium, a social system—any social system—must possess institutions of Type X." For instance, if it is to survive or remain in equilibrium, a society must possess conflict-resolving institutions. By general propositions of this sort the functionalists sought to meet Durkheim's demand for a truly independent sociological theory.

The problem was, and is, to construct deductive systems headed by such propositions. Take first the terms *equilibrium* and *survival.* If the theorist chose *equilibrium,* he was able to provide no criterion of social equilibrium, especially "dynamic" or "moving" equilibrium, definite enough to allow anything specific to be deduced in logic from a proposition employing the term. I shall give an example later. When indeed was a society not in equilibrium? If the theorist chose *survival,* he found this, too, surprisingly hard to define. Did Scotland, for instance, survive as a society? Though it had long been united with England, it still possessed distinctive institutions, legal and religious. If the theorist took *survival* in the strong sense, and said that a society had not survived if all its members had died without issue, he was still in trouble. As far as the records went, the very few societies of this sort had possessed institutions of all the types the functionalists said were necessary for survival. The evidence put in question, to say the least, the empirical truth of the functionalist propositions. Of course the functionalists were at liberty to say: "If a society is to survive, its members must not all be shot dead," which was true as true could be but allowed little to be deduced about the social characteristics of surviving societies.

Indeed the same was true of the other functional propositions. Even if a statement like: "If it is to survive, a society must possess conflict-resolving institutions," were accepted as testable and true, it possessed little explanatory power. From the proposition the fact could be deduced that, given a certain society did survive, it did possess conflict-resolving institutions of some kind, and the fact was thus explained. What remained unexplained was why the society had conflict-resolving institutions of a particular kind, why, for instance, the jury was an ancient feature of Anglo-Saxon legal institutions. I take it that what sociology has to explain are the actual features of actual societies and not just the generalized features of a generalized society.

I do not think that members of the functional school could have set up, starting with general propositions of their distinctive type, theories that were also deductive systems. More important, they did not. Recognizing, perhaps, that they were blocked in one direction, some of them elaborated what they called theory in another. They used what they asserted were a limited and exhaustive number of functional problems faced by any society to generate a complex set of categories in terms of which social structure could be analyzed. That is, they set up a conceptual scheme. But analysis is not explanation, and a conceptual scheme is not a theory. They did not fail to make statements about the relations between the categories, but most of the statements resembled the one of Marx's I cited earlier: they were not of the type that enter deductive systems. From their lower-order propositions, as from their higher-order ones, no definite conclusions in logic could be drawn. Under these conditions, there was no way of telling whether their choice of functional problems and categories was not wholly arbitrary. What the functionalists actually produced was not a theory but a new language for describing social structure, one among many possible languages; and much of the work they called theoretical consisted in showing how the words in other languages, including that of everyday life, could be translated into theirs. They would say, for instance, that what other people called making a living was called in their language goal-attainment. But what makes a theory is deduction, not translation.

I have said that the question is not whether, in general, functional theories can be real theories, for there are sciences that possess real functional theories. The question is rather whether this particular effort was successful. If a theory is an explanation, the functionalists in sociology were, on the evidence, not successful. Perhaps they could not have been successful; at any rate they were not. The trouble with their theory was not that it was wrong, but that it was not a theory.

AN ALTERNATIVE THEORY

Here endeth the destructive part of the lesson. I shall now try to show that a more successful effort to explain social phenomena entails the construction of theories different from functional ones, in the sense that their general propositions are of a different kind, precisely the kind, indeed, that the functionalists tried to get away from. I shall try to show this for the very phenomena the functionalists took for granted and the very relations they discovered empirically. I shall even try to show that, when functionalists took the job of explanation seriously, which they sometimes did, this other kind of theory would appear unacknowledged in their own work.

The functionalists insisted over and over again that the minimum unit of social analysis was the role, which is a cluster of norms. In a recent article, James Coleman has written: ". . . sociologists have characteristically taken as their starting-point a social system in which norms exist, and individuals are largely governed by these norms. Such a strategy views norms as the governors of social behavior, and this neatly bypasses the difficult problem that Hobbes posed."[5] Hobbes' problem is, of course, why there is not a war of all against all.

Why, in short, should there be norms at all? The answer Coleman gives is that, in the kind of case he considers, norms arise through the actions of men

[5] James S. Coleman, "Collective Decisions," *Sociological Inquiry*, 34 (1964), pp. 166-181.

rationally calculating to further their own self-interest in a context of other men acting in the same way. He writes: "The central postulate about behavior is this: each actor will attempt to extend his power over those actions in which he has most interest." Starting from this postulate, Coleman constructs a deductive system explaining why the actors adopt a particular sort of norm in the given circumstances.

I do not want to argue the vexed question of rationality. I do want to point out what sort of general proposition Coleman starts with. As he recognizes, it is much like the central assumption of economics, though self-interest is not limited to the material interests usually considered by economists. It also resembles a proposition of psychology, though here it might take the form: the more valuable the reward of an activity, the more likely a man is to perform the activity. But it certainly is not a characteristic functional proposition in sociology: it is not a statement about the conditions of equilibrium for a society, but a statement about the behavior of individual men.

Again, if there are norms, why do men conform to them? Let us lay aside the fact that many men do not conform or conform very indifferently, and assume that they all do so. Why do they do so? So far as the functionalists gave any answer to the question, it was that men have "internalized" the values embodied in the norm. But "internalization" is a word and not an explanation. So far as their own theory was concerned, the functionalists took conformity to norms for granted. They made the mistake Malinowski pointed out long ago in a book now too little read by sociologists, the mistake made by early writers on primitive societies, the mistake of assuming that conformity to norms is a matter of ". . . this automatic acquiescence, this instinctive submission of every member of the tribe to its laws. . . ."[6] The alternative answer Malinowski gave was that obedience to norms "is usually rewarded according to the measure of its perfection, while noncompliance is visited upon the remiss agent."[7] In short, the answer he gave is much like that of Coleman and the psychologists. Later he added the suggestive remark: "The true problem is not to study how human life submits to rules—it simply does not; the real problem is how the rules become adapted to life."[8]

The question remains why members of a particular society find certain of the results of their actions rewarding and not others, especially when some of the results seem far from "naturally" rewarding. This is the real problem of the "internalization" of values. The explanation is given not by any distinctively sociological propositions but by the propositions of learning theory in psychology.

The functionalists were much interested in the interrelations of institutions, and it was one of the glories of the school to have pointed out many such interrelations. But the job of a science does not end with pointing out interrelations; it must try to explain why they are what they are. Take the statement that the kinship organization of industrialized societies tends to be that of the nuclear family. I cannot give anything like the full explanation, but I

[6]Bronislaw Malinowski, *Crime and Custom in Savage Society*, Paterson, N.J.: Littlefield, Adams, 1959, p. 11.
[7]*Ibid.*, p. 12.
[8]*Ibid.*, p. 127.

can, and you can too, suggest the beginning of one. Some men organized factories because by so doing they thought they could get greater material rewards than they could get otherwise. Other men entered factories for reasons of the same sort. In so doing they worked away from home and so had to forgo, if only for lack of time, the cultivation of the extended kinship ties that were a source of reward, because a source of help, in many traditional agricultural societies, where work lay closer to home. Accordingly the nuclear family tended to become associated with factory organization; and the explanation for the association is provided by propositions about the behavior of men as such. Not the needs of society explain the relationship, but the needs of men.

Again, functionalists were interested in the consequences of institutions, especially their consequences for a social system as a whole. For instance, they were endlessly concerned with the functions and dysfunctions of status systems. Seldom did they ask why there should be status systems in the first place. Some theorists have taken the emergence of phenomena like status systems as evidence for Durkheim's contention that sociology was not reducible to psychology. What is important is not the fact of emergence but the question how the emergence is to be explained. One of the accomplishments of small-group research is to explain how a status system, of course on a small scale, emerges in the course of interaction between the members of a group.[9] The explanation is provided by psychological propositions. Certainly no functional propositions are needed. Indeed the theoretical contribution of small-group research has consisted "in showing how the kinds of microscopic variables usually ignored by sociologists can explain the kinds of social situations usually ignored by psychologists."[10]

What is the lesson of all this? If the very things functionalists take for granted, like norms, if the very interrelationships they empirically discover can be explained by deductive systems that employ psychological propositions, then it must be that the general explanatory principles even of sociology are not sociological, as the functionalists would have them be, but psychological, propositions about the behavior of men, not about the behavior of societies. On the analogy with other sciences, this argument by itself would not undermine the validity of a functional theory. Thermodynamics, for instance, states propositions about aggregates, which are themselves true and general, even though they can be explained in turn, in statistical mechanics, by propositions about members of the aggregates. The question is whether this kind of situation actually obtains in sociology. So far as functional propositions are concerned, which are propositions about social aggregates, the situation does not obtain, for they have not been shown to be true and general.

EXPLAINING SOCIAL CHANGE

My next contention is that even confessed functionalists, when they seriously

[9] See George C. Homans, *Social Behavior: Its Elementary Forms*, New York: Harcourt, Brace & World, 1961, esp. Ch. 8.
[10] C. N. Alexander, Jr. and R. L. Simpson, "Balance Theory and Distributive Justice," *Sociological Inquiry* 34 (1964), pp. 182-192.

try to explain certain kinds of social phenomena, in fact use non-functional explanations without recognizing that they do so. This is particularly clear in their studies of social change.

Social change provides a searching test for theory, since historical records are a prerequisite for its study. Without history, the social scientist can establish the contemporaneous interrelations of institutions, but may be hard put to it to explain why the interrelations should be what they are. With historical records he may have the information needed to support an explanation. One of the commonest charges against the functionalist school was that it could not deal with social change, that its analysis was static. In recent years some functionalists have undertaken to show that the charge was unjustified. They have chosen for their demonstration the process of differentiation in society, the process, for instance, of the increasing specialization of occupations. In question as usual is not the fact of differentiation—there is no doubt that the over-all trend of social history has been in this direction—but how the process is to be explained.

A particularly good example of this new development in functionalism is Neil Smelser's book, *Social Change in the Industrial Revolution: An Application of Theory to the British Cotton Industry 1770-1840.*[11] The book is not just good for my purposes: it is good, very good, in itself. It provides an enormous amount of well organized information, and it goes far to explain the changes that occurred. The amusing thing about it is that the explanation Smelser actually uses, good scientist that he is, to account for the changes is not the functional theory he starts out with, which is as usual a non-theory, but a different kind of theory and a better one.

Smelser begins like any true functionalist. For him a social system is one kind of system of action, characterized as follows: "A social system . . . is composed of a set of interrelated roles, collectivities, etc. . . . It is important to remember that the roles, collectivities, etc., not individuals, are the units in this last case." Moreover, "all systems of action are governed by the principle of equilibrium. According to the dominant type of equilibrium, the adjustments proceed in a certain direction: if the equilibrium is stable, the units tend to return to their original position; if the equilibrium is partial, only some of the units need to adjust; if the equilibrium is unstable, the tendency is to change, through mutual adjustment, to a new equilibrium or to disintegrate altogether." Finally, "all social systems are subject to four functional exigencies which must be met more or less satisfactorily if the system is to remain in equilibrium."[12] Note that by this argument all social systems are in equilibrium, even systems in process of disintegration. Though the latter are in unstable equilibrium, they are still in equilibrium. Accordingly they are meeting more or less satisfactorily the four functional exigencies. You see how useful a deductive system can be in social science? More seriously you will see that definitions of equilibrium are so broad that you may draw any conclusion you like from them.

But for all the explanatory use Smelser makes of it, this theory and its subsequent elaboration is so much window-dressing. When he really gets down to

[11]Chicago: University of Chicago Press, 1959.
[12]*Ibid.*, pp. 10-11.

explaining the innovations in the British cotton textile industry, especially the introduction of spinning and weaving machinery, he forgets his functionalism. The guts of his actual explanation lie in the seven steps through which he says the process proceeds:

> Industrial differentiation proceeds, therefore, by the following steps:
>
> (1) Dissatisfaction with the productive achievements of the industry or its relevant sub-sectors and a sense of opportunity in terms of the potential availability of adequate facilities to reach a higher level of productivity.
>
> (2) Appropriate symptoms of disturbance in the form of "unjustified" negative emotional reactions and "unrealistic" aspirations on the part of various elements of the population.[13]

I shall not give the other five steps, as I should make the same criticism of them as I now make of the first two. I think they provide by implication a good explanation of the innovations of the Industrial Revolution in cotton manufacturing. But what kind of an explanation is it? Whatever it is, it is not a functional one. Where here do roles appear as the fundamental units of a social system? Where are the four functional exigencies? Not a word do we hear of them. Instead, what do we hear of? We hear of dissatisfaction, a sense of opportunity, emotional reactions, and aspirations. And what feels these things? Is a role dissatisfied or emotional? No; Smelser himself says it is "various elements of the population" that do so. Under relentless pressure let us finally confess that "various elements of the population" means men. And what men? For the most part men engaged in making and selling cotton cloth. And what were they dissatisfied with? Not with "the productive achievements of the industry." Though some statesmen were certainly concerned about the contribution made by the industry as a whole to the wealth of Great Britain, let us, again under relentless pressure, confess that most of the men in question were concerned with their own profits. Let us get men back in, and let us put some blood in them. Smelser himself makes the crucial statement: "In Lancashire in the early 1760's there was excited speculation about instantaneous fortunes for the man lucky enough to stumble on the right invention."[14] In short, the men in question were activated by self-interest. Yet not all self-interests are selfish interests, and certainly not all the innovations of the Industrial Revolution can be attributed to selfishness.

Smelser's actual explanation of technical innovation in cotton manufacturing might be sketched in the following deductive system. I have left out the most obvious steps.

1. Men are more likely to perform an activity, the more valuable they perceive the reward of that activity to be.
2. Men are more likely to perform an activity, the more successful they perceive the activity is likely to be in getting that reward.
3. The high demand for cotton textiles and the low productivity of labor led

[13]*Ibid.*, p. 29.
[14]*Ibid.*, p. 80.

men concerned with cotton manufacturing to perceive the development of labor-saving machinery as rewarding in increased profits.

4. The existing state of technology led them to perceive the effort to develop labor-saving machinery as likely to be successful.

5. Therefore, by both (1) and (2) such men were highly likely to try to develop labor-saving machinery.

6. Since their perceptions of the technology were accurate, their efforts were likely to meet with success, and some of them did meet with success.

From these first steps, others such as the organization of factories and an increasing specialization of jobs followed. But no different kind of explanation is needed for these further developments: propositions like (1) and (2), which I call the *value* and the *success* propositions, would occur in them too. We should need a further proposition to describe the effect of frustration, which certainly attended some of the efforts at innovation, in creating the "negative emotional reactions" of Smelser's step 2.

I must insist again on the kind of explanation this is. It is an explanation using psychological propositions (1 and 2 above), psychological in that they are commonly stated and tested by psychologists and that they refer to the behavior of men and not to the conditions of equilibrium of societies or other social groups as such. They are general in that they appear in many, and I think in all, of the deductive systems that will even begin to explain social behavior. There is no assumption that the men in question are all alike in their concrete behavior. They may well have been conditioned to find different things rewarding, but the way conditioning takes place is itself explained by psychological propositions. There is no assumption that their values are all materialistic, but only that their pursuit of non-material values follows the same laws as their pursuit of material ones. There is no assumption that they are isolated or unsocial, but only that the laws of human behavior do not change just because another person rather than the physical environment provides the rewards for behavior. Nor is there any assumption that psychological propositions will explain everything social. We shall certainly not be able to explain everything, but our failures will be attributable to lack of factual information or the intellectual machinery for dealing with complexity—though the computers will help us here—and not to the propositions themselves. Nor is there any assumption here of psychological reductionism, though I used to think there was. For reduction implies that there are general sociological propositions that can then be reduced to psychological ones. I now suspect that there are no general sociological propositions, propositions that hold good of all societies or social groups as such, and that the only general propositions of sociology are in fact psychological.

What I do claim is that, no matter what we say our theories are, when we seriously try to explain social phenomena by constructing even the veriest sketches of deductive systems, we find ourselves in fact, and whether we admit it or not, using what I have called psychological explanations. I need hardly add that our actual explanations are our actual theories.

I am being a little unfair to functionalists like Smelser and Parsons if I imply that they did not realize there were people around. The so-called theory of action made a very good start indeed by taking as its paradigm for social behavior two persons, the actions of each of whom sanctioned, that is, rewarded or punished, the actions of the other.[15] But as soon as the start was made, its authors disregarded it. As the theory of action was applied to society, it appeared to have no actors and mighty little action. The reason was that it separated the personality system from the social system and proposed to deal with the latter alone. It was the personality system that had "needs, drives, skills, etc.,"[16] It was not part of the social system, but only conducted exchanges with it, by providing it, for instance, with disembodied motivation.[17] This is the kind of box you get into when you think of theory as a set of boxes. For this reason, no one should hold their style of writing against the functionalists. The best of writers must write clumsily when he has set up his intellectual problem in a clumsy way. If the theorist will only envisage his problem from the outset as one of constructing explanatory propositions and not a set of categories, he will come to see that the personal and the social are not to be kept separate. The actions of a man that we take to be evidence of his personality are not different from his actions that, together with the actions of others, make up a social system. They are the same identical actions. The theorist will realize this when he finds that the same set of general propositions, including the success and the value proposition mentioned above, are needed for explaining the phenomena of both personality and society.

CONCLUSION

If sociology is a science, it must take seriously one of the jobs of any science, which is that of providing explanations for the empirical relations it discovers. An explanation is a theory, and it takes the form of a deductive system. With all its talk about theory, the functionalist school did not take the job of theory seriously enough. It did not ask itself what a theory was, and it never produced a functional theory that was in fact an explanation. I am not sure that it could have done so, starting as it did with propositions about the conditions of social equilibrium, propositions from which no definite conclusions could be drawn in a deductive system. If a serious effort is made to construct theories that will even begin to explain social phenomena, it turns out that their general propositions are not about the equilibrium of societies but about the behavior of men. This is true even of some good functionalists, though they will not admit it. They keep psychological explanations under the table and bring them out furtively like a bottle of whiskey, for use when they really need help. What I ask is that we bring what we say about theory into line with what we actually do, and so put an end to our intellectual hypocrisy. It would unite us with the other social sciences, whose actual theories are much like our actual ones, and so strengthen us all. Let us do so also for the sake of our students. I sometimes think that they begin with more understanding of the real nature of social phenomena than we leave them with, and that our double-talk kills their mother-wit. Finally, I must acknowledge freely that everything I have said seems to me obvious. But why cannot we take the obvious seriously?

[15] Talcott Parsons and Edward Shils (eds.), *Toward a General Theory of Action*, Cambridge, Mass.: Harvard University Press, 1951, pp. 14-16.

[16] Smelser, *op. cit.*, p. 10.

[17] *Ibid.*, p. 33.

SOME EMPIRICAL CONSEQUENCES OF THE DAVIS-MOORE THEORY OF STRATIFICATION

Arthur L. Stinchcombe

Davis and Moore's theory of stratification,[1] though frequently discussed, has stimulated remarkably few studies. Perhaps this is due to the lack of derivations of empirical propositions in the original article. I would like in this note to outline some empirical implications of the theory.

Davis and Moore's basic argument is that unequal rewards tend to accrue to positions of great importance to society, provided that the talents needed for such positions are scarce. "Society" (i.e. people strongly identified with the collective fate) insures that these functions are properly performed by rewarding the talented people for undertaking these tasks. This implies that the greater the importance of positions, the less likely they are to be filled by ascriptive recruitment.[2]

It is quite difficult to rank tasks or roles according to their relative importance. But certain tasks are unquestionably more important at one time than at another, or more important in one group than another. For instance, generals are more important in wartime than in peacetime. Changes in importance, or different importance in different groups, have clear consequences according to the theory. If the importance of a role increases, its rewards should become relatively greater and recruitment should be more open.

The following empirical consequences of the theory are "derivations" in a restricted sense. We identify supposed changes in the importance of roles, or identify groups in which certain roles are more important. Then we propose measures of the degree of inequality of reward and openness of recruitment which are consequences of such changes. If changes in importance are correctly

Reprinted with permission of the author and publisher, The American Sociological Association, from the *American Sociological Review*, Vol. 28 (1963), 805-8.

This note was stimulated by a seminar presentation by Renate Mayntz, who focused attention on the problem of empirical investigation of functional theories.

[1] Kingsley Davis and Wilbert E. Moore, "Some Principles of Stratification," *American Sociological Review*, 10 (April, 1945), pp. 242-249.

[2] The theory holds that the most important positions, if they require unusual talents, will recruit people who otherwise would not take them, by offering high rewards to talent. This result would take place if one assumed a perfectly achievement-based stratification system. Some have asserted that Davis and Moore's argument "assumes" such a perfectly open system, and hence is obviously inadequate to the facts. Since the relevant results will be obtained if a system recruits more talented people to its "important" positions but ascribes all others, and since this postulate is not obviously false as is the free market assumption, we will assume the weaker postulate here. It seems unlikely that Davis and Moore ever assumed the stronger, obviously false, postulate.

identified, and if the measures of inequality of reward are accurate, then the consequences are logical derivations from the theory. If it turns out that generals are not more recruited according to talent in wartime, then it may be because the theory is untrue. But it may also be that generals are not in fact more important in wartime, or that our measures of recruitment do not work.

Consequence 1: In time of war the abilities of generals become more important than in time of peace. According to the theory, this should result in the following types of restructuring of the stratification system during wartime (and the reverse with the onset of peace):

(a) The rewards of the military, especially of the elite whose talents are scarce, should rise relative to the rewards of other elites, especially those which have nothing to do with victory (e.g., the medical and social service elite charged with care of incurables, the aged, etc.).[3]

(b) Within the military, the degree of inequality of rewards should become greater, favoring generals, for their talents are particularly scarce.

(c) Even standardizing for the increase in sheer numbers of high military officials (which of itself implies that more formerly obscure men will rise rapidly) there should be pressure to open the military elite to talent, and consequently, there should be a higher proportion of Ulysses S. Grant type careers and fewer time-servers.

(d) Medals, a reward based on performances rather than on the authority hierarchy, should behave the same way. They should be more unequally distributed in wartime within any given rank; new medals, particularly of very high honor, should be created in wartime rather than peacetime, etc.

Consequence 2: The kingship in West European democratic monarchies has consistently declined in political importance as the powers of parliament have increased (this does not apply, for instance, to Japan, where apparently the Emperorship was largely a ritual office even in medieval times). Modern kings in rich countries now perhaps have other functions than political leadership. Certainly the role requirements have changed—for instance, a modern king's sex life is much more restricted than formerly. Their rewards have also changed, emphasizing more ceremonial deference and expressions of sentiment, less wealth and power. It is not clear whether the ceremonial element has actually increased, or whether the rewards of wealth and power have declined. Investitures in the Presidency in the United States and Mexico seem to have nearly as much pomp as, and more substance than, coronations in Scandinavia and the Low Countries. Changes in the nature of the role-requirements and of the rewards indicates a shift of functions. At the least these changes indicate that some ceremonial functions of the kingship have declined much less in importance than the political functions. But to have a non-political function in a political structure is probably to be less important in the eyes of the people. Consequently, historical studies of the kingship in England, Scandinavia, and the Low Countries should show:

(a) The decline of the rewards of kingship relative to other elites.

(b) Progressively more ascriptive recruitment to the kingship. This would be

[3]This very interesting case is treated in Willard Waller, "War and Social Institutions," 478-532, esp. 509-511, in W. Waller, (ed.), *War in the Twentieth Century*, New York: Dryden, 1940.

indicated by (I) fewer debates over succession rules, less changing of these rules in order to justify getting appropriate kings, and fewer successions contested by pretenders; (II) fewer "palace revolutions" or other devices for deposing incompetent or otherwise inappropriate kings; and (III) less mythology about good and bad kings, concerning performance of the role, and more bland human interest mythology focussed on what it is like to occupy an ascribed position.

Consequence 3: In some industries individual talent is clearly a *complementary* factor of production, in the sense that it makes other factors much more productive; in others, it is more nearly *additive.* To take an extreme case of complementarity, when Alec Guiness is "mixed" with a stupid plot, routine supporting actors, ordinary production costs, plus perhaps a thousand dollars for extra makeup, the result is a commercially very successful movie; perhaps Guiness increases the value of the movie to twice as much by being three times as good as the alternative actor. But if an equally talented housepainter (three times as good as the alternative) is "mixed" with a crew of 100 average men, the value of the total production goes to approximately 103 per cent. Relatively speaking, then, individual role performance is much more "important" in the first kind of enterprise. Let us list a few types of enterprises in which talent is a complementary rather than additive factor, as compared with others which are more nearly additive, and make the appropriate predictions for the whole group of comparisons:

Talent Complementary Factor

Research Universities
Entertainment
Management
Teams in athletics and other "winner take all" structures
Violin concertos

Talent Nearly Additive

Teaching
    Undergraduate colleges
    High schools
    Manufacturing
Manual work
Groups involved in ordinary competition in which the rewards are divided among the meritorious
Symphonies

For each of these comparisons we may derive the following predictions:

(a) The distribution of rewards (e.g., income distributions) should be more skewed for organizations and industries on the left, whereas the top salaries or honors should be nearer the mean on the right. In organizations with ranks, there should be either more ranks or greater inequality of rewards within ranks on the left.

(b) Since the main alternative to pure achievement stratification in modern society is not ascription by social origin, but rather ascription by age and time-in-grade, seniority should determine rewards less in the systems on the left than on the right. There are of course many ways to measure it. For instance, men at the top of the income distribution in groups on the left should have reached the top at an earlier age than those on the right. There should also be a higher proportion of people whose relative income has declined as time passes in the talent-complementary industries and groups.

Other easily accessible empirical consequences of the theory are suggested by the increased importance of the goal of industrialization in many countries since World War II, the rise in the importance of international officials during this century, and the increased importance of treatment goals in mental hospitals. Since these consequences are easy to derive, we may omit their explication here.

Another set of derivations can be made if we add a postulate that a bad fit between functional requirements and the stratification system makes people within the group (and particularly those strongly identified with the group) perceive the system as unfair. For example, this postulate together with the others would imply that where talent is a complementary factor, those organizations with seniority stratification systems should create more sense of injustice than those in which the young shoot to the top. In addition, the alienation should be greatest among those *more* committed to group goals in seniority dominated talent-complementary groups, whereas it should be greatest among those *less* committed to the group where there is an achievement system. All these consequences ought to be reversed, or at least greatly weakened, for groups where talent is an additive factor.

It may be useful to present briefly a research design which would test this consequence of the theory. Suppose we draw a sample of colleges and universities, and classify (or rank) them on the importance of research within them. Perhaps a good index of this would be the number of classroom contact hours divided by the number of people of faculty rank on the payroll, which would be lower, the greater the importance of research relative to teaching.

Within each of the institutions we compute a correlation coefficient between age and income of faculty members. (Since the relation between age and income strikes me in this case as being curvilinear, some transformation of the variables will be appropriate.) The higher the correlation coefficient, the more seniority-dominated the stratification system of the institution.[4] The first hypothesis that we can immediately test is that this correlation coefficient should be generally smaller in research-dominated institutions. This is a direct consequence of the functional theory as originally stated.

Then we could divide institutions into four groups, according to whether they are research or teaching institutions and whether they are seniority-dominated or not. We could ask the faculty within a sample of such institutions a series of questions which would sort out those highly devoted to their work and to staying in the system, and those not highly devoted. At the same time we could ask them to agree or disagree with some such statement as "Most faculty

---

[4] An elimination system, in which young people are either fired or given raises, depending on their performance, will also produce a high correlation between age and income within an institution, and yet may produce (if the institutions with such elimination systems have markedly higher salary scales), in the higher educational system as a whole, a lower correlation. I doubt if the appropriate adjustments for this would substantially affect the analysis except for a very few institutions, but this is of course an empirical question. The adjustments could be made, theoretically, by including the people who have been fired, with their current incomes, in the institutions which fired them.

TABLE 1. Hypothetical Proportion Thinking "Most Faculty Promotions Go to the People Who Deserve Them Most"

	Institutions with			
	Substantial Research Functions and		Mostly Teaching Functions and	
	Achievement Systems	Seniority Systems	Achievement Systems	Seniority Systems
	Proportion Thinking the System is Fair			
Faculty with				
Strong commitments	High	Low	Low	High
Weak commitments	Low	High	High	Low

promotions in this school go to the people who deserve them most." According to the functional theory with the added postulate on the sense of justice, we could predict results approximately according to the pattern in Table 1.

But adding postulates goes beyond the original theory into the mechanisms by which the functional requirements get met, which is an underdeveloped aspect of functional theory generally.

I do not intend to investigate the truth of any of these empirical consequences of the theory here. The only purpose of this note is to point out that functional theories are like other scientific theories: they have empirical consequences which are either true or false. Deciding whether they are true or false is not a theoretical or ideological matter, but an empirical one.

9

An Overview

This final chapter consists of a paper that surveys methods current in sociology and that includes some suggestions for further development. James Coleman, like so many of the authors whose papers are included in this volume, is both critical and encouraging. He begins by considering some of the more recent trends in sociological method. First, he suggests a convergence in survey research and demographic research, with each now employing similar analytical tools toward a similar end. That is, the development of computer science has led the demographer and the research sociologist toward the examination of relationships between variables rather than simple qualitative description or index-construction.

Related to this development, suggests Coleman, is an increasing "convergence of statistical techniques." Formalization of cause-effect ideas has led to the possibility of treating categorical and continuous variables concurrently,[1] and to the increased comparability of cross-sectional and longitudinal data. A less promising development which Coleman perceives is the frequent resort to "indicators" of the "state of society," for which he suggests several avenues to increasing methodological sophistication. Comparative research, which sociologists have long extolled, and new approaches to experimentation in sociology are additional trends which Coleman suggests are of promise, although as yet inadequately developed.

A marked tone of pessimism invades Coleman's paper as he turns to a discussion of sociological output. He suggests that research problems are too narrowly defined and that sociologists are too intent on avoiding practical application. He suggests, for example, that although explanation is a legitimate goal of social science, so too

[1] See chapter 3 for Stevens' discussion of levels of measurement.

is prediction. Projections of future states have obvious policy implications, but are too uncommon in Coleman's view. Generally, in his concluding remarks, Coleman questions the infrequency of practical applications of sociological research.[2]

As Alan Mazur suggested in the first paper in this volume, perhaps our definition of a researchable problem should become more dependent on definitions of social problems. To assign such priorities need in no way detract from the rigorous application of good research procedure.

[2] For critical comments on Coleman's paper, by H. Blalock, P. Hauser, and H. Selvin, see "Commentaries on Coleman's Paper," in R. Bierstedt (ed.), *A Design for Sociology: Scope, Objectives, and Methods,* Philadelphia, American Academy of Political and Social Science, Monograph 9 (April, 1969), 115-28.

THE METHODS OF SOCIOLOGY

James S. Coleman

It is presumptuous to attempt to describe the current state of the art in sociological method, because of its variety and its rapidity of change; it is futile to attempt to predict the state of that art in the future, because of the unpredictability of innovations. But I shall attempt a little of both these things, for in an activity as rapidly changing as sociological methodology, it is useful at times to take stock of the current position and likely directions of the future. I recognize that my perspective will be biased by my own preferences, and ask that the reader recognize this as well, and be wary. He may use his own as an antidote to arrive at a more balanced view.

I would like to divide this overview of sociological methods into two parts. The first will describe the emerging developments and new directions in research methods, including not only the developments, but some of the problems that must be solved for such developments to proceed. I believe that the past few years have seen some extremely interesting developments, which have implications for the future, and I want to describe these. The second part will take a more skeptical look, examining some of the kinds of research methods that sociologists need, but do not have. These missing methods can, in some cases, be best seen merely by looking at the world around us, to ask what kinds of phenomena sociologists appear least able to examine successfully. In some cases, they can be seen by reference to sociological theory, and to the gulf that sometimes exists between research results and theory. In some cases, they can be seen by rare examples of work that illustrate what could be done. In all cases, these missing research methods truncate sociology, and cause some important problems of the discipline, and other problems important to society, to languish relatively unexplored.

Thus, the first part of this paper will give an optimistic and enthusiastic view of the current and emerging state of affairs in social research; the second will give a sobering view of the missing methods that continue to discourage work on certain problems.

PART I: EMERGING DEVELOPMENTS

The Marriage of Survey Research and Demography

In the development of sociological methods, two different sources of data,

Reprinted with the permission of the author and the publisher from *A Design for Sociology: Scope, Objectives, and Methods.* R. Bierstedt (ed.), Philadelphia: American Academy of Political and Social Science, Monograph 9, (April, 1969), 86-114.

both based on statistical surveys, shaped two directions of work. One source of data was the United States Census; the content of the data was demographic, and the analysis was based either on calculations from the simple cross-tabulations published in Census reports, or which could be carried out under Census auspices, or else on correlations across ecological units. The types of problems studied were those of deriving quantitative indices for different localities or different years, for demographic characteristics which showed the following property: they were not so simple as to be already tabulated in Census reports, but not so complicated that they could not be calculated from the published tabulations. An index of literacy did not qualify because it was already tabulated; an index of racial segregation did, because it was not tabulated but could be calculated from published housing-occupancy data; but an index of racial segregation controlled by occupation did not, because data were not published on housing occupancy by race and occupation.

The second source of data was the sample survey designed and executed for a particular analytical problem. The origins of such surveys in opinion-polling were more humble than this, but I prefer to begin at the point in history where this work had become, in the hands of sociologists, analytically oriented. The content of the data was often encyclopedic, though it specialized in attitudes, beliefs, and opinions, and the analysis ordinarily consisted of cross-tabulations designed to show the existence or nonexistence of a relationship. The unit of analysis was always the individual, and, even though the sample survey originated for obtaining a quantitative estimate of a population characteristic, in the hands of survey sociologists, it came to be used for making qualitative inferences about relationships among individual variables. The problems studied by these methods tended to be social-psychological, and the interest of the investigations was in obtaining deeper and deeper insights into such social-psychological processes.

One might have predicted that never would the twain meet; but one of the important current developments in sociological method is their meeting.[1] The meeting has occurred largely through the common meeting-ground and common method provided by computers. The demographer is not always limited now to census reports and desk calculators, but can sometimes work with unaggregated sample tapes, and computer programs, exercising a new flexibility made possible by computer methods. The survey researcher is not limited to the punched-card runs through counter-sorters of 101 machines, but instead works with magnetic tapes and computer programs. His proximity to the demographer has also been increased by the development of professional methods of survey data-collection. Samples are larger and better designed; interviewing methods are more professional. But probably the element of greatest importance in this convergence is the common use of a new tool for analysis, the electronic

---

[1] Philip Hauser in his comments on this paper argues that this supposed convergence is merely due to myopia, and disregard of the past when no divergence existed at all. My response is that if such a unity of methods existed then, those who followed in that tradition were unable to maintain it. The separation can be seen best in the work of Samuel Stouffer, who had a background in both demographic and survey research traditions. His survey research work, as represented by *The American Soldier* and *Communism, Conformity, and Civil Liberties,* did not incorporate those statistical techniques which are now coming into use in sociology.

computer. The programs used by demographers and survey researchers tend to be the same: either cross-tabulation programs that allow estimates of measures of association, or correlation programs that are followed by regression analysis. And the work that they do begins to look more and more alike. A paper of Dudley Duncan's and one of Peter Rossi's, coming from very different research backgrounds, are increasingly similar in the methods they use.

This common method has developed, not in the usual way that a common method is a least common denominator, but rather by forcing each to go *beyond* its previous ambitions. The techniques allow examining relationships, or sets of relationships that define a process, as done by the survey researchers. But they allow two other things as well: they allow multivariate analysis to an extent that previously existed only in imagination; and they allow quantitative estimates of population parameters, where the parameters are measures of a relationship, such as a multiple-regression coefficient. Thus, the survey researchers have been induced to go beyond qualitative descriptions of relationships, into quantitative ones, with statistical confidence intervals; and the demographers have been induced to go beyond their index-construction into the study of relationships between variables; and both have been led into the use of multivariate analysis with many variables.

This emergence of a new method that combines some of the best of survey-research and demographic techniques is making possible types of research that were not feasible a few years ago. A case in point is the recent massive survey by the United States Office of Education, covering four thousand schools and 600,000 students, which measured the characteristics of schools attended by different racial groups, the student achievement in these schools, and the relation between achievement and school characteristics. With increasing frequency, such research is going to be carried out, research that combines the analytical depth which the best survey research has carried for small samples with the scope, representativeness, and quantitative final measures that has characterized the best demographic research.

This development of a common set of techniques and capabilities is complemented by recent developments in social policy of governments, both within and outside the United States. Governments more and more frequently request research requiring exactly this combination of skills. Much of the social legislation in the United States in recent years has made provision for evaluation, and although this evaluation has been of variable quality, the best of it incorporates these new research methods, which are neither demography nor survey research, but some of both.

The details of this marriage between two traditions of research involves the examination of related changes in the methods and the goals of social research. I will discuss two such important changes, the first in methods and the second in goals, that are part of this new direction of work.

The Convergence of Statistical Techniques

Categorical data and continuous variables: A second current development is related to the preceding one: the convergence of different statistical approaches. For a long time, the statistical analysis of sociologists was confined to cross-tabulation. The controversies, and the advances, all centered around two activities: obtaining better "measures of association," and obtaining better tests of significance for these measures. The wide influence of the Goodman-Kruskal paper on measures of association is the result of the fact that it excellently fulfilled these needs. But as long as the focus continued on symmetric measures of association, there was little possibility of a convergence between analysis that uses categorical data and that which uses continuous variables. To see how the convergence began to occur requires going back to an earlier point in the story. In their early days of statistical sophistication, sociologists were captured by the approach to statistical data taken by statisticians. The sociologists' interest was in relations between variables, with a view to the attribution of cause. This way of thinking, however, the idea of causal relations, was something foreign to standard statistical modes of thought. The concentration of statisticians on the normal distribution and measures defined on it led the sociologists to compromise their goals, and to channel their interests toward correlation coefficients, zero-order and multiple. Thus, the relationships between categorical variables tended at first to be based on approximations to the normal distribution and product-moment correlations—with the only deviations from this arising through the authority of Yule and Kendall, and then later in papers like that of Goodman and Kruskal. But always they were symmetric, with no means of representing causal asymmetry.

The steps to a greater degree of independence began when sociologists attempted to formalize their ideas about cause and effect in mathematical models—and found that the symmetric measures of association which they used did not fit anywhere in those models, though other asymmetric measures could be derived from the models.

At about the same time, the advent of computers and the increasing statistical sophistication in the discipline began to lead to the use of regression-analysis methods, based on continuous variables. And with this, sociologists found that in regression analysis, statisticians did, indeed, have a model that expressed functional dependence, and thus was consonant with causal asymmetry; and, in fact, hidden in analysis of variance was the same linear model of functional dependence whose parameters could be estimated (though statisticians tended not to do so), and which could thus serve as measures of causal dependence. It then turned out that these asymmetric measures derived from the statistician's general linear model were identical to, or directly convertible to, the measures developed by sociologists from their causal models.

Furthermore, as sociologists gained in mathematical sophistication, they began to observe what some other disciplines had developed. Blalock's work on linear systems depended on econometrics through Simon; the work on path analysis encouraged by Duncan and others came from Sewell Wright's work in population genetics; and work in dynamic systems of equations has profited from controversies over recursive models in econometrics between Wold, Klein, and others.

A principal result of this statistical sophistication has been to bring about a convergence between statistical analysis based on continuous variables and that based on categorical data. This convergence makes possible the direct comparison of measures of relationship from different forms of data. One can begin by carrying out cross-tabulations, and then efficiently deriving his measures from these, or if his data are continuous or easily made so, he can begin with a correlation matrix and end with a multiple-regression analysis. In either case, he pays for the efficiency of his measures through the inability to examine complexities of non-linear relations. But even this payment can be reduced by obtaining measures of the effects of interaction (that is, multiplicative relationships) between the variables. His gain is that he can examine simultaneously the partial relationships of a number of variables to the dependent variable, and thus is far less likely to obtain a false picture of the true causal structure by failing to control simultaneously on a number of relevant variables.

Cross-sectional data and longitudinal data: There is a second result of the sociologists' increase in freedom from the normal distribution as the source of all virtue. This is the convergence between analysis based on longitudinal data, with observations on the same units at different time points, and cross-sectional data.[2] This convergence became possible only when sociologists began to derive their measures from causal models, because only in such models do time and other variables explicitly enter. An equation

$$\frac{dy}{dt} = a + b_1 x_1 + b_2 x_2 \cdots + b_n x_n,$$

expresses the dependence of y's change on the values of x_1, x_2, ... x_n; and from this equation, it is possible to express the assumptions of a static (equilibrium) situation and to derive the equation that allows the use of regression analysis with a cross-sectional survey data; and from the same equation, it is possible to derive an equation that allows the use of regression analysis with data at two or multiple points in time. In both cases, estimates of the same causal parameters, the b_1 in this equation, can be made from static or dynamic data (though the measures are only of relative sizes with the cross-sectional data). Similarly, with categorical data, an equation,

$$\frac{dp}{dt} = a + b_1 x_1 + \cdots + b_n x_n - (a + c + b_1 + \cdots + b_n)p$$

expresses the dependence of change in a dichotomous attribute (where p is the probability of being in the positive state on this attribute) upon other variables, $x_1, x_2, \ldots, x_n$. And, again, one can use either cross-sectional cross-tabulations or data from two or more points in time to estimate the parameters of effect b_1 — whether the independent variables x_i are dichotomies, ordered variables, or continuous variables. Thus, in both the case of continuous-variable data and the case of categorical data, there is a convergence between the statistical methods applied to (and the parameters estimated for) static and dynamic data. Again, it was the formalization of ideas about cause and effect in explicit models which made possible the convergence.

---

[2] This convergence began with Herbert Simon's initial uses of systems of differential equations for expressing certain work of Homans and Festinger in social psychology, and for explicating the idea of causal structures.

Through these two types of convergence—between categorical data and continuous variables, and between cross-sectional and longitudinal data-statistical analysis offers less impediment than ever before to the research goals of sociologists. It is true that these methods are only beginning to be known and used widely, but diffusion is much more rapid than only a short time ago—probably because of the computer, which forces the use of statistical techniques more sophisticated than those recently used by most sociologists.

One important consequence of these new approaches is an increased utility of the resulting measures obtained. In much sociological analysis of the recent past and present, the measures of association or dependence are used merely to provide the basis for qualitative influences—to strengthen the inference that x does affect y, or to show that x_1 has a stronger effect on y than does x_2. However, the asymmetric parameters of causal dependence from these models can be used in the causal models for a variety of other purposes—for making contingent projections, for obtaining expected values to allow the study of deviations, for allowing controlled indicators or studying combined conditions—as described in the section on social indicators below—and, in general, for beginning the transformation of sociological theory and research from qualitative to quantitative work. Because these research results are expressed as parameters in dynamic model, a whole new range of possibilities is opened. Although the models were introduced to provide a basis for appropriate parameters, they can come to play a different role in their own right, as described in other sections.

Social Indicators

There is one recent development in sociology which involves a combination of method and substance, that goes under the general heading of "social indicators" or "social accounting systems." The general thesis behind this movement is one arrived at by analogy from economics: since economic indicators have proved to be very important for the framing of government economic policy and for the discipline of economics as well, a similar set of social indicators which show the "state of the society" will be of similar importance for government policy and for the discipline of sociology. I subscribe strongly to this general argument, but feel, nevertheless, that the social indicators could turn out to be of little value for either policy or sociology. And the element that will make this crucial difference is the methodological sophistication used in their development. There are several points, of increasing sophistication, that need to be made.

(1) *Disaggregation:* First is the question of the kind and amount of disaggregation. The traps into which one can get are well shown by the use of economic indicators for policy. These indicators have, in general, remained highly aggregated. In particular, the concentration of unemployment within a hard core has not been measured until recent events have forced it. Yet, this would have been simple to predict some time ago, given age-, race-, and education-specific unemployment rates, rates of new job-formation, and rates of growth of different age-race-education groups. This absence of disaggregation, of knowledge about different patterns of unemployment, led economists to give what I believe was mistaken advice to the President, to the effect that unemployment problems could be dealt with by overcoming the deficit in

aggregate demand through a tax cut. Only more recently has the Bureau of Labor Statistics made detailed studies showing that unemployment in some groups, particularly young Negroes, was relatively unaffected by the general increase in employment. One might go so far as to say that the failure to disaggregate, to show trends detailed by types of occupations, by population subgroups, and by differing types of individual trajectories, caused policy errors with serious social consequences.

(2) *Combined conditions:* A second way to show the heterogeneity in the system appears to move in the opposite direction from disaggregation: to recombine data from several indicators. For example, it is one thing to know the proportion of families with incomes under $3,000, and the proportion with four or more children, and the proportion who live in dilapidated housing, but it is quite another to know the proportion who have incomes below $3,000, *and* have four or more children *and* live in dilapidated housing. Such partial reconstruction of the individual from the separate indices is particularly important for policy reasons: policies including welfare, income-maintenance, and rehabilitation programs apply to individuals as wholes, not to attributes of individuals. Consequently, a multidimensional profile of individuals, rather than a single characteristic, is important if one is to know how to apply policies. I see two ways of doing this. The first is by giving cumulative distributions of those who are at or below a given point in each of several distributions; for example, all those who are two standard deviations or more below the means on each of four characteristics, those who are one-and-a-half standard deviations or more below, those who are one standard deviation or more below, and so on. Such a cumulative distribution equates different characteristics through standardizing distributions. By comparing this cumulative distribution with the expected cumu- lative joint distribution, one has a measure of discrepancy which can be treated in much the same way as can an Engel curve with a different kind of data.

Another way to reconstruct a more conclusive picture of the individual from several indices is through regression analysis. After obtaining multiple-regression coefficients that show the partial relation of each attribute to a dependent variable in question (in this example, perhaps a variable such as performance of the family's children in school), the regression coefficients are used to standardize the variances of each of the independent variables:[3] that is, an increase of one standard deviation on each "standardized" distribution would have the same effect in increasing the dependent variable. Then a similar kind of cumulative joint distribution can be made, this time with the different characteristics (such as occupation, education, income, number of siblings, number of rooms, male head of household) weighted according to their relation to some outcome variable, such as achievement of children in school. Such weights give a measure of the "quality" (in this example, "educational quality") of the objective characteristics of the household, and thus make it possible to show the cumulative proportions of a population subgroup (such as Negroes in a given central city) with households below given levels of quality.

[3]An even more sophisticated way to carry out such a measure would be, instead of using regression analysis with a single dependent variable, to use canonical analysis, with several performance or behavior measures on one side of the equation, and several background or determinant variables on the other.

In short, I am suggesting that one must not only "break the population down" through disaggregation, if social indicators are to be useful, but must also "reconstruct the individual" through combining measures each of which gives only a fragment of information about his state.

(3) *Controlled indicators:* The reconstruction described above is designed to provide measures that show the joint consequences of several variables, and is thus useful as a way of summarizing the *conditions* in which people find themselves. The very concept of social indicators appears directed to this kind of question, as measures of the "state of the system." But if social indicators are going to be useful beyond this, they must lend themselves to analysis, to work that is designed to learn the causes of given conditions. For this purpose, one wants *controlled* indicators, which do not show the whole of a given condition, but only that part of it which can be attributed to a given cause. There have been several examples of this in recent years, by Cutright, Siegel, Duncan, Levenson, and others. For example, Siegel attempts to show the income differential that can be attributed to being a Negro, controlling an occupation and education. In order to assess the expected usefulness of different kinds of policies (for example, antidiscrimination, job-creation, or educational improvement), it is valuable to know how much of the income deficit experienced by Negroes can be accounted for by specific factors.

This, of course, implies exactly the kind of analytical activity which I suggested was emerging from the marriage of demography and survey research. Thus, the point is that if social indicators are to be useful as guides for remedial policy that directs itself to causes of given conditions (and not merely to alleviation of those conditions, through income-supplements or other supports), they must include controlled indicators that show the partial deficits of given population subgroups attributable to given causes.

(4) *Controlled indicators for combined conditions:* I will merely mention an approach which combines parts of points 2 and 3. This is the use of controlled indicators for combined conditions. It would show in a single measure the partial deficits experienced by a given group, not on a single outcome variable (such as income) but on a combination of them, such as income, housing, and illness. This is quite possible to do with current statistical techniques, through canonical analysis which allows the use of several dependent variables; but the important point is that the social indicators should be designed to include these controlled indicators for combined conditions.

(5) *Mechanisms and models of change:* In the long run, the idea of social indicators will probably give way to a concept of resources and conversion processes, with social change being the result of these conversion processes operating upon the resources . The set of resources (for the system as a whole or a given subgroup) include what are ordinarily described now as social indicators, but are not limited to them. Yet, for the model to be useful as a theory of social change, or as an instrument for guiding policy, measurement of the resources is only the first and simplest step. The conversion processes, to which much current sociological analysis is directed, constitute the more difficult and more important part. But this leads into the areas of research that are currently widespread, and it is not useful to discuss them in this section.

Cross-national Research

Recent years have shown increasingly the remarkably great potential of cross-national studies. Perhaps the best example of this work is that begun by Inkeles and Rossi some years ago on cross-national comparisons of occupational prestige. Despite the fact that occupational prestige itself would not appear to be a promising variable for research on social systems, this work has led into isolation of the subclasses of occupations for which prestige is similar across a wide range of countries, and those which differ from one type of country to another; and isolation of the types of countries which have similar prestige structures.

Quite recently, two cross-national studies in quite different areas have made initial reports of results. One of these is in school achievement in mathematics—by Husen and associates—and the other, in the distribution of time-usage. Neither of these studies has yet carried out much serious sociological analysis; but even the initial reports show the intrinsic value of these studies, and the one on mathematics (in which C. Arnold Anderson is the sole sociologist) shows a high degree of sophistication in design and analysis. Why is the achievement of Japanese thirteen-year-olds so high, and that of Americans and Swedes so low? Why are Rumania and Holland so high in the average number of hours worked per week, among the countries studied? Another cross-national study carried out by Kandel and Lesser (though not based on national samples, as in these cases) suggests that Danish children are socialized to independence at a younger age than Americans. If so, what aspect of American life delays independence-training? These studies certainly raise more questions than they answer; but they are questions quite relevant to problems of the functioning of societies; and they are questions that cross-national research can answer.

A major difficulty, of course, is that cross-national studies pose serious research problems that those in a single country do not. The analysis depends on strict comparability of data from different countries, for many of the inferences depend on inter-nation comparisons. Yet, categories of classification often differ, if the studies are based on existing data; and if new data are to be collected for the research, much greater care is necessary in sampling, data-handling, and, in fact, at all points in the research, than is true for single-country studies. The reason, of course, is that nearly all the sources of error are country-specific, and thus there is no possibility for randomization of errors. In such research, stories abound with the description of these country-specific errors. In one study, it was said that the key-punching errors reflected differences in national character: Germany showed a total absence of random errors in key-punching; whenever an error occurred, it was a systematic error that appeared in all cards; in Italy, the errors were scattered with apparent Latin abandon. Apocryphal though these stories may be, they point to the sobering fact that errors are highly correlated with country, and the cross-country comparisons on which such studies depend must be made warily. In the mathematics-achievement study mentioned earlier, it was discovered too late for changing proofs that all the results reported for Finland were incorrect, due to poor communication—so the book carries a note at the front that is a solemn reminder of the special methodological problems of cross-national studies. There has not appeared a literature on the specific methodological problems of cross-national surveys; it is clear that one is coming to be needed.

Laboratory Experiments and Related Activities

Some sociologists believe that the ultimate research tool for sociology is laboratory experimentation. Even Samuel Stouffer expressed such views in his presidential address to the American Sociological Society. I have never shared this view for a number of reasons, and do not share it now. I have been reinforced in this belief by a recent paper by Campbell and Stanley which shows some of the assumptions present in experiments of various designs and in "quasi-experiments"—the term Campbell and Stanley use to describe nonexperimental settings that have some attributes in common with experiments. Although their focus is limited to individual behavior, their paper is an aid in dispelling the myth that experimentation involves almost no perils of inference about cause and effect, while nonexperimental work always involves maximum perils.

I feel that there have been some problems concerned with small-group functioning, with leadership, and with the development of norms, for which laboratory experiments have been highly productive; but much laboratory experimentation has been of little value in sociology *per se*. This is not, I suggest, because of the usual reasons proposed, that is, the problems of extrapolation of results from small groups to larger social systems. The difficulties of making appropriate extrapolation with proper safeguards are great, but have not been the core of the difficulty for sociological experimentation. The core of the difficulty is rather this: most experimentation with groups in laboratories has taken as its dependent variable the behavior of individuals in the group, with the "group" acting as a surrogate for broader social influences. In short, these experiments have been extremely valuable for the study of psychology in a social setting, but less valuable for sociology itself. To see why this is so involves only examination of the design of many of the experiments. Individual behavior is, as I suggested, the usual dependent variable, but there has seldom been systematic variation of social-structural variables as independent variables; and even less frequently has social structure been taken as the dependent variable itself, except in the sense of "communication structure."

Three recent activities, however, have begun to rescue laboratory experimentation from its state of low sociological productivity. The oldest of these is exemplified by the field experiments of Sherif in camp settings, in particular, the Robber's Cave experiment. What Sherif did was to establish an ecological setting and some aspects of formal social structure, and then observe the development of the informal social structure. In this case, he observed the development of conflict. The important element in this experiment is that the dependent variable is not a characteristic of individuals, but of social organization or social structure. Social organization by its very nature is a synthesis or system of individual orientations, and Sherif established a setting in which this system could develop. Thus, the development of social organization itself is the dependent variable, and the ecological and institutional structures are the independent variables. In contrast, many experiments proceed by abstracting an element from social organization or social structure for study. The element abstracted often reduces the problem to one of individual psychology. One might expect, generalizing from the Sherif Robber's Cave example, that experiments which take the development of social organization as a dependent variable must always be field experiments, and complex to set up. But this is not so. An experiment performed some years ago by Mintz is at the extreme of simplicity. Mintz wanted to study the emergence of different forms of social organization under different conditions of contingency of individuals' rewards on one another's behavior. The subjects held corks suspended on strings in a narrow-necked glass beaker in which the water level was rising. Rewards depended upon removal of corks without getting wet, a task which involved some co-ordination to prevent bottlenecks. Mintz showed how this co-ordination (and thus the absence of a paniclike phenomenon) depended on the structure of rewards to individuals and group.

Recently experiments in non-zero-sum games, which involve both conflicts of interest and reinforcing interests, by Sawyer, Rapoport, Schelling, and others, have shown the emergence of patterns of co-ordination and contingency under different structures of reward. These experiments are beginning to bring work in the theory of games closer to a point of value for sociology than has been true in the past.

One direction, then, of highly fruitful and promising work in sociological experimentation is that in which social organization itself is the dependent variable. Such experiments are not always simple to perform; but they constitute a means of studying social organization that has been relatively infrequent, and they appear particularly appropriate for the study of some of the transient phenomena and insubstantial social units discussed in Part II.

A second promising direction of experimental work is that in which the focus of attention is on social structure as the independent variable. An example is recent work by Oscar Grusky, in which simple organizational structures were established, and the effects of different kind of mobility between positions studied—for example, promotion from within or from outside the unit. The dependent variables were, in some cases, individual behavior and, in some cases, emergent relationships; but the focus in this case is upon the independent variable: explicitly established formal organization. In Grusky's experiments, the specific variables were types of movement between positions in the organization; in the classic Bavelas experiments, it was the formal communication structure which was the independent variable (and those experiments were most sociologically useful where they studied the emergent patterns of communication as a dependent variable of interest). The general point is that this class of experiments has studied the effects of variations in the formally imposed social organization; and within this class, those most useful to the development of social theory have examined emergent social organization as dependent variables. Taking this class of experiments together with those previously discussed, the common element is that social organization constitutes either the dependent variable of the experiment, or the independent variable, or social-organizational variables appear both as independent and as dependent variables. Experiments in these classes differ from many in which only social-psychological concepts appear, either as applied to the individual or as applied to "the group."

A third development in laboratory experiments that appears to me particularly useful is one which is hardly a proper experiment at all. It is the game-simulation of a selected social process or set of processes in a laboratory setting. I mention such games in the second part of this article as an example of the kind of synthesis that sociology has neglected; but it is true, even so, that in the past several years, work on games that are social simulations has developed rapidly. The differences between most laboratory experiments and these games appear to be two: first, the laboratory experiment ordinarily abstracts a much smaller part of a social process for study, with the result that the activity is non-self-sustaining and non-self-regulating. A good game is self-sustaining and self-regulating. The players in a social-simulation game themselves constitute the micro-social system, which regulates itself without interference from the outside. The imagery of a simulation game is one of a self-contained system; the imagery of an experiment is one with a one-way process, with independent variables affecting dependent ones. The experimenter himself must be incorporated if the system is to be complete. As the examples of experiments which I have given indicate, some of the best experimentation in sociology goes beyond this imagery of a one-way process. Nevertheless, the game explicitly rejects that imagery in favor of a systemic one.

The second, and related, difference between sociological experiments and sociological games is that in experiments, the motivation for action must ordinarily be imposed from outside, through directives from the experimenter. In sociological games, the motivation arises as an intrinsic aspect of the miniature social system. The mark of a good sociological game, in fact, is that the individual goals which are induced by the rules bring about action which results in the system's functioning—just as the mark of good organization is that in which individuals in satisfying their own goals contribute to the functioning of the social organization.

It would be incorrect sharply to differentiate games from experiments in sociology. It is possible, in fact, that the direction of movement in sociological experiments is in the direction of games and the imagery of microsystems, and increasingly away from the stimulus-response imagery carried over from psychology.

Statistical Problems of Current Importance

Despite the statistical convergence described earlier, there are some statistical problems which if solved would aid sociological analysis greatly. The two most important classes of such problems are those involving structure, and those involving units of analysis at several levels of aggregation (for example, individual, classroom, school, city). The structural problems are of several varieties. Perhaps the largest class begins with data which involve relations between individuals or other entities, and the problem is to find the simplest structure that will adequately describe the relations. This problem is one to which factor analysis, multidimensional scaling, cluster analysis, analysis of sociometric networks into cliques, some applications of graph theory, and other methods have been applied. There have been a number of recent developments that make these problems more tractable, particularly in multidimensional scaling. Although these problems have not been fully solved, they are the most adequately solved of the various structural problems.

A different class of structural problems consists of those which involve analysis of the functioning of a structure. This arises in perhaps its simplest form in the study of social diffusion, where the problem concerns the effect of a given structure (for example, a sociometric friendship structure, or an authority structure in an organization) upon diffusion of the information or innovation. Only very small steps have been made toward the solution of these problems of diffusion in a structure. But even less progress exists in the solution of more general problems. Consider just one variant upon the diffusion problem: there is now not a single item being diffused throughout a system, but two competing items that begin at different points. How does one study the influence of the structure upon the final pattern that occurs, and the way that pattern becomes established?

Still another structural problem concerns the simultaneous study of multiple structures linking the same persons (friendship, respect, trust, authority in occupational organization). For example, if B trusts C, how does A's friendship with B affect A's tendency to come to trust C, controlling on A's trust of B and on the other relation in which he is indirectly involved with C? Computers have made the study of such complex structural problems simpler, but there has been relatively little use of the new technical capabilities.

The second statistical problem that needs serious attention is that of multiple-level analysis involving data at several levels of aggregation. This has been called "structural analysis," "compositional analysis," or "contextual analysis," and under these labels, techniques of analysis have been developed. More recently, techniques derived from explicit statistical models, in particular, analysis of covariance, have been applied to such data. One of the most important problems, however, is not solved by any of these approaches. This is the problem of inferring effects at the appropriate level. When a variable at a collective level is introduced to account for variations in a dependent variable, then how is one to know that the effect is not due to the individual-level variable? In research on schools in which I was recently engaged for the United States Office of Education (USOE), this question arose in the following concrete form: we related each child's achievement to the average level of educational background in the school. How could we tell what part of that is due to the child's own educational background, and what part due to that of the other students in the school? The standard answer, of course, is to examine this relation only after controlling on his own family background. But incomplete controls can produce spurious relationships. An incomplete control of the individual variable can produce spurious relationships at the group level. What is not so often recognized is that the reverse is true as well. An incomplete control at the group level can cause spurious relationships at the individual level. At present, the only method for guarding against such spurious relationships is to improve the control. For this purpose, multiple-regression analysis is a much better tool than cross-tabulation. For example, in the USOE research, six continuous variables were used to control for the child's own parental background before examining the relation of achievement to average background in the school. Even so, the possibility of a spurious component to the relationship exists. Some techniques are necessary to provide a better means of extracting all the effects at one level which might spuriously appear as a relationship at another level.

This is one statistical problem of multiple-level analysis. More complex problems arise when not only independent variables exist at more than one level, but dependent variables as well—for example, the variance in achievement in a school classroom, or the morale of a teacher, as a function of attributes of the children, and attributes of the organization of the school. These kinds of problems are important to sociology, and study of the problem is inhibited by poorly developed methods.

PART II: RESEARCH LACUNAE

I would like to begin this part of the paper by asking some sobering questions. Sociology is no longer an infant discipline, and it is presumably engaged in the advancement of knowledge. Yet, sociologists have astonishingly little to say, either from evidence or from theory or from both, on some of the most important sociological problems in the world. For example, sociologists appear to be able to say little about the genesis of the recent riots: quite apart from prediction, there is no background of data which sociologists can analyze to understand why they broke out where and when they did, to account for who participated in them and who did not, or to understand how they exploded from tiny beginnings. Furthermore, this is not simply a chance omission, which could be easily remedied. Methods as they have been developed in sociology are not especially well suited for the study of such transient social phenomena. Apart from the riots, research in the sociology of conflict, and in collective behavior generally, languishes, in large part because of the absence of appropriate methods.

It is not merely transient phenomena and collective behavior that sociologists have little to say about. Consider what is probably the most important locus of change in Western society today: changes in the relation of youth to adult society. These changes manifest themselves in numerous ways: in increased length of school attendance, in lesser contact across age-lines, in cultural and behavioral patterns among youth increasingly deviant from those of adults, in a greater frequency of psychological problems among the young, in an increasing alienation from the societal establishment, in an increasing identification with the age-group as a collectivity. There are many small problems concerning youth to which research is directed; but somehow we seem not to have a methodology, or perhaps not the vision to combine methodologies appropriately, to study this larger problem.

The same question might be asked more generally, about other "large" social problems—such as the problems of social change in places like Latin America, the problems of the social conditions and consequences of the increasing age-segregation of the aged in Western society, and the emerging patterns of social organization found in extremely open and individualistic social settings, such as California.

Is it the case that these problems are too large for sociologists' methodology? Are the methods appropriate only for small fragments of such problems, leaving us without a means for putting the fragments together? If so, then I suggest that innovations in method are urgently required, if sociological knowledge is to add up to more than a set of such fragments.

But as I will indicate, I believe that, although some of these problems present serious methodological barriers, not all do, and that some of the recent developments in methods give considerable promise for solving certain of these problems.

Synthesis

(1) *Contingent projections;* One of the reasons, I believe, that sociologists appear unable to say much about these phenomena is a perspective about research problems that is much too narrow. Sociologists and economists split into two disciplines on an issue that has separated them ever since: sociologists interested in ever more detail about the *causes* of some social phenomena or some type of behavior; and economists interested in examining the *joint consequences* of a rather simple and straightforward causal structure (that is, the utility-maximizing rational man). Sociologists were more interested in explaining; economists more interested in describing the functioning of a system. One major concomitant of this approach by sociologists has been the lack of any serious interest in problems of synthesis or the study of joint consequences. This lack of interest prevented the use of certain styles of work and certain methods in sociology, which seriously curtails the value of current work in sociology. I will mention two kinds of synthesis which can be done, each practiced by a few sociologists, but only in limited areas. The first of these I will call the development and use of contingent projections. There has been little interest among sociologists in joint study of the incidence of a phenomenon with the consequences, so that one can estimate changes in magnitude of the consequences. The example which shows this best by contrast—for it is the only area in sociology which is a major exception—is the study of population. Population studies are often concerned with projection, with showing the consequences of a decreased adult or infant death rate on population size and structure; showing the consequences of a birth bulge at one date for gross birth rates in the next generation, if age-specific birth rates remain constant, and so on.

To be sure, such projection is easier in population study than in other matters, where the data are less concrete and less regularly collected; but it is also a matter of the state of mind: there are numerous areas in sociology other than population for which such contingent projections are possible.

Certainly, one goal of any scientific discipline is to explain and to understand, but another goal is to predict. Sociologists appear to be so fully fixated upon the first goal that they seldom even ask what is necessary for the second. It is certainly not the case, as in some disciplines, that prediction follows directly upon explanation, and in some cases it is not even dependent on explanation. It is not the case that if sociologists knew the psychological and social conditions leading to a given form of juvenile deviance, they would automatically be able to predict the incidence of this deviance. They would need as well to know the incidence, and expected changes in incidence, of the relevant psychological and social conditions. On the other hand, they might well be able to predict the rate of this deviance, yet not have a good "explanation" for it in the sense of knowing the way the social and psychological conditions combined to produce it.

My argument is not that sociological research should neglect explanation, or even that it should give an emphasis to prediction. It is, rather, that sociologists should not completely neglect prediction or projection—for, both before explanations are found and after, one of the important fruits of sociological investigation should be its ability to predict.

The kinds of quantitative predictions that are feasible in the current state of social research are what might best be called contingent predictions—the estimation of what future state would be like *if* certain conditions obtain in the future. For example, Lieberson has done this in explaining what the occupational distribution of Negroes would look like in one generation *if* there were no direct effects of discrimination, and *if* current levels of educational attainment continue, and *if* the present relation of occupation to education continues. In a somewhat different application, I asked what rates of unemployment among youth would be in 1970 *if* current rates of new job-formation continued, *if* the rate of college attendance remained constant, and *if* the ratio of unemployment of youth (age 14–24) to that in the total labor force remained the same.

A different kind of projection, less quantitative but perhaps no less useful, is also possible. It is the sociological equivalent of "putting two and two together," to make possible a somewhat better idea of the future. If we know that communication from developed countries to underdeveloped ones increases the desire for a high material living standard, and if we know that the rate of communication is increasing more rapidly than the rate of increase of living standards, we can predict that dissatisfaction will increase. This is the sort of thing each of us does every day, in his everyday affairs. It is so much a part of the equipment we use for everyday living that we are seldom aware of it. In any case, sociologists have done nothing to construct systematic methods for doing it with more care and more sophistication. Were we to do so, the immediate capability of sociology for predictions would certainly be enhanced.

(2) *Games:* The second type of synthesis that constitutes a neglected but potentially profitable area of work is the development of sociological games. I hesitate to describe this as a research method—it might better be called a method of theory-construction. But, however it is described, it is a way in which a portion of a social system can be synthesized from the component processes. The construction of a game that simulates some aspect of social reality is a form of theory-construction and of research. One's theory about what motivates players in different roles, and the means which they have available to realize their goals, shapes the rules of the game; one's observation of how the players interact when they are presented with the hypothesized goals and means is the research that leads to theory-revision.

I will do no more here than mention the use of social-simulation games for theory-and-research, because I intend it principally to provide a second example of a kind of myopia that sociologists suffer through the intense concentration on explaining things. The relative absence of any serious attempts at synthesis—

whether through contingent projections, games, or formal systems like those of economists—points to serious weakness in the very way in which sociologists define their realm of endeavor.

The Observation of Social Behavior

One would suppose, if he were a natural scientist, that the principal research techniques of sociology are based on observation of behavior. Yet, most research techniques which analyze behavioral data take a short cut in data-collection, and base their methods on individuals' *reports* of their own behavior and, less frequently, on those of others. This is not to say that sociologists' analyses should be limited to nonverbal behavior, but, rather, that our study of both verbal and nonverbal behavior is often based on information obtained in settings outside the social frame under study: in interviews or questionnaires. This has been a boon, as one can see by examining the methods to which animal sociology is limited. But it has also been a handicap, for it has discouraged the development of techniques for studying behavior *in situ,* and it has also focused work on those problems easily studied by interview data and easily obtained records of behavior (often administrative records).

Let me give a simple example: some years ago, in reading the Ph.D. thesis of Arthur Stinchcombe, a study of a high school, I found most interesting a section on student attention, and the differing problems of control of attention that existed in different school activities: lectures, class discussion, laboratory work, school assemblies. Yet, the portion of the dissertation which was subsequently published did not include this, because it was based on casual observation, and contained no systematic data addressed to specific problems. Now, certainly, this would have been possible to study systematically, but not with the methods which sociologists are best prepared to use, and, in fact, only with some amount of work in the development of methods. This is only one example of a whole set of problems that depend on methods of observation in a social setting that are poorly developed. Work of Barker on the activities of children—where they are carried out, in what company, and what kind of activity—is of interest precisely because it begins to study problems for which interview techniques have not been especially appropriate.[4] Similarly, the interest of the work of Garfinkel and his students, in which the investigation presents verbal stimuli, not as an interviewer, but as a member of the same social system, lies in the fact that it shows the responses of people in a social system to a violation or disturbance of normative expectations.[5] More useful, however, than at least the existing disappointing results of Garfinkel's work is the work in participant observation carried out by such sociologists as Howard Becker, and work described by Webb, Campbell, Schwartz, and Sechrest in *Unobtrusive Measures.*

---

[4] It is true that in some of his research, Barker has depended upon questionnaire responses for reports of these activities. Yet, this, very likely, introduces biases that appropriate observational techniques would be without, and also limits the data to easily remembered aspects of the behavior.

[5] Eliot Chapple's work in developing methods for interviewing prospective sales clerks showed a number of interesting innovations in this direction. The interviewer would, for example, remain silent for a long period, and observe the subject's response to the pause.

Certainly, it is true that such observation is more difficult, even for problems in which it is most appropriate, than questionnaire and interview methods. And it is certainly true that several years ago, there were few aids for observation and recording of ongoing social behavior. Today, however, many problems initially in the way are solved. Time-sampling, space-sampling, and sampling of roles is well understood, and experience in observation is extensive. There is also now a wide range of electronic aids to such observation. Perhaps the association of such aids with covert surveillance has made sociologists hesitant to use them. But this is precisely the reason for a code of ethics: to provide collective protection to the subjects of sociological study through rules for the use of potentially harmful tools.

Measurement of Trust, and the Study of Social Movements

Here I will take the liberty of singling out one concept, that of trust, and one research problem, that of social movements, as two unrelated indicators of a general problem in research methods. The problem is the relative absence of certain important areas of research in sociology. The concept of trust is an attribute neither of individuals, nor of groups, organizations, or societies, but a relational attribute—an attribute of the relation between individuals and various social objects. Trust may not be the most important of these; some others are values, expectation, and attributions of legitimacy. But none of these concepts play a great part in most sociological research. Is this because of the problems that sociologists select, or because of their research methods? Or, perhaps, is it that these concepts are not really important in sociology?

I think that few sociologists would be prepared to grant the last possibility; certainly, in social theory of many varieties, these concepts appear. Trust, for example, stands at the base of monetary systems, and of systems of near-money and credit, as monetary theorists in economics are the first to point out. It is an inherent part of all social interactions in which there is a time difference between the gains of one individual and those of the others from the relationship: that is, most exchanges, economic or social, depend on the trust of one party. Thus, social organization itself involves networks of trust.

I suspect that the infrequent appearance of such concepts in sociological research depends on the fact that sociologists' research problems are often society-bound. Trust and many other aspects of the social system are overlooked by sociologists, because they vary so much less within a society than between societies. Yet, the variation within a society is certainly great enough to allow productive study.

When and if sociologists begin in some numbers to engage in such study, will research methods be appropriate? Probably so. The methodological problems are probably most pronounced at the stage of designing studies in which such concepts are necessary components. Their measurement itself appears to present few obstacles. Yet, their abundance in sociological theory, and their relative scarcity in sociological research, suggests that there is a failure of methods that facilitate study of the problems for which variables like trust are necessary. It is the infrequent appearance of such concepts in research that should sensitize sociologists to the limited research horizons that currently obtain in the discipline.

The relative absence of studies of social movements by sociologists is particularly distressing because of the frequency of such movements in current society. The neglect of such phenomena could be better understood in periods of social stability than at present, when there are many such movements to study. The current neglect leads one to suspect that the whole discipline of sociology (and not just certain theoretical positions, such as Parsons' and functional analysis, which have often been described as oriented to equilibrium) has evolved toward the study of social statics, and becomes impotent in the face of change. Whether this is the case, or whether it is merely that the study of social change, social movements, conflict, collective behavior, and other transient states is simply more difficult, the end result is the same. These are the underdeveloped areas of social research. They are not only backward at present; they are not catching up.

There are examples which show that research on transient phenomena can produce cumulative results. A case in point is the disaster studies of several years ago carried out under the auspices of the National Research Council, an excellent example of continuity which resulted in a cumulative product. Yet, it is true that methods for the study of social systems in states of change must be more flexible in time, place, and technique than methods for the study of stable states. Most of the methods devised for the study of stable states are also useful for the study of transient ones; yet their specific combinations, and the additional techniques required, have not been the subject of attention for methodologists. The special problems range all the way from the intellectual problems of devising appropriate statistical models for the study of change to the practical problems of personal safety in data-collection. It seems likely that, for several reasons, the time is appropriate for the development of appropriate methods for these studies: many of the methodological problems in the study of stable states have been solved; statistical models for the study of change are in a reasonably high state of development; and there is enough social turbulence, at all levels from community to international, to provide material for study.

With these problems as with others, the sociologists' vision of what they can do and what they should be doing seems to be narrowly restricted by what has been done. The inward-looking character that academic disciplines necessarily possess limits horizons and apparently inhibits sociologists from asking themselves fundamental questions about what problems are important ones to sociology, and how they might best be studied.

BIBLIOGRAPHY

Barker, Roger and Herbert Wright, *Midwest and Its Children.* Evanston, Ill.: Row, Peterson, 1954.

Barton, Allen H., *Social Organization under Stress:: A Sociological Review of Disaster Studies.* (Publication of the National Academy of Sciences—National Research Council, No. 1032.) Washington, D.C.: National Academy of Sciences, 1963.

Becker, Howard S., *Boys in White: Student Culture in Medical School.* Chicago: University of Chicago Press, 1961.

Blau, Peter M., "Structural Effects," *American Sociological Review,* 25 (April (1960), pp. 178-93.

Blalock, Hubert M., Jr., *Causal Inferences in Nonexperimental Research.* Chapel Hill: University of North Carolina Press, 1964.

————, *Social Statistics.* New York: McGraw-Hill, 1960.

————, and Ann B. Blalock, *Methodology in Social Research.* New York: McGraw-Hill, 1968.

Boocock, Sarane S. and E. O. Schild (eds.), *Simulation Games in Learning.* Beverly Hills, Calif.: Sage Publications, 1968.

Campbell, Donald T. and Julian C. Stanley, "Experimental and Quasi-Experimental Designs for Research on Teaching," in N. L. Gage (ed.), *Handbook of Research on Teaching.* Chicago: Rand McNally, 1963, pp. 171-246.

Coleman, James S., *Introduction to Mathematical Sociology.* New York: Free Press of Glencoe, 1964.

————, "Surplus Youth: A Future Without Jobs," *The Nation,* May 25, 1963, pp.439-43.

————, Elihu Katz, and Herbert Menzel, "The Diffusion of an Innovation among Physicians," *Sociometry,* 20, 1957, pp. 253-70.

Davis, James A., J. L. Spaeth, and Carolyn Huson, "A Technique for Analyzing the Effects of Group Composition," *American Sociological Review,* 26 (April 1961), pp. 215-25.

Duncan, O. D., "Path Analysis: Sociological Examples," *American Journal of Sociology,* 72, 1966, pp. 1-16.

Flament, Claude, *Applications of Graph Theory to Group Structure:* Englewood Cliffs, N.J.: Prentice-Hall, 1963.

Garfinkel, Harold, *Studies in Ethnomethodology.* Englewood Cliffs, N.J.: Prentice-Hall, 1967.

Goodman, L.A. and W. H. Kruskal. "Measures of Association for Cross-Classifications," *Journal of the American Statistical Association,* 49, 1954, pp. 732-64.

Guetzkow, Harold, *Simulation in Social Science,* Englewood Cliffs, N.J.: Prentice-Hall, 1962.

Harary, Frank, Robert Z. Norman, and Dorwin Cartwright, *Structural Models: An Introduction to the Theory of Directed Graphs.* New York: John Wiley and Sons, 1965.

Hovland, Carl I., Arthur A. Lunsdaine, and Fred D. Sheffield, *Experiments on Mass Communication,* Vol. III. Princeton, N.J.: Princeton University Press, 1949.

Husen, Torsten (ed.), *International Study of Achievement in Mathematics,* Vols. I and II. New York: John Wiley and Sons, 1967.

Inkeles, A. and P. Rossi, "National Comparisons of Occupational Prestige," *American Journal of Sociology,* 61, 1956, pp. 329-39.

Kandel, D., G. Lesser, G. Roberts, and R. Weiss, "Adolescents in Two Societies: Peers, School, and Family in the United States." Cambridge, Mass.: Harvard University, 1967. (Mimeographed.)

Keyfitz, Nathan, *Introduction to the Mathematics of Population.* Reading, Mass.: Addison-Wesley, 1968.

Li, C.C., *Population Genetics.* Chicago: University of Chicago Press, 1955.

Lieberson, Stanley and Glenn V. Fuguitt. "Negro-White Occupational Differences in the Absence of Discrimination," *American Journal of Sociology,* 73, No. 2 (September 1967), pp. 188-200.

Mintz, A., "Non-adaptive Group Behavior," *Journal of Abnormal and Social Psychology*, 46, 1951, pp. 150-59.

Rapoport, Anatol and Albert M. Chammah, *Prisoner's Dilemma.* Ann Arbor: University of Michigan Press, 1965.

Sawyer, Jack and William R. Morgan, "Bargaining, Expectations, and the Preference for Equality over Equity," *Journal of Personality and Social Psychology*, 6, No. 2, 1967.

Schelling, Thomas C., *The Strategy of Conflict.* Cambridge, Mass.: Harvard University Press, 1960.

Schreier, Fred T., *Human Motivation: Probability and Meaning.* New York: Free Press of Glencoe, 1957.

Sherif, Muzafer and Carolyn W. Sherif, *An Outline of Sociol Psychology.* New York: Harper, 1958.

Siegel, Paul M., "On the Cost of Being a Negro," *Sociological Inquiry*, 35 (Winter 1965), pp. 41-57.

Somers, R.H., "The Rank Analogue of Product-Moment Partial Correlation and Regression," *Biometrika*, 46 (June 1959), pp. 241-46.

Torgerson, Warren S., *Theory and Methods of Scaling.* New York: John Wiley and Sons, 1958.

Webb, E. J., D. T. Campbell, R. D. Schwartz, and L. B. Sechrest. *Unobtrusive Measures: Nonreactive Research in the Social Sciences.* Chicago: Rand McNally, 1968.

Editor's Note

In reprinting papers for this book, we have always retained the authors' references and bibliographies. Thus, each paper in itself includes references to additional readings. This bibliography does not include all such references. Rather, it is intended to provide a summary guide to the more frequently consulted sourcebooks in methodology.

ADDITIONAL READINGS

A. General Methods Texts

Ackoff, R., *The Design of Social Research*. Chicago: University of Chicago Press, 1953.

Blalock, H.M., Jr., *An Introduction to Social Research*. Englewood Cliffs: Prentice-Hall, Inc., 1970.

Blalock, H.M., and A.B. Blalock, *Methodology in Social Research*. New York: McGraw-Hill Book Company, 1968.

Cicourel, A.U., *Method and Measurement in Sociology*. New York: Free Press of Glencoe, Inc., 1964.

Duverger, Maurice, *An Introduction to the Social Sciences*, New York: Frederick A. Praeger, Inc., 1964.

Galtung, Johan, *Theory and Methods of Social Research*. New York: Columbia University Press, 1967.

Goode, W., and P. Hatt, *Methods in Social Research*, New York: McGraw-Hill Book Company, 1952.

Kerlinger, F.N., *Foundations of Behavioral Research: Educational and Psychological Inquiry*. New York: Holt, Rinehart, & Winston, Inc., 1964.

Lastrucci, C.L., *The Scientific Approach*. Cambridge, Mass.: Schenkman, 1963.

Lazarsfeld, P.F., and Morris Rosenberg, *The Language of Social Research*. New York: Free Press of Glencoe, Inc., 1955.

Madge, J.H., *The Tools of Social Science*. London: Longmans, Green & Co. Ltd., 1953.

Phillips, B.S., *Social Research: Strategy and Tactics*. New York: The Macmillan Company, 1966.

Riley, M.W., *Sociological Research*. New York: Harcourt, Brace & World, Inc., 1963.

Selltiz, Claire, *et al.*, *Research Methods in Social Relations* (rev. ed). New York: Holt, Rinehart & Winston, Inc., 1961.

Simon, J., *Basic Research Methods in Social Science*, New York: Random House, Inc., 1969.

Sjoberg, G. and R. Nett, *A Methodology for Social Research*, New York: Harper & Row, Publishers, 1968.

Thomlinson, Ralph, *Sociological Concepts and Research.* Random House, Inc., 1965.

Wakeford, John, *The Strategy of Social Inquiry: A New Progi Methods and Measurement for the Student of Sociology. ⅄* Macmillan & Co. Ltd., 1968.

B. Specialized Texts

Bales, R.F., *Interaction Process Analysis: A Method for the Study of Sm Groups.* Reading, Mass.: Addison-Wesley Publishing Co., Inc., 1950.

Blalock, H.M., *Casual Inferences in Non-experimental Research.* Chapel Hill: University of North Carolina Press, 1964.

Blalock, H.M., *Social Statistics.* New York: McGraw-Hill Book Company, 1960.

Blalock, H.M., *Theory Construction.* Englewood Cliffs: Prentice-Hall, Inc., 1969.

Bruyn, S.T.H., *The Human Perspective in Sociology.* Englewood Cliffs: Prentice-Hall, Inc., 1966.

Cochran, William, *Sampling Techniques* (2nd ed.). New York: John Wiley & Sons, Inc., 1963.

Conway, Freda, *Sampling: An Introduction for Social Scientists.* London: George Allen and Unwin Ltd., 1967.

Cotton, J.W., *Elementary Statistical Theory for Behavioral Scientists.* Reading, Mass.: Addison-Wesley Publishing Company, Inc., 1967.

Dornbusch, S.M., and C.F. Schmid, *Primer of Social Statistics.* New York: McGraw-Hill Book Company, 1955.

Edwards, A.L., *Techniques of Attitude Scale Construction.* New York: Appleton-Century-Crofts, 1957.

Fallding, H., *The Sociological Task.* Englewood Cliffs: Prentice-Hall, Inc.,1968.

Fishbein, Martin, *Readings in Attitude Theory and Measurement.* New York: John Wiley & Sons, Inc., 1967.

Franzblau, A.N., *A Primer of Statistics for Non-Statisticians.* New York: Harcourt, Brace & World, Inc., 1958.

Greenwood, Ernest, *Experimental Sociology: A Study in Method.* New York: King's Crown Press, 1949.

Hammond, P.E., *Sociologists at Work.* New York: Basic Books, Inc., Publishers, 1964.

Hempel, C.G., *Fundamentals of Concept Formation in Empirical Science.* Chicago: University of Chicago Press, 1952.

Hirschi, Travis, and Hanan Selvin, *Delinquency Research: An Appraisal of Analytic Methods.* New York: Free Press of Glencoe, Inc., 1967.

Hope, K., *Elementary Statistics.* New York: Pergamon Press, Inc., 1967.

Humphrey, G., and Michael Argyle, *Social Psychology Through Experiment.* New York: John Wiley & Sons, Inc., 1960.

Analysis. New York: Free Press of Glencoe,

ct of Inquiry: Methodology for Behavioral
.ndler Publishing Co., 1964.

e Sociology: A Codification of Cross-Sectional
.Aarcourt, Brace & World, Inc., 1967.

ok of Research Design and Social Measurement. New
.Aay Co., Inc., 1964.

e Sociological Imagination. New York: Oxford University

.W., *Readings in Cross-Cultural Methodology.* New Haven: HRAF
, 1966.

.er, C.A., *Survey Methods in Social Investigation.* London: William
Heinemann Ltd., 1958.

Nagel, Ernest, *The Structure of Science: Problems in the Logic of Scientific Explanation.* New York: Harcourt, Brace & World, Inc., 1961.

Northrop, Filmer, *The Logic of the Sciences and the Humanities.* New York: The Macmillan Company, 1949.

Rudner, R.S., *Philosophy of Social Science.* Englewood Cliffs: Prentice-Hall Inc., 1966.

Siegel, Sidney, *Non-parametric Statistics for the Behavioral Sciences.* New York: McGraw-Hill Book Company, 1956.

Stephan, F.F., and P.J. McCarthy, *Sampling Opinions: An Analysis of Survey Procedure.* New York: John Wiley & Sons, Inc., 1958.

Torgerson, W.S., *Theory and Methods of Scaling.* New York: John Wiley & Sons, Inc., 1958.

Webb, Eugene, *et al., Unobtrusive Measures: Nonreactive Research in the Social Sciences.* Chicago: Rand McNally & Co., 1966.

Whyte, W.F., *Street Corner Society: The Social Structure of an Italian Slum* (2nd ed.). Chicago: University of Chicago Press, 1955.

Zeisel, Hans, *Say It With Figures.* New York: Harper & Row, Publishers, 1957.

Zetterberg, H.L., *On Theory and Verification in Sociology,* (3d ed.). Totawa, New Jersey: Bedminster Press, 1965.